THERAPY
OF THE
SUBSTANCE
ABUSE
SYNDROMES

THERAPY OF THE SUBSTANCE ABUSE SYNDROMES

Henry Jay Richards, Ph.D.

JASON ARONSON INC.
Northvale, New Jersey
London

This book was set in 10 pt. Goudy by Lind Graphics of Upper Saddle River, New Jersey, and printed and bound by Haddon Craftsmen of Scranton, Pennsylvania.

Library of Congress Cataloging-in-Publication Data

Richards, Henry Jay.
    Therapy of the substance abuse syndromes / by Henry Jay Richards.
      p. cm.
    Includes bibliographical references and index.
    ISBN 0-87668-539-4 (hardcover) : $50.00
    1. Dual diagnosis. 3. Dual diagnosis—Treatment. I. Title.
    [DNLM: 1. Mental Disorders—psychology. 2. Psychopathology.
    3. Substance Use Disorders—psychology. 4. Substance Use Disorders—
    therapy. WM 270 R515t]
    RC564.68R53 1993
    616.89—dc20
DNLM/DLC
    for Library of Congress   92-48826

Manufactured in the United States of America. Jason Aronson Inc. offers books and cassettes. For information and catalog write to Jason Aronson Inc., 230 Livingston Street, Northvale, New Jersey 07647.

one is the song which fiends and angels sing:
all murdering lies by mortals told make two.
Let liars wilt, repaying life they're loaned;
we (by a gift called dying born) must grow
—e.e. cummings

Contents

II Treatment

III Special Topics

Acknowledgments

Many gifts were exchanged in the long process of revealing and recording whatever is of value in these pages. Most of these gifts stemmed directly from the generosity of patients and treatment staff in many settings who shared with me their journeys and the wisdom, vision, and human virtue that they gathered along the way.

During the first year of the development of this project, my staff at what was then the Psychiatric Substance Abuse Program (PASA), St. Elizabeths Hospital, Washington, D.C., provided the much-needed reality tests for my newly spun ideas and conceptual fragments. Edward Washington, L.C.S.W., substance abuse director for the Forensic Division of St. Elizabeths, was full of both encouragement and practical comments as the text began to emerge. Maxine Harris, Ph.D., helped me to gain a deeper appreciation of primary process on ordinary living, and an acceptance of the inexorable gravity of object relations in day-to-day life. Jonathan Fay, Ph.D., now at the University of New Zealand, was one of the first professionals outside the Washington, D.C. mental health community to review the early drafts of the first chapters. His remarks reflected a very close, thoughtful reading that helped me continue in the faith that I was on to something, and deepened my interest in bridging personality topologies with an understanding of the deeper levels of the self that are often crucial determinants of addiction.

As the writing process became more intense, I was pleased to discover that individuals at the cutting edge of our field are often open, accessible, and able to respond creatively to the ideas of others, despite their own demanding schedules. Leon Wurmser, M.D., was kind enough to offer comments and encouragement along the process of crafting the chapter on treatment issues and in sharpening my thinking on matters related to treatment in institutional settings. Arnold Bruhn, Ph.D., contributed written comments, permissions for reprints, and was generous with his time in discussing personality, goals, and cognitive processes. Arnold Wilson, Ph.D., at the New School, helped me to gain a better perspective of the scope of ideas I was trying to tie together, and more respect for the detailed and creative empirical work being done to make similar connections in the area of narrative productions. He also made highly illustrative case material available.

As this book became more oriented to developing ways of thinking about and working with the severe personality disorders who present with addictive problems, James Kludt, M.D., and Jay Casey, Ph.D., both at the Patuxent Institution (the state of Maryland's treatment-oriented correctional facility), provided much moral and intellectual support in the months of re-crafting chapters to suit this emphasis. Paul Montalbano, Ph.D., in addition to providing several clinical vignettes and insightful comments on large portions of the text, agreed to the task of collaborating on one of the most difficult chapters in the book, the chapter on criminality as a dual diagnosis issue. On this topic, J. Reid Meloy, Ph.D., provided information on assessment of psychopathy using the standard protective instruments. David Nurco, D.S.W., of Friends Medical Science Research Center, Baltimore, provided invaluable discussion of these issues as well as permission to reprint portions of his work.

I would like to thank my friends and family for accepting my postponements and apologies for absences that fell under the category of "the book." Throughout the process, my wife, Donna Cooper, remained a consistent friend, occasional editor, and constant voice for moderation and balance. She was able to accept my preoccupations when they were productive and to help me detect and break through them when they grew more like weeds than flowers.

Finally, the staff at Jason Aronson Inc. were persistent masters over a thousand details and respectful of my ideas both regarding form and substance. Their diligence has paid off in the form of a much more readable, energetic, and coherent book than would otherwise have been possible.

Introduction

This book had its inception in the late 1970s, when I first thought I had detected a meaningful correlation among the types of drug use, personality styles, and the various forms of psychopathology in patients at the psychiatric clinics and inpatient units of Michael Reese Hospital and Medical Center in Chicago. For some reason, the adolescent patients are still particularly vivid in my memory. Perhaps this is because of the resemblance that I now see between the dynamics of recovery from addiction at any age and the dynamics of the adolescent phase of development, especially for young people who are having difficulties with this life passage. Steve is one patient who comes to mind. In 1978, he was a 16-year-old inpatient who appeared to meet the classical description for hebephrenic schizophrenia. In addition to responding to voices and reporting bizarre hallucinations and delusions, he was extremely energetic, fanciful, dramatic, comic, self-centered, and exasperatingly intrusive. I found it enthralling to try to sort out the contribution made by schizophrenia to these aspects of his personality from the preferences, predilections, and family dynamics that clearly also contributed to his unique style of being.

Steve's drug history, which was extensive for such a young person, was viewed by most of the professional staff as important primarily as an expression of his acting out of frustrated dependency needs, an aspect of his rebellious impulsivity, and a contributing cause of the organicity detected in his psychological testing protocols. I was aware that my more abiding interest in the role of drug use in Steve's case, and in many other cases, appeared a bit disproportionate to these clearly more experienced clinicians who had taken on the burden of showing me the ropes. This interest was viewed as a quirk but was always tolerated by my betters and, as often as not, humored.

However, another view of Steve's presentation was provided by other members of the Michael Reese community. Due to that medical center's sensitive and humanistic staff and its community mental health oriented policies, many of the nursing assistants and housekeepers and some of the professional staff were in recovery themselves from either alcoholism, drug abuse, acute emotional decompensations related to intoxication, or from some physical complication of addiction. Many of these workers had first come into formal contact with the medical center by way of treatment for these problems in one of the center's many clinics or hospitals. These staff in recovery had in most cases completely terminated all formal treatment but remained extremely active in AA or NA, and other self-help and recovery activities. They also maintained frequent, if not daily, informal and friendly contact with some of the same clinical staff who had been crucial to making their recovery possible. In several unofficial discussions about various patients, these recovering workers pointed to the fact that on his intermittent leaves from the hospital, Steve had access to drugs and could continue to use intermittently while on the hospital ward due to what they saw as the naiveté of many of the staff concerning drug abuse and addictive behavior, and the ease of contraband procurement on the inpatient unit. Steve had routinely abused nearly all of the hallucinogenic street drugs then available and was a "huffer" of various psychoactive inhalants, from gasoline to liquid adhesive. Several of these recovering staff members complained that we had probably never seen a drug-free Steve, since he was always on heavy doses of prescribed psychotropics, even when he was temporarily free from the effects of street drugs. They suggested that addressing Steve's need to continue to abuse drugs should be the first priority in his treatment.

I found the subject of the relationship between mental illness and addiction in patients like Steve only slightly more interesting than the fact that the different views of these phenomena were being offered by what appeared to be two subcultures in the treatment setting: a formal mental health treatment culture and an informal recovery community. Retrospectively, after much more experience in other settings, I feel fortunate to have started my fascination with these subjects in an environment where these two subcultures interacted on a reasonably equitable basis and communicated with a good deal of mutual respect.

About the time that I was being introduced to these issues, Edward Gottheil edited the book *Substance Abuse and Psychiatric Illness* (Gottheil et al. 1980), which in many ways anticipated the importance of what was to become known in the middle and late 1980s by the term *dual diagnosis patient*, or the *mentally ill chemical abuser*. About the same time, Burt Pepper and co-workers (1988) began the documentation of the emergence of the young chronic mentally ill patient, which included an explicit underlining of the importance of the disruptive role of street drugs and the addictions in managing many of these patients. Like these earlier contributions, *Therapy of the Substance Abuse Syndromes* also has its origin in looking closely at the dual diagnosis patient, especially the chronic patient who has become a repeated treatment failure in both the substance abuse and mental health treatment sectors. However, the scope of this book has grown out of my attempt to come to terms with the dual diagnosis patient. Through addressing the treatment of dual diagnosis patients, a paradigm for what is required in cases with fewer and less severe complications slowly emerged. In its current form, *Therapy of the Substance Abuse Syndromes* provides a dual diagnosis perspective on the treatment of addiction generally.

The approaches to mental illness and addiction that are introduced and applied in this book are not limited to any one orientation or theory. My goal, however, consistently has been that of establishing coherence through the integration of diverse viewpoints and materials within an approach that is more than an eclecticism based on what is useful or merely fashionable or traditional. The first of these criteria, utility, is not such a bad standard, but it remains a surprisingly difficult one to determine in advance for the individual case. In regard to the criteria suggested in this book for treatment selection according to a patient's needs as they change over time, I have relied on my brief period of direct tutelage and a much longer period of studying the writings of Dr. Joseph Rychlak. I can only hope that both have helped me to make the philosophical inquiries and assumptions (biases) that support these selections explicit and coherent. Two of the most important premises that this book builds on are strongly supported by Rychlak's writings and work. The first is the importance of personal agency and free will in understanding human behavior, including psychopathology, and the second is the innate human ability of transcendence through dialectical thinking. In Rychlak's words, the transcendental dialectic is "the capacity all humans have to rise above their customary understandings of experience and—by thinking in opposition to it—bring it into question, analysis, and reinterpretation" (Rychlak 1981a, p. 829). Central to the methods employed in this book are an analysis of addiction and mental illness in terms of interacting opponent processes and the construction of an approach to treatment based on the union, or integration, of opposites.

Of all my goals in writing this book, the following three are probably the most important.

First: to provide an improved theoretical approach to understanding the connection between substance abuse and mental illness, both in terms of etiology and the fueling of a continued addictive cycle. Briefly described, the addictive cycle, introduced in Chapter 1, consists of a recurrent movement by the addict through three types of poorly modulated self-experience: inflation of the self, depletion of the self, and detachment of the self from others. For each of these positions in the cycle, parallels are drawn to a major mental illness that shares similar cardinal features. At least in regard to the general experience of self, mania or narcissistic grandiosity (inflation), major depression (depletion), and the schizophrenias and schizoid (detachment) disorders are shown to be exaggerated and fixated manifestations of positions in this addictive cycle. The addict (either consciously or unconsciously) experiences these self states in their extremes. On the conscious or manifest behavioral level of being, the addict may either become inflexibly stuck in one extreme position, or may experience and exhibit each of the three extremes sequentially. Either of these maladjustments contrasts with the normal experience of the self, which, although responsive to external vicissitudes and therefore somewhat susceptible to being blown in these three directions, is habitually anchored and redirected by a benign sense of identity. Any benign sense of identity incorporates positive and supportive memories of interactions with other persons, ideals, and ego-involving activities within a well-regulated emotional life.

Second: to provide the reader with a heuristic system for describing dual diagnosis problems. This system consists of plotting the patient's presentation on a three-axis matrix. The concept sets include: (1) a set of five symptom complexes, which in combination account for the primary sources of vulnerability to addiction, (2) a set of five biopsychosocial functions of addiction, which explain the major ways that addictive processes serve as temporary, substitute solutions to defects, deficits, and life problems, and (3) five drug-of-choice classes and related drug vectors (factors such as the route of administration, social situation of drug use, and expectancies and cognitions relative to the drug). These concept sets describe how the specific characteristics of various substances provide ersatz biopsychosocial functions by augmenting or bracing genuine but inadequate attempts at coping with situational or interpersonal demands, integration of experience, and the resolution of dynamic conflicts. This heuristic system de-emphasizes diagnostic groupings such as in the *DSM III-R* and stresses commonalities across diagnostic categories. Because the patients on which this system was modeled are repeated treatment failures, previous diagnoses are used as historical data about earlier treatment efforts.

Third: to provide alternative ways of approaching therapy with substance abusing or addicted patients, especially those with significant psychopathology. This book describes the dual diagnosis patient population as defined by repeated treatment failures, that is, an unusually difficult treatment group. I take the position that certain dynamics and relationships can be identified that are typical of this problematic group and can be fruitfully applied to the treatment of addiction in general. The discussion of therapy in Chapter 5 has both of these aspects in mind: general approaches to working with recurrent treatment failures and approaches that are more specific to the kind of dynamics found in the addictions, especially when complicated by mental illness. Chapter 5 also provides a theoretical framework for setting priorities and sequencing intervention strategies. It describes the process of the emergence of new psychological material in therapy and suggests ways to understand and support the creative process in psychotherapy.

Although this book does not shy away from difficult theoretical and clinical problems, I have attempted always to bring these issues back to simple ideas, analogies, images, or rules that will be of help to the clinician. Complicated ideas in the text are supported by tables, charts, or figures that are easy to understand.

Clinical applications are introduced through vignettes, both in the text and printed freestanding alongside the concepts they exemplify. A special effort has been made to bridge the varied training backgrounds, levels of sophistication, and informational needs of individuals involved in treating substance abuse and mental illness.

An administrator friend insists, half-seriously, half tongue-in-cheek, that if he had his way, he would always hire only one-handed mental health professionals, because the two-handed ones are always writing in their reports, "On the one hand we have this, and on the other hand. . . ." To freshen another clichéd figure of speech, it could be said that this book stands on two feet, so broadly spread apart as to almost belie its potential stature. On the one foot, it stands on an existential phenomenological orientation in regard to philosophical and theoretical understandings of persons, their experiences, and their behavior. On the other foot, it stands on a cognitive dynamic orientation in regard to treatment methods. The concept of self (and the related experiences of personal agency and identity) are used as the nexus, the body's trunk, the point of departure and return for both theory and clinical practice.

The book is divided into three sections. The first section (Strategies) establishes a theoretical basis for thinking about dual diagnosis cases and links this theoretical understanding to the empirical literature through several extended examples. The second section (Treatment) provides general assessment and treatment approaches and recommends several specific techniques and methods. The third section (Special Topics) covers several major areas of interest or need for individuals working with addicted clients, especially those with significant psychopathology. This final section contains two chapters emphasizing the importance of personality dynamics in substance abuse treatment. A chapter co-authored by Dr. Paul Montalbano, a forensic psychologist, is devoted specifically to the needs of clinicians, administrators, and policymakers in the area of forensic and correctional services. This section ends with a chapter that reviews the difficult issues that must be addressed in order to achieve optimal program design, program development, and administration of substance abuse programs with a mental health focus. For the reader's convenience, a glossary of 114 terms and an extensive list of references are included.

I hope that my long-standing interest in fiction and other forms of mythic and personal journey will help make the reader's experience of this nonfiction book an enjoyable, although at times challenging, journey. Although it contains sufficient amounts of academese, scholarly argumentation, technical jargon, empirical analyses, and all the other accoutrements of a professional text, this book is designed with the hope that the reader will take a small personal journey of sorts over several readings and brief excursions and will thus share something in common, although in only the most modest way, with works of fiction and with inspirational writings. The dominant explicit metaphor in this book is the image of two great rivers (psychopathology and addiction) converging and the challenge to health and the related opportunity for healing and growth that this convergence creates. The dominant implicit or covert image is that of the body (the ground), but especially of the hand stretched outward, as if to extend its grasp, or in a gesture of peace or praise. This book speaks to both heart and head, to the conscious and unconscious aspects of the reader enjoined in a co-creative process. I have tried to keep these aspects of the book as unobtrusive as possible. Only Chapters 1 and 5 contain explicit, modest experiential exercises designed to assist the reader in recreating the experience of self in the addictions. I have defined recovery as a spiritual movement of the experience of self from constriction toward freedom. Despite some complicated conceptual footwork here and there, the basic principle on which this book is founded is simple and straightforward: freedom (which rightly conceived also incorporates response-ability) is the highest value, the "drive theory" of this book and, I believe, of the human sciences and arts, including the art of psychotherapy.

I

STRATEGIES

1

Parallels and Paradigms

CONFRONTING THE PROBLEM

Suzanne arrived at the door of a specialty dual diagnosis program from the public hospital's psychiatric screening unit. Her dirty hair was disheveled, and her personal belongings were crammed into a black Hefty bag. She had been on the street for several days. Last year she had taken a housemate's pills in an attempt to kill herself, but nothing had happened. After that, she felt even worse, more desperate, and she began to fear she would do something more dangerous and violent to herself. She went to the screening unit to tell someone about her feelings of self-destruction. In a few minutes she would be interviewed by the dual diagnosis program's intake staff. This was an unusual way for her to gain admission to the program. Fortunately, the central intake psychiatrist had come to recognize over the years the cases that the dual diagnosis program director was apt to admit, and a developing rapport had led to earlier-than-usual specialized help for some patients in the dual diagnosis cycle. The intake psychiatrist was a mature, warm woman with grandmotherly charm who projected a sense of safe haven. Suzanne opened up enough to her to give a fairly candid interview. Despite this, relatively little of her complicated history would be discovered and documented in this one-session assessment.

Six months after this interview, a very detailed understanding of Suzanne's problems and background would emerge. She was 26 years old, from a working class Irish-American family. She had first started having problems in college, where she was studying to become a high school art instructor. In her sophomore year, she had fallen in love with her dormitory roommate. After sending the young woman a typewritten anonymous love letter, Suzanne realized how transparent her act was, since she had mailed the letter while on campus and referred to things that only the two of them would know. So she concocted an elaborate scheme to protect herself and her friendship with her roommate. She mailed several expensive gifts from a nearby town and constructed a

3

note from newspaper clippings claiming to be from male terrorists who threatened Suzanne's own life if she revealed the identity of the imagined anonymous suitor. Suzanne then staged an attack upon herself that left the entire dorm in an uproar along with various rumors floating over campus ranging from a rapist afoot to patent descriptions of her insanity. Before mailing a letter threatening her roommate with death should she attempt to move from the dormitory, Suzanne had carved a line with a letter opener from the nook of her right elbow ending with a flared arrowhead in her open palm. The dorm counselor knew that the wounds were only superficial, but after seeing Suzanne's inept attempts to care for them and realizing that the young woman lied about the origin of the cuts, she had insisted that Suzanne go for formal counseling. The dean of students, who already knew Suzanne because of her failing grades, agreed.

Suzanne had avoided the student counseling center. In her community mental health center, she was diagnosed as having bipolar disorder, based on her history of depressive symptoms and previously contained but somewhat bizarre hypomanic episodes. Suzanne lied about her drinking, although the center took enough of a history to determine that she would have to deal with the problems of having an alcoholic mother. She was started on psychotropics after refusing to enter a hospital voluntarily, although she agreed to a simple contract of not hurting herself in any way.

That was seven years ago. Since then, Suzanne had dropped out of school, performed clerical work in several widely separated cities, was in alcohol detoxification programs twice, and had had four brief psychiatric hospitalizations. She had been raped once while drunk but had not discussed this with anyone. The attack did not appear in any of her scattered records. She had had one debilitating bout with hepatitis after her male lover contracted the disease, probably from IV drug use. A close somatic examination, which she did not undergo at the time of the intake interview, would have revealed a swollen and distended liver. Her HIV status was also unknown.

Besides her hospitalizations and detoxification stints, Suzanne has been in several good outpatient programs for mental illness and others for substance abuse. She has never felt comfortable with the idea of being a psychiatric patient and has never complied consistently with any outpatient treatments for more than a few weeks. The medication has always made her feel bloated and sluggish. The one substance abuse program that engaged her interest (one with daily 2-hour meetings) had discharged her for poor attendance and too many relapses, and had referred her back to the mental health system. In periods of controlled drinking and when not depressed, Suzanne has made friends, lived in apartments or group houses with adults of her own age, and worked at various jobs, sometimes getting very favorable reviews of her typing skills. She had come to view her problems as being due only to her alcohol use, which she realized usually made her feel more depressed. She had also learned to avoid her family because they made her depressed and angry. She now rarely talked of them and rarely thought of them for more than a few seconds at a time, except when she needed something she could not get anyone else to provide.

Most recently, she had lived for several months in a house with three recovering alcoholics. Her AA sponsor of only two months had recently told her in a telephone conversation that she was too demanding and that it was a "selfish program," meaning that Suzanne had to look out for herself and she should get more out of the meetings she claimed to be attending and call her sponsor less often.

After two of the housemates became a couple and began doing things as a separate unit away from the house, Suzanne had started drinking in her room, spending days there watching television. She had received a message that she had been fired from her job. Her rent went unpaid for two months. Her hygiene deteriorated. Soon, her only contact with her roommates was to insist angrily that they leave her alone. Eventually, they asked her to move. She had wandered for several days weeping and trying to hold on to her belongings. Her main contacts with people were from getting drinks and a little food from strangers on the street. She felt miserable, then suicidal.

Now, Suzanne wanted help for these feelings and a place to stay. She did not want to be in another alcohol program by some other name, but this dual diagnosis program sounded better than a "regular" mental hospital.

Although most of this background information about Suzanne was not available to the program intake staff, they recognized that her case had come to their attention relatively early in the dual diagnosis cycle. After only six years of a clear symptom pattern and involvement in the health care delivery system, the constant stream of acute hospitalizations and aborted treatment programs had really just started. Yet, she had already became a treatment failure in three systems: the mental health system, the formal substance abuse treatment system, and the self-help alcoholism recovery community. Her point of entry was a coerced referral to the mental health system, where she was correctly diagnosed as suffering from a mental disorder with primarily affective features. After several forced detox hospitalizations, Suzanne had referred herself to the self-help programs of Alcoholics Anonymous. She had received help and support, but there remained an invisible wall creating distance and absence of real communication with her peers. In AA, her psychiatric problems had often been dealt with either harshly or with deep sympathy that later turned to exasperation and avoidance. People had tolerated Suzanne long enough for her to feel involved and hopeful, but they had always let her down. Even the things she heard in meetings—the life stories, the morals given to the stories, and the elaborations of the Twelve Steps—had confused her.

Sometimes people told her she should see a doctor or therapist; more often they told her that medication for mental problems was an unnecessary crutch, a way of denying a continuing dependence on chemicals. But when she tried to apply the things she heard, they never seemed to work for her, and she had sometimes left meetings wanting to drink more than ever before. Also, she more often than not met people who would exploit her or who seemed to have more emotional problems than she did. Being a treatment failure in this informal system had probably been the most bitter failure yet for Suzanne, because it had been intertwined into her daily life, her thoughts and feelings, and all of her relationships. Now, her denial and ambivalence about her problems with alcohol were returning, bolstered by her delusions.

Without yet having most of this information, the staff admitted Suzanne. How did they understand what had happened to her? What aspects of her clinical picture, other than the co-existence of her alcohol problem and her emotional symptoms, made her an appropriate candidate for such a program? What should such a program be able to offer her that either mental health nor substance abuse programs could provide? What was her prognosis? Was she apt to be labeled a treatment failure again?

Why does it appear that there are so many more individuals like Suzanne today as compared to two decades ago? The theoretical, clinical, and practical administrative questions and issues posed by the problems of patients such as Suzanne are the primary subjects of this book. The remainder of this chapter maps out the conceptual ground that must be covered before addressing specific clinical strategies and procedures. This chapter also attempts to provide the reader with an experiential grasp of the effects of mental illnesses and addictions as processes acting upon the total life of the individual, but especially upon the individual's experience of self.

DEFINING SYNDROMES

Suzanne and others like her (and still others very unlike her) suffer from an emergent psychiatric syndrome. A syndrome is a statistical concept. It relies on the probability of the occurrence of a pattern of divergent symptoms. This occurrence may suggest, for the various component symptoms, either common pathogenic mechanisms, common etiological clues, interactive patterns of predisposition, or vulnerability to various disorders. Suzanne's symptom complex is typified by the reciprocally reinforcing effects of psychiatric problems and substance abuse or dependence.

AN EMERGENT SYNDROME

In this book, the reciprocally reinforcing psychiatric and substance abuse syndromes, as they most properly might be named, are described as emergent in several senses. In one sense they are being recognized, dealt with consciously, and written about by professionals in a systematic way, after about a decade of unsystematic contributions. The dual diagnosis syndromes are emergent in that they are becoming more frequently encountered in clinical settings due to improved clinical sensitivity and because larger numbers of patients are developing the syndromes. (The plural is used here, because several different subtypes of the combined pathological processes of addiction and psychopathology will be identified.) In another sense, these syndromes are emergent because of the emerging social and health care environments that both cause more dual diagnosis cases and present opportunities for recognition and treatment. Several of these emerging environmental factors are located in the wider society, others are within the mental health system, still others occur in the boundary between that system and society.

Two contributing factors flow from the success and newly found effectiveness of the mental health system. The first factor is specialization. Growing demand for services and increases in knowledge and competency bases have permitted mental health care to be specialized into several separate training and treatment systems, each with its own particular traditions and cultures. Until recently this specialization had evolved into a pecking order that relegated substance abuse to either low status professionals, paraprofessionals, or self-help groups. These individuals, however well meaning, were the least prepared to deal with any coinciding psychopathology beyond mild character disorders or mild reactive depressions. The relegating of alcoholism and drug abuse cases to lay and paraprofessional attention had the unintended result of de-skilling core mental health professionals in the assessment and treatment of addiction. The division also produced a complex delivery system with more cracks to fall through for those patients whose needs and problems did not fit neatly into any of the specialty lines. The dual diagnosis case was likely to be called a treatment failure and referred out of several of these specialty delivery systems.

The second contributing factor resulting from a strength within the mental health system is the rapid growth of psychopharmacology, which made possible the humane deinstitutionalization of the mentally ill within modern society. Unfortunately, unrelated changes in political and social values put even more stark limitations on the extent to which one is personally or communally the keeper of one's brother. These values were less prevalent early in the deinstitutionalization movement. At that time, only heavy marketing, which presented overly optimistic views about medical maintenance and severe mental illnesses, and promises of sufficient funding to create a new community mental health network persuaded citizens to tolerate the dismantling of the asylum. Such dismantling, which in many areas of the United States was spearheaded by mental health professionals themselves, proceeded like Samson to bring down the temple, with only lip service given to providing community support for newly released patients. Once back in the community, expected to cope under relatively intense demands and stressors, and after being inculcated into a pharmacological model of problem solving, chronic patients participated in the social mores surrounding them and discovered their own drugs of choice. (This is the self-medication hypothesis in dual diagnosis problems, which we later revisit.)

For all members of the community, including the psychiatric patient, the rise of drug and alcohol use in society is an opportunity for addictive processes to be initiated more often. Sometimes increased drug use masks other pathological processes, while the resulting behaviors, because they are understood as drug effects, are met with more acceptance until they reach clearly dangerous levels. This can be seen as the dual diagnosis problem on the societal level, a process that provides a rich pool for the development of more dual diagnosis cases at the clinical level. Taken together, these trends have contributed significantly to the emergence of the syndromes described in this book. Finally, the syndromes described here are emergent in that they come into being and are defined by the new qualities that appear when addictive processes and patterns interact with other pathological processes in a reciprocally reinforcing manner.

DEFINING DUAL DIAGNOSIS POPULATIONS

In the mental health literature, the term *dual diagnosis patient* may refer to several groups of patients with more than one diagnosis on the primary axes of the diagnostic system. Here the term refers to those groups of patients with particular clusters of symptoms, usually resulting in two diagnoses: a psychiatric disorder and a substance abuse disorder. Using dual diagnosis as a population concept underlines the notion that there are possible subpopulations or categories *within* the dual diagnosis group and that the problems in the dual diagnosis subpopulation are, for the most part, continuous with those in the larger mental health population.

This broad population concept-based definition has the advantage of simplicity. Every patient with both a psychiatric and a substance abuse or substance dependence disorder may be easily pigeonholed by the dual diagnosis term. In one sense, it is no more than a shorthand way of describing a group of co-occurring diagnoses. In use, however, the term often implies that these patients have much more in common, either in treatment course, preferred management and treatment techniques, or perhaps etiologically. Defining the term more precisely will help to describe what is implied by this sense of commonality and will be one step toward identifying a treatment population or populations. Identifying meaningful population groups often results in refinements in research, theory, and clinical practice.

The widest definition offered in the literature reflects the view that any use of any psychoactive substance by any psychiatric patient (other than as prescribed) constitutes a dual diagnosis problem. The logic here is that such use may complicate or worsen an already tenuous psychiatric adjustment. More often than not, this may be the case, and this definition provides the heuristic advantage of warning patients and clinicians of the increased dangers of psychoactive drug use among the mentally ill. However, this definition lumps the dysthymic individual who occasionally uses cocaine with the paranoid who has active persecutory delusions, who is a severe alcoholic, and who has odd delusional beliefs about the antidemonic powers of alcohol and other drugs. It becomes obvious that so broad a definition defeats any useful attempt at classifying patients when we realize that the estimates of psychiatric patients with some significant substance abuse or dependence history ranges from 50 to 70 percent (Kosten and Kleber 1988, McKelvy et al. 1987).

The recent NIMH Epidemiologic Catchment Area (ECA) Study should be considered the watershed event in this field of research (Regier et al. 1990). With only limited space to deal with the wealth of statistical information that the ECA study has made available, readers are encouraged to obtain as complete a listing of the detailed statistics as possible and to check the study's findings against the assertions and theoretical speculations made in this text. Using a sample size of over 20,000, the study analyzed base rates of mental illnesses and addictive disorders to provide empirical estimates of their co-morbidity. Lifetime prevalence rates for mental disorders without substance abuse were estimated at 22.5 percent. Alcohol dependence/abuse and substance dependence/abuse had respective lifetime prevalence rates of 13.5 and 6.1 percent. For individuals diagnosed with a mental disorder, the odds ratio (subgroup base rate divided by the general population rate) of having some addictive process was 2.7, with a lifetime prevalence rate of 29 percent, which included a 22 percent overlap of mental illness and alcohol-related disorders and a 15 percent overlap of other drug disorders and mental illness. For persons with an addictive disorder, the odds for also having a mental illness were seven times higher than for the general population; 37 percent of alcoholics were found to have a co-existing mental disorder. Among other substance addictive disorders, 53 percent were found to have another mental disorder (a 4.5 odds ratio).

The ECA findings were even more dramatic for individuals in American institutions. Although the institutionalized population represents only 1.3 percent of the total U.S. population, being in an institution greatly increases the likelihood of having an alcohol, drug, or mental disorder (referred to as ADM by the study authors), with the lifetime rate being 71.9 percent, twice that of the general population. Mental hospitals, as expected, had the highest lifetime rate of 82.2 percent. (That means, of course, approximately 18 percent of hospitalized mental patients had no ADM disorder in their lives, using the NIMH research diagnostic instrument!) Prison inmates had a rate almost as high—82.0 percent. Nursing homes had a prevalence rate of 65.5 percent.

For individuals presenting for treatment in specialty mental health or substance abuse treatment centers, the ECA findings, based on 6-month prevalence base rates, give a closer picture of what clinicians working in these environments might expect. The co-morbidity of alcohol disorders and mental illness was 55 percent. For drugs other than alcohol, the co-morbidity rate was 64.4 percent. Looking at this rather impressive data base and using the wide definition of any co-existing mental illness with any substance use disorder, the majority of psychiatric patients clearly would have to be considered dual diagnosis patients.

A narrower definition than mere clinical and statistical occurrence is more useful. In the author's view, the most useful definition of the dual diagnosis syndrome or patient group must aid in establishing subpopulations based on clinical presentation, response to treatment, course of illness, or suspected etiology. Preferably, such a definition would reflect the relevant symptom dimensions or treatment issues that evolve in working with these patients. Optimally, such a definition would be informed by theoretical notions surrounding the most prominent feature of these cases, that is, the *persistence* of diagnostic occurrence despite active treatment for both disorders and the *interactive*, potentiating relationship between these disorders within the individual.

Several dimensions are key to forming relevant clinical subgroups from the apples-and-oranges population of those with both a substance abuse disorder and another psychiatric disorder. These conceptual dimensions have varying currency and usages in the clinical diagnostic and treatment literature and clinical practice. They are discussed in the next section before we return to refining our definition of the dual diagnosis population and to marking off the subgroups that may best be treated from the perspective offered in this book. The emphasis here is on the intractable patient, or the multiple treatment failure. In addition to patients for whom the approach to dual diagnosis work offered here is optimal, there are others for whom this approach offers only paradigmatic or heuristic value. Other ways of conceptualizing their cases will prove more efficient. The key dimensions discussed below will be useful in sorting cases into either of these two categories.

KEY DIMENSIONS OF DUAL DIAGNOSIS WORK

The concepts discussed in this section are not new. They are part and parcel of the clinician's everyday toolbox. In the current context, however, these concepts are delimited, providing additional connotations, elaborated or integrated with one another in a conceptual grid that helps to clarify and understand dual diagnosis problems. The key concepts are: acuity, chronicity, cyclicity, urgency, severity, and degree of reciprocity. Three of these concepts—acuity, chronicity, and cyclicity—relate to symptoms over time, and a fourth—urgency—relates to the subjective perception of time and priorities. The metaphor *clinical picture* is often used, but in their dependence on time, psychiatric disorders are closer to disturbing musical compositions than to crazed pictures. Psychiatric disorders exist in time; they have predictable courses and phases.

Acuity answers the question of how stable is the problem we are looking at. Did it just start? Has it reached its worst phase? What can we expect next? Often, the dual diagnosis patient reaches the health care system in acute distress from both a severe psychiatric problem (psychosis, suicidality, or dangerousness) as well as a severe substance abuse problems (intoxication, an overdose, or acute withdrawal symptoms). Just as often, in the acute phase the two pathological processes are not distinguishable as parallel or intersecting lines, but rather the lines appear superimposed. The symptom pattern may be explained as totally due to acute mental illness, or substance related effects. Acuity describes the expected acceleration, deceleration, or slope of the illness from where the patient is now, assuming that adequate care will be provided. Acuity often helps us to judge the level of severity.

Chronicity lets us know how long-standing or persistent the presented problems and symptoms are, how resistant they will be to interventions, how ingrained in the lifestyle, social functioning, and personality of the individual. Chronicity allows us to estimate how much anxiety will be produced in the patient and family (and sometimes, unfortunately, in the involved helping systems) should we be successful in changing the pattern. Dual diagnosis cases are usually chronic in either the substance abuse process or the psychiatric deteriorating process, or both.

Chronic illnesses are often cyclical. *Cyclicity* is a normal aspect of most biological processes (Sabelli and Carlson-Sabelli 1989). In periodic illnesses, such as seasonal affective disorder, premenstrual stress syndrome, anniversary depressions, and some levels of substance use disorders, an external driver (biological or situational) of the cyclical process may be easily identified. In other illnesses that demonstrate cyclicity, such as bipolar disorder, recurrent depressions, or cyclical exacerbations of schizophrenic symptoms, an external driver is not apparent and perhaps not present. As we shall see, biological and psychological processes grow out of the combination of opposing (or alternative but linked) processes often demonstrate cyclicity. Each repetition of a cycle, of course, involves differences from previous cycles, as well as the preservation of the basic pattern of illness. The shape of the pattern over time is more of a spiral helix than a circle. Knowing the degree of cyclicity of an illness, estimating where the patient is now in the spiral, and whether it is ascending or descending help in predicting the spontaneous or treatment-induced opening of windows of opportunity for various interventions. This information also provides clues to uncovering the external drivers, internal drivers, or drivers inherent to the pathological process itself, thus suggesting ways to short-circuit or ameliorate the cycle.

Urgency is a matter of perception of priority: what has to be dealt with first. Does the patient or the patient's family see the problem as the first priority? Does the treatment team (given their various disciplinary training backgrounds, counter-transference, and preferences) feel that some aspect of the case is really pressing and has to be dealt with now? The reader may notice that the problem of primary-secondary diagnosis has been deemphasized in this discussion by not being listed as a key concept. Although making the primary–secondary distinction in cases where both a substance use disorder and another mental disorder are present has been recommended as a modification of the *DSM* for future revisions; this recommendation was rejected due to the lack of empirical justification of the distinction and to the clinical problems with the required judgment (Rounsaville et al. 1987).

To the extent that primary–secondary diagnostic status may be established for any particular case, the case fits less neatly in the approach being offered here. Urgency on the part of the staff in regard to one symptom or problem versus others will usually reflect their judgments of primary versus secondary diagnoses or problems. This sense of urgency may be determined in part by factors somewhat external to clinical considerations, such as a forensic determination requiring proportional judgments of the contribution of the two pathological processes at the time of a crime, for example, or by the relative reimbursements offered by third-party payers for psychiatric versus substance abuse disorders. A clinical factor influencing urgency is the patient's tendency to powerfully engage countertransfer-ence issues of the staff. Urgency, at least in part, is a dimension that exists between the patient's needs and perceptions, and the needs and perceptions of involved others, especially family and treatment staff. Without separating urgency from other dimensions offered here and weighing it appropriately in the clinical decision-making process, most dual diagnosis cases will be dealt with almost exclusively in terms of the urgency dimension.

Severity may be described as how extreme the symptom pattern is when one combines the acute picture with the chronic pattern. Severity is a key concept, because it captures so much other data. The current course of the illness, the premorbid adjustment, the psychological structure of the individual, the typical level of functioning, the intensity and duration of continued treatment, and the predicted slope of a relapse are all reflected in an estimate of severity. Because it captures so much information and is a dimension easily traced for both pathological processes, we investigate the distinguishable levels of severity for both processes and project how these levels are apt to be interrelated in most cases. This leads us a fuller discussion of *reciprocity* as the pivotal dimension that reflects the interrelatedness of the severity levels of the two pathological processes and provides the most crucial criterion in defining the reciprocally reinforcing psychiatric substance abuse syndromes.

LEVELS OF SEVERITY FOR TWO PATHOLOGICAL PROCESSES

Life Space and Need-Related Motivation

Discussing abstract conceptual dimensions, population overlaps, and synergisms is a far cry from the heartfelt involvement that is the day-to-day work of the clinician or counselor. To assist the process of involving both the head and the heart in thinking about these issues, let us take a brief excursion into the phenomenology (the experience from the inside) of psychopathology and substance abuse as we discuss their various levels of severity. Two theoretical frameworks familiar to many mental health and substance abuse workers will provide a conceptual and schematic context from which to view the global effects of severity for two pathological processes. Slices of life will be sampled from various points along the addictive cycle and the cycle of breakdown from psychopathology. Kurt Lewin (1936) and Abraham Maslow (1962, 1964, 1970, 1971) both developed theories of motivation and personality based on need gratification or achievement. Both thinkers used visual schematics to assist in understanding human behavior based on responses to needs. Most introductory texts on personality or motivational theory include chapters or sections on these theories. Here, we outline only a few simple aspects of these theories in order to make explicit some of the relationships between the phenomenological effects of various severity levels of the two pathological processes focused on throughout this book.

Lewin's theories have influenced motivational concepts beyond those that directly use his terminology and methods. One of his key concepts was that of the life space. For Lewin, life space is a range of activity for the individual that can be depicted visually in a simple graph. A person moves toward or away from objects in his or her life space along vectors, or lines of psychological or motivational force. The strength and direction of these lines are determined by basic needs and values, or valencies, to use Lewin's terminology. We borrow these ideas and adapt them here to create some useful visual representations.

Figure 1-1 depicts a normal healthy individual balanced in a life space that

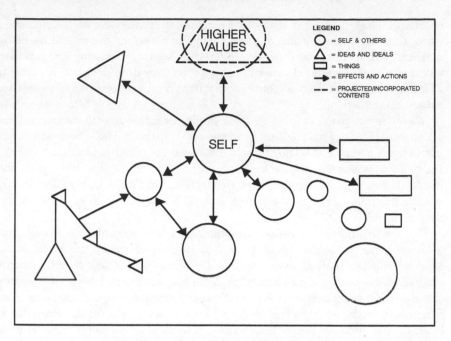

Figure 1-1. Balanced life space.

consists of persons (circles), things (rectangles), and ideas or ideals (triangles) connected by vectors (arrows). Size and distance are used here to represent importance and closeness to the self, or intimacy. Here, the vectors are drawn to show only how the individual person (self) perceives the influence or power of the relationship as either exerted toward or coming from him or her, or both.

The healthy individual depicted here is centered in the middle of the life space by his or her dynamic relationships with various objects, persons, things, ideas, or ideals. The life space is organized and meaningfully occupied, not cramped or empty. There is even an equally large other in this individual's life (lower right corner) who is acknowledged as a complete, unique, other person but who has no major significant relationship with the self. Here, the absence of vectors depict the healthy individual's understanding that others have their own autonomy in their own life space. The large broken circle at the top of the figure that partially contains a triangle represents this individual's internalized relationship to higher values, perhaps God, country, or humanity. Most of the vectors show influence or power moving in both directions, indicating mutuality.

An important aspect of the life space that is not easily represented in a paper figure is the aspect of fluidity, or change within continuity. This healthy individual's life space should demonstrate spontaneous change in organization and objects. A hanging mobile might better represent this aspect, if one could occasionally add or subtract objects from the mobile, change the color of the objects, or occasionally make a slight change in the length of the strings and wires connecting them. One might further imagine each hanging object in the mobile as being magnetic with a positive and negative pole, thus exerting attracting and repelling forces of various degrees on other hanging objects, creating dynamic movement. The line from which such a mobile would hang would pass through the higher values and the self.

We will return to this graphic analogue of the individual as we discuss the impact of increasing levels of pathological processes on the person. The concepts depicted in this figure and several related ones that follow it are numerous but simple. Take the time to try empathically to feel how a balanced life like this one is from the inside. (It may be useful to return to the sequence of figures several times while reading this book. They may also be useful visual aids in educating patients and their families.)

Our healthy individual, in managing the life space to meet his or her needs, has a good chance of beginning to achieve what Maslow called *self-actualization*. Maslow explained human development as a movement from basic need fulfillment (motivation) to the pursuit of higher needs (metamotivation). His view of needs is hierarchical in the conceptual and social senses. Conceptually, the achievement of functioning based on higher needs and values is dependent on achieving those lower on the pyramid. Figure 1–2 shows this stepwise relationship between need achievement and self-actualization as a pyramid, where each level rests on the achievement of lower levels of need-related functioning.

Society has often been compared to a pyramid. From the standpoint of need achievement, only a minority of individuals, at the pinnacle of the social pyramid, are able to spend their energies and resources in pursuit of higher goals and values. Most of humanity throughout history has been primarily engaged in meeting basic needs, or what Maslow called *D-needs*, or deficiency needs. Individuals at this level of functioning invest most of their energies in tension reduction, relieving frustration, and avoiding deficiency or pain. In doing this they are highly motivated, pushed, or driven. The ultimate goal of mental health systems should be to turn this social hierarchy on end so that most individuals are able to strive for what Maslow called the *B-values*, or being values. As opposed to survival and self-maintenance, these people would be engaged in self-actualization, which is self-directed and highly individualized. It reverses the direction of motivation, that is, the person will increase tension or stress, often frustrating lower needs, to approach an individual vision or goal (metamotivation).

Along the vertical dimension of the needs hierarchy, one might trace a spectrum of freedom/unfreedom (see Table 1–1).

When a person's need-functioning is optimal, that is, in the self-actualizing arena, the person experiences him- or herself as a prime mover, a source of power, the fountainhead of events in his or her own life. The individual has many high quality, complete objects in his or her world and is fairly well balanced between other persons, useful and valued objects, ideas, and higher ideals. A balance is

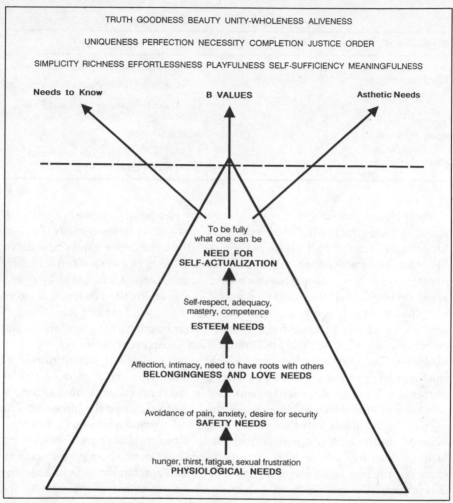

TRUTH GOODNESS BEAUTY UNITY-WHOLENESS ALIVENESS

UNIQUENESS PERFECTION NECESSITY COMPLETION JUSTICE ORDER

SIMPLICITY RICHNESS EFFORTLESSNESS PLAYFULNESS SELF-SUFFICIENCY MEANINGFULNESS

Needs to Know   **B VALUES**   **Asthetic Needs**

To be fully
what one can be
**NEED FOR
SELF-ACTUALIZATION**

Self-respect, adequacy,
mastery, competence
ESTEEM NEEDS

Affection, intimacy, need to have roots with others
BELONGINGNESS AND LOVE NEEDS

Avoidance of pain, anxiety, desire for security
SAFETY NEEDS

hunger, thirst, fatigue, sexual frustration
PHYSIOLOGICAL NEEDS

Figure 1-2. Maslow's need hierarchy.

struck between continuity and change in the organization of the life space, resulting in a fluid order. Such individuals experience both freedom and liberty. They experience freedom in that they have the internal ability to separate themselves to a certain degree from immediate environmental contingency (from the demands of the moment or of persons and situations), thus being able to make choices based on the integrity of their own values. They experience liberty in that they have in mind a virtually limitless number of environmental options that they have the capacity either to act on immediately, or for which they can create life space for future action. To return to our mobile representing the healthy life space, the self can act or be acted on anywhere in the life space, there is ample room for movement, and the position of the objects may move or shift somewhat, as directed by the self.

Table 1–1. Experience of Freedom/Unfreedom

Experience of Self	Constraints on Freedom
Being a prime mover: rich in objects, fluid order	Freedom limited only by higher values
	Freedom limited by law and social constraint
	Constraint by character limits and flaws
Being acted upon: few objects, or objects in disorder	Stuckness
	Unfreedom: life determined by internal drives and external forces

Pathological processes such as addiction or mental illness quickly result in lowering the level of needs that an individual can typically strive to satisfy. As need functioning decreases to the basic or deficiency level, the person experiences his or her self as being acted upon, a victim or pawn. Objects become fewer in number, poorer in quality, and there is less of a balance among persons and things. Ideas and ideals become either absent or irrelevant. The order in the life space is either atrophied and rigid, or overly fragile and easily disrupted. Freedom is quickly lost to undermined values and the habit of immediately reacting to or manipulating the current environment for rapid need gratification. Liberty may, ironically, appear to increase at first, due to the loss of prohibitions and inhibitions, but ultimately, at the lower levels of needs-related functioning, no liberty exists. *Stuckness* connotes the sense of being caught, mired down — as if in mud or quicksand — that accompanies the loss of freedom and liberty and the loss of balance in the life space. The parts of the mobile are losing magnetic charge, and no wind is stirring in the room. When a person's sense of agency is stuck, order is perceived as oppressive, allowing little space for free will, or, as the existentialists have pointed out, order is felt to have no inherent sense but is felt to be "thrown" or randomly (and unjustly) determined. The goal of both substance abuse treatment and treatment for psychopathology is to help individuals to move toward higher levels of the experience of freedom and to establish or re-establish balance and fluid change in the life space. This process is called *recovery* and is experienced as a movement up the hierarchy in Table 1–1. Movement down this hierarchy is the experience of the process of relapse.

The Psychiatric Severity Dimension

Let us take a closer look at the two pathological processes from which we are to help our patients to recover in dual diagnosis work and see how this phenomenological picture changes as these processes influence the life space. Table 1–2 outlines the

Table 1-2. Levels of Severity of Psychopathology

Self Experience	Severity of Psychopathology
Being a prime mover: right in objects, fluid order	Self-actualizing
	Normal
	Stress and adjustment reactions
Being acted upon: few objects, or objects in disorder	Neurotic
	Narcissistic
	Borderline
	Psychotic
	Florid psychotic

levels of severity of psychopathology ranging from low to high. These are the levels most often referred to in the psychological literature. Although psychodynamic meanings are implied, the severity dimension here is fairly useful across theoretical formulations. The different levels reflect differences in ego strength, adequacy of coping skills and mechanisms, structural level, range of behavioral freedom, and other ways of viewing optimal versus dysfunctional states and behaviors. The different categories reflect the typical psychological functioning of an individual, so that, for example, a person who is typically in the personality disordered spectrum of functioning may be psychotic for brief periods under stress, or display only mildly neurotic symptoms under pacific conditions.

At the top of the hierarchy is the high functioning individual characterized by reason, effective living, creativity and productivity, and spontaneous, modulated emotional reactions. The normal individual is usually described as being adequately adapted, free of crippling emotionality. Neurotics are not so lucky. Psychological factors often intrude on their emotional and cognitive functioning, which is typified by conflict, usually in specific sectors of living. The character-disordered individual demonstrates a pervasive pattern of impaired adjustment, deficient coping skills, and affective disruption or rigidity with usually intact reality testing and unimpaired perception. Such a person usually has a warped or severely limited interpretation of reality. The psychotic individual has lost close tracking of the external and internal environments. Behavior is usually disorganized, inappropriate, and inept. Affect is typically extreme, blunted, or inappropriate. In a florid psychosis, these psychotic traits are extreme, unremitting, and often unresponsive to medication or other intensive treatments.

When we superimpose this hierarchical dimension of increasing psychopathology over Maslow's hierarchy of needs, we find a close parallel between the level of psychopathology and the level of needs to which the individual's functioning is related. In turn, this need functioning level is parallel to the number, organization, and fluidity of relationships to objects in the person's phenomenal world, which together constitute his or her experience of freedom/determinism. As graphically represented earlier, the normal individual lives in a world of many things, persons, ideas, and ideals. The normal individual has a balanced relationship with these objects and with the self. These relationships are orderly, and the individual has a sense of spontaneity, leading to a fluidity or sense of flow among the various aspects of his or her phenomenal field. On the opposite extreme, the floridly psychotic individual's world is populated with few objects rigidly related, or with no really complete objects, but a multitude of distorted shadow objects. Such individuals have great difficulty even achieving a basic deficiency level of need-oriented functioning. We must return to similar descriptions in order to typify the most severe levels of the addictive disorders.

The Addiction Severity Dimension

Table 1–3 outlines the levels of severity of the addictive process disorders. The description, which is my integration of terms often used in the literature on substance abuse with my own experience, follows no single source or authority.

At the lowest level of severity is rational use of substances. The most obvious example is following a physician's orders for a psychotropic medication, or following a physician's or pharmacist's advice in choosing and taking over-the-counter

Table 1–3. Levels of Severity of Addictive Processes

Self Experience	Severity of Addictive Process
Being a prime mover: rich in objects, fluid order	Rational use of substances
	Controlled, appropriate use
	Insidious dependence
	One trial dependence
Being acted upon: few objects, or objects in disorder	Substance abuse
	Symptomatic dependence (Characterological dependence)
	Compulsive, accelerating addiction
	Psychotic addiction

medication. Cannabis use for glaucoma or morphine for hospice care are fairly clear examples.

The next level of severity is controlled, socially appropriate use. On this level, social and emotional factors are strongly present in the type, amount, frequency, and effects of the used substance. Obviously, local sociocultural norms determine what is appropriate to some extent. The qualifier *controlled* is added because when levels and patterns of use are within socially acceptable ranges but beyond an individual's personal control, a different pathological level has occurred. The two levels discussed so far are subpathological, but they present a context of use that may offer the opportunity for a pathological development. The threats come from three possible sources: external change, internal change, and interactions between external and internal events. External events may cause a change in the individual's physical, emotional, or social status quo. Subtle changes in these spheres may be due almost exclusively to the effects of the substance. More commonly, perhaps, synergistic effects among subtle changes in both internal and external status begin a potentiated emergent process: the addictive process.

Examples of the next level of severity, insidious dependence, are easy to find. An insidious dependence on a drug or substance develops slowly and without blatant early warning signs. The social drinker begins to have occasional party binges more than a few times a year. The cocktail to relax becomes two or three. A pathological process has been switched on that may or may not escalate. A decrease in freedom, perhaps imperceptible at first, has occurred. Dependence on caffeine and nicotine is usually held at this level. Alcohol and cocaine dependencies are less often stabilized indefinitely.

Near this level of severity is a somewhat rare form called one-trial dependence. This kind of dependence fits the age-old stereotype of the heroin addict who injects an unsuspecting victim who becomes immediately hooked for life on the first use or first trial of the drug. This popular view is more relevant to Dr. Jekyll and Mr. Hyde movies than to the typical addictive process, even for most highly addictive substances. One-trial dependence does occur, however, most often in alcoholism and is typified by a family history of alcoholism, early onset, and vivid memories of the first experience with the drug (especially the physiological and arousal level aspects of the effects) usually accompanied by an inability to experience emotion normally. (One-trial dependence often appears in the use of free-base or crack cocaine, although closer examination usually reveals that many trials of the drug occurred within several hours and days of first use, with no perception of an ego-alien addictive process at this early stage). One may hypothesize that this form of addiction has a very strong neuropsychological basis, probably related to the physiology of emotion and arousal. One-trial dependence is the pathological reverse, for example, of learning from one trial not to consume poisonous or emetic substances, and as such may be explainable by basic neuropsychological principles.

Substance abuse is placed further down on the severity scale than these forms of dependence. The rationale is that substance abuse is the lowest level of severity defined by social, personal, or other problems related to the drug. Any use of an illegal drug that may lead to arrest and loss of freedom and reputation is a form of substance abuse, at least from one point of view. Substance abuse is often a precursor to dependence, but dependence may occur with relatively few effects on the social and psychological functioning of the individual. However, in even mild dependencies a time bomb is often set ticking that may result in devastating physical and psychological effects, sometimes after a decade or more.

Symptomatic dependence is the level of severity that begins clearly to indicate a relationship with the levels of psychopathology already discussed. A dependence that is symptomatic of an individual's emotional problems, persistent conflicts, or pervasive pattern of self-defeating behaviors and thoughts is often qualitatively different from the levels of severity discussed to this point. However, chronic substance abuse is also usually symptomatic of these problems and often results in symptomatic dependence.

Individuals whose psychopathology is in the neurotic or character-disordered spectrum often demonstrate symptomatic dependence or symptomatic substance abuse. In this form of addiction, the uncontrolled, inappropriate use of substances is clearly a psychological defense against, an expression of, or an instrumental reaction to another psychopathological process. Notice that this is not often the case in insidious or one-trial dependence. Physiological factors and the psychophysiology of one-trial learning and allergic reactions are more relevant to these forms of substance dependence than are emotional and psychological factors. Examples of symptomatic dependence are often depicted in movies and novels about addicts and alcoholics who are strong characters. *The Great Santini*, Richard Pryor's *JoJo Dancer, Your Life Is Calling*, and the film *Clean and Sober* may be viewed as depicting individuals suffering from symptomatic dependence.

The difference between these two forms of dependence—symptomatic versus insidious—may be established by a history of accompanying life problems and, more importantly, by response to substance abuse treatment. Because addiction affects judgment through denial, insidious dependencies are often not initially addressed by the individual, but when they are challenged in treatment, the treatment progresses with relatively few obstacles. This is not true with symptomatic dependence; emotional factors independent of withdrawal, deconditioning, and relearning are constant obstacles to sobriety and continued progress. The urge to use the drug of choice does not follow simple, easily identified environmental, physiological, or even emotional cues. The patient's problems involve two related pathological processes. Using a film example noted above, the female character in *Clean and Sober* has an addiction that is more clearly symptomatic than that of the male character, who responds to treatment and begins to show recovery in social and personal functioning. The female character conforms only temporarily to the demands of the residential treatment setting, but upon discharge returns to her previous lifestyle, where emotional and interpersonal stress are managed through drug use.

Symptomatic dependence is the only category in this typology that by definition is a kind of dual diagnosis problem. Other kinds of addiction, including the two more severe forms discussed below, may not be the result of interactive pathological processes. The term *characterological dependence* might also be considered for what is here called symptomatic dependence. However, symptomatic dependence is preferred because although it usually involves long-standing, personality-based problems in an addictive process, personality disorders are not always present when an addictive process is related to a symptom or symptom cluster. Dependence may be the result of a more isolated symptomatic process such as reactive or endogenous depression, anxiety, or poorly suppressed anger due to adjustment reactions, or other emotional and behavioral patterns. These symptoms or symptom clusters are not necessarily organizing or disorganizing *principles*, or self-reinforcing pathological processes, as is always the case in personality disorders. Of course, although these more isolated symptoms may point to structural weakness in a personality, they do not in themselves constitute a pathological process in the personality. A later chapter addresses in depth the role of personality or character disorders in dual diagnosis problems.

Once dependence is established, its slope or acceleration is an important factor to consider. The levels of severity discussed to this point may be remarkably stable over many years. There may be a plateau of symptoms, dosage, and frequency of use. Personal impairment may be stable or may show a gradual, steady, predictable decline. To the nonclinical observer, disruption is apt to be noticeable only in selected areas of the individual's life. In a compulsive, accelerating addiction, the pattern is one of steep increasing decline, a rolling snowball gathering momentum. This may occur after only a brief period of substance use, such as in the case of one-trial dependence on free-base crack cocaine. Such an addictive course may have only a very brief stable period before converting into a rapidly escalating picture. The term *compulsive* reflects this level of an addiction's similarities with the compulsive disorders: the rigidity, absence of freedom, and the counterintentionality of behavior that typifies the compulsions. Needless to say, this level of severity is also accompanied by an obsessive preoccupation with the drug.

The term *addiction* indicates the most severe levels of substance use because of its connotations of loss of control and freedom and its associations with disease, evil, or the demonic, meanings that point to the radical isolation from or disruption of the self that occurs in addiction. Unlike the less severe levels of dependence, with addiction, no aspect of the person's life space is left fully intact. A compulsive, accelerating addiction may grow out of any of the other levels of severity due to an externally or internally based change in the person's life adjustment. It may be seen as the acceleration phase of the other types of addiction. Compulsive, accelerating addictions cause mental health problems but are not necessarily the result of them.

Special sensitivity to the drug, constitutional predisposition to addictive processes, or harrowing sociocultural conditions (as seen, for example, in the native American alcoholic) may result in this level of severity without an accompanying level of severe and pervasive psychopathology. Individuals who are typically normal in their psychological functioning do acquire addictions in this compulsive, accelerating range. However, now that our culture is more open to obtaining help and less moralistic about addictions, persons with lower levels of psychopathology may be less apt to allow this pattern to continue uninterrupted without seeking treatment.

If left to continue on this accelerating course, a person may develop what may be called a psychotic addiction. Reality testing, not simply judgments about reality, are grossly distorted. All thinking and emotion are in the service of the addictive process, to the extent that they are not disrupted by the effects of the drug itself. The best example of psychotic addiction is the cocaine addict who continually picks lint from carpets, upholstery, or garments, thinking that these light-colored specks are particles of the drug of choice. The same individual may dream only of drug use episodes. He or she may break down in tears following moments of great excitement and joy after viewing a news report about the confiscation of several tons of the drug in a warehouse as though this event was a great personal find followed by a great personal loss. Also, this individual might become more aroused about using from a bag from which another addict has just overdosed in front of him, thinking that it is "great stuff" and that his "friend" is no longer a competitor for the drug. This extreme distortion of cognition, affect, behavior, and values may be equitably described as psychotic.

This condition does not most often occur with individuals whose typical psychological functioning is psychotic. Individuals suffering from psychotic levels of psychopathology usually do not have the financial resources to maintain this level of drug use, or the interpersonal skills needed to conduct the complex social exchanges required to accelerate to this level. This addiction level is more common in severe character disorders than with normal or neurotic individuals.

In discussing levels of severity in the addictive process, drugs of choice are treated here as equivalent. But, this is only partially true. As noted, some drugs are more apt to lead to certain levels of addictive severity. Some drugs cannot be used in a rational or controlled, appropriate manner. PCP is the best example. Since its cumulative effects are unpredictable and the desired individual dosage and short-term effects are indeterminable, there can be no rational use of PCP. It could be argued that this is true of all hallucinogens.

Another aspect of the nonequivalence of drug of choice has to do with long-term physiological and neurological effects, which differ from drug to drug. Typical courses have been established for various addictions, especially alcoholism (Jellinek 1963). We will return to differences in the effects of drug of choice and some possible reasons why individuals choose different drugs in our later discussion of assessment, treatment, and the personality disorders.

Parallels in Experience and Needs Motivation

When we mentally superimpose this hierarchical dimension of increasing severity of addictive process over Maslow's hierarchy of needs, we find (as we did for psychopathology) a rough parallel between the level of addiction and the level of needs-related functioning. Again, we see the decline in freedom, the increase in being determined and driven, as severity increases. With each level, the number and quality of objects, their orderliness, and the balance between fluidity and rigidity in their interrelations are increasing disrupted. Figures 1–3, 1–4, and 1–5 depict common outcomes of both pathological processes.

They also represent experiential or phenomenological states, or ways of viewing the self from the inside, which often recur cyclically in both the addictive and psychopathology processes. The titles of each of these figures have two adjectives that describe the sense of self from the inside. The first adjective is the *less severe* form of the experience, the second is the *more severe*. The depleted (depressed or debased) self, the inflated (or grandiose) self, and the detached (or schizoid) self are both pathological endpoints and phase components in a pathological process over time. We describe them in the order in which they usually occur in the addictive process, which is somewhat more predictable than for increasing severity levels of psychopathology.

Although these processes and experiences of the self are described in a certain

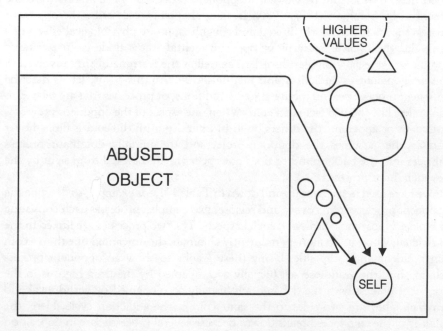

Figure 1–3. Depressed/depleted self.

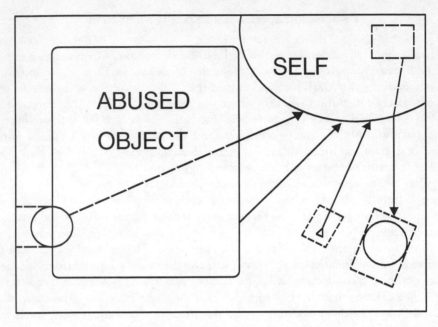

Figure 1–4. Inflated/grandiose self.

order here, they should be viewed as opponent processes in the manner of those described by Solomon (1977, 1980). In later chapters we describe the opponent process theory to discuss the linked and roughly opposite physiological effects of a drug and the cyclical patterns of opposite mental status findings in psychotic conditions (especially bipolar disorder), as well as the learning history involved in the development of addiction and mental illness. At this point, let us describe opponent processes as interactive states, conditions, or processes that are related to each other like the two faces of a coin. When one aspect of the opponent process is dominant or apparent, the others build in intensity until the coin is flipped over and another assumes the dominant role, and the initially dominant process subsides into the background or does not appear at all, blocked from sight by the new dominant process.

We have used movement up and down in Table 1–1, for example, to describe the opponent processes of recovery and relapse, two complex processes each consisting of biological, psychological, and social aspects. The two processes are linked in the individual, who can no more permanently eliminate the unwanted one than a coin can avoid having a flip side. Using these graphs to show an opponent process relationship, the grandiose self (usually accompanied by the drug high) is in the opponent process with the debased self (usually accompanied by withdrawal and craving). They are two sides to the same coin of the addiction cycle. Here, the analogy of the coin faces breaks down, because several processes are in opposition to one another simultaneously in the same individual, much as the six sides of a die are opposed to one another in coming up on each throw.

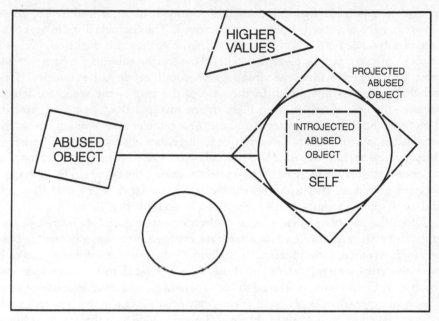

Figure 1-5. Detached/schizoid self.

In addictive processes where other pathological factors are only mildly present these opponent ways of viewing and feeling about the self may be experienced in a rough causal sequence. The usual pattern is for a healthy self first to become depleted or depressed. (This depletion process may be the result of recurrent drug abuse or the long-term effects of an insidious addiction.) In this experience (Figure 1-3), the self is pushed out of the life space by other objects, especially the drug of choice. There is less available space for motion, and fewer well-developed objects are in mutual interaction with the self. In Figure 1-3, the self is smaller in size and being acted on by other objects. The shadow of a sense of higher values is depicted as no longer effective in centering the self.

The depleted individual turns to the artificial defense of the drug of choice to avoid, interrupt, or obscure this process. The drug use results in a chemical bolstering of the self, and an inflated sense of self is established. In this experience, depicted in Figure 1-4, the self is primary, although not centered in the space, which may become occupied almost as much as the abused object as by the self. Others are either pushed out of the life space or are perceived as a means to obtaining the drug. The bolstering aspect of the abused object eventually becomes an internalized aspect of the self. This is both partially caused by and has later implications for the object relations (in the psychodynamic sense) and later object choices of the individual.

When the drug's physiological opponent process becomes dominant (creating the opposite effect to why the drug is sought) or when the chemical defense fails for some other reason, the self is left debased. This is not only experiential debasement or depletion but adaptive skills, stability of mood, physical health, and social networks have also been depleted or destroyed. The individual again seeks the abused substance both out of need for a defense against this depletion, and as a result of physiological or psychological craving for the substance that is, for the most part, separate from the drug's psychosocial or defensive function. The inflating process is intensified. In the case of the manic, the grandiose schizophrenic, the user of uppers when high, or the manipulative addict or character-disordered individual in a victorious phase, or a gambler on a winning streak, the self has become inflated and overextended, and balance is totally lost. There may be many objects, but they have lost normal object value because of the absence of order or a reasonable sense of relative priority among the objects. The individual becomes grandiose, that is, an unrealistic sense of victory over external threats and/or dysphoric feelings or self-perceptions is established.

Often the pathological experience of detachment (Figure 1–5) is an aspect of grandiosity but just as often it is a separate experience or component that is an opponent to others in the process. The individual separates him- or herself radically from the environment, except for those aspects related to the substance and securing it. Emotional indifference to life experiences, and even detachment from one's own experience – depersonalization – may occur. At times this is a predictable experiential effect of the drug of choice and may provide a motive for preferring it over other substances of abuse. As the addictive cycle repeats, the individual becomes further detached from reality until there is a breakdown in the ability to function, or until the individual is motivated to enter treatment by severe losses or threats of loss. At the worst stage of detachment, the hang wire of our mobile has been severed; the person has become literally debased, that is, the ground or basis for the self to grow and manage the life space has been undermined to the point of collapse.

Of course, the scenarios presented here greatly simplify this single causal path in the addictive process, which in most cases is the result of several causal lines intersecting and interacting, as in all the movements and eventual placements of the faces of two dice tossed in the air and coming up seven. Although the situation is even more complex for the experiential and causal sequences in mental illnesses, nonetheless, similar vicious cycles are clearly present. In Figures 1–3, 1–4, and 1–5, it is easy to recognize experience of the self in the major mental disorders of depression, mania, and schizophrenia. In each of these disorders, an individual resorts to less effective behaviors or less developed levels of psychological functioning in response to perceived threats until the self has become depleted, depressed, grandiose, or detached. Inflation, deflation, and detachment are decompensating processes of both addiction and mental illnesses.

These schematic concepts have been forged in the context of understanding dual diagnosis disorders, that is, treatment failures with severe psychopathology and addiction. For a similar scenario of self experiences that explains normal experience though the dialectical interaction of experience modes, the reader is referred to Ogden's (1989) description of the depressive, paranoid–schizoid, and autistic–contiguous positions as the basis for personality functioning. Ogden builds on the work of both Klein and Bion in his formulation of self states or modes. Klein had identified the paranoid–schizoid and depressive positions as phenomenologically distinct states, which, although tied to developmental stages, continue to exist as two different ways of relating to inner and outer reality throughout the lifespan (Klein 1952, Segal and Bell 1991). Klein viewed the more primitive paranoid–schizoid mode dominant only under stress-induced regression in normal adults. Ogden added a third state or position (the autistic–contiguous mode) to that scenario, to be discussed later at greater length in reference to the schizoid personality and the detached/schizoid position. Although this writer was unaware of Ogden's scenario while developing the addictive cycle positions, a good deal of similarity appears in the two theoretical constructions. Such serendipity does not necessarily indicate validity for the constructs, but it does suggest that both schematic systems reflect a relatively high degree of correspondence to clinical experience with primitive states and also suggests a general coherence of each system within the currently accepted paradigms of psychodynamic understanding and treatment.

A DEVELOPMENTAL VIEW

The experience of the self has so far been examined in its adult manifestation during addiction. The roots of these experiences, however, are in infancy before the development of speech. Wilson and colleagues (1989) have proposed failures in self-regulation as central to what they call the addictive self. These failures have their origin in preverbal experience that is incorporated into the adult person as a preverbal core self. In their view, misattuned caregiver–infant dyads produce the troublesome experiences of self that are later replicated by the addict through use of the drug and for which the drug is a home remedy. As in the model presented by Wilson and co-workers (1989), the life space figures presented here assume that addicts fall less into clear types—for example, the threefold typology by Adams (1978) of addictions based on symbiotic urges, management of rage, and failing self-cohesion—than into cyclical or related experiences of self that are expressed in the addiction. The reader familiar with dynamic views of the self, or the developmental psychology of the self, should view the presented figures as basic pathogenic positions in infant experience, as well as adult manifestations of the self under conditions of addiction. For the depressed self, the drug helps to unify experience after separation from the caregiver. In the grandiose self, the drug pacifies a globalized sense of threatened bewilderment related to traumatic overstimulation of the infant. For the schizoid self, the drug supports denial of interpersonal dependency related to failed attachment and repressed rage. The individual addict will emphasize one of these aspects of self over others, based on the predominant pathological position in the mixture of the addict's early parent–infant experiences. This will have important implications for the course of the addict's illness, its persistence during treatment, and the drug or drugs of choice.

Only the parallels to developmental Self psychology for the most extreme experiences of self are outlined here. For later developmental periods, the experiences may appear similar to the milder pathological views of self portrayed here and may have periodic or helixical relationships to the expression of more primitive infant experience. For example, the grandiose self may be seen in an addict's attempt to manage higher-level oedipal anxieties, that is, as an expression of power–powerlessness in response to disillusionment and defeat from an uncompromising, controlling parent.

Placing the two pathological processes on parallel scales in one table, as in Table 1–4, and keeping Maslow's hierarchy in mind as a contextual backdrop, we can mentally draw the lines across from typical level of psychopathology to typical level of addictive process, with the threatened need being the rough link between the

Table 1–4. Combined Levels of Severity and Maslow's Hierarchy

Psychopathology	Threatened Need	Addiction
Self actualizing	B-values	Rational use
		Controlled appropriate use
	Self-actualization	
Normal		Insidious dependence
	Efficacy	
		One trial dependence
Neurotic		
	Self esteem	Symptomatic dependence (Characterological dependence)
Narcissistic		
	Belonging	
		Compulsive, accelerating addiction
Borderline	Identity	
	Emotional regulation	
Psychotic		
	Safety needs	
Florid psychotic		Psychotic addiction
	Physiological needs	
———————————————————— General failure of life supports ————————————————————		

two processes. The lines are not drawn in on the table, however, to remind us that these relationships are only probable or suggestive and that many exceptions are apt to occur, such as the normal individual who gets caught in a chronic, compulsive, accelerating addictive pattern. Having the two processes on one table suggests that there are parallel effects from similar levels of severity on these two dimensions, that the two processes move toward common experiential and clinical endpoints, and that they have similar process components. The table also implies the possibility of interaction, reciprocity, or synergism that is really the key concept in dual diagnosis work. We have seen that at least one type of addiction—symptomatic addiction—must presuppose a related psychopathological condition or process.

WHY THE CHICKEN-OR-EGG-FIRST QUESTION IS ABSURD

One exciting aspect of the dual diagnosis problem is its ability to bring up some crucial theoretical dilemmas and controversies in new, practical, and important ways. For example, dual diagnosis issues have sparked the call for a substance abuse axis as part of the DSM diagnostic system and for officially recognized primary–secondary distinctions in dual diagnosis cases. These are both practical expressions of the chicken-or-egg-first discussion that is sometimes introduced in dual diagnosis problems. The question goes: Did the substance use cause the psychosis or depression, or did the psychopathology lead to the addiction? Such questions often seem academic, but the related question of what is the proper primary and secondary diagnosis has significant practical implications for treatment, administration, research, and reimbursement, as well as for theory construction. Some of the habits of thought that go unexamined and become codified in our diagnostic systems, and from there influence case formulation and treatment to the detriment of some cases, are brought to the light of closer examination by seminal problems and recurrent failures such as those found in the dual diagnosis patient group. In the language of Thomas Kuhn (1970), the dual diagnosis problem is useful because it challenges some aspects of our current paradigm of diagnosis, nosology, and etiology.

BIASES IN REASONING

The absurdity and humor in the chicken-or-egg first question come from its ability to point out the limitations inherent in demonstrative reasoning. This mode of thought, as useful as it may be, has led to many of the conceptual dead ends in dual diagnosis work. Demonstrative reasoning has been the dominant mode of thought in Western evidence and argument since Aristotle. Demonstrative thinking is based on premises that are assumed to be true. Their opposites are, therefore, necessarily false. In order to arrive at logical truth through demonstrative reasoning, all of one's premises must be true. Even when this is the case, logical truth may not jibe with reality. As Hegel put it, "The tree of life is greener than the tree of thought."

In the chicken-or-egg-first dilemma, one of the major premises, common to many attempts at demonstrative reasoning, is, in fact, a fallacy. The premise is that what comes first in a line of actions causes the subsequent elements on the line. The first form of the question assumes that temporal priority can determine causal priority and sequence, or, put simply, if the chicken was here first, it laid (caused) the egg, or if the egg was here first, it hatched (caused) the chicken. The tack-on assumption is one of value; the earlier cause takes priority, is more important, and presents the first term in a critical path that flows sequentially. This premise and its tacked-on value can easily be called into question, but that will not be necessary for the purposes of discussing theory building in dual diagnosis problems.

The second major premise in the chicken-or-egg-first question has proved more problematic for thinking about the problems at hand in this discussion, and it is a premise that is essential to demonstrative reasoning per se. The premise is that major categories are discrete and mutually exclusive. A chicken cannot be an egg and an egg cannot be a chicken when we attempt to reason demonstratively about chickens and eggs in a system of causality. Since we are aware that every chicken is in a sense an egg at an end point of development and every egg is a chicken at a starting point of development (and that we can view either alternatively as either end point or starting point), questions of causality in the sense of priority become absurd. Instead of straining at the logical absurdity in which we would be cornered if we had to live with exclusive discrete categories, we can concentrate on the biological process called reproduction (or at a higher level, emergent evolutionism), which defines the developmental relationship between chickens and eggs.

Demonstrative reasoning is preferred for thinking about problems where a small number of premises may be determined to be either clearly true or false and where categories are clearly established. It is at its best in situations where the categories of interest may be considered fixed, discrete, and relatively unchanging, and where all members of a category share the same defining features, that is, situations that meet the requirements of monothetic categorization. Recent revisions in the substance use disorders and personality disorders nosologies presented in the DSM III-R demonstrate a movement away from this kind of categorization. The new approach is toward dimensional models that place cases on a continuum or range of severity, and toward polythetic models of categorization, where no single feature or index is required for inclusion in a category. In polythetic models, categorization is accomplished by determining the overall goodness of fit of a case to a prototype description (Cantor et al. 1980). The approach advanced in this book combines dimensional and polythetic–prototypic methods.

Dialectical Thinking: A Corrective Alternative

The kind of thought that is designed to examine causality within process develop-ment (where categories are not exclusive or discrete) is called dialectical reasoning. It allows us to see many aspects of the dual diagnosis conundrum as aspects of both pathologies; it allows us to see both pathologies as mutually causal of each other and creating mutual effects in the form of what Bandura (1978) has called reciprocal determinism. From a dialectical point of view, once the dual diagnosis syndrome has emerged, each symptom is part of both processes, although it may be viewed in any given clinical formulation from the alternative perspective of one process or the other.

Another strength of the dialectical way of thinking is that it accounts for the phenomena of emergence. In demonstrative reasoning, a thing cannot be and not be at the same time. If it exists, it cannot be in two discrete, mutually exclusive categories. Dialectical reasoning allows for events and dynamics to be viewed as becoming or emerging. Events and dynamics can be latent, tending toward being in one category or the other, but in neither or both, depending on the emphasis given by the thinker based on the work at hand at the time an idea is struck. For the reader familiar with this century's developments in the world view stemming from modern physics, dialectical thinking will appear as nothing new, although it may not have been considered as applying to the dual diagnosis problem. It should be noted that theory constructed from either mode of thought must be operationa-lized to have scientific meaning and must be at least in part amenable to empirical tests. Such tests must result in modifications to the theory, and possibly to total rejection of the theory itself.

The interested reader should view Rychlak's (1981b) careful analysis of some of the philosophical issues that influence psychological theory building. Also, Sabelli and Carlson-Sabelli (1989) offer an integrated approach to psychiatry based on a elaboration of dialectical thought that they refer to as process theory. They follow Jung in emphasizing the union of opposites in dialectical change, but they add the general systems theory approach to levels of organization or description by stressing the flow of information from one level of organization to another.

For the current discussion, the point to be made is that cognitive biases related to exclusive reliance on demonstrative reasoning about dual diagnosis problems have influenced how these patients were dealt with clinically, and explain, in part, why theory construction in this area has been so slow getting off the ground. Effort was wasted on deciding whether patients were primarily addicts or primarily mentally ill, reflecting a need for discrete mutually exclusive categories and failing that, attempting to create a neat linear causal line of priority between the two disorders. Now we recognize that for a large group of patients, both disorders are primary, both are mutually causative. Effort had been spent on the order in which the two processes developed to determine treatment priority and etiology, when often both processes emerge from the same biological, psychological, and social vulnerabilities.

Perhaps the best reason for discussing these philosophical issues is that the prior equals primary fallacy has influenced treatment strategies in dual diagnosis work. In early dual diagnosis programs, patients in this population were treated in logical sequences, in part determined by the urgency criteria established by the management demands such patients place on a treatment setting. Patients first were detoxed chemically in a controlled environment, with the expectation that they would turn into normal mental patients. Then they were treated chemically for psychopathology or given psychotherapy. This consecutive or sequential strategy did not work after the acute phase of treatment, because of the interactive–emergent nature of the dual diagnosis problem.

The current dominant treatment strategy is more enlightened since the diagnostic problem has been partially resolved. Psychotic or severely depressed patients are now provided substance abuse interventions after brief detoxification and medication of the most severe psychotic symptoms in a simultaneous strategy. It is as though their two diagnoses were being treated separately but at the same time in the same person. This may at first appear to be an exaggeration of current practice and the criticism of it as a straw man, but the examination of a few treatment plans for the dually diagnosed will reveal this kind of strategy in spades. Addiction-related problems and mental health-related problems are listed separately with sensible, internally coherent interventions aimed at each. Such plans may be comprehensive and built on solid assessments. When all the various players are competent and well trained and communicating optimally, a level of integration of these interventions may approach the kind of reciprocal strategy advanced here. Minkoff (1989), for example, refers to the parallel treatment of the two disorders and parallel recovery processes.

The approach to treatment strategy suggested here and explored later in this book is described as reciprocal treatment for substance abuse and psychiatric disorders. It involves a concerted effort to determine the degree of interaction or reciprocal causality of the two pathological processes, the points of reciprocal origin and reciprocal current effects of the processes, as well as the relative extremity of the two processes on the other key dimensions outlined above. With this information, intervention plans aimed at both utilizing and decreasing the reciprocal interactions are constructed. The two disordering processes are both untangled and resolved simultaneously. The recovery process for one disordering process is used reciprocally to reinforce the other recovery process and to undermine and depotentiate the other pathological process.

Reciprocity as a Key Dimension in Dual Diagnosis Work

At this point, let us take a closer look at the kind of relationships that can exist between the two disorders of interest. Table 1–5 outlines the relatedness of the two

Table 1-5. The Relatedness Dimension

Degree of Relationship Addiction	Qualities of Effects/Causes
Co-existence	Cumulative impact of effects
Interacting effects	Additive impact of effects
Linear mediation	Catalytic relationships
	Geometric increase in effects
Linear causal paths	
	Shift in thresholds needed for change in quality
Reciprocal mediation	
	Potentiation of effects
	Complementarity
Reciprocal causal paths	
	Emergent qualities
	Synergism
	Cyclicity
Reciprocal reinforcement with reciprocal causal paths	
	Opponent process relationships
Dynamic unity	Union of opposites
	Synthesis
	Stable, self-replicating helix

pathological processes as a severity dimension in dual diagnosis cases. At the lowest level of relatedness, the two disorders are merely coexistent, presumably noninteractive. The fact that the two disorders are present only serves to give the individual more problems with which to deal. At the next level, the disorders are interactive, but do not spring from a common or related cause. The disorders are more closely related when causally linked in a linear manner (one causes or mediates the other, but not vice versa), or when their influences are additive or geometric in the same direction toward increasing pathology and life problems. At this interactive level, we are more interested in potentiating or catalytic interactions because they result in the most virulent cases; however, inhibiting, moderating, and depotentiating interactions also routinely occur.

When causal paths from origins to effects cannot be clearly separated for the two pathological processes, they are reciprocal in nature, and, again, it is, of course, the reciprocally reinforcing processes that become our focus. In fact, the syndromes

discussed in this book could be classified as one set in a class of emergent or synergistic disorders that are typified by potentiating interactions among established
disordering processes. If one takes the easily supported position that most psychiatric
disorders are primarily due to these synergisms, then the most appropriate class in
which to place the disorders might be that of second order psychiatric synergisms.

One way to make the synergism between two processes more tangible is to
return to the analogy of the throw of two dice in gambling games and examine some
trivia about how dice are constructed and played. We have stated that the two
processes are in a sense opponent or alternative processes within the same individual. As with a die or a coin, the alternative sides or processes are not necessarily
logical opposites. The numbers on opposing sides of a die are not logical opposites,
but they are logically linked, they always sum to a total of seven. When two dice are
thrown together, they are so constructed that when seven has been thrown, the
side facing down of each die is the value of the face that is up on the other die. In
relation to the number seven, the upper faces of the dice are in exact complementarity to the lower faces that are not shown. This bit of trivia provides an analogous
route to appreciating opponents, opposites, complementarity, and logical connectedness in interaction of the kind encountered in the relationship among processes
discussed in this book. One might further capture the destructive process of
addictive and psychopathological vicious cycles together by imagining each cycle of
drug use and decompensation as a throw of two dice. When the number seven is
thrown, a certain combination, the potentiating effects of the two illnesses, creates
a win for illness and a big loss for the individual. In these situations, decompensation is much more severe, more persistent, and the cycle itself is exponentially
ingrained. This process is called potentiation, or synergism. The process can most
clearly be seen when two drugs interact in the same individual, having a stronger
impact than the additive effects of either one alone; in effect, one plus one equals
more than two. The dice become increasingly loaded in favor of a loss for the
person and an increase in the pathological process.

The analogy to a game of chance, a gambler's game, is more than germane to the
issues here. Gambling is addictive in part because of the opponent processes related
to winning and losing, and to the illusion of control or predictability involved in
games of chance. Both of these factors have impacts on the perception and
experience of self that result in an addictive process and relapses from recovery. The
disorders discussed in this book have been termed reciprocally reinforcing psychiatric substance abuse syndromes. In the term *reciprocally reinforcing*, reinforcing
means both additive in effects as well as denoting the wearing the groove process
that the term has in behavioral theory, that is, both processes make behaviors
related to the other process more likely to occur and to occur with greater intensity.
Finally at the most extreme end of the continuum of relatedness, the disorders
become a synthetic unity or negative synergism, a closely tied vicious knot. This is
not the usual outcome of increasingly interrelated pathological processes. This is
because, as we have seen, at various severity levels on either pathological process,

the individual bottoms out, becoming incapable of maintaining the required behaviors to continue an addiction beyond a certain level of severity. Beyond this level, they are likely to suffer a collapse of the self into chaotic behavior and experience and to reenter the health care delivery system in a way that usually restricts their personal liberty. A prolonged synthesis of these two disorders that is allowed to go uninterrupted would probably be terminated by death due to somatic pathology related to drug use, drug overdose, severe withdrawal, severe neglect of self-maintenance behaviors, suicide, or provoked homicide. As in most opponent processes or oppositions, the most intense forms of the processes are incompatible, whereas the mild to moderate forms exist together in helixical stable states.

SYNDROME DEFINITIONS AND SUBPOPULATIONS

Let us return to our attempt to clarify the terms used throughout this book. We outline broad categories of dual diagnosis work. In addition, a tentative typology of dual diagnosis cases is presented. The supportive evidence for this typology is provided in later chapters, but enough of the required conceptual elements have already been covered to allow a preview in the form of a general typology.

DEFINING CATEGORIES OF DUAL DIAGNOSIS WORK

Programs or approaches to mental health or substance abuse that tend to avoid working with the other set of problems may be called single focus programs, or approaches. Not all approaches with a dual focus will be called dual diagnosis work, that implies at the least an integrated approach. Single focus and dual focus approaches are effective and most cost effective for many, perhaps most, patients. However, this book primarily focuses on patients who are usually treatment failures without highly integrated, reciprocal approaches, approaches which can profitably inform treatment with less extreme cases in single focus or dual focus programs, but may not be required for their effective treatment.

The term *dual diagnosis work* is broad enough to include the categories of treatment that follow. Within the confines of this book, the term refers to the integrated, reciprocally focused assessment, treatment, or management of patients who have a level of severity on the psychopathology dimension of character disorder or higher, as well as a level of severity on the addiction severity dimension of substance abuse or higher. The term is limited to these cases, primarily because all substance abuse treatment approaches are prepared to deal with the psychological and emotional problems of normal and mildly neurotic individuals. Acknowledging this by way of practice, mental health workers will typically refer normal or mildly neurotic individuals with substance abuse or higher levels of severity of addictive disorders to an addictions professional. At levels of psychiatric severity below the character disordered individual, simultaneous treatment of the individual by two treatment approaches is often effective, even without the coordinated, integrated, reciprocal approach offered here.

Almost in contradiction to the distinction stated above, however, we include in the category of dual diagnosis work the treatment of individuals who have some focal psychological or emotional problem that is not typical of their normal functioning, but that has in effect lowered their typical level of functioning temporarily to a level more common to disturbed individuals. Although patients with one or a few focal problems are usually dealt with successfully in many single focus or dual focus approaches, they may be helped more effectively and in less time by using dual diagnosis strategies. Like their deficits, the dual diagnosis work to be done with these patients is focal and relatively time limited. Table 1–6 outlines the categories of dual diagnosis work with respective sub-populations.

Table 1–6. Categories of Dual Diagnosis Work

	Major Symptom Clusters		
	Anxiety Arousal/Reward	Cognition and Context Dominance of Affect	Cognition and Context Sociability and Identity
N E U R O T I C	Stress-Related Problems	Anxiety Disorders	Socio-Cultural Problems
	Sexual Problems	Reactive Depression	Pathogenic Beliefs
	Schizoid Personality	Dysthymia	Dependent Personality
C H A R A C T E R D I S O R D E R E D	Psychopathic Personality	Depressive Personality	Obsessive Compulsive Personality
	Organic Personality (Sensation Seeking)	Histrionic Personality Passive Aggressive Personality	Narcissistic Personality
			Avoidant Personality Paranoid Personality
		Borderline Personality	
P S Y C H O T I C	Schizophrenia (Negative Signs)	Organic Personality (Affective Features)	Organic Personality (Cognitive Disruption or Paranoia) Schizophrenia (Positive Signs)
		Major Depression (Psychotic Features)	Paranoid Disorder Paranoid Schizophrenia
		Bipolar Disorder	

Symptomatic and Characterological Dependence Work

Working with individuals who show either a clear symptomatic relationship between an isolated emotional or psychological concern and a substance use problem (e.g., a brief reactive depression complicating treatment for alcohol binges) can be called symptomatic dependence work, or symptomatic substance abuse work. Symptomatic dependence work is based on an understanding of how the individual's use of substances is related to his or her focal problem or symptom.

The Greek root of the word *character* means to inscribe, as in engraving or carving. It connotes both depth and the signification of unique meaning to a written mark. Characterological problems are more deeply ingrained than isolated focal problems. When characterological problems, or character defects, are more pervasive, are incorporated in the personality, and intertwined in its organization (resulting in narrow, rigid, or invariant ways of viewing, judging, and acting), a personality disorder is present. Usually, distortions in the interpretation of life events and the demonstration of poor judgment surrounding such events have resulted in an accumulation of lost opportunities, undeveloped skills, and self-defeating routines. In addition, these cases have been resistant to routine methods of substance abuse treatment. Characterological dependence work is based on understanding the relationship between the substance abuse or dependence and the focal psychiatric problems and character deficits of that individual. The pathological experiences of the self and their developmental precursors described earlier in this chapter are of special relevance in this kind of work, because the self is essentially impaired and will fuel the addictive cycle more than in other cases where the core self is relatively intact. Obviously, more severe personality disorders and addictive problems will require more intense, longer term interventions. As with the categories of work to follow, the cases that demonstrate a high degree of reciprocity between the two pathological disorders will require the most intensity and length and will require a more reciprocal focus in the treatment.

Dual Diagnosis Work with the Major Mental Disorders

Several major mental disorders may result in psychotic levels of functioning. The most common of these major mental disorders are the schizophrenias, the paranoid disorders, and the major affective disorders, which include bipolar disorder and major depression. (Individuals with a single episode of major depression may be clinically distinct from those with recurrent episodes. These individuals may also not fit the treatment failure context of the usual dual diagnosis case.) Many intoxicants, including drugs of abuse, produce effects that mimic the syndrome patterns of one or several major mental disorders, depending on dose or conditions of administration, thus providing chemical models for these illnesses. As this would lead us to suspect, biological factors often are most prominent in driving these disorders. Working with individuals with major mental disorders is the primary focus of this book. The most severe, chronic forms of the major mental disorders, accompanied by a high degree of reciprocity with an addictive disorder comprise the greatest challenge in dual diagnosis work. This is especially true if, as is often the case, the individual also has a concurrent personality disorder.

Table 1-6 groups the major mental disorders into three categories: those in which regulation of mood is the predominant feature, those in which modulation of arousal level and various stimulus thresholds are implicated, and those in which the dominant features involve the production and quality of thought, especially in regard to the control of both the context and range of associations among mental contents.

Dual diagnosis work with the major mental disorders is based on understanding the relationship between the abused substance and the symptom pattern of the major mental illness, which together often implicate both a biological and a psychosocial function for the drug use. There will often be a complementary or opponent process biological relationship between the major mental disorder and the psychopharmacology of the abused drug, or the addictive function more generally. The escape hypothesis of addiction (that individuals use psychoactive substances to avoid certain feelings and thoughts) and the self-medication hypothesis of drug use (that individuals use drugs because of their positive effects on the symptoms of psychopathology) will often be relevant. The stimulus control hypothesis of addiction (that individuals use drugs to increase, decrease, and modulate the level of impinging environmental and internal stimulation) will be useful in some cases. The object relations and self experiences discussed earlier (always crucial in characterological dependence work) will be important for almost every case.

Reciprocally Reinforcing (Synergistic) Psychiatric Substance Abuse Syndromes

The synergistic syndromes may be defined as existing in those cases in which a chronic, severe psychiatric disorder is reciprocally causal and reinforcing of a substance use disorder resulting in a synergistic pathological process. One or both disorders will increase the severity and frequency of the other. One or both disorders will persist after an acute phase. One or both disorders will demonstrate cyclicity, often with the cycles between the disorders being linked in a helixical, progressive manner. Causal lines for both disorders will at times converge. Symptom clusters in the two disorders will either converge or demonstrate a complementary relationship, or an opponent process relationship. Opponent relationships or complementary relationships will often cycle alternatively between cause and effect among three major components and their subcomponents: a major mental disorder and its consequences, a personality disorder and its consequences, and an addictive disorder and its consequences. Consequences are, of course, social, cognitive, emotional, somatic, and spiritual.

CLUES TO TREATMENT STRATEGIES

The recovery process for the two disorders, of which formal treatment is only one aspect, may also be described as occurring in degrees of relatedness as in the manner outlined for the disordering processes. The proximal goal for dual diagnosis work is not to completely resolve either pathological process in itself, but to create a synergistic relationship between the two recovery processes while interrupting the synergistic relationship between the pathological processes.

To make this process more tangible, let us use an analogy taken from modern tourism and informed by pre-Socratic Greek philosophy. Heraclitus claimed that one can never step into the same river twice, pointing out the flux of nature and the pervasiveness of change within continuity. Modern tourists to Brazil spend an expensive and dangerous day on a river, actually the confluence of two mighty rivers. One of them is a bright yellow color from the mineral-rich clays that the river rakes from the highlands. The other is a dark sepia, from the rain forests thick with humus and lavish with microbial and vegetable life. The two rivers converge, and instead of mixing immediately, they flow in a parallel position for several miles before spilling into yet another river and dispersing toward the ocean. Two rivers become a third, but before doing so they remain intact, interactive, and potentiating of one another, each itself in constant change and flux. The analogy to the dual diagnosis problem is that both disorders are in constant flux, both make up one river, yet both are separate.

Since these are pathological rivers, or processes, our goal will be to go beyond marveling at their interaction and unity. We will use our understanding of their origins and interrelationships to redirect them both, make them less destructive, and, if possible, use the energy stored in them to some positive benefit to the individual. This process of marshalling these energies for life enhancement is called recovery. We will want to work on this confluence from both banks (recovery from addiction, recovery from mental illness) simultaneously, as in the parallel treatment approach cited above, but we will do so with a more informed strategy. When possible, we will ford the river at the areas that are shallowest and slowest moving, and narrowest at both banks, and those points will determine the placements of our dams and channels (interventions) to a great extent.

We may find it necessary at times to go upstream, to the sites above the confluence, to understand why they have intersected and, perhaps, to influence where they will meet to our advantage, if possible.

2

Mapping a Paradigm

DISTURBANCES IN FOUR SPHERES OF FUNCTIONING

Behavioral scientists have divided individual human functioning into three spheres: affect, cognition, and overt behavior. When physiological status and social functioning are added to these three, a fairly comprehensive description of an individual's functioning, or any part of it, may be made by assessing these spheres and their interactions. This chapter explores the relationships among representative functions from each of these psychological spheres in a prototypical dual diagnosis problem. Memory (a cognitive factor in personality and learning), depression (an affective factor), and alcoholism (a complex of overt behaviors) are shown in dynamic interaction. Obviously, this schematic presentation involves considerable simplification of a complex reality. Every term in this schematic can itself be described as consisting of interactions among several other elements from various spheres of human functioning. For example, alcoholism is more than a series of overt behaviors. Affective and cognitive defects and deficits result from and influence the behavioral patterns that lead to the diagnosis of alcoholism. Similarly, depression is more than an affective or mood disorder. Specific behaviors and cognitions accompany, perpetuate, or result from depression. In depressive disorders, cognitive factors such as memory and new learning are also clearly influenced by current mood, the presence of other distracting or competing behaviors, and that combination of all three spheres called attitudes. Despite this complexity, we adopt this simple schematic description of representative functions from somewhat arbitrarily separated spheres to show what the scientific literature and empirical research suggest about the interrelatedness between three aspects of one dual diagnosis problem.

The methods for investigating these issues in this chapter include a bit of informal analysis of popular songs about drinking, a brief review of a rather narrow wedge of the available scientific literature, a more detailed discussion of several seminal psychological experiments, and the presentation of empirical data comparing the daily emotional experiences of alcoholics and nonalcoholics. It is hoped that the information and ideas presented in this chapter provide an illustration of the kind of creative integration of scientific literature and clinical experience that is needed to further development of theory building and clinical practice in dual diagnosis work. This chapter also serves as a prerequisite to a more ambitious endeavor, which is the task of Chapter 3. The endeavor is to extrapolate from what is known about several such problems a general model, template, or paradigm that will be useful in approaching all dual diagnosis problems, including those with considerable complexity. While reading this chapter, the reader is encouraged to generalize the concepts presented in regard to alcoholism and depression to his or her own clinical experience of other dual diagnosis problems. In most cases, symptoms overlap, interaction of pathological processes, functions, or motivations for the use of a particular substance and the specific pharmacological effects and social consequences of a drug use are involved in a reciprocal, synergistic relationship.

In this chapter, we say much about the cognitive sphere, the foundation for many approaches to the treatment of addictions, and especially of the relapse prevention model of Marlatt and others (Marlatt and Gordon 1985). We focus on memory, learning, and the development of cognitive strategies. We informally define memory as what we directly *know about* (recall, reconstruct, re-experience) our own past experience, as opposed to learning, which is what we *know from* (deduce, infer, abstract, or form a behavioral posture toward) our experience, either past, present, or future. Cognitive strategies may be defined as learned or discovered ways of performing mental tasks effectively and efficiently, or methods of getting the optimal qualitative mental result (decision, answer, formulation, concept) with the least amount of time and effort.

These aspects of human cognition are hand-in-glove functions and not separate as in these informal definitions. Memory deficits as one aspect of impaired cognition are emphasized for several reasons. Most cognitive and dynamic theories of psychopathology and change stress memories for traumatic events, affect-laden events, or the distortion of memories due to childhood misinterpretations as fundamental to understanding adult behavior, although theories differ as to why such memories are important. Psychodynamic theories stress the energy required to repress, suppress, or otherwise control intrusions into conscious experience from memories and related impulses or wishes, as well as the distorting influence of defenses related to memories on otherwise rational or adaptive responses to the current situation. Cognitive perceptual theories stress the guiding and limiting functions of memories and related expectancies on the perception and organization of ongoing experience. Information processing theories stress the burden placed on processing capacity when emotionally laden memories are constantly recycled concurrent with demands to process new experience. Existential and phenomenological theories describe how memories and old learning are required for a genuine sense of integrity of the person, but may, nonetheless, seriously obstruct openness to meeting new experiences authentically. From a substance abuse perspective, the escape hypothesis of addiction stresses the motivation to use substances in order to escape painful emotions, often specifically related to painful memories. Finally, a psychopharmacological hypothesis suggests that some substances, for example, alcohol, specifically alter the storage or retrieval of emotionally laden memories and that this drug effect provides the motivation for drug abuse. Several of these theoretical lines converge in predicting special relationships among memory, negative affect, and substance abuse.

Let us begin our investigation of these relationships with a bit of very informal analysis of the psychological implications of a traditional aspect of American culture. Blues, jazz, and country and western ballads provide numerous examples of the lyrical theme that reflects a concern with loss, depression, and memory. Although the analysis below was developed from inspecting a jazz blues tune, "Drinking Again" by Johnny Mercer, the reader is encouraged to consider any of a number of songs that will be familiar in order to apply to the lyrics the informal psycho-cultural analysis suggested here. One could easily find song lyrics on the subject of drink that emphasize comradeship, cheerfulness, and an expansive sense of self that would reflect little psychopathology on the surface. However, clinical experience leads us to believe that, to a large extent, even these more positive expressions related to drinking cloak more pathological aspects of functioning. Positive expectations in regard to excessive drinking usually result in drinking to cope, and serve a defensive function against the experiences expressed in the bittersweet, savory-sad tradition of drinking songs. The mobiles discussed in Chapter 1 depict the various experiences of self in the addictions; lyrics that are more upbeat than this tradition of sad songs may reflect portions or single phases of a larger pathological process addressed by drug use. For instance, such drinking may provide disinhibition from a harsh conscience, or stimulation, general arousal, and pseudo-emotion in an individual with deficits in emotional discrimination and with a limited ability to modulate arousal level. If this is the case, the sad affect lyrics reflect the more fundamental pattern, or at least the one that is most apt to lead to presentation for clinical treatment.

Looking at this type of song from separate spheres of functioning we might find the following points.

1. *Affect* is primarily sad, depressed, and hurt, reflecting a sense of longing, abandonment, and alienation or estrangement. There is also a sense of being soothed by the drinking situation, some of which may be due, in part, to the easing of physiological craving for the drug and the removal of withdrawal symptoms.

2. *Cognition* is simple, dominated by preoccupation with the past, with losses, and with emotionally laden interpersonal memories. Representations of self and others are stereotyped and contaminated by simple primary affects and global evaluations. The idealized lost lover is seen as only positive, or as no good but longed for, with no attempt at integrating these contradictory reactions. Other characters are deprecated as fools, jokers, or clowns, including the self. Usually present is the context of repetition that the song both mimics and insinuates. The singer clearly fails to learn anything new from emotional experience and the lines repeat with little incremental change.

3. *Behavior* is stereotyped and compulsive, focused around drinking and dependent social interactions associated with drinking (buying or being bought drinks as determined by gender-related roles, borrowing other oral supplies such as cigarettes). Defensive behavior (as in laughing at jokes rather than crying about one's situation) is a prominent goal in social interactions. Mutual indulgence in drink (and probably the song itself and related memories) is used to provide a condition in which the mood states of the parties are attuned by direct influence of the drug and contagion of the familiar, stereotyped drinking environment rather than more intimate empathic processes. The resulting pseudo-intimacy is superficial and the parties involved are interchangeable or replaceable, although the external influences providing the state tuning (alcohol, the bar scene) are increasingly relied on.

The experience of self from the combined affects, cognitions, and behaviors is that of the "broken heart," or the depleted (depressed/degraded) self shown graphically in Figure 1–3. We cannot go much further toward an analysis of the mind and addictive state of the speakers in such songs, however. The existence of these elements and this particular view of self filtered though the traditions and conventions of popular culture tell us little about the speaker's typical level of psychological functioning, the severity of addiction, or the speaker's vulnerability to other experiential positions, or cycles of these positions. These elements cannot in themselves help place the speaker squarely in any of the dual diagnosis categories outlined in Table 1–6, since the characteristics may occur in all levels of psychopathology and addictive severity, and within most personality styles.

The speaker in these songs are usually clearly under the influence of alcohol, a patently important state for a problem drinker or alcoholic. We have relatively little data from naturalistic settings about alcoholics when intoxicated. Our very brief excursion into content analysis of popular songs leads to several crucial questions that are addressed in the rest of this chapter in a more formal and scientific manner. Do the affective, cognitive, and behavioral generalizations made from the song fit at least a subgroup of alcoholics during their sober periods as well as when intoxicated? That is to say, are these traits in some way characterological and not simply specific to the immediate effects of alcohol? Speculations on the anecdotal evidence in a popular song aside, is there a scientific basis supporting the existence of the kinds of relationships found in this explication of these lyrics?

Specifically, is there an empirical base supporting a higher incidence of depression and depressed affect in alcoholics, memory, and learning differences in alcoholics as compared to nonalcoholics, and a causal role for depressed affect in the etiology of alcoholism? The next three subsections review areas of psychological literature related to these questions. First, the literature on the incidence of depression among alcoholics is reviewed, followed by a synopsis of the literature on the role of depression, affect, and affective memories in the etiology of alcoholism. The final section of this sequence integrates these findings in a clinically useful way.

THE INCIDENCE OF DEPRESSION IN ALCOHOLISM

The effects of a depressed mood would be irrelevant to the study of memory in alcoholics if the incidence of depression in alcoholism were not substantial. However, the higher incidence of trait depression among alcoholics when compared to nonalcoholics has been a cornerstone of some theoretical and treatment approaches to alcohol addiction (Jaffe and Ciraulo 1986, Jones 1968, 1971, Keeler et al. 1979, Nerviano 1981, Nerviano et al. 1980, Wikler 1973, Woodruff et al. 1973).

Determining the incidence of depression among alcoholics and finding ways to screen for depression early in the recovery process have been of interest recently, since some investigators have suggested that among alcoholics, those who are depressed are most in need of intensive, long-term therapeutic programs (Willenbring 1986). Substantial evidence suggests that depressed alcoholics have longer histories of problem drinking, more previous treatments for alcohol misuse, more trouble in resisting use of alcohol, more marital problems, and more physical symptoms related to alcohol abuse than other alcoholics (McMahon and Davidson 1986). Some investigators, however, see no difference in treatment outcome and course of illness between depressed and nondepressed alcoholics (Hesselbrock et al. 1983, Schuckit 1983).

A recent study of depressed alcoholics found them to be more anxious, tense, restless, apprehensive, and having more somatic symptoms than nondepressed alcoholics (McMahon and Davidson 1986). There is also evidence that as a group they are more apt to be interpersonally detached with avoidant or asocial personality traits, to have disorganized and distracted cognition, and to have a negativistic self-image (McMahon and Davidson 1986). In an isolated study, depressed alcoholics were found to have a better outcome than other alcoholics. Reich and Green (1991) report a subgroup of depressed alcoholics diagnosed as having schizoid personality to be associated with better outcomes in group psychotherapy for alcoholics. This may be a subgroup of alcoholics whose depression is secondary to social skills deficits and avoidant traits related to a personality disorder. Group techniques, including Alcoholics Anonymous, would provide some remediation of these underlying deficits and result in a better outcome for these patients than for individuals with other types of personality disorder (Reich and Green 1991).

In their review of the literature on the relationship between alcoholism and depression, Jaffe and Ciraulo (1986) noted that the percentage of alcoholics considered clinically depressed depends on the diagnostic criteria and conceptual frames of the investigator, as well as on the point in the cycle of alcohol use and withdrawal in which the patients are assessed. In the view of Jaffe and Ciraulo (1986), depressive symptoms may be very common and very intense in alcoholics without warranting the diagnosis of a separate affective illness. One reason for not making the separate diagnosis is that these depressive symptoms may clear up very quickly after detoxification. For example, one study noted that as many as 98 percent of recently admitted patients reported depressive symptoms, which waned after a few days to several weeks to normal levels (Shaw et al. 1975). This has led some to the view that only a small percentage of alcoholics have persistent severe depression (Keeler et al. 1979, Schuckit 1979).

Studies that attempted to examine the occurrence of more stable kinds of depression than depressive symptoms after detoxification have produced a wide range of estimates (Cadoret et al. 1984, Freed 1978, O'Sullivan et al. 1979, Schuckit 1979, 1983). For example, Weissman and Myers (1980) found 44 percent of community alcoholics had major depression, 15 percent had minor depression, 6 percent had bipolar depression, and 18 percent were considered to have depressive personalities. Midanik (1983) found 33 percent of female problem drinkers and 17 percent of male problem drinkers to have a co-existent depression. When the same study examined persons who were alcohol dependent, 56.6 percent of the females and 19 percent of the males met the criteria for both disorders. Patients may also be divided into those who develop depression before alcohol use and those who develop it after chronic abuse, with the first group being considered primary depressives. In studies where primary depression was used as a criterion, estimates of the proportion of depressed patients ranged between 3 percent and 46 percent, with the incidence of primary depression consistently more frequent among female alcoholics (Beck et al. 1982, Hesselbrock et al. 1983, Schuckit 1983, Winokur et al. 1971).

In summary, various measures of depressive symptoms taken at different points in the recovery process have resulted in widely different estimates of the incidence of clinical depression and depressive symptoms in alcoholic subjects. Depressive symptoms appear to be most extreme upon admission for treatment, with some gradual decrease over the treatment period. Despite this gradual decline in depressed affect, there is strong evidence that a substantial number of alcoholics also have long-standing clinical or subclinical depression. It is also clear that many researchers have considered the depression–alcoholism connection as an extremely important area for investigation.

SORTING CAUSAL LINKS

The high correlation between depressed affect and alcoholism (as between many mental or emotional illnesses and addictions) suggests a possible causal connection.

Jaffe and Ciraulo (1986) listed ten possible causes for the high incidence of depression among alcoholics: (1) the direct toxic effects of alcohol on the brain, (2) indirect toxic effects, via other organs and body systems, (3) effects of alcohol withdrawal, (4) central nervous system (CNS) effects of drugs (other than alcohol) related to the treatment or use of alcohol, (5) CNS effects of injury or anoxia associated with alcohol-related trauma and/or suicidal gestures, (6) effects of social losses related to alcohol use, (7) psychological responses to physical impairment related to alcohol use, (8) a personality disorder antedating the alcohol use, and perhaps resulting in alcohol abuse, (9) effects of an independently transmitted affective disorder, and (10) effects of a genetically transmitted vulnerability to both affective symptoms and alcoholism.

Jaffe and Cirulo emphasized in their review the difficulty inherent in trying to investigate the relative importance of these possible contributing causes, underlining the difficulty in forming groups of alcoholics that are comparable in terms of the origins of their depressive symptoms, problems in the diagnoses of personality disorders, and problems in identifying the temporal order of onset in persons with both alcoholism and depression. To this list of difficulties can be added the differences in drinking history and length of abstinence encountered in clinical studies with alcoholics. This longer list might be applied to any dual diagnosis situation, both in its complexity of possible causes of comorbidity and in the quality of the two disorders being inextricably bound to each other, both in terms of clinical presentation and causality.

To continue with the goal of providing an extended but somewhat limited example of a representative dual diagnosis problem, let us concentrate on the aspects of a suspected causal tie among alcoholism, negative affect, and memory. We do this by reviewing several seminal experiments and related theories relevant to the relationships among these elements. A previously unpublished empirical study examining differences in negative affect and memory in alcoholics and nonalcoholics is also presented.

THE ROLE OF DEPRESSED AFFECT IN THE ETIOLOGY OF ALCOHOLISM

Several theories accounting for alcohol addiction suggest that in many cases alcohol is used primarily to escape or forget painful emotional experiences (such as depressed, tense affect) rather than primarily for its euphoria-inducing quality. These theories stress the role of predisposing personality characteristics, such as avoidance, unresolved rage, or unmet dependency needs in the development of alcoholism (Freed 1978). Focusing on the need to escape memories rather than a need to alter or escape current experience yields a related set of hypotheses about the origin of alcohol addiction. Let us pursue the work of several researchers who have empirically investigated this line of inquiry. Rather than trace the history of such research, we begin in medias res with a study that addresses directly a memory/alcoholism hypothesis and provides background from other studies that adds to the understanding of this seminal study's context and implications.

Cowan (1983), tested a set of very specific hypotheses related to the role of memory in the etiology of alcohol abuse. Among these was the hypothesis that alcohol may permit the drinker to forget previous feelings, both good and bad, and that this effect is an important motive in alcohol use. Cowan hypothesized that the primary action of alcohol on the emotional system may be to reduce the impact of past experience by blocking emotional memories and associated cognition, keeping them from intruding on current experience. This would allow current experience to change in accordance with the drinker's expectations and the drinking situation, rather than being dominated by emotional memories. According to Cowan (1983):

> Euphoric and dysphoric current feelings of various types, as well as increased emotional lability and "disinhibition," can all result from a drug-induced impairment (operationally, a decrease in *accuracy*) of memory for particular kinds of feelings. For the sober problem drinker, many of these memories are related to his problems, and are therefore unpleasant; forgetting these may be particularly reinforcing. [p. 41]

Notice that Cowan's statement can be taken to imply that the avoidance or impairment of memories may not simply lift the haunting shadow of previous experience but may also have the effect of intensifying current experience and behavior. Also, Cowan has defined the effect of alcohol on memory as one of impaired accuracy of memory for specific emotional states.

Cowan tested hypotheses related to his theory by using in vivo alcohol doses either during a learning session or a recall session. He randomly assigned thirty-two nonalcoholic students to one of four drug conditions over these two sessions: placebo-placebo, placebo-alcohol, alcohol-placebo, alcohol-alcohol. The Profile of Mood States (POMS) was used to measure the subjects' moods and mood changes (McNair et al. 1971). The POMS is a checklist containing sixty-five mood adjectives on six scales: tension-anxiety, depression-dejection, anger-hostility, vigor, fatigue, and confusion-bewilderment. Each subject's moods were measured five times over two separate sessions: during session one before ingestion of drink and at the end of the session; during session two before ingestion of drink, another for current mood at the end of the session, and a final measure reflecting the subjects' memory of their moods at the end of the previous session. In addition to this memory for moods task, subjects participated in several intentional verbal and pictorial memory tasks during each session. The tasks included free recall of a word list after one exposure, again after several exposures, and a task requiring the recognition of men's faces among four alternatives after only one exposure to the target faces.

When the results of this study were analyzed, none of the verbal and pictorial memory tests yielded significant effects due to alcohol before testing or before learning. Alcohol produced no significant changes in feelings of any of the POMS scales. In other words, in vivo doses of alcohol in nonalcoholics did not significantly influence relatively sensitive measures of new learning, memory for neutral visual stimuli (unfamiliar faces), or current mood. However, there were significant differences in affective memory, as measured by the subjects' accuracy in reconstructing their own previous POMS ratings. In examining the errors made on this task of recalling one's own mood states, Cowan divided the memory errors into two kinds: memory bias (or signed error in estimates of the intensity of previous emotions) and inaccuracy (or absolute error, without regard to whether the error was an overestimate or underestimate of the previously recorded POMS mood indicator). Both bias and inaccuracy effects of alcohol ingestion on affective memories were demonstrated. Persons given alcohol during session one (incidental learning of moods) reported exaggerated memories (biased overestimates) of angry affect on the reconstruction task significantly more than subjects who were not given alcohol in session one. Alcohol ingestion during the learning session caused significantly more inaccuracy on four of the six moods scales (confusion, vigor, depression-dejection, and tension-anxiety, in order of most inaccuracy). Alcohol given before the recall task increased inaccuracy for moods even more strongly, significantly effecting fatigue, confusion, and vigor, in descending order. When Cowan computed a Total Memory Inaccuracy Score by adding the absolute value differences between learning and test session POMs across the six scales, alcohol produced significant effects both during learning and testing.

The design of this study allows for the observation of possible state-dependent learning effects. A rough operational definition of state-dependent learning might be that state-dependent learning or retrieval has occurred if memory or learning efficiency is better when a subject is tested under the same state of drug influence, mood state, or state of consciousness in which the original learning experience occurred. The implied converse of this definition is also true, that is, state-dependent learning is also demonstrated by poorer testing performance when tests are administered in a different mood state than that present during a learning phase. State-dependent learning has been suggested as a powerful component in the development of some forms of pathological processes including alcoholism. The results of this study, however, which revealed a significant interaction of learning and testing states, were in contrast to what might have been expected if state-dependent retrieval had occurred. For example, the same drug condition groups showed less accurate memory for vigor than those that changed condition across sessions. The significance of this failure to confirm state-dependent learning may lie in the importance of incorporating into the state-dependent learning concept a greater appreciation of the specific characteristics of the drug, or other agent, that induces a given state. In this case, alcohol was shown to have powerful effects on memory that either prevented or obscured any coexistent state-dependent learning that may have occurred.

The other implications of Cowan's work are many. He considers it to be "the first study, performed with a well established and extensively validated mood scale, which demonstrates that alcohol directly affects memory for feelings" (1983, p. 45).

He cites five lines of evidence from his experiment indicating that alcohol has specific and selective effects on memory for emotional events beyond the general performance impairment known to be caused by alcohol ingestion: (1) alcohol's effects on memory accuracy are stronger than those on memory bias, (2) alcohol has a different pattern of effects on emotional memory than on verbal and pictorial memory, (3) alcohol's effects on both learning and testing conditions are specific to certain moods, (4) alcohol-induced inaccuracy for moods does not parallel the normal forgetting curve over time, therefore, alcohol does not merely potentiate the effects of time on memory for moods, and (5) alcohol does not alter current feelings while impairing memory for earlier emotional events.

Cowan's research is important in that it attempts to directly measure the psychopharmacological impact of alcohol on memory for moods in order to establish an etiology for pathological drinking that takes into account much that is known clinically about the personalities of alcoholics. However, this study is limited to nonalcoholics taking relatively small in vivo doses of alcohol and cannot easily be generalized to sober alcoholics or persons who are grossly intoxicated. Other procedural and measurement problems inherent in Cowan's research have been considered by some workers to cast doubt on his conclusions. His data have, in fact, been analyzed in a manner to support the hypothesis that alcohol enhances the memory for the affect current immediately before the ingestion of alcohol (Mueller and Klajner 1984), supporting the view that persons most at risk for alcoholism feel their best immediately before intoxication (Parker et al. 1981).

If Cowan is correct, however, alcohol use is at least partially motivated in some cases by the reinforcing effects of the specific memory impairments and distortions that it causes. The asymmetrical effects of alcohol on different kinds of affective memories may also have a role in the development of some variants of alcoholism. Depressed persons may be particularly vulnerable to the abuse of alcohol in order to take advantage of its specific effects on affective memories, which otherwise would intrude on ongoing experience. One can hypothesize that individuals with an inborn or acquired deficit in the biopsychological mechanisms that control the storage of negative emotion might be especially vulnerable to alcoholism as a form of self-medication or pharmacological coping device. This would be especially true if the basic deficit involved a predisposition to store negative affect more tenaciously than might others without such a deficit.

FAILURES IN SELF-PROTECTIVE BIASES

The line of research charted in the preceding section builds on the psychopharmacological effects of alcohol and lends itself easily to a biological interpretation of what may differentiate alcoholics from others. A less biologically based concept that might account for some persons relying on alcohol to inhibit the intrusion of memories into ongoing experience is the concept of depressive realism described by

Alloy and Abramson (1979). In regard to emotional memory, we might define depressive realism as the tendency to remember our feelings as they were, as opposed to distorting our personal emotional history in a way that might protect our view of ourselves as being competent, serene, and on the whole happy. According to Alloy and Abramson, depressed persons are less likely to apply self-protective distortions (or cognitive biases) than the nondepressed. Although their work is focused on depression rather than alcoholism, the high incidence of depression among alcoholics and the escape hypothesis of addiction elaborated by Cowan make depressive realism a likely candidate for the fruitful investigation of the particular dual diagnosis problem of this chapter.

Several of the early experiments by Alloy and Abramson were seminal to developing this concept and merit a fairly detailed exploration. In a set of four experiments designed to investigate the relationship between actual and perceived reinforcement, these researchers examined depressed and nondepressed students' abilities to detect the degree of contingency, or personal control, in a task under differing conditions. Severity of depression was determined by use of the Beck Depression Inventory (BDI) (Beck 1967).

In Experiment 1, the task was to make a green light come on by pressing a button. Each subject performed different "problems" in estimating the amount of control and rate of reinforcement (the lighting of the green bulb) in performing this task, having been told that the causal relationship between their button pushing and the appearance of the green light might vary between problems. Subjects were later asked to make judgments of the percentage of control they had over the light coming on. In Experiment 1, the rate of reinforcement was manipulated mechanically to be negatively related to the actual degree of control, that is, the green light came on less often when the subject had more control of it coming on. An earlier theory, the learned helplessness theory (Lewinsohn 1974, Maier and Seligman 1978, Seligman 1973), had predicted that under these conditions, more depressed subjects would believe that they were helpless and would therefore underestimate the amount of control in the situation. Contrary to the predictions of the learned helplessness model, however, ratings of contingency by the subjects were found to be highly accurate, with no significant differences between depressed and nondepressed subjects.

In Experiment 2, the subjects' task was the same, but the experimental goal was to assess judgments of noncontingency rather than contingency as in Experiment 1. The learned helplessness model predicted that depressed persons would be accurate in assessing lack of control, whereas nondepressed persons would overestimate contingency. The green light came on at different times in this experiment, but its lighting was not contingent on the subject's button pushing. It was found that depressed persons were, again, accurate in their assessment of the absence of control. Nondepressed persons, however, overestimated control when the light came on frequently, but not when the light seldom came on, thus apparently providing partial support for the learned helplessness model in that nondepressed persons perceived more control than depressed persons in either high or low reinforcement conditions.

Experiment 3 was designed to further examine the illusion of control found among nondepressives in Experiment 2. The task in this experiment was similar except that the green light was now associated with the gain or loss of money. In one problem, the light signified a twenty-five-cent loss from an initial five dollars provided by the experimenter (lose problem). In the other problem, the light signified a twenty-five-cent gain (win problem). Frequency of reinforcement was held constant across problems. The Multiple Affect Adjective Check List (MAACL) (Zuckerman et al. 1965) was used in combination with the BDI to form depressed and nondepressed groups. In addition, the MAACL was administered again both before and after each problem to assess changes in depression, hostility, and anxiety.

Depressed subjects accurately detected noncontingency of their responses, whereas nondepressed people demonstrated illusions of control. Both groups judged reinforcement to be higher in the win problem. Both groups showed significant change toward dysphoria in the lose situation, with nondepressed subjects showing greater change in the dysphoric direction in the lose situation, and depressed subjects showing greater change in the euphoric direction in the win situation. The investigators concluded that under conditions of noncontingency involving hedonistic rewards, nondepressed subjects err by overestimating both contingency and outcome frequency; they believe that they have more control over winning than they actually do and that they are apt to win more often than they actually do.

In Experiment 4, the learned helplessness model hypothesis that depressed subjects would underestimate control relative to nondepressed subjects under hedonistic reward conditions was tested, The procedure was similar to Experiment 3, but contingency was set at 50 percent in both problems. Depressed subjects were found to be more accurate than nondepressed subjects in judging contingency of reward. Nondepressed subjects overestimated control in the win problem (especially when the active strategy of pushing a button was most effective) and greatly underestimated control in the lose problem, whereas depressed subjects were accurate about the degree of control regardless of the amount of contingency or the kind of response that was most effective in gaining reinforcement (actively hitting the button, or passively not hitting it and waiting for reinforcement).

Across all four experiments the learned helplessness hypotheses that depressed persons will underestimate control and that nondepressed persons will overestimate control were not supported. Depressed subjects were consistently more accurate in their estimates of control, whereas nondepressed subjects showed both illusions of control and illusions of no control, depending on experimental conditions.

Alloy and Abramson (1979) proposed a revision of the learned helplessness model that would incorporate the findings of their experiments. The revised hypothesis maintains that there is a motivational deficit in depression that works without perceptual distortion, that is, depressives are less apt to initiate successful responses but are not less able to perceive what the required response would be. The revised hypothesis predicts that depressed subjects will initiate fewer instrumental responses when the required response is complex, due to their motivational impairment. The helplessness experienced by depressives, according to the new model, is not entirely due to the experience of noncontingency filtered through perceptual, attributional, and expectational processes, but may also result from hormonal and physiological sources.

An alternative framework was also proposed to account for the fact that nondepressives were inaccurate in assessments of contingency. Self-esteem maintenance and self-enhancement are the cornerstones of this alternative view. The results in all four of the Alloy and Abramson (1979) seminal experiments can be explained if one hypothesizes that nondepressed persons are motivated to maintain their self-esteem, whereas depressed persons are not motivated to protect themselves in this way. Precursors to this viewpoint include Bibring (1943) who argued that depressives are not motivated to retain self-esteem because the mechanism for self-deception has broken down. Depressives have taken off their rose-colored glasses and are "sadder but wiser," according to Alloy and Abramson (1979). The literature on self-esteem is consistent with the view that persons with low self-esteem lack protective perceptual biases. Zuckerman (1979b) concluded that self-esteem is maintained by the kind of self-serving attributional biases seen in nondepressed subjects. An attributional style of evenhandedness (willingness to attribute success or failure equally to either the task situation or to the self) has also been observed among subjects with low self-esteem (Fitch 1970, Ickes and Layden 1978).

The direction of the causal link between depression and helplessness is still under debate in the depressive realism literature. Building on the revised version of the learned helplessness model of depression, which emphasizes the perception and general expectation of noncontingency in the development of depression, Schwartz (1981a,b) has argued that it is essentially an "inferential handicap" that makes depressives appear "wiser." He cites a series of experiments by Reber (1967, 1968, 1976) demonstrating that incidental (passive and unintentional) learning of patterns and abstract principles can be superior to intentional learning of the same ideas, because of the distorting influences of hypotheses generated by subjects under intentional learning conditions. Individuals who expect to find a particular pattern will exert a confirmation bias that makes it more difficult to discover an unexpected or contradictory pattern. Schwartz views the depressed person as similarly operating permanently under conditions of incidental learning because of a failure to initiate hypotheses about the learning situation. At least one empirical study investigating the role of hypothesis testing in judgments of contingency by depressive and nondepressives supports Schwartz's view. Depressed subjects demonstrated the same biases as nondepressed persons after they were provided hypotheses to test in relationship to their judgments of contingency (Abramson et al. 1982).

Abramson and Alloy (1981) do not subscribe to the view that a failure in hypothesis generation in general is essentially what is wrong with depressives. They see the optimistic biases of nondepressives as a pervasive aspect of normal human cognition that accounts for their health-promoting inability to perceive an absence of control. To them the depressive does not possess a depressogenic bias, "but rather that he or she suffers from an absence of nondepressive cognitive bias" (p. 444). More recently, however, Abramson and Seligman along with other researchers (Raps et al. 1982) have presented evidence that a depressogenic attributional style (attributing causality of negative events to internal, stable, and global causes) may lead to both helplessness and to depression. This view is consistent with that of Beck (1967), who sees the self-reported preoccupations of depression in alcoholics as related to a depressive world view, that is, a system of cognitive biases, expectations, and self-constructions that are consistent with depressive feelings and experiences and are applied by the individual to all situations.

CLINICAL IMPLICATIONS

Several speculations about addictive processes may be generated from Cowan's findings on memory and alcohol and the depressive realism literature. For example, is it possible that individuals who are somewhat immune to depression due to their cognitive structure are somewhat more vulnerable to addiction to gambling? The rationale for this question is that Alloy and Abramson's depressive realism findings indicated that people who are predisposed to depression due to their cognitive structure may also be more realistic about both control and outcomes in games of chance. Are these depressives particularly vulnerable to addiction to alcohol for some of the reasons presented in the discussion on Cowan's experiments on the effects of alcohol on memory and mood, while at the same time being relatively immune to gambling addiction? Perhaps such a contradiction could be explained by relating the two ideas of depressive vulnerability to alcohol motivated by the need to forget with the idea of and nondepressive vulnerability to games of chance resulting from a self-protective bias. Linking these two ideas helps us to understand the frequently encountered case of the gambler who is also an alcoholic, although the explanation is in terms somewhat less simple and global than resorting to ideas like the addictive personality. Such an individual might use alcohol to interrupt intrusive feelings of low self-esteem and depression. When under the influence of alcohol, this individual might have the vulnerability to the false perception of control, or luck, characteristic of the nondepressed or even manic individual. A vicious cycle involving these two dynamics would be almost inevitable for our hypothetical alcoholic gambler.

The contradictions and interconnections among these theoretical constructs can help us to understand some of our contradictory clinical experiences of alcoholics. For example, many alcoholics often exhibit a depressed view of themselves and others, going beyond depressive realism to a depressed world view. When these individuals are not displaying this negative outlook, their insistence on avoiding the problematic aspects of their own lives is equalled only by their disparate dependence on alcohol. Understanding how cognitive mechanisms are influenced by alcohol and negative affects such as depression clarifies why denial is often seen as the cardinal feature of the addictions. Alcohol supplies the addicted person with a two-door escape system from painful realities and memories. The first escape is through the pharmacological interruption of negative affective memories; the second is through the interruption (disinhibition) of various self-monitoring mechanisms, such as those that lead to depressive realism, a depressive world view, feelings of low self esteem, and a damaged self-concept.

Regarding the need to escape memories, it should be emphasized that what is referred to is not always specific biographical events. For all of us, there is a certain amount of emotional fallout extracted from previous experience and stored in a relatively separate, negative affect storage subsystem of long-term memory, a Pandora's box of negative affects. For some alcoholics, however, this negative affect memory bin may be less integrated with other memory systems than is the case in other people; at the same time this bin may be more permeable to ongoing experience, either because of the intensity and amount of the affects it contains, or from some inherent weakness in its boundary, or both. These memories and memory fallout residues would be unacceptable to the sober monitoring self and would produce either irritating, tension-inducing distractions, feelings of conflict, or vivid re-experiences that are overwhelming. Some alcoholics may have learned to escape these affects (to close the lid on the box) by resorting to alcohol use, perhaps in some cases as the result of a particular biological vulnerability to the memory-altering effects of the drug. Other individuals may adopt this mechanism primarily due to the influence of parental or peer models, or the absence of other viable alternative escape or coping methods.

The second escape hatch provided by alcohol lies in the interruption of normal self-regulatory and self-reflective mechanisms. If one cannot avoid or completely distort an affective memory, it can be made less painful by altering various aspects of consciousness. Alcohol obviously diffuses attention, sedates, and causes tension reduction. Furthermore, it decreases the self-monitoring functions that produce conscious conflict and concern about dissonant elements in experience. Intoxication interrupts self-reflective mechanisms that might otherwise support integration of the personality by generating conscious conflict and thereby eroding unconscious denial. In intoxication, conflict-laden behaviors, regressive tendencies, and other aspects of the self that are usually repressed and isolated are simultaneously available to consciousness, although often with little inhibition and rational control. Access to otherwise "jammed" or repressed experiences and aspects of self is attained during intoxication. However, upon regaining a sober state, these fragmentary experiences remain insulated from the personality as a whole. During periods of sobriety, the benign processes of self-monitoring that are needed for the individual to initiate the integration of conflicting experiences and behaviors trigger intense negative affects such as anxiety, guilt, and—most importantly—shame.

In the emotionally avoidant alcoholic, these painful affects are quickly clouded by defenses and repressed, leaving only a sense of physical tension in consciousness that may be interpreted as a craving for alcohol. For alcoholic individuals with a different, somewhat defensive system, these emotions may be consciously experienced and then suppressed, leaving the sense of being bottled up or having stuffed or swallowed feelings, or a sense of being cornered by one's own emotions and inability to cope with them. These individuals often experience anxieties of impending explosion or attack and occasionally a conscious fear of impending death that fuels the experience of craving. Whether or not the sober alcoholic can consciously experience and discriminate among negative emotional states, the cognitive aspects of denial are further bolstered during sobriety by state-dependent learning effects, and the emotional experiences of the intoxicated state are not fully available for conscious examination.

In double-edge irony, the alcoholic's sober periods are incorporated within the illness, and drunken periods become failed attempts at integration and mastery. The first part of this irony is more than the well-known need for the addict to dry out, recuperate, patch up relationships, or otherwise attend to self-maintenance functions in order to support the addictive lifestyle. Clouded, repressed, or suppressed emotions generated during sobriety (such as those generated by being confronted by others with the addiction and its consequences) are added to the negative affective memory store to be later avoided or enacted within the period of intoxication. Thus sober periods serve to perpetuate the illness. Positive expectancies regarding alcohol use (escape, emotional freedom, social lubrication, etc.) perpetuate a fantasy of control in an individual who is at times painfully aware of not adequately coping with life's demands.

The other edge of irony in the addiction, the health-seeking aspect of the illness, is perhaps less familiar but is especially relevant to the dual diagnosis syndromes. The alcoholic may use alcohol in order to experience moments when elements are brought together that are discordant, dissonant, conflict-ridden or otherwise not apt to arise in consciousness. Rothenberg (1988) has documented how bringing such discordant elements together is a source of creative solutions in psychotherapy and the arts. Intoxication enables many persons to experience the coexistence of memories, experiences, and aspects of self that they otherwise could not tolerate in combination. The desire to experience these co-existences is an important motive, although rarely a conscious and intentional one, in the use of alcohol and other drugs. The perverse and self-defeating folly of this strategy for any important personal solution is obvious, since alcohol also inhibits and erodes the higher order brain functions needed to integrate and create anything out of a hodgepodge of conscious contents.

Another pharmacological effect of alcohol use is deprivation of REM sleep, which is required to properly consolidate experience and provide the psychic outlet and integrative functioning of normal dreaming, which plays a role in the management of conflicting or unacceptable emotions and impulses. In a certain sense, alcoholics are forced to act out their dreams, with the assistance of intoxication, but because they have disarmed self-monitoring and self-reflective functions, they learn little from the drama. This self-defeating attempt at self-healing and psychological resolution of problems may be behind the self-medicating and periodic relapses of many dual diagnosis patients.

A Greek myth provides a useful gloss to illuminate the situation of the alcoholic in regard to memory. Having awakened on the shores of the river Styx, in the realm of death, the ghostly traveler reviews his miserable life. Drinking of the fiery waters of forgetfulness allows for a return to the world of the living. However, if one drinks of this fountain, no aspect of the harrowing learning about life that has been gained in the underworld can be used consciously in the new life. One can view the life of the alcoholic, in part, as a perversion or a primitive and regressive re-enactment of this archetype in daily living. As long as the cycle is in place, the individual fails to learn from experience, because his or her failure to integrate memories and experiences continues to generate the cycle of avoidance and denial. Their agonies in the underworld are to no avail.

DAILY EXPERIENCES AND MEMORY FOR MOODS

This chapter pursues many theoretical lines, all so far converging on the relationship among alcoholism, depression, and cognitive processes, especially memory. The high incidence of depression among alcoholics suggests that some cases of alcoholism may result from depression. One line of investigation suggests that the specific influences of alcohol on affective memories may reinforce the abuse of alcohol among persons with intrusive negative emotional memories, including memories of depressed affect. Biased processing toward a depressive world view may occur, resulting in an increase of negative emotional contents in memory. The failure to produce self-protective biases may cause depressed persons (and therefore alcoholics who are depressed) to be more realistic about previous events than are other individuals in similar circumstances, resulting in more blows to their sense of well-being and competence. A vicious cycle is created of depressive memories causing depression in current experience, which contributes to poor coping mechanisms (most prominently, alcohol use) to avoid these feelings. These faulty coping mechanisms in turn invariably produce more depressive experiences and memories.

We conclude our investigation of these issues by looking at a sample of the daily emotional experiences of alcoholics and comparing them to experiences of nonalcoholics, keeping in mind the graphic depictions of self introduced in Chapter 1. We then examine differences in memory for emotional events between alcoholics and nonalcoholics in the light of the literature previously reviewed in this chapter. Our goal is to maintain an empirical and experiential basis for discussing the differences between alcoholics and nonalcoholics while allowing for clinically useful applications and speculations for future investigation.

One method for gaining the information we need for such a comparison is to carefully interview alcoholics and nonalcoholics about their experiences. Given the clinically based assumption that alcoholism is a disease of denial and that alcohol causes subtle, and eventually catastrophic, brain changes, this approach has obvious weaknesses. Even conceding that we might be able to find subjects willing to report their experiences as accurately as possible, we would conclude that at least some of the alcoholic subjects may have impaired memory functions, impaired judgment, and impaired ability to distinguish emotional states clearly. The interview approach would also assume that at least nonalcoholic, "normal" subjects could report their experiences with few distortions. As we have seen, this is not the case. The ability to distort the memory of negative emotional experiences in a self-protective way is one hallmark of the "normal" person.

To avoid some of these weaknesses, as well as to gain a sense of the flow of the individual's experience over time, the Experience Sampling Method (ESM) (Csikszentmihalyi and Larson 1984) was used to collect data for the empirical comparisons described in this chapter. This method was developed to study the subjective experiences of individuals in natural environments. It uses any reliable means of providing a signal to the subject at a point in time determined by the researcher. This signal is the subject's cue to complete a brief self-report questionnaire or rating scale, which records the subject's feelings, thoughts, interactions, activities, or other aspects of experience or behavior at the time of the signal. In some studies, the subject is asked to summarize, count, or otherwise quantify any of these aspects of experience since the last signal was received. In the United States, long-range pagers carried by the subject are the usual means to give the signal, hence the term *beeper study* to characterize the method. The pagers are activated by radio, usually at random times during the day, resulting in cues that are relatively unexpected (at that moment) by the subject. By examining the individual subject's self-reports over many "beeps," variations in his or her experience can be tracked. A profile of the subject's typical experience over a day, a week, or for longer intervals can be compiled from this data. Also, the subject can be grouped with others along some variable of interest, as in the studies reported here, to provide group comparisons. The self-report instrument used by the subject, the Experience Sampling Form (ESF), is designed to take no more than 90 seconds to complete in routine response situations. The modified ESF used in the current study, the Daily Activity Report, appears in Figure 2–1.

ESF data have been demonstrated to be highly consistent across time within the same individual while that person is engaged in similar activities or in similar

Figure 2-1. Daily Activity Report: Modified Experience Sampling Form

What were you thinking about? _____

_____

Where were you? _____
What was the MAIN thing you were doing? _____

_____

	Not at all	Some-what	Quite	Very
Did you have choice in selecting this activity?	+ ---- + ---- + ---- + ---- + ---- + ---- + ---- + ---- +		
Did you feel in control of your activity?	+ ---- + ---- + ---- + ---- + ---- + ---- + ---- + ---- +		
How guilty did you feel?	+ ---- + ---- + ---- + ---- + ---- + ---- + ---- + ---- +		
How vulnerable did you feel?	+ ---- + ---- + ---- + ---- + ---- + ---- + ---- + ---- +		
How self-conscious were you?	+ ---- + ---- + ---- + ---- + ---- + ---- + ---- + ---- +		
How much were you concentrating?	+ ---- + ---- + ---- + ---- + ---- + ---- + ---- + ---- +		
How satisfied did you feel with yourself?	+ ---- + ---- + ---- + ---- + ---- + ---- + ---- + ---- +		
	0 1 2 3 4 5 6 7 8 9		

Describe your mood as you were beeped:

	Very	Quite	Some	Neither	Some	Quite	Very	
Alert	0	o	•	—	•	o	0	Drowsy
Happy	0	o	•	—	•	o	0	Sad
Irritable	0	o	•	—	•	o	0	Cheerful
Strong	0	o	•	—	•	o	0	Weak
Angry	0	o	•	—	•	o	0	Friendly
Active	0	o	•	—	•	o	0	Passive
Lonely	0	o	•	—	•	o	0	Sociable
Adequate	0	o	•	—	•	o	0	Inadequate
Free	0	o	•	—	•	o	0	Constrained
Excited	0	o	•	—	•	o	0	Bored
Proud	0	o	•	—	•	o	0	Ashamed
Confused	0	o	•	—	•	o	0	Clear
Tense	0	o	•	—	•	o	0	Relaxed
Fat	0	o	•	—	•	o	0	Thin

situations. In contrast, ESF data differs significantly between individuals and for the same person when engaged in dissimilar activities or placed in different environmental circumstances. The ESF has demonstrated high concurrent validity and convergent validity with other psychometric instruments and physiological measures. It has shown strong predictive validity in distinguishing group membership based on item responses. Studies using the ESM have included those of the phenomenology of everyday life (Klinger 1978), changes in self-esteem (Savin-Williams and Demo 1983), variation in self-awareness (Franzoi and Brewer 1984), frequency and intensity of moods (Diener and Larson 1984, Diener et al. 1984), and—as is the case in the study reported here—recovery processes in alcoholics (Filstead et al. 1985). The best-selling book, *FLOW: The Psychology of Optimal Experience*, by Mihaly Csikszentmihalyi (1990), applies ESM findings to the problem of enhancing the quality of personal experience and was based in part on data obtained by using an instrument similar to the ESF found in this figure.

The data reported here were collected as part of the author's involvement with a larger study of recovery patterns in alcoholism. Because this larger study entailed a sophisticated, systematic investigation of many aspects of the recovery process in alcoholism and drug abuse, only aspects relevant to the smaller memory study are described here. The larger study began in 1983 at Parkside Lutheran Center for Substance Abuse, in Park Ridge, Illinois. This center is a private hospital specializing in alcoholism treatment. The study that is our focus on the relationships among alcoholism, cognition, and depression was conducted by taking a random sample of subjects from the larger study and adding an intensive investigation of memory to their research protocol.

Clinical subjects for the study were paid volunteers recruited from the inpatient population. They were all alcoholics in recovery after intensive treatment and they resided within commuting distance from the center. All subjects had a level of psychopathology that did not preclude their meaningful participation in this kind of study, and they were considered by their inpatient treatment team to be at minimal risk of relapse due to any additional stress caused by participation in a beeper study. Given this final criterion introduced out of concern for the uninterrupted recovery of the participants, this study, in fact, was inadvertently designed to rule out the dual diagnosis case. This exclusion process has important implications for the significance of the study's findings of a significant level of psychopathology in the remaining subject pool.

A community sample was recruited from the surrounding residential area to serve as a nonalcoholic comparison group. An attempt was made to obtain a reasonably representative sample across the age, gender, and socioeconomic status ranges typically served by the center. Once subjects agreed to participate, they were administered several standard psychological tests, including the Minnesota Multiphasic Personality Inventory (MMPI) and the Symptom Checklist 90 (SCL-90). The findings from these two instruments are also discussed later in this chapter. All subjects participated under a signed consent and all experimental procedures were reviewed and approved by the hospital's human subjects committee and were in accordance with the ethical guidelines for research of the American Psychological Association (APA).

Forty-four subjects constituted the memory study, twenty-two drawn randomly from the larger study's alcoholic subjects and twenty-two drawn randomly from the larger study's nonalcoholic control group. When compared demographically, both the alcoholic and nonalcoholic subjects differed significantly only in age, with the alcoholic subjects being older on average. Age was found to have only weak correlations with any of the variables of interest, as was expected given the kind of memory investigated. Age was statistically controlled, however, in analyses of group differences in order to avoid any confounding influence that might result from the age difference between the two comparison groups.

Subjects carried beepers while engaged in their day-to-day activities for 2 weeks. They were told not to turn off the beeper for any reason and to keep it nearby whenever reasonably practical in situations such as exercising, showering, or preparing for sleep. In short, the beeper was to be their constant companion for this 2-week period. The pagers were randomly triggered by radio signal four times per day between the hours of 8:00 a.m. and 10:00 p.m., 7 days per week. When beeped, the subjects paused as soon as possible in their activities and completed a Daily Activity Report, which included items composed of adjectives describing mood state opposites on each pole of a Likert scale. Subjects indicated their mood state and its intensity by placing a mark along the continuous scale formed between the mood extremes.

When this procedure is followed with a good deal of consistency, a fairly representative and random sample of the subject's moods and experiences can be compiled. In the present study, both groups were very cooperative, given the hassle factor involved in carrying a beeper and a Daily Activity Report booklet and pausing to respond in the entire gambit of personal and work circumstances. The alcoholic group subjects responded on average 86 percent of the time when beeped, and the nonalcoholic group responded on average 79 percent of the time. Table 2–1 summarizes this compliance data, along with data on other variables of interest discussed in this section. Perhaps the higher response compliance in the alcoholic group is due to a higher level of motivation for some expected gain from the study findings, or from the extra amount of self-absorption and interest in internal events that is related to the early phases of recovery.

At the end of 2 weeks of participation, subjects returned to the study site and completed a series of self-report inventories. They turned in their Daily Activity Reports and discussed their content with a graduate student interviewer. Later, each marking on the Daily Activity Reports was converted to a numerical mood intensity score. From these scores, simple arithmetic calculations can describe what the individual felt and how strongly he or she felt it over selected time slices, or on the average over the entire period of participation. The calculations of interest for the memory aspect of this study are group averages for the frequency and intensity of mood experiences over the entire 2-week period. The questions addressed by these data are similar to those posed earlier in the chapter: Are the experiences of alcoholics who are not currently drinking different on average than those of nonalcoholics? Does negative affect play a more significant role in the lives of

Table 2-1. Depression, Memory, and Strategic Processing Measures

Measures	Alcoholic		Nonalcoholic	
Depression Measures				
MMPI Depression	63.7	(16.3)	54.2	(11.0)*
SCL 90 DEP Scale	.85	(.686)	.63	(.631)
Accuracy Measures				
Error: Positives	15.7	(5.6)	16.8	(13.5)
Error: Negatives	11.5	(6.2)	8.3	(3.9)*
Relative Accuracy Scores	.80	(.18)	.83	(.15)
Bias Measures				
Self-Protective Bias	14.5	(8.7)	15.5	(9.4)
Underestimation: Negatives	7.0	(4.9)	5.9	(3.7)
Overestimation: Positives	7.5	(5.5)	10.0	(11.1)
Depression Bias	11.0	(8.7)	6.8	(5.7)
Overestimation: Negatives	4.7	(5.2)	2.3	(2.8)
Underestimation: Positives	6.5	(6.0)	4.3	(.9)
Behavioral Indices				
Performed as Presented	5.4	(3.2)	3.5	(2.0)*
Performed with Poles Switched	8.0	(1.3)	2.2	(1.7)*
Shift from Positive Pole	.3	(.5)	1.2	(1.1)*
Shift from Negative Pole	.5	(1.0)	1.1	(1.2)*

MMPI Depression Scale units are T-scores. DEP scale units are mean intensity scores. All other non-correlational variables are measured by percent of error.
*$p < .05$.

alcoholics? Do alcoholics process their own moods, both in memory and in ongoing experience, in ways that differ from nonalcoholics?

Before moving on to the consideration of memory, let us investigate differences in ongoing experience by examining the recorded mood experiences of the forty-four subjects. The moods and experiences of individuals in both groups can be easily summarized, compared, and contrasted. Both groups experienced positive mood states much more often than negative or neutral mood states. No significant differences between groups were found on any of the frequencies of these positive mood items. However, if one looks only at which group had the higher mean, the emerging impression is that the alcoholic group was more aroused, vigilant, and emotionally mobilized, and the nonalcoholic group was more relaxed. This view is also consistent with the higher (although not significantly so) compliance of the recovery subjects with the beeper response requirements of the study.

When we examine the frequency of mood experiences that were neither negative or positive, the alcoholic group had fewer affectively neutral experiences than did the nonalcoholics, with three of these items being significantly different. The findings on the frequency of negative moods show where this emotional free time went. The recovery group mean is higher than the nonalcoholic group mean for all ten negative mood items. More importantly, the alcoholics experienced significantly more negative moods such as irritability, confusion, tension, and shame.

Subjects abstained from alcohol use during the study interval. It is possible, however, that the higher experience of negative emotions by the alcoholic subjects might be due to their involvement in recovery processes. The Daily Activity Report item indicating the sharing of emotions and experiences with others indicates that the subjects in recovery shared much more with other persons than did the nonalcoholic controls. It is possible that the treatment effects of probing one's inner emotional life in a struggle toward recovery might increase mobilization, tension, and the experience of negative emotions while leaving positive experiences roughly unaltered.

A second source of data suggests that this treatment effect of generally mobilizing affect and affective vigilance probably does not account for all or even most of the negative emotion experienced by the recovery subjects. Psychological tests for state and trait depression indicated that the alcoholic subjects were more depressed as a group than the nonalcoholic subjects. For trait depression, that is, depression as a personality variable or an attribute that is apt to endure over time, the alcoholics scored a mean T-score on the MMPI Depression Scale of 63.7 (SD = 16.3), whereas the nonalcoholics scored a mean T-score value of 54.2 (SD = 11.0), a significant difference. Using the Symptom 90 Checklist Depression Scale as a measure of state depression, that is, depression in the immediate experience, the alcoholics again scored as more depressed, but this difference did not reach significance.

So far, our empirical excursion into the phenomenology of everyday life parallels some of the hypotheses generated by our analysis of simple song lyrics. Alcoholics are more depressed and experience more negative emotional states and less neutral time than do nonalcoholics. An analysis comparing groups on only extreme moods (very positive or very negative) revealed that the alcoholic subjects had significantly more extreme mood states in addition to less time that was "neutral," or where the mood poles did not apply.

To this point, our concentration is on negative moods, or what addicted persons experience in the absence of their drug of choice. However, it is important to assess what they do not experience as well. For the purposes of the model used in this text, which places a strong emphasis on freedom as a value required for the healthy self, this loss of neutral time to negative experience suggested in the ESM data can be seen as crucial. The highs and lows of emotional life provide a good deal of drive or push. During these times we may experience some loss of control or self-direction, albeit (it is hoped) with a gain of spontaneity. Neutral times, when external or internal demands are relatively low, can present valuable opportunities to rediscover direction, control, and an improved sense of the self as prime mover. For the individual with a well-developed self, these are not empty times to be avoided, or time lost to an experience of nonbeing. Often, they are times where the healthy individual can hang fire—in solitude or quiescent intimacy—and evaluate life, its prospects and implications, or bask in soothing memories or maintain a detached but pleasant sense of the connectedness and variety of their life experiences.

For the individual with a less structured and less well-ordered sense of self, this neutral time has a different quality. During these moments, the individual may be inundated with cravings related to the need for object supplies, basic emotional support, and soothing from important others, which has its origins in the suckling and holding of infancy. This object craving during moments of solitude or relative detachment is often consciously experienced as boredom or restlessness and is related to the need to reconstitute weakened narcissistic defenses, a condition described by Svrakic (1985) as a "pessimistic mood" state. For individuals with pathologies of the self, the experience of time may be distorted by the avoidance of these neutral periods. Fewer moments of this type may indicate less self-direction and more determinism in the individual's life. In regard to these speculations, it is important to note that the data presented here are taken early in the recovery process. One can hypothesize that later in recovery more of the experience of neutral time can be tolerated or even sought out or created by the person who has grown to value such moments as beneficial to the emerging self-directed sense of self. In fact, most thoughtfully designed treatment programs structure the treatment process in exactly this way, with the first month being completely structured, almost from rising to bedtime. Free time is restricted in the middle phase of treatment with aftercare and self-help activities, which also generate additional social time with others in recovery. In the later stages of treatment, there is a tapering off of activity and a concentration on introspection, on exploring one's own daily experience and how it is related to recovery processes.

Let us return to the internal record of time and experience for each of our subjects—their memories. At the end of the 2-week beeper participation period, subjects reported to the study site for interviews and psychological testing. In addition, they performed a memory task requiring estimates of the percentage of occurrence of their previously recorded mood states. In effect, they were asked to produce from memory the data generated by the researcher by hand-scoring and computer-keying their many Daily Activity Report forms. At first, it might appear unlikely that anyone could produce such data with any meaningful degree of accuracy from the mere memory of checking-off report forms each day. However, the kind of memory investigated with such a task, memory for frequency of occurrences, has been found to be highly accurate in most situations and to be fairly immune to the types of influences that otherwise influence memory or learning, such as age or intelligence. This study is the first to use the ESM to investigate memory for moods.

Estimates were collected from subjects by means of a paper and pencil instrument titled Memory Task Moment-to-Moment-Beep (Figure 2–2). This form divides the above described bipolar adjective items into three categories of mood occurrences: the percentage of mood occurrences fitting one adjective pole, the

Figure 2-2. Memory Task Moment-to-Moment Beep

Check one: ☐ Total Period   ☐ First 2 Weeks   ☐ Last 2 Weeks

General Questions:

1. What percentage of the time did you mark (fill out) your book on the EXTREME RIGHT of the mood rating form?   _____%

2. What percentage of the time did you mark (fill out) your book on the EXTREME LEFT of the mood rating form?   _____%

3. What percentage of the time did you mark the POSITIVE items on the mood rating form?   _____%

4. What percentage of the time did you mark the NEGATIVE items on the mood rating form?   _____%

Percentage of Responses

Mood Questions

	very 0	quite o	some •	neither –	some •	very o	quite 0	
alert	_____%		_____%			_____%		drowsy
happy	_____%		_____%			_____%		sad
irritable	_____%		_____%			_____%		cheerful
strong	_____%		_____%			_____%		weak
angry	_____%		_____%			_____%		friendly
active	_____%		_____%			_____%		passive
lonely	_____%		_____%			_____%		sociable
proud	_____%		_____%			_____%		ashamed
confused	_____%		_____%			_____%		clear
tense	_____%		_____%			_____%		relaxed

Percentage (%) of Responses

	Not at all/Somewhat	*Quite/Very*
How preoccupied were you with eating?	_____%	_____%
How preoccupied were you with drinking/using?	_____%	_____%
How confident did you feel about your ability to resist the urge to drink/use?	_____%	_____%
Did you share your feelings with someone close to you?	_____%	_____%

percentage of moods described by the opposite adjective, and the percentage of experiences recorded at moments when neither end of the bipolar adjective could accurately be applied by the subject to his or her emotional state. For example, the Alert-Drowsy bipolar adjective item on the ESF is divided into three ranges: (1) very to somewhat alert, (2) neither alert nor drowsy, and (3) somewhat to very drowsy.

The form was used in a structured interview format wherein the subjects were told to estimate the occurrence of their recorded moods in percentages, with 100 percent being the total number or times they had responded to the bipolar adjective over the 2-week recording period. Graduate-level research assistants administered the task according to written directions designed to impress on the subject that memory was to be used to perform the task, rather than some other strategy, such as guessing what one might have recorded.

For each individual, the estimates made on the memory form were compared to the corresponding recorded mood frequencies. Several measures of accuracy were calculated. Accuracy was conceptualized as having two components, error related to cognitive inefficiency and error related to cognitive bias. Cognitive inefficiency may result from various failures or incapacities of the subject's attention, memory, and/or ability to recall at the moment. On tasks that have the same level of difficulty, this source of error would be expected to apply evenly across items. Error due to cognitive inefficiency should be more evident in difficult tasks than in simple, less complicated tasks, and should not vary with the task content. However, errors related to cognitive biases are due to differential processing of information rather than failures to process information well. This type of error consists of processing some contents efficiently and others inefficiently when task difficulty is constant, or introducing systematic content-related distortions in the information.

Because here we are dealing with emotionally laden stimuli, we might suspect that both sources of error will contribute to each individual's accuracy. We can also hypothesize that our two groups might perform differently on the memory task due to differences in these two kinds of error. We can hypothesize that the alcoholic group will demonstrate more error due to cognitive inefficiency (due to residual brain dysfunction), although a large difference should not be expected, since the kind of task presented here is viewed by most memory researchers as very simple, requiring few demands on cognitive capacity. Given our description of the alcoholic experience from the analysis of lyrics earlier in this chapter, we should, however, expect significant differences in the cognitive biases of alcoholics and nonalcoholics.

We might hypothesize that alcoholic subjects, being more depressed and having more negative experiences as demonstrated by the ESF data, might demonstrate more depressive realism (i.e., less of a tendency toward self-protective defenses) than nonalcoholics. Conversely, if we were to follow the views of Beck (1967), we would hypothesize that alcoholics would demonstrate a depressive world view, that is, in addition to not showing self-protective biases, alcoholics would actually distort the memories of their emotional experience toward the direction of recalling it as more negative (and congruent with a negative self-image and a depressogenic world view) than indicated on their ESF records.

To test these hypotheses, several accuracy scores were calculated for each individual. These scores can be broken down into three types.

1. *Measures of relative accuracy.* Measures such as in a correlation coefficient indicate the degree of relationship between memory estimates and the recorded emotional events. Relative accuracy is important because estimates may have a close relationship with actual events without being on, or even very near, target, as when a estimate is always off by, say, five or so percentage points.

2. *Measures of absolute accuracy.* Signed difference scores indicate whether estimates are either "short" or "long" of their target, that is, they have a signed difference from the actual. The problem with signed differences is that they will to some extent balance each other out across items or in the calculation of group averages. Absolute difference scores, that is the difference of estimate and target without a sign, are more useful in that they do not have this liability. Signed error scores do contain very useful information, as we see in the development of measures of bias.

3. *Bias measures.* These are computed based on some operational definition of the type of patterned distortion or differential processing that may be occurring in the data. As such, bias measures are more theory driven than are the other measures of accuracy or error discussed here. Bias may be detected by examining the other types of accuracy measures as the affective content of the target item is varied. Using each subject's over- and underestimates (in percentage points) of both positive and negative moods, two composite measures of cognitive bias measures were developed: A self-protective bias measure (the overestimate of positive moods combined with the underestimate of negative moods) and a depression bias measure (the overestimation of negative mood events with the underestimation of positive mood events).

All three types of measures were calculated for each of the memories to record comparisons required by the Memory Task Form. Table 2–1 shows these measures along with the measures of trait (MMPI Scale 2) and trait (SCL 90) depression. Note that in order to simplify the discussion here, only the findings for positive and negative emotions are presented, dropping off the neutral range, which is less crucial to the theoretical issues at hand. The data in the table indicate that there was almost no difference in relative accuracy (discrimination coefficient) between the groups and that little support was found for either of the conflicting theories about the relative bias of alcoholics and nonalcoholics. Alcoholics did, however, make significantly more errors on negative moods (absolute error: negatives) than did the nonalcoholics, but not in the specific ways used to operationalize this either self-protective or depressive.

To fully interpret these findings, however, it is important to keep in mind that we are dealing with the interaction of three variables in regard to memory biases: alcoholism status, trait depression, and state depression. This pilot study consists of a small number of subjects. Subjects in both groups have some degree of state and trait depression. Table 2–2 shows the relationship of state and trait depression to the memory measures across groups, that is, for all subjects.

These data support the view that state and trait depression contributes to a depressive bias in memory. Higher levels of trait and state depression are related significantly to higher scores on the depression bias measure, with most of this relationship coming from the overestimation of negative experience rather than from the underestimation of positive mood events. Rather than demonstrating depressive realism, the depressed individuals in this small sample were more apt to exaggerate the negative in their experiences. However, when we looked at the scores for the alcoholic group alone in Table 2–1, we found that they both underestimated and overestimated negative events more than did nonalcoholics, a finding contrary to the depressogenic hypothesis given that the alcoholics were on the average more depressed. This finding is consistent with a psychodynamic interpretation that the alcoholic subjects have powerful conflicts in regard to negative affects, which involve alternately avoiding and immersing themselves in negative affects, especially depression (Khantzian 1980). An example would be an individual who uses alcohol to avoid feelings of depression and at times becomes overwhelmingly depressed while under the influence. What the pattern of findings

Table 2–2. Trait and State Depression Correlations

Measure	Trait	State
Depression Measures		
MMPI Scale 2	1.000	.351*
Frequency of Negative Affect	.217	.582*
Accuracy Measures		
Absolute Error: Positives	−.116	−.148
Absolute Error: Negatives	.406*	.290
Bias Measures		
Self-Protective Bias	−.091	−.244
Underestimation: Negatives	.015	−.032
Overestimation: Positives	.142	.211
Depression Bias	.347*	.339*
Overestimation: Negatives	.446*	.347*
Underestimation: Positives	.142	.211
Behavioral Indices		
Performed as Presented	.189	.285
Shift from Positive Pole	−.126	−.189
Shift from Negative Pole	−.025	−.217

Note. *$p < .05$.

suggests is that alcoholics do have a different relationship with negative emotional events than do nonalcoholics, but that not all of this difference can be accounted for by depression. This finding would be consistent with the cyclical view of the experience of self outlined in Chapter 1.

Before leaving the factors other than depression that are related to cognitive bias differences between alcoholics and nonalcoholics in this preliminary study, let us briefly examine a cognitive strategy measure that was also introduced in the context of the study. As the research assistants recorded the subjects memory estimates, they also noted the order in which subjects performed the sub-items for each bipolar memory item, using a standard format—see Figure 2–3. For example, in the memory item that requires an estimate of the percentage of feelings recorded as happy, neither happy nor sad, and sad, the subject could perform any one of the three sub-items first and could then choose either of the remaining two sub-items as a second choice. Two conflicting hypotheses were entertained. The first was based on the earlier contrasting of depressogenic and self-protective biases. Following this contrast, it was predicted that a depressogenic style would lead to alcoholics choosing the negative pole of the item first, whereas nonalcoholics would be primed by their self-protective biases to avoid the negative pole. It should be pointed out that the items were presented in balance so that positive poles alternated with negative poles as the initial sub-item to appear printed from left to right on the Memory Task form. A second hypothesis was that alcoholics, due to their depression, would simply show less of a tendency toward any use of a cognitive strategy, that is, since it requires energy and complexity to seek out any given sub-item pole, alcoholics would be more apt to perform the items as presented, without switching the order of subitems.

The findings were significant at the .005 level that the alcoholics were more apt to perform the sub-items as presented on the paper form than the nonalcoholics, who tended to make choices among the sub-items. Also, the nonalcoholics were significantly more apt (at the .005 level) to switch from the first pole presented to perform its opposite first and that (surprisingly) they were more apt to shift from the positive pole. The latter finding was due primarily to the alcoholic subjects' minimal deviation from the order presented on the form and the fact that when the alcoholics did deviate, they were more apt to switch away from a negative item. As was the case for some of the accuracy measures, the differences between groups for strategic processing measures were only partially explained by depression. The strategic processing variables had significant negative correlations with the total amount of negative experience recorded over the participation period.

Generally, this preliminary study adds to the growing body of research that points to an asymmetry of the effects of positive versus negative moods. The strategic processing findings suggest that defensive mechanisms can be reflected in both avoidance of a task (alcoholics tending to avoid the negative mood task) or preemption of a threatening task in a self-protective manner (nonalcoholics performing the negative mood sub-items first and then underestimating the

Figure 2–3. Behavioral Observation Record: Behavioral Observation of Memory
            Test

We want to observe and record the sequence of the answers to the mood
and preoccupation/confident/feeling questions.

As the subject fills out the form, observe how he/she completes these
sections and record that information as follows:

1 = FIRST CHOICE   2 = SECOND CHOICE   3 = THIRD CHOICE

	Columns		
	1	2	3
alert	_____	_____	_____
happy	_____	_____	_____
irritable	_____	_____	_____
strong	_____	_____	_____
angry	_____	_____	_____
active	_____	_____	_____
lonely	_____	_____	_____
proud	_____	_____	_____
confused	_____	_____	_____
tense	_____	_____	_____

Not at all/somewhat = 1
Quite/very = 2

	1	2
Preoccupied eating	_____	_____
Preoccupied drinking/using	_____	_____
Confident	_____	_____
Shared feelings	_____	_____

occurrence of negative moods, presumably to reduce information that was inconsistent with their self-concept).

We report here only preliminary findings from a single study that supports the
position that alcoholics and others suffering from depression may have a depressogenic world view that outweighs their more normal tendency toward a self-
protective bias. The data also suggest that alcoholics are more apt to have a passive,
uncreative way of processing experiences and memories. It is probable that depression does not fully cover the influence of negative affect generally and that other
affects (such as anxiety, tension, and anger) and psychological conflicts regarding
affective experience itself may be important to understanding the dynamics of

alcoholism. It should be noted that this study, like the chapter as a whole, does not directly address the effects of neurological impairments, which usually complicate cases of prolonged alcohol abuse.

THE DUAL DIAGNOSIS PERSPECTIVE

The moral to the many subplotted story of empirical and theoretical approaches presented in this chapter is that although dual diagnosis problems can be extraordinarily complex to conceptualize and difficult to investigate empirically, they can nonetheless be systematically charted or mapped, and the resulting maps provide useful clinical contexts and insights. For example, it is obvious that the one very limited study presented here does not weigh strongly against any of the alternative theories offered in regard to the relationship between depression and alcoholism. What should be clear to the reader, however, is the complexity of interaction among variables from separate spheres of human functioning in a specific, limited dual diagnosis problem. In addition, it is also apparent that it is not always possible to directly apply the solutions for one dual diagnosis problem to one that appears similar. What is required is an understanding of basic dynamics, interacting factors, and processes that are mutually causative. For example, the data presented in the preceding section confirm the escape avoidance hypothesis of addiction in that the alcoholics were depressed and had more negative affective experience during sobriety than did nonalcoholics, with little significant difference in the total amount of positive experience. One treatment implication of this finding might be to decrease stressors and negative affective events during recovery from alcoholism through the use of a protective environment and tranquilizers, a strategy that is often employed in the initial stages of most treatment programs, while designing interventions aimed at decreasing the patient's depressogenic cognitions. Recent evidence suggests that this would not be effective for cocaine addiction, where the capacity for positive emotional experience has been chemically undermined. The introduction of positive, high arousal events alternating with treatments designed to induce psychophysiological arousal and homeostasis such as meditation or reduced environmental stimulation might be more in keeping with the specific psychopharmacological impact of cocaine abuse on the capacity for the experience of pleasure. Concurrently, it might be necessary to confront the cocaine addict's cognitions that make periods of dysphoria or boredom intolerable, that is, their inflated self-protective biases. Specific psychiatric drugs may be developed to address the brain tissue damage and related pleasure center depletion caused by prolonged cocaine abuse. Whereas the complexity of these problems can be discouraging, the current knowledge base about the processes of addiction and psychopathology allows us to identify for each specific dual diagnosis problem a minimal set of crucial factors that must be integrated into a parsimonious theoretical approach, which can then be used to inform clinical work with specific patients at specific points in the recovery process.

3

Simplifying the Dual Diagnosis Dilemma

THE NEED FOR A GENERAL HEURISTIC SYSTEM

Every clinician or counselor has access to the *DSM-III-R* with its categories of mental disorders, which include the addictions. To anyone acquainted with this system, it is obvious that it would be highly time-consuming to review each diagnostic category for the types of dual diagnosis problems most likely to be encountered. To create such a cross-referenced catalogue or encyclopedia of dual diagnosis issues and suggested interventions, we would have to review for each emotional and mental disorder the key dimensions of dual diagnosis work described in the first chapter. In addition, each psychoactive substance has unique chemical properties and social consequences that may function in a multitude of ways within the context of a mental illness and an addictive pattern, making such an endeavor even more herculean. Another obstacle to such a task is the fact that the detailed knowledge about dual diagnosis problems is simply not available, due in part to limitations in theory construction.

Fortunately, by emphasizing the features of mental illnesses that are most relevant to dealing with addiction, it is possible to identify several symptom complexes that routinely occur across specific diagnoses. Similarly, psychoactive substances fall into well-known categories of psychopharmacological impact and action. Addictive disorders also may be described by a relatively restricted number of psychosocial functions that can be usefully applied to understanding most cases of addiction when other pathology is also present. This chapter outlines these three elements—symptom complexes, the dominant psychosocial functions of addiction when concurrent with other psychopathology, and the major categories of psychoactive substances—and identifies their typical relationships within dual diagnosis work.

By outlining these three sets of concepts, we develop a heuristic system for approaching dual diagnosis problems. By a heuristic system, we mean a theory or set of theories designed to guide observation and to generate hypotheses. In a sense, such a system is theory used as a tool to further investigation, rather than theory as explanation or an end point of thought. Perhaps it is best to include a definition from a theoretician not inclined to favor the developers of heuristics. Writing of the cognitive heuristic literature, Lora Lopes notes that the term is borrowed from computer science, perhaps suggesting that the concept maintains some of the garbage-in equals garbage-out flair of computerland. She goes on to inform us about the hopes and liabilities of heuristics applied to, or investigated in psychology:

> In broad terms heuristic methods are quick-and-not-too-dirty procedural tricks that usually yield acceptable solutions to problems at noticeably less cost than is required by alternative methods (called algorithms) that guarantee optimal solutions. In other words, heuristics are methods that achieve efficiency by risking failure. [1991, p. 68]

The heuristic system presented here has all of the advantages and problems of a computer-simulated expert system. As in such models, although the process of arriving at these heuristic elements is complex and requires some intellectual diligence to follow, the elements themselves and their recommended use are relatively straightforward. Unlike a computer model, however, the elements of the heuristic system are designed to be rich in associations to theories, clinical facts, and phenomenal experience available to most knowledgeable clinicians. The elements are few enough in number to enable a clinician to retain them in memory at all times, allowing their use as aids to guiding clinical observations and creating interventions on the spot, resulting in clearer formulations. When treatment results in either significant shifts in symptom presentation, or changes in the functions of addiction-related thoughts, feelings, or behaviors, the heuristic system can be reapplied to the case for a new formulation. In short, the system respects the data-processing limitations and virtues of the well-trained clinician. Although the purpose of the heuristic system is to simplify the dual diagnosis dilemma, like most clinical tools, its use at first is neither simple nor easy. With time, however, the system will begin to provide some sense of having a touchstone or landmark in an otherwise confusing and harsh landscape of problems and treatment setbacks where the dual diagnosis patient often eludes us.

In defining the major symptom complexes and addictive functions, there is no attempt to preempt the detailed and empirically researched canons of diagnostics such as the *DSM-III-R*. Nor are the symptom complexes described here synonymous with the factor analytic or structural dimensions of psychopathology that many researchers and theorists have tried to delimit, although this attempt does seek information by such earlier work. As far as possible, each clinician should have a close working knowledge of the diagnostic criteria, etiology, course of illness, prominent dynamics, and preferred mode of treatment for the diagnosis best fitting the patient in question. An understanding of the basic principles and conceptual issues in psychopathology and the addictions is also essential for anyone engaged in the treatment of dual diagnosis cases. In addition, an examination of the categories of symptom complexes and functions of addiction reviewed here should assist the clinician in conceptualizing the issues in the individual case. The reader who does not currently possess a fund of knowledge to evaluate the framework offered here should, with patience, find that this framework is a valuable starting point to increased understanding and interest while investigating the literature in both psychopathology and the addictions.

The symptom complexes and addictive functions described here are fuzzy sets, inclusive to various degrees of many diagnostic categories and behaviors. Similarly, the psychosocial functions of addiction require the application of more than one theoretical approach. Each complex and function is conceptualized as a continuous dimension that applies to some extent to each patient. The use of these heuristic concepts should, therefore, encourage dialectical and process-oriented thinking. Because of these integrative, relative, and eclectic characteristics, the utility of the symptom complexes and functions of addiction depends greatly on the judgment and experience of the individual applying them to a given case. Perhaps this heuristic system will minimize the overreliance on categorical diagnosis and will, therefore, help to reduce stigmatizing patients with labels that carry little specific information and often result in stereotyped intervention strategies and other treatment errors.

As with any heuristic system (and much of the content of this book), these complexes and functions are tools for learning and discovery. The goal is to help the user to find the appropriate questions, contexts, concepts, and methods that will be helpful in solving the problems presented by a specific case. The heuristic system application in itself is only a step in the process of discovery. Although a system helps to define a problem, it does not give a finished solution. Presupposing an easy solution will, even in a very well-designed heuristic system, result in a few remarkable successes and many more grave errors in diagnosis and treatment.

FIVE SYMPTOM COMPLEXES

The dual diagnosis heuristic system begins by temporarily leaving the question of diagnosis in abeyance. The dual diagnosis case—that is, the patient identified as involved with substance use and having some other significant psychopathology— is examined in terms of the totality of symptoms presented. The initial goal of the examination is to establish the symptom complexes that are most operative in the case, rather than obtaining a specific diagnosis.

The symptom complexes introduced here are composites from more than one generally well-known symptom cluster. A symptom cluster consists of symptoms of a similar nature, often having common origins or causes and often occurring together in the various clinical syndromes or single diagnoses. Both symptom complexes, and clusters consist of processes that affect the individual in similar ways, often negatively influencing the same sphere of behavior, or the same biological or psychological system. Symptom complexes, however, also contain symptoms with different origins and causal roots. In dual diagnosis problems, the addictive symptoms and the symptoms of a coexisting disorder have, at least to some extent, different points of origin and different causal roots. Symptom complexes arise when several symptom clusters interact and reinforce one another, and various unique qualities or characteristics emerge from this interaction.

Because we are limited here to dealing with dual diagnosis issues, symptom complexes are considered to be more important than symptom clusters due to the emergent qualities that spring from the addictive process interacting with at least one other kind of mental or emotional disorder. The term *addictive process* should not obscure the fact that in many cases one of the other disorders with which an addictive process may interact will be another form of addiction. Cocaine addiction and alcohol abuse, for instance, interactively constitute a form of poly-substance abuse.

Five major symptom complexes are identified across diagnostic categories: reward/arousal deficits, anxiety, dominance of affect, cognition and context, and sociability and identity. Each complex could apply to a certain extent to each dual diagnosis case, although in the majority of cases, only one or two complexes will be most relevant to the dual diagnosis problem of decreasing the synergy between the addiction and the psychopathology and increasing the synergy between recovery processes. Clearly, however, as the healthy functions that correspond to these symptom complexes are hand-in-glove functions, the symptom complexes themselves can be separated only by simplifying them.

The order in which the symptom complexes are presented here relates to Maslow's hierarchy of needs. Each complex roughly corresponds to a level of needs-related functioning at which the individual will become developmentally arrested if the complex is not adequately compensated for or neutralized. Viewed from a phenomenological perspective, the individual will experience strivings toward this corresponding set of needs. Viewed from a biological perspective, the complexes are presented phylogenetically and in the order of the degree of neurological complexity that is required for the optimal functioning of the system most affected by each complex.

Table 3–1 outlines each symptom complex. It provides a brief definition, identifyies the basic need threatened by the symptoms, gives clinical and lay terms often used to describe persons who clearly demonstrate the symptom complex, and

Table 3-1. Summary of the Symptom Complexes

Reward/Arousal Deficits
Extreme preference for either high or low levels of stimulation.
Threatened need: Optimal physical and psychological arousal level.
Descriptors: Type A/B personality, sensation seeking, reclusive/instrusive, demanding, "hyper," unmotivated, intractable.
Diagnostic categories: Autism, schizophrenia, psychopathy.

Anxiety
Symptoms are clearly related to the experience of anxiety.
Threatened need: Basic physical or psychological security.
Descriptors: Anxious, tense, jumpy, scattered, neurotic, avoidant, high-strung, overreactive, psychosomatic, fearful, rigid.
Diagnostic categories: Adjustment disorders, compulsive personality disorder, avoidant personality disorder.

Dominance of Affect
One or more emotional states dominate experience and behavior.
Threatened need: Emotional complexity, stability, and diversity.
Descriptors: Depressed, manic, euphoric, angry, rageful, impulsive, emotional roller coaster, emotionally out of control.
Diagnostic categories: Major affective disorders, dysthymia, adjustment disorders with affective features, borderline personality disorder, passive aggressive-explosive personality.

Cognition and Context
Thought or its appropriate context is disordered or impaired.
Threatened need: Rational basis for decisions and actions.
Descriptors: Psychotic, poor reality testing, delusional, out of touch, misses the point, weird thinking, paranoid.
Diagnostic categories: Psychotic disorders, primitive personality disorders, intellectual deficiency or organic personality.

Sociability and Identity
Sense of self and general interpersonal relatedness is impaired.
Threatened need: Identity, feeling understood, and belonging.
Descriptors: Narcissistic, lost soul, inadequate, antisocial, self-centered, impressionable, a follower, insensitive/fragile
Diagnostic categories: Adolescent adjustment disorders, borderline personality disorder, subculture participation.

---

lists representative diagnostic categories to which the symptom complex is particularly relevant.

We begin the description of these conceptual tools with the first two complexes, which represent primary psychophysiological predispositions gone awry, resulting in strivings toward psychophysiological homeostasis and basic physical security. They are reward/arousal deficits and anxiety.

Reward/arousal deficits is a complex related to sensation seeking, elimination of external stimulation, self-stimulation (including aspects of fantasy or hallucination) and abnormal responses to punishment or reward. The basic pathological process of this complex is a typical under- or overreaction to either stimulation or the factors that shape learned behavior. Stimulation may be environmental, social, or from sources within the body. Learning factors may include positive and negative reinforcers, secondary reinforcers, punishment, or specific learning conditions.

This complex may be the least familiar of the five discussed here; therefore, it is described more fully in Chapter 4, which outlines assessment techniques. As described here, the reward/arousal deficits has as its theoretical basis several important psychophysiological and learning theory concepts of personality and psychopathology that have been incorporated into the development of psychological tests. Specifically, they are optimal arousal and stimulation theory, as incorporated in Zuckerman's Sensation Seeking Scale (SSS) (Zuckerman 1979a) and biosocial learning theory as incorporated in the Millon Clinical Multiaxial Inventory (MCMI) (Millon 1983).

To identify some of the factors involved in this complex, let us note a few diagnostic categories where it is typically dominant. The reward/arousal deficits complex may be of special relevance to cases of schizophrenia when negative symptoms predominate and external stimulation and social contact are avoided. Conversely, primary psychopaths inundate themselves with stimulation and social contacts while overvaluing positive reinforcers and undervaluing negative reinforcers or punishments. Phobics typically avoid novel stimulation generally, and they overgeneralize and overreact to threatening stimuli. In many cases of mania, affect is less prominent than activity and sensation seeking. Similarly, in many cases of depression, manifest affect is not as pronounced clinically as withdrawal, inactivity, and a low tolerance of stimulation.

The *anxiety* complex of symptoms includes a range of responses to an undefined or polymorphous sense of threat with or without cognitive content. As the reward/arousal deficits threaten basic psychophysiological processes and the functioning of normal mechanisms of motivation, this complex threatens basic psychological security by imposing the awareness of, and psychophysiological preparation for, internal or external danger. This complex is obviously relevant to anxiety and phobic disorders and some paraphilias, but it also relates to many types of neurosis and psychosis where variations in anxiety appear to account for most of the vicissitudes of symptoms.

Although most nonorganically caused disorders of psychopathology can be taken as failures in anxiety management (and to some extent the failure to appropriately modulate arousal according to demand), this is not the approach here. Viewing all psychopathology as variant expressions of anxiety requires an overreliance on the analysis of psychological defenses, meaning that biological and learned capacities for coping with environmental and internal demands must be universally understood within the context of a single affective state. This places too much explanatory burden on too few concepts. In one sense, the model developed here deals with symptoms that result after such defenses against anxiety or demand have failed, rather than with the defensive operations themselves. The decision to separate anxiety symptoms as a complex is based on the qualitative differences between individuals whose problems are primarily focused around manifest anxiety and other individuals whose problems do not exhibit this focus.

These two complexes—reward/arousal deficits and anxiety—can be operationally defined by various measures of abnormal physiological and conditioning responses, such as an abnormal orienting response, unusual average evoked potential responses to affective stimuli, suppressed or heightened learned response to reinforcement, failure to learn under fear-conditioning procedures, overgeneralization of behavioral cues, failure to generalize learning, failure to decondition, and failure to respond to punishment. The third and fourth complexes discussed here involve disruption of the organism's basic systems of expression and information: affect and cognition.

Affect and cognition are thought of here as two subsystems of a single self-reflexive and interactive process for exploring the internal and external environments and for creatively adapting to and altering these environments. Given this view, it is of little consequence to consider the primacy of thought or emotion in personality development or psychopathology. Using a radio broadcast as an analogy, we may view the two complexes of reward/arousal deficits and anxiety as contributing to various sources of static, or background noise interfering with the reception of the broadcast signal. The symptom complexes of dominance of affect and cognition and context, in contrast, represent actual distortions, disruptions, or intrusions in the message or signal itself. The radio broadcast analogy is more appropriate if, for the dominance of affect complex, we imagine a performance by amateur musicians with poorly tuned instruments, tin ears, and bad taste. For the cognition and context complex, imagine the broadcast of an ill-informed, fuzzy thinking, or clearly prejudiced and biased news reporter whose sources are limited or highly suspect.

The *dominance of affect* complex is demonstrated by affect being the primary feature of the individual's clinical presentation. Intense and overwhelming depression, sadness, anger, fear, or an inflated euphoria are the most common affective problems. Another pattern related primarily to affect is found more often in substance abusers than in other patients. In this pattern, intermittent displays of intense primary emotion occur within an individual who more typically expresses overwhelming tension or stress and who usually demonstrates only a minimal ability to discriminate among emotional states. In cases where this complex is predominant, the source of the affect may be a higher biological predisposition toward a given affect or affectivity in general, may stem from an acquired biochemical imbalance, or may stem from the interaction of affective predisposition and psychological structure and defense.

Clarification of what is meant by overwhelming affect is to understand both affective dominance and its causes. To say that an emotion is overwhelming glosses over the specific personality functions or combination of functions that may be disrupted, impaired, or aborted by intense affect. Self-monitoring, general cognition, impulse control, discrimination of affective shadings, and somatic functions may be overwhelmed selectively or together. A specific overpowering affect or a tendency toward heightened affectivity in general may overwhelm these functions. Depression, bipolar disorder, borderline personality disorder, histrionic personality, and intermittent explosive disorder are diagnoses that often involve this complex of symptoms.

The related complex of symptoms involving *cognition and context* applies to pathologies where the process of ideation, thought content, orientation in the environment, and in extreme cases perception are distorted. The ability to establish and appropriately shift perspective in meaning or, in more severe cases, the ability to identify and maintain a single associational context for interpreting ongoing events is impaired. The clearest classes highly related to this complex are psychotic and paranoid disorders with psychotic features. However, compulsive personality, with its behavioral and cognitive rigidity and inability to shift context appropriately, also exemplifies the problems in this complex.

In most clinical cases, cognition and context is related to the affective complex in a complementary manner. Except in very severe cases of psychopathology, when one of these complexes is prominent, the healthier functions related to the other symptom complex are usually underdeveloped. Well-established physiological and psychodynamic processes link these functions into a reciprocally informing union of opposites, rather than independent personality functions. For example, in hysterical or histrionic persons, intense, inappropriate emotionality and action are hallmarks of the personality. Thought and perspective are often underdeveloped but not necessarily distorted. Another example is dysthymia, a mild affective disorder where thought processes are inefficient but otherwise normal.

In the fifth complex—*sociability and identity*—symptoms consist of defects and deficits in bonding, empathy, identification, self-formation, and relationship. The first four complexes presented here are related to impairments in functions that are prerequisite to developing the basic structure of the socially adapted self. This complex represents pathologies within the enterprise of self-development. The most severe personality disorders often show prominent impairment from symptoms in this cluster, although schizophrenics and the so-called schizoid personality often exhibit this cluster more prominently than any other. The psychopath and the schizophrenic often have prominent impairments in identification and social interaction. The psychopath often shows a pathological identification with the stranger or predator introject and, therefore, in effect with the unhuman (Meloy 1988), and the schizophrenic usually fails to make the basic differentiation of self from other on which healthy and stable identification and identity are predicated.

The five complexes introduced in this chapter are conceived as pathological processes within the context of the sequential development of the person based on a combination of developmental psychology and Maslow's hierarchy of adult needs-related functioning. The decision to emphasize symptoms rather than psychological structure in part is based on the desire to underline the importance of ebb and flow; psychological structure is usually abstracted from stability within change. Nonetheless, the same warning regarding other hierarchical categories or phases should be offered in regard to the symptom complexes. Like all forms of biological and psychological growth, the complexes represent changing processes more than stable traits.

The ebb and flow of a single symptom complex provides only limited assistance in dealing with the particular origins of a dual diagnosis problem. Although the complexes are roughly hierarchical in relationship to the developmental requirements that they jeopardize, pathology does not always build in such a strictly linear manner. There are three reasons why significant severity on one of the complexes does not imply more severe pathology on the next complex in the hierarchy. The first is the fairly obvious attempt to make the complexes relatively independent or orthogonal so that cases can be easily rated or classified by the dominant complex. The second reason is related to the eclectic manner in which these categories cut across etiological or causal lines and, therefore, cut across developmental eras where a symptom might have its origins. For example, anxiety due to a physiological or constitutional predisposition is combined here (and in most clinical observations) with anxiety due primarily to extreme personality conflicts that have a psychodynamic basis. Although we should expect a significant overlap of individuals who have both kinds of problems, with the predisposition contributing strongly to psychodynamic issues, there is no necessary causal tie between the two forms of anxiety that typically represent problems having their origins in different developmental eras.

The third reason that severity level on one complex does not predict severity on the others concerns the vicissitudes of development and growth. The dynamics of psychological development underline the process emphasis of these concepts as opposed to the end point or outcome emphasis of diagnostic categories. A complete, all-pervasive, and permanent blockage of development at any given stage, or in any single mental function, although theoretically possible, is extremely unlikely in any given case. In even the most impaired person, optimal conditions for growth sometimes prevail. For example, low levels of stress, interpersonal support, or other ameliorating circumstances may be timed fortuitously with the cyclical ebb in symptom severity, allowing an otherwise "stuck" individual to function at an untypical higher level. Some consolidation of learning or increased experiential range may occur during such occasions in a manner not totally conditioned by even very severe underlying pathology. A block in the flow of development is more like a sieve or a breakwater than a solid concrete dam.

As a reminder, the rough identifications and definitions for these five complexes are not meant to replace detailed and precise diagnostic work. Rather, the goal here is to identify prominent symptom clusters that take on relevance *in the context of addictive behavior*. Although these symptom clusters have some validity and usefulness in approaching psychopathology generally, they are meant for dual diagnosis work, that is, they are to be used in approaching a concomitant addictive disorder in order to understand it as a process that is reciprocal to the psychopathological process. Stated more simply, this approach is based on the assumption that the function of the addiction will tell us something important about the psychopathology in the individual and how he or she is trying to gain mastery over the illness. It is also expected that the psychopathology will inform us about the addiction, explaining to some extent why it is present and why it takes a given form. In any clinical case, several of these symptom clusters may be present, but only one or two will be of direct relevance in regard to the motivation and function of the addictive process as well as to its opponent recovery process.

FIVE BIOPSYCHOSOCIAL FUNCTIONS OF ADDICTION

Just as there is currently no fully satisfactory unified theory accounting for psychopathology, diversity is needed in a theoretical approach to the addictions to satisfactorily account for the range of addictive disorders that show up in clinical practice. Baker (1988), in several articles on empirical approaches to addiction, grouped promising models into four categories, which are limited by his focus only on experimental and empirical approaches and by an unnecessary and intense antimentalistic bias. In briefly identifying Baker's major categories of models, I loosely follow his substantially complete description while attempting to correct the bias.

The first model encompasses the traditional motivational concepts familiar to the behavioral learning literature, concepts such as conditioned response, conditioned stimuli, reinforcement history, and behavioral cues. To this, let us add physiological and genetic factors that specifically influence these learning variables. The second model, cognitive learning, and information processing models of addiction, have recently become increasingly concerned with the processing of memories and expectations involving negative and positive affective experiences. Within this broad umbrella of approaches, let us include the cognitive dynamic theories of self-psychology, to the extent that these intrapsychic theories are concerned with defenses that influence how information is handled, that is, the management of aversive or overwhelming affects, thoughts, and experiences. In clinical practice, existential approaches typically focus on these cognitive dynamic factors. The third model, interpersonal/social context of drug use, is attracting increasing interest. Let us add the related intrapsychic context of object relations theory. Finally, the model that covers the biology of addiction, especially genetics, has continued to grow in importance, as methods and guiding concepts for studying the gene-environment interaction (especially early formative environment) have improved.

Almost without exception, the myriad individual theories and explanations that enter into these four broad models seek to account for some cause or origin of addiction, the function of the addiction, or both. Function refers to the role played by the addictive process relative to the basic functions of the individual (healthful or pathological) which allows the addiction to continue in the face of aversive and life-threatening consequences. Since the focus in this book is treatment and the development of concepts that can guide clinical observation, we concentrate on the biopsychosocial functions rather than origins or causes of addiction. The remainder of this section describes five general biopsychosocial functions of addiction, each informed to some extent by the four models identified above. Although the function itself is emphasized here, an examination of the addiction in the light of the most prominent symptom complexes will lead to fruitful speculations concerning the origin of the addiction as well.

In concentrating on a few generalized psychological and social functions of addiction, some important information could be lost about the unique qualities of different drugs, the typical courses of dependence on various substances, or the social and legal consequences and implications of their use. Consistent attention to the key dimensions of dual diagnosis work when augmented with an understanding of the factors leading to the preference for a specific drug or for several drugs in an individual case, will prevent many of the liabilities of this focus. Attention to the symptom complexes outlined earlier and to the categories of psychoactive drugs discussed later in this chapter will provide important contexts for establishing the dominant function(s) served by the addictive process in the individual's dynamics, phenomenal world, and social sphere.

As indicated in the section on the symptom complexes, the functions defined here are concepts of addiction designed to relate to a concurrent process of psychopathology. They inform the clinician about the reciprocal pathology while guiding the detailed observation of the addiction.

Since hedonism and pleasure-seeking are motives ubiquitously attributed to substance abusers, an introductory note is in order critiquing the commonsense view of hedonism. The pursuit of pleasure and the avoidance of pain and unpleasure (the absence of a tension/discharge balance) should be automatically assumed as a dynamic operative in all human behavior. This basic assumption as a premise of philosophy or psychology is the correct formal definition of hedonism, as in the study of hedonics. However, in discussing addiction and its functions, the charge of hedonism against substance abusers relies on the moral and religious connotations of the word and calls up general social attitudes toward the irresponsible pursuit of pleasure and leisure. Ignoring for a moment its moral condemnation of the nonconformist or moral identification with the rebel, the common use of the term hedonism carries some other useful information. It most often indicates a failure in the subordination of lower values and needs to higher values and needs. The charge is similar to that of selfishness versus altruism as a motive. In reference to Maslow's hierarchy, the hedonistic individual consistently pursues goals at a lower level of needs-functioning than one would predict given his or her apparent developmental level. Hedonism in this context recognizes the existential value of striving (reaching toward that which exceeds one's grasp) in becoming human. This value emphasis is useful if we temper it with the knowledge that disdain for the underachiever is one of the most moralistically tinged, culturally bound, and unexamined attitudes in Western life. Given this critique, hedonism as a motive is replaced here by more specific references to pathological processes that might explain, rather than merely describe and condemn, the absence of well-coordinated values or the presence of misguided strivings. For example, the reward/arousal deficits complex and the symptoms of cognition and context often describe what appears to be simple hedonism. Hedonism is viewed here as a symptom rather than a function or motive for addiction.

In addition to avoiding concepts with overly moralistic connotations, the goal here is to avoid the use of concepts that are either too global or too specific to aid in the further refinement of ideas related to the function of an addiction. For example, some authors explain the use of substances as a faulty coping mechanism or a substitute for more appropriate coping skills. This is often clearly the case, but the simplistic conceptualization of coping skills, which often underlies such explanations may leave the question begging as to which skills are in deficit, why they have not developed, and how the substance use provides a partially effective compensation. Another example of an overly global approach is the concept of the addictive personality. Because of its generality and circular logic, this concept has added little to clinical understanding beyond a label that can be easily accepted by the general public or taught to people in recovery. Although the addictive personality label offers certain advantages to psychoeducational and self-help programs, it has not advanced clinical practice or scientific understanding.

On the side of the overly specific approach, many sophisticated formulations of drug use describe how specific affective states, self-representations, basic needs for control and mastery, object relations, reality-oriented threats, and other crucial factors mediate drug use. Fewer formulations address how drug use mediates the accomplishment of organismic and individual goals either contained in or resulting from these psychological factors. (For an example of an insightful and meticulously developed formulation of the function of substance abuse, see Wilson and colleagues 1989.) Such formulations become, in a sense, micro-theories of addiction. They do not provide a comprehensive framework for understanding addictive processes.

The functions of addiction outlined in this section are designed to improve on the formulation of addiction as being based on the capacity of many drugs to serve as general mediators of multiple personal functions and goals related to a wide range of psychological variables. The goal of proposing these functions is to strike the right balance between specificity and generality in order to provide an clinically useful framework for understanding the majority of addiction cases where other psychopathology is present. The proposed functions flesh out such concepts as *coping mechanisms* or *mediators* of basic deficits or defensive requirements and provide some sense of what is being coped with, compensated for, and how a particular substance accomplishes this in the total context of the person. Because of this comprehensive aspect of drug use, the functions described here are actually *bio*psychosocial functions, although the term psychosocial function or simply function is used here. These terms serve as convenient abbreviations.

The following biopsychosocial functions of addictive disorders often occur in the presence of other significant psychopathology: modulation, escape/avoidance, facilitation, repetition, and orientation.

Modulation as a biopsychosocial function of addiction includes the modulation of arousal systems, affect, and specific cognitions. Modulation of the level of general psychophysiological arousal or modulation of a habitually experienced affect is a frequently occurring function of drug use. When modulation is provided by psychoactive substances, the resulting shift in arousal level is experienced as a decrease in very general dysphoric experiences (such as the removal of a vague state of tension, fatigue, or languor) and an increase in very general euphoric experiences (such as a sense of well-being, vigor, physical or psychological tonus, or readiness). When affect is the focus of drugs used as modulators, it must be primarily ego syntonic (i.e., congruent with the overall strivings of the person) when experienced at some optimal level of intensity. Typically such a specific affect, or arousal, in specific systems is present in almost all the waking experience of the individual, or it takes on a clear cyclical pattern related to internal or external drivers or cues. This aspect of an ego-syntonic fit versus ego-dystonic discomfort often serves as the discriminating feature in regard to affect between modulation and the next function, where an affective situation is avoided in order to maintain equilibrium.

Escape/avoidance of painful, ego-dystonic affects, affective memories, or conflictual situations may involve conscious or unconscious defensive maneuvers involving drug use and may depend on either the chemical properties of the drug, the lifestyle involved in drug use, or both. Chapter 2 on alcoholism, depression, and memory gives a very detailed examination of some important escape/avoidance relationships. In all cases where this function is dominant, the avoided experience is perceived as so ego dystonic, ego alien, or so potentially overwhelming in its consequences that it must be totally avoided. The physiological symptoms of addiction, such as withdrawal, are often tied more to the function of modulation than to escape/avoidance. This is because contrary to the dread of withdrawal often claimed by addicts and immortalized in print and screen, "feeling sick" and having cravings or "a jones" for a drug is not entirely ego alien or ego dystonic when experienced at the appropriate intensity. These sensations and experiences, except in their most intense forms, must be interpreted by the individual as ego dystonic before they take on a clear dysphoric shading. To make an analogy to normal functioning, one must interpret low intensity hunger, subliminal sexual tension, or low levels of aggressive feelings as dysphoric. Typically, these low intensity drive-related experiences may produce an essentially pleasure-oriented anticipatory set of responses toward the object of the drive and enhance the pleasures of drive satisfaction. These experiences become clearly dysphoric with little or no individual interpretation only at high intensity levels in normal individuals. Similarly, drug-related cravings and early withdrawal symptoms often modify and increase the excitement, "rush," and "nod" of using a given drug and may enable a whole range of experiences and actions required by the addict for equilibrium of the self. This is also true for other states and experiences that are typically labelled dysphoric but become the object of modulation via drug use. For example, complicated bereavement cannot always be classified as related to escape/avoidance functions. Sometimes the modulation of sad, depressed, or angry affects is sought by the individual. In other cases, the drug may actually facilitate the ability to begin the grieving process, as in the third function.

Facilitation as a function of addiction occurs when drugs are used to facilitate the expression of, enactment of, or access to unintegrated aspects of self and self in relation to other. Facilitating drugs enable ways of being (however pathological, ego dystonic, ego alien, or painful) that would otherwise not be within the individual's repertoire of behaviors, experiences, or interactions. The facilitating drug may decrease inhibiting moral values or superego influences. The drug may serve to decrease conflicting or mutually exclusive affects, or other aspects of personality that decrease the ability to gain access to poorly integrated parts of the self. Conversely, the facilitating drug may increase drive states or affects that will enable action or experience. Probably the clearest conceptualization of the facilitating effects of drugs is described by Yochelson and Samenow (1986) in their work on criminal personalities who abuse drugs. Psychodramatists and dance therapists should be alert to the possibility that drugs sometimes enable primitive, psychological scripts and life motions to be acted out. The goal of decreasing social anxiety in order to facilitate social ease is a common, subclinical use of alcohol or cannabis. Decreasing reality orientation and impulse controls to facilitate psychotic acting out is a common function of drug use by psychotics. Illicit drugs often enable these patients to arrive at action-based, socially unacceptable but conflict-free or primary process solutions to problems that otherwise would be beyond their ability to solve. This is often the case with the psychotic who is not dangerous to self or others except under the influence of drugs. Facilitation refers to the enabling of access to parts of the self and part functions, rather than to situations where the drug is used to create the person's total social role definition and sense of identity. The latter process is viewed as forming the orientation function of addiction, discussed later in this section.

Probably one of the most common functions of addiction, and perhaps the most difficult to adequately define, is *repetition*. Repetition of the self and self–other representations from infancy or early childhood is a special form of facilitation by drug use that involves the facilitation, expression, or enactment of unconscious, preverbal representations. The function of repetition as used here is a fairly broad conceptual umbrella that captures many of the nuances of the term as previously used in the psychodynamic literature, with each nuance being a possible subtype of the function of repetition. Wilson and Malatesta (1989) provide an insightful review of the concept of repetition in the psychoanalytic literature beginning with Freud and ending with their own refinements based on developments in cognitive psychological theories of affect and memory. After reviewing Freud's early and later theoretical excursions with the concept of repetition and the temporary renunciation of the concept by psychoanalysts, they cite several developments since the ego psychologists, which have added to an understanding of what is repeated in psychological repetitions. The following summary of the development of the concept relies largely on their review.

Loewald's (1971) useful distinction between active and passive repetition defines active repetition as progressive and aimed at mastery through re-creation of traumatic or frustrating (fixating) events or situations. The hallmarks of active repetition are novelty and reactivation of earlier issues at a higher level of organization, with a movement toward resolution of the issue or conflict. The more passive type of repetition is more germane to our discussion of substance abuse. Passive repetition, called reproductive repetition in Loewald's terminology, simply duplicates the early conflict or trauma.

Klein (1976) further refined the understanding of what is repeated and some of the motives, aims, and forms of repetition. Some types of repetition that Klein identified include behavioral as well as psychoanalytically derived sources. For example, repetition of interrupted pleasurable tasks, repetition due to pleasure in functioning, imitation of a model's behavior resulting in repetition, and symbolic repetition through art are reminiscent of behavioral and cognitive behavioral theories. His categories of replica induction, or repeated aspects of an unconscious relationship, transference repetitions, and the repetition of repressed wishes of fantasies are more clearly psychoanalytic.

In reviewing the development of these concepts, Wilson and Malatesta (1989) remind us that repetition is a two-edged sword. It insures some fundamental continuities of interaction and experience, providing the comfort of the familiar. However: "When repetition is thus out of our control, when we are not conscious of nor can we discern the nature of the repetitive patterning, and especially when the fragment of repletion is beyond symbolic mediation, we may then speak of a repetition compulsion that can dominate our lives in subtle but telling ways" (1989, p. 266).

Wilson and Malatesta view the repetition compulsion, or what they call primary repetition, as the repeating of a specific aspect of experience. For them, "Primal repetition contains and carries the actual experiential content of the early dyadic interaction between caregiver and child, specifically the affectively laden content" (1989, p. 266). What is being repeated are specific (and in the case of substance abuse, pathological) interaction patterns that result in the formation of the individual's basic affective core. These basic interaction templates and their related self-representations are impressed on the individual prior to the development of verbal skills, and become the basic addictive personality core. Elsewhere, Wilson and co-authors (1989a) describe this basic core as consisting of the tendency to repeat certain favored, negative affective states with which the individual has become identified during early infancy. These states have become incorporated in the core of the personality structure itself.

Building on the elucidation of repetition (Wilson and Malatesta 1989) and integrating it with the emphasis of Wilson and colleagues (1989) on flux, variability, and instability in stable formations of personality, Chapter 1 introduced three basic positions of the addictive cycle that are roughly equivalent to the most frequently encountered addictive core selves: the depressed/depleted self, the grandiose/ manic self, and the schizoid/detached self. In the formulation in Chapter 1, although favoring or stabilizing for longer periods of time at one position rather than another during certain portions of the addictive cycle, the addicted individual is not described as repeating only one pattern learned in the infant–parent dyad, but rather as being prone to move experientially among various states that reflect specific self-regulatory failures. What is repeated is usually traumatic, unsatisfactory, or frustrating. In other cases, the repetition is an attempt at returning to a gratifying state/relationship, due to an overwhelming failure in current adaptation.

In the treatment of addiction, one sometimes encounters cases of patients using drugs to achieve a form of repetition, although a typical functioning level of these patients would suggest that either deficits in infant–caretaker experience had been minimal or significantly repaired prior to adulthood. However, severe trauma in adulthood either may result in regression to the preverbal modes of functioning, which prevailed prior to the repair, or may cause distortions after the fact in otherwise stable and relatively benign object and self-representations. Although perhaps controversial from a psychoanalytic object relations point of view, the idea that the encoded schemas of early objects and object relations might be altered by adult traumatic experience is consistent with cognitive theories of affective memory, memory for persons, and dissonant mental contents.

Repetition is often a subtle process that is difficult to identify and assess. The therapist's subjective experience of knowing clinically that events are occurring on more than one level in the transference relationship is often a crucial clue that repetition may be an issue in the patient's treatment. Repetition may be a predictable aspect of effective long-term treatment of severely ingrained addictions that have resisted treatment focused only on the substance abuse, or parallel treatments of emotional symptoms. To the extent that the regression and enactment result from the therapy, repetition is an iatrogenic phenomenon that must be understood by the clinician, who may use this understanding to prevent relapse to drug use and avoid treatment dropouts that would otherwise occur after a period of significant therapeutic engagement or respectable periods of abstinence.

Why would the repetition of early preverbal material, which might precipitate a relapse, be expected in intensive psychotherapy, which does not in itself emphasize investigation of early (infant) experience? Putting aside the special considerations of the termination phase of treatment, the answer is in the basic interpersonal form of intensive therapy of almost any type. The idea that special forms of regression, and therefore repetition, take place during intensive therapy is not new. Trevarthen (1979) described the intersubjective nature of the infant–caregiver relationship, which involves the experience of, for all practical purposes, shared mental states. Stern (1985) described a similar "dance of attunement" of caregiver and infant, which is organized around consistently providing the optimal level of arousal in the infant. Substance abuse treatment, especially to the extent that it is sensitive to the day-to-day and moment-to-moment regulatory needs of the dual diagnosis patient, is an almost exact replication of this kind of dance of attunement.

Working with repetition is one of the most difficult aspects of dual diagnosis work, in part, because the difficulty may increase when the patient has a typically higher level of functioning. That is, when the regression is very deep relative to typical functioning, the recurrence of relapse-oriented symptoms may be all the more bewildering to both the clinician and patient. In such cases it is often more difficult to identify the relevant object relations issues than in cases of more uniform and long-standing deficits. There may be intense resistance to treatment intermittently in an otherwise cooperative and not overly defensive individual who apparently has good ego controls. Without understanding repetition as a function of addiction, the temptation might be for the therapist to discredit these structural assets and to rediagnose the patient as more impaired than is actually the case. Due to the greater responsibilities and dispersed dependency network of these individuals, the personal and social consequences of the addiction may also be more severe, at least in the short run.

The final function of addiction is *orientation*, the use of substances to achieve or maintain a phenomenal, attitudinal, or social set, and/or to provide lifestyle context and identity. This function is operative when the drugs support the primary function of identity for individuals whose early development appears on the surface to have been relatively auspicious. More often this function of drug use occurs in the more seriously impaired patient. Adolescents and young adults who have major disorienting experiences (such as parental divorce, rapid onset of major psychopathology in a parent, or traumatic failures related to the normal orienting activities of group membership, achievement, and intimacy) may obtain orientation or reorient through drug use. In more than one sense, the drug epidemic in our cities spreads through a contagion of trauma. Young people who witness senseless violence or must see their parents or older youth they look up to become enmeshed in the drug culture are severely traumatized and disoriented. Drug use and adopting the drug culture as a lifestyle constitute one orienting response among the limited options available in our cities.

The use of substances as the result of traumatic disillusionments with self or significant others has its origins in the social referencing process, wherein toddlers use others, especially idealized adults on whom they are dependent, in order to appraise the emotional impact of events (Compos and Sternberg 1980). When the toddler is unable to permanently internalize these early social referencing events, and when the relationship with idealized adults is somehow abnormal, or when later traumatic disillusionment occurs, the ground is prepared for the replacement of appropriate social referencing in adulthood with orientation to the environment through the drug of choice. In the case of traumatic disillusionment, the idealized objects that were once the very context of evaluation and action are simply not available, or they produce severe conflict and feelings of loss when evoked as a guide to orientation.

Symptoms in this complex will most often be observed in the sphere of identity and social functioning. Interests, values, and sociability will all be tied to drug use or the drug culture. This function is sometimes mistaken as a superficial, simple hedonism and the need for peer acceptance on the part of the patient. These superficial symptoms usually mask other significant pathology. A pattern often seen in psychotics and severe personality disorders is that of using a drug-oriented lifestyle to obtain a social role, or *raison d'être*, or in a sense to "get a life." Not a small part of the effectiveness of a drug-focused lifestyle in meeting these needs are the social, sexual, and financial resources that other users are willing to invest in the situation, which on the psychological level is a self-construction or self-maintenance project. The immediate social consequence of the drug use is to mask over personal, maturational, and social skills deficits by focusing on the drug connection and the utility of the person as one who knows about drugs, can obtain drugs, or can be used in the drug procurement or sale process. The personal effect on identity and sociability ranges from the psychotic or mentally retarded user who concretely thinks "all real men use drugs, so I will use drugs to become a real man" to the narcissist who advertises to a select, chosen few his masterful means of safeguarding, acquiring, and distributing the substance, and thereby establishes a basic source of supply and repair of his narcissism.

The orientation function provided by the drug of choice is often compatible rather than incongruous with the underlying pathology in the case. For example, Meissner (1986), although describing a general dynamic found in addicted patients, provides a description that is strikingly similar to addiction functioning as a paranoid orientation that remarkably fits the case for many dually diagnosed individuals who are clinically paranoid:

> The paranoid construction, varying in degree in relationship to a variety of extrinsic social, cultural, or even political factors, plays a role in drug dependence. Projective transformation of the drug substance cannot simply stand alone; rather, the phenomenon and the experience of the taking of the drug must be embedded in a broader sustaining matrix. It is this aspect of the drug experience and the operation of the paranoid process which gives rise to the frequently observed phenomenon of the drug subculture and the often paranoid opposition which is directed against the surrounding society and particularly the authority figures within that society. [Meissner 1986, p. 361]

Having reviewed the five psychosocial functions of addiction, we can now examine more closely the relationship among them. Table 3–2 provides a summary of each function with the theoretical concepts most useful in exploring its meaning in most cases.

As with the symptom complexes, it can be argued that some of the distinctions

Table 3–2. Summary of the Psychosocial Functions of Addiction

Modulation

Use maintains an experience or function at the optimal level.

Needs addressed: Equilibrium of the personality.

Description: Getting just the right fix or high, relapse within therapeutic change, substance used to maintain functioning.

Theoretical constructs: Self-maintenance behaviors, defenses, familiar or favored states or situations, affective tolerance.

Escape/Avoidance

Use provides relief from a ego-dystonic experience or situation.

Needs addressed: Safety, avoidance of emotional or physical pain.

Description: Escapist, avoidant, inadequate, in emotional or physical pain, anxious, a sad drunk, lonely, angry, bitter.

Theoretical constructs: Self-medication hypothesis, escape hypothesis, coping skills deficits, self-esteem, self-monitoring.

Facilitation

Use enables an otherwise unavailable experience or behavior.

Needs addressed: Self-efficacy, removal of inhibitions, enactment.

Description: A different person when intoxicated, what is otherwise avoided or denied is manifest. Inadequate, lacking confidence.

Theoretical constructs: Conflict, defense (compensation, denial), social mores, dissonance theory, expectancies, self-concept, multiple selves theory.

Repetition

Use facilitates repetition of basic object relations.

Needs addressed: Working through of trauma, early experiences.

Description: Regressed or childlike, sense of two things happening at once, sabotage of therapy, unexpected outcome, unreasonable.

Theoretical constructs: Transference, object relations, acting out of therapeutic issues, regression due to trauma or return to point of fixation, psychological complexes.

Orientation

Use provides otherwise deficient direction, context, and identity.

Needs addressed: Identity, direction, belonging.

Description: Aimless, underdeveloped, immature, confused, burned out, cynical, impressionable, seeking to make an impression.

Theoretical constructs: Development of the self, value development, efficacy, role management theory, family systems theory.

made in regard to the functions of addictions are arbitrary. Let us look at this objection more closely. In any good tailoring job, the cloth must be chosen and cut to fit the contour of the customer and the use for which the garment is intended. The concepts used must both fit the facts of the dual diagnosis patient and provide assistance to clinicians in understanding basic issues, performing assessment, reaching clinical case formulations, and effecting treatment interventions. The functions and complexes are tailored to optimize descriptive specificity within a parsimonious set of concepts, each being a rather fuzzy set of motives, goals, functions, or symptoms. Taken together, these concepts form a theory-based network: an eclectic, rather loose heuristic system that may be usefully applied to dual diagnosis problems. This means balancing the value of specificity and precision that comes from generating many conceptual distinctions against the value of general applicability and efficient description that comes from consolidating concepts.

For example, the distinction between facilitation and repetition is based on the preverbal and primary object relations aspect of repetition as defined above. Obviously, repetition as a function of the use of addictive substances is a form of facilitation that would usually occur within patients whose typical functioning indicates severe psychopathology (character disorders with borderline structure and psychotics). However, repetition is a form of facilitation of special importance in many other cases of deeply ingrained addiction where selected regression to preverbal functioning must be seriously entertained as an explanation of the psychological circumstances surrounding relapses during treatment. Often such regressions can be otherwise clinically substantiated, such as by psychological testing or close inquiry into the patient's early development and significant events of infancy and childhood. The functional process referred to as repetition is also more difficult to detect and assess than most forms of facilitation. These two characteristics qualify repetition as worthy of a separate place in this heuristic system.

In contrast, for the sake of parsimony some functions that could be discriminated as separate and in addition to the five functional groups have been absorbed in one or more of the identified functions. For example, the particular qualities of the functions of addictions that are most often seen in significant causal tandem with neurotic conflicts (such as the rage, resentment, and power motivation of oedipal conflicts) are subsumed by the escape/avoidance and facilitation functions, rather than established as a separate functional category related to conflict or neurosis. The functions of drug use in regard to conflict or neurotic level of functioning are not so primary, distinctive, or difficult to assess that a description of them combining two broad functional categories (such as escape/avoidance and facilitation) decreases the usefulness of the heuristic system.

Another very rich arena of psychological issues that almost meets the criteria for a separate function of addiction is that of the various expressions, affective states, behaviors, and relationship patterns involving dependency and needs for being nurtured or cared for. Dependency needs and relationships that allow their direct or indirect expression are often facilitated via drug use, although modulation of the experience of dependence/independence is also a very common objective of substance use. Feelings of painful longing for a lost dependent relationship often fuel an addictive pattern when drugs are used to interrupt or dampen these affects. Drug use may mediate the experience of helplessness and neediness that provides repetition of early childhood abandonment. Despite the richness of these issues for understanding substance abuse and addiction, emotional and interpersonal dependency (such as depression or neurosis) can take on myriad forms, which are more profitably examined within the context of broader functions, such as those outlined in this chapter.

A few examples may help to clarify the kind of clinical observations that provide the rationale for the distinctions made among these admittedly interrelated and interacting functions. Let us compare the function of an addictive substance in the lives of individuals with very different levels of typical functioning and different severities of interfering psychopathological process. The schizophrenic's use of cannabis to escape or avoid persecutory voices has much in common with the overly stressed executive's use of alcohol to escape or avoid unusually extreme emotion related to competition and aggression in the workplace. An astute clinical observer might find that for both patients the primary function of drug use in regard to the specific symptoms of psychopathology is a fairly simple kind of self-medication that to some extent is effective in helping each one to avoid painful, ego-dystonic experiences. The avoided experiences, however, have very different origins and causes and are represented by two different symptom complexes: thought and context (for the hallucination) and dominance of affect (for the aggressive feelings).

Let us pursue a less familiar dynamic involving the same two diagnostic types. We might describe the function of addiction as modulation, if the executive and the schizophrenic used their drug of choice to perpetuate their symptoms at a certain level of intensity in consciousness, but not to totally avoid or escape the symptoms themselves. If such control of symptom intensity is the functional goal of drug use, the symptoms themselves could not be exclusively ego-dystonic, and we could assume that they are required at some optimal level for the equilibrium of each personality. For the executive, this might take the form of the drug functioning to modulate otherwise overwhelming aggression to an intensity where the aggression might be expressed in an ego-syntonic and pleasurable way though the verbalization or fantasy of insults toward work peers, or the telling of anecdotes that show his competitors in a negative light. In this example, a cathartic, expressive element is present, as in facilitation, but the primary affect is otherwise consciously available to the patient, is essentially ego-syntonic, but occurs with a wide range of intensity that is difficult to modulate.

In the case of the schizophrenic patient, cannabis might modulate the quality and intensity of auditory hallucinations, thus (in combination with inconsistent compliance to prescribed psychotropics) preserving familiar, mild, nagging voices. The hallucinated voices, although causing dysphoria and viewed as coming from a source external to the self, are similar to the nagging voice of the patient's mother. The hallucinations, although perhaps causing overwhelming anxiety, guilt, and distraction when intense, at a less intense level serve the equilibrium of the self by confirming a sense of merger with the mother and continually re-establishing a familiar self-with-other identity as mommy's bad boy. In periods of sobriety and relative compliance to medication, this patient's real mother and his exasperated treatment team will provide the same negative inputs to personality equilibrium, if held at the right intensity. During periods of sobriety, we might expect trends toward relapse if these negative social inputs were to shift toward more positive statements, or if they became intolerably harsh. We could note that in this example involving modulation, unlike the function of escape–avoidance, the symptoms have a strong ego-syntonic element, or ego-stabilizing function.

Separating the functions in any of these examples is a matter of degree and requires that the clinician make a judgment of the predominant role of the substance use relative to other significant pathology. In the earlier examples involving the function of escape/avoidance and modulation, the drug of choice (although involving complex dynamics) has an essentially simple relationship to a single representative symptom. We have intentionally simplified here, since an addiction usually addresses the needs threatened by one or more symptom complexes rather than influencing a single isolated symptom as in these examples.

To investigate situations where there is a more complex relationship of several functions that, nonetheless, result clinically in the observation of a primary function, we use as examples two individuals closer to the same level of psychological functioning and with major personality problems that can be summarized by the same symptom complexes. The socially inept person with prominent passive-aggressive traits (not quite rigid and pervasive enough to be considered a personality disorder) might use cannabis in every anticipated social situation because it helps him to experience the self as competent, assertive, and socially effective. Its use also represents a compromise in the breaking of social rules, which expresses his basic oppositionality and ambivalence. This patient's drug use is similar in function to the psychopath's use of crystal methamphetamine, or "ice," to facilitate the criminal activity he would not engage in otherwise. The psychopath blatantly and without ambivalence enjoys breaking a stronger social sanction against the use of this particular drug. Both the hip nebbish and the cowardly crook seek to avoid a certain experiential and dynamic relationship among fear, aggression, self-esteem, and social expectations: problems in the dominance of affect and sociability and identity complexes. The passive-aggressive person primarily avoids or escapes an internal neurotic conflict due to a harsh superego, although a reality-oriented concern with social skill development may also be avoided. The crook avoids experienced fear (with much less conflict than that experienced by the passive-aggressive patient) related to the reality-oriented concerns of apprehension by authorities, physical dangers involved in the enterprise, such as reprisals from criminal associates. Some internal inhibitions from a rudimentary sense of conscience and primitive moral values may also be present and disabled by the drug use in both individuals.

In this example, the drug users are engaged in the process of facilitating a desired enactment of the basic personality strivings toward self-esteem, specifically the self as effective and powerful in the face of aggressive impulses, inhibiting fears, and social prohibitions. For both individuals, the particular expression of a personality striving could not otherwise be realized without the use of the substance. The primary function of the drug use is facilitation rather than mere avoidance. Clearly, in both cases the enactment, once facilitated and realized, may be totally deficient regarding the demands of social reality and, perhaps even worse, will not create the psychological conditions for integration of the facilitated strivings with the rest of the personality. Both will be doomed to repeat this cycle unless there is intervention from without. With the passive-aggressive individual, feedback and reinforcement from a valued other might lead to change, both in the addiction and in the social skills base on which a sense of competence may be realistically established. With the psychopath such normal aspects of life will not prove to be sufficient, and professional and institutional intervention will be required prior to personality change. The above examples demonstrate the need to establish the dominant function(s) of an addiction though the careful, expert clinical observation of the total personality. This includes psychological structure, the conscious and unconscious strivings of the individual, and the symptom complexes and consequences of psychopathology most relevant to the drug use.

The following is a general description of the commonly recognized classes of drugs and their effects, as well as the most prominent factors contributing to drug choice. Following that, we can demonstrate more specifically how the three elements in the heuristic system are used together in the investigation of dual diagnosis cases.

THE DRUG OF CHOICE

There is currently very little empirical basis for classifying the use of specific drugs by psychological function in even a roughly accurate way. Most empirical attempts at establishing personality-based grounds for drug preference have proved relatively unsuccessful. The absence of empirical findings supporting speculations about the relationship between user characteristics and drug choice may be due primarily to the weak conceptual base that has informed the research. The theories guiding such research have either been too global and general or too specific and focused. At the one extreme, theories of personality type or traits sought to find the addictive personality, the alcoholic personality, dependency as a trait, and so on. At the other extreme, narrow biological or psychological theories tried to explain specific aspects of addiction while ignoring it as a pervasive, integrated process.

Examples of these extremes include studies of specific biochemical markers used to explain alcohol dependence, as though alcoholism were exclusively physical dependence, and conditioning theories used to account for the acquisition of drug habits, with little concern about the social and symbolic meanings of drug use.

Although some promising theories do exist, such as the opponent process theory of addiction or the sensation-seeking hypothesis of personality and addition, no conceptual model has linked clinically observed symptom complexes with the psychosocial functions of addiction as in this heuristic framework. By looking at this link, we may best discover the role of a specific drug's pharmacological and social utility to the user. This link should also aid in the development of criteria for forming homogeneous groups of drug abusers for research, development of differential treatment modalities, and program evaluation purposes.

McLellan and colleagues (1978) reported three studies that generally support the approach taken here. They looked at several hundred Veterans Administration hospital admissions for the presence and type of drug use and psychiatric diagnosis at the time of admission and examined the same subjects at subsequent admissions. Examining drug of choice, course of addiction, and the presence or development of significant psychopathology brought them to several conclusions. They found that drug-free treatment was unsuccessful by any criterion for all subjects in the sample and that instead of improving over the 6-year observation period, substance use and psychiatric severity increased despite interventions. When drug use was categorized as psychostimulant, psychodepressant, or narcotic use, an overlap with diagnosis was found such that schizophrenia, paranoid schizophrenia, and sociopathic personality dominated the psychostimulant category; cases of depression, anxiety reactions, and organic brain syndromes dominated the psychodepressant category; and psychopathic and sociopathic personality dominated the narcotic use category. They offered the following general conclusions:

> We are forced to conclude from the results of these studies that particular patterns of chemical abuse are intimately related to the expression and perhaps the development of specific types of psychopathology in chronic users. . . . It is our impression that although the patterns of drug use are a primary factor in accounting for the differential psychological symptoms found in the psychostimulant and psychodepressant groups, it is not possible to rule out the underlying psychological characteristics of the particular population. The fact that the majority of our subjects select and continue to use combinations of psychophysiologically similar chemical agents suggests that there may be specific underlying characteristics within these subjects that require or respond preferentially to theses chemical agents. . . . We would further propose that the regular, prolonged abuse of specific combinations of street drugs may have an active and direct role in the development and expression of these psychiatric disorders. [McLellan et al. 1980, p. 22]

Additional empirical support for hypotheses concerning diagnostic category and drug of choice is provided in the more recent Epidemiological Catchment Area

(ECA) Study described in Chapter 2 (Regier et al. 1990). Table 3-3 displays data on the relationship of drugs of choice and mental disorders taken from the ECA study. The data indicate for each diagnostic category the magnitude of increased risk over the general population for abuse or dependence related to specific drugs of choice. The numerical index of this risk is the odds ratio (OR).

We learn from the first cell of the chart that schizophrenics in the ECA study were more than three times more likely to have alcohol addiction or abuse than members of the general population with no diagnosable mental disorder. To the right of each OR is the rank order of that OR among the seven drug categories. For example, by reading across the row for barbiturates, we discover that this drug class is first in lifetime prevalence rank order only for the affective disorders and is second in rank only for the anxiety disorders. Comparing this with cocaine, only schizophrenics and antisocial personality disorder among the four mental health categories are most likely to show an increased risk for addiction to this drug over others. This is not consistent with what we would expect if lifetime prevalence rates of addiction were related only to availability of drugs due to market pressures or a general culturewide preference for a given drug during the time of the study. If this were the case, we might expect the rank order for drugs to be very similar in all four diagnostic groupings.

Although empirical investigations such as cited above are limited in number and scope, some useful observations can be offered regarding drug of choice (McLellan et al. 1983, McLellan and Druley 1977, Milkman and Frosch 1973). It must be stressed that probably the greatest determinants of indulging in any drug use and of the subsequent choice of a specific substance are primarily social in origin. The broad social influences of the degree of a drug's acceptability by the general society and by the individual's immediate reference group are probably at the top of this list of determinants. Cost in dollars, prestige or stigma associated with the drug's use, danger inherent in the drug connection, and, of course, availability are also crucial factors. The reference group's views of users, abusers, addicts, and persons in

Table 3-3. Mental Disorders by Drugs of Choice
Odds Ratios (OR's) and Rank Order by OR's

Drug Choice	Mental Disorders							
	Schizophrenia		Affective Disorders		Anxiety Disorders		Antisocial Personality	
Alcohol	3.3	7	1.9	7	1.5	7	21.0	3
Marijuana	4.8	5	3.8	6	2.3	6	8.3	7
Cocaine	13.9	1	5.9	2	2.9	3–4	29.2	1
Opiates	8.8	2	5.0	5	2.8	5	24.3	2
Barbiturates	5.9	4	6.6	1	4.5	2	19.0	4
Amphetamines	3.9	6	5.7	4	2.9	3–4	14.3	6
Hallucinogens	7.4	3	5.8	3	5.0	1	15.6	5

recovery have profound impact on user attempts at controlled use, treatment, and abstinence as a desired goal. These factors affect every drug user to some extent. The degree of acculturation to the mainstream society, social class standing, acceptance into a subculture, belonging to a racial or ethnic minority, and cultural and intergroup conflicts are extremely relevant to how these and other social factors will influence both the decision to use drugs at all, the decision to use them regularly, and which drugs will be chosen.

It should be clear that the position taken here in regard to drug use is that it is motivated behavior, meaning that drugs are used to get the person somewhere, to achieve some goal, to address some current concern, or in the language we adopted in Chapter 1, to move though or alter the life space. Addictions that are not motivated in this sense will be treated without complication, with few relapses, and are therefore of little significance to this task of discussing the most difficult types of substance abuse treatment cases. The description of symptom complexes and addictive functions has provided some sense of the liabilities, needs, deficits, and matching goals or current concerns involved in drug use. They have told us something about where the drug user wants to go, or needs to go, what he or she may be striving toward. This view of the motivation for addiction is similar to what has been described by Bruce Alexander (1988) as the Adaptive Model of Addiction, which he contrasts with the Disease Model of Addiction. In short, some people fail to "grow up" or to maintain adult integration:

> Failure to reach or maintain adult integration is a grave problem. It invites social ostracism, despair, mental disintegration, and ultimately suicide. Therefore, it creates an urgent need to search out and choose substitute ways to provide meaning, organization, and social support. Various "substitute adaptations" may be, consciously or unconsciously, adopted for this purpose. Substitute adaptations do *not* provide the abiding satisfactions of adult integration but at least provide a basis for survival and allow hope for the future. Therefore they are seized and held desperately when their availability is threatened.
>
> From an adaptive viewpoint, drug addiction or any other "substitute adaptations" are adaptive because the alternatives are worse. The substitute adaptations may be visibly harmful, but they provide something essential. For example, the despised identity of an addict is more bearable than the hellish void of none at all, and deep immersion in drug culture at least guarantees distraction from self-hate. In desperate situations, it is adaptive to choose the lesser evil.
>
> It might seem outrageous to assert that harmful addictions are adaptive. I believe this is because in the present atmosphere of a war on drugs, it is hard to see drug use in the same way as other actions. In a parallel case, regular use or crutches can produce painful blisters or bruises, but it is clearly adaptive for injured people. The alternatives to using crutches are worse—aggravating the injury or remaining bedridden. According to the adaptive view, drug addiction, like the crutch use is adaptive in spite of its drawbacks. [Alexander 1988, p. 47]

Although Alexander's use of search and choice as reflecting volitional aspects of addiction is fully endorsed, the view of addiction in this book emphasizes only the adaptive *motivation* involved in initiating and maintaining use and addiction. Our existence is only partially determined by our motives. Processes independent of the motive for repair and coping insure that addictive solutions to problems, inadequacies, or defects eventually become maladaptive and incapacitating, despite the original or sustaining motives. Self-destruction as a motive may exist, but if it does, it is much less frequent than this misplaced drive toward adaptation and mastery of deficits.

Several preliminary issues have to do with providing a sense of how psychoactive substances fit into the search and choice component of finding substitute adaptations or attempts at self-repair. Using the journey metaphor, the deficit provides a destination, and we must investigate how the abused substance appears to move addicts along in their quest for repair. Drugs compensate for liabilities, temporarily fulfill needs, and otherwise prove temporarily and partially effective in supporting psychological and interpersonal functions. Understanding these aspects of drug efficacy will give us important clues to factors informing and shaping preference of a given substance or set of substances.

We can identify several mechanisms or vectors through which drugs accomplish these ends. Substances vary in regard to qualities and intensities. A nonexhaustive list includes the psychopharmacological effects of the drug (which include tolerance and withdrawal), the route of administration, social context of use and procurement, and the interpersonal and self-concept consequences of the addiction. Let us briefly examine each of these.

The variance among substances is most obvious in regard to the *psychopharmacological actions and effects*. Drug effects can be described by noting their influence on the central, somatic, and autonomic nervous systems. Each substance has at least one profile of action and effect on each one of these systems and respective subsystems. Parameters of particular relevance to psychopharmacological actions and effects include dosage, route of administration, frequency of use, and purity of the substance used. Again, drugs vary widely in how much range exists in each parameter. The medical status of the individual is also of crucial importance, since physical health factors will determine the degree of dependence that the body will support, the amount of substance in the bloodstream or organs at any given moment with a certain use history, the half-life of the drug in the user's system, and to a great extent, the risks involved in detoxification and withdrawal. Genetic factors also exert influence on the drug action and effects vector.

The effects of the drug of choice do not occur only in a physiological context. Dependence, tolerance, and withdrawal have social and psychological components. In addition to direct chemical changes are the powerful classical conditioning effects that develop from and later support continued drug dependence. Some of these processes occur after drug ingestion and move the organism back toward homeostasis in response to the disturbance of the status quo caused by the drug. Other processes, which may be just as powerful, are related to the anticipation of, or preparation for, the drug effect and its consequences. In many cases, the anticipatory response is opposite to the effect, such as when opiate users experience an increased sensitivity to pain in anticipation of drug administration. An opponent process theory of opiate addiction rests on these opposite responses in anticipation of ingestion, which include measurable physiological changes (Solomon 1977). In addiction to other drugs, the learned anticipatory response is complementary to the effect and augments it, such as in the development to reverse tolerance with extended marijuana use. Siegel and colleagues (1988) have described these drug-mirroring and drug-mimicking conditioned responses (CRs) in addiction. Drugs that have primarily CNS effects are said to have mirroring CRs, and drugs that affect the peripheral nervous system more directly usually have mimicking CRs.

Both mirroring and mimicking CRs anticipate the drug effect and can be reliably elicited by the specific aspects of the environment that are present prior to and during the effect. These CRs are what may be called "feedforward" mechanisms, which augment the role of feedback mechanisms that occur after drug use. Feedforward mechanisms significantly contribute to the development of tolerance and withdrawal. The effect of any given dose of a substance is related to the environment of ingestion (environmental specificity). For example, heroin addicts who survive nearly fatal overdoses often report that such an incident had occurred in an unusual environment (Siegel et al. 1982). The opponent process explanation of these overdoses relies on the absence of conditioned stimuli in the novel environment. Without the familiar stimuli that reliably predict drug ingestion, there is no preparatory physiological response (feedforward mechanism). And without this preparatory response, which would otherwise counterbalance or oppose the drug's effects on crucial physiological functions, the desired dose becomes an overdose, that is, it has an unchecked and devastating effect. Similarly, newly released convicts often experience overwhelming withdrawal symptoms after first returning to environments in which they had used drugs. The familiar drug environment evokes an anticipatory response opposite to the drug's effect, causing withdrawal symptoms. Also, the low re-addiction rate of returning veterans who had been users while in Vietnam can be explained partly by the addiction-sustaining aspects of environmental cues. Without environmental cues at home similar to those in which drug use had occurred, the anticipatory responses related to craving and withdrawal did not take place.

The second vector overlaps somewhat the environmental and conditioned response processes discussed as feedforward mechanisms. The *route of administration* often becomes a conditioned stimulus that evokes the urge to use, and the CRs that prepare the addict for the drug effect, thereby increasing withdrawal symptoms. The method of administration, which may vary with the choice of drug and may be as crucial as the specific substance itself, often has significance beyond its influence on drug action, psychochemical effects, and conditioned responses in anticipation of use. Both psychological and social factors lead to preference in administration. For example, many drugs produce more direct and intense effects when administered intravenously or intramuscularly with hypodermic needles. Many users will avoid this route at all costs, although they resort to other harrowing acts in drug use and procurement. Other users prefer the needle, despite squeamishness about other aspects of a drug lifestyle or the unwillingness to suffer pain or see the blood of others. For many, if they avoid intravenous drug use, may convince themselves and those around them that they have not become too desperate in their quest for this forbidden satisfaction. Linking hypodermic administration simply to increased drug effect and the conditioned reactions to anticipation, however, does not tell the full story. At least in some cases, a prominent motivation includes the expression and enactment of total desperation and despair in dependence on a substance and isolation from others. Often, the shadow and counterphobic denial of death are represented in the administration ritual. Injection implicates the magical, primary process dynamics related to sharing and controlling blood and the very flow of life that it symbolizes. Conversely, injections can be used as a more radical way of relating to the body and brain as mere machinery, thus denying death its sting by implying that it is irrelevant of death to any existence stripped this bare. Psychotic patients may express these issues in their most basic and primary process forms, believing literally in magical qualities of the substances used, personifying the drug in a literal manner, or openly discussing which important person in their life or fantasy is causing them to take the substance, or who is being injected (read *introjected*) by the needle.

For several methods of administration, boundary and early developmental issues involving skin contact are amplified in some cases. For example, Meloy (1988) speculated about the emphasis that psychopaths give to the skin: skin contact, tattoos, self-mutilation, and IV drug use. Administration via absorption through the mucous membranes of the genitals, anus, or other erogenous zones has more obvious implications, both for sexual and sensation-seeking goals and for the developmental, depth psychological, and self concerns the drug use may reflect. Oral ingestion is the most socially acceptable route. However, clinical lore links orality and oral ingestion to aggressive expressions of basic dependency needs, such as the need for nurturance and soothing contact. The more pathological variants of orality are assumed to be related to reinforcement histories and/or expectations of painful consequences to experiencing these needs, such as rejection or abandonment by the caretaker, or frustration and deprivation by the nurturant parent.

Clearly, the same administration route may have different meanings for different drugs of choice, depending on user motivation. For example, clinical lore suggests that nasal users of heroin may have pronounced conflicts related to deception, seeing themselves and others as actors, and also may have pronounced tendencies toward psychosomatic illnesses. Nasal users of cocaine are viewed by clinicians as preferring this route primarily for intensity of effect and the social culture surrounding the drug, with little psychodynamic import placed in either the administration route or the psychosomatic-like symptoms they often display in the respiratory system during the first phases of postdetoxification and early recovery.

A useful generalization can be made about the probable addictive course of drug use that is related to route of administration: administration route often influences effective dosage, intensity, and duration of peak drug effects. Route of administration and typical dosage interact with the primary site of drug action to influence both the zenith of drug effects and the shape of the curve of drug effects over time. When the site of drug action is primarily on the CNS and the curve is very peaked, the use of the drug is more apt to result in accelerating addictive behavior. For the extreme of these effects, the best example may be the freebasing of cocaine, which results in a very intense drug effect on the CNS and a rapid decline and rebound to acute withdrawal effects.

When drug action results in proportionately more peripheral somatic and peripheral nervous system than CNS effects, fewer individuals will develop an accelerating addiction. This is also true when the curve peaks at a lower level of drug intensity and is more spread out over time with long plateaus. In these circumstances, drug use is more easily held to insidious dependence and to substance abuse addiction levels. This pattern is exemplified by the abuse of prescription drugs such as Valium, or by alcohol doses that do not catastrophically insult the CNS or the alcohol clearance system, especially the liver.

Any decision about preferred route of administration and psychological constructs is speculative, but the more social norm-based considerations are fairly reliable. The *social context of use and procurement* of a substance is also an important vector of drug efficacy. The social connection among other users, the sense of being in touch or "on the one" with a special group, the excitement of taboo and danger shared with others are all part of the drug experience. The expectations concerning a given substance, primed by those who introduce a user to a drug, are often crucial to interpretation of the drug effects. The meaning of solitude during use, experiences such as secrecy, hoarding, sharing, generosity, gratitude, expectations of reciprocity in relationships all intertwine. Preference for using alone or with others, for sharing a bottle or secreting a stash have powerful implications for treatment.

An extremely important mechanism of drugs that influences social dynamics is the ability of many substances to increase state tuning of mood or affect between individuals intoxicated at similar levels with the same substance. A contagious sense of empathy, understanding, and belonging is often established by a common shift in perception and sensation. Anxieties and differences are easily glossed over, facilitating the tuning of one individual's mental state with another's. Clearly, this is what is sought in the social use of cannabis and alcohol. Music or dancing, or even sharing the same topic of conversation, helps most normal individuals get in tune with others. This is not the case with many substance abusers, who require the drug as a facilitator of very basic forms of state tuning, a sort of concrete communion of users. (It might be noted here that the original meaning of communion such as in Christian rites involved ingesting the same substances to emphasize being at one with Christ and other worshippers. Religious observations often involve the use of wine or other psychoactive substances.)

Conversely, drugs can be used to cut off the longing for social contact at the physiological level. The opiates have been demonstrated to do this effectively in nonhuman primates. Drugs such as the hallucinogens or memory facilitating levels of alcohol can also fill the life space with soothing and stimulating objects of fantasy or memory, which compensate for the absence of safe and rewarding interpersonal relationships (Hofer 1983).

How drug use affects one's *self-concept* is also a crucial vector of drug efficacy, which must be evaluated in the context of the individual's entire life space. Concepts such as self-esteem and experiences such as shame, guilt, and self-adoration are relevant to this vector. A recurrent theme in this book is the effect that drug use has on the individual's sense of self as free, or unfree, defined, or lacking in identity and context. Drugs may influence these existential issues by converting them from open-ended to closed-ended questions. Under the influence of drugs, one may experience the self as having no options, or having infinite control, as being stuck in a specific role identity, or of being an amorphous blob of sensation. Often obliterated are all of the shadings between these extremes. For example, the feeling of being out of control of one's behavior while under the influence of an intoxicant has important dynamic and existential implications. Responsibility can easily become absolute or nonexistent for the drug-dependent person. A drug that will obliterate the most feared side of these false dilemmas, or accentuate the preferred side, will more probably become the drug of choice. Contrary to this process are the establishment and toleration of the many ambiguities and ambivalences required to build the realistic sense of responsibility and appropriate self-love that are the cornerstones of recovery.

DRUG EFFECTS AND DRUG CLASSES

This section gives a brief description of the major drug classes so that the reader who is not familiar with them will have some reference point for the ideas advanced later about the relationship between drug of choice and other components of the heuristic system. A detailed report of all effects, actions, and uses of various drugs, which is beyond the scope of this chapter, is available in such publications as Michael J. Gitlin's *The Psychotherapist's Guide to Psychopharmacology*, 1990.)

Drugs may be classified by their effects, mechanisms of action, or primary medical uses. The classes listed here are primarily based on effects. Where possible, observations are offered concerning possible connections with psychological functions and factors leading to a preferred drug or drugs of choice. The most commonly used drugs for each class are presented in order of decreasing potency. The effects that motivate drug use are noted before describing any unsought side effects and withdrawal symptoms. Important effects of route of administration are noted. Each class is then linked to one or more of the symptom complexes, usually by noting its use in medical practice. As stated earlier, it is not possible to link drugs clearly with psychological functions. However, where such connections have significant clinical support, these are also noted. Table 3–4 outlines the speculated connections among drug class, symptom complexes, and prototypic diagnostic categories.

Table 3–4. Summary of Drug Categories

Stimulants
Sought effects: Increased arousal, activity, efficiency, euphoria.
Unsought effects: Impulsivity, aggression, agitation, depression.
Functions: Avoidance of unpleasant affects, chemical support of self-esteem, self-stimulation, gain of social or sexual advantages.
Examples: Cocaine, amphetamine, Ritalin, nicotine, caffeine.
Ranked diagnoses: APD, schizophrenia, affective disorders.

Sedative-Hypnotics
Sought effects: Reduction in anxiety, pleasant sedation, euphoria.
Unsought effects: Severe withdrawal, dangerous disinhibition.
Functions: Often used to escape or avoid painful affects or situations, or to reduce anxiety to the point that other coping mechanisms can be affective. Disinhibition of self-monitoring.l
Examples: Barbiturates, alcohol, Valium, Serax, Xanax.
Ranked diagnoses: Anxiety disorders, affective disorders, antisocial personality.

Narcotic-Analgesics
Sought effects: Euphoria, detachment, affect blocking, sexual enhancement, avoidance of deprivation/withdrawal effects.
Unsought effects: Withdrawal symptoms, tolerance, impotence.
Functions: Controls primary affect, may decrease need for affection and social contact, has an antipsychotic effect, strongly promotes an emotionally detached and antisocial lifestyle.
Examples: Heroin, morphine, methadone, codeine, Dilaudid.
Ranked diagnosis: Antisocial personality, schizophrenia, affective disorders.

Hallucinogens
Sought effects: Pleasant heightening and distortion of perception.
Unsought effects: Psychosis, depression, confusion, impulsivity.
Functions: Escape from reality, enactment of identity and orientation issues, may support an asocial stance.
Examples: LSD, PCP, marijuana.
Ranked diagnoses: Antisocial personality, schizophrenia, affective disorders

Psychiatric Medications
Sought effects: Relief of diagnosed emotional or mental disorders.
Unsought effects: Many "side effects," primarily controllable.
Functions: Supports ego functioning. Maintains supportive input from or dependent stance toward caregiver, conflicts over advisability of use, or client noncompliance may split treatment team. Most effective within a broad treatment context.
Examples: Antidepressants, antipsychotics, antianxiety drugs.

Stimulants

The class of stimulant drugs includes: amphetamine, cocaine, methylphenidate (Ritalin), nicotine, and caffeine.

Administration of stimulant drugs covers the full range of routes, with injection of amphetamine and inhalant forms of cocaine providing the most intense effects.

These drugs primarily increase CNS arousal. They heighten energy level, decrease fatigue, induce sleeplessness, and stimulate motor activity and increase efficiency of selected mental and physical abilities. Propensities toward impulsivity and aggression are increased. Pleasure centers may be stimulated directly, causing euphoria and a chemically bolstered sense of competence and self-esteem. Irritability, increased tension, and loss of appetite and increased anxiety are often experienced. Decreased interest in sexual activity or impotence may occur after prolonged use. The stimulants cause little immediate interference with higher order brain functions. High doses and chronic use usually increase paranoia and may lead to psychosis. One study estimates that an addicted cocaine user is seven times more likely to have a psychotic episode than a nonuser (Tien and Anthony 1990). The high of stimulant use is often followed by a crash of psychological and physical withdrawal. These effects include severe depression, stuporous sleep, fatigue, extreme irritability, and agitation.

Stimulants are used in the medical treatment of obesity and narcolepsy, due to their ability to increase metabolism and induce a general brain and body wakening. In hyperactive children, stimulants such as Ritalin and caffeine decrease impulsivity and aggression while increasing concentration and mental composure. This paradoxical effect on hyperactive children (who appear to have clear arousal deficits) links the effects and actions of stimulants to similar mechanisms that account for the reward/arousal deficits symptom complex.

All five psychosocial functions are relevant to stimulant use. Facilitation of euphoria and confidence is perhaps most prominent in character disorders, whereas avoidance of negative affect is more pronounced in neurotics. Orientation may be the more pronounced function for psychotic patients who may use the stimulant to provide a sense of being, such as in schizophrenia with negative symptoms. Modulation may be more primary with other psychotic disorders, as in bipolar or schizoaffective disorder where drugs may be used to match psychophysiological pace with ego-syntonic mania and grandiosity. Increased vigilance and readiness for aggression, which are facilitated by stimulants, may be valued by paranoid individuals or those with conflicts about aggression, such as the passive-aggressive/explosive patient. Of course, a major use of stimulants is to avoid negative feelings and psychomotor retardation while promoting positive affect and psychomotor enhancement. Reactive depressions related to frustration of achievement needs, complicated bereavement, or low self-esteem are resolved temporarily by stimulant use. When used by those with more serious psychological difficulties, stimulants may provide the impulsivity and aggressiveness that may result in suicide or an attack on others. This takes on particular importance when we note that schizophrenia and antisocial personality disorder, or mild psychopathy, are two diagnostic categories where modulation of reward/arousal problems are often central to the motivation for continued stimulant drug abuse and dependence which may lead to violent acting out.

Sedative Hypnotics

The class of sedative hypnotic drugs includes barbiturates, alcohol, and the minor tranquilizers, or antianxiety drugs. (THC, the active substance in cannabis, is a hallucinogen, but in the doses encountered in marijuana smokers, the drug has many of the properties of this class.)

These drugs are general CNS depressants. Dose is an extremely important factor with this class. Small doses of more than one drug cause synergistic effects, often resulting in an overdose. A low dose of a single drug in this class reduces anxiety, emotionality, tension, or psychomotor agitation, that is, it produces sedation. At high doses, hypnotic effects appear, such as clouding of consciousness, psychomotor retardation, stuporous sleep, and, in the case of overdoses, eventually coma. Withdrawal effects are often more severe than with any other class of drug (including the opiates) and include overwhelming anxiety, sleep lag, anorexia, tremors, convulsions, seizures, hallucinations, delirium, and in extreme cases, death.

The barbiturates, unlike many other psychoactive substances, are fat soluble. Fat solubility is one factor that influences duration of drug effects. The barbiturates vary in fat solubility, have a wide range of effects curves, and are, in fact, generally classified by the duration of their action. Barbiturates include phenobarbital (Luminal), secobarbital (Seconal), and thiopental (Pentothal). Their medical application includes daytime sedative, antiepileptic, sleep induction, and anesthetic uses.

Alcohol is a sedative, although its use is often motivated by its disinhibiting, stimulantlike effects at low doses. (Alcohol and depressive and negative affects are covered in Chapter 2.). Although alcohol abuse and dependence are found in every diagnostic category, they have particular relevance for schizophrenia, bipolar disorder, dysthymia, panic disorders, and obsessive compulsive disorder. There is no medical use for alcohol ingestion, although some attempts (specifically those of Harry Stack Sullivan at St. Elizabeths Hospital in Washington, DC during the early 1920s) have been made to treat schizophrenics in group therapy while under the influence of prescribed alcohol.

The anxiolytics include diazepam (Valium), chlordiazepoxide (Librium), flurazepam (Dalmane), oxazepam (Serax), and alprazolam (Xanax). In addition to their medical use to decrease anxiety and agitation, these drugs are also used in controlling the symptoms of alcohol withdrawal. This is often a problem for individuals who are in early recovery and who may abuse both alcohol and, for example, Serax. The synergistic characteristic of these drugs with alcohol is often problematic for alcoholics.

The sedative hypnotics can be linked to the anxiety symptom complex. However, it is clear that any of these drugs can also be linked to other complexes, especially dominance of affect. The range of dose-related effects of these drugs allows their use for all of the psychological functions in a wide variety of diagnostic categories.

Narcotic Analgesics

The class of narcotic analgesics includes: heroin, morphine, methadone, codeine, anileridine (Demerol), hydromorphone (Dilaudid), and oxycodone (Percodan).

The more powerful of these drugs are the narcotics. Heroin is a semisynthesised narcotic that has three times the potency of morphine and was once touted as the cure for morphine addiction. The analgesics are milder and include common pain and headache medications. It should be noted that a dual diagnosis population is a group with many somatic complaints and a penchant for over-the-counter drug use. A dual diagnosis ward will need more somatic medications, especially antihistamines and pain killers, than other psychiatric wards, despite the relative youth and health of the population after stabilization.

The drug effects of the narcotics are dose dependent. At low doses, euphoria is induced and sexual performance may be enhanced. Higher doses result in clouding of consciousness, apathy, and decreases in self-preservative and self-maintenance behaviors. Side effects include constipation, nausea, loss of appetite, and loss of sexual interest. Routes of administration include oral, nasal, smoking, rubbing the drug on mucous membranes or perforations in the skin, and hypodermic needle. The naive users of narcotics often experience nausea, vomiting, and other extremely unpleasant effects upon first use. Withdrawal symptoms resemble a bad case of the flu and are not as severe as with the sedatives. Some users of low doses will relapse simply to achieve regular bowel movements rather than because of intense pain. It is possible that the narcotics do not completely block pain but primarily alter our emotional interpretation or reaction to it. Narcotic use is clinically related to intense rage, overwhelming depression, and prepsychotic personality structure (Khantzian et al. 1974). This suggests a link between narcotic use and both the dominance of affect and the cognition and context symptom complexes. Schizophrenics and persons with antisocial personality are at higher risk for narcotic addiction than other diagnostic groups. This may reflect the effective antipsychotic action of the narcotics. A subgroup of criminals dominated by affective problems, yet with the capacity for interpersonal bonding, are prone to narcotic addiction. The more psychopathic subgroup of criminals, more dominated by a need for modulation of arousal/reward deficits and with severe deficits in the capacity for interpersonal bonding, tend to have higher frequencies of cocaine and alcohol addiction.

Hallucinogens

The class of hallucinogens includes: LSD, Phencyclidine (PCP), and THC, the active drug in marijuana and hashish. The primary feature of this class is the distortion or impairment of reality testing. A heightened, selective sensitivity to the environment is combined with perceptual distortion, depersonalization, emotional confusion, and inappropriate, intense affect. The hallucinogens have been used as models for the psychoses, especially schizophrenia. However, there are clear differences between the effects of drugs in this class and psychosis. One hallmark difference is the occurrence of visual hallucinations in intoxication by these drugs and the relative rarity of visual hallucinations in psychosis that is not drug induced. Many of the hallucinogens are fat soluble and slowly metabolized, providing for extended drug effects. Flashbacks to drug induced states may be related in some cases to the release of small amounts of the drug from fat cells. It has been speculated that the hallucinogens may stimulate the pathological generation of enteric hallucinogens by the body, or disrupt brain receptor sites, and thereby permanently increase a susceptibility to psychotic states. Violence and general aggressiveness are often noted in PCP use, as are mania, paranoia, depression, spatial distortions, and identity confusion. THC is often viewed as innocuous in the case of marijuana use, although there is increasing evidence that habitual use causes significant cognitive disruption. This may be due to the reverse tolerance of the substance, wherein smaller and smaller doses of marijuana or hashish will result in stronger drug effects. A recent study found that individuals who used marijuana on a daily basis were at more than twice the risk for psychotic experiences as nonusers (Tien and Anthony 1990). Depressed individuals become more depressed with habitual use of cannabis. Individuals with psychotic disorders are more apt to deteriorate with habitual use of marijuana, although it is not clear whether the social withdrawal such use encourages is more important to this process than chemical effects. Even normal individuals may experience an increase in paranoia during cannabis intoxication.

There is currently no common medical use for the hallucinogens as such. However, some attempts have been made to treat psychiatric disorders through psychotherapy facilitated by LSD use. The effects of the hallucinogens appear to have a close parallel relationship to the symptom complex of cognition and context, and to some extent sociability and identity. Individuals with problems in these areas often seek out hallucinogens, suggesting that their symptoms are not ego dystonic. Under the influence of the hallucinogen, thought flow and shifts in context are attributed to the drug and not to the self, perhaps another secondary gain from hallucinogen use by individuals such as schizophrenics. Adolescents and young adults who have a poorly established sense of self may use the hallucinogen for enactment of issues related to identity and orientation. In regard to psychological function, escape–avoidance may be prominent for many patients. The finding of the ECA study that persons with an anxiety disorder had a higher risk for hallucinogen abuse-dependence than did other psychiatric diagnostic groups can be explained in the light of the escape provided by these drugs from the anxiety-producing context of the individual's life when not under the influence. Similarly, the stimulating perceptual distortions of cannabis and PCP appear to dampen dysphoric psychotic symptoms. The role of modulation of psychotic features in individuals for whom psychosis has significant secondary gain or for whom psychosis is not fully ego-dystonic must also be investigated.

Polydrug Abuse and Designer Drugs

Although this class of drugs cannot be classified by any set of effects or by action, poly-substance abuse and the development of new drugs with several qualities of the other classes have become more prominent aspects of drug use behavior. The days of a single drug of choice are probably over. Few pure alcoholics enter psychiatric clinics without some other form of substance use. This is due to a large extent to cultural attitudes toward drug use, the availability of many new drugs, and the increased affordability of a few old ones. Mixtures of sedatives and stimulants, stimulants and narcotics, hallucinogens and stimulants, and anything that will fit in the pot have become common. Also more common are psychotic drug reactions, pleas for persons not to be found criminally responsible due to drug use, and accidental death, homicide, or suicide related to polysubstance abuse. In addition to these do-it-yourself designer drugs, the ingenuity of criminal drug labs has increased to the point that drugs are designed for specific markets, taking into account class and financial considerations, current drugs of choice in the geographical area, and the nature of the local distribution system.

Due to the interaction of different addictive processes, we can state definitively that every polydrug abuser is a dual diagnosis case. Polypharmacy is an unfortunate trend both in somatic medicine, psychiatry, and the street. Barbiturates (such as Serax) and minor tranquilizers (such as Xanax) are often used by physicians to ease the withdrawal effects of alcohol or cocaine dependence. Since these drugs also have abuse potential, even greater withdrawal symptoms than those that they ameliorate, and because they may reinforce the patient's reliance on chemical solutions to problems, many addictions workers frown on this practice. Many physicians choose to medicate only the specific withdrawal symptom, as one would the symptoms of a cold or the flu, rather than providing a drug to avoid withdrawal effects overall. Until the use of medication in the interruption of addictive craving and withdrawal symptoms becomes more sophisticated, this is often the most reasonable course of action.

Since polydrug abuse is so pervasive, it is difficult to make useful generalizations about psychosocial functions. However, an extreme preference for a given drug (accepting no substitutions) or extreme propensity toward polydrug use (especially when hallucinogens and stimulants are combined) provides significant data about the range of probable symptoms and psychological functions. When only one drug is acceptable, the symptoms and functions are probably few. The reverse is usually true in polydrug use. One exception based on clinical experience should be noted. In adolescents and young adults with very fragmented family systems, polydrug use is more common, especially use that combines alcohol or a stimulant with PCP or LSD. This connection may be related to the repetition of early object relations that is enabled by polydrug use. The author has observed a similar pattern in cases of adolescence and young adults where the family history and developmental history from early childhood and infancy do not indicate chaotic object relations. In these cases, more recent family disruption is evident, such as in a divorce or the development of significant psychopathology in a parent.

Psychiatric Drugs

For the reader who is most familiar with substance abuse treatment and is relatively naive to clients who must use prescribed psychiatric medications, a short introduction to the psychiatric use of drugs is helpful. (However, any of several introductory books on psychopathology and therapeutic approaches, including psychopharmacology, is recommended.) Early on in one's involvement with the dual diagnosis patient, it is important to learn, and occasionally relearn, that these drugs have powerful main effects and powerful, highly undesirable side effects. Overdoses may be crippling or fatal. For some of these drugs, rapid withdrawal is hazardous. The patient is rarely oblivious to any of these facts, so treating professionals must be all the more aware of them. These negative aspects of psychiatric drugs are overshadowed by the effects of not taking them in cases where they are indicated. Acts of violence, suicide, severe psychological deterioration leading to hospitalization, and continual relapse to the use of street drugs are the usual consequences of noncompliance.

Supporting compliance with the total treatment plan, once it is adequately formulated, is perhaps the crux of dual diagnosis treatment. Mental health workers who have not dealt with their own ambivalence toward the need for psychiatric medication should not work with dual diagnosis cases. Working closely in consultation with the treating psychiatrist is the first rule of any dual diagnosis work. This is true even if the patient is not currently being prescribed a psychiatric drug. At any time, a consultation regarding diagnosis or the advisability of a prescription targeting either withdrawal symptoms or one of the symptom complexes may be in order. The failure to obtain a diagnosis and appropriate consultation when the course of treatment or symptoms warrant it is clearly unethical from the point of view of any professional discipline.

If medication is recommended, it is important that all parties involved are aware that this will require ongoing monitoring for symptoms and side effects. This will involve the prescribing psychiatrist, the primary therapist, the patient's family, and the patient. Some degree of compliance to dose administration, blood level appointments, dietary restrictions, and avoidance of substance abuse are required for the effective and safe use of all of these medications. Clearly, the maintenance of mental health through chemical means is usually a kind of necessary bargain with the devil. Many psychiatrists will treat only the most acute and dangerous psychiatric symptoms with medication if substance use is also present. Increasingly, however, the treatment of addiction is seen as a valid specialty in psychiatry, and more psychiatrists are being trained to become familiar with the psychopharmacological treatment of dual diagnosis cases.

Although the medical science and art of using these drugs are extremely complicated, even without the presence of an addictive disorder, the drugs themselves can be easily classified. The most basic categories are the antipsychotic, antidepressant, antimanic, and antianxiety drugs.

Antipsychotic drugs or neuroleptics (also called the major tranquilizers) reduce CNS arousal and decrease psychotic symptoms such as auditory hallucinations, delusions, or paranoia. Some examples in this class are haloperidol (Haldol), fluphenazine (Prolixin), and thiothinene (Navane). Most of these drugs have serious side effects, including permanent neurological change, which may result in involuntary movements. Most drugs of this type are administered in large doses initially and then are tapered off to an effective maintenance dose. Weight gain, urinary retention, and skin and sexual problems are side effects that generate the first line of resistance to these drugs. More serious effects occur later in treatment, including involuntary movements, muscle spasms, rapid heart rate, and muscular tremor and rigidity. Anti-parkinsonism drugs (Levodopa, Cogentin, Symmetrel) are used to mitigate or control these serious symptoms. In a very rare condition, neuroleptic malignant syndrome, some patients die with few warning signs. The rarity of this condition does not dissipate most patients' fears about psychotropic use. Although psychotic conditions usually implicate all aspects of psychosocial functioning, the use of antipsychotic medication is primarily targeted at the reward/arousal and cognition and context complexes outlined earlier.

Antidepressants can be divided into two categories: the cyclic antidepressants and MAO inhibitors. The first category is broken down into subcategories based on the number of rings, or cycles, of certain chemical components. All categories are primarily used to control severe depression, have serious side effects, and can cause death in high doses, such as in a suicide attempt. Fluoxetine (Prozac) is a bicyclic antidepressant first introduced in the late 1970s. This is probably the drug of choice for primary endogenous depression, that is, depression without any observable external precipitant. Prozac has become controversial of late due to its euphoria-inducing properties, possible addictive potential, and disinhibition among some suicide-prone patients. The tricyclic antidepressants are still in great demand. Patients may respond well to one of the tricyclics (Tofranil, Norpramine, Elavil, Sinequan) and not to others.

Atypical depressions, phobic disorders, and somatic symptoms often respond well to MAO inhibitors. Many of these drugs involve dietary restrictions and avoidance of alcohol. Since the drug may lift apathy and psychomotor inhibition prior to having any effect on the cognitive and emotional aspects of the depression, MAO inhibitors may enable a patient to act on suicidal or self-destructive urges that would otherwise not be translated into action. Clearly, the antidepressants are targeted at relieving symptoms in the dominance of affect complex, although effects on reward/arousal deficits and anxiety complexes may also be implicated. In psychotic depressions, these drugs decrease cognition and context symptoms, which are congruent with depressed affect.

In antimanic drugs, lithium (Carbolith, Lithobid) is the drug of choice in the treatment of bipolar disorder and mania. Manic depressive symptoms are eliminated in the vast majority of patients properly diagnosed and treated with this drug. Lithium is effective at modulating mood and arousal generally in manic depressives and in some cases of depression and alcoholism with affective features. The therapeutic level of this drug is very close to toxic levels, making frequent testing of blood lithium level crucial. Decreased sodium intake in the diet or the use of diuretics (such as alcohol) can seriously increase drug toxicity. Smoking marijuana while on lithium may increase some of the side effects as well as the probability of relapse to psychotic symptoms. Side effects include increased thirst, weight gain, muscle weakness, fatigue, frequency of urination, loss of appetite, decreased libido, inhibited erection, and hair loss. Clearly, lithium targets the dominance of affect, and reward/arousal deficit complexes. In regard to psychotic delusions, cognition and context and sociability and identity complexes are also ameliorated by lithium.

Ultimately, this author comes down on the side of an understanding of the drug of choice that includes its dynamic, social, and biological qualities in interaction. Perhaps this is expressed best by Meissner (1986) in describing how the paranoid process uses projective mechanisms to shape the drug of choice to meet the needs (functions required to meet the symptom complexes) of the addicted person:

> Our hypothesis is that the qualities and circumstances of the drug use provide a vehicle for the specific projective elements which are generated in and derive from the subject's intrapsychic frame of reference. The projective process does not commandeer the drug substance and bring it into the service of intrapsychic needs in any absolute or apodictic sense. The drug substance, in combination with the attendant circumstances of its administration and application, must provide a suitable substrate which allows the drug to be conjoined with the individual's projective elaboration. Consequently, in each case of addiction there is a specificity of drug preference which is based on the ultimate fit between the subjective needs and the pharmacologic properties of the drug, and the extent to which they can be successfully amalgamated to meet the inner needs of the drug-taking individual. [p. 360]

Accepting the premise that drugs are used to accomplish intrapsychic ends through projective mechanisms, the object-relational aspects of these ends can be described by Stern's (1983) outline of the three basic types of self-with-other schemata involved in infant–caregiver dyads. These are state-sharing, state-transforming, and state-complementing schema. We can expect to find that drug use, which includes the social context of drug administration and procurement, will roughly parallel these three kinds of interaction schema. That is to say that drugs will be used to the end of sharing states with others, transforming states, or creating states that are complementary to those perceived in internal or external objects.

FORMULATING DUAL DIAGNOSIS PROBLEMS

All of the major elements needed for the formulation of a dual diagnosis problem are surveyed earlier in this chapter. The first two steps involve identifying the relevance to the case of the various symptom complexes while investigating the primary psychosocial functions served by the addiction. The key dimensions presented in Chapter 1 — acuity, chronicity, cyclicity, urgency, severity, and degree of reciprocity to other heuristic elements — are used to explore both the psychopathology and the addiction. This will enrich the understanding of the primary symptom complexes and the most important functions of addiction operative in a given case. The drug of choice is then examined to discover how it effectively addresses symptoms and enables or supports the prominent functions of addiction, given its particular pharmacological effects and the specific social and personal consequences of its use. Putting all of this information together results in a formulation of the dual diagnosis problem or problems presented by the case. Although building such a problem formulation might at first seem a formidable task when spelled out so explicitly, in practice, arriving at clinical formulations of dual diagnosis problems using this heuristic system can eventually proceed very smoothly. Engaging in the process itself will help to guide and organize observation, even if no clear problem formulation is initially determined.

The complete clinical formulation for an entire case requires one element in addition to the problem formulation, which is an analysis of the recovery processes required by the case (described in Chapter 5). When the problem is formulated and an analysis of recovery processes is completed, they are combined with clinical expertise (such as assessment, refined diagnosis, and knowledge of therapeutic modalities) toward the purpose of designing a comprehensive approach to treatment. Skill, artistry, science, good luck, and good faith are then needed to successfully implement treatment plans generated by such approaches. More than in other forms of treatment, clinical formulations and interventions based on them must be seen as trial balloons. If these are shot down by additional experience with the patient, it is better to recognize this as quickly as possible and use the heuristic system to generate alternative formulations and interventions.

Often, the initial use of the system will result in more than one preliminary formulation. Focused assessment, a return to records of previous treatments, observations of responses to ongoing treatments, or diagnostic clarity (perhaps from response to medication) may eliminate one formulation in favor of another. The clinician must keep in mind that the dual diagnosis case has typically already been a multiple treatment failure. Although this involves some concern about repeating failure for the patient, it should not mean timidity on the part of treatment providers. The attitude assumed by the staff and projected to the patient should be pragmatic and hopeful: "Let's find out what will work, we have some very good bets on what will."

As an example of the heuristic system in use, let us return to the dual diagnosis case presented in Chapter 1. Expanding in a more clinical manner on the case introduced in that chapter, we identify the patient at admission as Suzanne, a 26-year-old woman of Irish-American ancestry with a diagnosis of bipolar disorder and alcohol dependence. She has a history of being sexually assaulted as an adult. The possibility of HIV infection must be investigated. She displays considerable identity confusion and has had at least one manic episode, which included delusional and paranoid thinking, with suicidal gestures. She is emotionally disorganized and labile, with depression being the dominant mood, accompanied by psychomotor agitation. She has had a poor adjustment history since age 18, but little history of problems before that time.

Two simple methods can be used to describe the severity of the pathology for each of the complexes relevant to this case. The first method is simply to rate each complex as high, moderate, or low in symptom severity level. Assigning the numbers 3, 2, and 1, respectively, to these levels quantifies them sufficiently. The second method is to rank order the complexes, thus indicating their relative importance. Suzanne has highly severe symptoms in three complexes (dominance of affect, cognition and context, and sociability and identity), a moderate level of severity on reward/arousal and a low level of severity for manifest anxiety. This would result in a numerical score of $(3 \times 3) + 2 + 1 = 12$, out of a possible 15 ceiling for severity scores.

Rank ordering the complexes is probably not very useful in this case, given the pervasiveness of symptom severity, but the following order is descriptive: dominance of affect, sociability and identity, cognition and context, anxiety, and reward/arousal. Although this case involves mania, affect rather than general arousal level appears to account for almost all of the manic symptoms, thus resulting in a low rank order for reward/arousal. Were hyperactivity, sleeplessness, sensation seeking, and increased activity during either cyclical exacerbation of the disorder or intoxication evident in this case (as in many other cases of bipolar disorder) the reward/arousal complex would be placed earlier in rank. Its last place here exemplifies how diagnosis alone does not give all the information needed to view the case comprehensively and how formulations based solely on diagnosis can be faulty, even when the diagnosis is correct. Assuming that symptoms that are typical of a given diagnosis are, in fact, present in this case and related to the addiction or substance abuse can lead to serious errors in conceptualizing and treating the individual. For example, we also find cases of mania where the affective component is minor on a manifest level, and arousal, sensation seeking, and pursuit of positive rewards explains most of the manic symptoms.

A case of this level of severity and variety of psychiatric symptoms requires judgments about the priority of various treatment foci, all of which are crucial to the successful treatment. The same difficulty was apparent in attempting to rank order the primary symptom complexes. We can note that Suzanne has been diagnosed as suffering from a bipolar disorder and assume that treating this syndrome medically is the first priority. We know that this is exactly what has happened to this patient in previous treatment episodes. We also know from her treatment history that global interventions, such as medication alone, have not worked. We need to be more sophisticated in our strategy. The type and sequence of our interventions, after the most urgent issues are addressed, must be based on a clear formulation of the problems presented by the patient's interacting addiction and psychopathology.

When this patient is medicated and detoxified, there will be significant residual symptoms. Nor can we consider all remaining symptoms as merely residual to the bipolar disorder. Taken together, the relative absence of arousal problems (sleeplessness, defatigability, etc.) and the fact that her manic episodes are not characterized typically by euphoric, expansive affect and behavior suggest that in Suzanne's case, the mood disorder should be quite controllable. Her history of poor response to psychiatric treatment and the intractability of the addiction to treatment suggest that other factors may be as significant in the long run as the bipolar disorder. After the manic depressive symptoms ebb, where should our psychotherapeutic interventions focus, especially if we are to prevent relapse to alcohol use and support her recovery from dependence on alcohol? Should the affective symptoms come first, or those related to cognition and context, or sociability and identity? How much attention must be given to the relationship between the addiction and the psychopathology?

When the information gained from the heuristic system is included, the picture becomes clearer. In some cases, rank ordering all five functions of addiction is useful. (Rating them is usually *not* useful, because only one or two functions are generally operative in a given case.) In Suzanne's case, however, two or three functions account fully for the tenacity of the addiction in relationship to the psychopathology. Escape/Avoidance of (depressive) affect and facilitation of relationships, which involve dependency and merger, are the primary functions of Suzanne's addictive use of alcohol. Alcohol is a sedative with disinhibiting effects and specific actions related to negative affective memory. Its side effects include increased negative affect, especially depression. Her history and observation of her behavior on the admissions unit suggest that this patient's use of alcohol both separates and connects her to others, via state tuning effects, disinhibition, and identification through drug use and social processes related to recovery (notice that the patient's previous use of recovery activities is included as part of the analysis of the function of the addiction).

Possible reasons for her choice of alcohol over other available substances can only be tested during treatment or with intensive psychological examination and directed clinical interviews. The drug suggests extreme oral dependency, which is somewhat supported by her history of adult relationships. Her difficulty in forming useful self-with-other representations without drug use or psychopathology suggests possible traumatic memories involving loss, rejection, or other such situations in early life. Her sexual history suggests that these memories may have been sexualized in nature or reconstructed as such in her mind. These experiences may have involved an alcoholic or depressed caretaker, probably a parent. If these speculations about the drug of choice are supported by evidence from other sources, her addiction might be treated as enabling repetition of object relations and repressed traumatic events.

Many of these aspects of this patient's problems—affective, interpersonal, and identity—could not be predicted from the Axis I disorder. No diagnostic formulation is complete without investigating the contribution of personality disorder or the basic personality style. Examining Axis II, a diagnosis of histrionic or borderline personality disorder clarifies the meaning of some of her symptoms and elevates them in our formulation. The diagnosis has been refined due to the analysis of which dominant functions are played by addiction. We might expect that were the primary symptom complexes resolved, say by lithium, the personality problems that are highly related to the addictive functions would, nonetheless, persist and become the new focus of treatment.

In Suzanne's case, some of the earlier speculations were confirmed, others were not. Her mother was an alcoholic, whom Suzanne experienced as alternately seducing her into playful intimacy as another child might or treating her in a warm maternal way. The appropriate maternal treatment was often followed by episodes of drinking, during which Suzanne perceived her mother as being rejecting and entirely oblivious to her needs. Although no sexual abuse was established, Suzanne had apparently generalized her expectations of her mother to males, who were her most typical, although not exclusive, love interests. Once sober and stable, Suzanne's own seductiveness toward others and her eventual rejection of them became a community issue on the admissions unit.

To summarize our findings in this case, Suzanne's addiction, bipolar disorder, and personality pathology were acute at admission with a chronic history of severe symptoms that demonstrated overlapping cycles of amelioration and deterioration. Although her personality problems were viewed as less urgently in need of intervention in the initial treatment stage, this shifted after stabilization and detoxification. The symptom complexes and addictive functions were complementary and indicated more than a simple one-way, linear causal path relationship, suggesting that they would be difficult to unravel.

We might formulate two basic dual diagnosis problems operative in Suzanne's case. In the terminology of the heuristic system, the problems can be described as (1) escape/avoidance functioning to address dominance of affect, and (2) facilitation (or repetition) of compensations (especially interpersonal relationships) required by deficits in sociability and identity. Her addiction provided an escape from painful affect and affective memories, especially those related to depression. It also facilitated relationships typified by merger, dependency, and (traumatic) rejection. These functions operate to support the equilibrium of a histrionic or borderline personality, which is vulnerable to decompensation to a bipolar psychosis. In this patient the depressive part of the cycle is more intense and prolonged than the manic, and unlike many manic depressives the manic symptoms themselves are, for the most part, ego-dystonic. Her personality style and personal history suggest that the addiction may also enable repetition of a early traumatic experience.

Most of this formulation would have been available to a well-trained clinician unfamiliar with the heuristic system presented in this chapter. However, the heuristic system guides clinical observation, helps to generate additional formulations, and makes assumptions more explicit so that they may be openly evaluated. It provides a way of communicating about cases and thinking about issues across cases and provides the seasoned clinician with a tool for teaching about and supervising dual diagnosis work.

II

TREATMENT

4

Reciprocal Assessment

ASSESSMENT STRATEGIES

A general heuristic system for conceptualizing dual diagnosis issues is outlined in Chapter 3, suggesting the starting and end points of a comprehensive assessment. In that chapter, the initial hypotheses needed to generate additional observation and the typical issues that tend to come together to create a dual diagnosis problem are outlined or summarized. The information required to use the heuristic system to generate hypotheses can usually be obtained in a structured interview after taking a good history from available records, informants, and treatment staff who are either familiar with the patient from other treatment episodes or have had the opportunity of extended observation of the patient.

This chapter fills in details of the middle aspect of assessment, the stage where initial hypotheses must be substantiated or rejected and where early working formulations must give way to clearer, more therapeutically fruitful refinements or corrections. The approach offered here is based on the interactive relationships described in earlier chapters. The assessment approach emphasizes the holistic nature of the problems that the patient faces, as well as the need for a comprehensive treatment program. Assessment is here conceptualized as a cyclical process that occupies at least some aspect of every encounter with the patient. By necessity, however, the emphasis here is on assessment material communicated formally to other treatment team members at specific points in the treatment, rather than on informal assessment activities that are more ubiquitous but more difficult to quantify.

The general approach to assessment in this chapter is similar to the "behavioral assessment funnel" proposed by Cone and Hawkins (1977), refined by Skinner (1981), and further detailed by Donovan (1988). At the top of the funnel is the broad-base assessment that must be performed as a screening; the next level is what Skinner calls basic assessment and involves detailed descriptions of addictive behavior. This is followed by specialized assessment to gather more detailed information to confirm or reject hypotheses developed at earlier assessment and treatment stages, or to provide information that will guide very finely tuned, focused interventions.

Although assessment is a cyclical process, its activities are more useful when synchronized as closely as possible with the recognizable phases of illness and recovery or the stage of treatment in which a patient is most intensely involved or about to enter. The terms *phase* and *stage* are used to distinguish between natural processes: relatively spontaneous process that occur in phases, and more rational, willful, and deliberative processes that are staged or occur in stages. This is consistent with Donovan and Marlatt's (1988) phases of addictive behavior and the "stages of change" model of patient participation in addiction treatment (Brownell et al. 1986, Prochaska and DiClemente, 1983). The concept of phases of recovery, however, guides much of the treatment and therefore assessment functions described in this book.

Regarding phase of illness or level of severity, Skinner (1981) noted that in early phases of addictions, or in low severity cases, the crucial issue is screening for individuals at high risk for more serious addictive behavior, thus targeting them for preventive interventions. A second phase identified by Skinner is early diagnosis and treatment, where assessment is needed to identify areas of impairment related to an active addiction and to provide information for ongoing intensive treatment. In Skinner's third phase, rehabilitation, the individual has experienced pervasive undermining of normal functioning due to the addiction. Very extensive and specialized assessments are needed to guide treatments that will be longer term and targeted at chronic problems and deficits.

Treatment is a rationally guided process occurring in, according to Donovan and Marlatt (1988), three major stages: preintervention (where motivation and commitment for change are developed), intervention (active engagement in treatment and initial behavior change), and postintervention (where maintenance of progress and relapse prevention are primary). Minkoff, in writing of dual diagnosis work, also identified three treatment phases: engagement, prolonged stabilization, and rehabilitation. Chapter 5 identifies other stages as well. But regardless of the specific concepts preferred, during the opening stage of treatment, the assessment goal is to collect enough data to begin setting priorities among treatment strategies, perhaps by applying the heuristic concepts to the case. In addition, an important goal of this stage is to build an alliance with the patient and the family system and to establish the basis for communication with other members of the treatment team who perform assessments or interventions from various disciplines or points of view.

In the stage of active treatment, the most crucial aspect is evaluating the impact of various interventions on continued participation in treatment and on specific problem areas identified as targeted for change. Consolidation of new identifications and learned behaviors is the focus of a long middle phase of treatment. Assessment of factors that can predict or help to prevent relapse or waning involvement in self-directed treatment becomes more pronounced in the latter portion of this phase. Teaching self-directed assessment or self-monitoring skills and assessing the match of personal goals and activities with recovery goals become more important for patients who have achieved stable recovery.

In addition to the assessment cycle, four related principles are the cornerstones of assessment with this patient population. Like the assessment cycle, they must continually address the rapidly shifting patterns of severity and urgency in client problems and the relative instability of treatment phases for dual diagnosis patients. The first principle is striking the correct balance between focused, problem-oriented assessment techniques and global, person-as-a-whole approaches. The second principle is changing the focus of assessment according to the focal problem, or the stage of treatment or recovery that is the current primary challenge to the client's continued development. The third principle is understanding the continual ebb and flow of transitory states or short-term behavioral reactions of the patient in the context of more enduring, stable characteristics. The fourth principle maintains that assessment must discriminate between changes that are related to the recovery/therapeutic process and those that are related to either pathological processes or major changes in environmental and interpersonal stress.

To provide a fuller understanding of these four general principles, we first outline the most important global assessment techniques recommended for the dual diagnosis patient population. Focused assessment instruments and techniques are then presented with the rationale for their use. Areas of attention often missed in a typical mental health-oriented assessment are reviewed. State and trait measures are discussed, along with several assessment instruments that help in tracking and understanding the relationship between them. How these principles are applied will depend to a large extent on the treatment context in which they are used; therefore, some suggestions are offered about tailoring assessments to the most common program and staffing characteristics. Finally, we explore how to evaluate the extent to which changes in assessment findings actually reflect progress, resistance to treatment, or retrenchment of one or more pathological processes.

Because the dual diagnosis area is relatively new, this chapter recommends some assessment instruments that are also new, with limited research available on their psychometric properties or clinical utility. Some, although developed primarily for research purposes, are introduced here in clinical applications. Other recommended assessment instruments are very familiar to some clinicians, especially psychologists, but can be used in new ways or with minor additions or modifications. Some assessment instruments are recommended because of their relevance or economy of resources in regard to assessing dual diagnosis cases. In all cases where a specific assessment instrument is recommended, other instruments that assess the same functions or factors might prove as useful, especially if a clinician is already familiar with a roughly equivalent instrument or technique. This chapter addresses several areas of assessment not adequately covered elsewhere and uses assessment findings to clarify some theoretical issues introduced in earlier chapters or perused in later ones. The reader is referred to the work of Donovan and Marlatt (1988), *Assessment of Addictive Behaviors*, for a review of many key issues of substance abuse assessment and a description of several specific instruments for measuring coping skills, expectancies, urges, and relapse vulnerabilities that are not covered here but can be usefully incorporated into ongoing assessment of addiction.

GLOBAL AND COMPREHENSIVE INSTRUMENTS

The Addiction Severity Index

Several requirements must be met by a global and comprehensive assessment of the dual diagnosis patient. Problems in almost every sphere of the individual's existence will require description. Since the treatment team members will most probably, and preferably, have backgrounds in a wide range of disciplines and have come to dual diagnosis work with varying degrees of familiarity with substance abuse or mental health issues, they should be able to fulfull an important aspect of any early assessment — to provide a common language for communication about the patient's problems, needs, and resources. Without this common language of basic information, staff members may duplicate efforts or disagree about basic assumptions concerning facts about the patient and his or her situation. Disagreement may occur under the best of conditions, but when it stems from garbled communication and poorly articulated or implicit assumptions that are not easy to examine, creative outcomes are extremely unlikely.

The *Addiction Severity Index* (ASI) (Fureman et al. 1990) is an instrument that provides a baseline of information and a means of communication that can be made accessible to all staff members and the patient. It is in its fifth edition after more than ten years of investigation and development. The ASI manual is a clear guide to administering the instrument for clinical purposes. It gives suggestions for use in treatment contexts, including cross-checking ASI items for accuracy, and instructions for a more brief follow-up reevaluation. There is a separate manual for using the ASI as a research and evaluation instrument, which relies on composite scores formed from objective ASI items, as opposed to the severity ratings, which are more clinically useful but include many subjective factors (see Composite Scores from the ASI, McGahan et al. 1986). The ASI is designed for use with adult populations, but several versions are in development aimed at adolescents (addresses of those working on these versions are listed in the ASI manual, fifth edition). The ASI is a good example of American tax dollars at work. It was developed at the University of Pennsylvania Veterans Administration Center for Studies in the Addictions and was supported by grants from the National Institute of Drug Abuse and the Veterans Administration.

The ASI, with minor modifications accommodating the informational needs and treatment parameters of a specific treatment program, is recommended for all patients participating in a dual diagnosis program. It is administered as a structured interview with sufficiently specific questions that cover seven basic areas of patient treatment needs. These status areas, which are the subscales of the index, include: medical, employment/support, drug/alcohol use, legal, family/social relationships, and psychiatric. The drug/alcohol subscale includes an exhaustive history of all drug and alcohol abuse, the longest period of abstinence, and previous drug treatment history.

The ASI relies on fairly basic interviewing skills. Its question-and-answer format allows the patient the role of expert on his or her life and behavior. It is important that the interviewer use terms that are familiar to the patient in asking questions, substituting commonplace terms for the technical ones, and asking as many follow-up questions as required for a full understanding of the issues. For example, asking about hallucinations is often less effective than asking about voices or seeing things that others cannot see. Depending on the interviewer's skill and the patient's defensiveness and mental status, the written question can provide a safe distance and professional atmosphere to early interaction, or in a more informal and intimate interview, printed questions may be reminders to get back to certain issues.

The undermining of denial for many patients often begins with their being confronted with these questions from one individual in a single treatment context. Patients often discover that their drug use has been more devastating than they had realized and more connected to problems that previous treatment contexts have labeled exclusively due to mental illness. Also, the ASI requires the patient to rate perceived need and importance of each assessed area. This provides useful information, promotes engagement, and constructs a basis for confronting denial.

Central to the ASI is the concept of severity, which is defined as the need for additional treatment, making the ASI ratings primarily need assessments. After obtaining information on each subscale, the interviewer rates the severity on a scale ranging from zero to nine, with nine being a life-threatening condition indicating an urgent need for additional treatment. For each subscale, a list of crucial items provides a standard weighing of each, so that across raters the most important items are given due emphasis. However, prior to performing the ratings for each scale, the clinician obtains two ratings from the patient for each, one as to how bothered he or she has been over the last 30 days by problems in this area, and a second indicating how important treatment for these problems is to him or her at the current time. The patient uses a zero- to four-point scale, with zero indicating "not at all" bothered or interested in more treatment, and four indicating "extremely" bothered, or that treatment in this area is extremely important. Using this information, the clinician will adjust his or her ratings on the nine-point scale by one or two points.

By incorporating the patient's own ratings in the severity scores, the ASI assessment establishes collaboration between patient and interviewer. Examining the difference between the patient's view of the severity and the view of a trained professional is an important start to the treatment process and may result in gentle confrontation fairly early. This is especially true in divergent views on the alcohol or drug scale for patients admitted with either one as a primary problem. Understanding why the interviewer sees alcohol use as a problem for a cocaine-addicted psychiatric patient can be an important early step in treatment. Because clinicians anticipate patients being in the process of denial, the more common pattern is for the interviewer to perceive more severity on various scales than does the patient. However, this is not always the case. For example, a patient may rate his family problems as very severe, although the interviewer's assessment indicates a moderate level. The patient is given the opportunity to explain his views in his own terms. He may or may not volunteer new information that would not otherwise have been elicited. Invariably in these situations, the patient will communicate important aspects of his or her values, priorities, anxieties, hopes, and aspirations, as well as personal diagnostic and treatment formulations, often informative in their own right.

After the severity rating, two additional judgments are made by the interviewer for each scale. The first is a simple yes or no judgment as to whether the information was significantly distorted by the patient's conscious misrepresentation. The second judgment is a simple yes or no as to whether the information was distorted due to the patient's inability to understand, for example, because of organic impairment, psychosis, or residual withdrawal. The interviewer is, of course, encouraged to make notes or comments directly on the ASI form to substantiate or clarify any of the ratings or to record any unique or notable aspect of the interview. In addition, any of the ASI scales can be corrected by information that is part of another treatment record, or corroborated by family members or other informants.

The ASI items are structured to inquire about specific intervals of time in the patient's life. For most items, the time intervals are the last 30 days and the entire lifespan. These intervals may be modified to better fit the needs of a dual diagnosis program. For example, patient problems experienced during the most recent 30-day period without hospitalization is often more informative than looking at the last 30 days, which may have been spent in a controlled environment. Adding an an interval is more useful than substituting one, and the contrast of the two intervals is often informative to the patient as well.

Although the content areas covered in the subtests are fairly well described by their names, a few comments are in order about some specific subscale items and their utility, because the responses to these items may provide information beyond the specific goal of assessing that content area. For example, in the employment/ financial support subscale, an item asks, "How many people depend on you for the majority of their food, shelter, etc.?" The interviewer may direct the patient beyond simply reporting a number, for example, by adding the follow-up question, "How is that going?" The answer may provide important clinical clues to the patient's feelings about dependency in general, having his or her own needs met, failure at providing, or a number of other emotionally charged themes. Items in the legal subscale may reveal important trends toward psychopathy, or feelings about the dangers encountered in a drug-oriented lifestyle. Asking the patient if he or she had been the victim of any crimes is an important item not in the current ASI but easily added in the context of the legal questions.

By mentally referencing responses across subscales, the interviewer can use the ASI to detect events and situations that are difficult for the patient to report in answering a single question. For example, until the most recent edition of the ASI, it was necessary to specifically inquire about sexual prostitution in the context of employment/support questions, or concerning the amount of money spent by the patient on drugs, as reported in the drug/alcohol subscale. Although prostitution activities have now been added to the legal status scale, asking about them in the above contexts can be a useful way of eliciting more accurate information. When working with patients who are motivated to distort or lie about their responses, it is often helpful to spread the interview over several days. After first finding as much information from other sources as possible, it is possible to confront the patient with inconsistencies toward the end of this process.

Although the ASI relies on fairly basic interviewer skills to be performed adequately, it does have its own clinical subtleties. Also, it should be noted that the psychiatric subscale requests a clinical rating of several important mental status items at the time of the interview, which require a basic level of familiarity with psychiatric conditions. When the initial ASI is completed, a fairly comprehensive and straightforward assessment of needs exists. Also, at least one member of the treatment team will have a good sample of the patient's emotional responses to a wide range of areas. The clinician severity ratings are recorded on the face sheet of the ASI in a graphic scale profile from zero to nine. This provides a quick way of reviewing important areas of concern for a given case and a means for staff members to compare and contrast their views of the patient. Comparing ratings by different members of the team at a later point in treatment is also often useful, as are updates of the entire ASI during established follow-up periods or prior to discharge. It is possible to use the ASI with little reference to these ratings, however, since it is basically a standardized guide to conducting an interview. Obsessing about the "actual" severity level on a given subscale is counterproductive, but the use of the ratings does help to encourage productive discussion of cases.

The ASI can greatly facilitate training in substance abuse and dual diagnosis work. Becoming familiar with and understanding the rationale for the items on each scale is in itself a kind of primer course on reciprocal causal connections between substance use and other aspects of the individual's existence. A good place to begin initiating trainees with some previous human services background in the substance abuse and dual diagnosis fields is to supervise them in the administration of the ASI accompanied by detailed case discussions of the results and process of these interviews. The structured ASI format often prevents the trainee from being inundated by clinical material or not knowing where to go when the patient is not forthcoming with information and engagement in the interview process.

Despite its many strengths and although it provides an important baseline of information and opens the process of investigation, confrontation, and therapeutic alliance, the ASI is not exhaustive even in its purely information-collecting aspects. Even with the 1990 edition changes that include route of administration, family history of drug use, sexual and physical abuse in childhood, and questions about the ability to form long-lasting relationships, the ASI is obviously designed only to discover if there is an iceberg out there to be dealt with, not to unearth how far such issues go historically or to fully understand their current dynamics. Of crucial importance early in the treatment process is the compiling of a good social history, preferably by a clinical social worker. A good social history that tracks cross-generational themes as well as individual development remains an invaluable resource for understanding the development of substance use and mental health problems, as well as a rationale for engaging family members early on in the treatment process. Armed with the information contained in the ASI (which may be compiled by counselors, nursing staff, or undergraduate level mental health staff) combined with a good social history and brief interview, a psychiatrist, psychologist, or clinical social worker familiar with dual diagnosis population can usually arrive at an adequate diagnosis and clinical formation.

The Millon Clinical Multiaxial Inventory

As a result of the Axis I mental disorders, the dual diagnosis patient often displays a very unstable pattern of symptoms, usually falling within one or a few of the symptom complexes outlined in Chapter 3. In addition, there is often a very stable pattern of personality pathology, which may be difficult to typify. Personality may be considered the most complex, subtle, and global level of individual functioning. After a good social and family history and an ASI, the assessment of personality dynamics is often more crucial to tailoring treatment interventions to individual needs and predispositions than almost any other type of information. The *Millon*

Clinical Multiaxial Inventory (MCMI) is extremely useful in assessing these three aspects of personal functioning: clinical syndromes, changing symptoms, and personality styles or disorders. It is based on a simple self-report questionnaire of 175 items, which the patient notes as either true or false for their behavior and experience.

The newer version of the test, the MCMI-II, is difficult to hand score, and the computer-scored format can prove expensive when administered to all patients as a routine intake assessment. Also, there is limited empirical research currently available on the newer instrument. Nevertheless, the MCMI-II does incorporate significant advances over the older instrument, although the original MCMI remains a highly effective assessment tool.

Either version requires an eighth-grade reading level to be administered in the questionnaire format. There is also a Spanish-language version of the test. Subjects are encouraged to answer all of the items. Like the Minnesota Multiphasic Personality Inventory (MMPI), the MCMI contains a validity index. The validity scale has only four items, which are highly implausible for examinees to endorse as true of themselves. Marking even one of these items as true places the validity of the test in doubt due to either random responding, careless reading of the items, or a florid psychotic process that might make the protocol invalid.

Again similar to the MMPI, several MCMI indexes adjust scores for various response biases. For example, these scales adjust for a subject's motivation to accurately disclose and to be viewed as socially desirable. Other adjusted-for biases include transient or ingrained tendencies toward self-debasement, denial of problems versus the cry for help, and the distorting effects of unusually high levels of depression or anxiety.

Although the MCMI is designed specifically to address the assessment of personality, its construction and theoretical base make it a starting point for assessing the full range of psychopathology. Users of the Minnesota Multiphasic Personality Inventory will note many commonalities between it and the MCMI. The two tests are, in fact, used very profitably in combination, in that the MCMI often can distinguish subtypes of MMPI profiles. There are several significant differences between the approach taken by these two tests, however. Whereas the MMPI was derived empirically and has accrued clinical lore and informal theory over time, the MCMI is a theory and concept-driven enterprise that has been validated and refined empirically. To understand and use the MCMI, one must explore and apply a comprehensive theory of individual functioning and of the nature of disfunction. In describing psychopathology, Millon (1983) differentiates among personality patterns, symptom disorders, and behavior reactions. For Millon, personality is the central concept in understanding psychopathology and normal functioning. By understanding the personality style, we are able to observe symptoms and situational reactions in their proper context. The MCMI symptom scales measure the degree to which the individual is distressed or is experiencing a commonly assessed range of psychological symptoms. From the severity of these symptoms viewed within the context of the personality style and an adequate history of the individual, an Axis I diagnosis can be derived.

In Chapter 6, we return to a discussion of Millon's theoretical views of the personality disorders. Here, we describe the MCMI as an aid to determining the basic personality style, with or without significant disorder, in accordance with a personality typology that is roughly equivalent to the typology used in the *DSM-III-R*, Axis II disorders. The basic assumption is that we all have a limited number of personality traits that dominate most of our functioning, at least to the point that these may be described as typical of our personality or as adequately assessing our personality style. When these traits are few in number and are rigidly applied across many situations, they become increasingly counterproductive for us personally and problematic for those around us. With the occurrence of these extremes, we can describe the personality style as a personality disorder.

Although personality styles are not in themselves pathological, the terms used to describe them usually have negative or harsh connotations. Millon labels the personality styles or disorders in somewhat different terms than those used in the *DSM-III-R*, in some cases reducing the tendency to stigmatize (Millon 1983b: manual). These less harsh labels are the parenthetical adjectives in several of the scale names in Table 4–1, which outlines the basic personality styles or disorders. The source for these descriptions is from Millon's own summaries in the MCMI-II manual, and the reader is referred to that source to flesh out the conceptual background and clinical distinctions that undergird the somewhat telegraphic descriptions presented here (Millon 1987). Several of the personality scales have the alphabetical subscript B (e.g., 6B). These scales are further refinements in MCMI-II over MCMI-I and do not correspond as directly with a *DSM-III-R*, Axis II diagnostic category.

Table 4–2 outlines the pathological personality disorders (or process disorders) and Table 4–3 outlines the symptom scales. In some ways, the pathological personality disorders have more in common with the symptom scales, in that these personality types are really more the result of decompensations, or failure in the development of the basic personality patterns, and are expected to garner a wide range of severe symptoms. Although the basic personality patterns are grouped by Millon in clusters of differing general levels of adaptation and effectiveness, and therefore can be seen as having various degrees of desirability, all are viable ways of functioning. However, the pathological personality disorders always indicate significant impairment in functioning and cannot be described as viable, adequate ways of organizing individual behavior.

MCMI interpretation begins with establishing the validity of the protocol, using the validity scale. Next, the scales are examined in three clusters: the personality styles, the pathological personality disorders, and the symptom scales. First, the personality style scales scores are examined. These scores reflect the probability of the examinee having both the intensity and number of traits to merit including

Table 4.1. MCMI Basic Personality Styles or Disorders

Scale 1. Schizoid (Asocial) Personality: behaviorally lethargic, interpersonally aloof, cognitively impoverished, primary defense mechanism is intellectualization, flat mood, complacent self-image, meager internalizations, undifferentiated intrapsychic structure.

Scale 2. Avoidant Personality: behaviorally guarded, interpersonally aversive, cognitively distracted, primary defense mechanism is fantasy, anguished mood, alienated self-image, vexatious internalizations, fragile intrapsychic organization.

Scale 3. Dependent (Submissive) Personality: behaviorally incompetent, interpersonally submissive, cognitively naive, introjected mechanism, pacific mood, inept self-image, immature internalizations, inchoate intrapsychic organization.

Scale 4. Histrionic (Gregarious) Personality: behaviorally affected, interpersonally flirtatious, cognitively flighty, dissociation mechanism, fickle mood, sociable self-image, shallow internalizations, disjoined intrapsychic organization.

Scale 5. Narcissistic Personality: behaviorally arrogant, interpersonally exploitive, cognitively expansive, rationalization mechanism, insouciant mood, admirable self-image, contrived internalizations, spurious intrapsychic organization.

Scale 6A. Anti-Social (Aggressive) Personality: behaviorally impulsive, interpersonally irresponsible, cognitively deviant, acting -out mechanism, callous mood, autonomous self-image, rebellious internalizations, unbounded intrapsychic organization.

Scale 6B. Aggressive/Sadistic Personality: behaviorally fearless, interpersonally intimidating, cognitively dogmatic, isolation mechanism, hostile mood, competitive self image, pernicious internalization, eruptive intrapsychic organization.

Scale 7. Compulsive (Conforming) Personality: behaviorally disciplined, interpersonally respectful, cognitively constricted, reaction formation mechanism, solemn mood, conscientious self-image, concealed internalizations, compartmentalized intrapsychic organization.

Scale 8A. Passive Aggressive (Negativistic) Personality: behaviorally stubborn, interpersonally contrary, cognitively negativistic, displacement mechanism, irritable mood, discontented self-image, oppositional internalizations, divergent intrapsychic organization.

Scale 8B. Self-Defeating Personality: behaviorally abstinent, interpersonally deferential, cognitively inconsistent, devaluation mechanism, doleful mood, undeserving self-image, debased internalizations, inverted intrapsychic organization.

them among individuals with a given personality style. These scores are derived from the base rate of each personality type among clinical patients, but they may also be interpreted as reflecting the intensity of traits related to a given personality type. Once the most probable personality style groupings have been determined, the pathological personality scales scores are examined in a similar manner. If significant elevations are found on any of these three scales, the presence of a disordering process must be integrated with an understanding of the basic person-

Table 4.2. Pathological Personality Disorders

Scale S. Schizotypal (Schozoid) Personality: behaviorally aberrant, interpersonally secretive, cognitively autistic, undoing mechanism, distraught or insentient mood, estranged self-image, chaotic internalizations, fragmented intrapsychic organization.

Scale C. Borderline (Cycloid) Personality: behaviorally precipitate, interpersonally paradoxical, cognitively capricious, regression mechanism, labile mood, uncertain self-image, incompatible internalizations, diffused intrapsychic organization.

Scale P. Paranoid Personality: behaviorally defensive, interpersonally provocative, cognitively suspicious, projection mechanism, irascible mood, inviolable self-image, unalterable internalizations, inelastic intrapsychic organization.

---

ality style or styles previously established. Finally, the symptom scales are examined to discover the likelihood and quality of either a moderate or severe Axis I clinical syndrome. The last step in profile interpretation is to integrate all of the information into a synthetic formulation of the personality, its dynamics, current symptoms, and diagnosed psychopathology.

In regard to the heuristic system for approaching dual diagnosis problems, the symptom scales are useful in corroborating a clinical impression of the prominent symptom complexes operative in the case. The personality style scales and the pathological personality scales help to understand the function of substance use that may be most important in supporting the individual's addiction. In fact, all of the spheres of behavior needed to reach a description of a dual diagnosis problem are tapped by the instrument and are presented as interactive and intercontextual. Chapter 6 on personality disorders contains examples of the entire process of working with personality-disordered individuals from assessment though post-discharge outpatient monitoring.

Although the MCMI is recommended as a comprehensive global assessment instrument that fits well with the emphasis here on reciprocal understandings of life events and dynamic developments, some caution is advised in its use. In most dual diagnosis programs, the alcohol abuse and drug abuse scales are not very valuable in that screening for a subtle problem (the purpose of these scales) is usually not necessary. If, however, the dual diagnosis program functions as a specialty group within a larger clinical matrix of other programs, the use of these MCMI scales to decide which individuals should receive closer dual diagnosis or substance abuse assessment can be valuable. A well-developed understanding of the personality styles can greatly increase the leverage of various interventions. Although a psychologist should usually be involved in MCMI interpretation, it can provide comprehensive information to nurses, social workers, counselors, or other staff members after only modest investments in staff training and becoming familiar with the concept of personality, its relationship to mental illness, how these concepts are codified and formulated in the *DSM-III-R*, and how they are operationalized through using the MCMI.

Table 4.3. MCMI Symptom Scales

Scale A. Anxiety: apprehensive, phobic, tense, indecisive, restless, hyperalertness to environment, wearisomeness, physical correlates of anxiety.

Scale H. Somatoform: hypochondriacal complaints, somatic conversion of psychological concerns, dramatic, vague, or exaggerated multiple physical complaints, overemphasis on actual physical problems.

Scale N. Bipolar: Manic: overactivity, distractibility, superficial elation, impulsiveness, irritability, intrusive interpersonal style, decreased need for sleep, flight of ideas, pressured speech, labile mood, expansive optimism.

Scale D. Dysthymia: persistent feelings of guilt, discouragement, low self-esteem, apathy, chronic fatigue, appetite problems, suicidal ideation, tearfulness, anhedonia, general pessimism.

Scale B. Alcohol Dependence: History of alcoholism.

Scale T. Drug Dependence: History of drug abuse, nonconventional behaviors.

Scale SS. Thought Disorder: Psychotic thinking, disorientation, hallucinations, unsystematic delusions, fragmented or bizarre thinking, high scores usually indicate a psychotic disorder.

Scale CC. Major Depression: Severe impairment in functioning due to depression, suicide risk, psychomotor retardation, increased somatic problems, difficulty in concentration, agitation, insomnia or early rising.

Scale PP. Delusional Disorder: paranoid thinking, persecutory, jealous, or grandiose thought content, ideas of reference, hostile mood, suspiciousness, vigilance, and alertness to betrayal.

The Epigenetic Scale for the Thematic Apperception Test (EPITAT)

Stories may not be what our lives are made of, but almost invariably our lives must become coherent, tellable stories if we or others are to make sense of, or even properly value our experiences, especially over time and perhaps over generations. Listening carefully to narratives and to the how, what, and why of the telling, is perhaps what therapists do best and most often. Therefore, it is unfortunate that some assessment batteries virtually ignore the verbalizations of patients. This section and the one that follows introduce techniques that emphasize narratives told by patients. The first technique, the *Epigenetic Scale for the Thematic Appercep-tion Test* (EPITAT) (Wilson et al. 1989) extends an older technique familiar primarily to psychologists. The second technique, the *Autobiographical Memories Test*, structures, extends, and enriches a recurrent interest of therapists from many training backgrounds in early or seminal events in the lives of their patients.

It is fairly obvious why professionals are tempted not to invest much structured assessment time in collecting and examining patient narratives. Our most impaired patients say so many things with so little structure and often make little sense that can be easily summarized and communicated, let alone integrated into a formulation of the individual and into the design of systematic interventions. It takes a good deal of time to slow down and listen to what patients have to say, especially if this must be done on a one-on-one basis. Finally, many therapists doubt whether important formative events and dynamics can be revealingly verbalized, especially by the severely disturbed patient, where the assumption is often made that significant psychic trauma or developmental catastrophes took place prior to verbal encoding of experience. Even so, it is of extreme importance that we make it possible to allow patients, regardless of severity level, to tell us what they believe their lives are about. This can be done directly in open-ended interviews, or in more structured interviews such as the ASI. What this leaves neglected, however, is what the patient will not, or more typically, cannot say directly. Projective tests or interview techniques can allow room for such expressions.

The *Thematic Apperception Test* (TAT) was developed by Murray and other psychologists to look at narratives in a structured way, specifically, to examine the needs or preoccupations that patients might project onto situations that are somewhat ambiguous. The technique is fairly straightforward. Subjects are shown standard drawings, most involving people, and asked to tell a complete story with a beginning, middle, and end and to tell what the people are thinking or feeling. Although the TAT is still considered an important aspect of psychologists' training, its use in routine clinical practice is on the decline for several reasons. First, it is time-consuming. The responses must be recorded in some manner, preferably written down verbatim or audiotaped for later transcription. Also, there is no single clinically relevant and scientifically validated system for objectively evaluating responses.

Although scoring systems for TAT stories have proliferated for research purposes in various areas of psychology, none has gained a consensus of general clinical utility. This is the opposite of the development of the Rorschach Inkblot Test over the last decade. John Exner's (1986) synthesis of several scoring systems has added to the Rorschach's value as a tool of clinical research. The empirical success of Exner's approach to the Rorschach has increased its use and perceived relevance, perhaps sometimes decreasing the use of other projective instruments such as the TAT. In part, this is because Rorschach practice and research have always tried to delineate and measure basic psychological and psychodynamic dimensions. Sometimes these measures were derived essentially from the test itself, but they were, nonetheless, directly related to a wide range of interest variables to any comprehensive psychological evaluation of complex human behavior. The goals of the TAT have usually seemed more modest and superficial and in some ways redundant to the early sessions of a course of psychotherapy. Identifying major conflicts, themes, and preoccupations or attitudes (the content area to which the therapist has immediate direct access and therefore needs little help from a diagnostician) seemed to be its strong suit. Although the Rorschach has usually been viewed as atheoretical, its synthesis of Gestalt psychology, psychoanalytic thought, and behavioral empiricism under Exner has extended its value as a bridge between traditions.

The kind of advance Exner accomplished for the Rorschach has been started in the area of narrative productions by Arnold Wilson and his collaborators with the *Epigenetic Assessment Rating System* (EARS), of which the EPITAT was the first application, using TAT stories as its data base. Two additional applications have been developed. EPI-LOG uses 5-minute speech monologues, and EPI-RAP uses relationship anecdote stories as their respective data bases. The discussion of EARS in this section is limited to the EPITAT.

Going beyond theme, content, and motivation, the EPITAT is designed to typify an individual's modal level of psychological functioning along ten crucial psychological dimensions. In addition, the EPITAT is designed to describe the specific situational determinants that will result in lower levels of modal functioning in an individual and the degree and type of deterioration that may be expected. All of this is accomplished using verbal narratives of the patient, which are produced within an interpersonal context with the examiner: conditions that simulate the typical psychotherapy situation. The EPITAT represents a theoretical bridge between the psychoanalytic view of the self (as encapsulating various stages of psychic development and interaction with others determined by past experience) and cognitive or phenomenological theories (emphasizing current needs, values, and expectations, as determinants of behavior).

The EPITAT scale is in several ways a synthesis of divergent sources of knowledge about personality functioning. The most basic source of the EPITAT procedure is the literature describing the qualitative observations that psychoanalytically oriented clinicians have made of the typical functioning levels of patients in therapy. These typical levels of responding, or modal levels of organization, are conceptualized as resulting from complete or incomplete structures acquired through mother–infant interaction during early development (Gedo 1979, 1980, 1988, Gedo and Goldberg 1973). Five modes (Wilson et al. 1989) are identified in the EPITAT, which roughly correspond with organizational levels familiar to most clinicians. These are the psychotic level (Mode I), the borderline level (Mode II), the narcissistic level (Mode III) the oedipal level (Mode IV), and the postoedipal level (Mode V). The five epigenetic modes are briefly described in Table 4-4, which outlines for each the typical level of psychological functioning, organization of self-other internalizations, prevailing defensive mechanism, principle experience of depression, and psychosocial functions of drug use. Although these concepts are largely consistent and additive to those presented by Wilson and his co-authors, Table 4-4 combines aspects of their thinking with the concepts presented in this text and is not a simple summary of their work.

An important element in the EPITAT synthesis is recognizing instability within stable personality organizations. This includes the observation that more effective, higher level personality organizations are inherently stable, whereas individuals with less effective personality organizations tend to show dramatic shifts toward lower modes of functioning when faced with stressful or overarousing situations.

Table 4.4. Epigenetic Modes of Functioning and Drug Use

Epigenetic Mode	Mode I	Mode II	Mode III	Mode IV	Mode V
Typical Functioning	Psychotic	Borderline	Narcissistic	Oedipal	Post-Oedipal
Self-Other organization	Presubjective: limited self-other distinction	Transitional: separate but attached	Self centered: parts of others used for self enhancement	Interdependent: others joined in mutual allegiances, competition, protective intimacy.	Autonomy: open, mutually rewarding collaborative relationships; co-creative intimacy.
Defensive operation	Denial	Projection	Disavowal	Repression	Renunciation
Depressive experience	Empty bewilderment	Abandonment depression	Self-esteem depression	Guilt-ridden depression	Appropriate grief
Typical function of drug	Modulates global unpleasure. Escape/ Avoidance of painful affects. Repetition of pathological infant–parent dyad, or trauma. Autistic-contiguous mode of consciousness.	Modulates affects and unacceptable self with other schemas. Orientation by way of drug role. Repetition of chaotic affects.	Facilitates narcissistic inflation of self. Orientation by way of role, control of environment and self.	Modulation of guilt, shame. Avoidance of interpersonal conflict. Facilitates enactment of poorly understood states or schemas.	Modulates specific reality oriented affects. Facilitates consciously desired and accepted states or schemas.

*Adapted in part from Wilson, Kuras, Passik, Morral, and Turner, 1989, and Wilson, Passik, Faude, Abrams, & Gordon, 1989.

The epigenetic principle integrates these two elements by explaining how more advanced patterns of responding can develop from more primitive patterns, how several levels of responding can remain available to the individual later in life, and how shifts between modal levels of response are related to both personality organization and stress, or situational demand (Kellerman 1983). The EPITAT, therefore, can be used to investigate what aspects of personality are most stable within a given disorder, or identify areas of contrast in regard to stability for various diagnostic groups. It can be used clinically to trace the progression and regression of an individual's psychological functioning as its quality varies with different levels of stress, demand, or threat.

Tracking the quality of psychological functioning described above does not occur in a simple global fashion. For each narrative presented by a subject in response to a TAT stimulus card, the EPITAT requires that a rater assign a modal level for each of ten psychological dimensions. These dimensions are: affect tolerance, affect expression, personal agency, centration/decentration, threats to self, defensive operations, empathic knowledge, use of an object, adaptive needs, and temporality. Table 4–5 briefly describes each dimension. The incorporation of several dimensions in a single global assessment tool in itself is a major advancement in the use of projective tests. Of special interest and almost unique to the EPITAT, the temporality dimension allows assessment of the patient's perception of time and ability to use it for planning and purposeful action, as well as expectancies in regard to effects of the passage of time. This is a much neglected area of behavior, which has far-reaching consequences for a treatment-oriented assessment. This whole sphere of behavior was tapped only crudely in the TAT, and not at all in a meaningful way by the Rorschach. The EPITAT's temporality dimension corrects this shortcoming. Another advance is in the dimensions of centration/ decentration combined with use of an object and empathic knowledge. Together these dimensions provide a conceptual basis for determining in a comprehensive way the relationship between identity processes, interpersonal issues, object relations, and social cognition in a given case.

For each of the ten dimensions, or areas of functioning, the EPITAT manual describes qualities of responses typically assigned to each of the five organizational/ developmental modes. An important aspect of these ratings is that nonverbal responses (gestures, pushing the card away, etc.) are considered in the scoring, allowing the EPITAT to tap material that may be related to preverbal modes of responding. Examples of the ratings of protocols are given. Although these ten dimensions are independent and the rating of each should be blind to the performance on other dimensions for the same story, it can be assumed that an individual with very stable personality organization will show a strong relationship among these dimensions under low to moderate levels of stress and will show only modest divergence in functioning under taxing or stressful circumstances. Individuals with less stable personality organization will show great divergence across stories and across psychological dimensions within a story.

Table 4.5. EARS Psychological Dimensions

Dimension	Description
1. Affect Tolerance	Ability to modulate the full range of affective arousal, including the management of depression and anxiety. Extreme or muted affect is noted.
2. Affect Expression	Range, depth, and differentiation among affects used as modes of communication and interaction.
3. Personal Agency	Sense and definition of self. Degree of relatedness, flexibility, creativity, and integration of aspects of the self.
4. Centration/Decentration	Egocentrism versus the ability to value, respect, and view others as separate persons.
5. Threat to Self	Nature of perceived internal and external dangers to the self. Realism, manageability, and adaptiveness of these perceptions.
6. Defensive Operations	Primary defenses ranging from discharge in activity to sublimation, renunciation, and conflict resolution.
7. Empathic Knowledge	Ability to know and empathize with the experience and feelings of others. Ability to see others as having both stable and changing qualities.
8. Use of an Object	Ability to achieve mutual self-enhancement through interpersonal relationship.
9. Adaptive Needs	Most pressing psychological needs. Similar to Maslow's hierarchy of needs related functioning.
10. Temporality	Ability to form time continua, and to separate past, present, and future. Ability to use flexible and creative thought in relationship to time, while maintaining order.

The EPITAT procedure obviously rests on the fact that the content of the TAT cards varies considerably in the amount of stress aroused in most subjects. Card 1, depicting a child looking at a violin, is considered a very low arousal stimulus. Card 13MF, which shows a man standing with his eyes covered by his arm while behind him a naked female lies on a bed, is considered a highly arousing stimulus. The EPITAT observes the progressive and regressive shifts in modal functioning in each of the ten psychological dimensions as the stimulus cards vary in degree of arousal.

Acceptable levels of interrater reliability have been established for the EPITAT modal ratings, using raters with relatively modest clinical training. EPITAT modal ratings validly discriminate between inpatients and nonpatients (Wilson et al. 1989). For high arousal cards, nonpatients regressed to Mode III, which is typical of inpatients when responding to low arousal cards. Under high arousal conditions, the inpatient group regressed to level II or level I.

Considering the attributes of the EPITAT, it should be relatively apparent why this particular procedure is advocated in the context of assessing the dual diagnosis patient. The narrative and interpersonal structure of the test makes it a good simulation of the therapy situation. The standard materials used provide a fertile yet well-explored field for investigating important themes, dynamics, content areas, issues, and sometimes relevant life experiences that can be translated almost directly to the therapeutic session. One of the problems that must be faced when working with dual diagnosis patients is that they often show dynamics under stress (or under the influence of drugs) that are otherwise not apparent. Shifts may occur in the salience of particular symptoms, or even more broadly, in the symptom complex that predominates. The relative sensitivity to various dynamic issues may also vary with the level of stress or stimulus arousal and may provide crucial indicators of which dynamics or issues most directly contribute to the relationship between the addictive disorder and dominant symptom complexes. The EPITAT is a safe way of inducing sufficient stress within a context where shifts in functioning can be carefully examined. These shifts will be reflected in the specific psychological dimensions, all of which can be closely related to the symptom complexes. For example, the dominance of affect complex to a large extent can be described in terms of lower modal functioning on the EPITAT's dimensions of affect tolerance and affect expression. The sociability and identity complex is reflected in maladaptive levels of functioning on the dimensions of centration/decentration, empathic knowledge, and use of an object.

An eleven-item scale based on the EPITAT system has been developed to measure self-regulation failures in substance abusers. Wilson and co-workers (1989) persuasively argue that a projective measure of self-regulation is the most appropriate for a population that cannot be expected to differentiate as well among negative affects as normal subjects may during self-report. The scale is applied to verbal and nonverbal responses to TAT cards 1, 5, 15, 14, 10, 13MF, 12M, 3BM, and 16. Responses are rated for each item on the Scale for Failures of Self-Regulation (SFSR) using a four-point rating scale (zero to three), indicating presence and severity of item content in the response. The method has differentiated normals from addicts on three subfactors of the SFSR: structural (nonverbal) thematic, and impulsive subfactors. The addicts who had the most pervasive problems with self-regulation also demonstrated the largest split between the nonverbal and the verbal subfactors. Table 4–6 lists the description of items from the SFSR (Wilson et al, 1989). A quotation below from the same article commenting on the nonverbal subfactor (SFSR-S) will clarify the implications of this seminal study based on the EPITAT method:

Opiate addicts differ from normal subjects in manifesting a constellation of dynamics that implicate failures in self-regulatory functioning. The particular items that load on the SFSR-S suggest that addicts, more than normal subjects, have particular difficul-

Table 4.6. Items from Scale for Failures in Self-Regulation (SFSR)*

Item	Description
1	A major theme of emptiness, aloneness, or helplessness is present.
2	Pathological guilt is either harsh, self-directed guilt or the absence of a sense of conscience.
3	Significant others are not introduced into the focal plot of the response.
4	A time continuum involving past, present, and future is not a primary dimension of the text of the story. When present, it appears to be tacked on in compliance with the test instructions.
5	The self-carrier is described as powerless or unable to cope with the task upon which he/she has been set.
6	Satisfaction or frustration of basic needs is the primary focus of the plot.
7	Intrusiveness, assaultiveness, abandonment, or pathological enmeshment are the primary interpersonal threats to the self (as opposed to jealousy or competitive conflicts).
8	Life-sustaining, parasitic, or fundamentally need-gratifying relationships are primary interpersonal enhancements to the self.
9	Self or other carriers are described as bored, listless, or feeling nothing.
10	The story resolution is vague or incomplete and marked by a predominant mood of bleakness.
11	One or more of the figure carriers possesses the potential for, or are in the midst of, an explosive expression of affect or impulsive action.
Score	Each item scored on a 0 to 3 scale for each TAT response

*Adapted from Wilson, Passik, Faude, Abrams, & Gordon, 1989, p. 395.

ties in mapping their experiences temporally, with the attendant difficulties of lack of planning and poor anticipation of consequences; impaired and idiosyncratic notions of cause and effect relationships; poor impulse control and affect tolerance; a marked tendency to construe interpersonal relationships in terms of either overt dependency on or exploitative intrusion by a need gratifier. Their narratives depicted, and were scored on the SFSR for, object relations with a quite literal, concrete quality in which physical proximity to a need gratifier is required to avert feelings of hopelessness and incapacitation and fears of abandonment and loss. [p. 397]

Although the SFSR is currently more a research measure than an assessment tool, its eleven items can be readily applied to the EPITAT protocol and clinically interpreted in the light of this early research. The EPITAT can provide a therapy-relevant, comprehensive assessment of personality that will assist in predicting vulnerabilities to regression, suggest which areas of functioning will most need bolstering by means of medication, coping skills training, or supportive therapies. Although learning the technique does require much time and effort, the investment is worth it, especially if the assessment measures to be used by a practitioner or agency include a projective component. Given its current stage of development, however, a psychologist competent in the use of tests and measures should be available to provide assistance with establishing local reliability data and to evaluate, report on, and incorporate into the assessment process the emerging research findings on the EPITAT as they become available.

Appendix A presents a complete TAT protocol for a 38-year-old female polysubstance abuser. This patient was significantly depressed at the time of narrative collection and complained of mood swings. The protocol clearly exhibits all the characteristics that result in high scores on the SFSR and especially on the structural subfactor. In addition, this protocol also demonstrates how modal level of functioning varies with stress, as can be seen by comparing EPITAT scores for each of the ten EARS dimensions for Card 1 (low arousal) with those for Card 13MF (high arousal). The visual and thematic contents of these cards are noted earlier in this subsection. The following scores and modal levels were observed in the responses to the two cards:

Low: 3,3,2,2,4,4,3,3,3,3 Mode = 3, or narcissistic
High: 1,1,1,2,3,1,2,1,1,4 Mode = 1, or psychotic/borderline

Ultimately, of course, clinical interpretation of this data is based on all available information, not simply the EARS scores for two TAT cards. Based on all EPITAT scores and other available data, this patient's most typical mode of functioning could be described as borderline/narcissistic, but under stress she will demonstrate psychoticlike decompensations. The content of her protocol and other narrative data suggest a histrionic personality with avoidant traits constituted at the borderline structural level. Dominance of affect and affective instability were demonstrated in the protocol, as were significant problems with sociability and identity. We can hypothesize that substance abuse functions in her case to modulate a self-esteem-related depression (usually triggered by actual or anticipated abandonment) and to facilitate positive feelings about the self, including a sense of control.

Appendix B provides scored EPITAT protocols for TAT cards 1 (low arousal) and 13MF (high arousal) for three additional depressed substance abusers. The individuals have little in common except depression, substance abuse, and failures in self-regulation as measured by the EPITAT, which are hypothesized to account for their addictions. Notice that only in the first of the three cases in the appendix is the regression very deep from low to high arousal levels and that this is the only individual capable of sustaining an oedipal level of development, even under favorable conditions.

The Early Memories Procedure

Throughout this book, the importance of memory in understanding personality functioning is emphasized. Memory, especially for affectively laden events, is at the heart of the therapeutic process as conceptualized from most mainstream orientations to treatment. Despite this, few systematic attempts are made during assessment to gain access early in the treatment process to the crucial memories of patients. One reason is the assumption that open-ended questions during assessment will lead both to uncovering principal dynamics and amassing any essential factual information, including autobiographical events that need to be addressed in treatment. This assumption places the burden of requiring almost omniscient insight and consummate communication skills on both patient and assessor. Patients usually do not know what would be relevant to a clinician to report meaningfully about their pasts. Clinicians cannot be expected always to know when to adroitly direct the interview to investigate nuances that may suggest an underlying, relevant autobiographical event. The ebb and flow of associations in an open clinical interview is highly sensitive to its interpersonal context and is thus ideal for determining mental status and identifying personality dynamics. However, the same process of association acts as strongly in omitting important autobiographical material as in directly providing any relevant historical content.

One way to rectify this problem is to ask the patient directly about important areas of previous experience. Clinicians are used to asking about symptoms or drug use history, becoming as systematic as the prestructured interview formats such as the ASI. However, there is the need to go beyond this, to look at the patient's priorities and interpretations of personal experience. The *Early Memories Procedure* (EMP) is a structured, systematic process for eliciting, examining, and introducing into the treatment process the important autobiographical experiences of the patient. Developed by a clinical psychologist, Arnold Bruhn, the EMP is based on more than eighteen years of research, experience, and application of the role of autobiographical memory in assessment and treatment (Bruhn 1990).

Before discussing the EMP and its use, let us look at some possible reservations concerning the statement that direct inquiry about autobiographical and childhood memories is an important assessment area and that it provides a global view of the patient's treatment needs. For example, the psychoanalytically minded reader might protest that what is important in memory is not what *is* remembered, but what *is not* remembered, that is, what is repressed. From this viewpoint, the memories reported by patients are screen memories. Much like dreams, such memories are thought to conceal a deep, latent content (the historical experience that is unacceptable, traumatic, and defended against) under the screen memory's manifest content (the memory as recalled and reported). Although the EMP does not deny the importance of repression, it does rest on the view that the memories available to the patient in the here and now contain important information; the manifest content of such memories is not all smoke and mirrors. Consistent with the methods used previously by the Adlerians, the EMP focuses on the manifest content of the memory and takes it seriously. The interpretive approach used is common to other projective techniques, which involve the presentation of ambiguous stimuli and the observation of responses to them. These techniques assume that any response to the stimuli has interpretative value, thus there are no right or wrong answers. Responses are interpreted as relating to the personality traits and temporary affect or drive states of the individual. In assuming the projective hypothesis in regard to reported memories, the EMP does not pass summary judgment as to the extent that such reports reflect independently verifiable historical events. Given this approach, the EMP can be thought of as a TAT with the stimulus being self-selected by the patient from the many possible memories or fantasies of memories that might be available to him or her.

Applying the projective hypothesis to autobiographical memories will raise objections from another camp. Freud is today often criticized severely for reducing his patients' reports of remembered sexual abuse to the level of neurotic fantasies, constructions based on their own primitive wishes. The reality of child sexual abuse is now well documented. Applying the projective hypothesis to early memory, it may be objected, also psychologizes away important experiences that may have critically shaped a patient's life. However, the EMP does not dismiss the importance of those memories by subjecting them to psychological analysis. Independent validation can be obtained for many aspects of most reported memories. Specifically in regard to traumatic memories, the peculiarities of personality structure, symptom severity, and extreme avoidant behavior may convince us of the powerful forces that were unleashed without the need for eyewitnesses to verify the occurrence. Similarly, the EMP is more concerned with the sequelae of events and their construction (traumatic and otherwise) than with the particulars of historical events or the many possible sources that contribute to the distortion, reconstruction, or re-interpretation of the actual experience.

The EMP is based on a what Bruhn has named the cognitive-perceptual theory of personality functioning. It holds that current thoughts, feelings, perceptions, and memories of the past are all strongly influenced by the individual's current expectations, attitudes, and belief systems. In examining memory or current perception, the theory dictates that how an event is interpreted, constructed, or construed by the person is more important than the external event itself. Another assumption is that the patient will automatically remember and select to report only those memories of current psychological relevance, which he or she is prepared to process in some way. Memory is seen as operating on the principles of utility and adaptation, that is, we remember what is useful to us in the here and now. And what we perceive as useful is based on our frame of reference, our guiding images of various aspects of our environment (schemas or cognitive maps) and our current goals and affects.

Cognitive perceptual theory, as developed by Bruhn, is more than an abstract explanation of memory processes, however. The EMP was created to help understand changes in personal functioning, especially as related to the therapeutic process. Rather than having a mechanistic theoretical base, the EMP is contextual, that is, it describes memory in the context of human striving toward growth, mastery, and positive change. Memories and early childhood experience in this context do not determine current personality functioning. Memory is constructed by the individual and chosen to further his or her current attitude, stance, or direction in the world. Early memories, therefore, represent the patient's unfinished business in life. Thus the EMP is very consistent with the existential phenomenological perspective that is the dominant theory type suggested for use with dual diagnosis. Patients are held responsible for their construction of reality and are not encouraged to be passive victims of the past as they have construed it. We see in the next chapter how deconstructing views of the past that have resulted in inertia and denial and then reconstructing or reconstruing the individual's identity are at the heart of the therapeutic process with the dual diagnosis patient.

Although the cognitive-perceptual theory can be used to richly elaborate an understanding of almost all components of the treatment process, it can be reduced to a relatively small set of key propositions. Among them are the following ten points:

1. Perception, and therefore memory, is selective not photographic.
2. The individual's frame of reference organizes cognition around his or her view of what is important, that is, as related to needs, wishes, fears, and expectations.
3. Schemas, or mental maps based on earlier learning, change only after they become significantly incongruent with current experience, and therefore lose utility.
4. Memory is based on schemas, or pictographic images of the past, rather than on recorded traces of sensory experience.
5. Memory tends to retain attitudes and impressions rather than facts.
6. Early memories reflect current concerns, attitudes, and needs.
7. The contents of long-term memory are continually reconstructed or justified to maintain considerable consistency with current attitudes and needs.
8. What is useful relative to the person's unfinished business or current needs is remembered, and what is not is forgotten.
9. What is perceived to be most useful is "highlighted, energized, and raised to a position of prominence in long-term memory" (Bruhn 1990, p. 58). This highlighting effect is operationalized in the EMP in the form of those memories that are rated by the patient as particularly vivid, clear, or affectively charged, or memories that are reported under more than one kind of memory inquiry.
10. Negative and positive affect memories are qualitatively different in the needs they reflect and the purposes they serve in personality organiza-

tion. Negative memories reflect the frustration of important needs and therefore often represent unresolved issues or unfinished business. Positive memories reflect satisfaction of major needs and provide a stabilizing and orienting function to personality.

Some of these propositions run counter to commonly held beliefs about autobiographical memory. Some of these myths are due to biases in psychology itself such as the bias introduced by psychoanalysis against the relevance of the manifest content of memory, or that introduced by some behaviorists against the projective interpretation of memories. Other myths are due to our own phenomenological confidence in remote, important memories. Our memories present to us with such obvious historical validity and personal relevance that we are very resistent to viewing them as in any way related to projection or some other distortion process beyond our awareness. Our memories are so closely related to our identity and sense of internal control that we become very uncomfortable with the idea that they constantly change and do not mirror a static historical reality. This close relationship between autobiographical memory and feeling that we are ourselves and that we are in control of our fates is creatively and playfully elaborated in the film *Total Recall* starring Arnold Schwarzenegger. The movie depicts a future world where memories can be bought and sold, where, for example, a memory of a vacation can be had for a fraction of the cost of the actual trip and time investment. All the savored events of such a vacation (which in fact never happened) remain permanent and vivid for future nostalgia. As the plot develops, the character played by Schwarzenegger is not the person he thinks he is. All of his available memories are fakes and his "real" identity has been concealed from him by others until he accidently regains "total recall." The film's rapid changes of identity and context reflect the basic fear that our memories for events might be dangerously unreliable and that our concept of stable identity can be placed in question.

Bruhn has created and compiled an impressive introduction to early memories in general, as well as the clinical use of the Early Memories Procedure in his 1990 book, *Earliest Childhood Memories: Volume 1: Theory and Application to Clinical Practice*. The forthcoming second volume compiles much of the background material needed for using the EMP in new research or for thoroughly investigating its already established reliability, validity, and usefulness in a variety of research and clinical contexts. Appendix C reproduces a previously published EMP for a depressed alcoholic patient with commentary by Bruhn (1992). Although diagnosis was not a major concern with the ongoing treatment of this patient, in addition to her alcoholism, she could be typified as a person with significant narcissistic damage within a personality style that contains both histrionic and aggressive traits, someone who at times will appear to be highly passive aggressive-explosive (i.e. a volatile mixture of the dependent and aggressive styles of personality, see Chapter 6). Dominance of affect, repetition of childhood abuse, and facilitation of anger appear to significantly contribute to her alcohol abuse.

FOCUSED ASSESSMENT INSTRUMENTS AND PROCEDURES

To this point, our discussion of assessment techniques concerns methods that will primarily yield a comprehensive or global view of the individual. These techniques reveal in a comprehensive way significant problems in specific spheres of functioning (the ASI), personality style and behavioral symptoms (the MCMI), critical life events and the resulting psychological issues (the EMT), or the individual's modal psychological organization and typical functioning under varying degrees of stress (the EPITAT). The purpose of instruments and interview procedures introduced in this section is to provide very specific and focused information about the patient that may be missed by using more global assessment techniques. Focused techniques are designed to measure specifically targeted traits, personality factors, or lifestyle characteristics that have special relevance to treatment issues with the dual diagnosis population. More important than the specific measure or technique recommended here is the trait, characteristic, or tendency that is targeted for measurement.

For all those in a dual diagnosis population, some brief measure of intellectual capacity is strongly recommended. It is necessary to determine if the patient will be able to use the written materials of a treatment program effectively and to gauge whether he or she has the ability to gain information from interactive group discussions. This is especially important because of the reliance on group modalities that is typical of many substance abuse and mental health treatment programs. These modalities do not contain the built-in safeguards against misunderstanding and gaps in communication that are inherently present in one-on-one counseling or sponsoring functions. Some means of screening for severe neuropsychological deficits that may seriously handicap a patient's program participation and compliance is also needed for a similar reason. The Quick Test (QT) (Ammons and Ammons 1963) provides a useful way of estimating verbal intelligence and of "breaking the ice" during the early phases of a psychological examination. The QT, which usually takes less than 15 minutes to administer, is a picture vocabulary test yielding several scores that are highly correlated with the WAIS Verbal I.Q. The Stroop Color and Word Test is a good neuropsychological screening instrument. In use for over 50 years, it consists of three kinds of stimuli to which timed responses are required: a list of names of colors, a list of colored nonverbal stimuli, and a list on which the names of the colors appear in varying primary colors (e.g., the word "red" is printed in green among similar combinations of verbal–visual matches and mismatches). The tasks involved include reading the verbal stimulus list, stating the colors of the nonverbal stimuli in order, naming the color of a printed color-word while ignoring the print, and reading the print while ignoring the color in which it is printed. The fact that color naming occurs at a slower rate than reading the printed word, or the Stroop Effect, is due to the automatic nature of reading. The Stroop requires a person to inhibit the verbal information that is almost immediately available in preference of the purely visual information that must be transformed into a verbal response. The Stroop, although usually used in neuropsychological screening, is also a measure of the ability to inhibit or disinhibit and can therefore add to an assessment of impulsivity.

Walfish and colleagues (1989) recommend the Shipley Institute of Living Scale in a general substance abuse population. The Shipley, which correlates well with many other standard measures of intelligence, allows comparison of old learning with the ability to develop new learning or abstraction, thus providing an intelligence estimate and a rough index of organic impairment that is relevant to the tasks of learning new material in therapy. Individuals with low I.Q. estimates, or who demonstrate a great disparity between Shipley Vocabulary and Shipley Abstraction scores will need special attention. These scores usually indicate a need for additional specialized assistance during treatment, such as audiotapes and videotapes instead of written materials, more frequent one-on-one counseling sessions to clarify or correct the patient's understanding of treatment activities and events, and the planning of lifestyle and living arrangements that are responsive to the individual's disabilities and strengths. These individuals should be administered a more intensive investigation of intellectual functioning, such as the Wechsler Adult Intelligence Scale-Revised (WAIS-R), or they should receive a complete neuropsychological battery.

Once the individual's intellectual functioning and minor residual neurological impairment have been ascertained through a screening instrument, several focused areas should complement a global assessment. Each of the areas introduced in this chapter is potentially rich in clues pointing to the primary symptom complex involved in the case, or the most prominent psychosocial functions of the addiction. These assessment areas also help to provide a means of predicting which treatment modalities will be most beneficial or which phases of recovery will present the most challenges. Figure 4–1 (see p. 165) lists these areas, along with focused instruments or subtests of global assessment instruments that can pinpoint more specific issues. Several areas are listed because they are either often neglected or inadequately performed, yet they may take on crucial importance in dual diagnosis work.

Optimal Arousal: The Sensation Seeking Scale (SSS)

This section presents more extensive coverage of the reward/arousal deficits complex introduced in Chapter 3. The concept of optimal reward and arousal responsivity as an individual difference is an important one, yet unfamiliar to many clinicians. Therefore, it requires more coverage of theoretical background and research findings than other assessment measures described here.

The goal is to clarify several key concepts in addition to introducing the Sensation Seeking Scale (SSS) as an assessment instrument. The reward/arousal symptom complex, modulation and facilitation as psychosocial functions of addic tion, and the concept of psychopathy rely heavily on the small number of concepts that can be explicated through SSS findings. Although the background concept of the reward/arousal complex is complicated, assessment of these problems is not necessarily difficult. This is because measures of sensation seeking and impulsivity are expected also to correlate highly with disorders of response to reward and abnormal learning curves under conditions of positive reinforcement or punishment. The Sensation Seeking Scale (SSS) developed by Marvin Zuckerman provides a sufficient, although not exhaustive, operational definition of the reward/arousal complex. (The complex is further detailed in Chapter 8 on psychopathy and substance abuse.)

The fact that a major concept in this book is based on biological theories, and even animal models of human behavior, does not mean an endorsement of reductionism or the view that human choice is secondary to biological predisposition. Even basic biological predispositions, such as those involved in setting the optimal level of arousal, can be expressed, experienced, or used by the person in an almost infinite number of ways.

The concepts in this section are primarily derived from biologically based theories that are intended to account for differences in activity level, environmental engagement, preferences for type and amount of stimulation, and learning performances under varying conditions of stimulus intensity and varying reward characteristics. Routtenberg (1968) proposed two arousal systems, one related to anxiety and fear, or the expectation of punishment (and, therefore, freeze, flight, or fight responses), and a second related to expectation of positive reward (and, therefore, to investigation, curiosity, and approach behaviors). Zuckerman (1983) sees sensation seeking as related to the second system, that is, arousal in the service of anticipated reward. He identifies norepinephrine and dopamine as the biochemical mediators of this system, with dopamine controlling readiness to explore and approach novel stimuli, and norepinephrine controlling the expectation of or response to positive reward.

Building on the work of Hans Eysenck, Zuckerman (1979a) has combined the concept of optimal level of stimulation and arousal with the related behavior of sensation seeking to develop a focused theory that describes and explains a generally applicable aspect of personality. In its most simple terms, this theory posits that an optimal level of arousal is built into the psychophysiology of each individual in a manner that is to a large extent genetically determined but that can be influenced by environment, experience, and other biological predispositions or learned personality patterns. Like many personality characteristics, this trait becomes evident and entrenched relatively early in life. When an individual is not experiencing the optimal level of arousal, he or she acts either to decrease the required threshold of arousal (internal adjustment) or to control the intensity and quality of stimulation impinging on the central nervous system (sensation seeking).

Zuckerman developed the SSS to measure behaviors and personality functions related to modulation of arousal levels though interactions with the environment.

The SSS consists of a general measure of sensation seeking and four subscales: thrill and adventure seeking, experience seeking, disinhibition, and boredom susceptibility. Currently, about thirty years of research have been conducted using the SSS. These research findings have been incorporated into a biopsychological model of sensation seeking, impulsivity, and anxiety (Zuckerman 1983). High or low sensation seeking as a personality trait is not viewed as a sign of psychopathology, but, as a behavioral predisposition, it may render the individual vulnerable to various disorders, including the addictions. It is fairly common in the general culture of today to speak of certain occupations or recreational activities as attracting sensation-seeking personalities without implying any kind of mental disorder.

In considering the relationship between sensation seeking and psychopathology, however, Zuckerman endorses a dimensional view. He identifies three major dimensions: neurotic anxiety, sociability, and impulsivity/activity. All three dimensions have a high genetic loading. Clinical syndromes display different degrees of elevation of these dimensions. Extremes on any of the three can result in psychopathology.

Neurosis is based on autonomic nervous system instability, making individuals high on this trait more vulnerable to emotional reactivity in general, but especially to socialization anxiety. Socialization anxiety is defined as the anxiety reactions produced by threats of social punishment, such as fears of failure and shame, embarrassment, and blows to self-esteem. Sociability is viewed as a dimension that is independent of neuroticism and consists of the ability to form interpersonal bonds, the ability to gain pleasure from interpersonal interaction, and an interest or desire to interact with others. The dimension of impulsivity/activity is most obviously related to sensation seeking. Clinical syndromes vary dramatically in the amount of activity produced by affected individuals. Impulsivity and risk taking involve impulse quality, quantity, and impulse control in addition to the degree of preference for dangerous situations and the quality of judgments involved in estimating danger or risk to self or others in various situations.

In thinking about the major mental and personality disorders, it is easy to see how these concepts can be used to characterize various pathologies. Ego-syntonic mania, for example, could be described as being high on activity/impulsivity, high on sociability, and low on neuroticism. Extreme depressives tend to be low on activity/impulsivity, high on neuroticism, and low on sociability. Primary psychopaths could be described as high on sociability, low on neuroticism, and high on activity/impulsivity. Schizophrenics (negative symptoms) might be characterized as low on sociability, activity/impulsiveness, and neuroticism. Regarding these various dimensions, sensation seeking is expected to correlate positively with activity/impulsivity and sociability and to have only marginal correlations with neuroticism (Andreasen 1982, Andreasen and Olsen 1982).

When we examine the SSS scores of individuals with various major mental disorders, Zuckerman's predicted pattern emerges rather clearly. For example, manics have high SSS scores, and depressed persons have low SSS scores. Schizophrenics and inactive psychiatric patients have low SSS scores, whereas psychopaths have high SSS scores. Manics demonstrate extreme sensation seeking, but depressed individuals are subnormal in seeking novelty and stimulation. Schizophrenia and psychopathy are two extremes on Eysenck's extroversion-introversion dimension. Psychopaths are seen as having a need for a higher level and variation of sensory inputs than normals in order to maintain a sense of equilibrium. Conversely, schizophrenics with intense, florid symptoms avoid environmental and social stimulation when their positive symptoms are occurring. McGhie and Chapman (1961) proposed an Input–Dysfunction Theory, which posits that selective and inhibitory functions of attention are disordered in schizophrenics, resulting in sensory overload. The effect of environmental stimulation is recognized in the way institutional environments are engineered and in the way that the psychopathology of their residents influence the use of those environments. For example, optimal hospital ward conditions for schizophrenics are almost intolerably boring to normals, who experience such places as monotonous and low in ambient environmental stimulation. On the other extreme, psychopaths in correctional environments inundate themselves with a full range of sensory stimulation, making such areas difficult for normals to adjust to, including incarcerated, nonpsychopathic criminals, whose need for external stimulation is closer to the normal level and, in the case of the mentally ill offender, may be below that of the average individual.

Zuckerman, again building on Eysenck, views neurosis as related to the degree of spontaneous autonomic nervous system instability and the level of spontaneous socialization anxiety experienced by the individual. That is to say, neurotic persons exhibit high emotional lability, especially in social situations. Overly controlled neurotics, such as obsessive compulsives, are expected to be low in sensation seeking. Expressive or acting-out personalities, such as subtypes of histrionic and borderline personalities, and, of course, psychopaths, are low in socialization anxiety and neuroticism and high in sensation seeking.

Data on gambling behavior, sexual experience, and eating are informative when discussing addictive behaviors in relationship to sensation seeking and the SSS. Zuckerman (1979a) views gambling as:

> a form of sensation seeking in which individuals entertain a risk of monetary loss for the positive reinforcement produced by states of high arousal during the period of uncertainty, as well as the positive arousal produced by winning. If we conceive of gamblers as risk takers, we would expect that they are likely to be high-sensation seekers. However, in some games of chance, there is a skill element (at least gamblers like to think so), so that the winning enhances a competency need. [p. 211]

Although the available correlational and experimental data concern college students rather than addicted gamblers, the expected significant positive correlation between the SSS and propensity toward gambling, choice of risky odds options, and the amount of token money waged in betting has been demonstrated.

In regard to sexual experience and activities, as expected, high sensation seekers are more permissive in their attitudes. Sexual activities with social disapproval are more highly related to SSS scores than more generally sanctioned sexual acts. In college student subjects, the SSS is significantly related to whether heterosexual activity had been experienced, homosexual experience in males, the number of heterosexual partners, and stated willingness to view erotic films. Mothers who breastfeed their children have significantly higher scores on the SSS than those who choose to bottlefeed (Berg-Cross et al. 1979).

Food preferences are significantly related to sensation seeking. When foods are divided into those that induce oral passive experiences (bland, sweet, and soft) versus those that produce oral sadistic experiences (spicy, sour, and crunchy), persons higher on the SSS were more apt to prefer the latter (Kish and Donnenwerth 1972).

Zuckerman has predicted that, similar to the data on sexual behaviors, the ability of the SSS to discriminate among participants in the use of any drug will depend on that drug's social acceptability. In several studies, the SSS best discriminates drug users from alcohol users. Generally, alcohol users and problem drinkers are not high sensation seekers, whereas drug users have higher scores than those who have not used drugs. Only the disinhibition subscale of the SSS has shown a relation to amount of alcohol use, suggesting the psychosocial function of facilitation through disinhibition as a motive for alcohol use among high sensation seekers. Among college students in the early 1970s, high and midlevel sensation seekers were more apt to use marijuana, hashish, amphetamine, and LSD in that order of preference. Only the high sensation group preferred cocaine. Correlations among drug of choice categories and the SSS tended to be significant (especially for the experience seeking subscale) and to follow Zuckerman's hypothesis that social acceptability predicts the relationship between SSS and drug experience. Although narcotic addicts have scores that are higher than nonusers of drugs, they tend to score lower on the SSS than other drug users, suggesting use motives other than sensation seeking. Polydrug users tend to score higher on the SSS than other drug users. Market availability, social acceptance of various drugs, and other factors may have resulted in significant changes since the 1970s in the relationship of drug of choice and the SSS. This is obviously the case with cocaine and LSD, whose market and social acceptance have radically changed over the last two decades.

Physiological measures relevant to the reward/arousal complex are worth a brief discussion, because they help to convey the pervasiveness of arousal and reward issues to personality functioning at its most basic and essential levels. Zuckerman has proposed a biological theory of sensation seeking based on physiological correlates (Zuckerman 1983). Physiological measures that have been demonstrated to be significantly related to sensation seeking include the orienting reflex (OR), average evoked potential (AEP), monoamine oxidase (MAO) levels, and endorphin concentrations.

The orienting reflex (OR) is defined operationally by the degree of an attentional response to a novel stimuli of moderate intensity. If the novel stimulus is repeated, the OR decreases and may cease. If a stimuli of high intensity is introduced, a defensive response (DR) is initiated. In animals the OR is followed by approach, investigation, or behaviors similar to curiosity in humans. The DR, in contrast, is followed by either flight or fight behaviors, indicating defense against a perceived threat. Subjects with strong ORs tend to be younger, have higher SSS scores, and demonstrate better performance on conditioned learning tasks than do subjects with weak ORs. Behaviorally inactive schizophrenics, who as a group have low SSS scores, demonstrate weak ORs and may not respond with any OR to appropriate stimuli. Psychopaths, whose SSS scores are typically high, demonstrate strong ORs only to stimuli that would evoke DRs in normals.

Clinical implications emerge when these differences in OR by diagnostic group are applied to the concept of optimal level of interpretation in therapy. This application assumes a strong relationship among SSS scores, OR responsivity, and psychological defensiveness. In uncovering, or insight-oriented therapy, many therapists agree that interventions that are targeted only at the conscious level and within currently acceptable cognitive-emotional frameworks result in little personality change. Although such interventions may be useful, they are more educational than psychotherapeutic. On the other extreme, otherwise accurate interpretations aimed at material that is fully unconscious are usually not understood, produce no emotional resonance for the patient, and may result in considerable confusion in a patient's attempt to understand what the therapist is getting at. In the worst case, these premature interventions targeted at unconscious or repressed material may result in the patient being overwhelmed with anxiety and fleeing from treatment, or more generalized acting out, or panic. Interpretations are optimally targeted at material that is preconscious or consciously present but undervalued or understood in a limited, self-constricting, or self-defeating manner. The data on OR suggest that interpretations may result in a curiosity or orienting response in normals or in a defensive response in persons with lower OR thresholds and lower SSS scores, whereas individuals with higher SSS scores may need considerably more confrontational approaches (therapeutic depth charges, so to speak), before they become genuinely interested in the dynamic issues that the therapist is trying to bring to their attention. Although the conceptual basis for current practice with substance abusers may be different, or absent altogether, the noisy, revivalistic atmosphere of many self-help groups and the confrontation and rapier-sharp interpretations applied with sarcastic wit used by many counselors who work with substance abusers are consistent with this line of thinking. With dual diagnosis patients, however, the depressed, schizophrenic, or anxiety-disordered patient with an addictive problem is likely to have low SSS scores relative to most substance abusers and will not need the same kind of therapeutic hammering to get his or her attention.

Another physiological measure associated with sensation seeking and psychopathology is the average evoked potential (AEP), a measure of the signal evoked from the brain in response to a presented stimulus. With moderate levels of stimulus intensity, the AEP is proportionate to the stimulus intensity. However, when high intensity stimuli are used, individual differences emerge. Augmenters show additional increases of AEP response to the additional increase in stimulus intensity, whereas reducers show a reduction or inhibition of AEP response to the higher level of stimulus intensity. Augmenters tend to have high SSS scores and low endorphin levels. Reducers have low SSS scores and high endorphin levels. Younger subjects are more apt to augment than older subjects. Schizophrenics tend to be reducers, along with inactive psychiatric patients. Psychopaths tend to be extreme augmenters. The line of speculation about OR responsivity and defensiveness can also be fruitfully applied to AEPs. Zuckerman's (1983) commentary about drug users and the AEP correlate to sensation seeking is worth quoting below:

> Sensation seeking has also been found to be high in drug abusers, both polydrug-user types (Kilpatrick et al. 1976) and young heroin users (Platt 1975). Despite the absent or weak association between sensation seeking and relative preference for stimulant or depressant drugs (Carrol and Zuckerman 1977), Murtaugh . . . found a relation between the AEP patterns and drug histories. Drug abusers who had a relatively preponderant history of depressant drug use tended to be augmenters, whereas those who primarily used stimulants (amphetamine and cocaine) tended to be reducers. Because alcohol and opiates tend to produce a reducing pattern and amphetamines tend to produce an augmenting pattern, it seems that the drugs preferred are those that serve a homeostatic function (i.e., return the extreme types closer to an intermediate level of stimulus regulation). If all drug abusers tend to be high sensation seekers, then those who are also augmenters need some protection against stimulus overload, whereas those who are reducers need high levels of arousal to process the stimuli they seek. Young alcoholics and heroin users do not usually use their respective drugs as sleeping potions; they use them to stay "cool" while engaging in a variety of social, antisocial, and sensual sensation-seeking activities. [p. 54]

MAO level and concentration of various endorphins have been implicated in mental disorders and drug use. These two biological factors correlate significantly with the SSS. Persons with low MAO levels are more apt to have high SSS scores, to be more prone to be AEP augmenters, to be younger subjects, male rather than female, and to demonstrate aggressive, sociable, domineering personality styles. Such individuals are at high risk for criminality and drug use. Low MAO levels are often seen in manics and their relatives, paranoid schizophrenics, schizophrenics in acute episodes (but not chronic), and alcoholics. High MAO levels are found more often among AEP reducers, older and female subjects, and depressed persons. High MAO levels are associated with personalities that are retiring, inactive, and reclusive. Most clinicians are aware of MAO inhibitors being applied to the treatment of depression. MAO inhibitors may induce mania in individuals with bipolar disorder if administered during the depressive phase, and overactivity and hypomania are side effects of these drugs even among persons with unipolar depression. The strong negative correlation of SSS with MAO level suggests that sensation seeking may be related to levels of catecholamines (particularly dopamine and norepinephrine) in the brain.

Endorphins and hormones are two biochemical factors significantly correlated with the SSS that have extensive effects on behaviors and conditions other than sensation seeking. There has been much said in the media about endorphins over the last decade. These endogenous substances have an effect on the body and mind similar to morphine in that they reduce the perception of pain, reduce general stimulation and activity, and modulate mood. Persons who have low endorphin levels tend to have high SSS scores and are AEP augmenters. High endorphin levels are associated with low SSS scores, higher Eysenck neuroticism scores, AEP reducing, and schizophrenia. Patients with organic pain syndromes have endorphin levels lower than persons whose pain is psychogenic.

Sex hormone levels are also significantly correlated with SSS scores. Testosterone, for example, is positively correlated with SSS scores, is higher in males than in females and higher in the young than in the old, and is associated with personalities that are aggressive, sociable, active, and dominant. Low testosterone levels are more common among persons with lower SSS, older people, female subjects, and those who demonstrate low sexual arousal, lower activity levels, reclusiveness, and submissive social behavior.

There are many implications for therapy from these SSS findings, such as the convincing evidence that persons high on the SSS are more apt to use and subsequently become addicted to various substances. In addition, these persons are more apt to be attracted to substances that are unusual and not approved in their social group. Because high sensation seekers more easily habituate to drug effects than other persons, they are more apt to graduate to other drugs or to seek out dangerous activities while under the influence of or in pursuit of drugs. Sexual involvement in combination with drug use is apt to be more frequent in high sensation-seeking individuals. Fortunately, the sensation seeking is, in Zuckerman's terms, a displaceable motive, which is to say that it can be satisfied by a wide range of activities. The therapist must recognize that unless the need for sensation is altered in some manner (through medication, relaxation methods, etc.) the needs that result in sensation seeking may continue to be a problem to an individual involved in recovery processes. Interpersonal relationships such as marriage are strongly influenced by the sensation- seeking needs of those involved. Similarly, the therapeutic process must not be guided by an ignorant or mistaken assumption about the meaning of sensory input requirements:

A lack of understanding of the sensation-seeker motive and its relationship to other motives, such as the needs for intimacy and security, may lead counselors to seek uniform solutions for unhappy clients that are inappropriate for the particular personality types. Clients with uncomplicated needs for new sensations may be judged as neurotic, and time and money may be wasted searching for the "insight" that will explain their "compulsive acting-out." Intractable low-sensation seekers may be urged to seek new experiences in order to become "liberated" or "self-actualized," and their feeble efforts at sensation seeking may lead to even more misery and unhappiness. . . . Some of the failures in the treatment of drug abusers may also be traceable to the failure to recognize the sensation-seeking aspects of drug abuse. The high-sensation-seeking drug abuser must learn new ways to find novel and stimulating experience, ways that are not illegal or as dangerous as drug abuse. [Zuckerman 1979a, p. 298]

The SSS exists in several forms, and norms for several of them are published. Form V consists of 40 two-option, forced choice items and is titled "Interest and Preference Test." Most of the items have obvious meanings, and conscious deception could easily confound findings where there is motivation to deceive. Each of the four subscales consists of ten items, which load only on that subscale and the total scale score. An example is item 38:

A. Sailing long distances in small sailing crafts is foolhardy.
B. I would like to sail a long distance in a small but seaworthy sailing craft.

The choice of B adds one point to the experience seeking subscale and to the total SSS score. Zuckerman (1979a) has defined the four subscales and the factors they purport to measure as:

1. Thrill and Adventure Seeking (TAS): items reflecting a desire to engage in physical activities involving elements of speed, danger, novelty, and defiance of gravity (e.g., parachuting, scuba diving).
2. Experience Seeking (ES): items reflecting seeking of novel experiences through travel, music, art, and a spontaneous, nonconforming lifestyle with similarly inclined persons.
3. Disinhibition (Dis): items describing the need to seek release in uninhibited social activities with or without the use of alcohol.
4. Boredom Susceptibility (BS): items reflecting an aversion to repetitive experience, routine work, or predictable people with a reaction of restless discontent when unavoidably exposed to such experience.

The concept of optimal arousal and sensation seeking has also been incorporated in several other assessment instruments that will yield a sensation-seeking index (see the discussion of the MAACL-R in a later section on negative affectivity). Preferably, however, a measure that yields a component breakdown of sensation-seeking motives should be used in the dual diagnosis assessment process.

Assessment of Impulsivity

A discussion of impulsivity naturally follows a discussion of sensation seeking and the SSS and should be expected in any text on dual diagnosis disorders, where impulsivity and disorders of intentionality are continual objects of assessment. Viewing impulsivity as a unitary concept is not very useful clinically and usually results in name calling and description rather than explanation of behavior. Monroe (1970) described a distinction between impulse and instinctual dyscontrol. Impulse dyscontrol involves a period of mounting tension, with debate and indecisiveness about the expression of an urge or impulse (usually rage or aggression) followed by abrupt, explosive expression of primitive affects, usually rage or aggression. Instinctual dyscontrol is not preceded by this tension and conflicted decision making. Eysenck (1978) described a four factor hierarchical structure for impulsive behavior: impulsivity in the narrow sense, risk-taking, nonplanning, and liveliness (behavioral tempo). Wangeman (1976) emphasized examining impulsivity as both a state and trait characteristic.

Barratt and Patton (1983) see impulsivity as part of action-oriented personality predispositions such as sensation seeking, extraversion, and a general lack of inhibition. They view this set of predispositions as orthogonal (not significantly correlated) to personality traits that describe mood, affective symptoms, and anxiety. The Barratt Impulsiveness Scale (BIS) (Barratt 1959) has been extensively researched and used to confirm this interconnectedness of impulsivity to other aspects of action-oriented behavioral traits and its relative independence to anxiety and emotion. Barratt and Patton describe impulsive persons as having a fast conceptual tempo, as tending to respond quickly (motor impulsivity), either when a quick response set is established or when no response set is dictated by external requirements. By conceptual tempo, they refer to the tendency for impulsive individuals to underproduce (or underestimate) time intervals. Timing and time judgment are, in their view, essential to understanding impulsivity.

The Time Score of the Stroop Color and Word Test correlates highly ($r = +.55$) with the BIS. The Stroop, described earlier as a neuropsychological screening instrument, may also be seen as a measure of impulsivity because it measures the ability to inhibit an automatic response.

Although the BIS is recommended here as an assessment instrument for measuring impulsivity, a history of major decisions and life events will reveal a good deal about the degree to which a person is impulsive intermittently or as a stable characteristic. However impulsivity is measured or assessed, it must be viewed not as the equivalent of sensation seeking or action orientation in that it involves inhibitory processes to a larger extent than do other traits in the action-oriented cluster. A good drug history will also include some probing about dyscontrol and impulsiveness while under the influence of the drug of choice, or the use of substances with the purpose of (to facilitate) disinhibition of restraints against acting on urges, wishes, or plans. Traditional Rorschach testing results in several good measures of impusivity, as does observing the patient in almost any structured or timed task.

Negative Affectivity: Depression, Anger, and Anxiety

Two symptom complexes introduced in Chapter 3 are primarily related to negative affectivity, which when combined with positive affect accounts for most of our experience of emotional states (Watson and Clark 1984). In fact, the anxiety complex and dominance of affect could be combined under the rubric of negative affectivity, if the latter did not include symptoms involving euphoria and elated mood, which are positive affects. Some variant of either depression, anger, and anxiety is involved in almost any treatment case. Most frequently patients present with a complex interaction of variants of these three negative affects. Global assessment measures, such as those noted earlier, often adequately describe the dynamics of these emotional factors. However, the need for focal assessment of these emotions becomes important in tracking treatment progress and in clarifying the style of experience or expression of negative affect. The emphasis placed here on negative affectivity should not disparage the importance of assessing positive affect in dual diagnosis patients. Patients who can spontaneously experience positive affects have a better prognosis of recovery from both addiction and clinical syndromes. Chapter 2 cites data on the positive and negative emotional experiences of alcoholics for this reason, and Chapter 5 discusses the importance of positive affect in the treatment of cocaine addiction.

Several instruments that can be used to measure or assess these affects and related symptoms are recommended, although only one is described here in any detail. For general measures of negative affect and affective symptoms, the symptom scales of the MCMI can be usefully interpreted, as can MMPI scores. However, there is a need in a dual diagnosis treatment program for assessment instruments that may be administered often, that are not burdensome for the patient, and that are easily scored and interpreted. The SCL-90-R (Derogatis 1977, Derogatis et al. 1978) can be recommended for its ability to examine general distress over relatively short time intervals and for its ability to be used in a continual retesting mode. Separate subscales exist for depression, anxiety, and hostility, although they are limited. A better choice might be the Multiple Affective Adjective Check List Revised (MAACL-R) (Zuckerman and Lubin 1990), which contains subscales for anxiety, depression, hostility, positive affect, and sensation seeking and can be used to measure both the state and trait aspects of these affects and predispositions. The MAACL-R is based on the finding that negative and positive affects, and vigor or surgency are the major components of emotional life. The importance of sensation seeking and level of arousal (related to the experience of vigor or surgency) occupies a major subsection of this chapter and is the basis of the reward/arousal symptom complex. Because of its comprehensiveness, theoretical basis, ease in administration and scoring, acceptable validity and reliability, and readily interpretable subscales, the MAACL-R is highly recommended for a general affective assessment.

For measures of specific affects, the Beck Depression Inventory (BDI) (Beck 1967) is a brief measure of depression well known in both the mental health and substance abuse treatment fields. The BDI has been well researched, is easily administered, and can be used in repeated testing. For assessment of anxiety and its changes over time, the State-Trait Anxiety Inventory (STAI) is useful and is similar to another measure designed by Spielberger to assess anger and its expression. Because these two measures developed by Spielberger are similar in format and application and because problems with anger are not typically assessed as effectively as those related to anxiety, only the anger measure is described in detail. In regard to any self-report instrument claiming to measure affective state in substance abusers, the reader is reminded of the caveat stated earlier of not expecting substance abusers to reliably discriminate among emotional states and shades of affect, since these individuals may experience negative affects as global discomfort rather than having better articulated emotional experiences.

The State-Trait Anger Expression Inventory (STAXI)

Anger is one of the more important negative affects to be assessed in dual diagnosis patients. It is often suppressed or its expression avoided during periods of sobriety, only for it to surface with a vengeance during periods of intoxication. Patients who cannot express anger are particularly vulnerable to narcissistic shame, which is pivotal in the dynamics of addiction. Like other negative affects, anger is often a precursor and cause of relapse to drug use. By being able to assess the role and importance of anger in the personality and in the dual diagnosis problems presented by a given patient, the skilled clinician will be able to intervene prior to early relapse related to the inadequate management of anger. In some personality types (the borderline, passive aggressive, or psychopathic, for instance), the presence of intense anger may be viewed as given, based on the diagnosis. The actual fact of angry experience, however, tells us very little about how it will be expressed typically by the individual. Other personality types (the dependent, avoidant, schizoid, for example) may mask anger that may fuel one or more of the psychosocial functions of addiction described in Chapter 3.

The State-Trait Anger Expression Inventory (STAXI), by Spielberger (1988), is a useful focal assessment instrument for determining the role and function of anger. It is designed to measure anger as independent of general anxiety. It incorporates the state-trait distinction and allows for the tracking of ebb and flow in state measures, which is encouraged throughout this chapter. The STAXI is an easily administered (10 to 15 minutes), self-report instrument with a relatively painless hand-scoring method and reasonable cost.

This inventory has its origins in the recognition that the experience and expression of anger can be usefully distinguished in clinical work. It is based on a relatively straightforward multicomponent view of both the experience and expression of anger. Angry experiences are viewed as consisting of both state and trait aspects. State anger is a subjective feeling that varies from "mild annoyance or irritation to fury and rage" (p. 1). It is accompanied by physiological tension and arousal, especially of the autonomic nervous system. The intensity of state anger varies with the individual's perception of frustration in goal-directed behavior, mistreatment, or injustice, or the perception of attack. The STAXI contains a ten-item state anger scale to assess the experience of anger at the time the inventory is administered.

Trait anger is a disposition toward easily perceiving these anger-inducing situations and the tendency to experience and express intense state anger in such circumstances. This predisposition is further refined by distinguishing between the tendency to become easily angered without provocation or external prompting (measured in the angry temperament scale) and the tendency to become angry upon criticism or perceived mistreatment from others (angry reaction scale).

The expression of anger is conceptualized in the STAXI as consisting of three basic components based on the direction and degree of exerted control on the expressed anger. Anger may be suppressed or held in without overt behavioral expression (anger-in) or it may be directed outwardly toward other people or objects (anger-out). Some individuals will have high scores on both of these scales, due to their ability to adjust the expression of their anger to differing circumstances. The degree to which the individual attempts to control the expression of anger (anger control) is also assessed. When combined these three measures of anger expression provide an anger expression score, which is a general index to the frequency that anger is expressed.

The STAXI manual contains normative data for more than 9,000 subjects from adult, adolescent, and college student populations. In addition, normative data for several special interest groups are provided, including prison inmates and medical-surgical patients. The STAXI has demonstrated reasonably good reliability and validity in the populations on which it was standardized. Studies with the STAXI have been heretofore concentrated in the area of health psychology. Although norms for psychiatric patients and dual diagnosis patients do not currently exist, the ease of using the STAXI makes the establishment of local norms at the clinic or treatment center relatively easy.

Assessment of Interpersonal Relatedness and Empathy

For psychologists, who will have access to the Rorschach and other projective tests that have sophisticated measures of interpersonal relatedness, the assessment of this important area is rather straightforward and is well described elsewhere. Empathy and interpersonal relatedness are crucial to the concept of psychopathy and are discussed in some detail in Chapter 8. Therefore, only an objective instrument (the FIRO Scales) that can be used to suggest interpersonal alternatives in treatment planning is described here. However, a few words are necessary about the conceptualization of sociability, intimacy, and empathy in relationship to substance abuse and psychopathology as they are encountered in the dual diagnosis case. Although we might find that most persons can be typified as moving toward, away from, or against others interpersonally, the substance abuser does not always fit this categorization. Interpersonal behavior and relatedness vary from position to position in the addictive cycle. In addition, behavior while intoxicated may be contradictory to the typical manifest attitude toward relationships. Intimacy may occur only under the influence of alcohol, for example, or aggressive and exploitative motives may be expressed only after the ingestion of cocaine. Drugs can serve as affective and interpersonal "switches," which temporarily modify what in the nonuser is a relatively stable aspect of personality functioning. The concept of the drug as a "switch" for personality and affect is adapted from research on switches from depressive to manic states or the reverse in the affective disorders, which are hypothesized to be related to endogenous biogenic amines (Bunney et al. 1971, 1972). Both the quality of interpersonal orientation and its stability will inform us about the function of addictive behavior, especially if the drug of choice appears to serve as a conduit, catalyst, or fulcrum for access to interpersonal behaviors that would otherwise be atypical of the patient. Of particular interest is the degree of object constancy with and without the influence of the drug of choice, or some other intoxicant. Literal failures in recognizing the identities of significant others while under moderate doses of an intoxicant are particularly pathognomonic and suggest the need to disrupt negative introjects. More common, however, are shifts in evaluation of significant others during intoxication. Knowledge of the qualities projected or extracted during such interactions can be useful in assessment of the function of addiction.

RELAPSE, DRUG "SWITCHES," AND COMPLICATED BEREAVEMENT

D. J. is a 33-year-old trucking supervisor from a tight-knit Christian family. He has had two outpatient treatments for cocaine abuse over two years. He is ashamed and embarrassed by his problem, especially now that his family is aware of it. He was evasive regarding his episodic use of alcohol, describing it as related primarily to the peer pressure he experienced from his brothers and cousins, who were heavy users of alcohol but to his knowledge suffered no adverse consequences from it. Like his relatives, he considered drinking a harmless diversion. In discussing his relapses to cocaine, D. J. revealed that when he was intoxicated with alcohol, his personality was significantly altered in either one of two directions. When drinking in public places, he tended to be loud, overbearing, argumentative, verbally aggressive, and capable of being physically combative, even toward his family. When drinking alone at home, he was prone to long bouts of bitter weeping, wherein he reported feeling mistreated and abandoned by his family and friends. Both of these conditions under the influence of alcohol were typically interrupted by cocaine use. They also contrasted greatly with his usual sober demeanor, which was polite, religious, and easygoing. While under the influence of cocaine, he was overactive and overconfident, but otherwise demonstrated little personality aberration.

In D.J.'s intake assessment, it was noted that one of his earliest memories was of being told of a beloved cat, Trudy, being run over in the street. Much later, in group therapy, D.J. mentioned in an almost off-hand manner that his brother's recently acquired pedigreed pup while under his care was killed by a car. The therapist, aware of the early memory, pursued the topic of loss and death. D.J. revealed for the first time in any formal treatment that his common-law wife, Dory, had been killed in a car accident four years earlier. Although he was not present at the time of the accident, he felt that if he had been there, the accident would not have occurred. Once it was established that D.J.'s alcohol use and cocaine addiction were complicated by his unresolved bereavement, his treatment was altered to pursue the unfinished emotional business with the lost loved one. Among the issues dealt with were his anger and disappointment with her family for not recognizing the common-law marriage and leaving him to carry the full weight of significant debts that Dory had accumulated prior to her death. He had in fact been abandoned and rejected by her family and had projected these feelings onto his own family. The therapist was now able to recognize how alcohol functioned for D.J. as a drug "switch" to problem affects and why the start of intimate feelings in the therapy had preceded and contributed to his first and only relapse in his third outpatient treatment. (The concept of the drug as a "switch" for personality and affect is adapted from the research on switches from depressive to manic states or the reverse in the affective disorders, which are hypothesized to be related to endogenous biogenic amines (Bunney et al. 1971, 1972).

The FIRO Awareness Scales

The Fundamental Interpersonal Relations Orientation (FIRO) scales (Schutz and Wood 1977) were designed to help individuals to increase their awareness of how they relate to others. Altogether, seven scales are available, which assess areas of typical interpersonal behavior: behavior (FIRO-B), child-to-child relationships (FIRO-BC), feelings toward others (FIRO-F), retrospective views of relationships with parents (Life Interpersonal History Enquiry, LIPHE), quality of relating to a love interest (Marital Attitudes Evaluation, MATE), educational relationships (Educational Values, VAL-ED) and the typical defensive style of an individual conceptualized from a psychodynamic perspective (Coping Operations Preference Enquiry, COPE).

Except for COPE, the FIRO scales yield subscores for inclusion, control, and affection. Inclusion is the degree to which a person associates with other persons; control is the assumption of responsibility or dominance over others in relationships; and affection is the emotional involvement experienced in relation to others. Each of these subscores is measured in terms of what the individual actually is able to express and in terms of desire for these interpersonal experiences, without regard to their ability to realize these wishes. The resulting typology consists of six FIRO types. Although the FIRO scales (with the exception of COPE) have relatively good reliability and criterion validity, reservations remain about the typology suggested by the originators. COPE, which claims to measure defensive style, cannot be recommended here, since the data obtained is not as valid or as useful as that obtained from more familiar assessment methods.

Several of the FIRO scales have specific uses, such as MATE and VAL-ED, that are outside the more typical dual diagnosis problem arena. FIRO-B is by far the most popular of the scales. LIPHE can be used to compare the subject's report on an objective measure to his or her projective responses concerning family experience using the early memories procedure. Overall, the FIRO scales can provide some prediction and understanding of a patient's probable adjustment to interpersonal activities, such as group therapy, individual therapy, group living, and self-help activities, all of which involve low dominance roles for patients during early phases of recovery.

Blind Spots

Most of the areas reviewed so far are the common stock and trade of mental health professionals. However, a few blind spots exist in relationship to dual diagnosis patients for most clinicians. These areas are sexual assessment, trauma and its interpretation, spiritual assessment, and imbedded cognitions related to substances. Such areas are not usually tapped by psychological testing and are not fully investigated in the ASI. No specific assessment tools are introduced for investigating these issues. Instead this section serves as a reminder of their importance. Obviously, what has been referred to as therapeutic and assessment blind spots are different for different clinicians. The subject of finances and money, for example, might be introduced as a blind spot here, given that the level of functioning and income of many dual diagnosis clients make getting into a hospital for a few weeks or having a cocaine binge the recreational equivalent to a few winter weeks on a tropical beach. It is well to remember that the context to therapy is the total person and that areas causing discomfort for the therapist are often as useful as more comfortable issues.

The area of sexual assessment and treatment is obviously a specialty in itself, and sexual dysfunction or activity as an addiction can be the primary focus of treatment. What is advocated here is not a highly specialized professional investigation of all aspects of an individual's sexual functioning and history with the goal of ameliorating a sexual dysfunction. What most therapists find imposing about the sexual assessment area is not so much a fear of inadequate competence, but the fear of being indelicate with patients, of introducing issues intrusively, and of appearing too "Freudian" in the eyes of clients and colleagues. Some clinicians, in contrast, easily discuss sexual dynamics without ever getting to the realities of sexuality for their patients.

For dual diagnosis cases, the minimum information that must be obtained early in the assessment cycle includes any history of sexual trauma or abuse, either judged by professional consensus or by the patient's own understanding. The patient's preference for gender of sexual partners and any major ambivalence or conflicts surrounding these issues must be known fairly early in treatment. Often a direct connection can be made between a persistent addiction and sexual abuse, sexual trauma, or anxieties about sexual preferences or gender identification. Motivated by the need to obtain drugs, addicted patients often become involved in prostitution, in sexual acts outside of their preference or range of comfort, and sexuality across gender preference. These are extremely common events in long-standing addictions, especially under conditions of weakened ego-strengths often found in the dual diagnosis patients. Trauma related to such activity is often hidden under a facade of indifference.

Sexual activity is sometimes an integral part of drug addiction in which the drug of choice is perceived as an extension the sexual encounter. Facilitation of sexuality is an important psychosocial function of addiction and drug abuse. Relapse potential in such cases is very high unless both the therapist and patient are aware of the relevant dynamics. Conversely, the period of sexual abstinence imposed either formally or by implication by many therapists and programs during the initial stages of treatment has unique consequences for some individuals who are overly identified with their role as a sexual person or object, a common pattern among those with low self-esteem or other narcissistic disorder. In an area related to sexual issues, the patient's gender identifications (an aspect of object relations that often requires months of therapeutic investigation to discern) can be especially influential in middle and late phases of recovery.

What is important in any stage of treatment is a willingness to ask the right questions in suitable contexts and the willingness to hear truthful answers. For example, asking about prostitution for drugs or about homosexual partners is appropriate during the interviews where the ASI legal, social, and family scales are administered. The Early Memory Procedure directly introduces the issue of inappropriate sexual experiences and sexual abuse during childhood and can be invaluable both for providing assessment information during the early stages of treatment or engaging the client in treatment of these issues regardless of treatment stage.

Although early childhood trauma, especially from sexual abuse, fits neatly into a developmental view of addiction and mental illnesses, adult traumatic experiences of other kinds are sometimes not given due attention when a developmental model is given priority. It is important to keep in mind that both global situational stressors and single event experiences can result in trauma or a breakdown in coping mechanisms. Addiction is often the temporary solution that becomes the persistent problem of a lifetime. Post-traumatic stress disorder subsequent to being a victim, losing a valued job, observing a catastrophe, or living in a chaotic urban ghetto are often underdiagnosed and fuel symptomatic addictions.

Spiritual assessment and therapy is an area that many scientifically oriented therapists may resist until it is understood that the concepts involved can be com pletely secularized if necessary. The emphasis on the patient's image of the future, his or her values and the ability to apply them in daily living, the ability to sacrifice lower needs for higher ones (as defined by the patient) need no support from supernatural concepts. Similarly, the patient's experience of meaning, the value placed on the self and the world, and his or her experience of freedom, individuality, loneliness, creativity, and finality are important issues in treatment. Gregory Bateson's (1971) classic article (formulated from observations of alcoholics who were also schizophrenic) describes addiction as being generated and supported by notions inherent in the Western view of individuality. Bateson advocated a serious clinical analysis of the theology of Alcoholics Anonymous and masterfully illustrated the point that the patient's understanding and sense of world view are essential elements in the recovery process. Yalom's (1980) description of existential issues such as death awareness, responsibility, isolation, and meaninglessness in therapy makes much the same point from within the mental health orthodoxy. Another perspective that encourages the assessment of the spiritual, valuative aspects of patients is Leon Wurmser's (1985) concept of split identity, in which addiction is seen as resulting from an overly intense investment in ideals that are in conflict.

The final blind spot discussed here is referred to as hidden or embedded cognitions concerning the drug of choice, or the relationship between the self and the drug of choice. Although the best way to discover these cognitions is through several months of intensive therapy and observation, a more direct interview technique might help communicate fairly efficiently what is meant by the concept. Before the conclusion of an extensive assessment interview, ask the patient to use his or her imagination to answer the question: "What kind of person is _____ ?" and fill in the blank with the drug of choice. If the individual has or has had several drugs of choice, ask the question for each drug. Sometimes patients will spontaneously start to compare and contrast these "persons." Although the material gained from this projective interview question must be interpreted dynamically and in the context of the phase of illness (for instance, someone who is debilitated by cocaine use would answer very differently from the same person interrupted earlier in the addictive process and coerced by external factors into treatment), the responses can yield crucial information about the function of the addiction. Other projective techniques include asking the patient to draw a picture of the drug of choice, being totally nondirective about what should be included in the drawing.

Expectancies about drug use held by dual diagnosis patients are often of two kinds, those encountered in the general population and more eccentric, sometimes psychotic notions. At times the absence of the normal expectancy is what characterizes the abnormal quality of what is believed. For example, some psychotic patients do not believe that alcohol *can* make them intoxicated. One patient who believed that drinking large amounts regularly would prevent her from getting pregnant referred to the drinks as "weed killers" and unwanted children as "weeds." Another patient viewed alcohol as a "spirit" but not in the usual sense. He believed that it had unusual magical powers, a personality, and astrological linkages. The eccentric cognitions described have been fairly stable beliefs that appear to the observer to be delusional or pseudo-delusional. However, the tendency to have transient cognitive distortions (which may result in relapse) related to drug use but not to other aspects of reality testing can occur among severe personality disorders and the severely addicted. Figure 4–1 is an outline of assessment components.

Figure 4–1. Summary Outline of Assessment Areas and Techniques

I. Sociability and Basic Relatedness
   A. Interpersonal Style
      1. FIRO-B
         a. Inclusion
         b. Control
         c. Affection
   B. Dependence/Independence and ambivalence, genuine empathy:
      1. MCMI Personality Scales
      2. EPITAT Narratives
      3. EMP Narratives
      4. Interview Impressions

II. Psychopathy (See Chapter 8)
   A. Life Style or Socio-cultural Factors
      1. Criminality Lifestyle Inventory
   B. Personality Dimensions
      1. Psychopathy Checklist-Revised
      2. MCMI Aggressive Scale
      3. Sensation Seeking Scale
   C. Arrest and Conviction History

III. Sensation Seeking
   A. Sensation Seeking Scale
      1. Thrill and Adventure Seeking
      2. Experience Seeking
      3. Disinhibition
      4. Boredom Susceptibility
   B. Life style from Clinical Interview
      1. Dangerous occupations or sports
      2. Promiscuity and sexual experimentation
      3. Drug use across drug categories

IV. Negative Affects
   A. Depression
   B. Beck Depression Inventory
      1. MCMI Symptom Scales
      2. EMP Narratives
   C. Anxiety
      1. MCMI Symptom Scales
      2. Hamilton Anxiety Scale
      3. State-Trait Anxiety Inventory (STAI)
   D. Anger
      1. The Anger Expression Scale
         a. Anger In
         b. Anger Out
         c. Anger Reflect
   E. Shame and Guilt
      1. Clinical Interview
      2. EMP Narratives
      3. EPITAT Narratives

V. Impulsivity and related controls
      1. The Barratt Impulsiveness Scale (BIS)
      2. Stroop Color and Word Test's Time Score

VI. Relapse Cues
   A. See Marlatt and Donovan (1988)

VII. Blind Spots: Use all available data, consider and inquire:
   A. Spiritual Assessment: Interview, Narratives
   B. Trauma and its Consequences: EMP, Interview
   C. Imbedded Cognitions and Affects: Guided projective interview

5

Reciprocal Treatment Strategies

Given the complexity of dual diagnosis work, treatment issues must be confronted on at least two levels. The first is the theoretical, conceptual, and to some extent, philosophical level. This general level of understanding informs and is followed by the second level, practical application. This chapter provides the broad view of approaches toward treating the dual diagnosis patient. Topics such as the basic metaphors that guide treatment, the relationship between treatment orientation and level of explanation involved in a given dual diagnosis problem formulation, the most generally applicable issues and treatment themes, and ideas with the most wide ranging implications for dual diagnosis work are reviewed. Finally, there are several perspectives on creativity in psychotherapy, such as an examination of the newly emerging psychological material and general methods of maintaining a creative approach to therapy with the difficult dual diagnosis patient.

ALTERNATIVE METAPHORS FOR TREATMENT

The basic metaphors that describe any important human institution or endeavor provide useful information about the way these activities are conducted and conceptualized. This is perhaps especially true for psychotherapy and other treatment enterprises, where metaphor often bears directly on the treatment process itself. Perhaps this is why we often find a combination of almost incongruous or mixed metaphors being used by those who represent the therapeutic process. It is important to make the metaphors we use explicit so that we can be as comfortable as possible with the ubiquitous, often unconscious influences that they exert in our work with patients and so that we can compensate for the liabilities involved in these influences. We discuss here several of the more prevalent and useful metaphors in the substance abuse and mental health treatment fields, making more explicit some of the metaphors incorporated in several major treatment orientations. The guiding metaphor of this book is also discussed in more detail.

Marlatt (Marlatt and Fromme 1988) described several advantages of using metaphors in therapy: heightening awareness and sensation, circumventing conscious resistance to an implied message, and promoting change by providing emotional experiences that are optimally incongruous with the individual's current mode of thought and behavior. One of the most important functions of metaphors describing any human enterprise is to strongly imply or specifically define role assignments for those in that activity. In many senses the physician–patient metaphor remains the most basic, almost archetypal, image of what takes place in psychotherapy. Teacher–student, sage–seeker, priest–supplicant, expert–client roles still serve powerfully as metaphoric guides to understanding the content and context of therapeutic enterprises. Most of these role dyads can be applied to any treatment approach. The full range must be used in treating the dual diagnosis patient, who is in need of understanding, medication, education, direction, forgiveness, and empowerment.

Almost as evocative as these dyadic roles has been the comparison of psychotherapy to a journey, often a heroic journey involving struggle toward some goal that involves trials and unpredicted detours as well as the hoped for, hard-won advances, a journey that requires a companionable and knowledgeable guide, the therapist. In Marlatt's work on relapse prevention, for example, this metaphor is elaborated through the image of the road map, which he uses to depict what must be given to the patient by the therapist (guide) to insure success in the journey of arriving at freedom from addiction. In this use, struggle is minimized since it represents only a failure to follow the map, or an obstacle not previously charted but, once encountered, easily penciled in. Marlatt also uses the familiar parable of teaching the hungry to fish rather than merely feeding them. The therapist begins to eliminate the need for outside intervention from the start by teaching the patient not only how to fish (i.e., provide for one's own recovery needs) but where, when, and under what conditions throwing out a line would be foolish and perhaps dangerous. Marlatt also compares the urge to use or craving for the drug of choice as being similar to an ocean wave that rises, crests, and subsides. The client is encouraged to view recovery as a kind of surfing activity, riding out the wave with grace and control.

Freud's writings contain a very complex interaction of metaphors, among them metaphors of journey and struggle. Analysis is viewed as a twofold journey: intellectual and emotional. The intellectual journey proceeds through uncovering and leads to ever increasing insight, much as a biologist's dissection or an archeologist's careful excavation may lead to new discoveries and new understand-ings. On the emotional side of this journey, we find Freud's use of the concepts of defense and resistance: basic metaphors of struggle (consciously borrowed from metaphors for disease processes) that are essentially military. The analysand, in part, responds to therapeutic efforts in much the same way a defeated nation responds to an occupying army's attempts to subdue a terrified, desperate, and resentful population. Both of these journeys, the intellectual and the emotional, move downward through strata of psychic functioning and structure and backward through the patient's autobiographic past.

In the self-help movement, we encounter many elements borrowed from Prot-estant revivalism in particular American variations. Perhaps most striking are the ways in which the Anonymous traditions preserve revivalism's emphasis on group process, its emotional expression of those personal experiences that have led to salvation ("testifying" to revelation), and its evangelical emphasis on the search for personal truths and a personal relationship with a higher power.

Many metaphors are incorporated in the cultural themes of these semireligious, self-help organizations. Perhaps most dominant is the barely hidden allegory of a contemplative, spiritual journey through time. The Protestant view of time as a recurrent progression, a sort of spiral staircase toward the final Day of Judgment, is seen in its emphasis on the here-and-now possibility of atonement and inspiration from God and in the preservation of the belief in a historical rapture and Second Coming. In the Anonymous traditions, we find this journey through time reflected in the Twelve Steps, which enumerate the hours in a clock (the modulated, regulated life), the disciples of Christ, and the stages of the cross. We also find another time metaphor as a recurrent progression in the deceptively folksy, yet profound motto "One day at a time." This motto implies the defeat of the dominance of the impulse toward flight or escape from painful affects and poorly modulated arousal, the removal of the negative dependency condition in which time takes on an essentially despotic, defeating character.

The approach in this book borrows from all these metaphoric sources. In addition, several metaphors are introduced that are not as pervasive in the mental health and substance abuse treatment literatures and cultures as those cited above. From Lewin, we take the metaphor of life as space and movement within space, a kind of journey of attraction and repulsion. From Maslow, we adopt the metaphor of ascent on a ladder of development, mirroring the ascent of the species as a whole toward an indeterminate future limited only by vision and self-imposed morality. To add to the range of metaphors available to work with the dual diagnosis patient, we add a somewhat more specific metaphor of journey and struggle. Addiction and psychopathology are compared to two rivers that intersect, intertwine, merge, bifurcate, and otherwise interact, sometimes increasing each other's depth and symptomatic expressions, at other times remaining relatively independent. Within each flow of pathological process, forces and influences combine dynamically and destructively, ultimately to cascade into increased pathology. Intertwined with these malignant forces are opponent processes, which we later identify as those of recovery.

The metaphor of two rivers can be elaborated in order to include the roles and activities of therapy in addition to describing the interactive, dynamic character of the dual diagnosis syndromes. In regard to role assignments for therapy within this metaphor, the therapist and patient together take on all the roles that might be assumed by a team of engineers, planners, and skilled workers involved in a grand land development scheme in the uncharted area where the two rivers wind. Not only must they map the terrain covered by these winding rivers, but they must know something of their depths, the sediments they carry, their origins and end points, the rainy and dry times of the year, in short, all of the relevant dynamics. They must be ready to move quickly to work upstream toward origins or downstream toward consequences. They must build structures that will direct energies and scarce resources. Some of these structures will be temporary and ad hoc in response to the unexpected; others will be permanent and well planned, making new features in the landscape. Occasionally they will have to demolish obstacles, including previously existing structures, recognizing that this is done only at considerable cost. Their overriding goal is to make potentially destructive forces productive or, at the very least, to manage their effects safely. Their work only prepares the field for other endeavors.

As with many of the more powerful metaphors, this one oscillates between an external (social, environmental) and internal (personal, intrapsychic) application. It allows for continual shifting among roles for all persons involved in the therapeutic enterprise: family members, therapists, patients. The many diverse roles are linked not only in complementary dyads. Issues and interventions, such as manipulation, control, neutrality, direction, support, insight, uncovering, and motivation for change, take on a different appearance in the light of this basic metaphor and its range of roles. Clearly, all of these stances are acceptable in at least some of the needed role assignments once all parties have agreed to participate in the overall project. Working within such a metaphor for therapy implies mastering many theoretical understandings as well as having a good empirical basis to guide the construction and application of theory.

IDENTIFYING RECOVERY PROCESSES AND PATTERNS

Chapter 3 develops a heuristic system for formulating dual diagnosis problems from an understanding of symptom complexes, functions of addiction, and the consequences and antecedents involved in establishing a drug of choice. Chapter 4 describes how information needed to continually refine and flesh out the dual diagnosis formulation could be obtained though relatively standardized assessment procedures. Even with this additional information, the heuristic system is incomplete, able only to hint at solutions, needing the processes of recovery and treatment interventions that support them. When an understanding of recovery processes is added to the formulation of a dual diagnosis problem, all of the elements are present to provide one or more complete strategies for conducting treatment.

The term *recovery processes* (or *process of recovery*) is meant to denote several things. Initially, one might argue that, like the term *rehabilitation*, the word "recovery" implies that the individual will return to his or her prior state. Here again we have the disease model implied (a return to health from disease), although in reality, returning to a prior state is often a very undesirable outcome for treatment. Should a suicidal alcoholic, for example, recover his dysthymic, isolated lifestyle? Most therapist would agree that one of the essential goals of treatment is to prevent patients from recovering too much of certain aspects of their previous ways of functioning. With that in mind, we define a process of recovery as a combination of factors that interact dynamically to assist the individual to move in the direction of increased freedom from a pathological process and toward personal growth. Given this emphasis on multiple factors in dynamic tension, a recovery process can contain pathogenic factors, but overall it will contribute to recovery. In fact, a basic strategy used here is to marshal isolated pathogenic factors, or vulnerabilities to them, in the service of recovery by incorporating them into larger dynamic processes.

Using Maslow's view of health, recovery processes involve movement toward higher levels of needs-related functioning and toward self-actualization. In Lewin's images, they are a correction, a re-establishment of balance in the life space. Although treatment interventions and stages often support and run parallel to recovery processes, they are not identical. Recovery processes have their own inherent direction. In a sense, a natural history of recovery would exist if organized treatment attempts did not. Maslow's basic assumption that people constantly (although often inanely) strive toward health, wholeness, growth, and meaning, even in their most pathological and behaviorally stupid aspects, is a perspective that dual diagnosis workers cannot abandon. The most productive strategy uses this assumption to the hilt. When analyzing or observing a pathological event or process, look for the often hidden "recovery" or adaptation-oriented motive or process that is linked to it, as the side of a coin not shown. Given this point of view, there are innumerable processes to be addressed in an analysis of recovery, which in a sense is another way of thinking about the entire assessment process. Some of the most important ones, fortunately, are present in almost every case and can be identified, anticipated, and strengthened or exploited in the treatment project.

Another important sense of the term recovery process refers to the predictable phases, struggles, and issues encountered by individuals who are actively engaged in establishing or maintaining stable remission from a specific kind of pathology. Here, the plural, recovery processes, is more appropriate, both because there is typically more than one line of development in recovery for any given individual and because these lines differ considerably depending on what is being recovered from. In the case of the dual diagnosis patient, what is to be recovered from is the specific problem or problems formulated by using the heuristic system in Chapter 3, that is, a specific interaction of symptom complexes, functions of addiction, and factors related to the drug of choice.

A simple rule is offered by way of identifying what recovery processes are apt to be dominant in a given case. Once a dual diagnosis problem has been formulated, it is usually best to deal with its elements in a specific order while attempting to identify recovery processes for each. After initial stabilization, an analysis of recovery should start with an understanding of the typical course and issues related to a specific drug of choice. Next, the analysis must deal with the function that this addiction has played in the individual's life and how it can be addressed more adaptively. Finally, an analysis must address the typical interventions and recovery sequences from the symptoms complexes (mental disorders) most prominently involved in the case.

This rule is not based on giving causal primacy to any one of these elements, but on the practical issue of the unsettling influence exerted on the personality by the start of treatment and recovery. Remember that dual diagnosis problems exist only because the person has reached a kind of equilibrium, albeit a pathological one. Hospitalizations, or their increased frequency, indicate a breakdown in this equilibrium.

The natural course for the patient (who has now had many treatments) is to reestablish this balance in essentially the same manner as before the current breakdown. Treatment must prevent this by providing medication, confinement, direction, hope, and insight, all in support of recovery. Nevertheless, the initial stages of recovery are experienced as a kind of disequilibrium. At first, specific psychological and physiological drug withdrawal effects, or more properly drug abstinence effects, take priority over other factors and will dominate the course of recovery. When these factors begin to ebb, the characterological issues that are usually reflected in the function of addiction and have made previous attempts at treatment begin to shape recovery more actively.

Thanks to the leveling effect of appropriate medication, the major mental illnesses exert more of an intermittent effect on recovery in a dual diagnosis case than a constant tug. The effects can usually also be mirrored in the function of the addiction, which is the nexus between personality dynamics and psychiatric disorders. As emphasized in Chapter 3, the formulation of a dual diagnosis problem should be based on dynamic, interactive, or dialectical thinking, and, similarly, the analysis of recovery processes is oversimplified by this suggested order of dealing with its components.

No absolute distinction can be made between treatment interventions designed to establish or enhance recovery processes and those primarily designed to ameliorate or interrupt pathological processes. However, some interventions fall more into one category than the other. For example, providing psychotropic treatment to a schizophrenic patient over his or her objection does interrupt the pathological affect related to the biochemical brain deficits. However, assisting the patient to alter his or her attitude toward medication and its side effects more clearly enhances recovery processes in several ways, besides increasing the likelihood that medication will be taken as directed. A relationship is built between the physician and patient and any other members of the treatment team. A sense of participation in the treatment intervention is enhanced. Finally, the patient's resistance to using the medication is explored realistically and without condescension, thus defusing the temptation to act out a cycle of struggle for control and the accompanied humiliation for the patient.

Coping with Specific Abstinence Effects

Let us look more closely at the initial effects on recovery of the drug of choice. The example used here is cocaine abuse.

Prior to examining the recovery processes most relevant to cocaine as a drug of choice, we must briefly examine the characteristics of cocaine addiction and its abstinence effects. In addition to the intense momentary euphoria, one of cocaine's basic effects is to intensify any other pleasurable events and to create a general sense of well-being and mental alertness. The user feels self-confident and has an expanded sense of mastery, much as in the inflated/grandiose experience of self depicted graphically in Chapter 1. These effects are due primarily to the drug's physiological influence on the central nervous system. In addition, cocaine has often been introduced as a status symbol and is accompanied routinely by other luxuries and expensive pleasures, especially those involving the breaking of social taboos related to the "opiates" of the working classes—morality and religion—providing further enhancement of pleasure in some personality types and in persons with negative attitudes or conflicts involving these social limits on acceptable behavior.

It is informative to look at the ECA study data (described briefly in Chapter 1) on drug of choice by diagnostic class, with the goal of understanding patterns of cocaine addiction. At the time of the study, schizophrenics were more apt to be addicted to cocaine (16.7 percent) than any other drug class, including alcohol, although they were less likely to have an addictive disorder than other patients. Antisocial personality disorders also favored this drug over others, with 42.7 percent having some lifetime occurrence of a cocaine-related diagnosis. (For both schizophrenics and antisocial personalities the second drug of choice was the opiate category, 11.4 percent and 36.7 percent, respectively. This correspondence in drug preference is congruent with the theoretical link between these disorders discussed in Chapter 3.) Cocaine ran a close second for preference in both affective-disordered and anxiety-disordered dual diagnosis cases, where the preferred drug category was the barbiturates and the hallucinogens, respectively. Across psychiatric categories, the lifetime prevalence rate overlap of an alcohol disorder and another drug of choice was highest for cocaine, with 84.8 percent of all persons with a psychiatric disorder and at least one episode of cocaine addiction abuse also having at least one episode of alcohol dependence/abuse (Regier et al. 1990).

These data suggest that a large portion of cocaine-addicted dual diagnosis patients will have an alcohol disorder and either schizophrenia, antisocial personality, an anxiety disorder, or an affective disorder other than major depression.

Most cocaine users who become addicted (about 10 to 15 percent of those who use) ingest the substance manageably for between two to four years before meeting the criteria for dependence. Compulsive accelerating addiction usually follows a transition to high-dose binges that become increasingly prolonged or after a switch to a more potent route of administration, such as from snorting to free-basing. As a parallel to the memory-based theory of alcohol addiction in Chapter 2, one theory of cocaine addiction holds that these binges contribute to the addiction through the formation of very intense memories of extreme euphoria. These memories later fuel the craving for the drug. Anyone who has treated a good number of patients for cocaine addiction has heard of "chasing a high" or "running after that first high." It means increased use in the attempt to regain some once-experienced level of euphoria. This is easily contrasted with alcohol use, or even narcotics, where the level of high is easily attained and most users are able to titrate dose and frequency almost exactly to reach the right high, even with only the roughest idea of purity of the dose.

Also contrasting with alcohol and narcotics as drugs of choice, cocaine abuse is accelerated by binges punctuated by periods of abstinence. Alcoholism, in contrast, is usually accelerated by daily, if not continuous use. In cocaine binges, which are more central to its addictive cycle than are alcohol binges to alcoholism, the individual almost totally concentrates on acquiring more cocaine. This is not a pattern usually found in alcohol intoxication where sufficient dosage results in loss of immediate craving and preoccupation with the drug.

Let us now examine the effects of cocaine abstinence on the early stage of the treatment process. Unlike alcohol or narcotic dependence, cocaine abuse and dependence usually do not produce extreme acute withdrawal effects on the physiological level. Until recently, this fact led many mental health professionals and those more familiar with alcoholism and narcotic addiction to interpret the difficulty that patients have in stopping cocaine abuse as due to hedonism, immaturity, poor motivation for change, or exaggerated estimates of concurrent psychopathology. When paraprofessionals who were former cocaine users began to work in substance abuse treatment environments, they introduced an understanding nearer to the mark. Now, research confirms the powerful addictive hold of cocaine on the severely dependent despite the absence of acute withdrawal effects.

Gawin (1991) recently outlined the phasic nature of cocaine abstinence effects based on a perspective of neurophysiological adaptation to chronic drug use. His conclusions are based on examining animal models of human cocaine addiction, assessments of outpatient and inpatient treatment, and positron emission tomography (PET) studies, which reveal brain functioning at the neurochemical-neuroelectrical level. His explanation for the primarily psychological nature of cocaine withdrawal effects is that tissue adaptation to chronic use is centered only in those brain structures that are responsible for higher psychological processes, especially those related to the experience of pleasure or hedonic responsivity. Gawin stipulates that this adaptation may be further perturbed by prior abnormalities of brain chemistry and functioning found in such disorders as depression, bipolar disorder, or schizophrenia.

Although Gawin's conclusions are tentative, due to the greater subtlety of cocaine abstinence effects than previous abstinence models built on other drugs of choice, they are nonetheless useful in understanding recovery from cocaine use. Gawin identified a triphasic withdrawal process from cocaine dependence. The sequence moves from the initial crash of cessation, through the middle phase of withdrawal, through extinction. Whether an individual will experience all three phases depends on two major factors. The first is the person's use history: amount, frequency of use, and route of administration. The second factor is the presence of psychiatric problems, which in Gawin's view (consistent with the basic assumptions in this book) results in increased probability of cocaine use spiralling into addiction, increased vulnerability to the negative symptoms that occur during addiction, and increased susceptibility to severe withdrawal effects on the psychological level when the drug is withheld or avoided.

The crash phase lasts from about 12 hours to 4 days and is more dramatic and prolonged when it occurs after a binge of high frequency, high dosage use. There is an immediate plummeting from the drug-induced mood and energy elevation of the binge. This elevation is replaced by craving for cocaine accompanied by depression, agitation, and anxiety. About half of all users also experience increased suspiciousness and paranoia. Over the following few hours (1 to 4), these experiences are supplanted by an increased craving for sleep and rest and aversion to further use of the drug. This is clearly the reverse of what is usually experienced in the early withdrawal phase from alcohol, sedatives, or narcotics, where craving is greatly increased when early physiological withdrawal effects, or even the fear of them, begin to exert their influence. During this phase, many cocaine dependent individuals will resort to other drugs, usually the sedatives and unfortunately alcohol, to induce sleep. However sleep is accomplished, it is often remarkably stuporous and reflects the physiological correlates of sleep deprivation. This hypersomnolence lasts for several days.

The second phase, withdrawal, which begins from a half a day to 4 days after the end of the crash phase, is marked by pronounced anhedonia and boredom. The withdrawal phase is a protracted period (2 to 12 weeks) of dysthymic experiences, which in a nonpsychiatric population are not severe enough to be described as a clinical mood disorder. The presence of a psychiatric disorder usually significantly intensifies these withdrawal effects on mood and cognition (Gawin and Kleber

1986). All previously pleasurable activities become uninteresting, and the individual is disinclined toward almost any purposeful behavior. Craving for cocaine is prominent, especially when environmental cues evoke vivid memories of euphoria and related pleasurable experiences. Due to the cloud of anhedonia under which the individual is functioning, these memories may be much more vivid and pleasurable than any directly accessible activity other than actual cocaine use. Relapse and resumption of habitual drug use often occur in the withdrawal phase in the presence of external cues and availability of the drug.

The last phase, extinction, begins after about the first 4 months of abstinence. In this phase, cocaine craving is episodic and typically induced only by external cues. A return to normal mood and appreciation of previously valued experiences provides some protection from temptation to relapse. Behaviorally, this is the period of extinction: the pairing of cocaine-related cues without relapse, leading to the decreased frequency and strength of craving and the temptation to use.

We can begin to analyze the implication of these three phases for treatment of dual diagnosis cases by paying close attention to the ebb and flow of cocaine craving between and within phases. It is also important to examine over time the degree to which craving is either primarily endogenous or related to external cues. In the first few hours of the crash phase, craving is endogenous and responsive to very generalized cues related to previous use. A piece of lint on the carpet, for example, may flood the individual with craving and memories of cocaine induced euphoria, causing the micro-delusion that the lint is in fact a particle of cocaine, or "rock." Such craving is very intense but typically lasts for less than 6 hours, followed by a period of noncraving and even aversion to use. High levels of craving return after a lag of up to 5 days, during the withdrawal phase. During this phase, endogenous cravings are related to anhedonia but can be resisted by most nonpsychiatric users. Cues associated with previous use may result in unexpected intense craving. Such cues include drug paraphernalia, sites where drugs were used or obtained, visits from individuals known to use drugs, mild intoxication from other substances, sexual activity, or specific events or times such as payday or the beginning of the weekend.

Of special relevance to the dual diagnosis population, pathological mood states, overload of coping skills, or other specific psychiatric symptoms or symptom clusters may also serve as cues. This cue-related craving usually lasts only a few minutes to a few hours. If the cue is internal and persistent, as with psychiatric symptoms as cues, the craving and resulting urge to use may be intolerable without outside intervention and interruption of the cue sequence.

In the extinction phase, craving can resurface without cues, as in spontaneous recovery of a conditioned response; however, such craving is greatly diminished and will quickly extinguish again if not rewarded. During extinction, the recovering cocaine addict is slowly desensitized to cues that previously elicited preparation for drug use and anticipation of euphoria. However, when external cues lead to frequent pairing of pleasurable cocaine memories with the internal sense of craving, a much more ominous situation is created. For this reason, the telling and hearing of "war stories" about drug-using situations is extremely countertherapeutic for cocaine-dependent persons.

Psychopathology can interrupt this component of the recovery process (coping with abstinence effects specific to the drug of choice) in several ways, some alluded to earlier. Psychiatric disorders may be accompanied by differences in otherwise normal physiological vulnerability to effects and/or chronic adaptation. Relative differences regarding acute effects could result either in early addiction after fewer trials and lower doses, or relative immunity from acute effects, which in turn might lead to increased dosage and frequency to reach the same level of intoxication. This has important implications for the likelihood of chronic adaptation to drug use.

Not all of these differences are physiological. For example, social detachment or deviant psychotic cognitions can render a person unable to experience cocaine's enhancement of drug effects by the social context of use and typical expectancies of its impact. Without such cognitive and socially mediated enhancements, the dose and frequency required to obtain the same high might be significantly increased. Psychopathology may increase the time needed to recover normal hedonic processes after the overload of a cocaine binge, especially in diagnoses such as depression, schizophrenia, or severe obsessive compulsive personality where pleasurable experiences are already depleted by other than stimulant addiction.

General character pathology can also interact significantly with the abstinence effects of cocaine. For example, the paranoia of the early crash phase can result in an intense refueling of the addictive cycle in an individual who is clinically paranoid, or it may result in panic or homicidal violence. These effects can also be related to the primary function played by the addiction. For instance, the extinction phase may be particularly difficult for an individual who has used the drug to provide orientation in response to deficits in the sociability and identity complex. Having become psychologically oriented toward drug-related cues and culture, these individuals will be faced with an abundance of situations that provoke craving and will face them without the buffers provided by competing interests, values, and preoccupations.

Psychopathology can result in differences in learning curves, such as the pronounced lack of response that psychopaths have to negative conditioning and punishment. A relative inability to learn from painful experiences places the psychopath (extreme antisocial personality disorder), for example, at extreme risk for relapse during the withdrawal phase, where more normal users are able to hold on to the negative consequences of relapse to help combat impulses to use. Obviously, the whole area of impulse management and control is another realm of psychological functioning directly related to surviving each of these phases of abstinence and is strongly influenced by most variants of major mental illness.

This section on the abstinence effects of a particular drug of choice does not exhaust the issues that must be investigated during treatment in this regard. For example, the entire intrapsychic and object relations dimensions must be addressed. Meissner (1986), in summarizing the role of the drug of choice in treatment, provides an overview of what must be accomplished on the intrapsychic level:

> The therapeutic work, therefore, entails a clear delineation of the projective dimension and its unequivocal connection with the patient's introjects. In cases of addiction, this would require a careful exploration in detail and understanding of the meaning of the drug, a systematic uncovering of its projective elements, and a linking of these elements with the introjects. [p. 363]

Meissner's emphasis on introjects echoes a concern with identity and its foundation, which is also informally embedded in the Anonymous traditions.

The Meaning of Denial

Denial is often discussed in both substance abuse and mental health literature. To discuss deconstruction of denial as a recovery process, we define denial here as the behavioral or verbal refusal to admit to the reality of a fact or situation regarding the self, whether or not that reality was ever consciously available to the individual. We, therefore, include conscious denial, deception, repression, and suppression. We do not, however, use the term *denial* as a catchall for any and all forms of refusal or resistance to therapy. Obviously, the concept of denial implies that the individual has sufficient data and intellectual grasp to acknowledge the thing denied were it not for the painful nature of such an admission. In short, denial is a defense and not due to limitations in perception or intellect. For example, retarded patients may exhibit denial, but more often they simply cannot make the logical connections needed to address abstract realities. Retarded patients are usually not in denial when they fail to acknowledge a subtle pattern of alcohol abuse; they just may not have yet grasped the concept. Retarded patients are in denial when they refuse to accept that what they have in their hands is a bottle of beer.

The symptoms held most in common between addiction and mental illness are various expressions of impaired judgment, most often resulting from denial. Gross denial, often a symptom of severe mental illness, indicates an impaired ability to tolerate affects and to cope effectively with reality. Denial is more central to the etiology of addiction and is not merely symptomatic of its severe levels. Addiction has often been called a disease of denial, but to say that denial is its cause is more the case of a description posing as an explanation than to say that addiction is a kind of repetition. Chapter 3 discusses the function of repetition and what is repeated in substance abuse when repetition is the primary function served by the addiction in the individual's life. Similarly, in discussing denial, we must discuss what is denied and why.

Linked with denial is the more global concept of narcissism, which denotes all of our feelings and values related to the self. Healthy narcissism consists of a set of cognitive and emotional biases in relationship to new information that supports a sense of self-esteem, competence, and worthiness without grossly compromising information about the self from the external world. However, as we see in Chapter 2 on the self-protective mechanisms in normal individuals, comparing these to the relative absence of such mechanisms in depressed persons, even healthy narcissism involves some distortion of experience. Pathological narcissism, however, exists when these biases are pronounced, usually due to basic feelings of low self-esteem or unworthiness, or from overprotection from or overexposure to frustration or criticism during infancy and childhood. One way to investigate narcissism as it exists in all of us, and more strongly in the addicted population, is to investigate the narcissistic disorders, especially personality disorders.

Psychiatrist and psychoanalyst Leon Wurmser (1984, 1985, 1987, 1990) has considerably extended our understanding of denial in substance abuse. He identifies shame, envy and spite, guilt, and rage as the central affects involved in the formation and maintenance of pathological narcissism and the addictions. Within this context, substance abuse can be seen as what Wurmser calls a "pharmacologically induced denial of affect" (1984 p. 44). Wurmser writes of the withering away of imagination, affectively based insight, and genuine empathy in substance abusers and others with severe neuroses:

> I believe that our patients give up this tool towards themselves; they cannot allow to feel themselves into their own affective world, and hence toward others, out of devastating anxiety. This giving up is denial. Moreover, they pick up external means—the pharmacon—to cement such denial. The defenses of denial and externalization bring about the characteristic "Verblendung," the self deception and blinding. They however, "learned" from their parents how and why not to use "empathy into feelings," not to accept emotions and conflicts, and how to cover them up. The sharing of such crucial defenses as a most prominent part of life style may be one of the most convincingly solid bridges between individual and family. [p. 44]

The process of learning denial in the family context, of course, begins in childhood. Erik Erikson's (1978) stages of development are useful in attempting to elucidate this process. They are expressed as bipolar opposite outcomes to the predictable challenges posed to the individual by the combination of emerging psychobiological potentials and ever increasing external societal expectations. The stages in Erikson's system of key importance to understanding substance abuse take place in early childhood (18 months to 4 years), childhood (4 years to school entry), and adolescence. Early childhood presents the ego crisis of autonomy versus shame and doubt, which if adequately resolved will result in the development of the ego strength of will. Childhood presents the ego crisis of initiative versus guilt, and provides the opportunity to develop purpose.

Adolescence resurrects all of the earlier crises with the demand either to form a sense of identity or to fragment and wallow in role confusion and identity fragmentation. If properly transversed, adolescence results in the ego strength of fidelity in regard to one's self, one's values, and a primary reference group. Clinically, we often find in substance abusers and the addicted, other prominent psychopathology notwithstanding, the atrophy of these three ego strengths: will, purpose, and fidelity to self, others, and values. We also see the origin of substance abuse occurring usually in the period of adolescence and find that our patients are permanently stuck in this period in terms of developmental issues and personal preoccupations, even after years of abstinence.

Given the family dynamics to which Wurmser alludes, the chance of transversing Erikson's developmental gauntlets unscathed is very slim indeed in families where addiction is already established. The parents not only demonstrate denial and avoidance of these developmental tasks and related affects in their own lives, but they also inadvertently or consciously oversensitize the child to the dangers of these tasks, or otherwise intrude upon the child (usually with negative consequences) in the midst of his or her own tenuous coping with some specific aspect of a developmental crisis. This is done through the display of the parent's own inappropriate or disproportionate affect, or by the actual modeling of denial or avoidance of relevant affect. In many cases there is also a direct or implied disapproval and rejection of the child at exactly those moments when partial aspects of the crisis situation (and therefore of its potential resolution) are being enacted or emotionally expressed by the child. Such parents will stimulate more shame and guilt during the childhood eras of their offspring and will pass on fewer adaptive mechanisms for dealing with these affects. Later, attempts at identity consolidation will be covertly undermined or actively sabotaged, sometimes by the parents' requirement that the corresponding ego strengths (will, purpose, and fidelity) be established, or even perfected prematurely, and that such pseudo-ego strengths serve the purposes of the parent. Combined with these dynamics of family pathology are innate predispositions toward poor affect tolerance or other symptom complexes that the child may share with the parents due to biological factors or by reasons of family culture.

The denial of anxiety and affect prevents in the adult what Wurmser has called a narcissistic crisis. We can see in the above analysis that at least three (and sometimes more) earlier narcissistic crises are telescoped, or re-experienced, almost holographically within the addict's adult narcissistic crisis. In a narcissistic crisis the denied and defended affects, realizations, and negative fantasies from adult life and earlier eras of failed development return at least partially to consciousness. These denied experiences surface amplified and without effective counterbalancing controls or buffering distractions. If the crisis is truly catastrophic, the usual structural divisions of the psyche (id, ego, superego) become permeable, with the ego left in shards, fragments of consciousness striving to pull things together. The resulting sense of collapse and impending doom is itself a severe narcissistic injury accompanied by shame, guilt, and fragmentation. There is an accompanied disorder in the sense of time, an experience of the eerie, or other forms of depersonalization. In the light of the childhood precursors to the adult narcissistic crisis, a fitting childhood equivalent is found in the nursery rhyme, "Humpty Dumpty sat on a wall, Humpty Dumpty had a great fall . . .", which combines grandiose and self-centered claims to supremacy (sitting above others in regal command; historically the character in the rhyme referred to a king) juxtaposed with images of extreme vulnerability and fragmentation. A review of Table 4–5, which outlines the characteristics of projective narratives produced by substance abusers who are prone to failures in self-regulation, will provide the reader with an adequate phenomenological description of the world view of persons vulnerable to narcissistic crisis.

Wurmser (1985) has outlined how adult attempts to avoid such a crisis can cascade into a spiralling cycle based on denial, reparation, and undoing:

> The sequence here is therefore: (a) hurt by, or fear of, rejection or shame; (b) anger about, and revolt against, such weakness; (c) such manifest rebellion supported by a triple denial: that those feelings of hurt mean anything: that time has any relevance and sway; and that the act of drug taking, dealing, law breaking, and breaking of all promises and commitments would have any long range consequences; parallel with the triple denial there are two events one cannot easily subsume under denial but are of very great importance at this point: the pharmacogenic suppression or blocking of disturbing affects, and the alteration of time experience; (d) the "crash" thereafter in form of contrition and remorse—a reassertion of the denied superego in form of massive shame and guilt; followed (e) by acts of reparation, expiation, and grandiose fantasies undoing the perceived flaws. [p. 93]

The central role of the superego in Wurmser's description of the substance abuser is counterintuitive for those who are not personally or clinically familiar with the chemically dependent. The stereotype of the addict as a devotee of pleasure or id experiences is more familiar. Even the descriptions in this chapter emphasize the ego weakness of the addict. This is an especially difficult trap to avoid when coexistent psychopathology makes the assessment of these deficits, such as those identified as symptom complexes supported by addictive functions, fairly straightforward. The same persistent messages are found in AA or NA groups, where it is not unusual to hear "Keep the lid on the id," and where almost any model that emphasizes the deficits of the dependent person are readily accepted. If Wurmser is correct, and the majority of clinical evidence seems to be on his side, inherent limitations in ego strength or the weakening of the ego by intense drives or impulses are no more important to understanding addiction than are the debilitating effects of an overinvested and primitive superego. The use of such mottos as "Just say no" shows how the dominance of the harsh, implacable, primitive superego aggression toward the addicted individual remains ubiquitous. When the addict is not castigating or punishing him- or herself, treatment personnel, correctional environments, media messages, or self-help groups are throwing the cheap and easy first stones of moral condemnation (e.g., the substitution of a slogan campaign for effective and available treatment) or dispensing actual punishment.

What is most easily observable in the addict, however, is usually not the sequence of emotions and self-perceptions described in the above quotation by Wurmser, whose work is based on hundreds of analytic hours with each patient. Instead, affects are submerged for most periods of the individual's life, and when they finally are expressed, they appear as impulsive outbursts of disproportionate or inappropriate affect accompanied by destructive or relatively chaotic behavior. What is most easily observable is the addicts' denial of consequences and their preoccupation and single-minded focus on procuring the drug of choice and related pleasures while avoiding any commitment or circumstances that would curtail this indulgence. Again, Wurmser has provided an invaluable insight into the meaning of this behavior, by identifying the phobic core of addiction. The addict's search for the external solution or substance and flight from containment and constraint are viewed as the antithesis of the phobic's (especially the claustrophobic's) flight from specific situations or objects. Unconsciously, the claustrophobic fears being contained because something internal cannot be avoided and may surface as overwhelming and destructive to self and others. "Dependency, superego strictures, and claustrum form one terrifying equation" (Wurmser 1985, p. 94).

The phobic core discussed by Wurmser is probably an adaptive and defensive response to the incorporation of the actual experiential content of the early dyadic interaction between caregiver and child, specifically the affectively laden content. As described by Wilson and Malatesta (1989) and discussed in Chapter 3 of this book, these basic interaction templates, which contain an overwhelming (usually negative) affective component, and related self-representations are incorporated in the emerging self prior to the development of verbal skills. The template is incorporated into, or shapes, the basic affective center of the person: the addictive personality core. This addictive core (an internalized, interpersonal schema combined with an overwhelming primary affect) can be seen as the precursor to Wurmser's phobic core. Following Wilson's description of pathological personality organization as consisting of instability between epigenetic levels of organization, the phobic core may emerge from the even more primitive addictive core, which remains as an underlying influence on behavior during moments of regression.

Meissner's (1986) description of paranoid process and projective mechanisms in addiction can be applied as a partial explanatory bridge between Wilson's internal, infantile world of the addictive core and the resulting core phobic defenses and split identity described by Wurmser. Paranoid process and projection explain how substitute coping behaviors in adulthood, such as drug addiction, serve to fend off, and yet eventually precipitate, a narcissistic crisis ultimately caused by childhood and infantile deficits. The physiological effects and drug ingestion scenario (the favored route of administration, interpersonal circumstances, etc.) of the drug of choice provide some sense of increased cohesion, soothing comfort, or supportive stimulation to the user. These experiences have an isomorphic (same form) resonance with early, preverbal symbiotic experiences. That is to say, drugs will be used to the end of sharing states with others, transforming states, or creating states that are complementary to those perceived in early internal or external objects. Most typically, the user unconsciously projects onto the substance the rekindled experience of the omnipotence of primary narcissism, the primitive awe of the parent, and the adoration of the soothing object. The user re-owns these qualities by ingesting the drug. Negative aspects of the parent–infant dyad are projected outside this isolated field of the self-drug dyad, that is, into the environment and onto other persons. These negative projections are viewed as haunting the environment and others and are experienced as in the self only with the loss of the drug effect. The drug becomes the external magical agent that wards off the internalizing of these demons.

Most of these elements of core personality functioning are preverbally encoded within the personality structure and are not available to adult conscious introspection. They do, however, result in repetitive experiences and self-talk, or scripts that guide behavior and provide the context of ongoing experience. The paragraph that follows is the conscious translation of the typical unconscious script of the addict. Any one aspect of this script might be consciously available and overtly stated by the patient, but in most cases, the majority of this material would be either preconscious or unavailable to conscious reflection. The reader should go over the paragraph several times ignoring the bold type at first reading (which provides explanatory concepts and the authors with whom they are most associated for the immediately preceding self-talk) before a reading that incorporates this more abstract didactic material.

In contact with a significant other on whom I depend and from whom I am only partially and intermittently separated, I am overwhelmed by a negative emotion or foreboding sense of tension (**the fear, sadness, anxiety, obliteration of the self through overstimulation, abandonment etc., of Wilson and Malatesta's addictive core**). I should not be this way and I am ashamed, guilty, and bad (**persecutory superego fragment leading to Wurmser's split identity, may be attached to a stranger introject – J. Reid Meloy, see Chapter 8 – leading to the psychopathic variant of split-identity**). I will panic and fragment, if I fail to avoid being captured in a space or interaction where this overwhelming situation will occur (**Wurmser's phobic core**). I cannot fully accept my condition and still survive (**denial**). Some external substances and situations (**drug use and contexts**) can magically transform me, or create charmed conditions where I am safe. I am drawn toward, and seek out, these substances and situations. I must submit to them in order to secure my escape into safety (**Meissner's paranoid-projective process, which is the opponent process to phobic dynamics, and which projects dominance/submission as an aspect of relationship to the drug of choice**). This quest results in my going through many changes (**moving through the phenomenal cycles of Inflation, Depletion, and Detachment of the addictive cycle**) until the dreaded overwhelming affective situation is realized and I am finally punished as I deserve (**Wurmser's narcissistic crisis**).

Extremes in Split Identity

A.M. is an African-American male in his forties, who has cycled in and out of psychiatric institutions for over 15 years. Although a medical school graduate, he has never been able to function for any length of time as a physician. Due to his father's career as an officer in the army, A.M. spent his early years in Japan, Germany, and throughout the United States. A.M. always felt closer to his mother and was convinced that he could never win the approval of his father, who favored A.M.'s older brother. A.M.'s first hospitalization occurred during his second year of medical school. He had snorted cocaine continuously in order to study for an important exam and became manic and delusional. Other manic episodes and hospitalizations followed, often precipitated or exacerbated by stressors such as breakups with his girlfriend or the suicide of his brother. Successful inpatient stabilization, treatment, and outplacement were inevitably followed by medical noncompliance, a manic episode, and hospitalization. Most often the manic episode was precipitated by excessive cocaine abuse.

A.M.'s extreme alternations in mood and energy level were paralleled by his vacillations in identification with various dichotomous parental introjects. His mother was viewed as soft, quiet, reassuring, caring, and seductive. His father, conversely, was perceived as hard, macho, rejecting, restless, and intellectual. His father was a light-skinned black who listened to country and western music and voted Republican; his mother was dark-skinned and held more liberal views. These polarized representations were closely entwined with A.M.'s own sense of gender and racial identity, sexuality, and social orientation.

A.M. recalled a memory of returning home after a hospitalization. He was sitting on his bed when his mother entered the room in her slip and whispered, "Let's do it again." A.M. was positive that he had been seduced by his mother previously and that she was again making advances. His fantasied oedipal victory induced feelings of triumph and guilt as well as fear of retaliation from his father. A.M. often felt trapped in a jumble of "mixed messages" from his parents, but especially from his mother. He viewed her as encouraging closeness or intimacy and then cruelly setting limits. Unfortunately, A.M.'s various identifications were often acted upon. In one instance, after alcohol and cocaine abuse, he interpreted an inadvertent touch from another physician as a homosexual advance and threatened the co-worker with a scalpel. Another hospitalization occurred after he began masturbating in front of his mother. His most recent hospitalization took place after he attacked and struck down his father.

Alterations in identifications and projections were repeated in the transference. These took the form primarily of the patient perceiving extremes in acceptance or rejection from the therapist related to either his sexual self (mother) or his intellectual self (father). The sexual aspects of this split were acted on outside of the therapy. His confusion around sexuality and gender issues was manifest in his attraction to and sexual encounters with transvestites, whom he simultaneously denied and accepted as males. He defined himself at various points in the therapy as heterosexual, homosexual, and bisexual. Drugs were frequently employed to facilitate liaisons with other males. After such experiences he often felt guilty and ashamed and would actively seek assurance regarding his masculinity. He reported dreams of being a hermaphrodite and delusions, when entering a manic phase, of having invisible female organs, after he read a warning on his lithium bottle regarding pregnancy.

A.M. was also intensely ambivalent about racial identity and skin color, alternating between feeling not "black" enough and not "white" enough. In the 1960s, he was the head of the Black Student Union at his school and he pictured himself as a black militant. He reported to his white male therapist, "Originally I wanted to help black people by becoming a doctor, but now I don't care. Black people are sick." Later, he related feeling crushed and reduced to nothing when his long-term relationship with a black female ended after she began dating a white male. His confusions around racial identity were mirrored by his religious conversions. He converted from Catholicism to Islam, but was soon disenchanted and eager to become Buddhist.

Unfortunately, A.M. tended to try on different therapies and therapists in a similar fashion and would abandon one when his shame, guilt, depression, and anger emerged in the relationship. In therapy he was acutely sensitive to how he imagined he was perceived by the therapist and tended to miss sessions when he felt like the therapist was "seeing through me" or "your eyes are too piercing" or "you're getting me to expose myself." Although A.M. made superficial progress in therapy, he tended to cloud the emotional significance of his insights with high energy and rambling monologues. Interpretations were frequently brushed aside or embraced with ingenuous enthusiasm. As his defenses were gradually broached, he became increasingly sullen and depressed. He felt that no one, especially his therapist, could accept such a morose side to his personality.

Effective interpretation of these transferences was complicated by the lack of a unified treatment approach within the institution. A.M. was successful in replicating the mixed messages of his family through the contradictory reactions he evoked from the various members of his treatment team. Given the medical model of the institution, his physician–patient status, and the unexamined racial and sexual dynamics of the staff, his unrelenting onslaught of projections and identifications proved impossible to contain. When confronted with his relapse to cocaine and alcohol use, he threatened to leave the hospital against medical advice, buy a gun, and kill himself in order to join his dead brother. A few days later, he successfully bolted from the ward but returned in a matter of hours, depressed and humiliated like a child who threatens to run away but only walks around the block. With this final humiliation, his tolerance for therapy, and for the therapist who knew so many of his contradictory selves, quickly dwindled. After approximately 18 months of therapy sessions twice per week, A.M. suddenly left his therapist a telephone message that was eloquent in its self contradiction: "I will not be in therapy anymore, because I have a new therapist."

Identity as Touchstone

Prior to the invention of specific chemical assay techniques, the purity of various metals was tested by the use of a touchstone. A hard black stone such as jasper was ground on one side to make a striking surface. When various metals were scratched against this surface, the resulting mark could be compared to marks made by an object of known purity, thus providing a reliable and fairly objective estimate of the unknown metal's identity and worth. The word *touchstone* now has the general meaning of a criterion or standard, especially of purity or worth. The touchstone of dual diagnosis work, the alchemist's standard, is the broad surface of identity issues that emerge while working with these patients. How a given intervention influences identity issues, especially over time, will be the most useful criterion for weighing its utility and impact.

Adolescence is the developmental era defined largely by identity issues and may result in an identity crisis. It is also the era that has the most obvious reverberations with the issues that appear most often in dual diagnosis work (Weider and Kaplan 1969). Working with dual diagnosis patients requires an ability to tolerate working with these issues, without regard to the age or apparent adult accomplishments of the patient. Although addictions are frequently related to infant and childhood developmental problems, these often do not show their full impact until the onset of adolescence, where a cumulative, snowballing effect can change what appeared to be slightly quirky children into teenage monsters. In adolescence, earlier childhood concerns regarding shame, humiliation, fear, and uncontrollable rage are reactivated in the adolescent's need to redefine the self in the context of the adolescent crisis. This crisis is due to the developmental revolution in body, mind, and social role, which marks the adolescent period. The powers of the adult body emerge precipitously, almost reaching their zenith at their first appearance. These powers include the new potential for physical force—including deadly force—and reproductive sexuality. Although these new powers of sexual pleasure, reproductive capacity, and effective violence take on different priorities for males and females, both genders darkly perceive that these forces contain an ominous threat of supplanting their parents and a transforming promise of liberation from childhood status.

At the same time a revolution in intellectual and cognitive abilities occurs. Emotional states become more intense and motivate behavior for longer periods. Changes in neural organization provide the basis for cognitive skills, which allow for greater reach and range of abstract thinking. Simultaneously, abilities that rest on experience, such as the ability to correctly discriminate appropriate contexts for ideas and the ability to achieve practical applications, remain relatively incipient. The social requirement of coming to terms with both the expectations of heterosexual adjustment and preliminary decisions about the world of work and responsibility is imposed with greater vigor from parents and teachers, who have their own anxieties to contend with related to the responsibility of helping the adolescent to channel and control these emerging powers.

Under unfavorable circumstances, the result of all these changes and stressors is the adolescent identity crisis. So far, this crisis is examined only in regard to internal and external responses to emerging adult characteristics. Other intrapsychic and interpersonal aspects of this process are just as crucial. One important change is a shift of the need of parents as self-objects to the need for peers to serve the same purpose. The result can be a painful teeter-totter between engagement and enmeshment, seduction and rejection, and the stimulation of jealousy and envy. All of this necessarily involves interpersonal triangles that may at any given moment involve parents, peers, adults outside the family, activities, and drugs in a dance of loyalties, conflicts, and powerful emotions. The parents may respond to all of this with any one of a full range of reactions that will either ameliorate or irritate the situation.

The adolescent situation that will usually result in a crisis of some degree is well described by Miriam Elson (1984), from a ego-psychological perspective:

> There is a vital, phase-appropriate thrust toward new self-objects in peers, cult heroes, and ideologies. The world of thought and the strength that lies in the mind become increasingly the focus of mastery and growth for some adolescents; for others, the focus is on the body strength and prowess in athletics. For still others, both worlds are available. There appears a simultaneous intensifying and loosening of the ties to primary selfobjects. Parents are put on hold, needed yet resisted. Their opinions and judgments are sought after, but their suggestions may be abjured even when they coincide with and confirm the adolescent's deeply cherished longings. They are tested against the values and standards of selfobject peers, or older selfobject mentors, which in turn must be vigorously argued with parents. The process attests to the intense scrutiny to which the adolescent subjects external and inner world in the struggle for confirmation of the self as center of perception and initiative.
>
> There can be a refreshing and vigorous increase in stream of ideas between the generations as the adolescent confronts cognitively and affectively, as if for the first time, those values, ideals, and goals that had earlier been laid down as psychic structure. Some they will jettison, others they will modify, and still others they will now include more firmly and enduring as *their* values, *their* ideals, and *their* goals. [p. 93]

Often when recovery begins in adult substance abusers, adolescent issues again become prominent. In part this apparent regression is due to the developmental failures and fixations discussed previously and to the opportunities and age-appropriate experiences that were displaced during adolescence and early adulthood by involvement in drug use, or by the need to cope with family co-dependency issues, in the case of transgenerational addictions. Just as in the adolescent crisis, recovery for the dual diagnosis patient results in increased biological vigor, a new sense of psychological clarity and emotional immediacy, the need for identity consolidation, and the need to assert one's privileges and prerogatives. Simultaneously, for the adolescent, and for the dual diagnosis patient in early recovery, these needs for assertion are met by increased expectations and limit setting from society and authority figures. Given these parallels, understanding the dynamics of normal and complicated adolescent development will provide valuable insight into the problems facing many dual diagnosis patients.

The difference found in the dual diagnosis patient from the healthy pattern of adolescence described above is that the patient (without regard to age or apparent level of functioning) has not adopted parental values, ideals, and goals in a manner that is relatively conflict free within the context of a self-regulating psychic structure *prior* to the adolescent crisis. Instead, as Wurmser has illuminated, the substance abuser with significant psychopathology has incorporated a painful relationship with primitive, harsh super-ego elements that turns goals, ideals, and values into harpies. When this is not the case in terms of surface behavior, Winnicott's (1960) concept of the false self is a useful way of understanding the bland affective and cognitive picture alternating with substance abuse and acting out that is a frequent alternative pattern in adolescents and in dual diagnosis cases. A grandiose archaic sense of self is present, but the harsh superego contents and the inability to integrate this persecuted grandiose self result in a horizontal split, a repression of the grandiose self and its primitive emotional contents. There is great denial of affect and conflict in emotionally arousing situations. This denial is maintained until the individual is emotionally overwhelmed and resorts to drug use or deteriorates to the point of having manifest symptoms of psychopathology. Both the resulting addiction, psychiatric condition, and dependence on institutions or other caretakers adds to the narcissistic wound (of guilt and shame) that remains unhealed from Erikson's early childhood and childhood phases.

The emphasis on identity stressed here is already reflected in the most common intervention in alcoholism and substance abuse treatment: the Anonymous traditions of self-help groups. Carole Cain (1991) has described from a psychological and anthropological perspective how Alcoholics Anonymous (AA) uses a body of culturally shared knowledge and practices to shape the identity of its members. She describes how personal stories, told and heard within the confessional atmosphere of the AA meeting, are used to redefine an individual's understanding of his or her self and the events that brought them to this point in life. These personal stories become the cultural vehicle for identity acquisition. Cain sees the process of identity acquisition as following the identity diffusion that takes place as the alcoholic approaches hitting bottom. The individual does not see him- or herself as an alcoholic but begins to know that he or she is not like others. The usual answers to the question Who am I? begin to work less and less well due to the role erosion caused by alcoholic dysfunction. Hitting bottom allows the individual to give up rigidly held beliefs about the self that perpetuate the addictive cycle. Hitting bottom overcomes denial, even if temporarily. Identity diffusion begins to occur; increasingly, the old self-definitions are not used to explain or rationalize behavior.

Cain describes the use of the personal story told in AA meetings as the mechanism by which a new sense of self emerges and is consolidated over time by the ritual retelling of the story. Upon each retelling the novice incorporates more of the traditional aspects of the personal story as a cultural genre containing a theory of alcoholism and recovery, and an understanding of relapses and their prevention. She also demonstrates convincingly how written versions of the personal story contain phrases (such as "I later understood," "like other alcoholics," etc.) which indicate that significant cognitive reframing of past experiences is done through the medium of the personal story. This process involves both a reinterpretation of personal history and a refining and consolidation of new aspects of the identity as a recovering alcoholic.

A similar transformation must take place in the dual diagnosis patient. The individual must relinquish the identity of being a chronic patient, "bizarre," a drug fiend, and such, and accept an identity based on a fairly detailed understanding of the fact that he or she is involved in a process of recovery from interacting mental and substance use disorders. The central identification is with the process of recovery, not with the pathology, just as in AA the central identity encouraged is "I am a nondrinking alcoholic who is working my program."

The basic self-other representations discussed earlier make such a transition in identity unlikely without extensive therapeutic intervention. The addictive cycle must be interrupted, denial must be confronted and minimized, older identifications must be acknowledged as previously operative and then relinquished. The patient must begin to feel worthy of recovery before the vast gap between cognitive understanding of new identifications and their incorporation on the affective level can be bridged. One important bridge in this process is provided by therapists, counselors, and "alumni" patients who have a history of successful recovery from disorders themselves. Although having had some form of psychopathology or addiction is not in itself a prerequisite for working with dual diagnosis patients, an understanding through personal experience of the recovery process can be a useful advantage in addition to the role modeling aspect provided to patients or treatment staff in recovery.

Family Dynamics and Split Identity

Eve W. is a 31-year-old elementary schoolteacher with a history of heroin dependence spanning her 25th through 28th years and intermittent use of heroin beginning at age 18. A mother of two children (6 and 2 years old), she is seeking help because her recent relapse to daily alcohol abuse has resulted in her husband, Sidney, insisting on her entering treatment under threat of divorce. They have been married for about two years; Sidney is not the father of either of her children, although she was pregnant with the younger child during their courtship.

Sidney, Eve believes, is not aware of her history of heroin use, to which she has also returned on an episodic basis. By the patient's report the marriage has accounted for her ability to decrease heroin use to only very occasional slips, until the 6-month period prior to the present treatment. In addition to her addictive disorder, Eve has many of the symptoms of borderline personality disorder and some of the features of bipolar disorder. She was referred to the dual diagnosis specialist at a substance abuse treatment facility after her second relapse while in outpatient treatment, and the program psychiatrist's refusal to prescribe for her emotional symptoms until she is completely abstinent from drugs and alcohol.

Unlike many other opiate-dependent individuals, Eve has never been involved in a life of crime to support her drug habit, which has always remained at under fifty dollars per day, with a quantity of alcohol costing less than five dollars per day. Her drug "friendships" with men, an ability to maintain jobs under the protection of people who have accepted her extreme dependency, as well as significant financial gifts from her maternal aunt have been adequate to fund her habit. Although she has been in two treatments for heroin abuse of short duration and was maintained on methadone about six months, she has had fewer than five weeks of total drug and alcohol sobriety since her addiction began. These were the first five weeks of her marriage.

Cognitive deficits were notable in the initial clinical interview even without the benefit of formal psychological testing. Her middle-class job, dress, and vocabulary no longer effectively concealed her distress and desperation. Her work in the elementary school setting had deteriorated to the point that her supervisor had assigned her to a class for the youngest students with severe learning problems. She was, in effect, functioning more as a baby sitter or teacher's assistant than as the kind of competent teacher that would be consistent with her education, which was achieved despite her alcohol abuse, limited family support, and chaotic interpersonal relationships during her college years.

In addition to obvious cognitive deficits secondary to drug use, alcoholism, and some residual effects from a severe infection contracted from an injection with a dirty needle, Eve's affective symptoms are dramatic. She had taken to verbally attacking her husband, a shy retiring man, without provocation, often demanding that he take her to expensive restaurants or shops that the couple cannot afford, although they live in her mother's home, due to the drain that her drinking and continued drug dabbling has placed on the family budget. In family assessment sessions, Sidney recognizes that her behavior has always been erratic but feels that both the emotional symptoms and her alcohol use significantly increased approximately a year before the current treatment. The continued use of heroin was the only major secret she has kept from her husband. It was fairly reliably established from individual sessions that the heroin she has taken over the past several months has been almost in token doses with no increase of dosage over time, despite clear availability for larger and more frequent doses.

In individual sessions, Eve reveals that her biological father, a bitter alcoholic and drug addict, was found mysteriously murdered due to a drug deal gone sour. She also recounts how her elderly uncle, whom she considered her emotional father, died of a heart attack while she was away at college. Her retelling of the event was enough to render her sobbing and unable to speak for the remaining 15 minutes of the session. His death had caused her to spend several weeks in a depressed stupor, punctuated with drinking binges. This was interrupted only when she left school for the remainder of the semester to spend the time grieving with and "helping" her widowed aunt. Although she has lived with her mother since her return from college, their relationship remains shallow and emotionally detached when compared to feelings for her grandmother who resides in a nearby town.

At the patient's lead, many of the following sessions were spent talking about her relationship to the lost uncle. Although she became increasingly aware that her husband's workaholic pattern and increased interest in a bowling league have led to some resentment on her part, she was not aware of the connection between these developments and her increased reliance on alcohol and heroin. Eventually, Eve was able to entertain fantasies about the loss of her husband to either death or divorce. She imagined that her life would be totally out of control and that she would lose her children and her job. She was unable to imagine herself exercising the strengths that had enabled her to achieve an education and to cope (albeit through drug use) with other traumatic losses. After several sessions examining her feeling of total dependency on Sidney, she discussed her concern about his developing a resentment toward their younger child. She admits to interpreting his absence from the home to his feelings about this child more than to the conflicts that her emotional outbursts may have generated. Eventually, she was able to link these thoughts and feelings to her sense of having been rejected and treated like a stranger by her biological father, who she believed suspected that she was not in fact his child.

In addition to the individual work, the marriage—the key to her tenuous sobriety and to her relapses—required continual shoring up. With clarification of his passive role in the family, Sidney began to assert himself more in the home situation and make plans for the nuclear family to move from the mother's house. He was able to relinquish the time he previously spent in relatively unprofitable part-time work and in unrewarding recreational activities without Eve. His ability to verbalize his gratitude to Eve for providing him with a family to care for was reassuring to her and also allowed him to deal more directly with the feelings of inadequacy that had prevented him from venturing further in life emotionally or professionally.

At the end of sessions with the dual diagnosis specialist, Eve was still considered at risk for relapse, but she had successfully integrated self-help activities in her recovery plan and was able to tolerate group therapy treatments with another therapist at the substance abuse center, who supplemented her group treatment with individual booster sessions twice per month.

WHY AA WORKS

The emphasis on identity and identity change provides the theoretical groundwork for understanding the success of Alcoholics Anonymous and other recovery self-help groups. We referred earlier to the problem of the two cultures in dual diagnosis work. These cultures differ significantly in their understanding and endorsement of AA. For purposes of clarification here, we exaggerate their differences and minimize their overlap in membership. On the one extreme is what we refer to as the mental health tradition community, which consists primarily of professionals from various disciplines who gain most of their knowledge from books, formal clinical training, research, and clinical practice. This community tends to see the culmination of treatment activities in the formulation of viable theories and empirical validation of gradual improvements in treatment technique based on these theories. On the other extreme is what for convenience we call the recovery tradition community, which consists largely of paraprofessional workers in substance abuse treatment and other individuals in recovery. The knowledge base of this community begins with personal experience of recovery and relies less on theories and empirical validation than on application of traditions and practices that have been validated by the recovery community as a whole. One aspect of this traditional knowledge base has been the belief that to divest oneself somewhat of professional discipline identifications is helpful, and perhaps necessary, to become fully engaged in recovery activities, either for oneself or for the benefit of others. To some extent this often has been interpreted to mean that there is a desirable distance for the recovery worker from professional procedures, practices, and beliefs, even when that worker is professionally trained.

Motivation for entering the treatment arena also tends to vary immensely between these two groups of workers. The mental health tradition community still remains motivated to work with substance abuse patients primarily out of scholarly, scientific, and altruistic motives. The motives of persons in recovery who enter the treatment field are more often ethical, evangelical, and above all practical. They often hope to spread the benefits of sobriety and, thereby, to strengthen their own recovery.

Career advancement is often an area of shared motivation and conflicting interest between these two communities, since individuals in both groups feel themselves uniquely qualified to provide treatment or to direct treatment enterprises. However, even this area of shared motivation is often viewed quite differently. Entry into substance abuse work, until very recently, was a step often taken at the beginning of a career for a mental health professional in a public setting. The eventual goal of these professionals was often to leave this setting and to gain access to the more prestigious, lucrative, and interesting neurotic client in a private setting. Often professionals were willing to relegate many of their substance abuse patients to the category of intractable pathology or treatment failures and were able to await the millennium of more effective psychological intervention strategies, increased social justice, or chemical antidotes to addictions. In contrast, paraprofessionals often entered substance abuse work after a tortuous climb involving personal recovery, de-centering emphasis from the self, and a passionate desire to help others with a similar problem. They are more often drawn to the most needy and down-and-out addicts or drunks, and (unless there is other significant psychopathology) they may be more able to contain countertransference responses with these individuals because of their basic conscious affirmation of connectedness and similarity to them.

Although these two communities can be contrasted in terms of degree of training, professionalization, and personal motives, perhaps the greatest difference between them is in regard to philosophy of the nature of addiction and the basis of recovery. These differences have become obscured to a large degree with the capitulation of medical practitioners to the practical advantages of incorporating AA and NA within a medical model. Despite shared interests in terms of public policy, patient recruitment, program management and operations, these two philosophical traditions, roughly dividing the two communities described here, are still largely intact and remain essentially incompatible ways of viewing addiction.

Even when these cultures agree on a specific course of action, it is often for divergent reasons and purposes. For instance, both mental health and recovery communities have emphasized the importance of group work with substance abusers in recent decades, with the mental health community being somewhat of a latecomer to this position. The mental health community stresses the importance of social networking and the effective use of professional resources in its emphasis on group methods. Within the recovery model the emphasis has always been on group work, because of the view that connection with others is essentially what supports the addiction and that it can break the addiction through the Twelve Step process.

It is not surprising, given these differences in origin, that rarely do these two traditions of training and practice have precisely the same meaning when using the same terms to describe addiction or recovery. For example, the term *denial* is used in both groups. The mental health tradition community often emphasizes what is repressed, whereas the recovery tradition emphasizes what is suppressed and avoided. The parallel exists in terms of treatment emphasis. The mental health tradition tended to emphasize specific ego deficits whereas the recovery tradition emphasized a basic disturbance in the entire pattern of personality and life. Complete repression is not an acceptable model of psychological functioning within the philosophy of the self incorporated in the AA/NA tradition. There must always be some element of awareness for there to be a valid sense of personal responsibility, or at least one that can be taken seriously by modern standards. This might have been otherwise if the Anonymous traditions had grown out of the Catholic Christian tradition. The emphasis on original sin and mediated relationships with the Divine might have allowed for responsibility for events totally outside of consciousness or awareness, for example, prehistorically in the fall, before the individual is even on the scene. In the Protestant tradition, however, the emphasis is on the relationship of the individual with God and of the ultimate free will of the soul.

Another primary difference in the two traditions is the view of personal agency. The mental health tradition tends to view the person as determined and mechanistic, with an emphasis on the analysis of the relationship between structure and function within the mechanism. The recovery tradition sees the individual as a nonreducible agent in the world and does not need to account for how that person has been determined, hemmed in, or structured in a certain way by mechanisms. All of these differences between the two cultures can be see in their different understandings of the recovery movement and the different values they have placed on AA or NA activities.

Ernest Kurtz (1979, 1982) attempted to provide historical and philosophical connections and implications that make Alcoholics Anonymous successes and limitations more understandable to those outside of that tradition. Kurtz asserts that AA is not generally accorded intellectual respectability because its core view of reality is based on essential limitation and on mutuality as opposed to the

Enlightenment insistence on objectivity and universality. He links AA to the same modernist bias that has impeded the serious acceptance of existential philosophies in America. Essentially, he argues that it is their overarching concern with the nature of human freedom that most deeply unites AA as a discipline of recovery and existentialism as a philosophy. Both movements are rooted in an affirmation of the reality, significance, and contingency or limitation of human freedom.

A brief outline of the history of AA shows its connection to existential philosophy and pre-Enlightenment views of the self. In late 1934, Edwin Thatcher approached William Griffith Wilson (Bill W.) with a message of salvation as preached by the Oxford Group. Thatcher had been led into recovery from alcoholism by a member of that group, who had himself been treated by Carl Jung. Jungian insight and emphasis filtered through the tinted glasses of a conversion experience and infused Thatcher's presentation when he told the story of his cure to Bill W. During his fourth hospitalization, Bill W. had a spiritual experience that he was able to grasp by combining his understanding of Jung with his readings of William James. In May 1935, he traveled to Akron, Ohio, on business and called Dr. Robert Holbrook Smith, a fellow addict associated with the Oxford Group, in the attempt to fend off overwhelming urges to use alcohol through "kinship in common suffering." Smith attained sobriety in the following month, an event that marked the birth of AA. Within two years, AA had split from the Oxford Group over the matter of religion and the expansiveness of the Group's aims. The Oxford Group wanted to save the world; Bill W. was only interested in saving drunks. In 1939, the book *Alcoholics Anonymous* was published, marking the true start of the AA movement. As its proponents proclaimed, the book outlines a simple program for a complex people, but the simplicity is one of action, not of intellectual connection and consequence.

AA is largely effective through its conceptualization of the self and its emphasis on identity. Although alcoholism is conceptualized as disease or malady, the alcoholic does not *have* alcoholism—he or she *is* an alcoholic. The AA recovery process begins with an identification of the self with an essential limitation, that is, the inability to relate to alcohol as a neutral, material substance with qualities that can be used rationally and hazards that can be avoided rationally. This identification with radical limitation is also applied to the AA model itself, not simply to the alcoholic. The AA model does not claim to be comprehensive, as do some models of human functioning. This recovery model claims that it applies only to addicts, not to everyone.

Control and its absence for the addict (as for all of us) are closely related to the experience of shame. Kurtz views AA as essentially a therapy for shame. Whereas guilt is associated with a wrong done to others, a debt that must somehow be repaid or harm for which reparation must be performed, shame is essentially about the self. Shame takes on many forms but is always at base about the self as being essentially by nature unacceptable, defective, inadequate, or worthy of disgust and hate. In a recent (1992) feature piece for *The Atlantic*, clinical psychologist Robert

Karen traced the emerging renewal of interest in shame, citing Leon Wurmser among others as pioneers in understanding this emotion's implications for the addictions and other personal and social pathologies. He cites how the popular recovery speakers and writers such as John Bradshaw (1988), have incorporated an understanding of shame in their works that reflects what has gone on routinely in the recovery movement over the last fifty years. Karen differentiates among four kinds of shame. All four forms may contribute to pathological narcissistic shame, the form most relevant to the addictions. Existential shame is a border experience; it places our lives in radical perspective, showing our extreme limitations, self-delusions, and pretensions for what they are, both on the individual level and on the level of being human. Class shame is associated with social power or power-lessness, as related to wealth, social class, ethnic and racial prejudices, and so forth. Situational shame, referred to by Kurtz as conditional shame, is a passing experience related to a specific humiliation or rejection, loss of personal control, or sense of being violated. Narcissistic shame, however, is of the most relevance to the addictions. It never goes away; it is constantly identified with the self.

All of the other forms of shame may contribute to narcissistic shame. Some experiences stimulate all of these forms. Civil rights, Black Power, and the women's rights movements are examples of social movements that have been as much about preventing racism and sexism from perpetuating shame in all of its various forms as they have been about ending specific social injustices. In a sense, the recovery movement has a similar function for the addicted. The addict experiences both class shame (as an addict or user) and situational shame (in using or the consequences of procurement and intoxication) directly related to his or her addiction. In addition, the addict is told (by society and by clinical experts) that there is something essentially different about him or her that is beyond choosing and control, a source of existential and narcissistic shame. This source of shame contributes to narcissistic shame, especially during sober periods of an addictive cycle.

The most basic form of the expression of narcissistic shame is the desire not to exist, or at the very least to be hidden, not to be seen or exposed to the self or others. To the extent that one is successful in avoiding being exposed and openly experiencing shame, there remains the anxiety of being found out or exposed, and the other characteristics of the split identity described by Wurmser. Both shame and its related anxiety fuel denial and addiction.

To return to Kurtz's (1982) analysis of alcohol addiction:

> Alcoholism—indeed, addictive dependence upon any psychoactive chemical—often arises from and usually is connected with the effort to conceal such weakness, to prevent its exposure *to oneself.* The alcoholic or addict uses his chemical in order to hide, and especially to hide from himself. The endeavor to hide reveals that the critical problem underlying such behavior is shame. . . . Guilt-oriented therapies, however sophisticated, fail because the addict or alcoholic cannot "mend his ways" or, by willing it, "grow up": he must maintain his addiction precisely to conceal his unendurable shame from himself. In any case in which the avoidance of pain—the

existential pain of shame—plays a basic part in the psychopathology, effective therapy must address itself first to the existential nature of that shame. [p. 51]

Kurtz argues that the Anonymous tradition effectively does this by placing an emphasis on openly and genuinely accepting one's essential limitation and inter-dependent connection with others:

> Anonymity implies, first others: one who knows who and what one is cannot be "anonymous" to himself. Through its own experience, A.A. learned that the necessity of "deflation at depth" and of some experience of "conversion"—as its sources referred to the process—impled something about the alcoholic's human need for others. [pp. 41-42]

Kurtz refers to the alcoholic affirmation of limitation as the denial of one's omnipotence, what he calls the not-God affirmation. The complex management of narcissistic issues is reflected on many levels in the containing affirmation that one is humanly limited and as a human *specially* flawed with alcoholism or addiction. This corollary of this denial of omnipotence is the ability to accept the nature of the human condition, which is limited control, limited independence, limited connect-edness. It is the full acceptance of radical limitation that takes the malignant sting out of narcissistic shame. It prevents the more natural (even desirable) forms of shame from contributing to pathological narcissistic shame.

With this new dynamic in process, control and independence take on new meanings for the narcissistically wounded and inflated individual who becomes genuinely engaged in the spiritual discipline of AA. Kurtz (1982) describes this process in language very similar to the opponent process theory of recovery advanced in this book:

> A.A., both in its suggestion of a Higher Power and in the dynamics of its meetings, invites and enables the living out of this mutuality between human dependence and personal independence. The First Step of the A.A. program establishes the founda-tion for this understanding: only by acknowledging continuing dependence upon alcohol does the A.A. member achieve the continuing independence of freedom for addiction to alcohol. This mutuality between dependence and independence also clarifies (because it undergirds) A.A.'s emphasis on limited control and limited dependence . . . These are, we now see more clearly, not two separate concepts, but obverse sides of the one coin of essential human limitation. Because of essential limitation, to be fully human requires the acknowledgement of both limited control and limited dependence; and it is the embrace of each that enables the attainment of its apparent opposite. [p. 64]

Although pathological forms of narcissistic shame and its consequences can often be dealt with most effectively within the context of expert guided treatment, the long haul of maintaining sobriety will depend on self-help movements such as

AA and NA. This is because they foster the establishment of appropriate self-love by the narcissistically injured addict, which defuses shame. They also have institutionalized mechanisms for ongoing identity change and consolidation. Finally, the practical realities of intimate social support and empathy from one's peers are not attainable within a fully professionalized model of care. Alternative self-help groups, such as Rational Recovery (a post-Enlightenment movement that stresses disengagement from religious ideas and from absolutist identifications on the part of individuals in recovery) will be successful to the extent that they can replicate these aspects of traditional Anonymous groups.

PHASES OF RECOVERY, STAGES OF TREATMENT

Followng an outline of some of the major issues involved in recovery, a discussion of stages and phases of dual diagnosis work is in order. It is not accidental that such a discussion should follow a description of identity issues in adolescent development and the similarity of these issues with those that surface during the recovery process. The approach to conceptualizing the epochs of treatment and change advanced here builds directly on this correspondence of normal identity consolidation in adolescence and dual diagnosis work. Other ways of viewing these sequential events have been advanced, however. Bean-Bayog (1986) divided treatment phases with dual diagnosis patients into three phases: achieving sobriety, maintaining abstinence and early recovery, and advanced recovery. In Bean-Bayog's phase description, only the final phase resorts to uncovering underlying issues; the earlier phases are almost purely directive and supportive.

Building on Bean-Bayog's phases, Kaufman (1989) provided additional detail to the expected activities of the first phase and commented on areas of therapist focus and technique in the succeeding phases. In the phase of achieving sobriety, Kaufman identified six major activities or goals: substance abuse assessment, assessment of psychopathology and psychodynamics, family assessment, detoxifications, beginning abstinence, and establishing a detailed treatment contract with the patient and family. In the phase of early recovery, directive therapies such as cognitive behavioral treatments should be emphasized in Kaufman's view, although these treatments should be informed by the psychodynamic assessments performed in the first phase. The final phase of advanced recovery may begin up to five years after initial treatment and relies on the patient's increased tolerance for defense analysis and experimentation with nonpathological relatedness to others.

Minkoff (1989), who describes what he calls an integrated treatment model for dual diagnosis, identified four phases of treatment for these patients: acute stabilization, engagement, prolonged stabilization, and rehabilitation. The acute stabilization phase places emphasis on dealing with detoxification in an inpatient setting. Engagement is initiated after the patient is stable and requires "a judicious use of leverage and confrontation by family and other caretakers or by the legal system," including forming a treatment alliance and educating the patient about the nature of his or her problems. Prolonged stabilization depends on symptom control through medication and abstinence from drugs other than those prescribed. This period lasts for up to one year and provides a time of needed convalescence wherein major life changes are discouraged to prevent relapses. Finally, the rehabilitation phase, which is ongoing once initiated, is a period of gradual growth.

A somewhat more detailed phase description has been offered (Osher and Kofoed 1989) and elaborated on (Kline et al. 1990), which includes the phases of engagement, persuasion, active treatment, and relapse prevention. These attempts to describe treatment phases in themselves indicate a growing maturity of theory building relative to dual diagnosis work. In part because of their generality, phase descriptions are a useful starting point for examining treatment and programming over time. However, the descriptions are not explicitly related to predictable processes of recovery from an illness based on any theoretical model of addiction or mental illness. Being focused primarily on treatment strategies, they do not distinguish phases that are intrinsic to the recovery process as a natural reparative mode from those induced and maintained primarily by treatment interventions. There is little description of what the patient is specifically working on *internally* during each phase, as distinguished from what interventions are required from therapists.

A phase typology suggested by Kathleen Sciacca (1990) provides some of the recommended recovery-based focus, although it remains at a very rudimentary level of development because of the focus on the single dimension of client denial. Sciacca identifies three phases related to changes in denial in the patient: client in denial, unfolding of denial, and movement toward abstinence. Unfortunately, like other phase descriptions, this one is is strictly sequential and linear in concept and therefore does not capture the cyclical nature of dual diagnosis problems. Such shortcomings seriously limit the utility of this kind of phase description in assisting clinicians in formulating treatment strategies that are fully responsive to recovery processes. Some of these problems can be mitigated by carefully sorting out where the descriptions concentrate on the patient as opposed to concentrating on the activities of the treatment staff and by establishing to what extent the phase describes events or developments that are primarily limited to a specific sequence or time during treatment, as opposed to being recurrent or cyclical. The phase of engagement, for example, introduced by Minkoff is a useful concept, although it is actually an attitude of the patient (and a corresponding focus for treatment with specific interventions related to patient participation), which ebbs and wanes throughout the recovery process and is not limited to a particular sequence of recovery or treatment. Engagement in each activity, mode, or phase of therapy must be continually evaluated and supported. Flapan and Fenchel (1987), for example, outlined how this cyclical process works specifically for psychoanalytically oriented group psychotherapy.

The phase approach offered here emphasizes the recovery process experienced by the patient in each phase. They are called phases of recovery rather than stages of treatment, the assumption being made that treatment should be built around and responsive to natural recovery processes and what we currently know of them. This approach is developed from the same level of observation that led to the "stages of change" model of patient participation in addiction treatment (Brownwell et al. 1986, Prochaska and DiClemente 1983). Phases and stages are hierarchical as well as sequential. Such phases in addictive or recovery also tend to progress in a cyclical or helixical manner, whereas treatment stages tend to remain sequential if not constantly adapted to the actual condition of the patient. Treatment stages are graduated both by intensity and extent of intervention (such as inpatient versus outpatient modalities) and in the degree of control exercised by the patient. They move from processes determined almost solely by the contexts generated by an emergency hospitalization or crisis intervention due to deterioration and break-down to a patient's growing self-direction in the recovery process. Treatment stages, then, are defined here as more related to what therapists and programs must do and the activities they must provide to patients, whereas recovery phases are more primary, inherent to the patient's own movement toward health and are only supported by professionally guided treatment activities.

The distinction made here is more than semantic. Ignorance of natural processes of recovery and the persistent refusal to acknowledge recovery processes that are not dependent on formal treatment interventions have contributed to the lack of communication and trust between mental health professionals and substance abuse workers, especially those from the self-help traditions. Defining interactive sets of phases and stages may help to promote understanding and respect between individuals who by experience and training believe in one or the other emphasis in understanding recovery.

Table 5-1 describes seven phases of recovery as they are supported by five treatment stages. As noted before, the phases have a kind of hierarchical and epigenetic relationship. Each phase is named after an internal process that is typically dominant at a given point in recovery. Although the phases are sequential, they are also viewed as graying into one another and as having the kind of opponent process relationship described in Chapter 1 for the positions of the addictive cycle. Although one kind of recovery process will be dominant at any given moment, others will also be present to some extent. In moments of regression, processes more typical of earlier recovery will surface. Because we are describing dual diagnosis work (that is, with patients who have been repeated treatment failures), even the most basic and earliest recovery phase may at times surface after the highest recovery processes are dominant. When pathology is not severe, however, regression will be only between the higher phases during advanced recovery. The treatment stages parallel the needs that are dominant in each recovery phase.

Because the middle period of recovery requires so much flexibility of therapeutic approach and covers the gauntlet of interventions, less discrimination is made

Table 5.1. Phases of Recovery and Treatment Stages

Phase of Recovery	Treatment Stage and Activities
1. Cooperation in Detoxification and Symptom Abatement: Follows "bottoming out." Accepting powerlessness and the need for external assistance is combined with an understanding of being a responsible co-participant in getting the help one needs.	**I. Stabilization** a. containment b. protection c. support d. pacification
2. Coping with Abstinence Effects and Loss of Secondary Gain: Specific after-effects of drug of choice. Growing awareness of new potential and energy, and harsh reality of consequences of previous behavior. Dependent role is questioned, but not relinquished.	**II. Orientation** a. instruction b. redirection c. focusing d. modeling e. clarification f. encouragement
3. Deconstruction of Denial/ Generating Motivation for Change: Identity diffusion, breakdown of earlier defenses. Growing understanding of limitations, vulnerabilities. Initiation of self-reliance and responsibility for change. **4. Identity Consolidation:** Acceptance of limitations, strengths, and vulnerabilities. Fidelity to values, new reference groups, and sense of self is initiated. Choices are increasingly consistent with new identifications.	**III. Uncovering/ Rehabilitation** a. containing dissonant material b. uncovering c. confrontation d. skill building e. modeling f. transference interpretation
5. Establishing Balance: External and interpersonal focus is re-established in ways that incorporate new identifications and understandings. Dependencies are diversified. Lifestyle changes and reconciling preferences, identity, and externals becomes primary focus. **6. Challenge to Established Recovery:** New identity is challenged, reassessed, refined, and reasserted. Appropriate protective, maintenance strategies are discovered.	**IV. Supporting Consolidation of Recovery** a. Skill building b. Life style design c. Practical focus in sessions d. Relapse prevention
7. Self-Direction of Recovery and Growth: Self reliance and appropriate dependency are established. Optimal division between maintenance activities and other life events is established. Energy, time, and personal focus are directed in new experience and personal growth.	**V. Aftercare/ Outreach** a. Maintaining access to care. b. Supporting repair by facilitating contributions to others in recovery.

among treatment stages than among phases of recovery. If identity is the touch-stone of dual diagnosis work, the isomorphic relationship between recovery from addiction and the dynamics of adolescence provides a valuable context for under-standing recovery phases. Similarly, attunement, limit setting, carrying of ideals, and supportive opposition that parents and other adults perform in supporting successful adolescent development can be used as a template for what treatment staff must accomplish to support recovery in dual diagnosis patients.

The first phase of recovery is marked by issues related to the patient's growing cooperation with the limits of detoxification and symptom abatement (coopera-tion). Many patients exhibit the depleted (depressed/degraded) aspect of the addictive cycle during this phase. With these patients, real commitment to change is low, whereas passive openness to help may be higher than in the next two phases, which occur only when old defenses are again partially in place. Patients in the detached (schizoid) or inflated (grandiose) phase of the addictive cycle will require extensive effort to achieve full cooperation. The treatment stage of stabilization parallels and supports the patient in early recovery by providing containment, protection from devastating consequences, and pacification of overwhelming affects or impulses. Lasting several weeks to several months depending on the severity of mental illness, addiction, and drug of choice, this treatment stage is conducted totally within an inpatient hospitalization setting for most dual diag-nosis cases. As in Minkoff's (1989) acute stabilization phase, coercion and external controls may be needed until cooperation is established.

Overlapping this phase is the phase of coping with abstinence effects and loss of secondary gain (coping). The patient is less passive, and personal health and energy are increased. At the same time, factors strongly in favor of continued drug use are active, including the resurgence of cravings for either the drug of choice or an affect trigger, renewed contacts with drug-related associates, and the stress of coming to terms with reality. Patients in the depleted or detached phases will not feel able to cope and will respond with passive dependency and helplessness, or avoidance of recovery tasks. Patients in the inflated phase are greatly endangered by a false sense of competence and invulnerability.

The parallel treatment stage is called orientation, because its most important result is the patient's total orientation to what will be required in a successful treatment and his or her realistic orientation to his or her predicament. This includes an understanding of diagnosis and the treatment team's assessment of the patient's strengths, weaknesses, and dynamics. Orientation is accomplished by psychoeducational techniques, detailed instruction, and highly structured envi-ronments with clear consequences for unacceptable behavior. External controls on behavior will be needed, and therefore the therapists must continually point out the consequences of specific unacceptable behaviors. Treatment staff will rely primarily on clarification, encouragement, and redirection as intervention tech-niques, with little need for uncovering. For therapists working with patients in the early phases of recovery, recognition of issues and dynamics must precede any form of effective confrontation.

Mild depressive experiences are usually operating at optimum levels during the early and middle phases of recovery, especially after abstinence no longer accounts for or causes a significant depressed affect. In stimulating mourning, self-reflection, and appropriate guilt and shame by pointing to loss, limitations, and negative consequences for previous behavior, therapists must be careful not to precipitate episodes of overwhelming depression or anxiety.

The next two recovery phases are closely linked and are supported by a single treatment stage, which is uncovering and rehabilitation. The phase of deconstruction of denial (deconstruction) is typified by a gradual removal of older identifications and defenses. Motivation for change becomes increasingly related to an acceptance of self limitations that may be adequately addressed with external help. This phase is marked by both global dependency and the beginning of self-reliance, similar to the conflict surrounding these issues that typically occurs in adolescence. Therapists will often need to confront patients in this phase with their misconceptions of themselves and others. Denial of unacknowledged aspects of the self or of unwanted consequences of behavior must be confronted by presenting the avoided or denied component in the context of support and acceptance. At the same time, the legitimacy of basic strivings must be affirmed by the therapist, especially at times when self-regulatory mechanisms have failed. Rapid cycling among positions in the addictive cycle may be expected. This is not the phase to expect consistency from the patient, but to objectively point to alternations in commitment to change and the resurgence of older ways of thinking and acting.

Consolidation of identity (consolidation) begins concurrently with deconstruction of denial, although it becomes fully dominant relatively late in recovery. Identity consolidation is typified by ego-syntonic affirmations of recovery goals. The patient is increasingly sensitive to role models, and the therapist is challenged to gauge the correct depth of interpretation of the idealization expressed toward such models. Some idealization is needed for consolidation to take place, but overidealization repeats the tendency toward projective identification and the paranoid process and can, of course, result in catastrophic disillusionment when the idols are discovered to have clay feet. Appropriate modeling, mirroring, and collaboration on skill-building efforts are the activities most required of the treatment staff.

The fifth phase, establishing balance (balance), places emphasis on the external world of the patient and on the diversity of needs and interests beyond those related to recovery and treatment. Dependencies become more diversified. Identity is consolidated by association with persons who are not idealized and by engagement in relatively conflict-free activities and settings. Work, leisure, and socialization activities become the focus of therapy, which is not interrupted by extremes in the addictive cycle of self-experience. The treatment stage that supports the fifth and sixth phases of recovery is called supporting consolidation of recovery because of this emphasis on supporting previously established gains, on relapse prevention, and on the development of a viable lifestyle that incorporates and goes beyond a recovery focus.

The sixth phase, challenge, takes place within stable recovery and could be viewed as a predictable event or events within the previous phase. Mental stability or sobriety is challenged by unanticipated exacerbations of condition, or by unexpected cravings or temptations. Unlike similar threats that have occurred in earlier phases of recovery, a reevaluation of the basis for recovery takes place in this phase, because the threat is viewed as ego alien, not consistent with the new definition of self. Relapse may or may not occur. Rapid cycling of positions in the addictive cycle of self-experience are expected. Dynamically, the challenge phase, which occurs squarely within a fairly stable period of sobriety, represents the need to test the ability to return to increased dependency and reliance on the treatment network. Relapse prevention work and support of appropriate defenses are crucial interventions. Successful management of this crisis leads to further consolidation of treatment gains, including appropriate reliance on treatment staff and community support networks.

Self-directed recovery and growth (self-directed recovery) is the final recovery phase, supported by the aftercare stage of treatment activities. Aftercare in some form is not expected to terminate fully at any point, although it may take on many forms over time. Although there is consistent, predictable contact with treatment professionals or self-help mentors or sponsors, these dependencies are not unique or overladen with significance, as is the usual case in earlier phases of treatment.

THE CLINICAL FORMULATION AND PROCESS THEORY

Building on the understanding discussed in preceding chapters of the most commonly confronted dual diagnosis problems, this chapter details the major psychodynamic issues that must be addressed by the therapist and gives an outline of the sequential healing processes involved in recovery and treatment.

Psychological treatment is never merely a practical endeavor. Therapists cannot help but encounter theoretical and philosophical issues in their work. This book tries to make many of these issues explicit and open for consideration. Its theoretical orientation is phenomenological-existential in that the author believes that a faithful description and empathetic understanding of the experience of another person from the inside (intraspective understanding, Rychlak 1981) constitute a basic starting point and point of continual return in psychotherapy. Both the logical (cognitive) and perceptual (experiential/emotional) aspects of the patient must be described faithfully, and these aspects of the therapist must be engaged in the observation and descriptive process, which is both active and co-creative. Cognitive-dynamic methods and concepts are given priority here for the task of grasping the patient's internal experience. This grasp, usually articulated first by way of an empathic response, is the fundamental step in the collaborative process of initiating change through the mutual action of therapist and patient.

The rest of this chapter addresses the outcomes of all these understandings: establishing a clear clinical formulation and choosing among intervention alternatives to address it. A full clinical formulation must somehow systematically map the specific problems presented in the case within a theoretical, empirically based, or consensually validated understanding of prominent dynamics. It must serve as a practical basis for generating treatment goals, setting priorities, and selecting effective interventions and establishing their sequencing. The clinical formulation provides an extraspective understanding of the individual, that is it helps us to understand the person from the outside by placing his or her experience and behavior within the context of what is generally known and ready at hand for the work of therapy. This is done at both the practical and abstract levels, that is, in the contexts of assessment findings, psychological theories, intervention methods that may be relevant, medication protocols, available programs and housing arrangements, and so on. It is from the understanding provided by the clinical formulation that treatment strategies, treatment plans, and specific interventions are selected.

This process of selection, sequencing, and assignment of relative priority among interventions builds on the clinical formulation, but it must itself also be guided by some method or theory. Theoretical orientation and professional training biases are not adequate or desirable as singular guides to this process, due to the complexity of dual diagnosis work. The treatment of the interaction of severe problems occurring within several different spheres of functioning is most appropriately conducted within a multidisciplinary setting. This also places strict limits on the ability to rely on the coherence of approach and clarity of communication that might be assumed to result from homogenous training and treatment traditions within a specific discipline or school of therapy.

Perry and colleagues (1987) have argued persuasively in favor of the brief written psychodynamic formulation as a guide to the treatment process. The kind of case formulation suggested here includes and expands this formulation. Process theory (Sabelli 1989) is described as an aid to constructing the clinical formulation because it assures a systematic consideration of sources that may result in the discovery of alternative hypotheses and the detection of submerged dynamic issues in dual diagnosis cases. Process theory is also suggested as a guide to the intervention selection process in that it provides a way of setting priorities among problems occurring simultaneously on different levels of organization or in different spheres of functioning, and therefore it does not lock the treatment process into a predetermined view based on theory, or on level of analysis most familiar to the therapist.

Before investigating process theory, let us briefly outline the psychodynamic formulation of Perry and colleagues (1987) to show how the approach suggested here incorporates and somewhat departs from their views. Perry and co-workers compare the psychodynamic formulation to the diagnosis: both succinctly conceptualize a given case, both are specific, brief, and focused, both incisively clarify central issues, distinguishing them from less essential characteristics and foci of treatment. Some common misconceptions concerning psychodynamic formulation identified by these authors are: that it is needed only in the case of long-term expressive psychotherapy and is less useful in more focused, briefer treatments; that the construction of these formulations, especially written ones, is primarily a training exercise to be abandoned after initial tutelage; that a psychodynamic formulation must be elaborate and time consuming; that an informal non-written formulation is as valuable as a written one; and that a written conceptualization is apt to bring rigidity into the clinical situation. Contrary to all these misconceptions, Perry and colleagues view the written clinical formulation as an efficient way of guiding treatments of any kind where dynamic issues are to be considered. Written formulations provide stability and clear departure points rather than rigid constraints. They require rigor in thought, imply ongoing evaluation of the conceptualization of the case, and support clear communication between therapist and patient and among members of a treatment team.

The psychodynamic formulation as described by Perry and his colleagues (1987) consists of 500–750 words structured in four parts: (1) a summary of presenting problems and life situation of the patient in the context of the patient's developmental history; (2) a summary of "nondynamic factors" contributing to the psychiatric disorder, including biological predispositions, childhood trauma, and social deprivation; (3) a psychodynamic explanation of the central conflicts, describing their role in the current situation and their genetic origins in the developmental history; and a prediction of how these conflicts are likely to affect the treatment and therapeutic relationship. The first part of their description of the psychodynamic formulation is similar to the first few sentences of a typical admission note. The second part includes many of the factors noted in a history and diagnostic impression. The third section is more clearly psychodynamic and requires a process similar to interpretation in therapy:

> Identifying the central conflicts requires both inductive and deductive reasoning. The aim is to find a small number of pervasive issues that run through the course of the patient's illness and can be traced back through his or her personal history, and then to explain how the patient's attempts to resolve these central conflicts have been both maladaptive (producing symptoms and character pathology) and adaptive (characterizing his or her general style of pleasure, productivity, and personal relationships). Conflicts are opposing motives and wishes, both conscious and unconscious; central conflicts are repetitive, link and explain a number of important behaviors, and usually contain elements that are hidden from the patient's awareness. [Perry et al. 1987 p. 546]

Once these central conflicts have been identified, they must be formulated within a coherent, prototypic model. The authors identify three such models within the psychodynamic perspective: the ego-psychological, the self-psychological, and the object-relational models. Although each stresses different aspects of mind and behavior and has different vocabularies and literatures, these three models can be said to communicate in that they share an assumption of dynamic unconscious mental activity that influences the conscious life and behavior of the patient. Because the models are interrelated, they can inform each other and can be mixed in the same formulation. This is because each of them uses data from the same psychodynamic level of explanation, rather than changing the basic data for consideration. If, for example, the case were to be interpreted in nondynamic terms such as in a behavioral or purely cognitive approach, observations concerning defenses in regard to central conflicts would no longer be relevant. Instead, reward history, reward preference, expectancies, and cognitive set would be appropriate data for the clinical formulation. Since all of these concepts come from more or less the same levels of organization (the behavioral and cognitive) they could easily be accommodated in a single model.

The fourth section of the formulation provides a statement of prognosis and the meaning of the treatment process to the patient, plus an assessment of the probable manifestations of transference, countertransference, and resistance in the case. These predictions will be significantly influenced by the dynamic model preferred by the therapist, or the one chosen as most appropriate to the issues presented in the case.

The formulation recommended as optimal for dual diagnosis cases expands on the model described above. It places less of a division between dynamic and nondynamic factors, which are viewed as constantly present and interactive as conceptualized in the heuristic system. It adds an understanding of recovery processes and phases to issues routinely confronted in therapy, such as general resistance to treatment and change, transference, and so on. A written formulation should include the following: (1) a summary of presenting problems, contributing situational factors, history, and diagnostic impressions carefully describing personality style or personality disorder if present; (2) identification, relative priority, and description of the most prominent relevant symptom complexes and related functions of addiction using the heuristic system presented in Chapter 3 (note that dynamic factors must be utilized to apply the system); (3) a psychodynamic formulation, which identifies and explains those central conflicts that are relevant to the factors identified in (1) and (2) within a coherent model or set of communicating models; (4) an analysis of recovery processes relevant to the case as outlined in an earlier section on that topic in this chapter; and (5) a prediction of response to treatment interventions, recovery processes and phases, including a dynamic and situational description of relapse issues.

Like the psychodynamic formulation of Perry and co-workers, the dual diagnosis formulation should be brief. It should reflect a process of winnowing: only essential, central characteristics and processes that are definitive, either causally or in terms of consequences, should be included, although others will be present and operative to some extent. The general heuristic system presented in Chapter 3 provides much of the cognitive shorthand for this process. Whenever a process or characteristic meets the criteria of centrality but appears parallel, that is, not causally interactive with other aspects of the case but having major consequences, this should be stated explicitly, pointing out the absence of full coherence in the formulation.

Once the comprehensive clinical formulation is constructed, systematic intervention selection and sequencing can begin. Process theory is recommended as a flexible approach to providing the needed guidelines to priority setting and to establishing the criteria for selecting among various treatment concepts and methods in dual diagnosis work. Process theory is rich in associations to other theoretical and philosophical contexts and is compatible with Maslow's self-actualization theory and the phenomenological concepts used throughout this book. Intervention techniques and concepts formulated from the point of view of process theory are introduced as helpful in all therapeutic work, but especially with the dual diagnosis population.

The work of Hector C. Sabelli and Carlson-Sabelli (Sabelli 1989, Sabelli and Carlson-Sabelli 1989), which describes what they refer to as process theory, is briefly noted in Chapter 1 as an elaboration of dialectical thinking. In Chapter 1, dialectical thinking is presented as an alternative approach to many of the dead-end concepts and chicken-or-egg questions in dual diagnosis literature. Let us now consider process theory as a useful innovation in thinking about clinical formulations, especially in regard to the question of treatment priorities, sequencing of interventions, and establishing the appropriate domain of treatment concepts and techniques to be marshalled in the treatment of any given case. Although process theory derives from sources somewhat broader than those of the phenomenological-existential orientation and cognitive dynamic methods favored in this text, it is viewed as an elaboration of a similar viable approach to the problem of dealing with complex processes in interaction across multiple levels of organization. This situation is crucial to the mental health sciences in general (Hinde 1989), but it has special significance in dual diagnosis work.

Process theory is derived, according to Sabelli, from the philosophical views of Heraclitus in the fifth century B.C., which have been incorporated to some extent in the intermittently dialectical thought of Freud and more directly and consistently in the work of Jung. The river metaphor, often elaborated on in this book, is closely associated with Heraclitus, who insisted that one can never step in the same river twice. Although the river maintains its integrity or objective status as "this" river, it is engaged in constant change.

Heraclitus was concerned with the issue of identity, reliable features in the flux of constant change. He called the tendency in nature for matter to take on definite, fairly permanent form or pattern, the *logos* of nature (Rychlak 1981). Heraclitus believed that the universal stuff of nature that *logos* "in-formed" (provided with form and structure to create discrete things and events) was fire—the symbol for dynamic energy. Using these two concepts (identity in change and structured energy as the common source of being), Heraclitus, like process theory, was concerned with accounting for how change, conflict, and opposition could result in both stability and creativity in organic or natural growth and in seeming permanence.

The title of Sabelli's (1989) book captures the essence of process theory: *Union of Opposites: A Comprehensive Theory of Natural and Human Processes.* Process theory has three major postulates that can be stated rather simply but require some explication:

1. Dynamic Monism: Inseparability of energy, matter, and information.
2. Union of Opposites: Processes are composed of and differentiate opposites.
3. Becoming (Bifurcation): Intercourse between complementary processes generate novel events, evolution, and emergent properties.

The first premise proved to be operative in the physical world by Einstein's demonstration that matter is energy bound. Monism in mental health has generally taken the form of materialism and reductionism to the biological level of explanation, but some therapists adhere to a psychic monism or idealism. The monism proposed by process theory, however, does not state that the body, the mind, and behavior are identical, only that they are ultimately inseparable and constantly distinguishable aspects of any human situation. The first premise has implications primarily for understanding the need for holistic and comprehensive understandings and shows how any literal dualism or nondynamic or reductionistic monism is essentially obsolete and inaccurate.

Modern views of monism, such as found in general systems theory, are usually accompanied by the concept of levels of organization. For example, a purely naturalistic monism (as opposed to theistic or supernatural) could state that physical, chemical, biological, social, and psychological levels of organization exist for any human event. This is similar to the organization implied in Maslow's hierarchy of needs. One weakness in Maslow's theory, however, is its difficulty in explaining how a higher value can be achieved when this requires the frustration of a more basic value. Sabelli's process theory avoids this problem by positing a bidirectional hierarchy of priority and supremacy among levels of organization. Complex processes are considered to have supremacy in local limited circumstances and for short periods of time (e.g., in the mind, psychological considerations are supreme). However, simple processes have priority of duration and extension, such as the biological processes that are preconditions for mental events to emerge. In Sabelli's hierarchy, which he acknowledges is similar to Maslow's, physical and biological processes have priority over social processes, which in turn have priority over psychological processes, whereas each type of process has supremacy within its own level of organization:

Our model is compatible with Maslow's conception of motivation, but its bidirectional aspect takes us beyond Maslow. Basic needs such as survival, respiration, and nutrition have priority in time but are dominated by the more complex levels as the simpler needs are partially met. This leads to a flexible approach, in which one level or another may be the predominant one at a given time. For instance, restoring breathing always has absolute priority, but once life is not threatened, taking care of the patient's emotional well-being may become more important than treating a respiratory difficulty. Conversely, attending to the emotional welfare of a dying patient has absolute supremacy. . . . This means addressing objective life circumstances before subjective feelings and conceptions, biological illness before interpersonal psychological disorders, social and family matrices before personal intrapsychic process and the facts as they appear before the meaning ascribed to them by interpretation. [Sabelli and Carlson-Sabelli 1989, p. 1550]

One implication of monism and levels of organization is that interventions are evaluated in regard to their impact on more than one level at a time. Ideally, interventions would give priority to lower levels and supremacy to higher levels at the same time. Helping patients to participate actively in medication compliance or assisting them in establishing responsible, caring, and safe sexual relationships with appropriate partners are two examples of such interventions. In the first case, physical and biochemical processes are corrected while considering the patient's self-hood and sense of control. In the second case, biological needs are combined with higher sociopsychological needs, such as the need for caring and being cared for over time and being able to value and love others appropriately.

When all important levels cannot be addressed effectively in one intervention or one set, Sabelli's bidirectional hierarchy helps to establish priorities for selection among interventions and their sequencing. This is done by determining from the clinical formulation which aspects of the patient's life situation has supremacy at a given moment and which aspects must receive priority for this supremacy to emerge. For example, a comprehensive clinical formulation for a patient who is a polydrug abuser in early adulthood and diagnosed as suffering from bipolar disorder may indicate that establishing his occupational viability and role consolidation through education or vocational training has supremacy. Medication, family therapy, and individual treatment can then be subordinated to this consideration. In this example, concentrating on an intrapsychic conflict experienced by this patient would be counterproductive, unless it specifically held sway over his educational adjustment. However, medication considerations and family dynamics that could support or interfere with educational achievement and establishment of vocational roles would be given priority. On the intrapsychic level, issues related to self-esteem through achievement and development of conflict-free interests would be given priority. (Notice that the self psychology model described by Perry and colleagues, 1987, is most appropriate to the need identified as having supremacy in this example.)

The second premise of process theory has to do with the component parts of any process. The word *opposite* in process theory, or in any truly dialectic theory, does not mean only one pole of paired contradictions or extremes, such as black and white or hot and cold. Opposites may be many in number; and the word *alternatives* might be more to the point, although bipolar contradictory opposites are frequently encountered in natural systems, partially because such systems are more available to analysis when this kind of opposition is dominant.

Process theory recognizes that opposites tend to be similar in many aspects and identifies four major patterns, or views, of opposition: harmonic, conflictual, separating, and hierarchical. These patterns must also be described as views, because often the appearance that a process is dominated by one or the other form of opposition is a bias of the observer, or an artifact of the level of organization that is of interest. An observer with different goals or interests would detect a different aspect of opposition fueling a given process.

Harmonic opposition is characterized by processes interacting in cooperative, complementary cycles, usually toward the same effect. Conflictual opposition is more familiar and is figured by struggle, competition, or conflicting ends or results. Separating opposites can be seen in the presence of an influence alternating with its absence, or in dichotomous theories, such as particle and wave conceptions in classical physics or in phobic/counterphobic reactions. Separating opposites are bound together in their separation, or they cease to fuel a process.

Hierarchical opposition, the kind most often implied in the tables and explanations in this text, are those oppositions that impose orderly priority among opposites. This priority is often expressed in the submersion or subsumation of one opposition within another. What has priority or is subsumed may vary at different levels of organization within the same individual. A clinically familiar example is the dynamic interaction of aggression and fear often found in borderline patients who act out violently. Unconscious fear of abandonment and obliteration may be subsumed by aggression on the behavioral level (further fueling the aggression and making it more sadistic in quality) while the conscious experience of aggressive feelings during the aggressive act may induce more unconscious fear of being overwhelmed or obliterated. This premise of process theory assists in the detection of submerged themes in treatment and in the formulation of specific interventions based on the understanding of opposition. One such intervention, partial contradiction, is discussed later in this chapter. Although common interactive patterns clearly exist, as outlined in the general heuristic system of Chapter 3, substance abuse and psychopathology can interact in any of these four forms of opposition and thereby create a dynamic, synergetic process, or what is referred to in this book as a psychiatric substance abuse syndrome.

The word *process* comes from the Latin and means to proceed or move forward. The third premise of process theory, bifurcation, or becoming, addresses this essential notion. Opposition and unity create change and novel events. All active processes consist of oppositions in interaction. Three patterns of change coexist in all active processes: movement toward equilibrium, oscillation between opposites, and bifurcation into new structures or processes. The dominance of any one of these types of change will depend on the degree of equilibrium between the opposing processes. In processes where equilibrium is nearly established between its driving oppositions, movement toward even more equilibrium is the most pronounced type of change. Farther away from equilibrium, alternation of opposites is most pronounced. When oppositions are extremely far from equilibrium within a process, chaos and emergence of novel events are expected.

Therapy based on process theory takes into account these notions of change and emergence by gearing interventions according to the type of opposition and the degree of equilibrium among the opponent processes involved in a given pathological situation. As noted in Chapter 1, the dual diagnosis work performed is different in kind when psychopathology and substance abuse are merely co-existent. A more difficult situation exists when these two processes are in a synergetic union, where each process is the co-creator of the other. Another index of equilibrium is the degree of defensiveness in regard to symptoms, or the resistance met by appropriate interventions. When pathological processes are in equilibrium, defenses are energized and resistance to treatment is high. When equilibrium is lost, such as in spiraling acceleration of either the addiction or the mental disorder, defenses either collapse or oscillate between being rigid and impenetrable, or being fragile and completely ineffective. This oscillation results in rapidly changing responses to treatment interventions.

A PROCESS THEORY INTERVENTION

This section introduces several specific treatment intervention concepts related to process theory.

The first concept, partial contradiction, was developed by Sabelli (1989). As a guideline to therapy, partial contradiction suggests that every intervention should be an empathic acceptance of the patient's feelings and behavior as well as a circumscribed, limited confrontation that suggests a small change. This is not a revolutionary concept for therapists involved in psychodynamically oriented therapy where the goal is to formulate interpretations that can be consciously considered by the patient. However, when the dynamically oriented therapist moves into other roles that require limit setting, direction, and instruction, the guideline of evoking only what is consciously available to the client is far from adequate in helping to titrate or evaluate interventions. Sabelli's partial contradiction technique accepts that a pathological process in equilibrium has also become part of the equilibrium of the personality. He quotes Spanish philosopher Miguel de Unamuno to make this point:

> We live in our memory and through our memory, and our life is our effort to preserve, the effort of our past to become future. To tell someone to change is to tell him or her to cease being who he is. Everybody defends his personality and only accepts change

in his mode of thinking or feeling insofar as this change can enter into the unity of his spirit and articulate his own continuity, insofar as change can harmonize and integrate with the rest of his mode of being, thinking and feeling, and can link with his memories. Neither a person, nor a people can be asked to make a change that breaks the unity or the continuity of their personality. One can change much, almost completely, but within continuity. To become another, breaking the unity and continuity of my life is to cease to be who I am. That is to say simply, to stop being. To this, I say "No; Anything before that!" [p. 399]

Sabelli quotes Unamuno to describe the individual who is in equilibrium, albeit an undesirable one. Perhaps it is this almost impenetrable resistance to change that exists while an addict is in equilibrium within his or her illness that has resulted in the folklore common in AA and NA, and among many clinicians, that hitting rock bottom in the addictive cycle is necessary before the willingness to undergo significant change can begin to develop. Piaget stresses a similar point in his description of motivation in animals and humans as being primarily related to various forms of disequilibria. Process theory concepts also imply that only individuals whose addictions and/or mental illnesses are greatly out of equilibrium are open to truly radical change. What we refer to here as deconstruction of denial and reconstruction of the identity (or consolidation of emerging identifications) does not require hitting rock bottom, however. It is a gradual, interactive process over a long course of recovery. Partial contradiction provides an explanatory concept for the methods required to initiate and maintain this process, which at times may result in dramatic breakthroughs and radical change, but is usually more typified by a cycle of barely perceptible movements of deconstruction, defense and resistance, and reconstruction.

However, Sabelli's partial contradiction is really more than a technique for dealing with stable, highly resistant pathologies. It can be seen as defining the whole context of psychotherapy. Therapy can be seen as a dialogue (dialectic) between the patient in his or her illness and the therapist who opposes their equilibrium in this position. From this point of view, every intervention is a partial contradiction. It must sufficiently follow the patient's situation, position, and understandings (and thus provides the minimal affirmation of acknowledgment and empathy) and must also provide an opposing thrust toward a more healthful position.

But how is the direction of this thrust to be determined? Usually in therapy what is considered healthy is determined by some theory or ideal of the nonpathological personality or of optional functioning. Although theories of personality, personality change, and therapy differ in the aspects of personality that are seen as exemplifying health, there tends to be much consensus on the actual process of therapy, especially when the field is narrowed to insight-oriented therapy. In psychoanalysis, the criteria for health have included movement toward mature sexuality, awareness and resolution of conflicts, and resignation toward the unchangeable or unresolvable. Maslow adopted criteria related to gratification of higher needs, expansion of freedom, and expressive creativity. Like Jungian therapy, the ideas related to process theory are consistent with choosing the criterion of a healthful movement in therapy as a change toward greater integration of unarticulated, submerged, or oppressed personal alternatives. These hidden alternatives may be seen as in opposition to the alternatives (often destructive or self-defeating ones) that are articulated, expressed, or relied on routinely by the patient.

Insight therapy in general consists of the patient being assisted in addressing these avoided, denied, underdeveloped, or unintegrated aspects of his or her life. The contradictory or opposing thrust provided by the therapist must always be toward these aspects being acknowledged, decided upon, and either actively and responsibly negated, or actively realized by the patient. Purely supportive therapy can be seen as opposing the client's self-destructive, self-neglectful, or incapacitating position toward life. One implication of this view is that psychotherapy that targets only one specific goal (e.g., to eliminate substance dependence) is inherently flawed, since opponent goals that might be the focus must at times be introduced to provide the necessary contradictory thrust toward integration and wholeness.

If insightful partial contradiction defines insight-oriented therapy as distinguished from other dialogues and conversations aimed at helping, how does the therapist keep pace with the patient, that is, remain in the correct position and equipped with the necessary understandings needed to formulate an opponent or contradictory thrust toward health throughout the constant changes of a course of therapy? This question goes beyond the technical issues of how to intervene and probes at the more essential question of how the therapist knows what needs intervention, and to what end, at any given moment. The answer for many therapists has been the ongoing discovery of emergent themes through active or creative listening and the application of equally hovering attention to the content and process of the sessions. Obviously, therapists also rely on the accumulation of wisdom about people and their problems that comes from the experience of struggling to help many people over many years. Yet there is a creative, inventive, interpersonal process in effective therapy that goes beyond discovery through listening and the accrual of conventional wisdom.

The premises of process theory, when enriched by concepts from a few other sources, can be used to illuminate this creative aspect of therapy. The answer to how therapy can follow and illicit new material that is relevant to healthful change begins in understanding how novel psychological material and processes emerge in the first place. Process theory implies that the psychological level of organization emerges in the individual (and historically evolves in the species) from the dynamic interaction of the social and biological levels of organization. This implication is consistent with the cognitive dynamic understanding that a stable personal psychological organization (core personality structure) emerges for the individual only when self with other representations is internalized. This internalization process is conditioned by the social level (the family, especially the caregiver) and the biological level (innate and constitutional predispositions and even nutritional status). The stability of the emergent process and related structures is radically increased and the new psychological person consolidated when these object representations can be evoked effectively through memory functions. Affective memories, such as the memory/phantasy of feeling soothed after contact with mother, are among the most formative of these stabilizing functions that gradually allow for the consolidation of the self.

Alcohol Expectancies and Thought Disorder

W.T. was diagnosed as having paranoid schizophrenia, although no one in the hospital where he had been for over a decade had ever observed him in a psychotic state. Although he used marijuana recreationally, alcohol was by far the most significant problem drug for him and his drug of choice. While intoxicated, he had been involved in the deaths of at least two individuals, and his behavior as described by arresting officers in both cases was patently psychotic, with symptoms of depersonalization, derealization, and delusional thinking. W.T. considered the first killing to have been accidental and the second a frame-up. The fact that he was found not guilty by reason of insanity for both deaths was, for him, evidence of a plot to prevent him from completing the design of an innovative computer language that would compete with those used in the defense industry. Although W.T. had an unusually high verbal intelligence, his formal education was limited. When confronted with the fact that he did not have the skills to produce a new computer language, W.T. replied that the conspiracy had been effective—so far—by preventing him from gaining these skills. W.T. recognized that his views of many things were unconventional, but he strongly felt that attempts to invalidate his views were expressions of the treatment team's self-righteousness and power striving, rather than based on any concern for his personal well-being.

W.T. identified himself as an alcoholic but in a rather eccentric way. He did not feel that the various treatments or self-help activities prescribed by the treatment staff would have any effect on him whatsoever, since he believed that alcohol as a "spirit" had certain spiritual reverberations with his own "spirit," which he had learned to master. In this mystical view, the drug and W.T. belonged to each other and were not separable and he would have to accommodate his life to this fact.

In investigating these meanings, the therapist discovered that the patient's adoptive grandmother, his strongest identification, was a Louisiana "roots worker," a person with knowledge of herbal magic among other forms of folk medicine and wisdom. The grandmother was also a moderate drinker. W.T. had his first childhood drinking experiences with her. These had not led to intoxication, but to feelings of warmth and intimate sharing. His alcohol experience with his adoptive grandmother contrasted with his experience with his mother, a cyclothymic alcoholic who had been alternately affectionate and seductive, or rejecting and even sadistic when intoxicated. She was an unpredictable figure, strongly associated with alcohol, whereas the grandmother was comforting and predictable, contrary attributes also strongly associated with the drug.

As with many addictive disorders, the issue of interpersonal dependency was prominent. The problematic identifications had been formed in W.T.'s most dependent childhood relationships, and the murders or accidents had occurred in two of his adult relationships where dependency was the primary aspect. Basic gender identifications were also involved. Males, such as his father, were viewed as ineffective and unable to realize a nature that was essentially more pure, disinterested, and benevolent than that of females. This natural superiority and goodness of males was never realized due to their emotional dependency on others, especially on women. Females were seen as ruling through intentional deception and manipulation, which included encouraging alcohol abuse. In the servitude of women, such men were expected to become jealous, defeated, and preoccupied with the ignoble aspects of life: sex, sexual competition, food, gross material wealth. Alcohol was the temporary escape from this slavery. Yet, the self-defeat that comes from alcoholism allowed this bondage to continue. W.T.'s view of the world was oddly tragic, filled with conflict and incongruities.

One of several challenges in this case was to prevent relapses to alcohol use by altering this idiosyncratic set of attributions and expectancies related to alcohol. These expectancies were deeply embedded in object relations and identifications that had been formed during the period of language mastery and gender role consolidation. There was a need to change both cognitive set and basic identifications, including those around what it means to be male and to communicate with and be close to another person. The patient's delusional interest in computer languages and alternative languages in general was viewed as a way of entering a dialogue about these imbedded meanings. Applying the method of partial contradiction, the therapist overtly accepted the limited validity of this way of talking about life, but also insisted that translation become the overt metaphor of the therapy. Experiences were expressed by the patient in concepts derived from many fields of discourse and containing varying degrees of eccentric content. The patient explicitly accepted the task of viewing his preoccupations with astrology, folk medicine, psychology, and computer analogies as mediums for expressing the meaning of events and feelings related to the meanings of the here-and-now relationship in therapy. As far as possible, little assistance was provided from the therapist, the exception being feedback about the clarity of the communication. The focus was not on alcohol use, relapse, or mental illness but on learning the language of interpersonal relationship in a new way.

The patient's improved ability to directly experience emotion and intimacy in relationship followed his feeling of competence in his ability to translate previously unshared experience into something understandable to the therapist and partially embedded in his semiprivate lexicons. Rather than being asked to abandon his delusions at the demand of the therapist, the patient was enabled to place them in perspective, allowing them eventually to become less rigid and pervasive.

THE EMERGENCE OF NEW MATERIAL IN PSYCHOTHERAPY

As this discussion moves toward explicating the emergence of novel psychological material, it only secondarily and incidentally explicates the permanent alteration of psychological structure. It could be said that the history of psychotherapeutic theories contains much more about the development of permanent psychological structure and the influence and reemergence of memories (again viewed as permanent structure) from formative periods than it does about the emergence of new psychological material and processes. The major exceptions to this generalization can be found in the work of constructivists such as Jean Piaget and George Kelly, and more recently (and from a different philosophical tradition), Sabelli's process theory.

As noted earlier, process theory implies that the emergence and construction of the psychological is not a one-time event that takes place in infancy and early childhood. Although psychological structures, once present, develop and condition experience thereafter, these structures are constantly supported by, and emerge from, the social-biological levels that support them. Psychological structure accrues over the lifespan, in a way that is analogous to, but not identical with, the learning of new skills, the development of cognitive operations, or the acquisition of new information. These changes can most properly be called structural when they are integrated within the self, that is, a cohesive center of experience, will, and behavior. This integration, just as the person, must be more than psychological. Accordingly, the most radical changes in therapy should be accompanied by changes in the biological and social aspects of the person. These aspects have priority over psychological processes, yet they remain subordinate to psychological supremacy at the level of experience and behavior. In turn, new developments in experience and behavior continue to reciprocally influence the person's biological and social existence.

Fortunately, placing a special emphasis on the continual emergence of psychological material and on creative functions of the psyche in therapy is not new in the therapeutic literature. Several therapists and theorists have developed ideas related to the continual emergence of the psyche into new being. The consequences of this emergence on the physical, social levels, as well its consequences for the development of stable psychological structure, have been identified. For example, Eugene Gendlin's (1979) experiential psychotherapy, which has its roots in existentialism, describes the *felt sense* as the total experience of any given situation in the here and now. The felt sense occurs in an "internal space," which is mental and experienced as in the body. It includes bodily sensations, perceptions, thoughts, a sense of history, and anticipations regarding the situation prior to these aspects becoming psychologically differentiated. The felt sense might be called the body's precognitive assessment of some aspect of the life situation. The felt sense is not identical with the psychoanalytic description of primary process condensations. The felt sense is prior to defensive action, although it may evoke defensive processes. It is, therefore, justifiable to equate Gendlin's felt sense with the experiential result of the emergence of a life event from the biosocial levels of organization to the psychological level.

Concepts similar to Gendlin's were developed by Silvano Arieti (1976) in his work on a theory of creativity, which he argued must include an understanding of the emergence of new psychological material. Arieti's *endocept* is an amorphous cognition "without representation—that is, without being expressed in images, words, thoughts, or actions of any kind" (p. 54). The endocept, therefore, can be characterized as nonverbal and preconscious and cannot be shared with others. Arieti described the endocept as being able to leave its mark on consciousness, however, by imparting a global experience of oceanic feeling, or other vague, primitive feelings and subliminal experiences. Creativity for Arieti consists of changing endoceptive experience or activity (which is vague and abstract, in the sense of not being particularized) into particular, clear mental productions or directed behaviors. That is, the endocept must develop into concept, image, or action for something new to emerge. Arieti viewed the problem of creativity as one of reducing the repression of the emergence of threatening new material from the endocepts. The emphasis here is on the emergence of the truly new, not the release of the repressed old material. (The reason for new material being threatening, however, can usually be found in repressed, unintegrated material.) The endocept is distinguished from Beardsley's (1965) earlier formulation, the incept, in that the incept is a much more specific mental content, a more finished cognitive product, and lacks the global quality and integrated multiple levels of organization, that is, abstract and concrete representations that are combined in Arieti's endocept.

Working from a concern with helping rather than creativity in the arts and sciences, Gendlin viewed psychotherapy as the problem of allowing the felt sense (here roughly equated with Arieti's endocept) to fully differentiate into contents (physical feelings, emotions, ideas, images) that could be carried forward into the person's life. By carrying forward, Gendlin refers to the capacity for a given experience of the felt sense to change through the emergence of specific particularizations, thus preparing the stage for even more emergent material. When the felt sense is not carried forward, a sense of emptiness, numbness, physical tension, or pain ensues, which then contributes, among other factors, to the development of psychopathology. Carrying the felt sense forward is inhibited by personal and cultural biases and identifications, which make the new material inconsistent with preconceptions of the self, others, or the world. Among these biases are those that view the body and its inherent knowledge as negative, or irrelevant, such as the cultural bias found in Western mind-body dualism.

Gendlin has described a technique called focusing, which allows for attending to the felt sense. The skill of focusing is taught to the client by way of simple instructions and guided practice. The patient learns in focusing how to attend to the felt sense and allow it to differentiate into specific contents without conscious willful effort. The therapist uses the focusing material verbalized by the client (as well as the therapist's own felt sense) as the basis of a helpful relational encounter. The existential idea of shared presence, or being-with, is implied in the assumed parallelism or isomorphism of experience in the encounter between therapist and client. "It can be assumed that whatever is felt by one party in an interaction is also in some sense relevant to the other. It may not as yet be clear just how it is relevant"

(Gendlin 1979, p. 358). At appropriate moments, the experiential therapist, according to Gendlin, should disclose the result of his or her own focusing experience with the patient.

Although Gendlin's felt sense concept is grounded in the context of an existential theory and technique of therapy, focusing, Arieti's endocept term is preferable, in part because it is not grounded in this way. Arieti's term does not imply an over-emphasis on seeing the body as the unconscious mind, as Gendlin's conceptuali-zation apparently does. The term endocept, therefore, allows for the nonbiological aspects of these primitive cognitions to be easily considered and affirms that the psychological level is not a derivative epiphenomenon of lower levels of organiza-tion. Although Gendlin's focusing technique can be used productively to assist therapists and their neurotic or stable personality-disordered clients to gain greater awareness of what he calls the felt sense, in the author's experience, the technique produces many of the liabilities of suggestion and directive techniques in therapy. More regressed patients, such as psychotics and borderlines, may become further regressed. Some patients become paranoid or have counterproductive experiences of the loss of boundaries between themselves and the therapist during focusing.

What is of most value in the focusing technique, and Gendlin's theoretical exposition of it, is the attention it gives to psychological emergence during therapy. In their incipient, emergent forms, both Gendlin's felt sense and Arieti's endocept could be easily mistaken from a psychoanalytic point of view as pure condensa-tions, where previously experienced emotions, memories, concrete and abstract attributes, and proximal and loose associations are all pooled in a single percept as an ineffective primary process defense. However, what characterizes the endocept is the integrity of representation and perception (prior to defensive distortion) that it entails, albeit in a vague, diffuse way. The endocept is available to both primary and secondary process activity. The endocept has the experiential status of an object of knowledge. It is in fact a type of presentational knowledge, that is, something intuitively known about a general context or situation that is important to the person. Unlike procedural knowledge, presentational knowledge does not require supporting evidence or argument in support of its validity. The appropriate validation approach to presentational knowledge is to locate its appropriate context and place the new information in perspective, that is, to use Piaget's view of cognition and knowledge, the validation of presentational knowledge is inherent in its appropriate assimilation and accommodation.

When the patient can be helped to creatively differentiate among the potential specific contents of the endocept and hold them simultaneously in consciousness, increased insight and integration take place. This process is interrupted in dual diagnosis patients. In these patients endoceptive activity does not lead to differen-tiation and integration. Due to stable personality characteristics, the process of differentiation of the endocept from the bio-social context of experience is pre-empted by symptom formation, that is, drug use or dysfunctional thinking and behavior. When either treatment interventions or recovery processes begin to alter this habitual preemption, disequilibrium of the personality (which was previously adjusted to addiction and psychopathology) is also initiated. Extreme imbalance results in bifurcation, or new experience. Typical defenses and resistances to treatment are enlisted by the personality to maintain its familiar maladjustment and ward off new experience. When these defenses fail to reestablish equilibrium, endoceptive experience is again intensified, increasing the need for more defensive action. Without support, containment, or assistance in developing endoceptive activity into concept or insight, relapse to drug use or psychopathology or both is the predicted result, since this has been the habitual way to handle emergent psychological material.

The therapist can help with the process of particularizing and developing material emerging from endocepts by relying on the principle of partial contradiction. The content (thought, idea, feeling, behavior) of emergent material is affirmed in part and confronted with alternative ways in which the endocept might have been particularized by the patient. The ability to have a range of alternatives to present to the patient depends on several factors. A detailed extraspective understanding of the patient and his or her life goals, values, and experiences is primary. This information is used in the light of an understanding of the dynamic oppositions that may be present in any given interaction. An intimate intraspective understanding of the patient based on the therapist's awareness of his or her own emergent material at the level of the endocept shapes the interpretation. The degree of affirmation or confrontation required to effectively move the patient forward, either gently or radically, determines which alternative is presented at any given point in the therapy. By consciously holding several alternatives simultaneously (perhaps using the therapist as a container for one or more alternatives in order to accomplish this), the patient is able to differentiate existing and emergent psychological material and begin the process of building psychological structure. Above all, the capacity for creativity on the part of the therapist is required in this orientation to treatment. This capacity must be supported by the therapist's theoretical understanding of the process of therapy, as well as the therapist's own engagement with life.

Prior to further investigating the creative process in therapy, which is a primary focus of the view of treatment that results from process theory, the relationship between the preceding discussion and more traditional formulations of therapy should be briefly considered. In many ways the view of therapy presented here is a cognitive existential description of how parallel processes in client and therapist (the ebb and flow of primary process and countertransference phenomena in the broad sense) must be understood and used creatively by the therapist for effective therapy to take place. Although the more traditional explanatory concepts are useful, advantages exist in alternative descriptions (a position concerning theory construction that is consistent with process theory postulates). For example, the emphasis of the discussion here is away from impulses and drives (such as sexuality and aggression), which are usually associated with primary process. Only minimal presumptions about psychological structure are made (that is, no use of id, ego, superego etc.) and no complicated theory of repression is required. At the same time, this interpretation of the emergence of psychological material from a process theory point of view de-emphasizes the importance of distortions in perception and communication in the therapeutic situation, which are imposed from the past (such as found in transference and countertransference reactions) and has moved toward affirming the co-creative, reality constructive components of the therapeutic relationship.

Although this book relies on dynamic and cognitive dynamic formulations, other orientations to personality and therapy can be conceptualized in ways that are consistent with the ideas and approaches derived from process theory. The language of process theory is relied on because it is the most general theory, states the philosophical and conceptual issues explicitly in ways that are clearly applicable to treatment of the dual diagnosis population, and because it is less tied to a specific therapeutic method or research agenda than, say, Piaget's constructivism. However, other valid starting points could have resulted in similar conclusions and recommendations.

For example, readers who are interested in a well-developed, behaviorally oriented theory of psychotherapy and personality that is in many ways consistent with process theory should investigate Rychlak's logical learning theory (1981b). Its principles and basic concepts include the notion of dialectical thinking and the carrying forward of the person's phenomenal perspective through the imperatives of coherent logic, as opposed to viewing the person's behavior as being shaped by external objective rewards. Logical learning theory acknowledges that in each action or thought the person particularizes one out of an infinite array of response possibilities and thereby places heavy emphasis on human self-direction and freedom. Rychlak's concept of the affective assessment has some important similarities to the endocept concept. In addition, Rychlak introduced the term *telesponse*, to describe the goal-directed, essentially free, and idiographic nature of primary human experience and behavior.

CREATIVITY IN THERAPY

A deeper understanding of creativity in therapy will assist the therapist in using partial contradiction and the opponent process view of therapy derived from process theory. Rothenberg's (1988) *The Creative Process in Psychotherapy* is aimed at providing such an understanding and is highly recommended for its presentation of a theory of creativity in therapy that in many ways is consistent with the process theory view of treatment. Consistent with an emphasis on creativity and with understanding that the roots of change lie in opposition, Rothenberg emphasizes interventions that incorporate metaphors derived from the therapeutic process: paradoxical and ironic interventions. He provides an analysis of error and empathy in therapy based on the view that differentiation of mental contents (in his language, articulation of experience) are based on processes involving simultaneous opposition. The reader is referred directly to Rothenberg's book for a detailed description of these specific techniques and analyses of therapeutic empathy and error. Here, we summarize and critique his general analysis of creativity in therapy and show how his analysis can be enriched by the concepts and ideas previously introduced.

Rothenberg introduced two major processes as essential to the creative process in the arts, sciences, and psychotherapy. The first, the *homeospatial process*, consists of bringing more than one image into consciousness at the same time, resulting in creative synthesis. His second, the *janusian* process, describes how opposites or contradictions can increase consciousness and result in creative solutions. Taken together, Rothenberg's processes explain creativity in therapy in ways similar to how such a description would be formulated from the process theory premises of the union of opposites (i.e., that processes are composed of and differentiate opposites) and the premise of bifurcation or becoming (i.e., that intercourse between complementary processes generates novel events, evolution, and emergent properties).

Rothenberg (1988) defined the homeospatial process as "actively conceiving two or more discrete entities as occupying the same space, a conception leading to the articulation of new identities" (p. 7). His homeospatial process is a special type of secondary process that can be learned and encouraged but occurs more often as a personality trait in creative individuals. Unlike primary process, the homeospatial process is conscious, deliberate, and reality-oriented. It is more than reality-oriented, however, because it is reality transforming or transcending:

> Unlike primary process condensation, the homeospatial process involves no spatial substitutions or compromise formations, but sensory entities are consciously and intentionally conceived as occupying an identical spatial location. This produces a hazy and unstable mental percept rather than the vivid images characteristically due to primary process, because consciously superimposed discrete spatial elements cannot be held in exactly the same place. From this unstable image, a new identity then is articulated in the form of a metaphor or other type of aesthetic or scientific unity. Also whereas in primary process condensation aspects of various entities are *combined* in the same spatial area in order to represent all of those entities at once, the homeospatial process involves no combinations but rather whole images *interacting and competing* for the same location. [p. 8]

The second creative process identified by Rothenberg, the janusian process, is named after the multifaceted god Janus. As Rothenberg points out, Roman doorways often had four or six entryways, and the god Janus was often depicted as having four or six faces, each oriented to different directions. The first month of the year is named after Janus because of the assessment of past and future that simultaneously is demanded at the pivot point between the old and new year. Although Rothenberg has not explicitly conceptualized it as such, his janusian process appears to be a special case, or subcategory, of homeospatial process, which places emphasis on opposites or contradictions being held simultaneously in consciousness, resulting in an expansion of the field of consciousness and, therefore, an enrichment of meaning and the possibility of novel solutions. Using Sabelli's categories of opponent processes, it appears that Rothenberg has separating and conflictual opposites in mind when considering janusian process and stresses harmonic and hierarchical opposition when describing homeospatial process. Homeospatial process (which is more general and has less of an impact on the total field of consciousness than does janusian process) does not rely on logical or emotional oppositions or contradictions in mental contents, but rests on superimposition or juxtaposition of any two or more well-articulated mental contents that are related to the creative problem. Janusian process is defined by Rothenberg (1988) as:

> . . . *actively conceiving two or more opposites or antitheses simultaneously.* During the course of the creative process, opposite or antithetical ideas, concepts, or propositions are deliberately and consciously conceptualized side-by-side and/or as coexisting *simultaneously.* . . . These formulations within the janusian process are waystations to creative effects and outcomes. They interact and join with other cognitive and affective developments to produce new and valuable products. . . . The janusian process usually begins with the recognition and choice of salient opposites and antitheses in a scientific, cultural, or aesthetic field, progresses to the formulation of these factors operating simultaneously, and then to elaborated creations. [pp. 11–12]

In his conceptualization of the homeospatial and janusian processes, Rothenberg's thinking is congruent with what has been described heretofore as dialectical thinking or process theory, although he stresses the conscious, deliberate aspects of thought. Rothenberg reports empirical studies indicating that janusian process, as manifested by rapid opposite responding on word association tasks, is higher in creative persons (such as creative students, executives, and Nobel laureates in science) than in normal or psychiatric patient control subjects (Rothenberg 1973, Rothenberg and Sobel 1981). Other empirical studies have found support for improved creative productivity when mental superimposition is introduced experimentally in creative writers and visual artists (Sobel and Rothenberg 1980).

Rothenberg describes creative endeavors, including psychotherapy, as beginning with the conscious perception of what the aesthetician Beardsley (1965) termed the *incept.* Beardsley's incept is more of a finished, processed product than either Arieti's endocept or Gendlin's felt sense. The incept consists of a specific mental content (word, image, color, shape, metaphor, puzzle or mathematical equation) that has unconscious significance for the creator. Three sources of motivation draw the creator into engagement with the incept. The first is the unconscious significance of the incept (related to the creator's conflicts, fears, and wishes, that is, his or her own dynamics), which leads to a playful, creative involvement with the incept that involves both anxiety and minimal uncovering. A second motivation is in the pleasure derived from the materials of the creative work. The love of the familiar material of the incept (words for poets, colors for painters, formulae for physicists) leads to combinations of homeospatial process and generation of new alternative views of the original incept due to the janusian process.

Finally, the creative results of these activities is a kind of knowledge or resolution (aesthetic, emotional, or intellectual) and provides a sense of pleasure or accomplishment. Specifically in psychotherapy, the therapist's incepts of empathic views of the patient (which may take, e.g., the form of specific insights into the patient's problems and dynamics) also have unconscious reverberations for the therapist. The conflict-free pleasures found in interaction with the patient, in arriving at a clinical formulation, and in creating and delivering interventions combine with this countertransference element to fuel the janusian process (creating new alternatives) and homeospatial process (deepening the meaning and context of specific insights by simultaneously considering them with one or more alternatives).

Rothenberg begins his description of the creative process too late in the game, that is, after much of the material has become conscious and objects of the creative will. His description is considerably enhanced if the meanings of Arieti's endocept or Gendlin's felt sense are substituted for the incept. Rothenberg's use of the term incept does give due consideration to the fact that a very deep bias exists for almost all individuals for the way in which emergent psychological material will be particularized. The incept, however, does not address the likelihood that global apperceptions and general precognitive assessments occur prior to the articulation of such specific mental contents. These processes (referred to earlier as endocept activity and equated roughly with Gendlin's felt sense in becoming) have crucial significance for a theory of creativity or change in therapy.

Granted, some individuals will prefer the articulation of emergent psychological contents into visual images, others into emotional responses or attitudes, but these preferences are often an aspect of the problem situation itself, especially when personality disorders are present. In many substance-abusing patients, the direction of articulation will be from endocept to action or behavior, with very little intervening mental representation reaching consciousness. The bias referred to in the incept is exactly what must be countered in these cases. The patient must be assisted in learning how to articulate the emergent material in new useful ways. Histrionic personalities must be helped to develop clearly defined articulated cognitions. Compulsives need assistance in articulating emotional experience and weighing the appropriate affective value of elaborate ideas and overly precise perceptions.

Partial contradiction can be used to evoke the emergence of reflection, emotion, relevant memories, or alternative views of world or self rather than allowing the emergent material to be preempted by being transformed into the urge to use drugs, or into other forms of acting out, or any other imbalance in emphasis. The understanding of endocept activity in therapy, which is primarily preconscious, can lead to a more fruitful exploitation of the secondary homeospatial and janusian processes. In fact, the homeospatial and janusian processes describe the method used throughout this book for exploring dual diagnosis issues. In each chapter the goal is to consider dual diagnosis problems from two points of view simultaneously (as addictive process and as psychopathology) to provide the opportunity for the reader to form a creative synthesis of these issues on the level of theoretical and experiential understanding. The emphasis is consistently on creativity. To resort once again to metaphor, all preceding pages are the setting up of an easel and the arrangement of the paints and brushes. The overt discussion of creativity and emergence in psychotherapy presents the more important invitation to the clinical reader to join in the process of painting, that is, finding ways of remaining creative and engaged while working with the difficulties of conceptualizing and providing treatment to patients who suffer from these complicated and often exasperating disorders.

III

SPECIAL TOPICS

6

The Basic Personality Disorders

PERSONALITY AND PSYCHOPATHOLOGY

Throughout this book, the importance of personality structure and dynamics is emphasized. The personality style or disorder of a patient usually presents a much more pervasive and consistent problem over time than does the waxing and waning of symptoms related to Axis I disorders. Also, the faulty adaptation to normal stressors and frequent failures in self-regulation, which account for continued addiction in the face of negative and even catastrophic consequences, can usually be attributed to deficiencies or disturbances in the sphere of personality. The favored position in the cycle of addiction is often determined by the personality style. Response to various treatment modalities and types of interventions are somewhat predictable if the personalty style is known. This chapter reviews some of the more significant theoretical issues involved in conceptualizing and working with personality disorders. The most common and moderately severe basic personality styles and disorders are reviewed in the light of dual diagnosis work.

The continually revised and constantly evolving work of psychologist Theodore Millon provides the most comprehensive and systematic approach to understanding personality disorders. Since personality disorders are diagnosed on a separate axis from the major clinical syndromes, let us start the discussion of personality disorders by investigating the relationship between Axis I disorders (clinical syndromes and symptoms) and the personality disorders or personality styles.

Several models explain the relationship between Axis I disorders and personality disorders (Dorcerty et al. 1986). Personality disorders may be seen as causing a *predisposition* to Axis I disorders. A personality disorder may be viewed as a *consequence* of another clinical syndrome. The personality disorders may be viewed as being *attenuated* versions of Axis I disorders. Finally, the coexisting disorders may be seen as sharing *causative* factors, that is, being different expressions of underlying problems. All four of these models are discussed in this and the following chapters, although the fourth model—causative factors—is cited most frequently.

Millon differentiates among personality patterns, symptom disorders, and behavior reactions as expressions of psychopathology (1973, 1977, 1983). These three concepts differ in regard to the extent that they are inherent in the individual, rather than related to the specific circumstances in which the individual is placed. They also differ in the level of complexity and the degree to which they are ingrained in the individual. On all these dimensions, symptom disorders (roughly equated with the Axis I disorders) fall between the behavior reactions and the personality patterns.

Behavior reactions are simple responses to situational demands. Individuals learn to favor some reactions over others in a given situation, although several alternatives are usually available. Behavior reactions, even when ineffective, are usually understandable strategies in that they have a logical or reasonable quality to an external observer and usually occur under conditions that could be objectively viewed as inherently stressful. For example, an individual who develops a headache on the day an important work assignment is due, misses work, and thereby is not present for the deadline, is exemplifying a behavioral reaction to the stress of the workplace. Behavioral reactions occur only in the environmental circumstances to which they are a reaction, and, therefore, they have a now-you-see-it, now-you-don't quality. The individual who missed work might "recover" in time for a party or sports event later that same day.

Symptom disorders (usually coded on Axis I) are usually viewed by others, and often by the patient, as even less rational responses. They are less directly linked to the individual's current life situation. Symptom disorders carry the stamp of the unresolved past. As a result, when a symptom disorder is operative, there is usually a disproportionate response to an environmental situation, and the response itself may appear contradictory or irrational. Symptom disorders represent an unusual vulnerability of the individual in that the observed distress and irrational response are not expected from the normal individual under conditions that are even remotely equivalent. To use the previous example, the developing headache to avoid facing a deadline may become a symptom disorder if the same individual is unable to hold a job because of frequent somatic decompensations due to the expected stress of the workplace.

Personality patterns are on a different order of organization than either behavioral reactions or symptom disorders. They are highly ingrained, systematized, and pervasive behavioral predispositions that are not specific to a given situation. The personality styles and disorders are behavioral and structural nodes. This is true in two senses of the word "node." The first sense can be applied to the individual case. In the individual, several developmental lines or behavioral themes come together in the formation and expression of the personality. Subsequently, almost all further developments or adaptations must be expressed through the personality. The personality disorders and styles are also nodes in the statistical sense of high density peaks in the multivariate distribution of various pathological traits or symptoms. Put more simply, personality consists of many predispositions and behavioral tendencies coming together in an interactive, coherent pattern; similarly, personality disorders represent the mutual interaction of several pathological trends in development and adjustment.

Again to build on the earlier example of somatization, this trait may be more pervasive to the individual's life and not limited to the workplace. The individual may present physical complaints to avoid sexual demands or social expectations and may be unable to work any job, regardless of stress level, because of this personality pattern. Avoidance and escape may begin to characterize the individual over a large number of circumstances, and methods or strategies other than somatic complaints will also be employed to effect this avoidance. Procrastination may be used, for instance, to avoid environmental demands without recourse to somatic symptoms. The traits of somatization and procrastination can easily become interrelated and self-reinforcing while creating more problems than they solve for the individual, thus causing more situations where these faulty coping mechanisms will be ineffectively employed. Prescribed medication and, later illicit drugs may be used as a coping mechanism to escape or avoid the consequences of somatization and procrastination. The resulting addiction will predictably contribute to more avoidant behavior. An individual with several prominent and interlocking coping mechanisms that have the effect of avoiding or delaying stressors rather than addressing and resolving their causes could be described as having avoidant personality traits.

Once established, personality patterns influence almost all situations and provide the context for understanding and action for the individual. Unlike symptom disorders, personality patterns or traits, even when pathological, tend to be ego-syntonic, that is, the individual views these traits as consistent with or part of the self and experiences the pathogenic trends as normal, adaptive aspects of daily functioning and coping. In fact, the trends may be assumed as givens, and it is often difficult to make patients aware of the fact that there are other ways of coping than those that are ingrained into their characters.

The relationship between these three aspects of psychopathology (behavioral reactions, symptom disorders, and personality patterns) is crucial to understanding Millon's view of psychopathology and the one advanced in this book. For Millon, personality is the central concept in understanding psychopathology and normal functioning. Under very stressful conditions, which may largely be caused by the individual's interpretation of the environment and previous interactions with it, behavioral reactions emerge, which may be easily resolved by introducing new coping strategies (alternative behaviors that are more effective) or by changing the objective situation. Symptom disorders occur when an individual's typical style of coping is overwhelmed by environmental demands, disrupted by internal or external influences, or intensified to the point of being grossly ineffective. These failures in typical coping style are sometimes due to a disease process following the medical model (e.g., by damage to the brain or by an abrupt pathological alteration in biochemical factors), but symptom disorders are more often due to the accumulation of ineffective, uncreative responses to one or more recurrent situations or life problems. Although symptom disorders can be addressed in much the same way as behavioral reactions, they are more difficult to correct, largely because there is no direct link between the current life situation and the type and degree of disordered behavior that is expressed. The indirect links, often in the individual's past learning history, must also be addressed. When personality patterns are disordered, the task of inducing change is exponentially harder, because of the pervasiveness of interlocking, mutually reinforcing patterns of traits.

All three aspects of psychopathology are typified by adaptive inflexibility, vicious circles, and tenuous stability under moderate stress. Adaptive inflexibility is exhibited by the rigid use of the same coping mechanisms without regard to the type of situation or stressor being dealt with. Vicious circles exist when the individual's typical style of reacting and coping intensifies already existing problems, forever digging the pit of personal difficulties deeper and deeper. Tenuous stability is reflected in the susceptibility to failures in coping under conditions that are managed adequately by most persons and in a tendency toward more severe regressions, more maladaptive responses, and longer recovery periods after failures in coping than would be experienced by most persons in the same circumstances.

Having set the stage for understanding the relationship between personality and psychopathology, we must distinguish between personality styles and personality disorders. Personality disorders are typified by interactive patterns of severe adaptive inflexibility, self-defeating or destructive vicious circles, and tenuous stability. Personality styles are predispositions toward particular styles of coping, feeling, thinking, and behaving that, although ingrained and systematic, do not exhibit the extreme rigidity, exclusiveness, and self-defeating or destructive quality of personality disorders.

We may speak, then, of a compulsive personality style and a compulsive personality disorder and expect significant commonalities among individuals who exemplify these ways of coping and being. What are the main differences between the individual with the compulsive personality style and the one with the compulsive personality disorder? The latter is unable to use noncompulsive ways of responding, is unable to avoid increasing personal difficulties because of the extremity of compulsive behavior, and suffers frequent deteriorations in functioning and inability to cope effectively. The person with a compulsive personality style, in contrast, is able, for example, to at least intermittently express feelings of warmth, caring, or joy within a close interpersonal relationship such as a marriage and to be somewhat flexible about the role assignments within the relationship. The style of the compulsive person may actually effectively enhance the relationship, such as by religiously remembering anniversaries with ceremonious celebrations. The person with a compulsive personality disorder, however, typically will be unable to express emotion except by great indirection, will rigidly concentrate on the role assignments for husband and wife, being disturbed by and intolerant of any deviation in these roles. The personality disordered individual will be largely unaware of how these personality traits contribute to exacerbating marital discord. Such a person, for example, may insist that the same relatives or work associates participate in a holiday meal each year, despite the spouse's intense dislike for and disapproval of these guests.

To explain how these personality patterns develop and eventually combine to become either styles or disorders, Millon follows what he calls a biosocial learning approach to understanding infant and child development. He assumes that the child's constitutional predispositions both shape and interact with his or her social reinforcement experiences, which in turn will either strengthen or mitigate these predispositions in later behavior and may contribute to the development of significant central conflicts. The biological and genetic contributions to these predispositions provide the focus for several major research agendas in the human sciences. The child's social environment, however, is crucial in determining the expression of these predispositions. Of special importance are the amount and quality of what Millon calls stimulus nutriment. This includes the experiences of being loved, being given attention, being held, talked to, or having one's actions reflected and either praised or punished, and so on. An optimal quality and quantity of stimulus nutriment is needed to allow the child's native endowments to unfold in a healthy manner. Too little or too much stimulus at sensitive developmental phases may result in maladaptive consequences. Millon's theoretical approach to psychopathology is epigenetic in that it involves hierarchy, sequence, and continual interaction of factors, both in seminal phases of development and throughout the lifespan.

In developing a typology of personality types and disorders, Millon stresses three key dimensions of behavior acquired in early childhood: the *nature* of reinforcement sought by the person (pleasure or pain), the *source* of reinforcement (self or others), and the *style* of instrumental behavior used to obtain the reward (passive or active). The source dimension is roughly equivalent to an attachment dimension and describes coping styles as either dependent, independent, ambivalent, or detached. Dependent persons see others as the source of reward and move toward other persons. Independents rely on the self for reward, such as through accomplishment or self-admiration, and tend to move away from, or against, others. Ambivalent persons are in conflict concerning the safe or optimal source of reward and demonstrate approach/avoidance behavior toward others. Detached persons are unable to process rewards normally and become socially isolated and self-alienated. When the source of reward dimension is combined with the active/ passive dimension, eight personality types are derived, which closely approximate the major personality disorders described in the *DSM-III-R*. The reader may refer back to Table 4–1 for a brief description of the MCMI's operational definition of each of these disorders. Table 6–1 lists Millon's styles and the corresponding *DSM-III* disorders grouped by source and instrumental style dimensions.

While drawing correspondences between the personality styles and disorders it is important to stress that the styles themselves are not essentially pathological. All individuals favor some coping mechanisms and strategies over others. When there is a noticeable commonality among these preferences, we can refer to a coping style as a personality trait, and when these traits are relatively consistent and frequently relied on we can refer to a personality style. Although the basic personality styles do differ in overall effectiveness and may be favored or disapproved of in a given culture, subculture, or situation, individuals with any of the basic eight personality styles may lead relatively healthy, productive, and happy lives. One factor that distinguishes a benign personality adjustment is that a range of traits or coping styles is available as alternatives or adjuncts to the primary style. An established personality style is often a sign of personal maturity, to the extent that the style is bolstered by alternative styles that are used in situations more appropriate to the alternative than to the favored style. A narcissistic individual may, for example, rely primarily on compulsive traits to achieve goals and accomplishments that realistically support narcissistic entitlement. A histrionic individual, dependent, socially active, and assertive, may go through an extended period of social avoidance (behavior more typical of an avoidant personality) while trying to gain personal clarity on life priorities or to achieve some specific, time-limited goal. This flexibility of access to divergent coping mechanisms within an effective preferred coping style is the hallmark of the healthy, mature personality.

Table 6–1. Millon's Basic Personality Types and Disorders

| Attachment | Instrumental Style | |
	Passive	Active
Dependent	Submissive (Dependent)	Gregarious (Histrionic)
Independent	Narcissistic (Narcissistic)	Aggressive (Antisocial)
Ambivalent	Conforming (Compulsive)	Negativistic (Passive-Aggressive)
Detached	Asocial (Schizoid)	Avoidant (Avoidant)

Personality-disordered individuals, when confronted with situations that demand coping mechanisms other than the favored style, will demonstrate an increase in the extremity and exclusiveness of the favored style. When this fails to be effective, either a collapse ensues or even more primitive and less effective alternative styles are employed. These alternative styles are also inappropriate to the specific situation and bear the stamp of the past, rather than reflecting a comprehensive grasp of the current reality. When this vicious cycle is uninterrupted, it leads to what can be referred to as a character psychosis, in effect, a loss of reality orientation due to ineffectiveness and rigidity of personality functions.

To round out this brief discussion of personality styles and disorders, it should be noted that the diversity described as inherent to the healthy personality can also be seen in the personality disorders. Many personality disorders, like the healthier personality styles, are combinations of more than one basic type. In the personality disorders, however, combinations that are often found in normal individuals (such as narcissistic, histrionic, and compulsive traits combined) are typified by an extreme of one of these patterns (usually the least effective one) and an ineffective integration of the alternative styles. As in most clinical topologies, the mixed types best represent the most frequently met clinical reality, and Mixed Personality Disorder and Personality NOS (Not Otherwise Stated), followed by a short list of trait descriptors is the most common diagnosis on Axis II.

Regarding trait combinations, incongruous combinations of alternative patterns of personality is a much more frequent pattern in substance-abusing patients than in other individuals. For example, dependent and paranoid traits are found often in alcohol-abusing forensic patients. Extreme narcissistic, avoidant, and histrionic traits are often poorly integrated in novelists and poets. In these two groups, alcohol is often used to modulate the conflicts and extremes of the incongruous traits. Both consistent and incongruous mixtures of personality traits reveal the link of trait acquisition with object relations through the mechanisms of introjection and identification. The modeling of coping mechanisms by those with whom we identify, or introject aspects of, profoundly increases the likelihood of acquiring and favoring the modelled trait and of it becoming available under specific circumstances, such as during intoxication. Selective and unintegrated introjects of this type may account for the occurrence of incongruous combinations within the personalities or intoxication behavior of persons whose parents were incompatible or in conflict, in regard to coping style, actions toward the child, and other forms of cooperation.

In addition to these basic personality styles and their combinations, which in their extremes can develop into personality disorders, Millon identified two types that represent extreme developmental departures from two more basic or common styles and that invariably involve a more malignant personality adjustment. The aggressive/sadistic personality type is a more pernicious variant of the antisocial personality. The self-defeating personality, similarly, represents an inversion of the passive-aggressive personality.

Table 6–2 describes the pathological variants of several personality styles and three personality process disorders. The disorders are viewed as deteriorations of the personality, or distortions in normal personality development. Millon describes them as severe personality disorders at the borderline level of organization, that is, they indicate frequent decompensations to psychotic states due to failures in the basic reality and regulating functions of the personality. Table 6–2 indicates the coping styles (related to the basic types) from which these disorders are likely to decompensate or developmentally deviate. The table also indicates the behavioral system or symptom complex most involved in the decompensation or developmental detour.

Dealing with underlying personality disorders in addicted individuals with major mental disorders is a major bane of the modern mental health system. Although an Axis I disorder may contribute to the development or worsening of a personality disorder by the exertion of additional stressors, or the breakdown of previously effective coping mechanisms, more often than not the personality style contributes more powerfully to the recurrent insurgency of Axis I symptoms.

In the Chapter 1 example of Suzanne, it is possible that her bipolar disorder reciprocally reinforced and channelled her histrionic traits into a more malignant expression. If so, the Axis I disorder could account for her detour from a basic style of an active dependent personality development to the borderline or cyclothymic personality process disorder with which she presented at the clinic. To accept this, we would have to overlook the exogenous factors, such as her parenting, which clearly contributed to her anguished ambivalence toward herself and others. In treatment, however, it quickly became clear that Suzanne was a repeated treatment failure primarily due to her personality. Personality factors alone could account for her failure to comply with treatment team recommendations and her disruptive sexual involvement with other patients. After her bipolar disorder was fully controlled through medication, Suzanne was even more aggressive in pursuing her need to repeat a chaotic, exploitative, rejecting, and retaliatory parental relationship by cyclically seducing, rejecting, and provoking the treatment staff into complementary stances through her frequent relapses.

Table 6–2. The Decompensated Types and Process Disorders

Disorder	Primary Symptom Complex	Decompensation From
Cycloid (Borderline)	Dominance of Affect Socialization/Identity	Dependent or Ambivalent Orientations
Paranoid (Paranoid)	Cognition, Anxiety (regarding basic security)	Independent or Ambivalent Orientations
Schizoid (Schizotypal)	Context and Cognition	Detached Orientations

The development of the symptom complexes and functions of addiction introduced in this book was, in part, spurred on by the perceived need to acknowledge
and take advantage of the way that these interactive Axis I and Axis II problems
blur together in the dual diagnosis situation. Clearly, describing in detail the
relationship between the major mental disorders and the personality disorders
could be the subject of several books. The reciprocal relationships and process
theory-based ways of thinking described should, however, help the reader to begin
making these connections in regard to their relevance to the treatment of addictions. In each case where a major mental disorder exists with both an underlying
personality disorder or pronounced personality style, the type of opponent process
relationship (harmonic, conflictual, separating, or hierarchical; see Chapter 5)
existing between the two disorders should be determined. This involves examining
the symptom complex dominant in each disorder and determining if the function
of addiction addresses only one complex, the complexes in both disorders, or if
more than one function of addiction addresses each complex differently. For
example, in the case of Suzanne, the relationship between the Axis I and Axis II
disorders is primarily harmonic or hierarchical in that the symptoms of both her
bipolar disorder and her borderline personality disorder have similar effects
(dominance of affect) and can be subsumed under either disorder, depending on the
symptom picture that is dominant at any given time, or depending on the purpose
of the diagnostician.

Suzanne's borderline personality disorder was exhibited in significant problems
with sociability and identity as well as affective symptoms. She used alcohol to
escape or avoid overwhelming negative affect (both disorders) and to facilitate
chaotic, exploitative interpersonal relationships as a repetition of object relational
deficits (borderline personality disorder). She was prone to relapse due to both of
these psychosocial functions of addiction. Once she was on her feet again after a
treatment episode (i.e., not psychotic and not suffering from conscious emotional
pain from intrusive memories), she would become increasingly preoccupied with
her recent failures and interpersonal losses. Soon, she would resume her favored
way of propping up her freshly damaged self-esteem—involving herself in dangerous, chaotic, and abusive relationships during periods of sobriety, which could be
easily explained by her borderline style of self and other representation. These
relationships often led to her involvement in drug or alcohol use, influenced by the
new partner. When this was not the case, these relationships consistently ended
badly (and quickly), resulting in split loyalties, severed attachments, hurt feelings,
deflation of her self-esteem, and her eventual relapse to alcohol use. Although
overlapping in regard to affective symptoms and self-medication though alcohol
use, in regard to relapse dynamics, Suzanne's personality and Axis I disorders were
in a separating opponent process, with the two pathologies eclipsing each other
episodically. Each episode primed the pump, so to speak, for a different kind of
relapse and for making the subsequent interval (dominated by the alternate
process) even more dramatic and pernicious.

In the case of a patient with compulsive personality disorder and schizophrenia (positive symptoms), the relationship between Axis I and Axis II disorders may be described as conflictual if both sets of symptoms are present simultaneously but with mirroring behavioral expressions, as when the compulsive symptoms are used to defend against the more psychotic disruptions of schizophrenia. An example of this is a patient who obsessively counts and recounts his clothing articles as a way of fending off psychotic intrusions. The personality style can be used as a means of coping with the psychotic process; however, the outcome of faulty or insufficient coping may not be a simple partial containment of psychotic symptoms and exacerbation of compulsive rigidity and obsessive behavior. Some forms of delusional ruminations and delusional systems in schizophrenia appear to result from conflictual opposition of an obsessive compulsive cognitive style and the psychotic disruption and related depression and anxiety stemming from a schizophrenic process. These processes combine in a conflict, creating and sustaining a paranoid compromise, which defends against anxiety and depression through the obsessive projection of the awareness of threat. In a case where explosive or bizarrely disorganized psychotic outbreaks and overcontrolled compulsive behavior alternate over time, the same two disorders could be said to be in a separating opponent process relationship, which may increase the severity of each kind of symptom episode.

In addition to establishing the kind of relationship between the Axis I and Axis II disorders, the relationship of the personality disorder or preferred coping styles to each of the phases of recovery and the stages of treatment should be similarly considered to form a prognosis of response to treatment interventions and make a prediction concerning the course that recovery will take. In more than one sense, the personality style or disorder reveals, more than almost any other factor (including drug of choice and severity of addiction), what will be the course of least resistance for the patient in each aspect of treatment.

PERSONALITY AND ADDICTION

Personality has been described earlier as a pattern of coping strategies or mechanisms typically used by the individual that are pervasive, interlocking, and relatively invariant over time. Since the view of persistent addiction advanced in this book is related to failures in self-regulation, factors which influence the effectiveness of a personality style are of particular importance. This is because the most available and important mediator of self-regulation is the personality, i.e., the self is regulated most frequently and most effectively through personality mechanisms.

At the broadest level, cultural factors have a significant impact on the effectiveness of personality and, therefore, on both vulnerability to addiction and the form of addiction. Cultures determine to a large extent the instrumental value of having a given personality type. Cultures that reward competition and divergence, such as modern American culture, provide a haven for the aggressive and narcissistic personality types, which are often viewed as most effective within this cultural context. Cultures that do not prize diversity, but instead reward productivity within the context of consistency with established cultural norms and submission to central authority, such as many Oriental cultures, are arenas where conforming (compulsive) and dependent personalities are favored. Societies that place high value on communal experience and provide influence and power primarily through interpersonal affection and family influence, such as many African cultures, provide special rewards for histrionic and dependent personalities.

Healthy societies give rewards and advantages primarily to the more effective personality types, preserving specific, narrowly defined social roles for the less effective types. Cultures dealing with unfavorable social, political, or economic trends may inadvertently give more rewards to the more pathological personality types. Historical examples are easy to cite. The Inquisition and Imperial Spain clearly rewarded certain sadistic personalities. What were once the Iron Curtain countries tended to reward and engender passive aggressive, avoidant, and mildly schizoid personalities because these types could accept the inefficiency, alienation, and duplicity of the political/economic system with less stress than persons with fewer pathological orientations.

None of these patterns is fixed for a given culture. For example, American culture rewarded passive–aggressive and dependent behavior in African-Americans during the slavery period because of the context of chattel slavery. In modern America, rewards related to personality type are provided differentially according to social class as well as race. Lower class African-Americans may find rewards through aggressive and narcissistic behaviors often involving crime and the drug trade, whereas middle and upper-class African-Americans are rewarded for compulsive (conforming) and dependent traits, the exact reverse of the ways these rewards are distributed to nonblack Americans. A similar analysis could be made for differential perception and reward of personality style by gender, age, or sexual preference. These cultural dynamics are crucial to understanding the epidemiology of substance use and addiction from a psychosocial perspective. Drugs and alcohol are often used to facilitate compliance with the dominant social expectation, to moderate conflicts related to the absence of a fit between one's personality style and the social reward system, and to escape the negative consequences of having a culturally defined stigma.

Sheer cultural relativism in regard to personality is not being advanced here, however. Under conditions of extreme stress, the various personality styles prove to be more or less effective in coping. However, the advantages of one style over another in regard to a specific sphere of demand (such as technical competence, competition, cooperation, interpersonal influence, etc.) disappear under conditions of extreme stress. Under very harsh conditions, factors related, but not identical, to personality style become more important. Such factors as ego strength, intelligence, integration of personality traits, level and coordination of drives, previously acquired skills and competencies, and the strength and neutralization of drives and impulses become more important than coping style.

In short, self-structure (and the cognitive and affective resources available to the self) is more basic and more pivotal to adjustment than personality style. The self-experiences making up the addictive cycle introduced in Chapter 1 are related to instability and inadequacy of self-structure and can be observed among persons with any personality style. The addictive core self, phobic core, and split identity aspects of the self identified in Chapter 5 are partial descriptions of the self-structure and, therefore, are prior to and more pivotal to ongoing adjustment than personality style. Ultimately, the self-structure places some limits on personality development. To again employ the river analogy, personality is to self-structure as surface is to depth. An individual with severe disturbances at the level of what is referred to here as the self-structure is unlikely to develop an effective personality style, although such a development is possible. If one of the more benign personality styles does develop in such an individual, situational stress, like rapids on a river, will churn up the bottom, revealing that the personality is fraught with lacunae, fragile, prone to decompensations to less functional alternative styles, or to becoming rigid, extreme, and self-defeating, that is, a personality disorder. Except under conditions of bottoming out of an addiction, or during the acute phase of a psychiatric decompensation, the personality style or disorder is the surface consciously experienced by the patient and most easily discernable by others.

This surface–depth distinction between self structure and personality accounts for the distance between the description of psychoanalytically derived concepts of addiction (Wurmser's phobic core or split identity) and what is seen in less intensive, less uncovering oriented forms of therapy. It also accounts for the failure to find a true addictive personality. What should prove more productive are attempts to identify individuals with a susceptibility to failures in self-regulation who, therefore, tend to rely on substitute adaptations such as the use of addictive substances for specific self-maintenance and psychosocial functions.

The surface of personality provides the first line of defense and also marks the line of least resistance for the individual. The particular position in the addictive cycle that the individual is most apt to rest at or bottom out at is highly related to personality. By "rest at," we mean the tendency for the individual to feel most comfortable in, to try to maintain, or to naturally gravitate toward a given experience of the self. The position of rest is the most ego-syntonic. Narcissistic and aggressive individuals are more apt to rest at the grandiose/inflated position and feel in charge of the addiction most of the time. Dependent, and to a lesser extent, histrionic personalities will rest at the depleted/depressed position, often viewing themselves as victims and eliciting helping or exploitative behaviors from others.

The detached types (schizoids or avoidants) will rest at the detached/schizoid position. They tend to refuse to acknowledge the reality or meaning of the addiction to themselves or others and often rely on a purely perceptual defense, that is, experiencing the stimulation of the here and now in detachment from others, the core self, and future consequences.

The ambivalent styles tend to cycle more frequently, having less of a resting place and a somewhat less stable self-structure. Accordingly, tenuously adjusted compulsive and passive–aggressive personalities should show the most frequent transitions in self-experience and behavior over the course of an addiction among the basic personality style. This certainly is consistent with the experience of many clinicians.

Deviations from the basic styles (sadistic and self-defeating subtypes) display coping variants of the resting places found by the narcissistic/aggressive and dependent/histrionic types, respectively. The sadistic personality rests within the grandiose/inflated position (perhaps triumphant or predator position would be more descriptive in these cases) through cruelty, subjugation, and vanquishing of others. The self-defeating personality rests in the depleted/depressed (surrendered or martyred) position by arranging the defeat of the self, a maneuver that still avoids realistic self and other appraisal and the possibility for repair. It is interesting to note how these two extreme variants of more basic styles stand dependence and independence on their heads. The sadistic individual is totally dependent on the victim or person over whom victory is gained. The self-defeating character constantly places the self first in experience (and in most external situations), albeit in a negative or victimized guise.

When we apply the same concepts to the more pathological personality disorders, we find the conscious fixation of the paranoid in the grandiose position, which could also fairly be described as the paranoid position because of the dominance of denial by way of projective mechanisms. The schizotypal personality also is fixated in the unreality of the detached/schizoid position. In the cycloid or borderline, we find a rapid, chaotic, darting alternation among the positions, which in severe cases begin to lose their sequential quality.

In each case the kinds of underlying defects are quite similar (addictive core, phobic core, split identity) and the failures in self-regulation account for the addictive process. However, just as the favored resting position varies by the more superficial personality style, so do the frequency and severity of decompensation, and, typically, the severity and specifics of the underlying psychopathology of the self. A close analysis of the addictive cycle reveals that the depleted/depressed position, for example, is less pathological than either the grandiose/inflated or the detached/schizoid, because it depends less on denial of basic negative affective experiences of the core self. It is the position from which reparation, repair, and healing can occur. Using this essentially Kleinian criterion, the detached/schizoid position is the most pathological resting place, because it denies external and internal reality and the experiential nexus of the two within the self. This line of thinking is compatible with Millon's grouping of the personality disorders and styles by level of functioning (Table 6–3).

In regard to vulnerability to substance abuse, it is fair to say that all the personality disorders that exhibit fragility have an increased proneness to using drugs as alternative solutions to life problems, due to their more frequent failures in self-regulation. This caveat of fragility must be stated, because although the vast majority of personality disorders are prone to failures in self-regulation, some may be remarkably resilient to forming substitute solutions, which involve drugs, such as the higher level narcissistic, antisocial, and compulsive types who dynamically resist external dependency or dyscontrol. The low functioning triad of process disorders (paranoid, borderline, schizotypal) are especially prone to failures in self-regulation. Some personality types are prone to addiction because their defensive dynamics closely parallel the dynamics that account for addictive processes. For example, projective and introjective mechanisms have been identified as crucial to addiction. The one extreme along this dimension is the paranoid personality (often derived from narcissistic, antisocial, or compulsive individuals who have decompensated), which relies on the projection of aspects of the self in order to maintain a sense of identity, connectedness, and to regulate the self. This process of externalization of self contents (especially object relational needs) accounts for much of the potency and addictive effect of substances over many persons. For some paranoids, drug use is a kind of purgative, a way of more effectively eliminating the negative aspects of the self by reinforcing projection onto others. On the opposite end are the dependent personalities (and to a lesser extent histrionic individuals) who rely on introjection of aspects of others to stabilize the self and often find in substances a substitute solution for the unavailability or inconsistency of other persons. For these persons, the taking in of the drug provides solace, security, and general pacification.

Antisocial personalities and lower level narcissistic personalities are often very prone to substance abuse and addiction because of their need for a high level of stimulation or sensation. Borderline personalities often exhibit all three of these sources of vulnerability in the form of sensation seeking as a perceptual defense (i.e.,

Table 6–3. Personality Styles and Disorders by Severity

High Functioning	Moderate Functioning	Low Functioning
Narcissistic	Compulsive	Borderline
Histrionic	Passive-Aggressive	Paranoid
Antisocial	Schizoid	Schizotypal
Dependent	Avoidant	

sensation used to ward off thought and feeling) and the primitive mechanism of projective identification that combines projection and introjection in the process of splitting. Splitting involves keeping opposite identifications or introjects separate in order to avoid internal conflict. These identifications or affects (usually involving aggression) are projected outwardly while the person maintains an empathic tie to the projection. Projective identification may occur within an addiction by the borderline projecting certain aspects of the self onto the drug or use situation while attempting to maintain control over these self-fragments. The drug of choice, or the consequences of its use, will also be instrumental in controlling the person or persons involved in the splitting maneuver, such as a treatment unit or a family. In cases of clearly self-destructive drug use, the borderline patient is sometimes motivated to use *because* the drug is seen as destructive. By ingesting the dangerous drug, the borderline externalizes, controls, and internalizes dangerous aggressive impulses and introjects. Because of the identity diffusion of the borderline, addictions in this personality disorder can be very resistant to treatment because the identity exists to a large extent in the drug–self dyad.

Vulnerability to addiction in the other personality disorders is primarily related to two factors. The first is the disorder increasing the likelihood of deficits in one or more of the five symptom complexes. The second factor is that the defenses characteristic of the disorder may allow one or more of the five functions of addiction to serve as relatively viable, ego-syntonic substitute solutions to both self-regulatory failures and symptoms. Cognitive style, affective temperament, activity level, interpersonal style and object relations, and affect tolerance are all areas of behavior and experience that are mediated through the personality style or disorder and provide for specific vulnerabilities to addiction and to other psychopathology. In the next section, each personality disorder is reviewed in regard to these factors. Comments regarding prognosis, preferred intervention modality, key dynamic issues, drug of choice, and such are provided in the context of discussing these vulnerability factors.

Table 6–4 maps the personality disorders against both the functions of addiction and the symptom complexes. Although the table is merely suggestive, it provides a schema for beginning to think through the role of personality style or disorder in the establishment and maintenance of addiction. Table 6–5 describes the typical relationship between personality style and the various positions in the cycle of addiction.

THE BASIC PERSONALITY DISORDERS
IN DUAL DIAGNOSIS WORK

Personality disorders are discussed in the following sections in order of severity of psychopathology as shown in Table 6–3 and by type of attachment as shown in Table 6–1. Severity of psychopathology can be established along two dimensions,

Table 6–4. Personality and the Heuristic System

Function	Reward/Arousal	Anxiety	Dominance of Affect	Cognition Context	Sociability Identity
	Most Prominent Symptom Complex				
Modulation	Antisocial	Compulsive Borderline Histrionic	Borderline Histrionic Passive Aggressive	Schizotypal	Avoidant
Escape/ Avoidance	Avoidant	Avoidant Dependent Compulsive Narcissistic	Narcissistic Compulsive Antisocial	Paranoid Narcissistic Compulsive	Schizoid Narcissistic
Facilitation	Antisocial	Self-Defeating Borderline	Antisocial Narcissistic Compulsive Histrionic	Schizotypal Paranoid Antisocial	Schizoid Dependent Avoidant
Repetition	Narcissistic	Borderline Histrionic Compulsive	Borderline Dependent	Schizotypal Borderline	Narcissistic Paranoid Schizoid
Orientation	Antisocial		Borderline	Paranoid Schizotypal	Paranoid Narcissistic Antisocial

internal psychological structure and external coping mechanisms and their effi-ciency. The work of Otto Kernberg stresses the former, whereas Millon's emphasis on learned behavior led to his stressing the latter. The quality and form of interpersonal attachment fortunately provide an overlap between these two per-spectives, in that interpersonal relatedness is an expression of internalized object relations. The first personality disorders discussed are the higher level types, which have nonconflicted attachment styles: the dependent styles, including dependent and histrionic personalities, and the independent styles, including narcissistic and antisocial types. These are followed by personalities whose interpersonal attach-ment style is basically in conflict or not coherent, that is, the ambivalent styles: compulsive and passive–aggressive types. The detached schizoid and socially isolated avoidant personality types are then discussed. They are at a qualitative level of functioning below the other basic styles. Their tendency toward decom-pensation, aberrant untenable style of attachment, and enhanced inclination to manifest Axis I disorders place them in close clinical affinity to the decompensated personalities covered in Chapter 7.

Table 6–5. The Addictive Cycle and Personality Disorders

Cycling Style	Favored Position or "Resting Place"		
	Grandiose	Depressed	Detached
Fixated	Paranoid Sadistic < Narcissistic >	Self-Defeating Dependent	Schizoid
Stable with Intermittent Cycling	Narcissistic Antisocial	Compulsive < Avoidant >	Avoidant
Rapid Cycling	Histrionic	Passive Aggressive < Histrionic >	
Erratic "Hops" in position	< Histrionic > < Borderline >	Borderline	< Borderline >

THE DEPENDENT STYLES

The Dependent Personality

The *dependent* personality is the basic passive dependent personality type. The dependent person views others as the primary source of reinforcement, which most typically means that he or she takes a sense of security and support from others, who are viewed as more powerful and more competent. Dependents are interpersonally submissive and will avoid situations that require responsibility for self or others, or where they are expected to take the lead in competence, competition, or self-assertion. Dependents strive to be pleasant, agreeable, "nice gals" and "yes men." Internally, they may be insecure, plagued by doubts about their abilities and security, and very anxious about how they are regarded by significant others. Dependents can be very involved and affable in situations where the social atmosphere is undemanding and emotionally supportive. Accordingly, dependents tend to avoid or deny harsh realities. Although they can easily be moved to self-deprecation, criticism of significant others is very difficult for them. The dependent tends to rely on feelings and empathic attunement with others rather than on thinking, neutral analysis, and problem solving. The dependent is very adept at determining what others will reject in them and in identifying any threat to their support system. The dependent style can be very effective within families, workplaces, and other groups where rewards are based on compliance with expectations and acceptance by authority figures and where constant interpersonal contact is available.

Although any personality style may be vulnerable to any Axis I disorder, those most relevant to the dependent in regard to addiction are anxiety and depressive disorders and phobic reactions. Accordingly, these patients are often placed on antidepressant medications or on the benzodiazepines (Gitlin 1990). The symptom complexes of most relevance are typically anxiety or dominance of affect where ego-dystonic problems are prominent. An examination of the sociability and identity cluster will often reveal ego-syntonic deficits. Loss of a supportive person, new environmental demands, or severely suppressed anger or critical thoughts toward the relied on object or system may precipitate any of these disorders. Surprisingly, dependents, who usually have low activity levels and barely detectable aggressive drives, can become quite paranoid and even violent if their basic dependency is threatened. Mortal attacks on family members by intoxicated dependent types are not rare. Because of their avoidance of adult activities, immaturity, and self-identity as a child, sexual offenses against children are sometimes committed by inadequate dependent personalities, especially during periods of abandonment or rejection by another adult.

Drugs or alcohol may provide a release and emotional expression that are suppressed or denied out of fear of losing security and support or as a substitute solution to unmet interpersonal needs. Drugs may play a role even at the level of a spouse's daily coming and going, resulting in the need for self-medication for separation anxiety.

Highly dependent persons are prone to chemical dependency due to their tendency to rely on introjection of significant others internally as regulators of the self. Positive and self-soothing functions of the self and early introjects are projected onto significant others, environments, and substances. Although no clear correspondence between personality style and drug of choice exists, alcohol and other sedatives are very effective in addressing anxiety symptoms. Oral routes of administration may be favored by the oral dependent type, following traditional psychosexual typology. The preference for drugs other than sedatives may suggest counterdependent modulation and displacement of dependency needs, such as heroin use through nasal administration. Intravenous injection of opiates may indicate the need to escape or avoid feelings of emptiness, loss, or abandonment, which are related to a failure of introjection processes in infancy and childhood. Clinically, this is often related to the literal or emotional unavailability of the primary object of identification. In these cases dependency needs are closely meshed with rage at the abandoning parent and with a incipient anaclitic depression.

Some immunity to addiction will be present if significant others are very disapproving of drug use, but more often such disapproval will lead to secretive use and greater anxiety, depression, and self-loathing. At times the dependent person will use an addiction to facilitate the acting out of hostility and self-assertive longings in an interpersonal relationship. In other cases, the addictive pattern provides an escape from competency demands and a bid for total dependency.

Accordingly, dependents often do well in inpatient treatments and in early phases of recovery, since the stabilizing and supportive aspects of the treatment process correspond with their essential personality style.

Not surprisingly, the dependent tends to stay in the depressed or depleted position of the addictive cycle and to resist movement through it. In this position, the dependent strives to maintain the soft and mushy feelings of being attached and secure, weak and provided for, rather than suffer the pain and anxiety of independence and abandonment depression. According to the hypothesis that the depressive position is optimal for treatment, the prognosis would be positive were it not for the external reinforcement that this personality style often receives. Substances can facilitate the attachment experience through state tuning and can modulate feelings of abandonment through direct chemical effects (as heroin does in experiments with socially isolated primates). Drugs may provide escape or avoidance of pain. The isomorphism between drug and interpersonal dependency is obvious and results in the high frequency of repetition of early infant experience through drug dependency.

As noted earlier, the dependent style is difficult to change because it is easily supported and reinforced externally. In fact, the initial phases of recovery hinge on using the dependent's needs for attachment, security, and support. Uncovering of co-dependent and pathological family systems may lead to the dependent dropping out of treatment or becoming extremely anxious and depressed, thus precipitating a relapse to drug use. Since dependents will follow the lead of those around them, especially significant persons whom they perceive as powerful, assessment of the dependent's social environment is especially important to locate areas of peer pressure or the social orientation function of drug use. Establishment of NA and AA contacts will be easy for the dependent, but there is no assurance that these individuals will seek out and attach to the healthier and more sincere members of such groups. More often than not, they are prey for more aggressive or narcissistic social players in almost any system. Therapy must be centered on diversifying dependencies across a full range of social and activity domains. Specific guidance and reinforcement of preferred interpersonal attachments are often crucial to the treatment of dependent persons with an addictive disorder.

The Histrionic Personality

The histrionic personality contrasts with the dependent by its active strategy of establishing dependent ties and rewards. This personality type, and to some extent the dependent type, has historically been described under the hysterical personality grouping and was considered to occur primarily in women, or men with strongly feminine characters. This is probably due primarily to the fact that the prevalent culture during the origin of these clinical descriptions rewarded women for exhibiting histrionic and dependent traits.

Histrionic personalities are always on stage, winning attention, and providing a dramatic experience to themselves and others. They are very gregarious, even when that is not apt to provide inherent rewards. Even under conditions when one would try to avoid attention (e.g., during a plane hijacking by terrorists), the histrionic person will do something in an attention-getting manner and probably become the focus for some action, regardless of the threat to self. Like the dependent personality, the histrionic personality views other persons as the primary source of reinforcement, particularly attention, admiration, sympathy, or passionate involvement. Unlike the dependent, however, the histrionic is unwilling and unable merely to accommodate and submit in a passive manner to win interpersonal support and can quickly replace objects of dependency needs. The histrionic person is particularly astute at manipulating others by becoming the other's desired object. This strategy of adopting the characteristics required to be attractive or admirable leads to the histrionic person being essentially without real commitments and exhibiting an emotional fickleness and inconsistency across situations and relationships.

Histrionics rarely favor cognition over affect and generally evaluate individuals, ideas, and situations in terms of a rather fleeting emotional impression, rather than detailed analysis. If the primary fear of the dependent is to be abandoned because of rejection, the primary fear of the histrionic is to be abandoned through neglect. Active, engaged negative contact is preferred by most histrionic persons to noninvolvement and neglect, even by relatively nonsignificant others. In extreme histrionic personality types, it is sometimes difficult to determine who is significant and who is not (a pattern rarely found in the dependent personality), because of the pervasive pattern of histrionic interpersonal seduction. The histrionic person tends to sexualize nonsexual relationships and to resent the professional relationship stance taken by a therapist, viewing it as a defense against romantic or sexual attraction, an expression of envy and hostility, or a form of disfavor. Overreaction, overexpressiveness, and an overly demanding interpersonal style are typically present. Although the activity level in histrionic persons tends to be erratic and undependable, with a good deal of emotional liability, their hedonistic, sensation-seeking, involvements in numerous sexual liaisons and get-rich-quick schemes and their constant interpersonal confrontations and seductions in many ways mirror behavior typical of mania.

The histrionic style is highly effective in situations requiring a good first impression, interpersonal attraction, the communication of an emotion or the gist of an idea, or where the support of other persons can result in success. Histrionic individuals do less well in situations where individual merit is evaluated by objective measures or where competence, diligence, thoroughness, and depth are required. The histrionic style, however, is able to deal with competition more effectively than the dependent and often perceives competition, especially for favor or attention, where there is none. Acting, marketing, politics, and the arts are fields where the histrionic personality may manage competition effectively.

In regard to the Axis I disorders and symptom complexes, conversion disorders and hypochondriasis are common, as are dissociative disorders and affective problems such as dysthymia or cyclothymia. Ego-dystonic symptoms are apt to occur in the reward–arousal (sensation-seeking and high arousal levels alternating with low arousal), anxiety (especially related to abandonment and separation), and dominance of affect (cyclothymia or dysthymia). MAO inhibitors often are useful in modulating these affective problems (Gitlin 1990). Ego-syntonic deficits are found in the management of close interpersonal relationships and core identity issues. In some cases the sociability and identity complex will be dominant, with severe dissociative phenomena such as fugue states, amnesia, or multiple personality disorder. More commonly, the histrionic personality exhibits dissociation by experiencing memory, affect, and values as essentially context dependent, that is, as changing according to the patient's perception of who is to be won over or seduced in a given situation.

As in the dependent personality style, the histrionic reliance on introjection creates an additional vulnerability to addiction. The shallowness and absence of integration among the introjects of the histrionic personality are mirrored in a superficial involvement in the details of life, with little ability to integrate emotional experience across situations and persons. The isomorphic relationship between the histrionic person's poorly integrated and alternating identifications and the suddenness and distinctness of chemically induced mood states increases this vulnerability to addiction. In regard to specific affective experiences, sexuality and aggression are frequent problem states for the histrionic individual, because expressions of such feelings can undermine, establish, or defend dependent ties. Also, exaggerations of these states may account for the faulty identification process that leads to the development of the histrionic personality. During childhood, integration and full incorporation of introjects may fail in the budding histrionic personality because of the irreconcilable emotions and perceptions of parents. Extreme attraction and aggression, which are inconsistent with stable identification, may be generated by a sexualized competition with the same-sex parent, which the histrionic continually attempts to win. Alcohol and drugs often are used as substitute solutions to this failure of integration. This use is temporarily effective because drug use facilitates dissociative behavior through the expression of two or more sets of alternating emotions or self-states. An example is the histrionic who is indiscriminately sexually provocative only under intoxication, but while sober the same individual is childlike and dependent, even asexual, in his or her approach to interpersonal attraction.

The histrionic personality is apt to rest at either the grandiose or depleted positions, depending on external circumstances. The histrionic would prefer to be carefree and hedonistic, enjoying the attention and admiration of others, but this is a difficult position to maintain both intrapsychically and in the external world of harsh realities related to drug use and trade. Rapid cycling between the role of enraptured user and a victimized person suffering from the illness of addiction are typical. Antianxiety drugs are commonly abused by histrionic personalities, but stimulants also provide the dramatic mood boosts they seek.

Histrionic personalities will be greatly influenced by what is "in" or fashionable, even in regard to their drug of choice and its route of administration, and to treatment centers or movements. These individuals will rarely use drugs in a asocial context. Dependents may use drugs to substitute for interpersonal support or to avoid anxieties related to interpersonal situations. Histrionics usually will use drugs as part of an interpersonal scene or in preparation for the role they intend to play in an interpersonal drama.

Accordingly, chemicals may play a significant role in the sexual and romantic behavior and fantasies of histrionics. Although the view will rarely become conscious, some extreme histrionics will perceive the therapist and the drug of choice as two jealous lovers competing for his or her exclusive attention and will relate to this situation with the same degree of conflict and relish as they might in such an interpersonal triangle. In such cases, the function of addiction is repetition, and the expectation will be for the good parent (the therapist) to rescue the patient from the bad parent (the drug), usually by seduction or being seduced. For histrionics who are closer to a borderline level of organization, the good and bad aspects of this drama will be attributed to the self or to the therapist in an alternating fashion and may be rapidly reversed, with the drug becoming the soothing rescuer from either a punitive, rejecting, or neglectful therapist, or from a demeaned, depleted self. Even without this level of pathology, the histrionic patient will insist on specialness and will engage the therapist in as many roles as possible to accomplish this sense of being special and winning favor over other patients.

Histrionics find it difficult to commit to change. Because they rely so heavily on repression, constant interpretation of their behavior is required for it to become more consciously determined. If there is enough of a dependent bond between the therapist and the histrionic patient, the patient may be highly motivated to respond to specific interventions. Although it is easy to win a battle with an infatuated or dependent histrionic, the war is probably most often lost. Because of this ability to win attention and admiration by temporarily responding favorably in treatment (becoming the therapist's desired object, the ideal patient), there is always the danger of a histrionic patient becoming the special or star patient in a treatment group, later to become the center of attention for being the problem child due to relapses. Histrionic patients will have extreme difficulties in the end phase of recovery, especially the challenge phase, which signals separation from close dependency on the treatment staff and the beginnings of self-directed recovery.

Because of its effectiveness in interpersonal control, the histrionic style is often the secondary coping style for antisocial and narcissistic personalities and other styles that are not essentially dependent but can adapt to situations where interpersonal influence and dependency are rewarded.

THE INDEPENDENT STYLES

Two independent styles complete the high functioning group of personality styles and disorders that are oriented toward psychosocial rewards in a viable and relatively conflict-free manner. The narcissistic and antisocial (aggressive) types derive rewards primarily from the self and view others only as instrumental to self-gratification. As noted earlier, the active independent type, the antisocial personality, especially in its most deviant expressions of the psychopathic and sadistic personalities, are discussed in Chapter 8.

The Narcissistic Personality

As with the borderline personality, many theoretical views have proliferated over the last few decades to account for the narcissistic personality. Considerable confusion has resulted from this growth of clinical and theoretical attention, in part because various theorists do not always clearly differentiate their basic terminology from the same terms used somewhat differently by others. The type of patient to which they refer may vary widely from theory to theory under the rubric of narcissism. All of these confusions and contradictions cannot be clarified here, but a few of the major positions can be briefly delineated.

Freud described narcissistic personalities as extremely self-centered individuals who gravitated toward leadership roles in relationships and in society and who were prone toward homosexuality, the perversions, hypochondriasis, and, at the extremes, megalomania and paranoid delusions. In the psychoanalytic tradition, Freud introduced an approach toward understanding the narcissistic orientation by stressing frustration in the infant–parent dyad. Narcissism in this view results from an abandonment by the infant of any hope of comfort or reward from the parental object due to the parent or parents' unreliability and/or inaccessibility. The narcissistic person is defensively turned toward a focus on the self because of expectation of frustration from the external world.

Within the analytic tradition, Kernberg (1967) placed special emphasis on the role of aggression in this turning toward the self. Accordingly, the narcissist has an inadequate internalization of objects and places, a focus on the self as a defense against oral rage toward frustrating others. Kernberg's narcissist is seen as primarily suffering from feelings of rage, indignation, and frustrated entitlement. In Kernberg's narcissist, dependency feelings are ego alien and produce more rage and grandiose inflation of the self.

Kohut (1971, 1976) posited a two-pronged course of self-development involving two sets of idealized internal representations: the grandiose self and idealized parental imago. In normal development, both of these sets of internal representations would gradually change through the infant's/child's accommodation to optimal frustrations. In pathological narcissism, either set of self-objects has failed to develop beyond this primitive stage of idealization, probably due to traumatic disillusionment. In adulthood, Kohut's narcissist is prone to disappointment or disillusionment (traumatic deflation of an idealized internal representation) and to feelings of low self-esteem, somatic complaints, emptiness, and depression. Kohut differentiates the narcissistic from the borderline personality by the kind of transference they are able to establish. The borderline is essentially unable to tolerate a transference-related regression to the intersubjectivity of experience in therapy that replicates the early infant–parent dyad. In the borderline personality, this inability results in various iatrogenic disorders of analysis such as a transference psychosis or severely destructive acting out of regressed states.

Kernberg's evaluation of prognosis for the narcissistic personality is much different from Kohut's self-psychological view. Kernberg sees severe narcissism as the result of essentially flawed psychological structure, whereas Kohut views the development of the grandiose self as a normal maturational hurdle that leads to increased ability to self-regulate. To oversimplify the positions for our purposes, Kernberg's is a defect view of psychopathology, calling for basic structural change in the self, whereas Kohut's stresses maturational deficits that can be more easily remediated. In both cases, these theorists stress factors that are probably more fundamental than personality and extend to the area of the development of the core self, described earlier as the depth of the individual, as compared to the presented surface level of personality.

Millon's social learning theory approach views narcissistic personality disorders as resulting from a more obvious source: unrealistic overvaluation by the parents, which engenders an unrealistic self-image. This approach is not inconsistent with psychodynamic formulations of the problem of narcissism, because the process of overvaluation identified by Millon as pathogenic can be pathogenic in ways consistent with unavailable objects, traumatic frustration, and catastrophic disillusionment of early idealizations. Patents who overvalue children usually do so by using the child as a self-project, or extension of themselves. In doing this they are unavailable to the child to the extent that the child forays out toward independent development. Overinvested parents may be harsh and punitive toward any failing in the child and may offer either an ideal image to be followed exactly or a negative example to be avoided and overshadowed through the child's accomplishments, which serve as compensation for the parent's own frustrated life goals and ambitions.

Regardless of how one evaluates the various theoretical explanations of the narcissistic personality, for treatment purposes of substance abuse disorders, it is useful to distinguish between those who are prone to conscious experiences of low self-esteem, guilt, and depression, and those typically without such conscious experiences. All things being equal, the depressive narcissist will have a better prognosis over time than the more defended type, although in the early phases of recovery the reverse may appear true. The grandiose/inflated self of the addictive cycle could stand as the emblem for the narcissistic personality. In fact, the grandiose/inflated position echoes early descriptions of the narcissistic personality:

> If narcissism is considered not genetically but with reference to its actual meaning it should, in my judgment, be described as essentially self-inflation. Psychic inflation, like economic inflation, means presenting greater values than really exist. It means that the person loves and admires himself for values for which there is not adequate foundation. Similarly, it means that he expects love and admiration from others for qualities that he does not possess, or does not possess to as large an extent as he supposes. [Karen Horney 1939, quoted in Millon 1981, p. 162]

Narcissistic individuals view themselves as the center of concern in almost all situations and often grossly overestimate any positive self-attribute. They see themselves as the source of rewards and distort events in a manner that results in confirmation of their superior knowledge, wisdom, moral purity, power, and influence over others, and their unfettered abilities. At the same time, negative aspects of the self, including any weaknesses or inconsistency with socially approved or self-endorsed values and standards, are met with denial or rationalization. Accordingly, narcissistic individuals usually experience expansive positive moods, especially while their fantasies about personal specialness or self-aggrandizing exploits are unchallenged by other individuals or by reality testing. Successful confrontation of a narcissistic personality with such weaknesses or shortcomings usually results in an enraged sense of entitlement and demands to be made whole by someone who has caused the defect or deficiency, which is only apparently their own. Often fairly transparent prevarication is supported by the narcissist's air of superiority and authority and an implied threat of retaliation or retribution. This maneuver is often effective in dealing with compliant, dependent, and other nonconfrontive individuals. If disillusionment should occur (meaning that the narcissist is forced to abandon a prized self-representation, self-project, or self-object), personality disorganization, explosions of rage, severe depression, and inconsolable feelings of humiliation and emptiness may result.

The narcissistic personality relies heavily on rationalization and fantasy to self-regulate. This is often not evident to casual observers because of the skill with which the narcissist is able to obfuscate the distance between the projected self-image and reality. In addition to blatant lies, distortions of the truth, very creative autobiographical sketches, and nonchalance in the face of any challenge, the narcissist uses real accomplishments and talents to defend against acknowledging deficits and to perpetuate inflated experiences of self. Narcissists tend to rely on cognition more than affect, although upon close examination both cognition and affect are shot through with spurious, fictional elements. An example of this spuriousness is in the instance of an accomplished administrator who effectively won an argument in an important multidisciplinary professional meeting by citing (in the most arrogant, aggressive, and indignant manner) a research finding from investigators from within the discipline in which he claimed competence. The study was cited as a well-known seminal work in the field. The administrator in question, although a consummate orator, was not licensed or properly credentialed in the field over which he had merely arrogated the right to an authoritative opinion. Not only had he not corrected those who mistakenly referred to him as "doctor" in the sessions, but he later tried to ensure that the distinction between qualified and unqualified individuals would be obscured, both in that session and in the official record of the meeting. His intimidating style and apparent confidence had effectively prevented qualified persons from volunteering that the cited study, if it existed at all, was apparently known to no one but the administrator. Because the meeting was multidisciplinary, the sessions ended before he was confronted with that fact or before his true background and qualifications were made known to the membership. In this example, both real and imagined talents, skills, accomplishments, were marshalled successfully by the narcissistic personality to accomplish a self-project; that is winning an argument over highly qualified experts and getting others to reflect his conscious evaluation of himself.

The reader will, of course, note the similarity of this behavior to psychopathic actions. The distinction is that on some level, the narcissistic person in this example believed himself entitled to an authoritative view on the subject and probably could not have consciously *in advance* examined the factors that led to the distortion of scholarly and professional reality. The psychopath, in contrast, would be aware of the deception as it occurred, could have prepared for it in advance, and would have gained an additional personal reward from the success of the conscious deception. Such an individual would suffer no sense of shame, either upon reflection, or if the manipulations and distortions had been exposed.

Needless to say, the narcissistic style can be highly effective and rewarding in a competitive society that relies heavily on self-marketing and surface impressions, such as media sound bites in political elections. However, long-term interpersonal relationships and work situations where responsibility for error or failure, or the mere consequences of behavior cannot be deflected or obscured are problematic for narcissistic persons. These liabilities can be mitigated when the narcissist is able to attach to very dependent partners and when his or her real base of interpersonal and occupational skills is relatively sound or realistically superior within a limited arena.

In regard to Axis I disorders, the narcissistic personality disorder is very vulnerable to dysthymia and depression and may present as depressive personalities, that is, individuals with lifelong depressive orientations. Often hypomanic episodes will punctuate a generally depressive presentation. MAO inhibitors and lithium are sometimes useful in managing these symptoms (Gitlin 1990). Narcissists are relatively immune to many other disorders because of the effectiveness of rationalization and denial. However, somatic complaints are often expressed, because these are not seen as part of the self. Narcissists are usually very unaccepting of any psychological interpretation of these illnesses. Delusional beliefs and outright paranoia may be exhibited while under attack from valued others or in the face of a series of severe failures or disappointments. Pathological jealousy and the fear of conspiracies are often easily developed in such individuals, who typically cut themselves off from open confidences and honest feedback from others, due to their inability to accept constructive criticism or tolerate others viewing them with disappointment.

The narcissistic personality is vulnerable to substance abuse because many drugs support an inflated sense of self, or interrupt or moderate feelings of low self-esteem and depression, which are the reverse side of the narcissistic way of being. Most narcissistic persons prefer the grandiose/inflated position and under optimal circumstances will use drugs only to enhance feelings of vigor, power, or euphoria. Stimulants such as cocaine are very effective for facilitating this goal. To use the concepts introduced in Chapter 5, the narcissistic personality is the most vigilant in warding off intrusions from the addictive core through the establishment of the phobic core defenses. If the depressive aspects of experience stemming from these more basic injuries to the self do intrude on consciousness, drugs may be used in an attempt to avoid rotating to other positions in the cycle that threaten to precipitate the narcissistic crisis described by Leon Wurmser. Generally, the narcissist prefers the manic defenses of denial, flight, and overcompensation, and these are supported behaviorally by increased activity, overproductivity of thought, and grandiosity. In the extreme, these defenses comprise an agitated schizoid detachment preferred by most narcissists over the depleted/depressed position. Some narcissists will present as more detached than independent, especially after the effects of a long-term addiction have resulted in a narcissistic crisis and disillusionment with the idealized self. In one sense, the fully inflated narcissist is (interpersonally) detached due to the atrophy of independent objects in the life space, other than the self and the drug of choice. Alcohol and other sedatives often help provide this isolation, although for some patients the autistic stimulation provided by the hallucinogens is preferred. Narcissists who show dominance of affective factors, specifically the affect of rage as noted by Kernberg, may be more prone to heroin addiction, which specifically addresses affects related to attachment, which has faltered after bonding has become a viable developmental option for the individual. In the context of discussing the drug of choice for narcissistic personalities, it should be noted that the consummate skill required to manage the drug situation (especially as a high rolling dealer) and the centrality to others that drug dealing fosters may be more rewarding to the narcissist than any drug use in itself.

Narcissistic persons are very prone to hidden or secret addictions, since an addictive problem or even the use of a drug may be very inconsistent with their self-image and the image they project to others. The fear of detection by admirers is often a source of significant motivation for change. Their tendency toward rationalization and fantasy provides very strong supports for denial of loss of control over substances, however. Their "one-down" view of the patient role in a therapeutic relationship often prevents them from entering substance abuse treatment until after they have reached some major personal catastrophe related to drug use. Even after several DWIs and accidents, for example, the narcissist will enter therapy only under court order. Because of the ease with which these patients will experience themselves as special and resist direct feedback from others, group therapy is the preferred modality for engaging the narcissistic person. In group work, the therapist must prevent the narcissist from dominating the group with his or her concerns, from allowing the patient to become a co-therapist, and must at times be prepared to protect the narcissist from the worst consequences of his or her insensitivity toward other group members.

In regard to repetition of early experience as one psychosocial function of addiction, an interesting pattern of addiction is related to the denial and projection of dependency in the narcissistic personality. Some narcissists are great benefactors and givers, apparently devoting large amounts of time and care to others, on whom they project their own (unconscious or suppressed) sense of inadequacy and dependency. Drug dependence in such cases is rationalized as "the only thing I do for myself," and on the unconscious level is the return of the repressed need for emotional dependency and narcissistic supplies from others. The use of the drug denies the primacy of other individuals, that is, dependency on drugs is more acceptable (and safer) than dependency on other persons, a pattern mirroring infant or childhood experience of self with caregiver.

Given that there is some success in breaking through the denial and rationalization of the narcissist in the deconstruction phase of treatment, these patients will, nonetheless, remain especially vulnerable to relapse in the middle phases of recovery. They are apt to be free of any fear of relapse factors or to feel that they will be able to reassert controlled use because of the knowledged gained from the first round of addiction. Any lapse in the challenge phase will often result in permanent relapse and avoidance of any further contact with treatment staff or recovery peers in order to escape fears of overwhelming shame and humiliation. Narcissists may use self-help groups to further advance their self-aggrandizing agenda, which at the same time will exacerbate a more basic sense of defectiveness. Successful treatment of the narcissistic personality will involve the encouragement of appropriate dependency, if possible, and the development of toleration for dysphoric states related to increased acceptance of personal limitations and emotional connection with others.

THE AMBIVALENT STYLES

These personality styles are less effective than the dependent or independent styles discussed in the preceding sections. The ambivalent styles display an an essential conflict in regard to sources of reward. They live in an eternal Catch 22 because they cannot feel secure or content in anticipating rewards either from the self or others. This is not the healthy situation where the individual will at times choose internal and at other times external sources of reward. The ambivalent type spoils all rewards by his or her conflicted experience of self and others. For example, power, status, and control are crucial issues for ambivalent types because of the intense conflicts generated within them by these aspects of relationship. Dominance and submission are two alternative, complementary ways of structuring power or leadership roles so that social rewards and task achievement can be optimized. In healthy social situations, at least some degree of alternation occurs between participants in regard to dominant or submissive behavior. Despite this natural give and take, most people are fairly clear (at least on the behavioral level) as to the general desirability of being either domineering or submissive in interactions with others. Healthy individuals are typically *very* clear as to which of these behavioral modes they desire in a specific interaction with a specific other or set of others. However, for the ambivalent individual, none of the possible role prescriptions is satisfactory, because each one generates a basic conflict over whether to be submissive or dominant. The vacillation, erratic behavior and mood, contradictory cognitions, and general inconsistency of the ambivalent style are expressed passively by the compulsive (conforming) personality and actively by the passive-aggressive (negativistic) personality.

The Compulsive Style

To understand the compulsive style, Millon (1981) advises thinking of it as being comprised of qualities from the antisocial (aggressive) style and the dependent (submissive) style. The conflict is obvious. Whereas on the behavioral level, the compulsives are conforming and submissive, they also experience strong impulses toward self-assertion and independence. Defending against aggressive impulses, the compulsive person becomes extremely submissive, overcompliant, and uncreative and relies on external rules and prohibitions to determine his or her actions. The compulsive carefully identifies which persons in the environment are dominant or assigned to authority and follows those individuals doggedly, often to absurd lengths. Compulsive individuals are very emotionally restricted, largely out of fear of their own potential outbursts of aggression or self-assertion, but also out of fear of rejection from significant others. Although compulsives are very concerned about control and productivity (a dynamic linked psychoanalytically with anal retentive and anal expulsive issues), they are commonly mediocre performers in any situation demanding something beyond merely repetitive tasks, careful planning, or attention to detail. This is because of their unconscious resentment of task demands, which they perceive as being forced on them, their overconcern with orderliness, which results in missing the forest for the trees, and their fear that their efforts will not be acceptable to themselves or others. Compulsives often behave in a passive-aggressive manner. In fact, passive-aggressive personalities can somewhat humorously be described as compulsive personalities with "an attitude," that is wanting everyone else to share in their conflictual dilemma.

Compulsives can find very secure niches in bureaucracies and large organizations, where lines of authority are clear and power is exerted from the top down. Compulsives are often concerned about prudence and may impose very close restrictions on others to prevent any potential foolhardy action from them, a projection of their own repressed fear and desire for aggressive abandon. Compulsives are disciplined and perfectionistic and harsh toward self or others when idealized standards are not met. They are unusually attentive to ceremony, correctness, and the relative social standing of individuals. Although they prefer cognition to affect, their style is constricted and lacking in confidence and variety.

Compulsives rely on sublimation and reaction formation to regulate the conflicting aspects of their personalities. These defenses can be greatly supported when encouragement is provided by an idealized person with whom the compulsive has identified. It is not surprising that compulsives are particularly vulnerable to obsessive compulsive disorders, which often express their buried aggressive and sexual impulses in more acceptable but repetitive and incapacitating ways. Excessive grooming, for example, may sublimate sexual urges, or provide a reaction formation against the resentment felt about being required to appear a certain way in a given situation or for a certain person. Anxiety disorders are very common among compulsives, because all situations are potential sources of disapproval and rejection for them. Somatization of problems is relatively common as well, largely because these disabilities are socially acceptable ways of expressing hostility or resentment and of avoiding responsibility and therefore catastrophic anxiety concerning potential failure. Depressive personality traits, dysthymia, and/or episodes of recurrent major depression are frequently experienced by compulsives who perceive themselves as having failed some perfectionistic standard, or who find themselves in a secure niche that allows little room to externalize their anxieties.

The relevance of the split identity concept is clear in the case of the compulsive, who attempts rigidly to compartmentalize aggression and other unacceptable impulses within a submissive, compliant, conscientious, and mature surface experience and presentation. In assessing the compulsive personality with an addictive problem, it is important to ascertain whether the addiction supports this compartmentalization by shoring up defenses (as in escape/avoidance or modulation), or if the addiction provides an outlet for expressing otherwise partitioned and unacceptable aspects of the self (as in facilitation). Whatever may be the case, compulsives tend to have more muted expressions of the addictive cycle than other personality types discussed to this point, and they remain functional addicts for long periods of time. They tend to cycle slowly, primarily resting in the depressive position until the addiction escalates. At full tilt, the extremes encountered in the antisocial and dependent personalities are seen in the compulsive, with aggressive grandiosity alternating with intense humiliation, shame, and guilt. With some compulsives these traits will alternate simultaneously with episodes of sobriety and intoxication.

The symptom complexes usually most relevant to compulsives are anxiety and dominance of affect, with mood congruent obsessive cognitions (usually of a depressive nature). In some cases obsessive compulsive disorder will also be present, which may be addressed medically with clomipramine or fluoxetine (Gitlin 1990). The function of addiction involved is usually escape/avoidance or modulation of painful affect or haunting thoughts. It is important to note that affects, cognitions, and experiences that would be totally avoided by less ambivalent types will be modulated or facilitated in compulsives through drug use. Some compulsives, however, will repeat conflicted infant–parent relationships by relating conflictually with the drug of choice. The drug chosen by the compulsive will usually be alcohol or a prescribed medication, because of the minimal social opprobrium with these substances. Compulsives easily acquire ingrained habits, perhaps because of their basic passivity, the relief afforded by any repetitive behavior on their overloaded nervous systems (due to the pervasiveness of their conflicts), and their constant search for external rules to guide their behavior. Drug use can, therefore, easily become a compulsive accelerating addiction in compulsive personalities. Distinguishing this kind of repetitive use of substances from repetition of basic object relations is sometimes very difficult and may not be possible without data concerning circumstances surrounding lapses or episodes of intense urges to use the drug of choice.

Compulsives are good followers of advice, guidelines, and programmatic efforts that require note taking, records, measurements, and specific steps or sequences. Psychoeducational efforts with compulsives are important ways of avoiding the stimulation of resistance. Identification with a sponsor or therapist can very often provide important ego controls to otherwise fragile compulsive personalities. Authority figures can aid in breaking down the compulsive's resistance to deconstruction of denial phase of recovery. Extreme confrontation as an intervention with the compulsive is often unnecessary, and redirection by an authority figure is usually quite effective. Compulsives usually work too hard cognitively at gaining insight and need to be instructed that working through of emotions and reactions is more important than cognitive understandings. The term *working through* is apt to be appealing in itself to the compulsive, who will then dutifully try to work through, with more emphasis on *work* than on *through*, since continual striving is more congruent with compulsive ambivalence than is fully resolving any issue.

The phase of recovery the compulsive will find most difficult is establishing balance. The compulsive's idea of balance is unbalanced and rigid, with a focus on work, following rules, and very limited ability to form an adequate range of appropriately mutual dependencies. Because of the compulsive's ability to make use of guidelines and rules, the challenge and self-direction phases are relatively nonproblematic. An important caveat to this generalization is the fact that should a lapse occur, it may result in overwhelming guilt (Marlatt's abstinence violation effect), complete loss of control, and quick spiralling into relapse.

Compulsives are not usually fun people to work with, which can result in some significant countertransference problems. The therapist may begin to favor less conflicted members of a treatment group, for example, or may adopt a routinized, uncreative way of relating to the compulsive client, accepting and mirroring the client's own stereotyped and constricted self-presentation. Compulsives can demonstrate extreme gratitude and admiration toward their therapists in appreciation of progress that is rightly attributable to either self, family, or group processes. Underlying the compulsive's gratitude is often a hint of hostility or aggression, especially a "yes, but . . ." which may stimulate the therapist's aggression. Since progress with the compulsive is usually slow and uneven, countertransference reactions of this kind are less hazardous than those related to the compulsive's rigidity and seeming predictability.

Passive–Aggressive (Negativistic) and Self-Defeating Styles

As noted earlier, the passive–aggressive personality could be described as a compulsive personality with "an attitude." Rather than submerging his or her basic ambivalence, the passive–aggressive person expresses it openly. This may be due to less effective internal controls related to constitutional factors. Another explanation is that when compared to the compulsive, the passive–aggressive person was exposed during infancy and childhood to more severe conflicts between intense and extremely incompatible or conflicting parental injunctions and behaviors. The compulsive constricts affect and establishes rigid controls to avoid aggressive outbursts and thereby hopes to gain safety and reward by submission and conformity. The passive–aggressive, in contrast, expresses an irritable or sour mood and reveals aggression usually by pouting and complaining, but also at times in explosive outbursts. Millon's use of the term *negativistic personality* is apt in that passive–aggressives are often either depressed or sulking and gain perverse pleasure by raining on everyone's parade, including their own. The self-destructive and perverse aspect of the passive–aggressive personality is present because the souring discontent that they express toward the world is also internalized as an attitude toward the self.

In extreme cases, the passive–aggressive personality may develop into the more pathological variant, the self-defeating personality, formally referred to as the masochist. The debates in the various *DSM-IV* committees have revealed a general absence of consensus about the distinction between the passive–aggressive and self-defeating type. Although Millon has clearly distinguished structural and behavioral differences between these personality types, they are discussed here as a cluster of disorders.

In the context of dealing with substance abuse issues, the label of *self-defeating* could be applied to almost any abuser, and the identification of a specific personality of this type could lead to additional labeling, misdiagnosis, and confusion. Generally, the statements made here about the passive–aggressive type also apply to the self-defeating type, who usually will demonstrate an extreme version of the same behavior or characteristic.

Whereas the compulsive achieves consistency by internal partitioning, restriction of affect, and disciplined behavior, the passive–aggressive is actively inconsistent and contrary. The opposite of the behavior called for in any given situation is the one most likely to be expressed by the passive–aggressive person, hence the term *negativistic personality*, or perhaps even better, *oppositional personality*. The negativistic personality is fickle and impulsive, like the histrionic, but this is because of internal ambivalence projected outward and then acted upon, not because of the need to ingratiate, as is most often the case with the histrionic.

Inconsistency or incongruity of thought and affect, even within a single expression, is common with the negativistic personality and its variants. The negativistic person favors neither thought nor affect, but maintains a consistent attitudinal set toward the self and world. This spoiler attitude is something like Murphy's Law ("what can go wrong will go wrong") being used to justify fatalism and nihilism, rather than rational planning and intervention. Although this is not an effective personality style, passive–aggressive behavior is tolerated well in highly conflicted family systems. Passive–aggressive persons may find niches in work environments that are riddled with conflicting cliques, or where there are relatively few consequences to nonproductive behavior, where lines of authority are blurred, in settings where rewards are distributed arbitrarily, or where there are simply very few rewards to distribute

The individuals described in this cluster use displacement and devaluation as a means of establishing balance. There is no form of excellence or good fortune that the negativistic person cannot disparage or demean. The stubbornness, intentional ineptitude, and exasperating quality of interacting with these individuals are qualities related to the very thin veneer of resentful compliance that masks their aggression toward others and disdain toward themselves. Although these individuals may appear disgruntled or declare that they have been handled improperly by others, they are just as likely a few minutes later to express feeling unworthy of good fate and to minimize their inherent worth or personal rights. This is due to a basic conflict concerning self-worth, an oscillation between self-loathing and entitlement or moral superiority. Either side of this internal oscillation of self-experience may be projected outward toward others or the environment at any given moment in any one of the styles of oscillation described in Chapter 5, that is, the contents projected outward may be in harmonic, conflictual, separating, or hierarchical relationship to the internal self-perception at any given moment. This chaotic and seemingly indecipherable complexity is extremely crazy-making for others, who usually begin to avoid or minimize contact with the negativist out of self-protection.

In regard to Axis I disorders, the passive–aggressive personality is especially prone to anxiety, including panic attacks, probably due to his or her anxiety-generating attitudes and cognitions. Dysthymia, cyclothymia, and major depression with agitation are commonly experienced by these persons. Many chronic pain clinic patients have passive–aggressive personalities. It is not unusual for forensic or correctional environments to have a concentration of passive–aggressive personality disorders who have committed explosive acts of violence or who have become psychopathic in the expression of their negativity and opposition to the normal view of things. Carbamazepine, lithium, and in some cases stimulants can be used to help contain these symptoms (Gitlin 1990).

In regard to the symptom complexes, the negativistic personality is prone to problems in the anxiety and dominance of affect complexes. This is perhaps the most miserable of the personality styles, and they inflict a good deal of discomfort on others through the use of their anxiety and emotional symptoms. In many cases, the negativistic person will become socially isolated due to his or her destructive attitudes and the almost negligible rewards he or she can provide to others. Negativistic persons also exhibit problems with reward/arousal, but these are usually expressed by an hypomanic agitation and anxiety, or a depressive stupor and inertia, and can best be subsumed by the respective complexes that refer to affect and anxiety.

Because of its active ambivalence, the negativistic personality is even more likely than the compulsive to use drugs to modulate mood states and experiences that other personalities attempt to escape entirely. The negativistic person feels entitled to an external solution to his or her problems, but also feels entitled to having the problems, because the suffered wrongs place him or her in a morally superior position. Vicious circles created by drug use are congruent with the negativistic person's expectations from life and help to provide a forum for repetition of the conflicting internalizations of the infant–parent dyad. Accordingly, passive–aggressives are apt to display their addictions in a loud uproar, rather than in secret as in the compulsive personality. Almost any of the drug classes will suit the needs of this cluster, although the more severe types will be more prone to the drugs with more devastating personal and social consequences. The stimulants are not usually preferred because additional stimulation can make the subjective experience of ambivalence intolerable. Prescribed pain killers, antianxiety agents, in combination with alcohol, are probably the most common pattern of abuse. Oral administration is most likely preferred, consistent with the oral aggression that is common in this personality type.

The contrary object relationships of the negativistic personality result in a basic instability of character and behavior and in a rapid cycling through the addictive cycle. Negativistic persons are prone to use their addictions interpersonally, either to justify and facilitate the direct expression of anger, and even violence, or to provide a rationale for their own nonperformance, incapacitation, or inaccessibility, or to place a guilt trip on significant others. The negativistic person is apt to rest at the depressed/depleted position but will experience moments of vigor and grandiosity if the depleted or debased components can be successfully unloaded onto others. Substance use may trigger the change from stubborn minimal compliance to aggressive defiance and demands or active self-loathing and self-sabotage.

As noted earlier, the negativistic personality pessimistically applies Murphy's Law to everyone and everything. This also applies to their attitude toward recovery and treatment processes. They will feel passively entitled to recovery but will refuse to work toward it because they believe life owes sobriety and normalcy to them and are convinced that recovery efforts are doomed to failure anyway, or that treatment staff are incompetent or have flawed motives. Because of these attitudes, the passive–aggressive is extremely difficult to motivate and maintain in substance abuse treatment. They are particularly prone to Marlott's Principle of Immediate Gratification (PIG). They are so easily demoralized that they will consider themselves as having sinned by the mere thought of using illicit drugs. In effect, they may relapse due to a kind of abstinence violation effect when there has been no actual first use. After actual use, they will feel entitled to being demoralized and abandon recovery efforts. Similarly, they may feel entitled to relapse because of their unjustly being cast into temptation by the cruel forces of fate.

Passive–aggressive persons have been described as highly oral aggressive and oral incorporative. Both characterizations are true, and treatment staff will feel that their resources and selves are being eaten up in one way or another by the passive–aggressive person. (We see later in this chapter that the avoidant person is attempting to prevent just this kind of oral aggression at the object level; this is what he or he specifically avoids.) The treatment staff's experience will be either that the patient is using others and showing no progress or mutuality in return, or that the patient is in an orally destructive manner undermining the efforts, morale, and good faith of both staff and other patients. Often when these patterns have been established in the experience of a treatment setting in regard to a passive–aggressive patient, the patient will begin to unctuously praise the staff and show inordinate affection to and admiration of other patients, in effect trying to kill them with kindness while preventing the total rejection that they sense is forthcoming. In this context, constructive criticism, jokes, and humor of the negativist can be particularly devastating to dependent types in a psychotherapy group, because their more sadistic remarks often take naive group members by surprise, whereas the unconflicted aggressive and sadistic types are discovered relatively early in group life, and this awareness of threat provides some protection from their aggression. The members of a working psychotherapy group must learn when to respond in partial contradiction to the negativist, when the negativist should be silenced, and when to provide these co-members with rewards on a relatively unilateral basis. All addicts have a negativist somewhere within, however, so it is important for treatment settings to insure the possibility for negativistic personalities to participate in treatment activities without debunking or demeaning treatment, and without being unduly scapegoated when their negativism is un-covered.

The cooperation and coping phases of recovery are particularly difficult for the negativist, who may resist help in a self-destructive manner in early treatment. Often coercion is needed to obtain the required level of compliance, and the assistance of family members and the few social supports who have not been alienated by the patient's behavior can be marshalled as additional leverage to a court order, a medical ultimatum, or a threatened divorce or removal from employment. Clear consequences and specific, well-articulated limits are unusually necessary in family therapy with the passive–aggressive patient. Drug testing is of crucial importance with this group of patients, who are second only to the psychopathic personality in insisting that they are abstinent, despite daily use. Care on the part of psychiatrists must be taken that all sources of medication are known and centrally tracked or controlled. Involvement in self-help groups will be self-defeating without parallel counseling on how to use these groups. Attendance should be regularly monitored in all phases of treatment. Low credibility should be given to self-reports of behavior. During the phase of coping with abstinence effects, the negativist is very prone to seek immediate gratification of urges to use and feels entitled to avoiding any discomfort from withdrawal symptoms, which they will greatly exaggerate, often in an attempt to obtain pain medications. Since the negativist uses an attitude of depression and any identified weaknesses as a defense against change, an emphasis on attitude development and appropriate self-esteem is crucial in their treatment.

THE DYSFUNCTIONAL DETACHED STYLES

The least effective of the basic personality types are the detached styles. These individuals are very ineffective at gaining interpersonal rewards and usually have marginal adjustments in work or creative tasks. These personalities have aban-doned the attempt to obtain secure and rewarding attachment. Although the schizoid and avoidant personalities have this detachment in common, the schizoid is passively detached, whereas the avoidant is actively withdrawn from relation-ships. Millon advanced the idea that what has come to be called negative and positive symptomatic differences in schizophrenia research may be related to active versus passive styles of detachment in schizophrenics. According to Millon, many schizophrenics with negative symptoms (underarousal, undermotivation, and in-sensitivity) have decompensated from a schizoid personality style. Schizophrenics who display the positive symptoms of overarousal, overmotivation, and hypersen-sitivity and floridly bizarre symptoms are more likely to have decompensated from the avoidant personalty style. Extreme and unstable forms of the schizoid and the avoidant personality disorders may be seen as precursors to the more pathological schizotypal personality decompensation and to various manifestations of schizophrenia. Many persons with these detached styles, however, stabilize due to more benign family conditions, greater intelligence, or ego-strength and never exhibit the more extreme symptoms of either schizotypal personality or schizophrenia.

The Schizoid Personality Style

Almost all personality topologies have included a basically seclusive, asocial type. Early in the history of modern psychiatry, the asocial type was linked to a prepsychotic or to a healed or sealed-over psychotic condition, especially schizophrenia, hence the term *schizoid*. Autism is another major mental disorder that this personality type appeared to mimic in milder fashion. The biological relationship of the schizoid personality to either schizophrenia or autism has been questioned, however. Some investigators minimize the genetic contribution to schizoid disorders (Kety et al. 1978). Classically, the schizoid has been described as passively uninterested in social relationships. Kohut and Wolf (1978) considered this type as a contact shunning personality prone to using social withdrawal, fantasy, and omnipotence during periods of narcissistic distress. More recent formulations have acknowledged the clinical evidence that, with an empathic interviewer, most persons diagnosed as schizoid will admit to an underlying desire for social contact, but only with a degree of acceptance and understanding that is ordinarily impossible to obtain.

Schizoids are behaviorally inert or lethargic with flat affect. They are often perceived as boring or empty, totally lacking in spontaneity or inquisitiveness about others. The lack of interest is sometimes interpreted as overt hostility or haughty aloofness, especially by persons who require attention and centrality from others. Schizoids are often without noticeable emotional reactions, and their thought processes are typically sparse as well. When a response is required, its content is apt to be poorly connected, filled with digressions, and generally inept. Nevertheless, schizoids are described as intellectualizers, probably because of their adherence to the objective, purely factual aspects of any situation. They tend not to embellish abstractions with complications, perceptually rich images, emotional overlays, or other sources of texture as do most other personality types. Although the schizoid is viewed as empty or bored, this is often ego-syntonic. The schizoid is relatively self-satisfied and complacent and demonstrates little of the rich internal life and conflict of other personality styles. Object relations can be described as sparse, rigid in form, extremely stable, and poorly articulated.

Thomas R. Thompson (1990), in reviewing the literature on the schizoid style, developed some interesting ideas concerning the nature of its deficits and conflicts. He notes that studies of Asperger's syndrome (slow, withdrawn children with schizoidlike parents) do tend to grow up to be schizoid, but that only one in twenty-three becomes schizophrenic. The trend in both adult and child psychiatric literatures, according to Thompson, suggests that schizoids are actively phobic rather than passively disinterested in regard to social relationships, making the clinical reality closer to Millon's avoidant type. The biological or organic deficit suspected in schizoid development is not, judging by the weight of evidence in the literature reviewed by Thompson, related to the same biological deficits that result in schizophrenia or autism.

Thomas and Chess (1977) described a group of children at risk for schizoid development as "slow to warm up" in that they take significantly longer than other children to adapt to new situations and are more apt to cling to a parent, hide, or withdraw from a new social situation. Thompson (1990) hypothesized that such children are prone to develop schizoid traits, especially if the parent is narcissistically wounded by the child's seeming rebuff or rejection of parental approaches during infancy:

> At some point the parent fails. The schizoid child withdraws further and the parent rejects further. A vicious cycle is set up that leads to the schizoid deterioration. The schizoid, knowing she cannot adapt quickly or well enough to please anyone in the environment, chooses to please no one and retreats to isolation to protect her fragile sense of self. In this isolative world there is no criticism or rebuff but also no opportunity for any positive emotional experiences with others that would compensate for this low self-concept. The pathology has become self-perpetuating. Narcissistic injury becomes increasing damaging with the length of isolation. [p. 233]

This situation leaves the slow-to-warm-up child starved for love. Guntrip (1967) underscored the psychological reality in this cliche by describing the schizoid problem as "love made hungry." Guntrip noted the similarity of the schizoid to the narcissist (lack of empathy for others, air of superiority, dependence on fantasy) while noting the schizoid's contrasting withdrawal from, and rejection or abandonment of, threatening objects. This response toward objects starkly contrasts with the narcissist's attempts to control the object. The schizoid prefers to be hungry for love rather than to be poisoned, or to be a destructive cannibal out of his or her overwhelming emptiness and neediness. The flip side is the narcissist, who has eyes bigger than his or her psychic stomach and who attempts to incorporate, subsume, or consume all threatening objects by enveloping them within his or her span of control.

Thompson identifies the roots of these feelings in our primate heritage, specifically in the evolution of socialization through troop behavior, which is controlled by adult primates who mimic predators in order to herd in juveniles. Without this fear induction, the younger members would wander away from the troop. Thompson cites the work of Bowlby (1969, 1973) to describe how these early primate behaviors remain crucial to human socialization:

> Bowlby states that the major reasons that man is a social animal are based on survival in a more primitive world and include (1) protection from predators and (2) cooper-

ative hunting and food gathering. In the context of a troop of ground-dwelling apes, secure social attachments assure (1) that members of the troop will not be preyed upon and (2) that members of the troop will have enough to eat. These primitive oral issues haunt the schizoid. [Thompson, 1990 p. 239.]

Using a richer source of mythology, Thompson more convincingly traces these oral themes in childhood fairy tales, such as "Little Red Riding Hood," and "Hansel and Gretel." These tales describe the primitive fears of eating and being eaten related to schizoid conflicts over close interpersonal contacts, which can be summed up as the perception of love as destructive or devouring of the object. In Thompson's view, the schizoid world is one in which protectors and predators are constantly confused.

A true schizoid personality might qualify as an exception to the surface–depth analogy for the relationship of core self to personality introduced earlier in this chapter. It is possible that an individual's core self could incorporate a fear of being devoured as the basic infant–caretaker dyadic sense of self. The schizoid personality dynamics on the surface of such a person would simply reveal the deeper self-structure with an almost one-to-one correspondence. Although such schizoid personalities may exist, the pure type is rarely encountered in clinical practice, perhaps due to the fact that such people have few complaints and would not seek an interpersonal context for solving their difficulties. Schizoid *traits*, however, or the schizoid style as a behavioral fallback position under stress, are commonly found in treatment populations. The detached/schizoid position of the addictive cycle is covertly present even in the most active, engaged, high-rolling (inflated) addict, who may be seen as phobically counterschizoid during most of the addictive cycle.

The schizoid style is a very ineffective way of being and usually coexists with some other major form of psychopathology. Dissociative disorders such as depersonalization are common, and (despite statistical data to the contrary) clinicians often suggest anecdotally that decompensations to various forms of schizophrenia are not uncommon. Brief reactive psychoses and hypomanic panic attacks may occur under stress, especially due to excessive stimulation, or as the end point of a spiral of self-imposed social and sensory deprivation. Schizoids are apathetic under almost all circumstances and demonstrate a profound underresponsiveness to stimulation. In regard to the symptom complexes of most relevance to the schizoid type, reward–arousal and anxiety provide the major ego-dystonic symptoms, whereas examination of the sociability and identity complex will usually reveal significant ego-syntonic deficits. These patterns suggest a possible psychophysiological link of schizoid personality with schizophrenia (negative signs) and psychopathy.

Addictions in schizoids usually provide escape–avoidance or modulation of anxiety. Orientation and a sense of identity may also be provided by drugs to schizoid persons (or those in the detached/schizoid position of addiction). One aspect of this process is the isomorphic link between the schizoid's view of relationship and the kind of relationships fostered in drug subcultures. As in Bowlby's primate troop, the drug world is held together by a fear of loss of supplies, and the fear of being consumed or used is the emotional stock in trade. A more important aspect of addiction that provides for substitute orientation and identity, however, relies on the ability of drugs to simulate or produce an internal environment that will support a very primitive sense of self established through continuity of simple sensation or perception, with very little emotional or symbolic elaboration. The detached/schizoid position of the addictive cycle represents a regression to this primitive sense of self.

Thomas H. Ogden (1989) described a mode of primitive experience that he calls the *autistic-contiguous mode*, which helps to provide insight into the extreme expressions of the detached/schizoid position. The autistic-contiguous mode also explains how drugs provide orientation and identity to socially detached personalities. In other personality styles, orientation and identity through drug use is either effected through social relationships (being part of the "scene," etc.) or though deviant shadow identifications with the drug of choice (e.g., feeling affirmed and gratified by the self-statement "I am a crack fiend!"). The autistic-contiguous mode used by schizoids or persons decompensated to a schizoid state is presubjective and essentially asocial, although it provides the basis for object relatedness. Ogden's autistic-contiguous mode is a sensory-dominated, presymbolic way of being. The sense of self is established through the experience of rhythmic sound or motion, the feeling of skin-to-skin molding, or other repetitive or contiguous sensory experiences. Building on the work of Klein and Bion, Ogden views the autistic-contiguous mode as the most primitive of self experiences. In normal individuals, according to Ogden, this primitive mode is in dialectical alternation and balance with two more advanced modes, the depressive and the paranoid-schizoid.

In Ogden's schema, collapse into the exclusive use of any these modes is a sign of decompensation or arrested development. The schizoid is most prone to decompensate to this primitive position and to rely on drug-induced stimulation, perception, or contiguity of sensation to provide a minimal experience of self. Since the experiences required are minimal, drugs may be used to avoid or modulate any source of anxiety or any affect that might result in the impingement of a hungry-desirable object upon the schizoid's preferred empty emotional life. Sedatives and alcohol often meet the requirements of such inadequate personalities and facilitate their basically autoerotic stance in the presence of what they would perceive as intrusive, externally impinging temptations and attractions toward contact with others. Given Thompson's concept of schizoid orality, one could speculate that schizoids would prefer the oral route of drug administration. However, many narcotic addicts who are otherwise fairly low functioning also have a highly schizoid style of relatedness, or rather nonrelatedness, and in my experience have no preference for oral, nasal, or intravenous ingestion. Perhaps these inadequate addicts are too ineffectual and passive to demonstrate a strong preference in any arena.

Although the prognosis for insight-oriented therapy with the schizoid is very poor, there are fortunately very few pure schizoids. If the addictive core self has incorporated a basic fear of contact with others, counterphobic defenses against this core may also provide some attraction toward attachment, unless there is some severe biological or organic incapacity. Therapists working with these strongly schizoid persons should be patient and accepting of the withdrawal and should be careful not to respond to it as a rejection of help or as a personal rebuff. Joining more severe schizoids or individuals in the schizoid/detached position in activities that involve aspects of the autistic-continuous mode of self will provide a basis for the patient beginning to experience empathic contact from the therapist. For example, being openly sensitive to the temperature of the room (an example given by Ogden in a case report), listening to music, walking at a regular pace without conversation are all basic ways of establishing primitive, nonthreatening contact with the schizoid.

Knowing when this level of interrelatedness by way of state-tuning in the autistic contiguous mode is functioning as a ongoing resistance to be interpreted or otherwise interrupted is also crucial to making progress with the schizoid. Although ultimately the therapist will have to appeal to the healthier aspects of the patient rather than to his or her schizoid core, one study (Griggs and Tyrer 1981) found a *better* outcome for such personalities involved in group therapy than other alcoholic patients. Perhaps the structure and engineered veneer of intimacy of focused therapy groups can allow some socially inept and fearful schizoids to come out of their shell enough to profit from these contacts. Also, schizoid persons may have an inherent tendency to be relatively impulse free in regard to action in the external world, as opposed to the more impulse-ridden, acting-out addicted person. With few social pulls from without toward substance use and fewer drive pushes from within, relapse (as with all other behaviors) may be less frequent in the schizoid after a successful initial treatment.

The Avoidant Personality

Recognition of the distinction between the schizoid and this avoidant, more active type is relatively new. Millon first coined the term *avoidant personality disorder* in 1969. Unlike the schizoid, who is viewed as passively detached and unconcerned about obtaining social rewards, the avoidant individual is so overly concerned about the consequences of social interaction that he or she desperately withdraws from interpersonal situations. The difference between these styles illustrates why an introspective understanding of human beings must complement an extraspective analysis of behavior (Rychlak 1981b). Although the observer might see exactly the same behavior in both personality types (e.g., not coming to the office Christmas party for example), the motivation is directly antithetical in the two cases. The schizoid avoids parties out of apathy, boredom, or the ability to obtain the minimal reward requirement from nonsocial activities. The avoidant, however, is terrified of the thought of going to the party out of fear of rejection, humiliation, and the conviction that his or her basic worthlessness and social incompetence will be exposed to others. The term *avoidant* in describing this personality is specifically in the area of social relations and internalized object relations. The passive-aggressive, and dependent styles are often pervasively avoidant of behavioral demands, and this is also true of histrionic and compulsive personalities. Narcissistic persons avoid facing personal limitations. Although it is true that substance abusers are often behaviorally avoidant, this is not the case in terms of the specific social and object relations usages of the word, which are directly applicable to the avoidant personality.

Avoidant individuals are filled with internal and interpersonal anguish. They desire acceptance, approval, and attachment, but they are convinced that they will receive only aversive experiences from others. Painful self-loathing and self-pity provide a background of constant distraction and emotional disruption. Their constant punitive introspection makes these emotions even more poignant. Consequently no sphere of behavior is ever fully developed. Although aggressive or affectionate relationships may be fantasied, they are never dared in reality. Because every interaction is a potential bomb waiting to explode in the avoidants' faces, these people are hypersensitive to any sign of disapproval or rejection and are often viewed as fragile, guarded, overly defensive, and even paranoid in the layperson's view because of the tendency to detect slights and insults where none are intended.

The painful social phobia and anxiety of the avoidant personality can sometimes be ameliorated with MAO inhibitors or benzodiazepine management (Gitlin 1990). Because the avoidant individual has few outlets for expression or gratification and because avoidant behavior greatly atrophies any potential skills or talents, this is a particularly fragile and incompetent way of being. Like the compulsive personality, the avoidant is easily labeled neurotic in social circles they are forced to endure, such as workplaces, where they are apt to be overcontrolled, constrained, and rigid. In family life, in contrast, the same individual's neurosis is seen as one of extreme sensitivity, self-flagellation, and distrust. The avoidant person, in contrast to the usual description of the schizoid, is consciously aware of painful affects of loneliness and alienation. In regard to overt behavior, avoidant individuals do avoid action out of fear of showing their hand and having it openly attacked or rejected. In relationships, they are always ready to cut their losses early in the game, since the expectation is one of inevitable loss.

Millon described the avoidant as one of the personality styles most vulnerable to Axis I symptoms. Social anxiety and self-deprecation usually underlie these disorders, which may be expressed as manifest anxiety symptoms, panic attacks, and somatic complaints. Long-standing depressive disorders are also common. In regard to the symptom complexes, anxiety and affective dominance describe the majority of ego-dystonic symptoms. Hyperarousal and overreactivity to social stimuli produce significant pathology in the reward–arousal complex. The avoidant can be contrasted to the psychopathic individual in this specific area of sensitivity to aversive social stimuli. Psychopaths fail to learn avoidant behavior from aversive social events, and avoidants fail to learn anything else from interactions, since they interpret almost all social consequences negatively. Unlike many other personality disorders, deficits in the sociability and identity complex are consciously available to the avoidant patient and may be consciously ego-dystonic, but the avoidant is rarely convinced that these aspects of self could possibly change. Unfortunately, this extra awareness usually contributes further to the avoidant's sense of self-alienation.

Addiction in the avoidant provides escape/avoidance of painful affect, anxiety, or situations that evoke these experiences. Modulation of hyperarousal and of self-deprecatory thoughts and feelings is also a prominent function of addiction. At times, avoidants will use their addictions to repeat the experience of feeling initially accepted, but later disappointing to, and betrayed or rejected by the caretaker. The tension of disappointed/disappointing is often exhausting between client and therapist in these cases of addictive repetition of infantile experience. Surprisingly, avoidants may often prefer mild hallucinogens over other drugs, perhaps due to their facilitation of escape into fantasy and the generation of perceptual/sensory distractions from their constant self-absorption. Sedatives and antianxiety agents are probably the drug of choice in most of these personalities, however, especially those that can be obtained with a minimum amount of social exposure and interpersonal risk.

Avoidants tend to rest in the depressed/depleted position of the addictive cycle, although they may do so in an agitated, frantic manner rather than with overt depression, which is also common. They tend to cycle rapidly between this position and the schizoid/detached stance. Ironically, when some of their interpersonal needs are met, they may shift from the depleted to the schizoid/detached position out of the fear of rejection that will follow any sign of social acceptance.

Because of their painful style of being, avoidant persons may often be more impaired in surface functioning than the schizoid. The motivation to use drugs may also be much higher because of the increased strength of drives and the paucity of outlets and rewards. Secretive substance use must be guarded against, although the avoidant is not otherwise an acting-out treatment case. A treatment team working with an avoidant personality, especially during brief inpatient contacts, has a good chance of establishing enough trust for the patient to being to perceive some social rewards. Very careful and nonconfrontive approaches are required so that this early trust is not betrayed. Tolerance of the patient's disappointment with staff and with self is crucial; not becoming disappointed with slow recovery is even more important.

This patient type must be carefully guided through any involvement with self-help groups. Early prompting to speak up in AA or NA or early confrontation by more aggressive types could be devastating to recovery and adjustment. As noted earlier, sadistic individuals will have great disdain for the avoidant, and in some group treatments it will be necessary to prevent these personality styles from having much contact with each other. Not surprisingly, the early phases of recovery are not as trying for the avoidant as are the later phases, where real personal and interpersonal risks are involved. The danger of the middle and late phases of recovery lies in the avoidant's fear that all support, progress, trust, and accomplishment during earlier phases are really a sham and will disintegrate with the least external pressure or personal failure. Complete termination of treatment activities with the avoidant person is highly inadvisable. Treatment teams may require additional sessions over those requested by the patient in order to maintain stability and a sense of belonging, since the avoidant expect the staff or therapist will want to "dump" them as soon as this can be done without losing face.

7

Personality Decompensation and the Spectrum Disorders

This chapter introduces the concepts of personality decompensation and spectrum disorders in psychopathology. The treatment of addictive behavior in the schizoid and avoidant personalities is discussed in the context of the schizotypal personality, which represents a decompensation of these two more basic dysfunctional styles. Dual diagnosis work with the schizotypal, borderline, and paranoid decompensations are described here as representative samples of work with individuals whose problems can be arranged into three broad spectrums of disorders encompassing Axis I and Axis II. Each of the three spectrums can be prototypically defined by one of the three personality decompensations. The schizotypal-schizophrenic, the cycloid-affective, and the paranoid-narcissistic disorder spectrums are prototypically defined, respectively, by the schizoid, borderline, and paranoid styles of personality decompensation.

THE PROCESS AND SPECTRUM DISORDERS

Two concepts of psychopathology are linked and used in this chapter to discuss some of the more severe problems encountered in clinical work with the addictions. The first concept is Millon's view (1981) that dysfunctional personalities may progressively decompensate from personality disorder to the more severe schizotypal, borderline, or paranoid styles of decompensated personality. This progressive decompensation reflects the activity of what is referred to here as a process disorder of the personality. The second concept, that of spectrum disorders in psychopathology, has been advanced by several theorists, researchers, and nosologists (Cloninger 1987, Eysenck 1967, Grinker 1966, Meel 1962, Millon 1969, Siever and Davis 1991, Stone 1980, Zuckerman 1984). In discussing personality and addictions related to personality dynamics, these two concepts mutually inform one another. Millon has explicated the centrality of personality to overall functioning and the process by which nodal expressions of personality and its pathology develop and deteriorate under stress. The idea of spectrum disorders illuminates our understanding of why severe personality problems are inclined to develop certain Axis I disorders and why, under unfavorable conditions, they are likely to disintegrate along certain fault lines of structure and functioning into a few categories of severely decompensated personality. Just as geological fault lines are zones of weakness that lead to somewhat predictable geological upheavals, certain underlying constitutional or structural aspects of the individual provide the dotted lines along which the personality tears most easily under stress.

Millon (1981) described personality deterioration as proceeding to two levels of severity beyond that of personality disorder proper: the level of advanced personality dysfunction and the level of severely decompensated personality. The first level is marked by severe deficits in social competence and periodic, reversible psychotic episodes. The second level is typified by developmental immaturity, social invalidism, enduring cognitive disorganization, and extreme feelings of estrangement. Individuals who have severely decompensated personalities are apt to need continued hospitalization or institutionalization. Although individuals whose personalities have decompensated are also highly vulnerable to Axis I manifestations, personality decompensations are more devastating than most Axis I conditions. This is because the latter most typically involve only one sphere of functioning and can be time-limited, especially with appropriate medication and psychological treatment. Personality decompensation, however, may cover most of the lifespan, is pervasive to every sphere of functioning, and any symptom relief provided by medication is apt to be very fleeting. Medication alone fails to address the essential causative factors, which are intrinsic to the personality.

One way of viewing the personality decompensations is to see them in terms of their relationships to several identifiable spectrums or continuums of disorders that span Axis I and Axis II, that is, which exist across the behavioral reactions, symptom disorders, and personality disturbances. The spectrum approach to understanding psychopathology is one expression of a movement toward dimensional models of categorization in psychopathology described in Chapter 1. Dimensional models place cases on a continuum or range of severity of a given trait or manifestation of a particular pathological process. In addition to using dimensional categorization, the spectrum approach may stress the similarity of various disorders to a unifying clinical prototype, which consists of more than one dimension or factor and presupposes one or more causal mechanisms accounting for the similarity across cases. Prototypes are models, ideals, or paradigms, and very few actual cases perfectly exemplify a given prototype. The prototype may be seen as an early or original type, a precursor, or an exemplar by which subsequent adaptations or versions of a disorder may be evaluated. Spectrum formulations are usually applied polythetically (Cantor et al. 1980). This means that no single feature or index is required for inclusion in a spectrum, rather the sameness of the overall causal and clinical Gestalt—the overall goodness of fit of a disorder to a schematic paradigm description—recommends inclusion in the spectrum. The approach advanced here combines dimensional and polythetic-prototypic methods. Dimensional constructs have been used for *descriptive concepts* of psychopathology and addiction as in the symptom complexes and psychosocial functions of addiction. The spectrums, as conceptualized here, are *nosological/etiological* constructs used to define, explain, and connect various clinical manifestations.

Ideas describing some kind of unifying biosocial connection among various disorders, which results in a range or spectrum of severity in presentation, are recurrent in the history of psychopathology. It will be worthwhile to follow some of these early descriptions because they shed considerable light on the proposed relationship between the more severe variants of the personality disorders and the Axis I major mental illnesses.

In a classic paper, Paul Meel (1962) carefully spells out the biological and environmental connections that he believes link schizoid behavior, schizotypal behavior, and schizophrenia in a complex of vulnerabilities called schizotypy. According to Meel, these disorders hold in common four cardinal traits: associative dyscontrol (thought disorder), interpersonal aversiveness, anhedonia, and ambivalence. He surmises that these traits are biologically based in a genetically determined neural integrative defect. Given this constitutional hypothesis, Meel works out a paradigm of the relationship between a major mental disorder and personality aberrations that can be applied to the severe personality disorders and pathological personality process disorders discussed in the rest of this chapter.

> Summarizing, I hypothesize that the statistical relation between schizotaxia, schizotypy, and schizophrenia is class inclusion: All schizotaxics become, *on all actually existing social learning regimes*, schizotypic in personality organization; but most of these remain compensated. A minority, disadvantaged by other (largely polygenically determined) constitutional weaknesses, and put on a bad regime by schizophrenogenic mothers (most of whom are themselves schizotypes) are thereby potentiated into clinical schizophrenia. What makes schizotaxia etiologically specific is its role as a *necessary* condition. I postulate that a nonschizotaxic individual, whatever his other genetic makeup and whatever his learning history, would at most develop a character disorder or a psychoneurosis; but that he would never become a schizotype and therefore could never manifest its decompensated form, schizophrenia. [p. 830]

Although the term *schizophrenogenic* applied to mothers marks this as a passage from an era with different assumptions and sensitivities, the logic of Meel's piece is still sound. He suggests that a constitutional deficit can be conditioned by environmental input to result in either fairly normal adjustment, a personality disorder, or a major mental illness. Deficits due to this constitutional defect could be predicted to occur along specified dimensions of functioning.

In short, Meel introduced the concept of a biologically based and environmentally conditioned spectrum of disorders to contemporary psychopathology. Using the guiding prototype of schizophrenia (an Axis I disorder), his analysis forged a descriptive and causal loop between several distinct disorders (including an Axis II disorder). These disorders represented different degrees of impairment to overall functioning and consisted of varying details of expression. Nonetheless, Meel tried to demonstrate that they shared several distinctive, cardinal features and an underlying causal unity. The disorders constituting his spectrum all involved disturbances in sociability, arousal systems, and cognition and were all hypothesized as expressions of an underlying constitutional weakness in basic neuronal functioning.

Chapter 3 argues in favor of a link among several very different diagnostic categories based on their similarity in regard to patterns of severity on various symptom complexes. This primarily monothetic dimensional view of unity across disorders was advanced due to the descriptive purpose of the heuristic system, which is used to formulate dual diagnosis problems and related treatment interventions. In discussing the spectra advanced here, however, the goal is to elucidate how several major clinical prototypes unify various Axis I and Axis II disorders in such manner that each individual disorder may be seen as a manifestation of one level of severity, pervasiveness, and exclusiveness of the defining prototype. The prototype and its manifestations are presumed to share at least one underlying cause. The concepts of the heuristic system ignore, to a large extent, diagnostic prototypes and instead focus on large clusters of symptoms or psychosocial functions associated with the onset and continuation of addiction. The spectrums, in contrast, examine the goodness of fit between a given clinical presentation and a unifying prototype (a specific diagnosis) that is clinically significant in terms of severity and frequency of occurrence and fairly easy to identify.

Both methods of examining specific cases and disorders are valid but have slightly different goals. The heuristic system is primarily descriptive and assessment oriented, with a practical application always in mind. The spectrum approach is more abstract, explanatory, investigative, and discovery oriented, always pointing beyond the practical concerns of the specific case. The tension between these two kinds of approaches can provide space for creative thinking about any specific case to which they are simultaneously applied. Accordingly, the spectrums are introduced here because of their ability to provide an alternative window to the heuristic system for exploring many dual diagnosis cases from the vantage point of a few unifying clinical prototypes and related pathological processes. Similar formulations that link specific personality disorders with a spectrum of Axis I pathologies have proved useful in providing guidelines for the use of medications in controlling symptoms in individuals with personality disorders (Gitlin 1990).

The three personality organizations discussed in this section—the schizotypal, borderline, and paranoid—are viewed as manifestations of three disorder spectrums: the schizotypal-schizophrenic, the cycloid-affective, and the paranoid-narcissistic. The format of their labels reflect the combined dimensional-prototypical approach. Each spectrum name is hyphenated, being composed of a personality decompensation (the prototype for the spectrum) followed by the pathological process dominant in that group (the dimensional aspect). These terms, each with a severe personality disorder as the defining prototype, are consistent with the view that personality is more central to overall functioning than behavioral reactions or symptom disorders. The vulnerability of these personality disorders to deterioration and disintegration along certain fault planes to other levels and types of disorders is also encompassed by these terms. The personality decompensation is seen as the median case in the spectrum, both in terms of general impairment in functioning and severity of the dimensional pathological process. Viewed as a spectrum, behavioral reactions and personality disorders of moderate severity fall below this prototype median. The severe Axis I disorders which are related to the spectrum are above the prototype.

Two of the three proposed spectrums—the cycloid-affective and the schizotypal-schizophrenic—have a psychobiological foundation and have been advanced in slightly different forms elsewhere. In the paranoid-narcissistic spectrum, the primary underlying causal factor (narcissistic pathology) is intrapsychic rather than biological. The range of potential expressions are both broader and more subtle (and debatable) than the other spectrums. A recent heuristic schema providing a psychobiological perspective on the personality disorders identified four spectrums across Axis I and Axis II disorders (Siever and Davis 1991): the cognitive/perceptual organization, impulsivity/aggression, affective instability, and anxiety/inhibition spectrums. They have obvious similarities to the symptom disorders in Chapter 3 and to the three spectrums proposed here, but they suffer from the absence of a prototypic, polythetic focus. In dealing with the relationship between Axis I and the personality disorders, however, their psychobiological model indirectly approaches a prototypic method. The paranoid disorders and the narcissistic personality disorder are notably absent from the discussion. Perhaps this is because self-structural defects at the psychological level spawn the paranoid and narcissistic disorders. Although the developmental paths leading to these defects are legion, only a few can be accounted for in a purely biologically centered heuristic system such as the one proposed by Siever and Davis.

Each of the three severe personality decompensations is discussed in the context of a related spectrum of disorders, which presupposes some underlying trait or process that in part accounts for decompensation to this level. Discussing the personality decompensations in this light helps to explain some aspects of personality functioning of someone who is recovering from schizophrenia, bipolar disorder, or paranoid disorders. In many cases, residual effects of these Axis I disorders make the individual's behavior reminiscent of schizotypal, borderline, or paranoid disorders, even when they are not the underlying basic orientation. In many cases of substance abuse, the fault lines, or areas of weakness, exposed by the effects of continued drug use can be as effectively characterized by reference to one of the spectrum disorders and its style of decompensation as by the use of the symptom complexes. This is especially true in cases where the effects and consequences of addiction, which produce some degree of end-stage decompensation, are not the same or even similar to the symptoms or vulnerabilities that account for the initiation or maintenance of the addiction. For example, a socially anxious alcoholic who drinks to escape or avoid anxiety related to threats to self-esteem may develop, as a consequence of drinking, a dementia resulting in pathological jealousy, paranoia, and aggressive behavior. The relationship of this individual's problems to the paranoid-narcissistic spectrum may be more easily discerned at first than the predecompensation dynamics of escape/avoidance or anxiety, which supported the addiction prior to organic decompensation.

For most dual diagnosis cases, at least one of the personality decompensations and related spectrums will have some degree of applicability. Since dual diagnosis work is defined by recurrent treatment failures, some decompensation is inevitable, and its style can usually be considered in some way to significantly exhibit the cardinal features defined by a spectrum prototype or to demonstrate the influence of a pathological process typifying one of the spectrums. Clearly, this means that many cases or disorders can be fruitfully considered from the vantage point of more than one spectrum, although this overlap is not as great as for the more unidimensional symptom complexes.

THE SCHIZOTYPAL-SCHIZOPHRENIC SPECTRUM

The schizotypal personality disorder is characterized by oddness of thought and behavior. Although these people demonstrate misapplied understanding, poor reality testing, inappropriate affect, and illusory perceptions, these symptoms are not severe enough to warrant the diagnosis of schizophrenia. Developmentally, the schizotypal personality may be seen as the result of decompensation from the less severe detached personality styles, that is, the schizoid and avoidant styles. Although Millon (1981) views this deterioration as stemming primarily from extreme social isolation, a schizophrenia-like process may also account for this level of the decompensation. Given the latter view, the schizotypal personality may be seen as a nonpsychotic form of schizophrenia. Concepts such as pre-schizophrenic, latent-schizophrenic, sealed-over or residual schizophrenic, and borderline schizophrenic have often been applied to individuals who fit the DSM criteria for this disorder. The schizotypal-schizophrenic spectrum ranges from brief reactive periods of bizarre disorientation and psychosis, to schizotypal adjustment, and on to schizophrenia in its various forms. The schizophrenic process that unifies the spectrum is probably a small group of processes that are all exhibited to some extent in the spectrum prototype, schizotypal personality. Current conceptualizations of schizophrenia include the view that more than one hypothetical disease process or factor must be used to account for the various manifestations of the disorder. This view is well summarized by a recent review of the factor analytic studies that suggest three factors as active in schizophrenia. According to Mukherjee (1991), the three factors are:

> A negative symptom factor (affective blunting, anhedonia, abolition-apathy) a positive symptom factor (hallucination and delusions), and a third factor, which showed high loadings of attentional impairment, alogia, bizarre behavior, and thought disorder. This factor was significantly correlated with neuropsychological deficits that implicated early neurodevelopmental compromise. [p. 1751]

This book makes several references throughout to the positive and negative factor views of schizophrenia. The third factor in Mukherjee's work cited above is the most dominant in uncomplicated cases of schizotypal personality disorder and is usually present to some extent in most cases of schizophrenia. In terms of positive symptoms, schizotypal personalities are more apt to experience illusions, depersonalization, and derealization rather than hallucinations and to demonstrate magical thinking or bizarre speech rather than rigid delusions. All of the negative symptoms cited for schizophrenia may be present to a milder extent in the schizotypal personality.

Schizotypal personalities appear to others as odd, eccentric, and aloof. Their symptoms change constantly, indicating a chaotic internal organization. If the case represents a deterioration from the schizoid personality, affect will be blunted. In schizotypal personality decompensations whose original orientation was more avoidant prior to deterioration, affect may be expressed primarily as diffuse anxiety and/or through odd thoughts and behaviors. The thoughts and feelings of schizotypals often appear autistic. Personal associations and symbols are combined with more commonly shared ideas with little regard for the difference between these two kinds of symbolic expression. In a sense, the schizotypal individual is constantly speaking or acting out a kind of bad poetry, an autistic play on ideas, words, and feeling states. This is an effective social distancing mechanism for the detached schizotypal, who establishes an impersonal, detached dependency on institutions and other social settings that will tolerate their marginal involvement. Schizotypal personalities self-regulate by means of magical undoing and resort to a sparse but overinvested fantasy world of imagined persons and events.

In regard to the symptom complexes, schizotypal individuals demonstrate most of their deficits on the cognition and context, and sociability and identity complexes. Whereas these deficits are primarily ego-syntonic, occasionally schizotypal personalities will experience ego-dystonic depression and anxiety and will complain about problems with modulating arousal and energy levels. Episodes of derealization and depersonalization are common experiences. Other than decompensations to schizophrenia, overwrought, avoidant schizotypal types may develop panic attacks and anxiety disorders.

The organization of the schizotypal is so chaotic that the drug of choice is likely to be determined by random, or autistic factors. However, cocaine and the opiates are often preferred. Cocaine provides direct stimulation for patients with primary negative symptoms. Heroin provides direct relief from positive symptoms such as hallucinations. The psychotropic effect of Methadone is well documented. For example, Feinberg and Hartman (1991) report a case that suggests that self-medication of schizophrenic symptoms by use of heroin could be replaced by prescribed Methadone if ethical considerations can be appropriately addressed. The case involved a 34-year-old man with a longstanding history of psychotic symptoms, mainly positive in nature, with significant alcohol and heroin use. The patient verbalized a self-medication view of his drug use. After several unsuccessful attempts to wean him from Methadone treatment by substituting neuroleptics, Methadone was tried as the only medication for both his drug dependence and his psychotic symptoms. At a three month follow-up, the patient was taking 80 mg of Methadone, but was functioning much better and was without other drug use. In addition to exemplifying the effectiveness of opiates in alleviating psychotic symptoms, this case also demonstrates the typical recurrence or treatment failures in a dual diagnosis case until the treatment process is directed at the function of the addiction (including the selection of a particular drug of choice) within the context of the psychopathology dominant in the case.

In addition to providing relief from either positive or negative symptoms, drug involvement may provide a significant social role through the function of orientation to the schizotypal personality who is otherwise devoid of motivations and social contacts. Stimulants and hallucinogens may facilitate flight into fantasy and illusions, thus supporting the schizotypal defenses. Alcohol may sedate anxious schizotypal individuals and will allow for escape/avoidance of realities that otherwise impinge on the sanctuary of detachment and unreality. For the decompensated schizotypal, stimulants and hallucinogens will provide a basic sense of cohesive self through the autistic/contiguous mode of experience described earlier (Ogden 1989). Low doses of the antipsychotics may provide relief from symptoms for individuals whose problems are located within the schizotypal-schizophrenic spectrum of disorders (Gitlin 1990).

The schizotypal individual rests primarily in the detached/schizoid position of the addictive cycle. As with the other decompensated styles, the schizotypal will cycle rapidly during periods of exacerbation. Early phases of recovery are rarely traversed smoothly. Schizotypals usually relapse during the coping phase of recovery. In part this is because of the difficulty of substituting social rewards over the immediate gratification of drugs. Also, the drug of choice may be more effective and have fewer immediate negative side effects than prescribed medication. Schizotypals have little sense of time perspective and little cohesive identity to work with. Confrontation and direction may only result in a shifting of the internal sands rather than producing enough conflict or consolidation to begin to build a treatment alliance. It is sometimes useful to provide the patient with a more cohesive sense of personal history by carefully exploring autobiographical events until he or she can make productive, sequential sense of them. This is also true of events in therapy, which are often lost in the wash of the patient's fantasy and undoing. Since stabilization activities are required of the staff working with the schizotypal in almost all points of contact, the countertransference temptation to avoid is the perception that it does not matter whether the patient remains abstinent and strives to be symptom-free. The therapist must continually avoid slipping into hopelessness and apathy in regard to the case.

THE CYCLOID-AFFECTIVE SPECTRUM

Much has been written over the last few years about the borderline personality. One major confusion in this literature is, unfortunately, now codified in the *DSM* by use of the term *borderline* rather than other terms or Millon's preferred "cycloid" or unstable personality disorder. Although Millon (1981) has openly expressed disagreement with the borderline label, he has endorsed major aspects of the *DSM-III* conceptualization of the borderline disorder:

> Although the term *borderline* was retained, its evolution in the deliberations of the *DSM-III* committee reinforces the notion that it is a specific diagnostic entity that has stabilized at an advanced level of dysfunction. More importantly, its clinical characteristics are not only those of a personality syndrome but one that falls within the broad spectrum of *affective disorders*. In this sense, it parallels the schizotypal syndrome, which was also conceived as an advanced level of personality dysfunction but within the schizophrenic disorder spectrum. [p. 332]

Although Millon's use of this approach is limited and remains one-dimensional, as opposed to prototypic-polythetic multidimensional, in this quote he has explicitly linked the process and spectrum disorders. Millon views the borderline as a form of advanced decompensation of the basic dependent and ambivalent personality styles. Like the description of dual diagnosis populations as treatment failures advanced in this book, Millon's decompensated personalities are failed personality styles. Millon views the borderline as a developmental failure, or end point of deterioration from the more basic dependent and ambivalent styles. Accordingly, avoidant and passive–aggressive personalities are most apt to decompensate or experience developmental detours toward the borderline personality disorder. This is more likely to take place in avoidant and passive–aggressive individuals with an inherent predisposition toward affective disorders, which would constitute the fault line along which this personality type would tend to break down.

Although the *DSM-III-R* provides an very adequate description of the borderline, the most prominent aspects are repeated here as a context for discussing addictions among this group. Perhaps the most prominent trait is affective lability and rapid cycling of a full range of intense moods. Under stress, minipsychotic episodes are common, but most borderlines reconstitute quickly with pacification and support and are able to recognize their earlier crazy period. Borderlines typically have intense dependency anxiety and separation concerns (fears of abandonment, rejection, etc.). In addition, a symptom of cognitive-affective ambivalence is manifested by intense and conflicting beliefs, attitudes, or emotions experienced simultaneously toward persons or other objects. Not surprisingly, borderlines experience very little by the way of a consistent, coherent sense of identity.

Borderline personalities are extreme acting-out types. Self-condemnation and even self mutilation are not uncommon ways for these individuals to express inverted aggression and to reestablish some sense of order or control over the self. Suicide attempts, destructive relationships, and drug overdoses are also common outcomes of poor self-management, which eventually result in hospitalization.

Interpersonally, the borderline is seductive and manipulative, and at the same time resentful and retaliatory. These paradoxical behaviors often draw others into an initial fascination with the borderline which quickly leads to distrust and rejection. Regression under threat or stress is another hallmark. Impulse control, cognitive style, affect, and anxiety tolerance are often more characteristic of a child than an adult. The borderline splitting is a reflection of an underlying incompatibility of basic introjects. Affective dyscontrol prevents any integration of these conflicting elements. In one sense the term *borderline* does apply aptly to this group. Internal structures tend to blur into one another, with little differentiation among levels of consciousness, degrees of reality, associations, and memories. Millon's formulation of these disorders as due to the breakdown of dependent and ambivalent personalities along an affective fault plane makes this combination of traits remarkably coherent when compared to the confusion that the borderline condition once generated.

Although the full range of Axis I disorders may occur in the borderline decompensation, affective and anxiety disorders are perhaps the most common. In regard to the symptom complexes, dominance of affect (depression and anger) and anxiety (especially related to separation or rejection) are the most pronounced ego-dystonic symptoms. Constant arousal due to the these more essential symptoms may also be problematic. MAO inhibitors, carbamazepine (Tegretol), and (with caution) stimulants are sometimes useful in medical management, and the antipsychotics may provide improved ego cohesion and cognitive functioning (Gitlin 1990).

The sense of self is often impaired and may play a role in substance use. Using the characteristics of addictive dynamics described in Chapter 5, the borderline is the best candidate of all the personality styles for developing addictive disorders. Split identity is essential to the disorder, narcissistic crises are recurrent, and the addictive core of the borderline consists of highly charged negative affects regarding the self-other dyad. In addition, the borderline is typified by acting-out affects and by projective identification, a mechanism that can be easily be accommodated in co-dependency relationships and in introjections related to the drug of choice. The borderline is a rapid cycler in the addictive cycle (cycloid personality is an apt description from a substance abuse perspective). The borderline rests by not resting, that is, he or she is most familiar with the constant change of affective disruption. Although borderlines do this naturally due to their affective lability and contradictory split introjects, their drug use will often facilitate this change and disruption by triggering opponent affects or behaviors. The concept of drugs used as a "switch" for personality and affect is very relevant with this group. The concept is adapted from research on switches from depressive to manic states, or the reverse in the affective disorders (Bunney et al. 1971, Bunney et al. 1972). Holding the borderline in any one position (preferably the depressive) will result in over-whelming anxiety and will require an intense interpersonal involvement to main-tain. Nonetheless, holding and containing the patient within the depressive position are usually prerequisites to further progress in treatment of the borderline (Druck 1989). Personal equilibrium resulting in consistency both across and within sessions is the quality most demanded of the therapist with this addict. This is particularly difficult to achieve when the borderline demonstrates the Friday 4:50 P.M. pathognomonic sign, that is, suicide gestures, uproars with treatment staff, or the revelation of relapse information, which occurs only minutes before the weekend begins for resented normal people.

All of the functions of addiction are relevant to the borderline, but perhaps repetition is most crucial. These patients quickly regress to infantile levels and have been characterized as developing a transference psychosis. Early trauma involving real or imagined child abuse or abandonment will often become the focus of therapy, and the drug of choice will be used to replicate the traumatic relationship within the treatment. Because of the split and contradictory introjects of these patients, almost any drug of choice and route of administration will be used. In fact, the borderline tends to use any pathogen at hand to worst advantage. Fortunately, higher level borderlines will avoid the most disruptive substances and instead use sedatives and alcohol to self-medicate. Prescribed medications are often abused, however, and may be hoarded for suicide attempts or gestures.

Every phase of treatment is filled with dangers for borderlines. Unambivalent cooperation is not within their range, except when extremely regressed to almost infantile levels. Impulsiveness and self-destructive behavior from this type of patient result in the need for constant restraint and coercion in the coping phase, which should preferably be conducted in an inpatient setting. Deconstruction of the patho-logical elements of identity is almost impossible for this type, since the deconstruc-tion in itself stimulates fears of personal fragmentation and because the personality is already incredibly diffuse. Part of the borderline's denial, in fact, exists in this diffuse personality style, where protection exists because no one can quite put a finger on what is happening. The famous splitting of staff and the borderline's pan-sexuality add more management problems. The sexual acting out of the bor-derline must be treated as one aspect of his or her addiction and personality prob-lems, especially given the high rate of HIV infection among drug users. Engagement at the phase of identity consolidation is perhaps the maximal expectation. Complete discharge from treatment is not possible or desirable, since the borderline requires ongoing therapeutic support, even without an addictive dynamic.

Modalities of treatment with stress clarifying cognition, following through on realizable commitments to change, and that avoid excessive affective expression or action are preferred. Because of the tendency to split, a single case manager-therapist model is sometimes effective with the borderline, although exasperating and exhausting for staff attempting to apply it. Open-ended psychodrama or therapeutic help with getting in touch with deeply repressed emotions is contraindicated. Confrontation with the borderline can consist mainly in providing ego assets like clarity about consequences of behaviors, pointing out ambivalence, and labeling self-destructive action. Supportive work will involve much personal contact on a one-to-one basis and redirection from self-destructive trends. The rollercoaster ride or Marlatt's surfer metaphor can be used fruitfully to help the borderline (or other patient in the affective spectrum) to understand the proper relationship of the self to brief endogenous affects. Understanding that there are enduring aspects of the self beyond immediate affect is one of the crucial treatment goals with patients in this group of disorders.

THE PARANOID-NARCISSISTIC SPECTRUM

Perhaps the least self-explanatory of the three spectrums discussed here is the paranoid-narcissistic spectrum, which is based on disorders of the management of narcissistic feelings and development. A related practical complication is that at the extremes of the personality and Axis I disorders, the identifiable differences between both the spectrums and specific disorders begin to break down. At these extremes, paranoia (just as feelings of depression) exists to some extent in almost all disorders. Paranoid personality disorders, however, are characterized by pervasive mistrust of others and extreme vigilance in protection of the self. Cameron (1963) has identified the cardinal defects of the paranoid as the absence of basic trust and the internalization of a sadistic attitude toward the self. The self-directed aspect of these internalizations is defended against in a manic, counterphobic manner. The self is, therefore, seen by the paranoid as the center of all contexts, and all contexts consist of some kind of danger or threat. Affect is typically very stable in the paranoid, and reality testing outside of the area of self-interest or self-protection is almost always intact. In fact, even in these affected areas, the paranoid's perception of reality may be uncontaminated, although the interpretation of the significance or meaning of that reality is at the same time extremely warped or idiosyncratic.

Early descriptions of the paranoid personality were remarkably similar to those of the psychopath and narcissistic personality disorders, to which they are now often contrasted or compared. In discussing the relationship of the paranoid personality disorder to other personality styles, Millon (1981) notes:

In mixed cases, the paranoid dimension is often an insidious and secondary development, fusing slowly into the fabric of an earlier and less dysfunctional coping style.
Although paranoid-like features may be exhibited in almost every other personality
disorder, they tend to become integral components of only four of the patterns
previously described: the narcissistic, the antisocial (aggressive), the compulsive, and
the passive-aggressive. [p. 375]

Millon views the paranoid as a decompensation of the independent and ambivalent
styles and implies the possibility of a spectrum of disorders in his use of the term
paranoid dimension.

In the view of this chapter, the specific narcissistic vulnerability of these
disorders accounts for their tendency to decompensate to the paranoid style. The
paranoid personality disorder is cast here as the prototype of extreme pathological
narcissism, of which the narcissistic and psychopathic personality disorders are two
less extreme developmental variants. The paranoid-narcissistic spectrum also includes brief reactive paranoid states, many delusional disorders that protect the self
from projected threats or dangers, and paranoid psychosis. Both narcissistic issues
and paranoid-projective processes have been linked earlier in this book to the
dynamics of denial in addiction and the intrapsychic and object relational aspects
of drug use as a mode of self-regulation.

The paranoid's superficial certainty about perceptions of the environment and
his or her overt self-aggrandizement and self-centeredness serve as manic defenses
against uncertainty about the basic security and benevolence of the environment
and against feelings of humiliation and shame. Despite the paranoid's attempt to
detect and contain externally observable signs of their internal states and motives,
and the general rigidity of character that results from this strategy, paranoids are in
several senses extremely brittle characters behind a stable persona. Their overcontrolled style can lead to an ostensibly lethargic and rigid style of coping. Nevertheless, apparently impulsive, explosive, and energetic behavior can be quickly
unleashed when they feel under direct or immediate physical threat, when they feel
that their autonomy will be permanently compromised, or when a paranoid "plan"
is executed. Paranoids are very quick to take personal offense, to feel betrayed, and
to sense a conspiracy. Accordingly, it is not advisable to plan confrontative
"interventions" involving families and employers with paranoid clients. These
interventions are extreme confrontations and, in fact, often involve initial secrecy
and unilateral planning, factors that stimulate paranoia in almost anyone. If
coercion is to be used to initiate or maintain treatment with the paranoid, it must
be effective and inexorable and present at least one acceptable alternative course of
action that will be experienced as a conscious choice by the client.

Forced medication may at times be necessary and can lead to considerable
improvement in orientation and mood in decompensated paranoids. However,
once reconstituted, these patients are highly litigious and can rationalize their own
beliefs, behaviors, and indictments of the actions of others in a disarmingly

convincing manner if the observer loses or is never provided the overall context of things. The paranoid prefers cognition over affect. Although cold or indifferent to others, the paranoid often feels that his or her own hurt feelings provide sufficient cause for justifying almost any retaliation.

Breaking through the denial and projection of the paranoid is often almost impossible. Getting the paranoid into substance abuse treatment is only less difficult than maintaining him or her in treatment. However, paranoids often see the world in terms of competing sides, with individuals, treatment programs, and themselves as sovereign powers in a cold or warm war. They are, therefore, constantly seeking allies and can be joined in an alliance of sorts against something, which can result in tenuous cooperation with treatment requirements. In treatment, the paranoid will maintain a provocative stance and will routinely attack staff and other patients for their shortcomings or out of paranoid fears of various kinds. Among all the disorders, paranoids require the most interpersonal distance, probably because of their fears of the consequences and hidden motives of attachment. In this respect they are similar to the avoidant personality and may establish a very brittle dependency on others if optimal conditions prevail, although this will be predictably followed by the perception of disloyalty and betrayal by the momentarily trusted object. In the paranoid's own mental life, he or she is always connected, albeit in a negative and threatening relationship with others.

Since the paranoid is seen here as a failed narcissistic or antisocial personality, decompensations related to addiction, intoxication, or substance abuse related stressors will increase the probability that these individuals will develop paranoid features or paranoid disorders, without regard to the drug of choice. Some drugs of choice increase paranoid dynamics (cocaine, marijuana, amphetamines, and extreme alcohol intoxication or chronic alcohol abuse) and may be sought out by paranoids, narcissists, and antisocial personalities *because* of their facilitation of paranoid vigilance and self-aggrandizement, which they experiences as an empowering ego-syntonic boost. Recent research indicates that individuals who succumb to paranoid states or psychosis after cocaine use have pre-addiction tendencies toward magical thinking and other expressions of projective process. Primitive object relational aspects of self-maintenance are often represented in the use of drugs to repeat the basic traumatic experience that resulted in mistrust and the internalization of sadistic representations of self and others. Paranoids will often be motivated to use drugs in institutional settings or restrictive families because they are forbidden, and thus represent an infringement of their sacred autonomy, and the dynamics of secretiveness and attempts at detection are isomorphic with their narcissism and extreme persecutory internal dynamics and object relations.

The rationale for the historical link of these disorders to the anal expulsive period of psychosexual development and sadomasochism can be seen in the paranoid's preoccupation with control and maintaining autonomy under threat of coercive intrusions that are simultaneous with concerns about shame, defeat, and jealousy. The traditional linkage of paranoia with homosexuality is made somewhat more coherent by deemphasizing hypothesized fears/wishes of anal penetration and emphasizing instead the need for narcissistic mirroring, incorporation of a similar object, and mastery over autonomy issues. It is nonetheless clinically accurate to view the drug and needle sharing among some addicts as a form of displaced or altered sexual activity. Either the sexual connection, the drug connection, or both may serve the narcissistic requirements of paranoid individuals. Premature interpretation of these behaviors may increase paranoia.

The paranoid typically rests in the inflated/grandiose position of the addictive cycle. The paranoid style appears independent or even detached on the surface, but it masks a profound negative and fearful dependency on others. If the paranoid marshals manic defenses to remain in this position while under significant stress, a manic disorder may develop. Although usually very stable in the grandiose position, extreme paranoids may cycle rapidly in the addictive cycle as they decompensate and may experience manifest depression and anxiety and ego-dystonic alienation and self-estrangement, that is, they begin to appear like their less stable borderline and schizotypal counterparts. Panic attacks are not uncommon in paranoids upon realizing that they have lost autonomy to an inpatient treatment setting, where they anticipate having their vulnerabilities sadistically exposed.

In contrast, delusions that the addiction has been externally imposed by a conspiracy may develop in order to avoid personal accountability or acknowledge the narcissistic wound of being dependent on a substance. For example, a very paranoid patient believed that his father, whom he had murdered while under the influence of drugs, had provided him the money for the drugs in order to bring on the patient's psychotic break. Thus the delusional patient believed that the parent had engineered his own murder for mysterious motives.

Another paranoid patient insisted for weeks that he had been kidnapped by "scientists with white coats" and forced to ingest alcohol, after which he became suicidal and homicidal. In the patient's delusions, only a superficial displacement to a "white-coated scientist" obscured the patient's feeling that the therapist was responsible for the relapse and, therefore, the resulting adverse behaviors. Consequently, the patient became indignant with the case manager when informed that he was required to suffer all the consequences of the relapse, his delusions notwithstanding, in terms of lost hospital privileges and such. Actually, there was a grain of truth in the patient's delusions concerning the therapist's contribution to his relapse. The therapist did not correctly interpret the patient's expressed concern in the pre-relapse group session about overspending at the fast food shop over the coming weekend as a concern that he would overspend by buying alcohol at the same establishment. The therapist had interpreted the concern as the patient not having enough, or feeling emotionally deprived by the therapist's absence over the weekend. The therapist had missed the fact that the patient was concerned about not having enough self-regulatory control and personal freedom to avoid buying alcohol. The therapist had also been aware that the shop mentioned by the patient was officially out of bounds, but he had not confronted the patient with this paranoid provocation. The patient may have felt that his hands were tied by the therapist into acting on his semicovert dare and cry for help.

If such massive defenses are somehow mollified or, more probably, circumvented and the cooperation phase is traversed successfully, the phase of coping is usually not a problem. The paranoid will be able to leverage considerable self-control against urges to use after initial stabilization. As recovery progresses, helping the paranoid to reconstruct a more benign and less self-defeating identity is much more productive a strategy than attempting to accelerate deconstruction of denial and diffusion of old identity constructions. Not only do paranoids deny their own problems, they have an inherent difficulty in identifying empathically with the problems and accomplishments of others. In deconstruction work, aggressive uncovering and confrontation from treatment staff or other patients can be catastrophic for the paranoid and provide a clear rationalization to drop out of treatment and/or relapse to reestablish autonomy. It should go without saying that workbooks, self-report measures, note taking, and homework assignments, which may be very effective with compulsive and narcissistic patients, will be counterproductive with paranoids. Group activities and group psychotherapy can eventually proceed smoothly after a long period of trust building and testing, unless the paranoid is an aggressive, attacking type, who can rarely be integrated in an ongoing group. Psychoeducational materials such as films or autobiographical stories told by other addicted persons are not usually helpful to the paranoid, who has a hard time identifying with the impairments and problems of others. Materials that show how some historical figure or unusually accomplished person struggled against an addiction and other obstacles may engender some motivation for superficial identification of the self as a chemically dependent person.

The paranoid's cynical misgivings and narcissism can be used to the advantage of recovery processes. The paranoid has a philosophy of personal responsibility and a contradictory attitude of blaming others for all problems. Paranoids see themselves as central to all contexts, yet they do not believe that they are more than of instrumental value to others. Given their cognitive bent, they are sometimes willing to entertain the meanings of these contradictions. In the proper affective climate established by the therapist (one where sadomasochism and power issues are not the primary tensions), this dialogue can proceed in a way that builds the therapeutic alliance and expands tolerance of inherent contradictions in the patient. However, if this is pressed too far, paranoids will feel betrayed and invaded and will either retreat or retaliate. Similarly, too much empathy or insight on the part of the therapist into the patient's internal process will be seen as a sadistic intrusion and will increase the need for flight or fight. If the technique of partial contradiction is used, it is not unreasonable to share with the patient the reason why the therapist will often be taking the other side of issues or situations than the one presented. In that way, the patient will not detect a hidden agenda of psychological manipulation in this technique, which does not hinge on the client being an unwitting participant.

Psychopathy, Criminality, and Substance Abuse

This chapter provides a dual diagnosis perspective on the treatment of addiction in individuals with significant criminal involvement and/or antisocial or psychopathic personality dynamics. After surveying the most relevant of the many issues and subjects involved, the relationships among crime, substance abuse, and the treatment of addiction as a crime prevention strategy is investigated. Such strategies may be made much more practical and coherent when the concept of psychopathy is introduced as a significant mediator of some, but not all, criminality and drug abuse patterns. The psychopathic personality is described here prototypically and in contrast and comparison with the other pathological variants of the independent personality styles (the narcissistic, antisocial, paranoid, and sadistic disorders). The assessment of psychopathy and psychopathic personality disorder as distinct from both criminal behavior and antisocial personality is presented, along with several clinical examples of substance-abusing psychopaths and antisocial personalities. These personalities are described in terms of the heuristic system introduced in Chapter 3. The descriptions encompass their vulnerabilities to Axis I disorders, common deficits in each of the five symptom complexes, the principal psychosocial functions of their addictions, their favored positions in the addictive cycle, and their typical responses to various treatment modalities and interventions.

Building on all of the information, a tentative procedure is set up for assessing degree of risk for future criminal behavior of substance-involved offenders. Selected clinical, program design, and social policy implications of these relationships are discussed in the process of critiquing several existing correctional and forensic

---

Note: This chapter was co-authored by Paul Montalbano, Ph.D.

models of substance abuse treatment. The severity of psychopathy is shown here to be highly predictive of response to treatment and recidivism, providing a valuable criterion, in combination with others, for improving decisions about preferred treatment approach, triage of scarce substance abuse treatment services to correctional and forensic populations, assignment of security levels in institutional environments, and assessments of risk for future criminal behavior in regard to consideration of conditional or early release (parole) programs.

Some discussion of terminology is an important introduction to this chapter. Such terms as criminal personality, antisocial personality, sociopathic personality, and psychopathic personality, among others, have been used to describe a personality type or behavioral trait that includes the following hallmarks: a propensity for criminality and antisocial behavior, sensation seeking, and hedonism, including the abuse of mind-altering substances. In clinical practice and common parlance, most of the terms that describe this personalty type and its related behaviors have been used interchangeably, resulting in confusion about their original senses and preventing further development of the specifics and coherence of their meanings, which greatly limit their utility in constructing viable and generative theory.

As used here, criminality refers broadly to involvement in acts that are punishable by law, but especially those that violate the property or personal rights of others. Antisocial behavior is broader than crime and includes a wider range of social rule breaking, destructiveness, gross immorality, and other behaviors that reflect undue disregard for the rights and dignity of others and general animosity toward socially prescribed behavior. Antisocial personality disorder (APD), as defined in the DSM-III-R, relies primarily on legal and behavioral characteristics. Building on earlier work, especially that of Cleckley (1941), Robert Hare (1970) developed a biologically based conception of the psychopathic personality, which includes malfunctions of inhibitory mechanisms in the central nervous system, deficient emotional arousal, stimulus seeking, and behavioral modes believed to result from these characteristics. J. Reid Meloy (1988), integrating psychodynamic understandings with Hare's psychophysiological perspective, designated the psychopathic personality as a malignant subtype of the narcissistic personality disorder, which exhibits the effects of an inordinate amount of instinctual aggression and the absence of a capacity to bond and appropriately identify with others. According to Meloy, in addition to behavioral and psychophysiological characteristics identified by Hare, these effects include an incapacity for genuine empathy, remorselessness, an absence of guilt or shame, and a malignant mode of self repair that relies on humiliation or sadistic behavior toward others.

The acronym APD is used in this chapter to refer to the DSM-III-R diagnostic description for the antisocial personality disorder. The terms psychopathic personality, psychopath or psychopathy refer to the formulations of Hare or Meloy or to similar or congruous formulations. Because of their limited utility and specificity, the terms sociopathic personality and criminal personality are not used in this chapter.

PSYCHOPATHY AND DUAL DIAGNOSIS WORK

In the broadest sense, the use or distribution of illegal substances, by definition, constitutes antisocial behavior. An addictive pattern of use would therefore automatically lead to a chronic pattern of criminality. Such broad terms as *criminal*, *illegal*, or *antisocial* obfuscate the crucial individual differences among the many motivational factors that contribute to use or addiction in each individual case. A more exact classification scheme provides important information about such individual differences that is indispensable in making decisions regarding amenability to treatment, type of treatment recommended, relapse rate, and risk for future criminal, and specifically violent, behavior. Criminal or antisocial labels, which are rife with moral condemnation, also contribute to a pejorative, judgmental, and punitive orientation that may taint clinical perception and complicate treatment.

The persistent, addictive use of substances other than alcohol or prescribed medications has long been seen by many mental health workers as an indicator of antisocial, sociopathic, or psychopathic tendencies, with these terms being used interchangeably and without much formal definition. When either alcohol or prescribed drugs were the drug of choice, however, it usually took a criminal conviction, especially for violent crime, to generate a suspicion of APD or psychopathy. That suspicion would have surfaced much sooner had other drugs of choice been the issue. Once formed, the perception of significant psychopathy or the formal diagnosis of antisocial personality generated fear, wariness, and moral distance, if not disdain, on the part of many clinicians. These reactions account for no small part of the sometimes officially sanctioned "refer-them-out" policy held by many in the mental health care system regarding dual diagnosis patients. Despite this tendency to overpathologize the psychopathy of the substance-abusing patient, psychopathic dynamics are often left undetected in the treatment of many nonusing patients, where they are often much more relevant than is generally recognized by therapists.

Providers of substance abuse treatment have been less apt than mental health workers to view the mere fact of addiction or drug abuse as tantamount to evidence of psychopathy or antisocial behavior. In part, this is because many providers are themselves in recovery and know the process of addiction and heterogeneity of the drug culture from the inside. Also, these providers make fewer mistakes in overpathologizing psychopathic trends because they have more clinical experience in dealing with the real thing. Although recognizing heterogeneity of motive in substance abusers, paraprofessionals are, unfortunately, much less likely to accept heterogeneity of treatment modalities and needs. Motive may predict outcome in their perceptions, but it should not influence the methods used to support recovery or undermine denial. As we see later, this blanket approach to treatment is least likely to be effective with psychopathic individuals; nonetheless, substance abuse programs heavily staffed by paraprofessionals with these attitudes are often the penultimate repository for those truly psychopathic and antisocial individuals referred out by the mental health system and courts.

These programs, except for highly structured therapeutic communities (TCs), are not essentially designed to treat psychopathy, and most have very limited tolerance for psychopathic personalities once identified. These patients quickly subvert benign and nonauthoritarian treatment environments. Their rule-breaking behavior often results in rapid discharge from residential and inpatient programs after detoxification reestablishes their manipulative skills, hedonistic motives, and narcissistic entitlements. In outpatient programs, the patient with significant psychopathy who is coerced into treatment by court order or threat of termination of employment is often allowed to remain at the periphery of the program and to be relatively noncompliant with treatment. This happens out of the therapist's realistic fears of retaliation if the patient is directly confronted and out of the therapist's desire to protect the treatment culture from a psychopathic group member who simulates the role of pseudo co-therapist. Such patients often successfully become ensconced as a leader in competition with the therapist and in covert opposition to legitimate treatment goals. Ironically, these patients are sometimes tested less frequently for drug lapses, and their many excuses for nonattendance, passive participation, or sabotage of therapeutic dynamics are vigorously defended by staff members who unwittingly identify with the aggressor out of fear of retaliation or their own suppressed psychopathic traits.

In inpatient or correctional settings, such individuals will go to great lengths to ingratiate themselves with those in positions of power and often trade valuable information—"snitch"—in exchange for hints about urinalyses to evade detection or entrap those who have crossed them in some way. The more structured authoritarian TC model programs intended to deal with antisocial personalities often exclude by policy patients requiring medications. In that way, the programs exclude most patients with both a major mental illness and an antisocial personality or significant psychopathy. These programs also rely extensively on highly confrontational and defense-penetrating modalities, which lead to the decompensation and referral out of patients with major mental illness or tenuous personality structure (such as lower level borderlines and narcissistic personality types) and pronounced psychopathy.

The end of the line of such referrals is the correctional environment (prison or court-ordered treatment) or the forensic hospital. By definition, drug treatment programs in correctional and forensic environments are all, in a sense, dual diagnosis programs, because the majority of the clients have significant personality pathology, usually with mixtures of antisocial or psychopathic personality. In addition to the overlap between criminality and the personality disorders, there is increasing evidence of a growing criminalization of major mental illnesses. Individuals who previously would have been diverted to the mental health system for ongoing treatment and asylum are often instead arrested and prosecuted for crimes and are now disproportionately represented in offender populations. Most mentally ill offenders also meet the criteria for a substance- or alcohol-related diagnosis. This trend for co-morbidity among offenders, which does not vary with the nature of the offense, is especially strong in the case of the severely disturbed offender. As many as 72 percent of severely disturbed offenders meet the criteria for co-morbidity of alcohol or drug disorders in addition to a major mental illness (Abram and Teplin 1991).

In discussing their recent findings of a high prevalence of co-morbidity of mental illness and substance abuse among jail detainees, Abram and Teplin (1991) identified two primary conclusions that may be drawn. One conclusion focuses on the offender and another on the interface of the criminal justice and mental health systems. Ample support for both conclusions are found in this chapter.

> The extremely high rate of co-occurring disorders among both misdemeanant and felon jail detainees suggests two interpretations. First, two of the most common co-occurring disorders—drug abuse or dependence and antisocial personality disorder—have a criminal component. . . .
>
> An alternative explanation lies with the interstitial nature of our health care delivery system. Many programs will not accept patients who have multiple problems. . . . Because of the narrow parameters of each of the various caregiving systems, arrest becomes an alternative for handling cases that fall thought the cracks. Jails, unlike many treatment facilities, have no requirements or restrictions for entry.
>
> . . . Both interpretations suggest complementary rather than contradictory policy: Treatment systems must be redesigned to deal with the codisordered mentally ill, both in jails and in the larger health delivery system. [p. 1042]

Like dual diagnosis programs in the general community, drug treatment programs in correctional and forensic facilities, which are currently called upon to do what others have judged either impossible or beneath them to do, are often incredibly overworked and understaffed. Despite the attempts to increase service delivery in correctional environments, most incarcerated offenders have no access to formal substance abuse treatments. As Ellis MacDougall, former director of corrections in five state systems, stated in his 1976 article, "Corrections Has Not Been Tried," in the *Criminal Justice Review*, before the last decade and a half of sky-rocketing prison populations:

> The staffing of these institutions further has ensured their failure. In many cases even the security forces were either understaffed or underorganized to achieve their objectives, and where there were treatment staffs, their caseloads and teaching loads were so large that they were doomed to failure. [p. 67]

Given this situation, it is painfully clear that, whereas other sectors of society may feel comfortable with faulty notions regarding the relationship of criminality, psychopathology, and drugs (including distribution as well as addiction), correctional and forensic workers and agencies that often refer clients to them cannot afford these luxuries. Among the false beliefs are the equating of all criminality with psychopathy, acceptance of the blanket statement that all criminals are untreatable and unchangeable, the blind faith that rests on the occasional miraculous cure or spontaneous conversion from a criminal lifestyle, and the foolhardy notion that the psychopath is just like anyone else but suffers from a poor family, inadequate background, faulty education, and so on.

The abilities to recognize and accurately assess psychopathy and to adjust the approach to treatment accordingly are important skills for any therapist, but especially those working in dual diagnosis settings and correctional or forensic programs. These clinicians can be expected to encounter many individuals who adopt antisocial styles out of addiction-related needs and those who have a more primary antisocial and psychopathic orientation to life. Such clinicians are faced with an overwhelming demand for service accompanied by very meager resources of programming space, staff, and materials. This scarcity requires a careful triage of existing service capabilities. In any treatment environment, judgments in regard to the severity of psychopathy may largely determine the direction taken by the therapist. In addition to the emotional and countertransference motives cited earlier, a rational basis does exist for attempting differential treatment depending on the level of psychopathy in a case. For example, severe psychopathy is a strong contraindication for traditional psychological and correctional treatments aimed at rehabilitation and crime prevention. However, many individuals engaged in criminal behavior as an extension of their addiction do respond positively to aggressive intervention and long-term follow-up. In isolation from other data, an inspection of the criminal histories of these treatment-responsive offenders is often rife with high frequency predatory crimes, some of which may have resulted in violence. Superficially, on the basis of criminal history alone, these offenders may appear remarkably like the psychopathic offender. Differentiating between the two is an integral part of rational treatment programming and public policy in regard to substance abuse treatment strategies for individuals in the criminal justice system.

Outside the criminal arena, less severe manifestations of psychopathy, such as manipulation of the therapist or family, social rule breaking, hedonism, and mimicking of aggressive and even frankly criminal lifestyles, are often the results of positive developments in the treatment of certain immature, counterphobic, and negativistic (passive–aggressive) personalities. Similar dynamics are also almost inevitable in the normal development and routine treatment of relatively healthy adolescents or substance-dependent adult patients whose addictions are driven by identity and socialization deficits originating in late adolescence or early adulthood. Determining the severity of psychopathy, estimating its probable amenability to treatment, and establishing the relationship of substance involvement to psychopathic and other personality traits are crucial steps toward deciding on an effective treatment strategy. Assessment and analysis may result in the decision that the treatment context (private practice, clinic, residential program, or correctional program) is not adequate to effectively treat the case, or that radical modification of the usual treatment regimen will be needed to provide interventions with any hope of success.

THE RELATIONSHIP BETWEEN DRUG USE AND CRIMINALITY

Some commonly held but faulty beliefs related to this chapter are based on a confusion of terms. Part truths and exaggerations that become dislodged from broader perspectives account for a good deal of the confusion. For instance, assessment of the severity of criminality can easily become falsely equated with decisions of the court (number of convictions and incarcerations or sentence length) or police officers (arrests). One severely violent offense (without regard to analyzing the circumstances) is easily equated, again falsely, with a high risk for future dangerous behavior. Similarly, a history of frequent nonviolent criminal acts (again ignoring the degree of potential risk for violence) can be mistakenly interpreted as reflecting a low risk for danger. Recidivism measures are as much indicators of a system's ability to closely monitor and usefully interpret its own methods and operations as measures of the objective behaviors of offenders. Studies that compare recidivism rates across treatment and nontreatment groups are, therefore, usually catastrophically confounded, especially if conducted across systems or components of a system.

In the same vein, it is assumed in both clinical and public policy forums that drug use and addiction cause predatory or instrumental crime (i.e, crime for gain) and that drug use accounts for most instances of expressive violence. A recent review of the research demonstrated convincingly that such assumptions are based on misinterpretations of partial realities (Tonry and Wilson 1991). The correlations between substance abuse and crime is high, but this is not proof of the presence or the direction of a causal tie. Both substance abuse and crime begin in puberty, although most studies find that delinquency usually precedes drug abuse (Greenberg 1977). High rate users are also high rate predatory offenders with long-term involvement in both activities. Most serious offenders use both alcohol and drugs (Petersilie 1980). Chaiken and Chaiken (1991) corroborate the view that for most criminals predatory criminality more commonly occurs before drug abuse. However, a subgroup of drug-abusing offenders becomes increasingly deviant over time and may eventually cross the threshold, or "graduate," to heroin addiction or frequent polydrug abuse. The intensity of their criminal behavior then escalates dramatically. For this group of offenders, the rate of offending is directly related to the severity of addiction. Frequency of predatory crime is two or three times higher when they are using versus when they are in treatment or voluntarily abstaining for some other purpose. Most commonly, arrestees are either low frequency inept offenders (usually emotionally disturbed and substance involved) or heavy polydrug users who engage in a high volume of opportunistic criminal activities. Approximately one-third of these opportunistic criminals used heroin as juveniles and report daily heroin use prior to the last arrest (Chaiken and Chaiken 1985). In an important sense, our understanding of the relationships among substance abuse, mental illness, and crime can be easily confounded by the high arrest and conviction rate of the inadequate, unsuccessful criminal, who is more often mentally impaired or drug dependent, than more successful criminals who are less frequently apprehended and convicted.

In regard to violent crime, substance abuse and aggression have some common antecedents in personality origins. Wurmser and Lebling (1983), for example, have emphasized the role of violence and sexual overstimulation in the family backgrounds of more than half of substance abusers in psychotherapy. Jessor and Jessor (1977) described both substance abuse and violent crime as having origins in a failed transition from adolescence to adulthood. The classic Cambridge-Somerville Youth Study (McCord 1983, 1988), which began in 1936 and continued for 40 years, found that subjects rated as aggressive by teachers at ages 7 and 8 were significantly more likely to be classified as alcoholic as adults:

> The results showed that aggressiveness in childhood predisposed subjects to adult criminal behavior, and that alcoholic subjects were convicted of more crimes regardless of their early childhood aggressiveness. Moreover, alcoholism and early childhood aggression were associated with different forms of adult aggression. Alcoholic subjects who were aggressive during childhood more often were convicted of interpersonal crimes as adults than nonalcoholic subjects. In other words, early childhood aggressiveness and alcoholism as an adult were found to interact and predict the highest levels of interpersonal violence. [J. Fagan, quoted in Tonry and Wilson 1990, p. 262]

For violent crime among adults, a pattern has emerged that is similar to that for predatory crime, with criminal violence preceding drug abuse (Collins et al. 1985). The essence of the growing consensus in the literature is that there is considerable variety in the relationship between criminal patterns and drug use. Some of this diversity is explained by examining the drug of choice and the severity of addiction. Chaiken and Chaiken (1991) summarize this point succinctly:

> In short, no single sequential or causal relationship is now believed to relate drug use to predatory crime. When the behaviors of large groups of people are studied in the aggregate, no coherent general patterns emerge associating drug use per se with participation in predatory crime, age at onset of participation in crime, or persistence in committing crime. Rather, different patterns appear to apply to different types of drug users. But research does show that certain types of drug abuse are strongly related to offenders committing crimes at high frequencies—violent crimes as well as other, income-producing crimes. The observed relationship applies

to various population subgroups, including groups defined by age, race, or sex.
[p. 205]

If there appears to be no simple general relationship between high rates of drug
use in itself and high rates of crime for groups of offenders, the same complexity can
be found at the individual level for most offenders. Narcotic addicts and high
frequency polydrug users may be more predictable. For most offenders, changes
over time in the use or nonuse of drugs are not systematically related to changes in
the frequency or types of their criminal activity. However, for heroin addicts with
a pattern of high frequency criminality, intensity of criminal activity varies directly
with intensity of drug use. This apparent causal tie is intensified by long durations
of involvement in drug use and predatory crime and is strongest for individuals
with early onset of cocaine or heroin use. Apparently, drug use serves more to
intensify or facilitate criminal behavior than being the cause of criminality:

> In sum, use of illicit drugs may be a primary cause for initial participation in predatory
> crime for some offenders; however, for the vast majority of offenders who commit
> predatory crimes, use of illicit substances appears to be neither a necessary nor a
> sufficient cause of onset of predatory criminal behavior. Even onset of narcotic
> addiction often does not appear to be causally related to onset of involvement in
> property crime. Rather, the onset of heroin addiction is often a key point in
> accelerating an existing criminal career. [Chaiken and Chaiken 1991, pp. 218–219]

In regard to specific offense categories, Anglin and Speckart (1986) found that
theft more frequently precedes than follows addiction. Burglary and robbery are
more likely to follow than precede addiction. Heroin addicts in particular are
exceptionally diligent in their criminal efforts. The average heroin addict offenders
spend more days per year (228, according to Chaiken and Chaiken 1991) working
at their profession than does the typical factory worker. Obviously, there are no
scheduled holidays, weekends, or vacations on an addiction. Heroin addicts
typically have between five to ten times the crime days per year (days where a crime
is committed) as do offenders who do not take drugs. A similar pattern may be
emerging for cocaine addicts. The absence of a pattern of increased drug use
resulting in increased crime in groups other than heroin and cocaine users has
important policy and treatment implications. Reducing drug dependence on
substances other than heroin and cocaine and targeting criminals outside the high
frequency group are strategies not likely to reduce instrumental crime. On first
examination, this analysis appears to provide an important guide to resource
allocation in crime prevention activities. Its logical implication is that criminal
justice programs should target the high rate predatory criminal with high substance
use rates. As usual, however, things are never as simple as they first appear. Drug
sellers, who often do not use drugs on any ongoing basis, and commit a high rate
of predatory and violent crimes, are often excluded from treatment efforts. The

term *substance-involved offender* is much more comprehensive and meaningful than a conceptualization of the drug-crime connection, which largely excludes the dealer. Also, as we see later, a large proportion of high rate criminals are psychopathic, that is, they have personality traits that predispose them to be recalcitrant to psychological and correctional interventions and prone to constant rule-breaking and exploitation of others.

Criminologists have relied more on topologies of criminals based on criminal history than on those based on individual differences related to inferred internal characteristics, either learned or inherent. In addition to the poor specificity of topologies not based on overt crime, psychological and psychiatrically based topologies have in the past proved to be tautological and overly simplistic in regard to classifying offenders (such as labeling them as antisocial personalities because of the criminal behavior). Some have been based on the findings of a single psychological instrument not designed specifically for an offender population, such as MMPI offender classification schemes (Megargee and Bohn 1979). Still other psychological topologies of offenders have required intensive clinical training and extensive background and behavioral data before categorizing any individual case. This chapter shows that the criminological and psychological approaches to offender topologies can be fruitfully combined.

An example of a criminologically based typology relevant to substance-abusing offenders can be found in the work of Dr. David Nurco and colleagues (1984, 1991), which demonstrates the importance of weighing factors such as criminal frequency, history of violence, and pan-criminality in developing public policy or in designing treatments aimed at reducing crime. Although this system identifies ten categories of offender, we focus here on the category called the Violent Generalists, which has the most significance for correctional policy and substance abuse treatment. For Nurco, the Violent Generalists (like Megargee and Bohn's [1979] Foxtrot group, or Chaiken and Chaiken's [1982] Violent Predators) are offenders who are actively involved in criminal behavior in preaddiction and nonaddiction periods. Their criminal behavior and addictions begin early in life. In the sample used to develop the typology (N = 250) Nurco's Violent Generalists were only 7 percent of the sample but accounted for more than 52 percent of the violent crimes and 76 percent of the auto thefts. Nurco suggests that handling such offenders differently from others is essential in an effective strategy of reducing drug-related crime.

> With regard to crime reduction strategies, we recommend that among the addict types, the Violent Generalists be considered the most appropriate candidates for incapacitation and the least appropriate for rehabilitation. This recommendation is suggested not only because of the seriousness of their crimes, but also because they tend to persist in committing serious crime when they are no longer addicted to narcotics. Thus any efforts to reduce their crime through traditional treatment for narcotic addiction would more likely be ineffective.
>
> It appears that the higher the decline in crime rates from addiction to nonaddiction periods, the more likely rehabilitation would serve as a reasonable crime

reduction strategy. A large difference generally indicates that an individual is heavily involved in serious crime when he is addicted, but minimally involved when he is not addicted. Therefore, if the addiction to narcotics is eliminated, his crime is likely to be significantly reduced. Based on this, a reasonable crime reduction strategy for this type of addict may be rehabilitation in the form of conventional drug abuse treatment with a focus on the elimination of narcotic addiction.

Given the enormous amount of crime committed by drug abusers and the pressing need to selectively incapacitate the most serious criminals, we recommend that more attention be paid to measuring levels of seriousness of crime among narcotic addicts. Such a measurement is crucial to making distinctions with regard to the type of intervention to be employed. [Nurco et al. 1991, p. 444]

Nurco's Violent Generalists category is based on heroin users and may generalize in only a limited way to other drug-involved offenders. Although some of the individuals described in the Violent Generalists category may be psychopathic, the choice of heroin as a drug of dependence may contraindicate severe psychopathy. As shown later in discussing the drug of choice in relationship to psychopathy, individuals with the most extreme forms of psychopathy favor the stimulants, especially cocaine and the amphetamines. However, Nurco and his colleagues have contributed significantly to the area of substance abuse treatment of offenders and public correctional policy by empirically demonstrating that an identifiable subcategory of substance-involved offenders accounts for a large percentage of predatory crime, but those people are not likely to be amenable to traditional interventions and represent the preferred long-term occupants of expensive incapacitation strategies such as imprisonment.

In addition to the emphasis on severity of crime and criminal history in relationship to substance abuse, psychological and personological variables can significantly improve judgments of risk for future criminal behavior and prediction of a favorable response to treatment. Although these variables can be viewed as controversial because they go beyond the question of the legality of an individual's behavior, neither treatment efforts nor public policy agencies can afford to ignore such information. Much of the rest of this chapter focuses on psychopathy, one of the few scientifically validated concepts shown to predict course of criminal behavior over time.

PSYCHOPATHY IN THE CONTEXT OF THE PERSONALITY DISORDERS

So much confusion surrounds the meaning of psychological terms related to aggressive and criminal individuals that it is perhaps best to begin with a historical review and definition of terms. More detailed reviews are contained in Meloy's

(1988) *The Psychopathic Mind* and Millon's (1981) *Disorders of Personality. DSM-III: Axis II.*

The evolution of the clinical and scientific concept of the psychopathy has been long and uneven for several reasons, including the confusion of criminal behavior with criminal personality attendant with all the diversity of biological, psychological, and social variables asserted as relevant to criminal behavior. One of the most important obstacles to theory building in this area, however, has been the strained dialectic between clinical and moral perspectives. Clinical descriptions often became infused with moral reproaches. Scientifically oriented clinicians tried to disentangle the jumble of clinical and moral imperatives, only to have others retie the knots.

This pattern of confusion began early in the nineteenth century. For example, in 1801 Pinel introduced the term *"manie sans delirium"* to clinically describe patients who acted impulsively and destructively, yet appeared to manifest no marked deficits in reasoning. A few years later, Benjamin Rush (1812) noted the same contrast between apparently intact reasoning and chronic irresponsible and impulsive behavior, which he attributed to an innate, preternatural moral depravity. The pendulum continued to swing just as society vacillated between hospitalizing or incarcerating these puzzling and destructive individuals. Mental health professionals, reflecting the moral outrage of the public, used such terms as *moral insanity* (Prichard 1835) and *morally insane* (Gouster 1878, Kraepelin 1887) to describe and at the same time censure this population. Daniel Hack Tuke (1892) proposed dropping the term *moral insanity* and replacing it with *inhibitory insanity* to reestablish scientific objectivity and moral neutrality. Theorists continued to wage the familiar debate concerning the relative contributions of genetic and environmental factors to psychopathy. Birnbaum (1914), for example, introduced the term *sociopathic* to emphasize the influence of environmental factors and social learning.

Psychoanalysts initially focused speculation on the contribution of psychodynamic factors in infancy and early childhood to the development of psychopathy. Aichorn (1925) noted the contribution of narcissism, oedipal configurations, and the failure of early identifications to psychopathy. In the 1940s, renewed interest in the narcissistic aspects of psychopathy led to several elaborations of these earlier insights. Karen Horney (1945) eloquently described the use of exploitation and sadism to increase a sense of power and importance. Wilhelm Reich's (1945) explication of the arrogant, aggressive, misogynistic "phallic narcissistic character" serves as prototype for an extremely dangerous variant of the psychopath, the sexual sadist. By 1950 this line of theory stressing narcissistic pathology in the development of psychopathy was well established, with Levy (1951) foreshadowing Millon's aggressive and narcissistic subtypes of the independent personality by distinguishing between individuals who had experienced the two extremes of narcissistic injury: the deprived psychopath, who often experienced a harsh upbringing, and the indulged psychopath, who often experienced parental overvaluation.

Other themes were explored as well in the 1940s. Fenichel (1945) emphasized the distortions of early identifications and spoke of "instinct ridden characters." Later psychoanalytically oriented clinicians emphasized the superego deficits in psychopathy (Johnson 1949, Schmideberg 1949). Hervey Cleckley (1941), in his hallmark book, *The Mask of Sanity*, attributed psychopathy to a type of concealed psychosis. Cleckley (1976) postulated: "a selective defect or elimination that prevents important components of normal experience from being integrated into whole human reaction, particularly an elimination or attenuation of those strong affective components which ordinarily arise in major interpersonal and social issues" (pp. 230–231). Cleckley also introduced sixteen behavioral criteria that formed the basis for Hare's Psychopathy Checklist (Hare 1991), a standardized measure of psychopathy as a dimensional behavioral trait.

It was not until the late 1980s that these themes matured to provide a coherent and convincing explanation of the psychopathic personality, which integrated both the line of theoretical development implicating failures in narcissistic processes and the line of development related to innate predispositions toward impulsivity and aggression. Building on Kernberg's (1984) subtype of "malignant narcissism," J. Reid Meloy, in his seminal (1988) work, *The Psychopathic Mind*, elaborated the concept of the psychopath as a severe, malignant variant of the narcissist. Meloy combines these lines of development in his definition of psychopathy as a "deviant developmental disturbance characterized by an inordinate amount of instinctual aggression and the absence of a capacity to bond" (p. 5). Meloy acknowledges the biological factors that may contribute to the development of this disorder. In his words, "psychopathy is psychobiologically predisposed, but there are necessarily deficient and conflictual primary object experiences that determine its phenotypic expression" (p. 6). Psychodynamically, psychopathy may be understood as "a virtual failure of identification" (p. 441) and on a broader scope as "a fundamental disidentification with humanity" (p. 5). What occurs instead, according to Meloy, is an identification with the stranger self/object. Meloy cites Grotstein (1982), who defines the stranger self/object as "the unconscious pre-awareness of the enemy which is believed to be both within ourselves and to have an external counterpart" (p. 63). The identification with the stranger self-object entails projection and re-incorporation in a process similar to the paranoid processes described in previous chapters as a crucial component in many addictive patterns.

These contributions are noted to form a general context for the understanding of the concept of psychopathy. It is important to keep in mind that many of the factors that contributed to the confusing evolution of the concept continue to exist. With the theoretical framework of this book, psychopathy may be viewed as a severe form of the active-independent or aggressive personality as defined by Millon, resulting from failures in the management of paranoid-narcissistic processes. It is viewed both as a distinct clinical entity (in the form of a personality disorder) and as a dimensional trait with degrees of severity. Developmentally, psychopathy represents a failure in attachment and bonding and therefore can be compared and contrasted to both schizophrenia and autism. In regard to object relations, we concur with Meloy (1988) that psychopathy is characterized by pathological identification with the stranger, perceived as predator or enemy, and Millon (1981) that this essentially constitutes a sadistic object orientation.

Throughout this chapter, the basic independent personality styles (narcissistic, antisocial) and their more deviant variants, the paranoid, psychopathic, and sadistic disorders) are contrasted and compared to draw light on the relationship between criminality and substance involvement. In discussing the more malignant variants of the independent styles which are the focus of this chapter, it is important to stress that these categories are theorotypes (Rychlak 1981b), that is, stylized, professional terms that are in effect sophisticated stereotypes meant to illuminate behavior and not intended to demean or dignify the individuals described and that only a minority of individuals will exhibit the type fully or exclusively. In addition, psychopathy is presented as a dimensional trait exhibited to a greater or lesser extent in many individuals, but especially in the population of identified offenders.

The independent personalities as outlined by Millon (1969, 1981) derive basic rewards principally by relying on themselves. Millon identifies two basic subtypes of the independent personality style: the narcissistic style and the antisocial (aggressive) style. For both of these, the interpersonal sphere is entered primarily to gain selfish rewards that could not be procured in isolation. Narcissistic personalities, to the extent that they are engaged in interpersonal relationships, use them in order to support their inflated sense of superiority through stimulating and accepting the admiration of others, by privately or publicly devaluing others, or by avoiding exposure or the need to acknowledge their own limitations or imperfections. The narcissist pursues these goals passively in the sense that the premises of independence and superiority of the self are assumed and consistently acted upon. The effect on others of these actions is important only to the extent that these consequences reflect on and influence the self. The more active aggressive personality also demonstrates instrumental motivation in relation to others. In addition, however, the aggressive individual is driven by a need to actively attack, conquer, dominate, or devalue others. Millon (1981) describes the core of the active independent personality as composed of the following traits:

1. *Hostile affectivity* (e.g., pugnacious and irascible temper flares readily into argument and attack; frequent verbally abusive and physically cruel behaviors).
2. *Assertive self-image* (e.g., proudly characterizes self as self-reliant, vigorously energetic and hard-headed; values tough, competitive and power-oriented life style).
3. *Interpersonal vindictiveness* (e.g., reveals satisfaction in derogating and humiliating others; contemptuous of sentimentality, social compassion and humanistic values).

4. *Hyperthymic fearlessness* (e.g., high activation level evident in impulsive, accelerated and forceful responding; attracted to and undaunted by danger and punishment).
5. *Malevolent projection* (e.g., claims that most persons are devious, controlling and punitive; justifies own mistrustful, hostile and vengeful attitudes by ascribing them to others). [p. 198]

It is important to emphasize the distinction between Millon's aggressive personality and APD as defined by *DSM-III-R*. Millon's conceptualization grounds the antisocial personality within a framework of personality theory and is not simply a behavioral checklist. As Millon notes, such a personality structure may or may not interface with the criminal justice system. Millon does not view the antisocial (aggressive) style as inherently pathological. Only when the five traits listed above are sufficiently extreme and pervasive and begin to result in severe adaptive inflexibility, self-defeating or destructive vicious circles, and tenuous stability should they be referred to as a personality disorder. Millon (1981) points out that many antisocial personalities are successfully employed "in the rugged side of [the] business, military or political world" (p. 182).

Millon has also identified a pathological variant of the active independent type, the sadistic personality. Whereas the narcissistic individual has a contrived sense of self (which may often be essentially benevolent or neutral toward others when not directly threatened), and the aggressive individual has a rebellious, resentful, and revengeful sense of self, the sadistic individual's sense of self is pernicious, cruel, sadistic, or malevolent. The antisocial is an acting-out character who impulsively loses control and is shortsighted, lacking in planning ability or insight into consequences and alternatives. The sadistic individual often shows the opposite of this impulsiveness and cognitive inadequacy. Nonetheless, the sadistic individual is not deterred by possible consequences that involve punishment or pain, and remains fearless and unflinching in striving for sadistic rewards despite sound insight into reality and social processes. Whereas the antisocial individual is callous and irresponsible in disregard of others, the sadist is actively hostile, cruel, and mean-spirited. At the level of object relations, the antisocial individual has incorporated a self-other schema involving autonomy of the self and resentment of the other, who is viewed at best as a withholding obstacle to his or her needs being met. More malignantly, the sadistic individual has incorporated a self-other schema involving opposition or competition of the self with others and brutality toward the other, who is perceived as either threat or prey.

Millon's sadistic personality disorder and antisocial personality disorder represent two active, aggressively independent styles, the latter being the more malignant variant. The remainder of this chapter uses the term *antisocial personality* to refer to his basic active aggressive style, with a level of severity indicating a personality disorder. The term *sadistic personality*, however, is not relied on as a general category of personality. The term *psychopathic personality* captures some of the same attributes but has greater generalizability and a history of connotations that are not overly identified with sadomasochistic dynamics, as is the term *sadistic personality*.

Within the group of individuals described here as psychopathic personalities, however, a more narrowly defined subgroup does exist where the dynamics of sadomasochism are so pronounced and pervasive that the use of the term sadistic personality disorder does seem warranted. Together, disorders comprising a paranoid-narcissistic spectrum is introduced in Chapter 7. This spectrum is viewed as resulting from various pathological developments of narcissism. Listed from mild to severe manifestations of narcissistic pathology, the paranoid-narcissistic spectrum includes extreme vacillations in self-esteem, brief paranoid states, the narcissistic personality disorder, Millon's aggressive personality, APD as outlined in *DSM-III-R*, the psychopathic personality, paranoid personality disorder, and paranoid psychosis. Table 8–1 shows the relationship among these disorders in this spectrum. A dynamic of the paranoid-narcissistic process is identified and related to vulnerabilities to Axis I disorders, significant antisocial behaviors, personality styles, personality disorders, and their decompensations.

Table 8–1. The Paranoid-Narcissistic Spectrum

Sub-Process* Emphasis results in the following:	Contrived Self Inflation	Rebellious Contempt	Self Protection against Treat	Identification with the Predator/Enemy	Sado-masochism
Vulnerability to Axis I Disorders:	Depression Psychotic Episodes	Emotional Dyscontrol	Somatoform Disorders Paranoid Disorder	Phobias Rage Reactions	Sexual Disorders
Significant "Antisocial" Behaviors:	Interpersonal Exploitation	Instrumental and Expressive Crime	Provocation and Preemptory Attack	Planful Conquest and Predation	Victimization and Dehuman-ization as Reward
Personality Styles:	Narcissistic	Antisocial	**	**	**
Personality Disorders:	Narcissistic PD	Antisocial PD	Paranoid PD	Psychopathic PD	Sadistic PD
Decompensated Personalities	Paranoid Schizoid	Borderline Schizotypal	Paranoid	Paranoid Psychopathic	Borderline Sadistic

*The table identifies dynamics within the paranoid-narcissistic process. Severity of pathological process and deviance of outcome increases from left to right in the rows and from top to bottom in the columns.

**Process almost always results in disorder or compensation to a pathological personality pattern rather than to a viable personality style.

In this discussion of criminality and addiction, we refer to the antisocial personality (APD), the psychopathic personality (PPD), or both. This limitation occurs for several reasons. Narcissistic and paranoid personalities are discussed in previous chapters. The sadistic personality is, we pray, too rare a variant to merit separate consideration in this context. More important, however, is the fact that although all of the personality styles, disorders, and decompensations discussed here are capable of a criminal lifestyle (as are individuals of almost any other personality style or disorder), only the antisocial and psychopathic types are inherently motivated to maintain such a lifestyle in the sense of Nurco's Violent Generalists. Other disorders may resort to criminality to achieve specific rewards, but this is usually done in an opportunistic manner or for clearly instrumental purposes. Such is not the case with the antisocial and psychopathic personality disorders. Only these two are motivated to indulge in criminal behavior per se in an addictive pattern. Although all these types are vulnerable to addictive disorders because of the paranoid process and basic failures in self-regulation, only antisocial and psychopathic individuals are specifically motivated to routinely use drugs or abuse substances to facilitate criminal behavior.

Our focus here on antisocial and psychopathic types also implies several significant assumptions. First, if we are to learn more about the relationship of criminality to addiction, we must concentrate on those individuals who are motivated to combine the two rather than on those who are ineffective criminals. Second, violent crime, although it occurs in all personality styles, is more frequently performed by those with a criminal lifestyle, that is, individuals whose lifestyles provide frequent or daily opportunity and motive for apparently coherent instrumental or expressive violence.

Let us now further elaborate our earlier definition of the psychopathic theorotype as a personality disorder and, as a psychopathy, as a dimensional trait of other personalities. Psychopathic personality is characterized by a pervasive lack of genuine attachment, which manifests itself in an inability to experience authentic empathy, remorse, and love. There is an overall constriction in the depth and range of affective experience and a general lack of anxiety. Studies that support significant genetic contributions and the growing body of research indicate that psychopaths are autonomically hyporeactive. They tend not to display normal arousal when faced with aversive consequences and may be predisposed toward sensation seeking to compensate for their hyporeactivity (see the Sensation Seeking Scale in Chapter 4). Behaviorally, psychopaths are thrill seeking, impulsive, antisocial, and irresponsible. They do not appear to learn to alter their behaviors, and punishment appears to have little effect in deterring future recklessness or amorality.

Interpersonally, the psychopath's lack of genuine attachments contributes to deficits in empathy, remorse, guilt, and tenderness. Often there is a callous disregard for the feelings of others and/or sadism toward others. The external world of humanity becomes a smorgasbord of experiences to be tasted and then tossed aside. There is delight in deception and manipulation. Sexual relations tend to be promiscuous and lacking in depth. Attempts to engage in genuine and heartfelt interpersonal exchanges are marked by superficiality and hollowness. Goodness in others is often resented and envied, and the psychopath will consciously or unconsciously seek to destroy or compromise such goodness. Psychodynamically, the psychopath constantly seeks ways to maintain, recapture, or inflate his or her underlying grandiosity. Devalued self-aspects are projected onto others and rigidly controlled. However, the psychopath, in contrast to the narcissist, is often not content with benign or passive modes of narcissistic repair but appears impelled to aggressively devalue others, often violently, in order to establish superiority and a position of relative strength in a world viewed exclusively in terms of a hierarchy of raw power. The world of the psychopath is a hostile, alien place, characterized by competitiveness and a ruthless, dog-eat-dog mode of thought. In such a feral realm, assertiveness, self-reliance, boldness, pugnacity, and vindictiveness are valued assets. The projection of one's own hostile impulses onto the surrounding world often contributes to a paranoid's red alert mentality characterized by a readiness for preemptive attacks (the best defense is a good offense). If caught off guard or humiliated, the antisocial personality will characteristically retaliate with unusual vigor, often with sadistic overkill, in order to reestablish his or her reputation among peers and his or her own sense of power. Often, any word or action toward the psychopath that implies his or her passivity or inferiority is enough to unleash extreme physical retaliation or carefully laid traps to accomplish disproportionate revenge.

Clearly, it is imperative that psychopathy be differentiated from APD as defined by *DSM-III-R*, which is essentially a less malignant type. The confusing overlap is currently being addressed by the Axis II Work Group of the American Psychiatric Association's Task Force on *DSM-IV* (Hare et al. 1991). APD has been targeted for significant revision with the objectives of simplification and incorporation of items related to the traditional concept of psychopathology. The current criteria for APD are based almost entirely on the presence of certain antisocial behaviors. Lack of remorse is the only criteria that measures an emotional response instead of a behavior. Although the behavioral checklist approach may yield good reliability, the underlying personality structure, including motivational and emotional dynamics, is not taken into account. Individuals who fulfill the criteria for APD may have a diverse range of underlying motivations and varying capacities for attachment, as well as for the emotional heirs to attachment; namely, feelings of remorse, guilt, compassion, and love. The concept of psychopathy provides a method of winnowing out the more dangerous, callous, recalcitrant individual from the more emotional, impulsive one, both of whom may satisfy the criteria for APD. This is a crucial distinction, for these are very different individuals with very different prognoses for treatment. Individuals with a capacity for attachment are more likely to form a therapeutic alliance and, therefore, more likely to benefit from treatment, especially when the modality is centered on this relationship. Gerstley and colleagues (1989), for example, found a significant correlation between the ability to form a working relationship and positive treatment outcome for APDs.

Hare and colleagues (1991) estimated that 25 to 30 percent of federal prisoners and about 15 percent of forensic psychiatric inpatients are psychopathic, and less than half of individuals diagnosed as having APD are also psychopathic. Hare and colleagues (1989) found that a diagnosis of psychopathy was significantly correlated with a diagnosis of APD. Computations of positive predictive power (PPP), defined as the conditional probability of having one disorder given the other, clearly indicated that a diagnosis of psychopathy was highly predictive of APD (PPP = .90), but that APD (PPP = .23) was not predictive of psychopathy (Widiger et al. 1984).

To summarize, psychopathy is emerging as a distinct clinical entity related to, but not identical with, other mental disorders. When psychopathy is objectively quantified by the Psychopathy Checklist, it can be correlated with other personality disorders. One study has empirically demonstrated that psychopathy "tended to be associated with the absence of an Axis I principal diagnosis and with the presence of substance abuse (other than alcohol)" (Hare et al. 1989, p. 214). In fact, these researchers found that patients with a diagnosis of psychopathy were about nine times less likely to receive any principal Axis I diagnosis than patients who were not psychopathic. This research tends to disagree with those who view psychopathy as a direct variant of a major mental illness.

In regard to personality disorders other than APD, they found a modest but not significant correlation between psychopathy and histrionic personality disorder. Total PCL scores were positively correlated with ratings of histrionic and narcissistic personality disorders and negatively correlated with avoidant personality disorder. The positive correlations with narcissistic personality disorder are congruent with this book's perspective of viewing narcissicism and psychopathy as subtypes of the independent personality. In regard to the correlation with histrionic personality, the first factor of the PCL measures affective and interpersonal processes that are often of importance in histrionic individuals, such as glibness, lying, callous indifference, conning, and factors that can result in superficial or pseudo-empathy. Interestingly, Meloy (1988) has noted high frequency for the interpersonal pairing of psychopathic males with histrionic females. Histrionic traits (related to the dependent cluster of personality style) are often developed by psychopaths as an alternative style that greatly increases their effectiveness as persuaders and manipulators and often provides a means to lure and maintain victims into their orbit.

In regard to the empirical data on psychopathy and addictive behavior Hare and colleagues (1989) found that total PCL-R scores were correlated 0.24 with diagnoses of alcohol disorders and 0.31 with diagnoses of substance abuse. Smith and Newman (in press) found that total PCL-R scores correlated 0.34 with the number of alcohol-related symptoms and 0.33 with the number of drug-related symptoms.

Hemphill and colleagues (1990) found that total PCL-R scores were not significantly correlated with alcohol abuse/dependence; however, total PCL-R scores were correlated 0.35 with drug abuse/dependence. These findings are consistent with the view that antisocial personalities tend to indulge in alcohol, whereas psychopaths do not. The Epidemiological Catchment Area Study described in Chapter 1 confounded antisocial and psychopathic personalities. Nonetheless, they found that APDs preferred stimulants above other substances. Personal clinical experiences support the hypothesis of Meloy (1988) that "the illicit drugs of choice for the psychopathic character appear to be cocaine hydrochloride and the various forms of amphetamine and methamphetamine" (p. 294). Analyzed in terms of the heuristic system, this choice of drug category (the stimulants) is consistent with deficits in the reward–arousal complex and with the pathological narcissist's motivation to rest within the inflated/grandiose position of the addictive cycle.

ASSESSMENT OF SEVERITY OF PSYCHOPATHY

In addition to the emphasis on a personality prototype, psychopathy can be defined as a dimensional continuum from mild to severe. The Revised Psychopathy Checklist (Hare 1980), used in much of the research cited earlier, is the preferred instrument for the objective assessment of this dimension. The checklist was initially derived from Cleckley's (1941) original sixteen criteria for psychopathy. Hare (1985) developed and refined a twenty-item checklist that has demonstrated high reliability with criminal populations. In his revised manual (1990) he outlines the growing body of research that supports the content, criterion and predictive validity of the instrument (Hare 1980, 1982, 1983, 1984, 1985, Kassen et al. 1990). The items on the checklist are:

1. Glibness/superficial charm
2. Grandiose sense of self-worth
3. Need for stimulation/proneness to boredom
4. Pathological lying
5. Conning/manipulative behavior
6. Lack of remorse or guilt
7. Shallow affect
8. Callous/lack of empathy
9. Parasitic lifestyle
10. Poor behavioral controls
11. Promiscuous sexual behavior
12. Early behavior problems
13. Lack of realistic, long-term goals
14. Impulsivity
15. Irresponsibility

16. Failure to accept responsibility for actions
17. Many short-term marital relationships
18. Juvenile delinquency
19. Revocation of conditional release
20. Criminal versatility [Hare 1990, p. 16]

Items that do not apply to an individual are scored 0. Items that are a good match are scored 2. Items that apply to a certain degree or for which there is uncertainty score 1, such as when the scorer is unable to resolve conflicts between different sets of data. Items not applicable to the subject are omitted. Scores for the twenty items are totaled. Hare (1985a) recommended that a cutoff score of 30 be employed to differentiate psychopathic from nonpsychopathic individuals. Meloy (1988), arguing for a continuous rather than dichotomous conceptualization of psychopathy, suggests three groupings of mild (scores 10–19), moderate (scores 20–29), and severe (scores 30–40) levels of psychopathy.

Proper use of the PCL requires training in scoring the checklist, which uses a structured interview and review of objective information, as recommended by Hare (1990). To increase reliability, different individuals should score different items, especially when the subject of the rating is in ongoing contact with the scores and may, therefore, influence their ratings. Average composite scores can then be used for the final assessment. It is important to emphasize that this instrument has not been demonstrated as empirically valid outside of its application to offender populations. Although psychopathy may be fundamentally manifest at an early age, a diagnosis should not be made until the age of 18.

Empirical research in progress is striving to lay the groundwork for utilizing other forms of psychological testing to assess psychopathy. Gacono and Meloy (1991), investigating psychopathic indexes in the Rorschach, found in a sample of forty-two subjects, all meeting the criteria for a diagnosis of APD, that severe psychopaths (those who scored 30 or higher on the PCL) produced significantly fewer texture and diffuse shading responses than the moderate psychopaths (those who scored below 30 on the PCL). Texture responses have generally been interpreted as indicators of interpersonal attachment or affiliation (Exner 1986a, Klopfer 1938) or a fear and discomfort around skin contact (Schachtel 1966). Diffuse shading responses have generally been interpreted as indicators of anxiety and helplessness (Klopfer et al. 1954, Rapaport et al. 1946, Schachtel 1966, Viglione 1980). Gacono and Meloy (1991) emphasize the presence of texture as a contraindicator of severe psychopathy. They note that of Exner's nonpatient adults, 90 percent produced this type of response (texture), whereas only 5 percent of their severe psychopathy group produced a texture response.

Such research has led Meloy to formulate a tentative goodness-of-fit index based on predicted psychopathic indices on the Rorschach, when scored according to the Exner Comprehensive System (1986a). Detailed information on the early version of this evolving index can be found in Meloy (1988). From these indicators, Meloy is in the process of formulating a tentative psychopathy index based on the structural summary of the Rorschach when scored according to Exner's (1986) comprehensive system. In a personal communication (1991) with one of the authors of this chapter, Meloy indicated that the index would tentatively include the following components: (1) texture = 0; (2) reflections > 0; (3) pairs > or = 3; (4) egocentricity index > 0.45; (5) diffuse shading = 0; and (6) personalizations > 3. Considered as psychopathic constellations, these indicators would reflect the lack of attachment (1), lack of anxiety (5), and the grandiose, narcissistic self-focus of the psychopath (2,3,4,6). Gacano and Maloy (1992) have proposed the addition of four aggressive indices for Rorschach scoring: aggressive content, aggressive potential, aggressive past, and sadomasochism. Nomothetic comparisons between groups of moderate and severe psychopaths yielded mixed results; however, sadomasochism, defined as "any response in which devalued, aggressive, or morbid content is accompanied by pleasurable affect," was significantly higher in severe as opposed to moderate psychopaths (p. 110). This suggests that evidence of sadism may be an important indicator of a high level of psychopathy and that staff observations of patient or inmate laughter or enjoyment in response to the suffering or misfortune of another should be carefully noted and considered when making decisions regarding that individual. The nature of these indicators is tentative, but they point to the important, evolving role of psychological testing in the detection and severity assessment of psychopathy.

Although the concept of psychopathy has been around in varied forms for more than a century (Koch 1891, Kraepelin 1896) and its origin can be traced even further back, one may wonder why clinicians have taken so long to accept and utilize it, or to develop valid and reliable measures for its assessment. Putting aside general social and political resistances to the concept of psychopathy, perhaps significant countertransference issues account, in part, for the halting progress in this field of behavioral science and clinical practice. Individuals who pursue the mental health disciplines tend to share certain characteristics, attitudes, and values. To generalize, mental health workers tend to be what may be called benign narcissists. They like to help and change others and derive satisfaction and a sense of efficacy from doing so. This helping in many cases may be a means of narcissistic repair, compensating for the therapist's own narcissistic liabilities. It is perhaps especially difficult for such persons to acknowledge and identify patients who might inherently be unable to benefit from the therapist's kindness, attention, or diligent investment, or whose mode of narcissistic repair might be the obverse of the therapist, that is, destructive and victimizing toward others, rather than constructive and helpful. Especially for therapists not sufficiently aware of their own sadism and aggression, their kindness and desire to help may obscure their ability to detect the complete lack of compassion and attachment in others. Therapists whose level of narcissism compromises their ability to assess the limitations of their methods and skills may not recognize the possibility that (given currently available understandings and treatment techniques) the severe psychopath for all intents and purposes may not be treatable. The dynamic interaction of the therapist's and psychopath's preferred mode of narcissistic repair (the former being a malignant perversion of repair), along with identification with the aggressor as a defensive and protective mechanism, might account for the perplexing, strange—and dangerous—over-identification by therapists with their most severe psychopathic patients. This is a far from uncommon observation in institutional settings where clinicians should otherwise be assumed to be savvy to psychopathic manipulation. Without the kind of cautious assessment process described here, it is much more likely that these distorting influences and unrecognized countertransference issues will result in the faulty management and treatment of psychopathic individuals.

SYMPTOM COMPLEXES AND FUNCTIONS OF ADDICTION

Here we apply the heuristic system for problem formulation in dual diagnosis work to the pathological personality types that are the focus of this chapter. Unless noted otherwise, the text applies more to the psychopathic than to the antisocial personality, although to varying degrees the data are applicable to both. Symptom complexes overlap, as do psychosocial functions of addiction and are treated separately here only for expository convenience.

Reward–Arousal Symptom Complex

Level of arousal is of primary importance for the psychopath. A growing consensus of research points to psychopaths as autonomically hyporeactive. The autonomic baseline activity, as measured by the Galvanic Skin Response (GSR), has been found to be consistently lower for psychopaths than nonpsychopaths (Hare 1978). The hypothesis of electrodermal hyporeactivity for psychopaths has been supported by a wide range of studies (Hare 1972, 1975, Hare and Craigen 1974, and Schalling et al. 1973). Psychopaths also appear to demonstrate less autonomic arousal than do normals when faced with an impending negative experience (Hare 1978, Hare and Craigen 1974, Lykken 1956, and Wadsworth 1975). Psychopaths seem to have a slower skin conductance recovery, indicating that they return more slowly to their autonomic baseline after arousal. Collins (1984) developed a maturational lag hypothesis of psychopathy on the finding of abnormal EEG test results in violent offenders. He argued that the bilateral theta activity in many adult psychopaths represents a delay in cerebral maturation, since his slow wave activity is commonly found in children and not in normal adults. A similar pattern of desynchronized resting EEGs is often noted in alcoholism, schizophrenia, and other psychiatric disorders. Hare had earlier hypothesized that excess theta activity might indicate cortical underarousal and that the daring behavior of the psychopath might be aimed at self-stimulation.

The foregoing provides a sample of the now extensive scientific literature that describes psychopaths as individuals with marked differences from normals in factors that constitute the reward–arousal symptom complex. These psychophysiological differences have profound consequences for general personality adjustment as well as for the propensity and nature of substance abuse and addiction. Meloy (1988) speculates that this autonomic hyporeactivity may predispose the psychopath to "lead a sensation-seeking, extroverted life-style" (p. 30). The psychopath compensates for the low level internal arousal by a ceaseless chase of external stimulation. Thrills, kicks, and excitement are pursued with relentless vigor. Although many psychopaths may avoid drug use because it constitutes an area of narcissistic vulnerability and exposure, or prevents them from being as adept in various manipulations or stalking of prey, use of drugs is more commonly an aspect of their sensation-seeking behavior. Logically, the drug of choice for the psychopath is the stimulant, with cocaine or amphetamine abuse probably most preferred. Empirical data supporting this conclusion are found in the Epidemiological Catchment Area (ECA) Study described earlier (Regier et al. 1990), showing that cocaine was the drug most often preferred by individuals with antisocial personality. The psychopath is able to modulate and increase his physiological arousal level through the use of stimulants. In addition, his or her internal sense of grandiosity is heightened by the euphoria and stimulation. The sense of thrill and power is enhanced by the illegality and potential danger of illicit drugs. For the psychopathic drug dealer, the criminal lifestyle that accompanies the dealing may become as or more rewarding and exhilarating than the actual drug abuse. As observed by Yochelson and Samenow (1986):

> The primary factor in craving drugs is the desire to do the forbidden. The desire for drugs and the desire for action go hand in hand. The user craves the excitement of a "big score" in crime, of a sexual conquest, or of involvement in some other form of activity that will provide him with a build-up in which he will emerge on top. [p. 172]

It may be that the psychopath can tolerate higher doses of stimulants without a significant diminishment of functioning. Such a capacity may be viewed within the drug culture as a special talent to be respected and revered. Such respect would further inflate the psychopath's already exaggerated grandiosity. Similarly, his or her capacity to tolerate risky, dangerous situations without significant anxiety, situations that would elicit considerable fear and anxiety in even moderately antisocial individuals, often earns the admiration and fearful allegiance of criminal colleagues.

The treatment implications of the psychopath's deficits in the arousal/reward complex are manifold. Programs must be aware of the amount of stimulation provided to psychopathic clients. Stimulants have been used as prescribed medication to help modulate arousal levels with some psychopathic patients, hyperactive children, and some adult alcoholics (Gitlin 1990, Reich and Green (1991).

Since psychopaths do not experience or anticipate painful, aversive stimuli in the same way as do nonpsychopaths, they are less likely to learn from negative reinforcement or punishment and appear to be more primed for, or oriented toward, reward and pleasure than others. Activities that would be experienced as highly aversive by most persons can be highly or mildly rewarding to psychopaths, even when such activities involve physical or psychological discomfort and pain. Psychopaths, for example, appear to enjoy more aggressive, confrontational forms of treatment, especially when they are able sadistically to vent their aggression by confronting, belittling, or demeaning others. Their predatory predilection may express itself in therapy by catching others in their inconsistencies or lies. It does not follow, however, that the psychopath's natural gravitation and praise of such treatments indicate that any essential benefit is gained by them from engaging in activities that they find essentially pleasurable and ego-syntonic.

Anxiety Symptom Complex

When patients in a correctional or forensic environment express pervasive anxiety and a history of substance abuse related to anxiety symptoms (especially related to social situations), the likelihood of meeting the criteria for primary psychopathy is almost nil. Nonpsychopathic offenders, however, are often anxious individuals, especially those who ultimately are apprehended and convicted. These people typically have low normal intelligence and experience some degree of conflict related to their criminal activity, albeit this conflict is most often related to fear of apprehension or punishment rather than out of moral compunctions.

Dominance of Affect

The psychopath may be conceptualized as dominated by chronic anger and irritability. This is analogous to what Millon (1968) labelled the "hostile affectivity" of the "active independent personality." Many psychopaths will strike out angrily with little provocation. The dominance of anger and the propensity to act it out illustrate another parallel between the psychopath and the histrionic personality, two actively oriented, socially adept types. In both disorders there is affective dominance and an incongruity of verbalizations and actions in affectively charged situations. Verbally, the psychopath may deny anger, which is frequently projected. However, his or her actions and gestures belie the underlying hostility. Sometimes, the anger is revealed by the overwrought vehemence of any denial. Drugs may modulate and dampen aggression and irritability (narcotics and sedatives) and thereby ease interpersonal relations or heighten the experience or facilitate the enactment of aggression and the rage (alcohol and stimulants). When these enactments replicate a preverbal, motorically encoded, self-other representation, or severe trauma, repetition is the relevant psychosocial function of the drug use. Antisocial personalities may be more apt to modulate or escape/avoid aggressive impulses through substance use, whereas psychopaths may be more likely to use substances either to facilitate or modulate these states. Significant numbers of individuals in the independent cluster may be unaware of primary affective states during periods of nonintoxication (alexithymia). These states remain, nonetheless, strong determinants of behavior and may be overtly observable only during intoxicated periods.

Several classifications of aggression, which may or may not lead to violence, have been developed. Miczek and Thompson (1982) distinguished between offensive and defensive aggression. Moyer (1968) identified different neural and hormonal determinants for each of the following types of aggression: predatory, intermale, fear-induced, irritable, maternal, sex-related, and instrumental. In Moyer's typology, the term *predatory aggression* should not be confused with *predatory crime* as used in the literature to denote crimes committed for material gain. Instrumental aggression and violence are often important aspects of predatory crime as opposed to expressive crime (crimes of passion) or consensual crime (such as prostitution). Although both the antisocial and the psychopathic personalities are aggressive individuals and can be expected to engage in aggressive behavior and violence more than others in the same circumstances, the psychopath is distinguished by a high degree of predatory aggression and violence. Moyer's predatory aggression evokes the kind of instinctual hunting behavior observed in predatory animals, including stalking and an absence of signs of defensive aggression, that is, no anticipation of threat. Meloy (1988) has described the quality of predatory aggression in the psychopath as similar to that seen in animal predators involved in instinctually directed stalk, attack, and kill sequences toward natural prey. This can be contrasted to the affective and instrumental violence that is more typical of antisocial personalities.

Cognition and Context

Affect and cognition must be considered together to fully illustrate the peculiarity of the psychopath. Whereas these individuals are often impulsive and hostile and their emotions may be incomplete and lacking in depth and subtlety, their reality testing may appear completely intact. However, some emerging research findings indicate that psychopaths may have a mild, but pervasive thought disorder. Form quality on the Rorschach is typically poor and affect appears to exert undue influence on cognitive processes (Gacono and Meloy 1991). Distortions also occur in the psychopath's sense of time. The psychopath appears locked in the present, unable to learn from previous emotional experience or to fully consider the consequences of current actions on the future. The psychopath's proneness to boredom may also be related to this distorted sense of time. Meloy (1988) cites

Hartocollis (1983) who hypothesized that boredom is in part a distortion of the sense of time, where individuals are unable to fully comprehend a past or future orientation. The continual pursuit of novelty may be the psychopath's principal means of altering the present, since he or she is impaired in the ability to recall the past or anticipate the future. Some of this timelessness quality is found in Cleckley's identification of a failure to follow a life plan as a hallmark of psychopathy. Many anecdotal stories of psychopaths read like fantastic novels. The psychopath careens through life responding impulsively to his or her present array of stimuli and making little effort to adhere to any long-range goal. Drugs that alter the user's phenomenal sense of time may be especially appealing to such a person. The moment can be phenomenologically expanded into infinity, especially through the use of hallucinogens, such as LSD, PCP, or, less intensely, with cannabis. The search for novelty will impel the psychopath constantly to seek out new drugs or higher doses, new combinations of drugs, and new routes of administration. His or her drug menu tends to be unendingly expanded and altered.

Sociability and Identity Symptom Complex

The psychopath has been described as identifying with the stranger, enemy, or animal predator, rather than with the loving caregiver, friend, or benefactor. This lack of normal identification, almost paradoxically, results in abnormally low social anxiety and extreme extraversion. The psychopath is at home in a brutal world. Identity as a member of a criminal subculture or underworld is inherently appealing. Although many psychopaths are lone wolves, the need to establish narcissistic repair through mirroring of their grandiosity, deception, dominance, and sadism is usually best met in a loose interpersonal web. Given that the psychopath perceives relationships as expressions of power, he will frequently be drawn to assume a power position within antisocial milieus, for example, as a drug lord or enforcer. Drug dealing, for example, has a rigidly defined hierarchy from the street hustler to the large-scale dealer. Within such a specific chain of command, there is little need to feign attachment and emotions of love, remorse, sadness, guilt or regret. Proficiency in deception is frequently overtly valued. This paramilitary, pseudo-war environment is highly appealing, since interpersonal exchanges are guided by codes based on submission/dominance rather than affiliation, and the general pervasiveness of threats and potential enemies is ego-syntonic with the psychopath's expectations and identifications. At best, the shared use of substances provides a mask of affability to ease the artificial strain of interpersonal interactions. More often drug use provides a primitive mode of state sharing and boundary crossing between otherwise separate individuals. The drug also serves as a strong screen for projecting identifications related to power, denied dependency, and perceptions of good and evil.

Psychosocial Functions of Addiction

Modulation

With major disturbances in the reward–arousal complex, the psychopath and antisocial personality will often resort to drug use to provide additional stimulation in a world they perceive as otherwise devoid of significant pleasures and rewards. Drugs provide only one source of sensation seeking, which in psychopaths is viewed as modulation because of their predisposition toward physiological and psychological hyporeactivity.

Escape/Avoidance

Escape/avoidance is not typically a significant function for the psychopath, at least in regard to escaping or avoiding conscious experiences that may be emotionally painful. Nonpsychopathic criminals, including some antisocial personalities, often resort to substances to avoid or escape anxieties related to apprehension by authorities or intrusive memories of painful experiences. Unconsciously, the psychopath avoids experiencing ego-dystonic feelings of envy, inadequacy, and worthlessness by splitting them off and projecting them onto others. He or she then attempts to control and manipulate (projective identification) these individuals, who are used as self-objects. This process usually parallels the facilitation of an inflated sense of self through the use of substances. These dysphoric feelings related to narcissistic injuries and a loss of self-esteem, which are presumably present but not consciously available to the psychopath, are often consciously experienced by the antisocial personality. The power of drugs to provide temporary escape/avoidance of these emotions and self-states may be a major motive for substance abuse and addiction, indicating a potentially better prognosis for treatment.

Facilitation: An Extreme Psychopathic Inversion of Recovery Activities

At 28 years of age, B.G. is securely exiled to the criminal justice system after a long history of criminal and aggressive behavior. His personality structure combines a moderate to severe degree of psychopathy with features that are characteristic of the borderline personality. Petty stealing, truancy, fire setting, and cruelty to cats and dogs by age 14 were overt warnings of the blossoming sadism, aggression, impulsive sensation seeking, irresponsibility, and indifference of the prepsychopathic adolescent that he was to become. By age 17, B.G. was abusing cannabis and alcohol on a daily basis; beginning at age 19, he used PCP daily for 4 years. Starting at age 23, he began free-basing crack cocaine, which instantly became his drug of choice, another predictor of psychopathy. He reports smoking over $200 worth of the drug daily. Running like an ominous, parallel stream to his escalating substance abuse was his escalating criminal activity, which included drug distribution. His dealing progressed rapidly from the sale of small quantities of marijuana to the high stakes of large-scale cocaine distribution. By self-report he was able to "move" about $1,000 worth of cocaine daily at his peak. He carried a .25 millimeter automatic and was enthralled by the round the clock danger, action, and suspense. Criminal charges and convictions advanced in severity from trespassing and theft to weapons charges to violent crimes, including rape and kidnapping, crimes clearly not instrumental to supporting a drug habit.

As his sense of self swelled, B.G. was successful in mentally reducing the outside, straight world into a petty object he could outwit and manipulate at will. For B.G., addiction, dealing, and crime had combined in a terrible confluence of psychopathic grandiosity. He revelled in the identity of a powerful, invincible warrior-outlaw, who commanded respect and fear in a violent subculture. All of his criminal, drug taking, and dealing activities promoted a high level of autonomic arousal on the physiological level and maintained his ego with constant sources of inflation. A deeper, unconscious sense of inadequacy and vulnerability were revealed by his hypochondriacal preoccupation with potential illness. Even a preconscious awareness of such deflated and vulnerable psychic states were usually enough to trigger free-basing, aggression, or a new adventurous criminal enterprise. With the diminution of the outside straight world and the reduction of its individuals to increasingly insignificant objects, B.G.'s aggression and sadism accelerated, with his narcissism approaching paranoia. As he said, "If I trust somebody, it's like giving them ammunition." To protect against such projected aggression, he compensated with sadistic acts of violence and deception toward others.

As his web of addiction and criminality spun out of control, he fell into the embrace of the criminal justice system. Drug treatment and parole supervision were abysmal failures. To B.G such systems represented oppressive, controlling authority figures. To the extent he submitted, he became deflated and depressed. The deflation was heightened by imposed abstinence from his ego food: cocaine and criminal versatility. Within treatment programs, whenever he dared to openly defy treatment staff or values, his sense of self again momentarily became inflated and grandiose. Such inflation precipitated lapses to substance abuse, especially cocaine, which further augmented his grandiosity. Frequently "getting over" on treatment staff by not being detected for his many violations or by having his flimsy excuse violations accepted naively by the staff intensified his grandiose sense of control and his fantasy of having vanquished an opponent.

B.G. often attended NA meetings or treatment groups while the cocaine coursed through his system. His success at brandishing the slogans of recovery (complete with depictions of his previous pitiable state as an addict) while remaining undetected in his current drug use facilitated an exhilarating contemptuous delight, further fanning the flames of his psychopathic self-inflation.

Eventually, B.G. did not have the ego strength to maintain these flames. He is currently incarcerated for robbery and kidnapping, offenses that suggest a loss of reality orientation, although his reality testing apparently remained intact. Having again been released on parole to a treatment program despite previous parole violations, B.G. had lured a friendly acquaintance into giving him a ride under the pretense of wanting companionship at an NA meeting. Once in the car, B.G. pulled out a large kitchen knife, placed it at the victim's throat, and robbed him of over $3,000 in cash and jewelry. The fear of being controlled by the straight system (represented by drug treatment and his victim, a former addict struggling to maintain his abstinence) was aggressively and brutally reversed in this crime. B.G. was able to regain the illusion of total control over the straight world and over himself as long as he brandished the knife. His triumph of successful deception and aggression was immediately celebrated by an orgy of cocaine use, which ended only with apprehension by the police at the same address at which he had been picked up by his victim.

Two months after he was excluded from participation in a correctional substance abuse program because of his elevated PCL-R scores (a fact not revealed to him), B.G. was convicted of stabbing another inmate with a makeshift knife over a drug stash.

Stimulants are often used by psychopaths to facilitate an inflated sense of self, giving them the confidence to enact more daring feats of aggression, deception, or malevolent control over others. Alcohol and cannabis may be used as disinhibitors, allowing any remaining semblance of morality to be easily discarded. In addition to the direct facilitation of an inflated sense of self and the easy enactment of otherwise difficult acts of daring or sadism, addiction maintains the split identity found in many antisocial and psychopathic individuals. Like the histrionic, borderline, and other personality types prone to dissociation, the psychopath uses drugs to facilitate the enactment of unintegrated aspects of self while solidifying the partition of these aspects.

Although it provides enactment and expression, the intoxication or addictive pattern as a whole gives no movement toward integration and actually helps to prevent such movement. This facilitation of split identity (Wurmser 1985) allows the individual to view him- or herself as basically good, kind, sensitive, and responsible, despite actions and emotions to the contrary.

The relationship of criminal activity to substance use goes beyond the need to support a habit in the psychopath, and crime itself becomes a primary mode of narcissistic repair, which is usually both pleasurable and ego-syntonic. The most extreme form of drug facilitation of psychopathy can be seen in Meloy's (1988) description of how drugs, particularly stimulants, may be used in the private ritual that precedes predatory sadistic violence, such as found in the serial rapist or killer. He characterizes the symbolic function of drugs in these rituals as "quintessential transitional objects":

The transitional object as a symbolic link prior to or during predatory violence has both a progressive and regressive side. It facilitates both distancing, or disidentification, with reality and the imagined object of aggression, while at the same time ensuring that the imagined object is perceived as a further extension of the grandiose self-structure, a selfobject imbued with certain projective characteristics that heighten the predator's sense of omnipotent control. [pp. 225–226]

This primitive mode of paranoid process is probably closer to the repetition function of addiction than mere facilitation of a desired, partitioned, or dissociated self-state. We should also note that the victims of the predatory and sadistic violence are often drugged with substances that have an opponent effect to the stimulants. Sedatives, very high doses of alcohol, and occasionally hallucinogens render the victim immobile, easily controllable, and literally depersonalized and dehumanized, that is, less uniquely defined as a personality and more obviously a body, part object, or animal. The stimulation of aggression, sadism, and narcissism in the psychopathic victimizer and the facilitation of docility, weakness, and submission in the victim are often combined in the same crime. A remarkable historical and cultural parallel exists to this dynamic of predatory violence in the rituals of ancient Mexico, brilliantly described by Inga Clendinnen (1991). Anyone interested in the psychology and anthropology of predatory violence will learn much from her description of the culture of sacred predatory violence systematically inculcated by the Mexica, the ancient people of Tenochtitlan, in what is now modern Mexico. Clendinnen describes the Mexica capital city as a society obsessed with personal restraint and control, simultaneously dominated by the centrality and preeminence of evil and chance personified in their most important deities. She describes their public rituals as addictive in themselves, although also involving the use of psychoactive substances, which facilitated the ritual violence and killings. The Mexica carefully controlled the use of their main intoxicant beverage, pulque, made from a specific cactus. Public drunkenness outside the frame of ritual could incur a death sentence, except for the very elderly. However, this society's victim management system involved the use of pulque mixed with other intoxicants. Prior to the ritual climax of victim torture and extraction of the still beating heart, pulque and other psychoactive substances (in addition to psychosocial measures) were carefully administered so that the victim would be docile and appear to exhibit willful participation. The priests performing these rituals, although remaining clearheaded enough to be professional in their actions and bearing, prepared themselves for the violence with stimulants and hallucinogens.

Repetition

As noted earlier repetition is a special form of the facilitation function of addiction involving the compulsive enactment of early object representations and identifications. Millon described the object relations of the aggressive personality as sadistic and the basic identification as rebellious and rejecting of the sadism toward the self. The more severe psychopathic could be described as also having a sadistic quality to object relations, but the most basic identification is predatory, with sadism enacted toward the other. Whereas the passive narcissistic is content with more "benign modes of narcissistic repair" (Kernberg 1984), the psychopath must actively devalue, demean, and control others in actuality. Traumatic experiences of abuse or neglect are reversed and acted out with virulent ferocity on victims, who may, but need not necessarily, remind the psychopath of abusive parental figures. Acute and chronic use of cocaine or amphetamines may induce a psychotic episode characterized by paranoia and mania. The particulars of the delusion will provide clues regarding the primary object relations issues. Primary fears of dominance or annihilation may contribute to violent, paranoid rage reactions. Meloy (1988) speculates that chronic abuse of stimulants may induce the psychopath to acts of predatory violence, since the constraints of reality testing have been loosened to the degree that persecutory introjects may more easily be projected onto others and perceived as real persecutors. The stranger self-object is projected and then attacked.

Compulsive criminals who are also addicts may be utilizing both activities in synergistic fashion to reenact an early trauma that they attempt to master through an unconscious repetition compulsion.

Let us consider the severe example of a habitual criminal exhibiting a pattern of compulsive nighttime burglary with occasional opportunistic sexual offenses or violence against residents. He almost always vandalizes or defaces some aspect of the home, once by his own excretion. This pattern is combined with an addictive use of cocaine by injection. Both the criminal and substance use activities involve penetration (of the self, a house boundary, or, in the case of rape, another individual). Both are illegal. Both result in euphoria and excitement. Both involve the use of various tools or equipment. Both combine the possibility of control with the vicissitudes of chance (uncertainty about quality of street drugs and of what will be encountered at night in the selected home). Further, the excitement of one may be augmented by adding the excitement of the other. The rush of breaking and entering can be heightened by injecting cocaine prior to the offense, which can be further intensified by additional cocaine purchased with the stolen goods.

What type of early issue might be enacted by these repetitive dramas? Let us peruse a family background profile that is commonly encountered in almost any correctional or forensic environment. The individual was an unwanted child raised by violent, alcoholic, and neglectful parents. The father regularly beat his wife, who abused and neglected the defenseless child. The mother typically held him abruptly without caresses and was eager to relinquish her child rearing and return to selfish, hedonic pursuits. At other times she was overly loving and physically affectionate in an attempt to compensate for earlier neglect. He was rarely fed or nurtured adequately and alternated between periods of neglect, abuse, and overstimulation. He had no control over these alternations. He was exposed to the primal scene on many occasions during childhood. His experiences of contact with parental figures were harsh and erratic. In his primal drama of crime and addiction, he penetrates the facade of the house or the surface of his skin. In this new drama the contact results in the wished-for euphoria. He need not depend on anyone. He has all the tools. He has a sense of control over the site of contact (of the chosen home to be burglarized and of his skin for needle penetration) and unconsciously exacts revenge for his lack of nurturing, especially against the settled homes of others, whom he resents and envies. The drug-crime connection in this case provides for a repetition of very primitive levels of experiences perceived as sadistic and defended against through identification with the aggressor. Not all of this behavior is dynamically determined in the intrapsychic sense. This individual also learned important aspects of the drug-violence dynamic by direct modeling of his defective parents.

Psychopathic Repetition in a Case of Cocaine Dependence and Compulsive Burglary

E.P. is a stocky, balding, Caucasian male with graying, brown hair and a thick long beard and mustache. Like many other psychopaths, his sallow skin is covered with tattoos. On his back is a tattoo of a skull with crossbones and on his right arm is a large tattoo of a red-tinted devil with a pitchfork; these images are perhaps emblematic of the poisoned family dynamics in which he was first nurtured and the acceptance of evil as his lot in life. At 39 years of age, he presents as a recalcitrant, intimidating scoundrel, whose only source of pride is an aggressive reputation in prison and an extensive criminal record. By age 15 he had a record of thirty-nine arrests and thirty-one convictions. He has spent approximately 27 years of his life in some form of institution, usually prison. When he is not incarcerated, his adult record reads like the resume of a criminal, revealing a string of arrests for burglary, theft, assault, unauthorized use of a motor vehicle, bad check, malicious destruction, escape, assault on a police officer, resisting arrest, harassing communication, and various violations of parole and probation. His personality structure is an amalgam of paranoid and severely psychopathic features. E.P. is an impulsive, chronically angry individual, who has never functioned with any success in an unstructured environment.

While incarcerated, he functioned as an addictions counselor. E.P. related with considerable amusement (contemptuous delight at his successful deceit) that he had used the money earned from this position to purchase "jump steady," institutionally brewed alcohol. His psychopathic impulsivity and failure to learn from punishment were evident in his behavior after early release from a lengthy incarceration. By self-report, he was out for less than an hour before he impulsively reached into a cash register and stole money when the cashier went to a back room. Within eight hours, he had borrowed his brother-in-law's car, smashed into another car, and sped off for 17 months on the run before being rearrested. Official reports estimate that he committed over 400 burglaries during this time. E.P. scoffs at this estimate and boasts of committing up to eleven burglaries a night. In his lifetime, he estimates committing over 5,000 burglaries.

His compulsive burglary may be viewed as motivated by an unconscious repetition of basic object relationships. His early history was marked by instability and parental acrimony. At age 6 he was apparently institutionalized for emotional problems. E.P. terms this an "abandonment." His alcoholic father physically abused him, his mother, and his five siblings. Each parent took custody at different points, as the children were caught in the crossfire of their animosity. E.P. shuffled from parent to parent, and from aunt to aunt, then to foster care before entering juvenile and adult institutions. He described the time spent in various juvenile facilities as "living in a hell-hole with animals." The trauma of being the helpless victim of various placements is reversed with the attempt at mastery by continually reenacting the experience through an identification with the aggressor. Rather than being shipped from house to house, he now moves from house to house; rather than depending on caretakers to supply him with what he needs, he now takes what he wants. Wearing sneakers and targeting houses with the air conditioning running, he boasted that he was in and out the house within 10 minutes and that "I never woke anyone up." Before he robbed jewelry stores, he would send away for brochures on their alarm systems. During this crime spree, his pattern of cocaine abuse escalated rapidly. He began free-basing daily and reports with a smirk that he received $180,000 for stolen jewelry, which he spent all on cocaine. The drug was used to energize himself for his criminal activities and to augment his rush after a successful night of theft. The secret energizing food of cocaine provided E.P. the kind of boost or support that was always lacking in his life, which he perceived as a constant process of abandonment and vicious struggle for survival.

After his capture, E.P. conned his way into a treatment program, deftly exploiting his advanced age and traumatic childhood to pull the heartstrings of the clinical evaluators to give him "one last chance." Within a few months of being accepted he tested positive for cocaine. At his disciplinary hearing he vehemently denied ever using such a substance but argued that if he were found guilty he should not be sentenced to segregation because of his diabetic medical condition and past suicidal ideation. He was sentenced to a lengthy term on cell lockup, which is a considerably less aversive setting. Knowing the rules and regulations of the institution better than the disciplinary board, E.P. appealed the sentence on the ground that it exceeded the limit of time an inmate could spend on cell lockup. He managed to avoid any time on segregation and spent limited time on lockup. One can imagine his exhilaration at having "gotten over on" the disciplinary committee. E.P. was eventually discharged from treatment without any attenuation of his psychopathy.

Orientation: Drug Dealing as Orientation, Cocaine Dependence as Escape, An Antisocial Personality with Complicated Bereavement

Most psychopaths find orientation in the manipulative cycle that may or may not result in a criminal lifestyle. However, orientation may be provided to the aimless, drifting psychopath with goals of drug procurement and use. Priority of place among other drug users or dealers provides grounds for meaningful achievement and action in an individual incapable of following a life plan. As with many other addicts, orientation usually addresses important deficits in the sociability and identity symptom complex, with identity issues being more prominent in the psychopath and issues of social contact and anxiety more prominent for antisocial personalities.

J.M. is a 26-year-old single female with an Axis II diagnosis of antisocial personality disorder with histrionic and narcissistic features. In therapy, a higher level of dependence and relatedness was revealed than this initial diagnosis might have suggested, although at intake her level of psychopathy was assessed by the Psychopathy Checklist Revised to be only in the mild range. J.M. was separated from her mother at 9 weeks of age and raised by an alcoholic father with a history of psychiatric problems. She was sexually abused by her uncle and probably by her father. During adolescence, she caroused through a meandering path of indiscriminate polysubstance abuse including amphetamines, cannabis, PCP, and LSD, although cocaine became her drug of choice. A close relationship to a male ended abruptly when he left her for another woman. She watched her own father die on the front porch before she was able to express her love and her regrets. Her mourning process was complicated by her anger toward her father and by her numbing polysubstance abuse. Prior to her father's death, J.M. had an extensive history of abusing and dealing drugs dating back to the age of 13. After his death, her guilt and shame intensified, as did her cocaine addiction. In her words, "I didn't give a fuck anymore."

In her despair, J.M. discovered a drug of choice and a lifestyle as a drug dealer. By age 18, she was buying several ounces of cocaine to distribute. At her peak at age 24, she estimates netting over $15,000 in profits in a week. Her dealing appeared to be motivated primarily by the need to supply her own expensive addiction to cocaine and to fulfill narcissistic needs for attention and admiration. Her dealing also provided an identity and position of respect within the drug subculture. She admits to having a "tough" image on the streets with a reputation as the "crazy white girl." She gained a sense of mastery over her anger around unmet dependency needs by her sense of power as a dealer and the sense that her clientele was dependent on her. Her addiction enabled her to avoid feelings of shame and rage, which always haunted her just under the surface of concentrating on external activities demanded by dealing and using. In addition, the high from cocaine facilitated the experience of her self as independent and self-sufficient, a source of nurturance (in the form of drugs) to others, thus supporting her denial of dependency. Her climb up the ladder to midlevel dealer within the nefarious underworld of the drug game served as a way of mastering her sense of being "dirty," which was engendered by her sexual abuse. Whereas the sense of guilt, shame, and being tainted lowered her self-esteem, her rise to power vindicated her.

Once incarcerated, J.M. worked hard in therapy to access her underlying feelings of rage and shame. She initially tended to split off and project the anger, which she feared would increase the guilt she felt around her relationship with her father and his death. She was gradually able to differentiate anger from depressive affect and to hold together her positive and negative feelings toward her father and mourn his loss in deeper fashion. Several strip searches in the prison (performed by female correctional officers) were constructively dealt with to explore and work through her rage and shame around her sexual abuse. J.M. achieved her GED, a socially approved accomplishment that she had barely imagined was possible. After less than a year in treatment, she obtained a court-ordered release to a long-term inpatient drug treatment program, which she could use to consolidate her therapeutic gains while re-entering society.

DRUGS OF CHOICE AND ROUTES OF ADMINISTRATION

The stimulant category was identified earlier as the drug class most often preferred by psychopaths. Alcohol, other sedatives, and the opiates are more typically drugs of choice for other independent personality types. In offender populations, nonstimulant drugs are preferred by antisocial personalities as opposed to psychopaths, with the exclusive use of opiates considered highly contraindicative of primary psychopathy (the exception to this rule being the psychopathic individual who is a high-frequency polysubstance abuser and prefers heroin over other substances).

These conclusions are based on reports of many psychopaths encountered in our own clinical experiences and reports from colleagues as well. They are also consistent with the Epidemiological Catchment Area Study (see Chapter 3), which found that a lifetime occurrence of any addictive disorder was highest for cocaine dependence and second highest for opiate dependence for persons diagnosed with APD. As noted earlier, we view the APD prison population as consisting predominantly of individuals fitting Millon's aggressive personality type with less than half of the APD group fitting Hare's criteria for psychopathic personality (Hare et al. 1991). Although several other interpretations are also viable, the finding that these two drug categories with drastically different effects are the most frequent causes of dependence in APD can be explained if we view the APD group as consisting of two essentially different subtypes of aggressive, rule-breaking individuals.

A third source of support for these conclusions lies in the theoretical explanations for vulnerability to opiate addiction and alcoholism. The anger-frustration hypothesis of opiate addiction and alcoholism appears to have some merit, both for antisocial personalities and other anger-prone individuals such as passive–aggressives, borderlines, and those in the dependent cluster who are frustrated within their primary relationships. The anger-frustration hypothesis of vulnerability to opiate addiction presupposes conflict within the individual between a desire to conform to the requirements of acceptable behavior within a potentially positive attachment that also generates overwhelming rage. Opiate addiction, this hypothesis supposes, chemically dissipates interpersonal rage and provides a compromise substitute for a lost or conflicted primary attachment. (The analysis of personality dynamics of addiction in earlier chapters describes the avoidant, passive–aggressive, and compulsive personality styles—typical neurotic styles—as having intrapsychic and interpersonal dynamics more consistent with this kind of vulnerability to addiction.) The experimental data on opiate effects on socially isolated primates suggest that the drug is effective in reducing distress related to object loss, separation anxiety, and social isolation. These are feelings more often experienced—and viewed as aversive—by almost all personality types other than the psychopathic. (The analysis of the schizoid personality in Chapter 7 demonstrates that this personality is phobic to attachment and should not be driven by attachment motives to addictive behavior, since detachment is not an aversive experience). In our view, the exclusive opiate abuser, although often engaged in criminality, adopting a criminal lifestyle, and developing prominent aggressive traits, more often does so adaptively or instrumentally, that is, in order to survive the demands of his or her addiction, which may fit the anger-frustration vulnerability scenario. This conflict and attachment-based hypothesis of opiate effects, however, does not come close to explaining recalcitrant cocaine or amphetamine addiction in highly independent individuals with a tendency toward criminality and hyperaggression, that is, psychopaths.

A fourth source of support for the view that psychopaths might be more inclined to prefer stimulants lies in the psychopath's preference for inflated grandiose self-states and constitutional hyporeactivity. These characteristics are complementary and isomorphic to the hyperarousal, euphoria, and super-optimism induced by stimulants. This line of reasoning is pursued in more depth in an investigation of the addictive cycle and psychopathy later in this chapter.

The aggressive personality is typified as an acting-out character who is impulsive, but who, nonetheless, is capable of experiencing primitive forms of social anxiety and even intrapsychic conflict in regard to criminal or destructive behaviors. Although psychopaths may not genuinely have these capabilities, these individuals may simulate such characteristics quite artfully. The theorotypes discussed here are rarely encountered in clinical practice and the mixed type is the most common actual reality, but individuals with strongly psychopathic characteristics will achieve relatively little gain (when compared to stimulant use rewards) from the mellowing, dampening effect of opiates or from opiate effects on central psychophysiological mechanisms related to interpersonal attachment and dependency. In regard to mixed personality types, however, drugs can be tailored to suit the physiological and object relational requirements of the user. For example, some drug abusers with antisocial features and with a clear need for primary attachment to others may prefer the combination of heroin and cocaine ("speedballing"), which can be exactly titrated. They utilize the cocaine primarily to increase alertness and reduce vulnerability to attack, thereby countering the narcotic tendency to "lay back" and avoid the interpersonal deficits or traumas for which only partial compensations have been achieved.

Regarding preferred routes of administration, an investigation of them can shed considerable light on the overall meaning and purpose of an addictive pattern. Several administration routes involving basic boundary issues are pertinent to the psychopath. Oral and other natural orifice routes are probably more typical of antisocial (highly dependent and oral aggressive and incorporative) individuals. We discuss here syringe use and inhalant methods for the psychopath because the first involves controlled violation of a natural boundary, and the second highlights the contrast between the seen and the unseen, the superficial and the deeper structure, which are often unconscious obsessions of the psychopath. In addition, rather than placing drug dealing as a drug of choice, we consider it under the logistics and personal strategies of self-maintenance connected with procuring and administering substances, although this categorization is arbitrary. The discussion here is highly speculative, but the subject of route of administration illustrates several concepts more central to an understanding of psychopaths, their attraction to addictive patterns, and their responses in typical treatment situations.

Intravenous Administration and the Skin as Psychological Boundary

Several aspects of any discussion of the psychopath involve boundary issues in general, but especially the body envelope, the skin. Developmental concepts provide a powerful key to understanding the importance of skin to the psychopath (both of his or her own and that of others). Chapter 6 noted that cultures are biased in the way they reward various personality styles. To return to the culture of the ancient Mexican, it may be argued that a psychopathic view of the world was dominant in that culture when the Spanish arrived. (We are well aware that perhaps a more convincing analysis of psychopathic dominance is found in Spain's Conquistador subculture, since it also utilized deception and simulation in addition to sadistic aggression.) In commenting on the Mexica view of the sacred as evoked in ritual costumes, Clendinnen (1991) notes:

> Despite the importance of behavior, for the Mexica—as for Amerindians more generally—it was the skin, the most external and enveloping "appearance," which constituted a creature's essence, and so stored the most formidable symbolic power . . . This power of skin extended through the secondary "skin" of the sacred garment, to face and body paint masks, and adornments.
>
> Mexica conviction of the transforming capacity of a donned skin or magically charged regalia threads through all their ritual action, and much of their social action too. In the text of the painted world a human being was less than impressive: a featherless biped indeed, with no precedence or privilege. He had to construct himself, to make a "face"; borrowing power though his capacity to "take on" an appearance: a skin, a costume, a mask, insignia, a characteristic movement or cry. [pp. 228–229]

No better source of this power over surfaces/essences and acquired identities could be obtained than from the newly flayed skin of human beings. The flaying of human skin was an important public ritual act among the Mexica, which reflected on the narcissistic identity and power of the captor who provided the victim.

> The offering warrior was projected into a terrible and enduring intimacy with his victim: having proudly tended and taunted him though the days and weeks of his captivity, and watched his own valour measured in the captive's public display, he had seen life leave the young body and its pillaging of heart, blood, head, limbs, and skin. Then he had lent out the flayed skin to those who begged the privilege, and pulled it on over his own body as it went through its slow transformations: tightening and rotting on the living flesh; corrupting back into the earth from which it had been made. Powerful emotions must have been stirred by these extravagant and enforced intimacies with death, and more with the decay and dissolution of the self, but there is no indication that pity or grief for the victim were among them. (Clendinnen 1991, p. 96)

The flaying of the victim was followed by ritual cannibalism. Although a culture of mercy did not exist for the Mexica, the ability of fairly normal individuals to pursue these rituals depended on the otherness of the victims (foreigners or outcasts), the split identity of referring to the "flowery death" of the killing stone, and chemical and psychological intoxicants. In the light of these once widely practiced cultural rituals not uncommon in prehistoric Europe, the private skin rituals of psychopaths, briefly explored here in relationship to drug use (hypo-dermic needles, tattoos, and inhalants) seem mild indeed! However, some of the same basic intimacies with death, and more with decay and dissolution of the bodily self, cited by Clendinnen are clearly involved in many addictive patterns, as is the search for a more solid identity in a world of surface illusions and primal threats.

The roots of the psychopath's fixation on the skin can be found in the earliest eras of development. The envelope of the skin functions as the boundary between the organism and the world and as the boundary between intero- and exteroceptive sensations. The skin of the infant is a primary source of sensation and stimulation and the medium of contact between infant and mother. The cognitive and affective integration of such sensations forms the basis of attachment and a coherent sense of self. Attachment to and identification with the primary caretaker is commonly conceptualized to be of primary importance for the development of a stable, positive self-structure. The psychopathic process can be conceptualized as a developmental disturbance that is "fundamentally a virtual failure of internalization" (Meloy 1988, p. 44). The psychopath typically resorts to a fixation on the grandiose self (Kernberg 1975). Meloy hypothesizes that "the psychopathic process crystallizes toward the later subphases of separation-individuation with the failure of object constancy and a primary narcissistic attachment to the grandiose self-structure" (p. 54). Such disturbances of internalization and identification are overtly manifest in particular nuances of the psychopath's interactions around the skin boundary.

Prisons abound with men adorned with tattoos. (Less artful self-mutilations with razor blades and cigarettes are also very common in prison populations.) These images of women, heroes, knives, insignias, flowers, and demons (often in incon-gruous combinations suggesting fragments of a split identity) are vivid reminders of the failure to internalize, as though the wearers are following the logic that since the abiding, coherent, psychological structure of a primary caretaker had not been internalized, why not have one painted on? In addition to their value as narcissistic adornments, tattoos constitute a distorted and ultimately doomed attempt at symbolically achieving identity formation. The fragments of self–other representa-tions are projected onto the skin in an attempt to consolidate, objectify, and take possession of them. Although the thematic content of such tattoos can often be interpreted given an account of their selection and meaning to the wearer, their presence is generally more significant than what they depict. Perhaps the seduc-tiveness of the idealized mother is captured by the tattoo of the curvaceous, naked female. Such tattoos might also hint at a confused gender identity, which is counterphobically masked with sinewy musculature, phallic knife tattoos, or tattoos of power figures such as super heroes or motorcycles. Similarly, the insignia or letters of a gang imbue the tattoo carrier with some sense of identity. Beyond specific content, in all cases, fragments of a potential self are projected and forcibly injected onto the skin surface.

The process of obtaining tattoos through the pricking of the skin is not coincidental; the pricking in itself provides additional motivation for the procedure that is analogous to the unconscious meaning of injecting veins with a syringe. The continuous use of intravenous drugs may be understood on one level as a repetition and attempt to master painful, early infant and mother interactions. Tustin (1981) speculates that premature separation of the caretaker from the infant or a "predominance of 'hard' or uncomfortable sensations could result in the excessive projections of 'hard not-me' sensations outside the nascent self-boundary" (p. 190). Meloy is careful to note that such maternal separation or discomfort may result not only from the irresponsibility of the mother but could in part be a result of the psychopathically predisposed infant's low autonomic arousal and aggressiveness. If the infant is generally less able affectively to mirror the emotional advances or replies of the mother, the mother may withdraw or handle the infant with some trepidation or discomfort. Meloy (1988) says, "This harsh sensory-perceptual experience with the mother may combine with an atavistic fear of predation and predispose the formation of a narcissistic shell" (p. 43). The preference of the psychopath for the intravenous route of administration may reflect unconscious motivations stemming from a repetition of primary object relational issues. The psychopath strives to master the harshness, unpredictability, and pain of those early dyadic experiences by carefully reconstituting a painful moment of contact that ultimately leads to euphoria. The needle may represent both infant and mother. This time the needle (self) is cradled with care and handled with deft skill. This time the outer "hard not-me" is under the control of the sensation receiver, who controls the dosage and point of contact. This time the recipient will be quickly suffused with a pleasurable "soft-me" interoceptive sensation, perhaps represented what was wished for in the early dyadic interactions.

Boosting the autonomic level of arousal with stimulants, in particular, reinforces the grandiose self-structure. Repetitious piercing of the skin boundary also serves as a concrete reminder of the existence and identity of the self.

Sadomasochistic dynamics may also be represented in the ritual of intravenous drug use. If the primary caretaker is unreliable, sadistic, seductive, or suffocating, but remains the sole or primary source of gratification, the infant's internalization of this relationship may turn passive into active, such that the sadistic wish to dominate or destroy the object prevails. The wielding of the syringe may represent this wish to dominate or destroy, which is enacted each time the needle punctures the skin. The obverse, masochistic wish to be dominated may be represented by the turning of the needle against the self and perhaps the enjoyment of the pain of the injection. The turning of the needle against the self and the using of the self as a target may represent an enactment of additional psychopathic dynamics. Millon (1981) describes malevolent projection as a key psychopathic mechanism. Mistrust ful, hostile, and vengeful motives are ascribed to others. If the psychopath expects to be the target of such evil intent from the world, he or she may preemptively strike out at others or symbolically strike out at him- or herself first in what may amount to a inoculation against attack: "If I can withstand this violation of my skinboundary, I am ready to deal with whatever you throw my way." The effects of the drug may also imbue the abuser with a heightened sense of power and invulnerability to attack or actually heighten his or her alertness to detect such an attack.

Inhalant Drugs and Boundary Issues

Smoking as a route of administration may appeal to the psychopath, in part because of its sense of control over blurring the boundary between self and environment. The deep inhalation and exhalation of smoke constitute a deliberate trespass and retreat across this fundamental boundary and, in part, an unconscious form of fusion. A jogger may seek the same fusion as the air sacs rhythmically take in and expel air from and to the outside environment. Psychopaths tend to concretize the process and to derive satisfaction from observing it visually through smoking. The smoker can watch the substance pass outside and disintegrate into the surrounding environment. Engulfed by deep exhalations of nicotine-laced, cannabis-laced, or cocaine-laced haze, the abuser exalts in the annihilation of the boundaries between self and world and the apparent symbiotic merger. The smoke is a palpable reminder of this achievement. The audible sounds of such deep inhalation and exhalation, the sights of the smoke and the cigarette, joint, or pipe, which may be an elaborate creation specifically designed for this purpose, the somatosensory warmth or harshness, and the sweet, pungent, or acrid smells exuded in the ritual all combine to swathe the user in a blissful symbiotic bath.

Smoking tends to be a more social phenomenon than intravenous drug use for practical and psychological reasons. The sharing of a joint or pipe envelops the users in a ritual of communion. Through the joint or pipe, they all come into contact. Once the effect of the drug takes hold, a bond of shared experience is established. Some abusers enact rituals that serve unconscious wishes for merger, which have little to do with getting high per se. The smoke, for example, may be blown directly from one person's mouth into another by mouth-to-mouth contact. As the addiction heightens and the supply diminishes, however, the joint or pipe is viewed as a coveted source of nurturance and in primitive fantasy becomes the longed-for breast or breast-penis. Obviously, these speculations are directed to a primitive mode of awareness, not likely to become conscious even in the psychopathic user. Schizophrenic drug users may have more direct access to the meanings of these paranoid-schizoid modes of experience (Ogden 1989). Nonetheless, such meanings are relevant to the unconscious motivations of apparently high functioning patients with severe personality pathology and addiction.

Dealing as an Addiction

Drug dealing holds an irresistible allure for many psychopaths. An excellent ground for practicing the active modes of narcissistic repair, drug dealing may be particularly fertile ground for the malevolent or sadistic mode. As drug abusers are drawn like moths to the magical sources of their addiction flame, the dealer is imbued with a sense of control over the substance and the user, a master of illusions in many senses. In the 24-hour, nonstop adventure of scoring, wheeling, and dealing, the psychopath is drawn to and undaunted by the constant threat of danger or capture. Unable to form genuine attachments, the psychopath functions well in a brutal culture where all transactions are conducted according to a hierarchy of dominance and power and where ruthlessness is a respected asset. The psychopath is freed of the troubling distractions of a range of complex or subtle affective states. The grandiose self may swell to gargantuan proportions. He feels "on top of the world." He views with superior contempt the straight world whose pitiful inhabitants slavishly adhere to droning routines. Sadistic and libidinally fused impulses are gratified by extorting sex for drugs. Sadistic impulses are satisfied deeply with the sense of triumph and control attached to meting out the drug to the dependent throng. Imagine the sense of power when addicts seek the dealer at all times of day and night to beg for a tiny piece of his omnipotence. The sadistic, psychopathic dealer may revel in watching of the physical, emotional, and spiritual decline of his customers. As their addiction worsens, his sense of control over them heightens. Note, however, the denial and projection of dependency and vulnerability. No matter what level of status the dealer attains in the keenly psychopathic culture of drug dealer, he too remains dependent on someone else for the substance. The role of the gangster/dealer provides the psychopath with a sense of identity consonant with his inflated narcissism. Although the emphasis on dealing here is on the psychopath, many dealers fit more benign narcissistic personality characteristics, and have a better prognosis for relinquishing this addictive mode of repair.

Although most dealers also use at least some of their products, the addictive cycle can be complete without significant use. The power of controlling the drug and the wealth that flows from it help maintain the dealer in the inflated/grandiose position. The dealer actively tries to disown identifications with the user's dependency, stupidity, and powerlessness. Both his interpersonal detachment (a job requirement) and his attempt to detach from basic identifications with the user provide the detached/schizoid position and complete the cycle of self-states.

RESPONSE TO TREATMENT

As described earlier, the addict maintains psychic equilibrium through the ongoing cycling of the three basic positions: the depressed self, the grandiose self, and the detached self. Often, he or she alternates between the grandiose and depressed positions, where the drug of choice is used to avoid or retreat from the conscious experience of the depressed position. Within this phenomenological framework, the psychopath may be understood as an individual who is basically fixated at, or rests in, the grandiose position. Drugs, and in particular the stimulants, fuel this inner sense of power, strength, and omnipotence. Bursten (1973) explicated an analogous cycle, called the manipulative cycle, which the psychopath uses to maintain a sense of grandiosity. The process may be intrapsychic or interpersonal. For the psychopath, it is frequently both, as this personality type exhibits a propensity to act out inner schemata. In the manipulative cycle, according to Bursten, shameful or devalued self-representations are projected onto a victim, who when successfully deceived induces a feeling of contemptuous triumph and superiority in the deceiver. According to Bursten (1973), there is an internal reunion of actual self-object and ideal self-object at the moment of deception or triumph. In the language of the addictive cycle, the idealized grandiose sadistic self is the self as experienced in the moment of deception. Due to their essentially sadistic object relations, such manipulative cycling is the typical mode of narcissistic repair for the psychopath. Psychopaths are often not content with merely the internal drama of successful deceit and control but are driven to act out such dramas on the stage of life. Lying, shoplifting, breaking and entering, clandestine drug purchases and use, and the deceitful luring of unwary prey are among many examples. For some of these types, such as the sexual psychopath, the drama may play itself out in internal fantasy many times in recurring images of bondage and penetration (thus involving imposition of constrictive boundaries or violation of the natural boundaries of the victim) before the psychopath finally crosses the threshold and acts out the fantasy with brutal effectiveness. Often, drugs, especially disinhibiting drugs such as alcohol, facilitate this dangerous leap.

For the psychopath, devaluing others helps to maintain and boost a sense of superiority. Successful deception is part of a repetitive cycle that imbues the psychopath with a sense of triumph and contemptuous delight. Treatment facilities that try to ameliorate moderate or severe psychopaths must consider the opportunities within the program for enactment of this manipulative cycle. For many psychopaths, the covert goal of treatment is simply to "get over on" the treatment staff. This is especially true when there is a desired reward such as placement in a less restrictive setting or access to addictive substances and less restrictive drug monitoring. The psychopath will find out what is expected and set about to provide it with the semblance of positive change or recovery. It is probably an impossible task for therapists to winnow out individuals making genuine change from those who are simply "faking it" (Woody et al. 1985). To many psychopaths, the treatment institutions themselves represent oppressive, rigid, controlling authority. To "get over on" such an impressive representation of authority induces an exhilarating sense of triumph. To the extent that the psychopath submits to treatment, he or she becomes deflated and depressed. Deflation may be heightened by abstinence from drug use. To the extent he or she does not submit but defies or deceives treatment personnel, the psychopath's sense of self becomes inflated and grandiose, and narcissistic repair is accomplished, but in a way that effectively negates the goals of treatment. Such inflation can be augmented by substance abuse, especially stimulants. Psychopaths in treatment for substance abuse will often covertly use drugs and are often extremely adept at evading detection. Failed attempts to uncover them will actually increase their pleasure in subsequent drug use. Such patients will enjoy secretly passing drugs to one another during a session and exchanging private smirks at the therapist's naiveté and gullibility. They may relish the sense of being undetected as they feel the effects of the drug while interacting with treatment staff and peers, thus finding even withdrawal effects narcissistically rewarding. Glibly paying lip service to the various cliches of reform while experiencing or anticipating the next high will augment the sense of successful deception.

In general, all of the deception and potential danger of exposure and punishment involved in the illegal purchase and use of drugs are simply additional motivators for the psychopath, whereas for other users, these factors serve as powerful deterrents and provide motivation for abstinence and self-referral for treatment. Additionally, destroying the "goodness" of treatment settings or the family home, which is unconsciously envied by the psychopath, may be motivation to undermine treatment programs and family stability, not only for themselves in a self-destructive fashion but for innocent others, whom they resent. Psychopaths, therefore, may not only be essentially unable to benefit from conventional treatments, but they may pose a risk for undermining any treatment enterprise that harbors them. On a practical level, psychopathic drug dealers have a concrete investment in their clients maintaining their addiction and have considerable experience in spreading or promoting addictive behavior and relapse. This is especially worth considering in long-term inpatient settings such as prisons or forensic hospitals, where the psychopathic dealer's power and prestige is contingent on his dependent, addicted consumers. When such an individual is placed in a group, for example, he will do everything in his power to disrupt the treatment process. Individuals who dare to risk being genuine, especially with regard to ongoing substance abuse, run the risk of psychological and physical intimidation and retaliation. This same process, while attenuated, probably occurs rather frequently in other settings. The more psychopathic clients tend to encourage an atmosphere of concealment, deceit, and superficiality, especially with regard to ongoing drug urges and relapses, which opposes the establishment of openness and honesty within which genuine progress is more likely to occur.

Psychopaths are also adept at deceiving professionals who provide treatment. They will attend carefully to the narcissistic vulnerabilities of therapists and counselors and will stroke those areas with deft skill. If the therapist wants to be seen as a helpful, sensitive professional, he or she will be given the message in many different ways that he or she *is* helpful, professional, or empathic. Meloy (1988)

notes that "individuals who deny their own narcissistic investments and consciously perceive themselves as being 'helpers' endowed with a special amount of
altruism are exceedingly vulnerable to the affective simulation of the psychopath"
(p. 140). If the therapist is confrontational and aggressive, the psychopath will
mimic this behavior toward his peers. Professionals working in the field of substance abuse should develop an awareness of their own narcissistic vulnerabilities
and be trained to detect psychopathic clients. Training in discriminating forms of
identification with the manipulative patient or patient offender that are legitimate
and consistent with appropriate therapeutic goals, roles, and their limits from
inappropriate identifications is of particular importance, since psychopathic patients often evoke countertransference reactions of either disidentification or
overidentification in therapists over the course of treatment. Severe psychopaths
should be eliminated from treatment programs not specifically designed to manage
their typical use of the therapeutic situation.

A crucial question that has not been adequately addressed is whether some
traditional psychological treatments (including models such as the Therapeutic
Community, which has at times claimed to be effective with offenders and
antisocial personalities) can actually increase the risk posed to society by psychopaths. This possibility was hinted at in the discussion of Harris et al. (1991) about
the only study investigating the use of the Psychopathy Checklist to predict violent
recidivism in a population of violent offenders:

> Finally, the subjects of this study were all graduates of an intensive treatment program
> aimed at altering psychopathic traits. It is possible to argue that the performance of
> the Psychopathy Checklist in prediction violent recidivism is at least partially the
> result of differential responsiveness to treatment. Such an argument would run that
> the therapeutic community (counter to the expectations of everyone involved)
> differentially reduced the rate of violent recidivism for the nonpsychopaths, but did
> not change or perhaps increased the rate for psychopaths. . . . The present results
> suggest that the observation that psychopaths burn out after age 40 is not true for
> violent offenses. . . .Interestingly, there were only two psychopaths with opportunity
> to fail over 60 years of age, and both committed violent offenses. All of these data
> point to the conclusion that *if* an effective treatment for psychopaths were found, it
> could have the possibility of being extremely cost-effective in reducing violent crimes
> committed by psychopaths upon release and/or in reducing the cost of very long
> incarcerations and supervision that would otherwise be required to prevent their
> future offending. [pp. 635–636]

It seems unlikely that effective treatment for psychopathy utilizing interpersonal
and verbal methods will be available in the near future. Treatments that increase
social skills, interpersonal persuasiveness, awareness of superficial expectations,
and the ability to simulate genuine emotion, especially remorse and empathy, can
provide the psychopath with an instrumental mock histrionic or compulsive style
of relatedness. Individuals unable to penetrate this acquired facade to perceive

the basic narcissism and hostile detachment of the psychopath are unable to view this polishing as the potential sharpening of a blade that it may be. The new improved psychopath who has received substance abuse treatment often goes on to dominate and misdirect self-help and recovery efforts, leading to disastrous consequences for others, if not for himself. In correctional or forensic settings, the long period of incarceration, monitoring, and liberty restriction required to provide traditional treatments to such individuals (with an appropriate balance between concern for public safety and respect for human potential for change) is usually combined with a promise of conditional release or other positive reward at the end of treatment. Although the carrot of early release, return to work or to family life may be a powerful motive for temporary conformity on the part of the psychopath, it may also increase the resentment and desire for retaliation against others after termination of treatment, or when the promised reward is either not delivered or proves frustrating. The term *treatment* is used advisedly throughout this section. In fairness to aggressive types (including many offenders) who strive to change in therapy, it should not be even inadvertently implied that severe psychopaths are ever engaged in the reciprocal, ego-syntonic, conflict-ridden, and co-creative process suggested by the term. They tend to view treatment as the attempt of a therapist or treatment organization to act upon them, and they in turn resist and covertly attempt to act on their captors with new weapons. Usually they learn to have their actions take the form of words, interpersonal manipulations, or induction of feelings through projective identification. This new narcissistic-sadistic sublimation is how they perceive the ongoing process of treatment.

To the extent that psychopaths do genuine work in treatment, other complications often arise. Uncovering primitive rage, abandonment fears, or feelings of inadequacy in individuals who are unable to contain conflicts intrapsychically but who retain access to either an addictive or manipulative cycle during treatment may result in a deepening of these ingrained addictive expressions and the surfacing of unbridled rage and retaliation after treatment. Examining the psychological protocols of many severe psychopathic offenders pre- and postparticipation in long courses of insight-oriented group psychotherapy shows that posttreatment protocols reflect improved cognition (especially in verbal skills), decreases in overtly expressed grandiosity and impulsivity, an increase in ego strengths (especially those that result in improved stress tolerance), and an increased awareness of what is socially expected behavior (especially in the areas of verbalizing emotions and making empathic or altruistic statements). The projective material, however, maintains a narcissistic focus on the self, a tendency to demean or humiliate others, and an expectation of harm or aggression in the environment. Narcissistic focus on the body typically moves from experiences and activities that maintain or reflect a sense of bodily perfection to hypochondriacal themes and themes of physical repair or recuperation. (This shift in focus does not appear to be merely a function of increased age between observations.) Aggressive reactivity remains high, as does stimulus seeking. Attachment behavior is essentially unaltered, and a sense of entitlement in relationships may be somewhat heightened, with resentment and rage toward those not meeting these expectations very superficially veiled. Risk factors for vulnerability to addictions as described in the symptom complexes remain high, although direct manipulation of the social environment and delay of immediate gratification in favor of more planful behavior may provide some resilience against addiction as long as external factors make abstinence to the advantage of the individual (i.e., constant drug monitoring, or a serious health issue). In sum, there is a strengthening of the resources available to the individual without a basic change in structure, basic values, or interpersonal orientation. In some cases, it is reasonable to suspect that these increased resources may be used in the service of criminal activity and that the offender may, therefore, present a greater threat to society after treatment than before.

Facilitation of Sadistic Enactment and Ritual

L.K. is a 32-year-old male convicted of murder. He has been diagnosed as a sexual sadist and as having a borderline personality with significant narcissistic, antisocial, and passive–aggressive features. He was dependent on alcohol and cocaine and episodically abused cannabis, LSD, and barbiturates.

L.K. was placed in foster care and subsequently adopted at an early age. After his first night in his new adoptive home, he was found sleeping on the floor. His mother eventually discovered that L.K. had a pathological fear of mattresses with buttons. Beneath a quiet and secretive surface adjustment, deep feelings of anger and alienation developed. As far back as age 5, he recalls images of mature women in bondage. By age 10, L.K. was regularly masturbating to sexual fantasies, especially those involving the anal penetration of women, where sexual and aggressive themes violently merged. Later in adolescence, he began to write down sexual fantasies. In college where he dabbled in theater and philosophy, he regularly abused hallucinogens, marijuana, and alcohol. He interpreted his altered perceptions as an expansion of consciousness and a symbiotic merger with elemental forces. To further bolster his narcissistic grandiosity, he began to deal drugs and to act on stage. He strove to master his core identity disturbance and concomitant lack of substantial identifications by simulating the roles of characters. He even changed his name to phonically echo a favorite stage moniker. He viewed his unstable relationships and erratic behaviors as the exhilarating consequence of his unique and expanding talent.

After dropping out of school and skirmishing with the law, he began to drink to excess and to deal and abuse cocaine. Cocaine was introduced to his nightly ritual of returning home in the early morning, securing his basement apartment, procuring his stash, undressing, lying on the floor, fantasizing and writing. The stimulation was so intense that he would persist in this activity for up to four hours. Elaborate fantasies, increasingly violent, of rape, sodomy, and bondage were imaged and transcribed. His narcissistic self-absorption became so intense that reality tended to be ignored or arbitrarily forced to conform to his idiosyncratic wishes. After one night of intense alcohol and cocaine abuse, he called a former lover and friend, requesting a ride home. She was eventually found dead, gagged, naked from the waist down, having apparently been bludgeoned to death. Writings were uncovered that revealed the planning of this victim's murder as well as the planned kidnappings of other women. Given the severity and chronicity of his sexual sadism, his intense grandiosity, and thinly veiled rage, L.K. was considered beyond the scope of available therapeutic endeavors aimed at eventual release to the community.

RISK ASSESSMENT OF SUBSTANCE-INVOLVED OFFENDERS

Future criminal behavior cannot be predicted with any degree of certainty for any particular individual. Criminal behavior is determined by many factors, including the biological, psychological, and social, as well as the complex interactions of all. Most of the variability in specific criminal acts and in relapse to criminality probably is due to situational factors.

Following is a list of twelve factors to be considered in evaluating risk in substance-involved offenders. This list is intended only as a guide for formulating an informed clinical contribution to the decision-making process, which may ultimately, and properly, hinge on nonclinical considerations. It is not designed for use without reference to other information and clinical judgment. Specific types of criminal behavior, such as violent predation, drug use, and so on, can typically be predicted by taking into account more specific factors. Obviously, for any individual case, any given factor may or may not be significant. Many of the categories overlap, which at this formative stage of development of clinical risk assessment provides an appropriate consideration of the same data from different vantage points during the assessment process.

1. *Severity of Psychopathy.* Central to assessment of psychopathy is the use of Hare's Revised Psychopathy Checklist (PCL-R), an instrument with good reliability and impressive content, construct, and criterion-related validity. Scores range from 0–30, with a score over 30 generally considered as valid evidence of significant psychopathy. Current research indicates that the instrument can be used to predict recidivism. Serin and colleagues (1990), for instance, found that psychopaths reoffended crimes four times more frequently than nonpsychopaths after release from incarceration and reoffended at significantly shorter intervals. Hart and colleagues (1988) reported similar findings. Harris and colleagues (1991), conducting a 10-year follow-up study, found that PCL, an isolated predictor variable, indicated violent recidivism as well as any other variable or combination. Psychopaths also tend to commit more violent crimes after release. Harris and colleagues (1990) found that 77 percent of the psychopaths, but only 21 percent of the nonpsychopaths, committed a violent crime following release. There is mounting evidence that psychopaths commit a disproportionately high percentage of criminal and violent offenses (Hare and McPherson 1984, Jutai and Hare 1983, McCord 1983).

2. *Age.* In general, criminal behavior peaks in late adolescence and early adulthood and decreases over time. Violent crimes are most likely in the 15- to 24-year-old age range. In 1980 the per capita arrest rate for violent crimes for individuals in this age range was three times the population average for similar crimes (FBI 1980). Age takes on a different significance for psychopaths versus nonpsychopathic offenders. Hare and colleagues (1988) found that psychopathic criminal activity peaked at a later age than other offenders, around age 35 to 40. They also found that psychopaths' violent recidivism rates increased between the ages of 35 and 40, and they continued to recidivate at a higher rate than nonpsychopaths even beyond the age of 40, tending to refute the notion of psychopathic burnout, a concept that may apply to antisocial and impulsive offenders. Harris and colleagues (1991) found in their sample of treated psychopaths that violence increased after age 40. In fact, the two offenders in the sample over age 60 both reoffended violently during the at-risk interval. Early onset of substance abuse with tapering off over time may be considered as favorable to continued abstinence in older offenders. A caveat to this is that significant interpersonal losses and physical deterioration may lead to relapse in older offenders.

3. *Sex.* Violence, psychopathy, and aggression appear disproportionately in males, probably reflecting biological as well as psychological and social factors. Wilson and Herrnstein (1985) found that in the United States, nine out of ten individuals arrested for violent crimes were male.

4. *Instant Offense Risk.* Clinical assessment of risk should be tempered by an awareness of the national data, and if available, local and even institution or agency data on rates of recidivism or rearrest for the offense categories most relevant to the case. The instant offense category may be given priority, but the categories of most severe and most frequent offense often provide crucial information. The role of substance involvement in the offense history should be carefully investigated.

5. *Prior Criminal History and Lifestyle Criminality.* A clinical review is needed in addition to use of the Lifestyle Criminality Screening Form, an empirically based instrument developed in the federal correctional system. The instrument provides four subscores and a total score: (a) irresponsibility (score 0–6); (b) self-indulgence (score 0–6); (c) interpersonal intrusiveness (score 0–5), best predictor of future violent behavior; (d) social rule breaking (score 0–5). Total score (0–22). A score of 10 generally is viewed as the cutoff point determining a significant criminal lifestyle.

6. *Substance Abuse and Addiction.* Assessment of substance abuse history includes duration, severity, and variety. Relapse rates for specific drugs of choice and the relationship of the addiction to instrumental or violent crime should be established. Assessment of the dominant psychosocial functions of addiction and the symptom complexes they address is crucial to this process. Classification of the offender into a drug-criminality system has several advantages for both ongoing treatment and risk assessment. Several systems exist. David Nurco's typology of

narcotic addicts has been briefly described earlier. *The Drug Offender Monograph* (National Association of State Alcohol and Drug Abuse Directors) provides a comprehensive overview of many screening instruments currently in use in various state criminal justice system. Several of these go beyond needs assessment and include criminal-use pattern topologies. Of particular interest is the Drug Offender Profile Evaluation/Referral Strategies (unfortunately, the acronym is DOPERS) developed by Nancy Powell Bartlett (1989) at the Texas Adult Probation Commission. Although like many of these instruments, the psychometric qualities of the DOPERS interview is unknown, it yields a profile for each inmate on a four-category addiction-criminality typology. Offenders are typified as either chronic compulsive users, chronic impulsive users, poly-situational (prosocial) users, and poly-criminal (antisocial) users. Of these types, the chronic compulsive and poly-situational groups are seen as having the best prognosis for treatment, and they pose the least posttreatment risk to public safety. The polycriminal user is at the other extreme. This category reflects a polymorphous use of substances within a more psychopathic criminal pattern, which includes drug mixing, violent offenses with deadly weapons, lower probability of drug dependence, criminal value system, and predatory aggression. Comprehensive relapse prevention assessment and intervention should be conducted with the offender as part of the re-entry plan (see Donovan and Marlatt 1988).

7. *Interpersonal Relationships/Attachment.* This includes assessment of ability to maintain appropriate attachments; assessment of depth, commitment, quality, and stability of relationships. In addition to a careful history by self-report, records, and independent verification of relationship data, direct observation of interactions with significant others should be obtained if possible, preferably in informal or naturalistic settings. Significant evidence of sadistic themes in relationships should be viewed as strongly predictive of risk for future violence.

8. *Self-Esteem and Identity.* An appropriate level of self-esteem is viewed clinically as predictive of optimal community adjustment and resilience against other substance abuse relapse factors. Extremes in self-esteem reflect high risk for relapse and reoffending. Low self-esteem is usually ego-dystonic and masked; a grandiose sense of self is often ego-syntonic and potentially more predictive of reoffending. Consolidation of a stable, realistic sense of self, including stable identity in the areas of sex role, occupational role, and standard of living, suggest a better prognosis. Information should be sought from staff, especially those who work most closely with the individual and have an opportunity to observe him or her in daily living situations to help determine the genuineness of a positive prosocial sense of self. Objective and projective psychological testing provides additional sources of data. High egocentricity scores on the Rorschach provide a tentative operational definition of pathological grandiosity.

9. *Mood/Affect.* Positive predictors include stable mood, full range of affect, and appropriate affect. Induction of various moods in the clinical interview can provide helpful clues in detecting psychopaths who are simulating emotional maturity,

remorse, and empathy. Psychopaths often demonstrate the ability to move quickly from one deep expression of emotion to another with a rapid change of topic, such as in a guided early memories interview (see Chapter 4). Nonpsychopaths tend to stay with a favored emotion (other than anger) or to linger with an emotional state triggered by an autobiographically relevant memory or subject.

10. *Ego Strengths.* This covers several clusters of psychological assets, which may be assessed by educational record, staff observations and psychological testing. The clusters include: (a) overall coping skills including impulse control and stress tolerance assessed by behavioral record, staff observations, and psychological testing; see the EARS Psychological Dimensions for a fairly comprehensive list of factors reflecting ego strengths (Chapter 4); (b) cognitive resources including intelligence, information processing, judgment and decision making; and (c) flexibility and creativity within an established set and the ability to change set or context appropriately.

11. *Vocational Readiness.* The offender should be assessed in relation to prior job history, demonstration of a work ethic, and the development of marketable skills for obtaining a livable wage. Jobs should be evaluated in relation to self-esteem issues, level of sensation or arousal provided, nature and degree of social contact involved in the work, concentration of ex-offenders in the worksite, and criminal opportunity provided by the job. Jobs with high turnover, although often available to offenders because of this characteristic, may come with significant liabilities for offenders at risk. Delivery jobs are not advisable, for example, for sexual offenders, whose whereabouts should be determinable at all times, both for public safety and as a reinforcer of the limits internalized during treatment. For a different reason, the samel is true for cocaine and heroin offenders, who are very vulnerable to external environmental and social cues to use. Another example is the job of garbage collector, which provides an adequate income in many cities. Community reentry plans should take into consideration the effect on the offender of the low status of the job and the ability of the worker to use the job as an opportunity to "case out" homes, neighborhoods, and potential female or elderly victims for later criminal activity.

12. *External Support Systems.* This must include an assessment of community conditions in the area in which the offender will be living. A list of community contacts obtained from the offender should be matched against historical visitor lists. Individuals on each of these lists should be discussed with the reentry planner and within community supervision.

PROGRAM MODELS FOR CORRECTIONAL AND FORENSIC POPULATIONS

Given that the understandings advanced in this chapter are judiciously applied, the approaches and techniques noted elsewhere in this book are generally adaptable to forensic and correctional populations, including the principles of program design and administration discussed in Chapter 9. Nonetheless, these environments differ from other treatment sites in several significant ways, most importantly, the way in which these settings circumscribe the goals of treatment and the approach to evaluating its effectiveness. In most treatment settings, among the most important goals is the improvement of the quality of life for the individual, especially assisting the patient to realize the value of freedom. These values are so universal as almost to be taken for granted, even to the absurd extent of allowing the homeless mentally ill to die with their rights on, instead of their boots, as someone phrased it. Assessing the intrinsic value of treatment in most settings, given these values, properly focuses on the perceptions of the person being treated or the individual's ability to exercise personal freedom in a practical sense. In contrast, addressing the perceived and legitimate needs of individuals per se is often seen as a luxury in correctional and forensic environments, where public safety must take first priority. Treatment, especially for substance abuse, as a public safety strategy has more of an external focus than improving quality of life, although an improved quality of life can generally be expected from these applications. An example of this divergence from most treatment settings can be found in the report of Harris and colleagues (1991) concerning the apparent effectiveness of forced (involuntary) treatment of both insane and sane offenders (this practice was at one time considered ethically acceptable and legal in both Canada and some U.S. states). It is hard to imagine an area outside of the criminal justice arena where forced treatment would be seriously entertained, not simply because of the legal and ethical constraints, but also because of the almost universal importance placed by clinicians on personal freedom and on the patient's subjective valuing of therapy.

The discussion of psychopathy, criminality, and addiction in this chapter has several primary implications for program design and implementation of substance abuse interventions aimed at reducing recidivism of those involved in correctional and forensic settings, where the freedom of others (especially potential victims) must always be at the forefront, over and above the personal freedom of the offender. This is the essential ethical implication of incapacitation versus rehabilitation or retribution, as one among several goals of incarceration. Maintaining this public safety focus, as correctional and forensic programs must, will at times lead to conclusions and actions that would appear harsh or even countertherapeutic in other settings. This is especially true concerning decisions that are now the equivalent of triage choices in a hospital emergency room after a disaster. With so much need and so few resources, who gets what help and when?

These issues become even more starkly drawn when we focus on violent crime and drug treatment as an attempt to prevent it. Although nonpsychopathic offenders do commit violent crimes, psychopathic offenders commit them 3.5 times more frequently (Hare and McPherson 1984), and they continue this violent aggressive pattern while incarcerated or in treatment settings (McCord 1982, Wong 1984), and later in life than other offenders (Harris et al. 1991). In correctional settings, psychopaths are more likely to be referred to treatment, both because of the problems they cause and because of their ability to manipulate themselves into more rewarding, less harsh environments, where other participants and treatment staff are viewed as easy marks. This higher rate of referral occurs despite the general consensus that psychopathic criminals are not treatable using conventional techniques (Ogloff et al. 1990, Wong et al. 1988). Despite what is known about their higher recidivism rates, their tendency to simulate change in order to acquire rewards through manipulation of individuals in authority is apparently effective in correctional and forensic systems, since they receive conditional releases at rates similar to those awarded to nonpsychopathic offenders (Wong 1984). The need to interrupt this pattern of equally high conditional release rates for psychopaths under traditional supervision regimens is the first major implication of this discussion. On a practical level, this means screening severe psychopaths out of many treatment programs at the point of admission, especially when those programs involve early releases from incarceration, which are contingent on rehabilitation.

An important caveat must be offered here, however. Meloy (1988) has warned against what he calls therapeutic nihilism toward the psychopath, that is, the stereotyped judgment that this class of individuals is untreatable by virtue of their diagnosis. We must be careful not to behave psychopathically toward the psychopath out of our fear of being deceived, or our desire to withhold from the psychopath the rewards of the manipulative cycle. We must respect the psychopath's humanity, although we cannot assume that he or she will consistently understand, identify with, or express this humanity. As one forensic and correctional administrator reminds us, we do not cease attempts to understand and treat other untreatable diseases such as some forms of cancer or genetic disorders. Many conditions that once fell in the category of untreatable are now treated or almost eradicated. As with other disordering processes, psychopathy is only one aspect of any individual and should be viewed as a matter of degree, ranging from mild to severely malignant. Other factors may provide justified hope for profit from treatment—even with our current armamentarium—especially in moderate levels of severity, or when psychopathic traits are mixed with more therapeutically responsive personality characteristics. We agree strongly with Meloy's warning that judgments such as exclusion from treatment activities must be made on an *individual* evaluation of all available data. A minimum data base must include the findings of at least one competent clinical interviewer's face-to-face investigation of treatability issues with the candidate.

In addition to assessing the severity of psychopathy of an individual, an assessment of the psychosocial functions of addiction and the symptom complexes that the addiction addresses is crucial in making treatability and risk assessment judgments, especially when combined with an analysis of the relationship of criminal behavior to the addictive pattern. A careful analysis of these factors can contribute to increasing the confidence of judgments that treatment for substance abuse in any given case will have an acceptable likelihood of being effective, will result in reduced frequency of targeted criminal activity, will not result in an increase of other criminal or antisocial activities, and will provide useful information for the future supervision, monitoring, and relapse prevention for the individual upon release from confinement.

Escape/avoidance of specific forms of affective dominance, for example, represents a highly treatable addictive pattern in most cases. Individuals with this pattern are more apt to have adopted a criminal lifestyle out of the need to survive within and support their addiction, and/or out of sociocultural factors such as peer pressure, scarcity of options, poor education, or inadequate vocational skills. Although individuals with this addictive pattern and a history of primarily instrumental crimes (perhaps combined with a few violent crimes reflecting only instrumental or affective aggression) are unlikely to be assessed as severely psychopathic, even a moderately high level of psychopathy may not contraindicate treatment in this type of user. The same scenario combined with occasional predatory aggression or sadism toward a victim would probably tip the scales against treatment as a public safety strategy. An illustration of a pattern of addiction that would be less auspicious for treatability is found in the facilitation (or repetition) of sadomasochistic goals or identifications (part of the sociability and identity complex) through the use of substances. This pattern, often found in serial rapists, for example, is highly resistant to treatment. Any elevation of psychopathy in an individual with this pattern of addiction and criminality would strongly contraindicate conventional treatments, unless the goal of those treatments was primarily to improve the quality of the offender's own life.

Given the scarcity of resources available to this population and the enormity of the need for services, enabling programs to make valid and reliable judgments of treatability and the appropriateness of specific treatments to subgroups of treatable offenders are among the most important responsibilities facing policymakers and executive administrators responsible for these people. When we look at correctional and forensic models of treatment, we typically find a poorly conceptualized application of these principles to client selection and matching of treatment modalities employed, even in programs deemed to be relatively successful. After over 100 years, it would appear that the concept of psychopathy did not exist, at least in the awareness of many correctional and forensic program directors. In her review of four in-prison programs considered successful (all reporting improvements in recidivism rates over nontreatment populations, with one program reporting a rate of only 16 percent), Marcia R. Chaiken (1989) found that they had several prominent characteristics in common. In general, as one might expect, these successful programs followed the basic principles of design and administration. The programs maintained some fiscal independence from the correctional institution or hospital that sponsored them, and inmates were housed separately from the general population, thus establishing program boundaries as clearly as possible. All of the programs drew from professions other than correctional personnel, although staff were viewed as being sensitive to security needs and had realistic goals for program participants, factors that prevented them from alienating the correctional staff. The expected length of stay in these programs was high, ranging as long as 36 months.

In regard to participant selection, the programs focused efforts on heavy users who were also high frequency offenders, a strategy that we believe is effective if a causal relationship of high frequency criminality and addiction can be established, and there is an absence of severe psychopathy. None of the programs were selected on this basis. However, two of the four programs excluded sexual offenders and those with severe mental illness. One excluded any inmate with a violent infraction within 8 months. Most of these programs tended to accept inmates with higher or average IQ scores. We would note that these criteria might eliminate a significant percentage of psychopathic offenders, or at least select for the intelligent, nonimpulsive psychopathic, who could be expected to better simulate treatment-related changes in behavior. These criteria would also be expected to result in a racial bias in program participation, favoring white and higher SES inmates, a generally reported finding regarding correctional treatments.

Within treatment, all of the successful programs require written documentation of change from both the clinician and the inmate. All of the programs maintained confidential treatment records, which were not available to correctional personnel and not used for parole decisions. In regard to general approach to problem formulation, all programs used the comprehensive approach typical of free-standing substance abuse programs in the community:

> All four program regard participants' histories of drug use as only one element of their criminal lifestyle. The programs focus on enabling participants to review all elements of their entire style of life—including destructive interactions with family members, friends, and employers; participation in criminal activities; and use of drugs. Rather than merely attempting to persuade participants to give up drugs, program staff provide opportunities for learning and practicing more constructive and responsible patterns of behavior. [Chaiken 1989, p. 15]

All of the programs attempted to develop ownership among participants in various ways, most of them building on the therapeutic community concept. At the end of treatment, all of these programs provided follow-up and aftercare services for participants. One program, Cornerstone in Oregon, utilizes a surrogate family concept, dividing its thirty-two inmates into two family groups of sixteen. Cornerstone parolees are given lifetime privileges for mental health services and participation in graduate groups.

In addition to common traits that might account for claims of effectiveness by these programs, Chaiken identified several common barriers to successful program implementation, which had been encountered to some degree at all four program sites. These were shifts in program priorities due to pressure applied by the large custodial environment, constraint on resources, staff resistance to change, and inmate resistance to change. She suggested open negotiation with all parties prior to program implementation and the introduction of some aspect or program component to match this negotiated consensus. Of special importance is the need to design programs to complement other existing ones, such as educational or vocational efforts. Competition for inmate time or for the participation of highly intelligent, talented inmates desired for other programs was problematic. Space for treatment activities was a crucial issue, with one program housing inmates who were not program participants due to overcrowding.

> Negotiation of space for program activities occupied a substantial portion of all program directors' time. In many institutions such negotiation may be needed because of actual space limitations and overcrowding. However, the struggle over space may be exacerbated by symbolic issues, based on power struggles between program staff and other administrative staff or other concerned parties. Each program has its own set of issues but the essential issue is: who is in control? [Chaiken 1989, p. 45.]

The latent concern that drives the custody-treatment conflict so often encountered where the two co-exist is not mentioned by Chaiken. This is, of course, the fear that the answer to the question of who is in control is that the inmates are. Even in these well-designed and well-administered programs, participant characteristics tend to drive the treatment process. For example she found that motivation for treatment on the part of inmates was at best short-sighted and instrumental:

> Almost all inmates are less interested in improving themselves while incarcerated than in finding the best way to do time. Prison programs that provide pay or privileges are preferable to programs that do not. Several of the programs are finding fewer participants because other seemingly more desirable programs have become available. . . . Although program directors and staff tried to select inmates they thought sincerely wanted to change their behavior, they were aware of the factors that attracted the inmates and encouraged this attractive image. [p. 47]

In effect, Chaiken found that inmates continued their selfish, hedonistic motives and incorporated treatment participation within these preexisting attitudes. To return to the theme of morality versus science in approaching offenders, G. L. Little and K. D. Robinson (1988) attempt to correct the defective moral reasoning of inmates though a seven-step process, which they refer to as Moral Reconation Therapy. Its principles are very similar to many of the treatment strategies and stages of treatment described in Chapter 5. The elements of Moral Reconation Therapy are:

1. Confrontation and assessment of self (beliefs, attitudes, behavior, and defense mechanisms.
2. Assessment of current relationships.

3. Reinforcement of positive behavior and habits designed to raise awareness of moral responsibility.
4. Facilitation of positive identity formation through exploration of the inner self and goals.
5. Enhancement of self-concept though ego-enhancing activities and exercises.
6. Decrease the hedonistic orientation of clients by developing delay of gratification expectations.
7. The development of higher stages of reasoning. [Little and Robinson 1988, p. 144]

Little and Robinson have developed a simple typology of offenders based on Kohlberg's (1980) six stages of moral reasoning as operationalized by Rest's (1986) Defining Issues Test:

Stage 1. Punishment and obedience (pleasure and pain).
Stage 2. Instrumental relativists (backscratching).
Stage 3. Interpersonal concordance (seeking approval).
Stage 4. Law and order (the rules are the rules).
Stage 5. Social contract (what is best for society).
Stage 6. Universal-ethical-principle (following one's conscience). (Little and Robinson 1988, p. 85)

Moral Reconation Therapy is typically applied to substance abusers who become involved in the criminal justice system. It is designed to be used in close coordination with Anonymous traditions groups and other traditional recovery activities. This approach has some of the appeal of taking the bull by the horns. As they state clearly:

It is our conclusion that antisocial behaviors and inability or unwillingness to act in accordance with accepted societal standards of conduct are mediated, at least significantly, by low levels of moral reasoning . . . Educational and traditional treatment programming for adult offenders does not facilitate moral growth. The incarceration experience in itself does not facilitate increases in moral reasoning. It is recommended that correctional treatment providers focus their attention upon methods and experiences that raise offenders levels of moral decision making. [Little et al. 1990, p. 1387)

Although these researchers report promising recidivism rates for drunk drivers, whom they see as antisocial, it is hard to generalize beyond this group of relatively mild offenders to severely antisocial or even psychopathic offenders.

Again, classification of offenders and match of treatment to offender characteristics is at the heart of the matter. Moral reasoning, if rightly conceptualized, goes beyond understanding and applying principles of ethical action. Such principles are founded on two essential prerequisites. First, a consolidated identity is needed, which will result in the very ability to establish personal values, personal integrity, and to experience conflict or dissonance about actions that do not concur with these integrating processes of the self. Second, an empathic understanding and valuing of others is needed, that is, an intraspective understanding of the experience of others and of the intrinsic value of these experiences separate from the effects they have on the self. Both of these prerequisites rest on identification with benevolent (caretaking) others during infancy and early childhood. This is exactly the area of deficiency for the psychopath. Whereas cognitive approaches such as Moral Reconation Therapy may prove highly effective for antisocial individuals and neurotic criminals, such approaches should not be expected to be effective with individuals whose basic identification is with the stranger, the predator, or the enemy. Such approaches come too late in the game. Perhaps parent effectiveness training, a few nutritious meals every day, and a kinder, gentler family and society prior to cataclysmic narcissistic injury in infancy or early childhood are the proper prescriptions for the psychopath, but these prescriptions rely on the society as a whole, not on generally understaffed treatment programs.

It is not at all clear at this point in the evolution of therapeutic understandings that even long-term intensive therapy can result in the kind of drastic reidentification that is required in the case of the severe psychopath. To place the prognosis of the psychopath in perspective, the attempt to encourage identity formation within the fragmented, merged, or overidentified schizophrenic patient appears to have a much better prognosis than does the attempt to abolish and replace the psychopathic way of being, which in its own terms is highly rewarding, even addictive (as in the manipulative cycle) and is also usually supported by strong physiological underpinnings, for which we currently have no magic psychotropic bullet. Psychopathy, unlike schizophrenia, is also supported by a pervasive criminal subculture, which (like the biblical poor) apparently will not only always be with us, but apparently will continue to increase in number and influence. It is appropriate that this chapter, dealing psychodynamically with issues usually seen as sociocultural, ends on a sociological note. Narcissism and psychopathy result from narcissistic injury, which has two primary sources. First are the biological predispositions that create additional vulnerability to such injuries, including factors so easily captured in the last century by the term *inheritance*, but which we now know are in fact powerfully influenced by diet, the amount of stimulus enrichment in the environment, environmental pollution, prenatal maternal health and drug abuse, and "systems" factors such as access to health care and treatment services. The second source for these injuries is in the caretaking activities of significant others, beginning, of course, with the mother and the family as a whole, but extending— for the still emergent and impressionable identity and sense of self of the child—to the child's growing comprehension of the school, the media, and the workplace. The effect on identity of the child's dim apprehension of the potentially caretaking, indifferent, or predatory society and culture they must face, and their place within such a world, is simply to sculpt the contours of their adult faces from the raw materials of predisposition and potential. In the 1980s (the age of passive and relatively benign narcissistic repair and benign neglect of the shadow side of American life), older, more frightening psychological and cultural themes emerged, which in part account for the renewal of popular and professional interest in the psychopath. America in the 1990s has two options. It must begin to choose between owning its shortcomings and negative projections (including those concerning addiction and criminality) and, thereby, face the national narcissistic crisis, or it must choose by default to move even further from the helter-skelter violence of the streets of cities such as Washington, D.C., toward the more controlled, institutionalized ritual forms of violence such as the "flowery death," which flourished atop the temples in cities such as Tenochtitlan in ancient Aztec Mexico.

9

Program Design
and Administration

BRIDGING TRADITIONS

Although the approaches to substance abuse assessment, formulation, and treatment introduced here may be fruitfully applied in almost any setting, the description of dual diagnosis patients as repeated treatment failures implies that most of this work will take place in a program or institutional setting. Given that the current delivery system is bifurcated and categorical, both alcohol/drug and mental health programs will typically be involved in working with a single dual diagnosis case. Chapter 1 advanced the view that the dual diagnosis patient was, in a sense, the creation of a faulty delivery system, which was well prepared to deal with uncomplicated cases of psychiatric disorder or addiction but not with complications arising from their combination. Dual diagnosis programs specifically developed from a cogent rationale have only recently emerged as ventures designed intentionally to address these inadequacies. This chapter reexamines the problems that have led to the emergence of dual diagnosis patients and programs and describes the major issues of program design and administration. It also addresses the crucial issues of staff selection, development, and training, especially in regard to the competing and often contradictory perspectives held by substance abuse workers and those held by professionals trained primarily in the mental health disciplines.

SERVICE DELIVERY IN A BIFURCATED SYSTEM

Although many of the most important issues regarding dual diagnosis patients and programming needs were identified more than a decade ago (Gottheil 1980),

347

problems inherent to a bifurcated, categorical system of health care delivery remain endemic. For example, in an attempt to increase delivery of services to family members of dual diagnosis patients, researchers found that essential inadequacies remained in the delivery of services to the patients themselves (Menicucci et al. 1988). The original goal of Menicucci and colleagues (1988) was to deliver psychoeducational services to family members and close friends of dual diagnosis patients. Their hope was that the delivery of these "knowledge packages" would greatly increase these persons' involvement in treatment efforts. This goal in itself is laudatory and represented an advancement in programmatic dual diagnosis work. However, when the researchers interviewed eight program administrators (including inpatient and outpatient psychiatric and drug/alcohol units and a psychiatric emergency unit), the administrators revealed that service delivery lagged far behind the clinical sophistication and sensibilities of the researchers. The consensus of these administrators probably reflects the general condition of delivery of services to dual diagnosis patients on the national level. The administrators reported the following perceptions based on intimate knowledge of their respective programs, personnel, and treatment populations:

1. The routine underreporting of dual diagnosis patients.
2. The absence of a cogent, articulated plan for the combined treatment of psychopathology and addiction.
3. The limitation of family contact by budgetary constraints, heavy clinician workloads, and the training biases and knowledge limitations of the clinicians.
4. A very inadequate referral system for placement or follow-up care for this patient group following treatment.

Today, individual clinicians and administrators are increasingly aware and concerned about the problems:

Our findings support the concerns of individual treatment providers regarding the inadequacy of existing health care delivery systems for dual-diagnosis patients. From intake, the dual-diagnosis patient is stratified by a primary diagnosis, and ancillary services are relied upon for the "secondary" problem. Outpatients fare no better than inpatients with regard to coordination of care; many treatment providers resort to two separate services to treat the substance abuse and psychiatric difficulties. The splitting of treatment in this manner taxes the abilities of patients to follow up on appointments with multiple treatment programs, attend to a variety of therapies, and take the variety of medications administered. Thus, lack of coordination among providers can result in diminished quality of patient care and, ironically, the criticism of patients for "noncompliance." [Menicucci et al. 1988, pp. 620–621].

Bureaucratic organization of facilities, limitations of perspective due to professional specialization, and the perceived status, stigma, or deviance of particular diagnoses (e.g., alcoholism, heroin addiction, psychotic disorders, affective disorder) were viewed by these researchers as contributing to this state of affairs.

As pointed out by Alfonso Paredes (1980), administratively placing dual diagnosis patients in either segment of a bifurcated system presents problems from an organizational, administrative perspective:

> . . . categorical programs foster replication and redundancy of services. Different professions will evaluate and treat the patient depending on the suspicion that the primary problem is alcohol, drugs, or "mental." Even information systems become categorical and idiosyncratic. The coordination of categorical services with other services becomes a formidable task full of political traps. On the positive side, such a system will receive increasing public support and will experience a concomitant growth. The price is increasing polarization of opinions and irrationality. The most serious risk inherent in such a categorical system is that the complexity of the human being in need of help might not be properly appreciated and effectively addressed. The provider of services is bound to be guided by a set of assumptions influenced by his affiliation to the categorical system rather than by the actual experiences and behavioral complexities of the patient. [p. 122]

Since two systems of care currently exist and compete for limited funding, constituencies, competent staff, and such, the question arises as to where lies the most desirable administrative locus of dual diagnosis programs, in the drug/alcohol system or in the mental health system. Until recently no additional funds followed this especially problematic group of patients, so the answer was usually rendered by default. Although neither system was eager to receive these patients, they were almost always relegated to mental health programs.

Substance abuse facilities are often heavily staffed by paraprofessionals who accurately view the level of severity of the dual diagnosis patient as beyond their competence. Programs with a strictly AA or NA orientation have been hesitant to accept patients whose problems were not directly attributable to addiction and who might require psychoactive medications for daily maintenance, a fact seemingly at odds with a strict abstinence philosophy. Legal issues also contributed to placing the dual diagnosis patients in the mental health sector. Substance abuse programs are not usually statutorily required to care for noncompliant individuals, or persons without primary resources. Such programs also do not receive the emergency admissions and court-ordered evaluations that are routine service demands on the mental health care sector. Mental health care facilities are required to treat the committable patient or the patient in an acute emergency presentation. Since many dual diagnosis patients have often worn out their welcome and resources over multiple hospitalizations, the public sector hospital or mental health service became the most frequent unwilling recipient, simply such programs could not effectively resist accepting these patients.

Having somewhat begrudgingly been awarded the dual diagnosis problem, the already overburdened staff of public mental health facilities tended to ignore all but the most obvious consequences of substance abuse in psychiatric patients. Typically, workers in these settings learned that addressing substance abuse issues in a hospitalization resulted in more difficult initial outplacement and referral, longer hospital stays, and larger caseloads, since no one else wanted to deal with a substance-abusing psychiatric patient and most community resources could refuse to do so. The short-term rewards weighed heavily in favor of minimizing the secondary substance abuse diagnosis.

The development of managed care strategies, such as reflected in Diagnostic Related Groupings (DRGs) used for federal reimbursements may have reversed this trend to some extent and encouraged the development of dual diagnosis programs, since a dual diagnosis justifies longer stays. These developments, combined with increased clinical sophistication, resulted in the formation of coordinated dual diagnosis programs, usually within a general psychiatric ward with consultation from substance abuse specialists or coordination with a substance abuse treatment unit. Eventually small wards specifically dedicated to dual diagnosis patients were viewed as clinically necessary and organizationally viable. Now, they are community-based resources (case management, day treatment, supervised housing) specifically tailored to the needs of substance-abusing psychiatric patients. Ironically, the deinstitutionalization of mentally ill patients has meant both the expansion of the dual diagnosis problem (due to increased exposure of mental patients to substances, stressors, and addiction-oriented attitudes) and an expansion in the resources and knowledge bases required for effectively performing dual diagnosis work in the community.

COORDINATED OR LINKAGE MODEL PROGRAMS

Preliminary efforts at developing dual diagnosis programs often tried to improve referral and evaluation services between components of a delivery system that remained essentially bifurcated and categorical. Such attempts have been called coordinated programs (Weinstein and Gottheil 1980) and, more recently, linkage model programs (Kline et al. 1990). Weinstein and Gottheil described a coordinated program for treating dual diagnosis cases as exemplifying a movement away from two entirely separate delivery systems involved in a dual diagnosis case. In designing a countywide program for dual diagnosis issues, they considered the advantage of centralized components of care (mental health care and substance abuse care in separate programs) as consisting primarily in improved efficiencies within each component. However, they noted that this may be only a perception of an advantage that must be balanced against the disadvantages of multiple staffs, multiple appointments for the patient, the burden of coordination and communication requirements between two programs, incompatible treatment approaches between centralized programs, and the tendency for specialists to find in the case what fits their particular specialty.

Ultimately they decided to assign a substance abuse counselor to each district service team. It was the job of this counselor to admit substance abuse cases, consult on dual diagnosis cases, receive mental health consultation from other staff on their own cases, and to meet with the service team on a routine basis. Administratively, the counselors continued to report to and provide records to a central substance abuse administration staff. The counselors were, therefore, not under direct control of the team leader, an aspect of the program that the local administrators were reluctant to accept. The program was clearly at an early stage of development: In the authors' words: "We have termed this a coordinated, rather than a combined or integrated, program since the services treat different diagnostic populations and have remained administratively distinct (Weinstein and Gottheil 1980, p. 54).

Nonetheless they report that the program did significantly improve the number and quality of referrals and admissions between the two systems. The biggest problem was that the counselors had difficulty maintaining their sense of identity under the mental health umbrella. This initial success demonstrated that coordinated systems can be effective if properly administrated and if respect for different perspectives and knowledge bases can be maintained in both treatment sectors. Such collaborations, however, are often based on the temporary overlapping of needs between programs. Programs are notoriously reluctant to relinquish or share power, control, or resources, especially in times of budgetary restraint. Administrators and managers often view such coordinated efforts as the least painful first casualty during mandatory retrenchment of services caused by budget cuts or staff shortages.

In coordinated programs, the emphasis must be placed primarily on staff development, mutual consultation, and—most vigorously—on appropriate referrals. Regarding referrals, Ottenberg (1980) has reported criteria identified by Bernard Sobel for deciding whether a given drug/alcohol program should accept dual diagnosis cases. Among the factors to be considered are:

1. Intensity and nature of the patient's symptoms.
2. Ability of the milieu to tolerate deviants.
3. Competence of the staff in dealing with persons needing specialized, individualized care.
4. Availability of specialized therapeutic techniques.
5. Availability of specialized, qualified staff for prompt diagnosis, treatment, and referral in emergency situations.
6. Willingness and ability of the treatment community to allow and support the use of psychotropic medications for selected patients.
7. Proportion of psychiatrically impaired or symptomatic persons within the whole treatment population.
8. Prearranged referral agreements and working relationships with psychiatric facilities for proper and prompt referral of patients. (Ottenberg 1980, p. 58)

Ottenberg strongly disagrees with the recommendation that homogeneity of patient type should be maximized to whatever degree possible. The dilemma of choosing to form either homogeneous or heterogeneous treatment populations faces most mental health treatment efforts and is usually conceptualized as related to typical level of functioning (psychotic, character disordered, neurotic) and sometimes by specific diagnosis. In the substance abuse treatment sector, this dilemma is usually viewed in terms of the drug of choice (alcohol, cocaine, or heroin), which is often seen as a major determinant of required care. In linkage model dual diagnosis programs, homogeneity of patient population is often encouraged to protect schizophrenics and other fragile patients from more predatory character-disordered substance abusers. However, an overemphasis on homogeneity can support the denial of the so-called higher functioning patients that they share significantly in similar symptoms, habits, and personality traits with the more impaired psychotic level patients. Also, even seriously impaired patients can contribute meaningfully to ward and group process if the environment is held fairly constant as a safe, nonpunitive arena for pursuing recovery.

These advantages to a mixed population notwithstanding, homogeneity becomes imperative if differential treatments cannot be provided in the general program setting. For instance, the differential response of fragile patients to highly confrontational techniques requires traditional therapeutic communities that rely on the imposition of group responsibility and the use of interpersonal confrontation and exercise of punitive authority to be highly homogeneous, consisting primarily of highly defended narcissistic personalities and moderately psychopathic individuals.

Ottenberg reports a more patient-focused list of factors (developed by Angelo Zosa) for considering the involvement of a dual diagnosis patient in a substance abuse program which can also be used to evaluate whether a patient should be referred to a purely homogenous mental health-oriented substance abuse program:

1. The degree of psychopathology.
2. The level of functioning on various areas.
3. The need for supervision, and the ability to live independently.
4. The need for potent psychotropic medication.
5. The effects of medication on daily functioning.
6. The relationship between psychiatric symptoms and drug-taking behavior.
7. The patient's ability to deal with stress and social pressures, particularly in a therapeutic community setting. (Ottenberg 1980, p. 61).

This list was developed primarily to ensure that fragile dual diagnosis patients are not harmed by being placed in programs oriented toward higher functioning individuals. It is equally important that character-disordered patients not have their recovery significantly impeded and their narcissism and psychopathy stimulated by being placed in a program that is too accepting, nonconfrontational, or full of easy prey. Heterogeneous programs are workable if confrontational work is limited to small group settings and if the staff is well trained in following the ebb and flow of psychological stability in the treatment process. They must be able to avoid being split by manipulative patients, which usually means that they will have established effective means of communicating information, subjective impressions, and events suggesting changes in stability or level of functioning in patients. Also, heterogeneous programs must be able to provide patients with transfers to homogeneous programs if the challenge of the environment proves too great for a given fragile patient. They must also be willing to terminate the treatment of disruptive, intractable nonpsychotic patients who can make the heterogenous linkage model totally unworkable.

HYBRID OR INTEGRATED PROGRAMS

The next step in the development of dual diagnosis programs was toward integrated and combined systems. Such programs aim for treatments related to both addiction and mental illness within the same organizational framework and treatment environment, with a team trained to understand the relationship between these disorders. Almost all these programs have their base in an inpatient psychiatric unit or residential care setting. Levy and Mann (1988) described a mature integrated approach toward dual diagnosis programming in a state hospital. The program was first established in 1973. The general environment of care and the factors that have resulted in the formation of the Special Treatment Team for dual diagnosis patients they have comprehensively described unfortunately apply to many settings where dual diagnosis work must take place:

> Our Special Treatment Team is part of a large state hospital, where several conditions complicate the clinical task. The patients are numerous (over 300 admissions per year), and they come through quickly (average length of stay about 30 days), so that time often does not allow proper diagnosis or treatment. Also the patients tend toward clinical extremes. Many have done poorly in treatment elsewhere, entering the public sector as "treatment resistant" or even "treatment failures," a population more challenging (and more frustrating) than most. Many of them are chronically ill, not only with obdurate illnesses but with multiple complications of alcohol and drug abuse, of mental illnesses, and of prior treatments for both. Most of the patients are hospitalized involuntarily, requiring careful evaluation of their competency to accept or refuse treatment, and of their need for continued hospitalization, and so forth. Many come directly from the courts, to be evaluated for their competency to stand trial, for criminal responsibility, for ability to serve penal sentences, and for related matters. Resources, in general, are scarce here. Laboratory work, nursing care, the time and attention of a good clinician—all are in short supply. Yet, being a state hospital, we cannot say no. We must treat all who present in need of care. In this

atmosphere of overwork and privation, only patients and dilemmas abound. [Levy and Mann 1988, p. 220]

Admissions to the Special Treatment Team occur directly through the psychiatric emergency room or via court order for medicolegal concerns. The authors do not detail the inpatient resources available to the team (number of beds, wards, staffing, etc.), although their description reflects considerable control of patient management resources and treatment modalities by the team. On the day after admission, patients are seen in team rounds. In these discussions, the patient's presenting intoxication behavior is not ignored:

> Like hypnosis, the amytal interview, and other states of narcosis, states of intoxication and withdrawal do reveal much that patients generally hide, from themselves as well as from others. Unconscious contents and defenses may be revealed, and may prove helpful in formulating psychodynamics. As a general rule, however, in these the presenting mental status is an unreliable basis for psychiatric diagnosis. [Levy and Mann 1988, p. 222]

The team director conducts a structured interview with the patient during rounds. Tentative treatment planning and assignment of a primary clinician follow this encounter. Routine admission work includes laboratory screening for organ damage and nutritional deficits. For alcoholic patients where liver damage is suspected, acute withdrawal syndrome is diminished with lorazepam (ativan) because of its shorter half life than chlordiazepoxide (librium). Benzodiazepines abusers are weaned away from these drugs on very small doses. Other drugs are cleared naturally, with oral vitamin C and fruit juices assisting PCP clearance. Cocaine withdrawal is sometimes assisted with desipramine (a cyclic antidepressant). Symptomatic treatment for specific withdrawal symptoms, such as constipation, vomiting, and gastric distress, is also routine. The authors warn of the problems of detoxification and stabilization associated with the general poor health, dietary deficiencies, drug intoxication, and habilitation posed by the dual diagnosis patient. Even the basic absorption and metabolism of medications though usual oral means may be very problematic.

Drug screens for all drugs of abuse and blood alcohol level on admission are used in later treatment planning, since patients are not expected to be accurate or truthful about such histories. Contacts with families and friends, as well as with other treatment and social services agencies familiar with the patient, are considered during treatment planning. AA and alcohol discussions are built into the inpatient regimen. Patients are encouraged to join AA and outpatient treatments before discharge. Although not very specific about treatments utilized in the inpatient setting, the Levy and Mann 1988 article does address the constantly reappearing problem of getting the right inpatient-outpatient balance with the dual diagnosis patient and the dilemma of when maximum benefit from a hospitalization has been reached:

One of our constant struggles is to give patients enough time in the hospital, while at the same time, encouraging them to begin making a transition back to the community. Too lengthy hospitalization may make any eventual transition to community life more difficult. On the other hand, encouraging a patient to return to the community before ready, generally results in yet another failure, taxing the hopes of all concerned. [p. 224]

Ward restrictions are titrated to shape the behavior of unmotivated or noncompliant patients. Those who do not meet the criteria for involuntary commitment are discharged upon multiple relapses while in treatment. Discharge of patients is often to "wet shelters" with mental health orientations developed specifically for dual diagnosis patients in coordination with social services agencies:

Without this program, patients uninterested in treatment but not in need of hospitalization could not be discharged, which would have a devastating effect on the milieu of our program. No one could get effective treatment in the presence of a few patients who continued to drink or otherwise refused active treatment. This program thus serves—in Winnicot's sense—as a "transitional environment" where those unable to tolerate either treatment or sobriety can be "held" loosely enough to protect them from the worse consequences of their behavior, but tightly enough to keep them from sabotaging the course of their colleagues who are attempting sobriety. [Levy and Mann 1988, p. 225]

Even for patients discharged sober and stabilized, housing remains a problem. Reflecting another theme common to these programs, a large amount of the team's resources is absorbed by the need to develop and maintain viable placements in the community for reentering patients. "Selling" the dual diagnosis patient often means offering day hospitalization services, intensive case management with ambulatory community providers, and emergency backup and consultative services to community programs. The payoff is in more frequent successful referrals, better adjustment of patients upon reentry, and continual contact (although often indirect) of the patient with the dual diagnosis program.

The Special Treatment Team administrators are sensitive to the stress this work presents daily to their staff but becomes critical around treatment failures and early discharges. ALANON participation is encouraged for all staff as a means of preventing burnout. A disease model of addiction is propagated, in part as a preventative of staff negativity and providing some additional buffer to burnout.

In their overview of a workable combined dual diagnosis program, Levy and Mann provided little detail to the process of treatment planning and contracting. Chapter 5 describes the clinical information that must provide the foundation for the plan. Treatment contracts can be used to communicate and commit the plan to patients and serve as a basis for engagement on the part of the patient and the family. Kaufman (1989) has identified many of the key elements in an viable dual diagnosis treatment contract. A detailed treatment contract is developed with the patient and family and should include an agreement on methods of detoxification, medication compliance, and aftercare treatment for the patient. Family members should commit to specific participation in the identified patient's therapy and to involvement in self-help for their own support and education. In some cases, explicit behaviors or attitudes to be expressed by the therapist should also be stated in the contract.

If the patient or family does not agree to the contract or fails to implement it in good faith, Kaufman recommends terminating treatment in hopes that at some point they may be able to comply with a workable treatment program.

PROGRAM DESIGN IN THE INTEGRATED MODEL

The intent of describing integrated systems and programs as more advanced than coordinated or linkage model programs is not to minimize or exaggerate the potential effectiveness of either approach. A sophisticated, client-focused perspective on the utility of the two models has recently been advanced, which matches well with the practical realities faced by clinicians and administrators dealing with patients in a bifurcated, specialized system of care delivery (Kline et al. 1991). In this view both dual diagnosis program models have advantages and disadvantages, are in some ways complementary, and may be used sequentially:

> The models are not mutually exclusive. They have applicability depending on the individual characteristics of a referred client. The degree of willingness of clients to engage within an agency setting, bond with a case manager, and accept intensive treatment determines the appropriateness of referral to one or the other treatment approach.
>
> These models may also be used sequentially. The less demanding, more diffuse substance abuse treatment approach of the linkage model can provide the only tolerable form of treatment for clients who are actively abusing substances in a state of denial about their negative consequences. As the commitment to abstinence grows, the integrated approach can then be utilized to provide the intensive treatment and support clients may need to remain abstinent. As clients become more committed to abstinence and more engaged in AA, they may once again benefit from the linkage model in its emphasis on utilizing generic substance abuse treatment resources in the community. [pp. 104–105]

This complementary, sequential view of two models may help clinicians to optimize the use of all available resources to provide benefits and services to a given client at a particular point. However, multicomponent integrated programs, by definition, can contain all of the important aspects of the linkage system in addition to the more integrated, intensive treatment approach required to use the reciprocal assessment and treatment strategies advanced in this book.

Free-standing substance abuse programs for patients with neurotic and mild character disorders and long-term asylum wards are two extremes in setting that can profit from the dual diagnosis perspective on treatment of addiction. However, patients with moderate levels of severity of psychiatric functioning and moderate to severe addictions are apt to show the most progress applying the approaches offered here. These patients can be best served in a program designed specifically for their needs as dual diagnosis patients. The danger of advocating for the development of such free-standing dual diagnosis programs, however, is that within larger systems they can easily become therapeutic dumping grounds where all impossible patients are labeled dual diagnosis and where minimal resources are invested in their care and treatment. On the other extreme, a few programs have become exclusive, high resource pilot programs, with low case loads, low patient turnover, little staff interchange with other programs, and little overall contribution to a larger system. The obvious limits in generalizability of such pilot programs and their luxury status within overburdened systems have contributed to retarding progress in the development of more reproducible and affordable programs.

Developing well-formulated, integrated dual diagnosis programs is one of the major challenges facing the treatment community in the 1990s. Whether these integrated programs are free-standing with dedicated staffs and facilities, consist of special consulting teams and referral systems, or a combination of these two approaches, several issues must be dealt with in their design and implementation. These areas include the establishment of a treatment philosophy and related goals of treatment, the definition of a target population and the development of related admission and discharge criteria, the levels of care available to the program through either direct control or referral, the preferred modalities of treatment, and the phasing and coordination of these modalities. In addition, issues related to staffing and maintenance must be addressed. These include staff selection and development, self-help activities, outplacement and referral development, and the development of outreach and self-referral work. Each of these areas is briefly discussed in the following pages. Examples from several dual diagnosis programs are offered, including that of PASA (Psychiatric Alcohol and Substance Abuse Program), an integrated residential dual diagnosis program once located on the grounds of Saint Elizabeths Hospital complex in Washington, D.C., which the author redesigned and directed.

Establishing Treatment Philosophy and Goals of Treatment

Although there is always room for many opinions, it is usually advisable to restrict divergence of goal-related action in any coherent treatment program. A dual diagnosis program is no place for clinical loose cannons or for staff who are in doubt about the direction of the treatment endeavor they are joining. The goals must be specified—at least to the extent that both addictive and mental illness components are addressed—and mutually exclusive positions in regard to several major issues must be decided. A strong philosophy of treatment in regard to total abstinence or rational use of substances, the use of psychotropic medication, the status of Twelve Step groups, and the degree of applicability of the disease or medical model to the program's activities and methods should be explicitly stated for the benefit of staff and patients.

In reviewing five published reports of dual diagnosis programs, Evans and Sullivan (1990) noted that all endorsed concurrent treatment of addiction and substance abuse, the use of psychotropic medications, involvement in AA/NA for their patients, and a generally supportive therapeutic approach as opposed to a highly confrontational one. Only one of the five programs did not endorse a disease process model of addiction and mental illness, although one program was silent on the issue. Evans and Sullivan state that their program was (at the time) unique in the advocacy of stepwork within a dual diagnosis program. Working with a very explicit program philosophy, they have required physicians to sign a "dual diagnosis treatment agreement" outlining specific behaviors for their professional practice. The agreement endorses an abstinence model and a team concept of patient management, as opposed to a physician-guided model. They state that this practice of signing agreements screens out physicians not in accord with their philosophy and clarifies the program's mission to all team members, providing a basis for resolving conflicts. Although the use of an explicit program philosophy and practice guidelines for professionals is highly recommended, such interventions should not be limited to one professional discipline group in the dual diagnosis setting and need not be authoritarian or unilateral. It is unreasonable and counterproductive to require prospective employees or consultants to endorse a treatment philosophy or agreement as a condition of employment. Developing and periodically reviewing the philosophy and guidelines should be used as noncoercive opportunities for staff orientation, development, guidance, and conflict resolution. Participation by the staff in the development of program philosophy and guidelines eventually results in improvement, based the entire staff's awareness of the program's history and the growth of the staff's experience and knowledge base over time.

In a dual diagnosis program directed by the author for the District of Columbia, the treatment philosophy statement included reference to the origin of dual diagnosis disorders in recurrent treatment failures, the organizational basis for these failures, and the shortcomings of sequential treatment of these patients. The multiple causal mechanisms in reciprocal interaction that result in dual diagnosis problems were described as requiring reciprocal or cyclical treatments. Complete abstinence as a goal of treatment specifically for dual diagnosis patients (not necessarily for the treatment of uncomplicated cases of addiction), the need for psychotropic medication in the management of many patients, the role of NA/AA in the program, and the expectation of clients to be involved in Twelve Step work were also specified. The philosophy explicitly favored supportive approaches with patients other than the highly defended character disorders and explicitly expressed the program's need to have as its employees and program associates staff members and patient alumni in stable recovery. Whatever the stance taken by a program on these issues of philosophy, the more explicitly they are stated, the more clearly they are promulgated among staff, patients, and referral sources, the more unified and coherent will be the treatment processes within the program. Programs guided by such explicit, detailed statements of philosophy are also open to examination of their mission, purpose, and general approach to treatment and therefore are more available to planned and environmentally responsive organizational change. This openness increases the likelihood that the program will survive as the external environment changes and will mature over time.

Establishing Target Populations and Patient Mix

The purpose, mission, and treatment philosophy of a dual diagnosis program are largely conditioned by the targeted population. Reviewing the categories of dual diagnosis work identified in Chapter 1 will help to provide the context for deciding on target groups. The acuity, chronicity, cyclicity, urgency, severity, and degree of reciprocity involved in the dual diagnosis situation were used to define the reciprocally reinforcing (synergistic) psychiatric substance abuse syndromes. For cases where the level of psychiatric severity is moderate (i.e., cases below the level of severe personality disorder), a less sophisticated and intensive approach was described as adequate, although not ideal. For cases in this range of severity, sequential treatment of either disorder or simultaneous (parallel) treatment of the individual by two treatment approaches and different therapists is often effective. The integrated, reciprocal approach offered here was shown to be required for work with the major mental disorders. This approach was also highly recommended for dual diagnosis cases where the addiction has a strongly characterological or symptomatic basis. Characterological basis for addiction is demonstrated by the presence of a personality disorder and at least one failure in traditional substance abuse treatment. Symptomatic basis for addiction is demonstrated by clear evidence (after detoxification) that the individual has suffered some focal psychological or emotional problem that is not typical of normal functioning and that has, in effect, temporarily lowered his or her functioning to a level more typical of disturbed individuals. A failure in at least one traditional treatment episode by such an individual usually is sufficient to confirm a symptomatic addiction.

No single program (unless it consists of several coordinated programs under a central umbrella) should be expected to provide comprehensive treatments for all the categories of chemical dependence. In most cases, it is advisable to target either dual diagnosis work with the major mental disorders or characterological and symptomatic dual diagnosis work within a single ward or for a single treatment team. If several treatment environments and teams are available, optimal patient population mixes can be established by targeting both dual diagnosis work with the

major mental disorders and dual diagnosis with a characterological and symptomatic basis, with each kind of work centered in a different ward or residential unit. A
practical matter making this second approach (mixed programs) more desirable is
the assessment and diagnostic rigor required to clearly differentiate cases. The
distinction between types of dual diagnosis work is impossible to make during
detoxification and often remains difficult during the first month of stabilization and
evaluation of early response to treatment modalities. Dual diagnosis programs that
have the luxury of admitting patients only after detoxification and stabilization in
another setting, can minimize, but not eliminate this problem.

In the program directed by the author, five different ward environments
(ninety-eight beds) were available. Patients were admitted only after inpatient
hospitalization, detoxification, and stabilization. Nevertheless, the admissions unit
still found detoxification and stabilization procedures necessary, in addition to its
primary tasks of patient orientation to the recovery and treatment process and
other initial psychoeducational interventions. After 21 to 30 days on this ward (at
least 40 to 60 days into a treatment episode), patients were designated for either one
of two wards doing mixed dual diagnosis work or to a ward working exclusively
with the major mental disorders. Cases that primarily involved symptomatic and
characterological work with dependent personality styles and moderately severe
ambivalent and independent styles were provided differential treatments on the
mixed wards, and then usually transferred fairly quickly to a less medically
oriented, community living environment with less intensive staff supervision. Most
individuals with severely ambivalent personalities and highly defended independent and aggressive personality styles were referred to confrontational and uncovering therapies earlier in treatment. They remained on the mixed wards where their
behavior could be closely monitored and only later in treatment were moved to the
less supervised community living setting. Severe psychopaths without a major
mental illness were usually eliminated from the program relatively quickly, due to
the staff's intolerance for their manipulative and rule-breaking behaviors. In effect,
three program tracks existed: one for the major mental illnesses, one for nonacting-
out symptomatic or characterological addiction, and one for acting-out, or highly
defended, personality disorders. All three tracks were fed by the admissions unit
and in turn eventually fed into the community living unit.

Developing Well-Defined Admission and Discharge Criteria

Whatever population is targeted by the program, it must be well defined and clearly
reflected in admission criteria. The criteria must be understood and endorsed by
the staff and clearly communicated to everyone in the referral pool. If there are
several components of a program, each should have explicit admission and
discharge (entry and exit) criteria. Authority for determining admission must rest

ultimately with the dual diagnosis program director. To the degree that this authority rests elsewhere (such as in the courts, a central admitting unit for a large mental health system, or any other mandatory referral system), the program is very likely to have an undesirable mix of patients. On the one extreme there will be too many patients in the extremely severe end of major mental illnesses and behavioral disorders. On the other extreme, psychopathic and narcissistic patients will gravitate toward the easy victims, "soft" staff, and relatively gratifying ward milieu required for the more impaired dual diagnosis patient. This is the worst possible mix in a single component program, and these extremes of the referral process can also eventually overburden a multicomponent program's ability to the optimal mix. At PASA, for instance, prior to extended information sessions with the staff of referring programs, nonpsychopathic, nonviolent, compliant patients were severely underreferred to our dual diagnosis program, although we were occasionally called in to provide on-ward or residential consultation. As a result, only the severely impaired and psychopathic acting-out patients were referred for special programming, which caused the de-skilling of the dual diagnosis staff and the staff in the referring agencies. In addition, patients in the middle range of severity of dual diagnosis problems (those most apt to respond favorably to specialized interventions and to have fewer relapses and decompensations) were the least likely to receive specialized treatment, although such treatment would clearly optimize benefits to both the patient and the system. The quality of referrals was greatly improved when referring staff were better trained to understand dual diagnosis issues. Another quantum leap in quality occurred when patients who had progressed enough to be managed effectively at their referral site—ward, community residential facility, day treatment—were returned with continued support from PASA staff and programming.

The population targeted by PASA was defined prototypically. The prototypical patient was described as a person with an active substance problem and a stable psychiatric condition, except for deterioration related to substance use. Usually patients with this profile will reconstitute rapidly after brief periods of abstinence from substances. The psychiatric condition was expected to actively complicate substance abuse treatment, making the patient inappropriate for facilities without a mental health orientation. Cognitive functioning was expected to allow the patient to profit from a combination of psycho-educational interventions and insight-oriented interventions. When stable, the PASA patient was expected to exhibit the activities of daily living skills (ADLs) appropriate to a residential setting and be capable of functioning in an open ward environment. From this description, admission criteria were developed after factoring in several administrative considerations. They included the scarce treatment resources in the entire mental health care system, patient "dumping," lack of sophistication on the part of referral sources regarding addictive behavior, and the mix of voluntary and committed patients in the referral pool.

1. Patients must have a dual diagnosis defined as a major mental illness (specifically schizophrenia, bipolar disorder, paranoid disorder, major depression with psychotic features) and substance dependence. Cases of hospitalization for depression or recent suicide attempts with long-standing dysthymia and substance dependence proven resistant to treatment may be admitted for a specific length of stay, based on severity
2. Patients must not be in need of detoxification at the time of admission.
3. Patients must be capable of profiting from a mainly psycho-educational, cognitive, didactic program.
4. Patients must be capable of complying with program requirements for participation, including an initial ward restriction of 21 days without casual social visits.
5. Patients must not be actively violent, disruptive, suicidal, or homicidal at the time of admission.
6. At the time of admission, patients must not be so emotionally labile that they are unable to take in new information or exercise minimal self-monitoring and self-control.
7. Voluntary (noncommitted) patients must demonstrate the ability to develop motivation for substance abuse treatment and have the willingness to comply with treatment recommendations.
8. Admissions are accepted only from mental health care settings. Patients ordered into treatment due to involvement with the criminal justice system must meet all clinical criteria for admission as determined by program staff.

Most of these criteria required further operational definition, for example, in terms of Addiction Severity Inventory (ASI) mean scores, frequency, and recency of disruptive ward behaviors, urine screening prior to admission, and behavioral ratings at the time of the admission team's prescreening interview. In addition to personality assessment, motivational factors were determined by self-reports of distress and value of treatment (ASI items) as well as by analysis of the available leverage that could be applied by the family and social network of the patient.

Defining Treatment Goals

For the severity levels recommended for the target population in most dual diagnosis programs, the most important treatment goals to be shared by staff and patients are:

1. Total abstinence from nonprescribed psychoactive substances.
2. Patient engagement in the treatment/recovery process.

3. Rational, informed compliance with medication regimens and active participation in other major treatment modalities.
4. Compliance with a mutually agreed upon, written treatment contract.
5. Management or abatement of symptoms.
6. Increased self-direction within a recovery-oriented lifestyle.

The goals of treatment outlined here emphasize the importance of programmatic support of opportunities to increase motivation for change in the client. Because of this general emphasis, there is little need to differentiate between goals and objectives. This distinction is necessary, however, at the level of the individual treatment plan. The first goal in the list establishes the groundwork for continued treatment. Some substance abuse programs may have rational use as a goal (i.e., absence of dependence or abuse), although this is not a workable alternative for patients at the levels of severity recommended for targeting by programs for dual diagnosis patients.

Levels of Care and Length of Stay

Because of the range of potential problems (often in the some individual at different phases of recovery) a dual diagnosis program must have access to treatment environments that vary in the dimensions of protection for self and others, degree of expected self-control and compliance, and sequestering from substances that might be abused. Dual diagnosis programs must either contain several levels of care or be able to refer patients easily to different levels in the mental health and substance abuse care systems. Guidelines must determine the proper point in recovery or regression at which a shift in care level should be made.

Highly structured protective and restrictive environments that support the patient's need to avoid abused substances are essential in early phases of treatment and during relapse. Locked units, seclusion, restraint, and involuntary medication regimens may be required in these difficult and dangerous phases. Initially, dual diagnosis patients need intensive orientation and education related to their problems and their recovery process, while they function in an environment that demands new ways of structuring time and relating to others without access to substances or external cues that provoke the desire to use them. Later in the treatment process, patients require the gradual easing of structure and the introduction of opportunities for new personal choices and responsibility. As they enter full recovery, patients must be supported as they begin to face the same stresses and predispositions that brought on the substance abuse. Education, psychotherapy, medication, and rehabilitation activities must all be coordinated to take into account the patient's gradual steps toward abstinence, self-reliance, and recovery. Such modulated structure, support, and treatments are best provided in an organization that allows quick access to all levels of care. In every phase of treatment, ward cultures must be created and maintained that will assist the recovering patient in identifying with an abuse-free lifestyle and becoming account-able for his or her own behavior. Often patients must be moved to the appropriate environment in a relatively brief period of time due to decompensations. In other cases the patient must be moved because he or she has reached a higher level of functioning than is viable in a very restrictive setting. Such settings tend to promote dependency, regression, and sometimes resentment and rage, which will undermine the treatment alliance.

Lengths of stay should be longer in the dual diagnosis program than in most psychiatric programs and substance abuse programs. Complete termination should probably not take place, except for repeated noncompliance (treatment failure), geographic relocation, or more suitable treatment arrangements identified (patient transfer). In a comprehensive program (with inpatient, residential, community living, and outpatient components), the length of stay in some components may be fixed and should vary in others. At PASA, for example, the orientation/education unit was limited to a 30-day stay under most circumstances. Patients in either of the two mixed wards—major mental illnesses and personality disorders—were dealt with in a track system. Those with characterological or symptomatic addictions or psychotic patients who responded unusually well to medication were expected to enter a residential setting within ninety days of admission to the mixed ward setting. Medication nonresponders were not given a specific length of stay on these wards. Unit coordinators on each ward provided the director with detailed justifications for any stay beyond that described in the component description, for the patient's track, or the estimated length of stay specified upon admission.

Programming to Correspond to Recovery Phases

Program design should take into account both the cyclical and sequential nature of dual diagnosis treatment and recovery (see Chapter 5). The high frequency of relapse, spontaneous exacerbation of symptoms, and inconsistent sources of sup-port require ongoing assessment of the patient's current phase of recovery. Changes in individualized treatment plans and immediate intervention by staff are some-times an adequate response to changes in the recovery phase. Program components designed for patients in middle or advanced phases of recovery can, for instance, manage a single lapse into substance use or a brief period of relapse through these means. Multiple relapses probably signal a return to a less advanced stage and the need for transfer to an environment with more structure, closer supervision, lower expectations for independent functioning, and a more directive therapeutic ap-proach that relies less on the patient's ability to cope with uncovering and confrontation in therapy. Assessment of the phase of recovery in which a patient is currently engaged should be a routine staff activity. Substantial consensus among treatment staff concerning the patient's phase of recovery and level of functioning should be reached prior to moving a patient from one component to another, or before expanding the types or intensity of treatment modalities applied to the case.

Although the PASA program was based on a relatively early and less sophisticated version of the phases/stages schema discussed in Chapter 5, its structure and functioning provide a useful example of a treatment program with multiple components and tracks. Each component addressed phase-specific treatment needs, with movement between the components based on ongoing assessment of the patient's recovery progress. A brief description of the program's structure emphasizes the relationship between treatment activities and phases of recovery.

In the PASA program, three major treatment components were spread over five wards. All served both men and women. A closed (locked) ward admission unit housed the orientation/education component, which was designed for an inpatient level of care and a fixed length of stay. Its mission was to prepare patients for intensive treatment in one of three residential wards. The intensive treatment/ rehabilitation phase was housed in three contiguous but separated residential care wards. In effect, three tracks existed in this program component: one for the major mental illnesses, one for nonacting-out symptomatic or characterological addiction, and one for acting-out, or highly defended, personality disorders. One of these wards was designated for very impaired chronic patients with major mental illnesses who responded poorly to medication, and/or patients who demonstrated low compliance with medication regimens. Only this ward and the admission unit had access to seclusion or restraint. The ward functioned as an open or closed space, depending on the characteristics and behaviors of the patients at any given time. The medical, behavioral, and educational foci of the admission unit was retained on this ward, although with a longer term approach, such as placing emphasis on acquisition and maintenance of basic social skills and activities of daily living rather than on stabilization of symptoms and coping with abstinence.

The two remaining residential units were mixed (major mental illnesses responsive to medication and personality disorders) with open ward environments. The patient mix on each was monitored and controlled by selecting appropriate candidates to improve the ward mix from the admission unit, or patient transfer from one ward to the other. Such transfers were usually related to a specific patient behavior in regard to others, that is, an inappropriate counterproductive sexual or romantic relationship, a unresolvable interpersonal conflict, or a countertherapeutic alliance with one or more patients on that unit. Each of these wards provided modalities tailored to their patients' specific needs. One ward prided itself on exceptional work with highly defended, moderately psychopathic patients and tended to have a higher proportion of these people in its mix. Uncovering or insight-oriented therapies, expressive therapies, cognitive restructuring programs, and transition to formal education or community work activities were centered on these two wards. These activities took place in either treatment or common spaces or in areas designed for shared program component treatments. For example, a highly confrontational group therapy was provided in the shared component space to highly defended patients from both of the mixed open wards and from the community living ward.

The community living ward was located in another area of the large Saint Elizabeths Hospital campus. This ward was similar to the community residential facilities (CRFs) to which most patients would eventually be discharged. Although this ward was on the hospital grounds and therefore had access to medical support and was familiar to previously hospitalized patients, it was run like a loosely supervised rooming house. The ward housed the preparation for aftercare component of the program, which included simulation of community housing, alumni activities, and program based AA and NA groups. Patients on the community living ward were expected to maintain a schedule of 35 hours of staff-approved, structured activities consisting of a combination of paid or volunteer work, school, therapies, self-help tasks, and religious or spiritual activities.

Each ward, regardless of the program component centered there, had a graded privilege system. Privileges were related to the respective phase of recovery targeted by that component. Patients were awarded privileges based on the staff's assessment of their current phase of recovery, their ability to follow program rules and requirements, and endorsement of the treatment team. As in most treatment programs, removal or award of privileges was often tied to behavioral interventions. In addition, individual behavior was related to group consequences in several ways. For example, finding any illicit substance on one of the open wards could result in the ward being temporary locked so that all participants could be searched and informally screened for mental status.

In addition, patient privilege meetings and ward rounds were used to grant privileges and establish staff consensus on the progress of each patient. Meetings between program components were held once per week to discuss general issues and to assess the readiness of individual patients to move to the next step. In these meetings, staff members occasionally expressed the view that having patients move between treatment components was counterproductive. They usually felt that the loss of continuity in treatment, which sometimes occurred in the move from one component to another (primarily staffed by treatment personnel relatively unfamiliar to the patient), or the disruption of relationships between patients could delay or abort progress. Often, countertransference issues or the desire to maintain a stable, familiar caseload contributed to these feelings. For the most part, however, staff were very accepting of the increased assessment and engagement opportunities presented by the multiple component system. Patients had to provide evidence for behavioral and attitudinal changes when they requested a move. When staff initiated a move, the patient was consulted and later given the reasons for the final decision, including an assessment of their current recovery level. To build on what patients had learned in AA and NA, these explanations were most often expressed as equivalents to step work. Patients involved in step work often understood the ebb and flow of progress within recovery and were usually less resistant to understanding and using information that the staff conveyed about their current phase of recovery.

Selecting and Improving Modalities

Dual diagnosis programs must be willing to utilize innovative treatment methods and should have an active evaluation and research component to evaluate such innovations. Group treatments that are educational, supportive, expressive, uncovering, or a combination of these approaches are the stock in trade of substance abuse programs. Individual therapy is an important adjunct in dual diagnosis work, as are individualized case management services. Family therapy is perhaps essential in almost every case.

Relaxation techniques, meditation, and other experiential techniques, physical exercise, and values education and clarification are well worth investigating as options in a dual diagnosis program. The PASA program, for example, reduced its seclusion rooms from five to two by converting three of the areas to meditation rooms and training interested staff and selected patients in Transcendental Meditation (TM) through a grant that funded this training for substance-abusing patients. Although the number of patients involved was small, data collected on them indicated a trend toward decreased stress and a general improvement in symptomatology. All patients and staff, including the program director and those not involved in the TM grant project, were encouraged to use these rooms for solitary relaxation, religious meditation, or for timeout under stress. Incidence of violence and the need for seclusion or restraint decreased significantly. On one occasion when one of the rooms was used as a temporary housing assignment, patients insisted that it be reinstated as a meditation space. Seclusion rooms were eventually required only on the ward for chronic patients with major mental disorders and the admissions ward where many were completing detoxification or adjusting to program requirements.

Often, innovation in treatment simply means finding a new use for or new way to conceptualize already available resources and activities. Treatments must also be culturally relevant and ethnically sensitive. Another innovative treatment program at PASA involved patient participation in a gospel choir group. This counted as a treatment rather than a religious activity on the staff-approved list of structured activities. Many of the patients were of African-American ancestry and a Protestant-evangelical religious background. It was hoped that the participation in a music group with an interested local church would provide continuity with familiar cultural and spiritual themes that would support an abstinence ethic, as well as provide social support during reentry into the community. Several of the psychologists associated with the program also hypothesized that the catharsis, state tuning, stimulation, and stimulus modulation function provided by this activity would give some additional resistance to relapse. Participation in a positively oriented rap group would have met the same analysis. Staff members were convinced that positive results were produced, but unfortunately there was no formal evaluation. Innovative use and conceptualization of activities and connections already available and attractive to patients maximize patient involvement and extend program resources.

Staff Selection, Training, and Development

A reasonable expectation of any staff member in an intensive treatment program is that he or she be able to maintain a high degree of emotional stability or equilibrium in the workplace, which implies some minimal degree of adjustment in the employee's own life situation. Ziegler-Driscoll and colleagues (1980) identified three other selection criteria for dual diagnosis work staff. The first criterion relates to the personal characteristics of the prospective staff member and includes an evaluation of:

1. Empathic capability
2. Nonjudgmental, accepting attitude
3. Communication skills, especially congruence of verbal and nonverbal communications
4. Stable boundaries between self and others
5. Absence of an intimidating or overdemanding interpersonal style.
6. Comfort with setting appropriate limits.

Many of these factors can be the result of prior training or clinical experience rather than personality style. Prior experience with a broad spectrum of clients and settings is highly recommended by Ziegler-Driscoll and colleagues, who also recommend that this experience should be accompanied by a motivation to improve one's professional status and not simply to serve in a helping capacity. If helping is the primary motive, especially if the prospective staff member is not in personal recovery, vigilance concerning countertransference issues and suitability based on several of the traits cited above would be appropriate.

Training for staff selected in a dual diagnosis program should include as goals the development of role competencies according to Ziegler-Driscoll and colleagues (1980). These roles include student, teacher, colleague, leader, counselor, community liaison worker, supervisor, and change agents. To this list should be added the ability to function as a case manager or system negotiator for the patient, the ability to work cooperatively in a team, and the ability to work toward organizationally approved goals and objectives that may have only limited personal endorsement. Also implied in the idea of dual diagnosis work is the ability to view events and dynamics as multiply determined and to understand them from more than one viewpoint simultaneously.

Once staff are selected, their development is no longer an individual matter. Regularly held staff development activities are a must in any treatment setting, but this is especially true in dual diagnosis programs. Academic courses, discussion groups, and individual study and supervision designed to develop skills and understanding related to dual diagnosis patients are highly recommended.

Brown and Backer (1988) identified ten aspects of an effective dual diagnosis professional training and education program:

1. Knowledge and skill of mental health professions on specific substance abuse issues.
2. Team teaching by mental health and substance abuse specialists.
3. Specific topics related to substance abuse introduced in the curriculum. Topics such as addictive personality, multiple addictions, assessment instruments for dual disordered patients, and suicidality in dual diagnosis patients.
4. Participation in self-help groups: AA, Alliance for the Mentally Ill, Alanon, etc.
5. Rotation through drug and alcohol treatment facilities during internships or practica.
6. Changing attitudes toward working with dual diagnosis patients.
7. Team teaching with family members, delivering "knowledge packages" to the involved family.
8. Establishment of task forces and interdisciplinary training models at universities.
9. Noncategorical conceptualizations that deemphasize diagnosis.
10. Rapid knowledge transfer, including computer information exchanges and informal publication methods.

They also identified obstacles to implementing such training. These included not enough respect for different perspectives and knowledge bases within each delivery system; "pseudo-collaborations" between systems based on temporary needs, such as to staff a program or gain funding; reluctance of delivery sectors to relinquish or share power, constituencies, budgets; and fundamental disagreement about the use of medication in ongoing treatment.

Use of Self-Help and Volunteers

The PASA program arranged for special AA and NA groups to be lead by community volunteers and staff in stable recovery. In addition, AA and NA meetings known to staff in recovery were groomed to deal with psychiatric patients on a routine basis. Patients were instructed in the use of AA and NA in the first stage of treatment and were expected at each stage thereafter to verbalize the stage of step work in which they were currently engaged. Thus, involvement in self-help groups was viewed as a parallel and coordinated treatment to those offered by the staff. Since several key staff were also part of the local recovery community, an intimate relationship evolved between formal treatment and self-help activities. Although this is clearly only one way of relating to self-help groups and the special category of AA and NA, every dual diagnosis program should take an active stand in regard to participation in such activities. At the very least, verification of frequency of attendance should be expected from patients who have agreed to participate in their treatment contracts.

Although religious volunteers and even students in training for the various mental health or substance abuse professions must be carefully screened and oriented, they are also an invaluable source of support, new ideas, and resources in the community. For example, PASA had the advantage of a highly motivated, well-trained chaplain intern completing his training as a substance abuse counselor. He was able to provide reality testing and orientation to both patients seeking magical solutions and to community religious volunteers who were sometimes prone to offer quick-fix miracle cures. Improper supervision and direction of volunteers, however well meaning, can be very defeating and demeaning to the paid staff's attempts at a coordinated, consistent treatment program. Volunteers and students should be taken on only if the appropriate quality and quantity of supervision is available.

Outplacement and Referral Development

Programs must develop a sound grounding in community housing and social service resources. Dual diagnosis programs should be prepared to provide community consultation services to other programs and community resources, and highly proactive case management services must be made available to patients who are placed in residential settings. Housing resources are scarce today for any patient. Dual diagnosis patients are often explicitly excluded from some CRFs. The continual involvement of the program with a housing site is usually necessary to maintain the site as a referral source. The development of "wet shelters" with mental health orientations such as those described by Levy and Mann (1988) is essential to provide a humane way of preventing patients who refuse to comply with treatment requirements from destroying the treatment milieu. At the same time, "wet shelters" help the program to maintain some contact with these patients and provide a source of reliable information about them when they return for another episode of treatment.

Formal or informal interagency agreements regarding assessment, referral, and treatment of dual diagnosis cases require considerable effort and aplomb on the part of program administrators. Such agreements can be established in a manner that mutually enhance both parties and improve service delivery to patients. An initial start toward appropriate referrals and interagency agreements is in training opportunities provided to staff of other agencies by dual diagnosis program staff. Offering several months of on-site training to a substance abuse program's counseling staff on a rotating basis, for example, builds an understanding of program goals, methods, and appropriate referrals.

Outreach and Self-Referral Activities

It makes good sense to involve dual diagnosis patients as early as possible in appropriate treatment. One way of doing this is building in self-referral opportunities for dual diagnosis patients in general psychiatric settings. Kofoed and Key (1988) advocate using any psychiatric hospitalization as an opportunity to recruit, indoctrinate, and motivate patients for substance abuse treatment. They use a 30-minute, twice-weekly substance abuse group experience (SAGE) held on the psychiatric ward to provide self-referral opportunities and psychoeducational services. Conceptualized as an adjunct to AA and NA, SAGE also has a 15-minute break in each session to accommodate the limited energy and attention span of psychiatric patients. SAGE is co-led by therapists and patients in recovery. Some component of substance abuse orientation and education should exist on every inpatient treatment unit and can be easily modified for use in outpatient settings.

Community Case Management Services

Intensive case management has increasingly become the tool for enabling mental health systems to begin to realize the vision of an effective delivery system that is less centered on the institution. Specially trained workers with small case loads have proven invaluable in providing patient advocacy and helping patients to negotiate complex systems to obtain basic resources and services. Case managers provide early crisis and preventative interventions, help to maintain patient engagement during all phases of recovery, and can ensure the optimal use of rare resources, such as hospitalization or supervised housing. Although this chapter advances the superiority of integrated or hybrid models of treatment based in dedicated dual diagnosis programs with an inpatient or residential component, these programs do not have to be dominated by the program center, and this center does not have to be housed in the residential component. Instead, the goal should be a careful balance of centralization and decentralization, with most services being delivered outside the program center in the community to patients and their families (or surrogates) or in residential settings linked to the center by informal agreements, staff consultations, or staff sharing across programs. Coordinated or linkage model programs that emphasize parallel treatments can deliver superior results over hybrid programs, if the case management component is strong in the former and weak in the latter. Long-term family contact and even formal family therapy can usually be accommodated only within an aggressive case management model. This is especially true in the case of patients and families with minority backgrounds, low incomes, or single-parent responsibilities, for whom the practical strain and distant professionalized aura of the office visit quickly become tiresome.

Many mental health professionals who are unfamiliar with dually diagnosed patients may initially demonstrate a lack of interest and devaluation of case management services. This attitude can be changed by requiring all staff to have some level of case management responsibility, even if this means for some having only responsibility for the clinical supervision of the case managers. The model of case management is somewhat more congruent with the self-help and sponsorship models familiar to staff in recovery from addiction, and these staff members will usually meet the idea with less resistance. Case management can be better understood by these workers as a professionalized and aggressive form of sponsorship and support. Whatever method is used to allocate and train staff, it is of crucial importance that all members have an appreciation of these services as the most effective preserver of the progress in any phase of treatment and the likely source of new assessment data and the early warning, early intervention system for almost all dynamic change in patients over the long haul of treatment.

ISSUES IN PROGRAM ADMINISTRATION

Program design and development interact and overlap with administration. Essentially, programs can develop (or fail to develop) only through administrative execution of philosophies, goals, policies, and procedures. The realization of any programmatic vision is always imperfectly executed by the actions and omissions of staff members and leadership. This realization process meanders through myriad formal and intentional processes and through powerful covert and unacknowledged (even unconscious) pathways.

Routine administrative work most often takes the form of applying clinical and political instincts, common sense, good judgment, and a few general organizational and procedural principles to specific cases and situations. The higher art of program administration, however, could be defined as planning for and dealing with those aspects of service delivery that should not occur if design and development were accomplishable tasks. Management by exception, management by way of creative divergence from established parameters, and management of crises or emergent opportunities all fit this kind of half tongue-in-cheek definition. Several areas of special difficulty predictably face the dual diagnosis program administrator and can be dealt with only partially by program design. A confluence of problems— stemming from the dual diagnosis syndrome itself, from the two treatment cultures in conflict and partial communication, and from a delivery system that remains for all practical purposes bifurcated and categorical—makes these issues more the province of dual diagnosis programs than others, although the issues are increasingly relevant to the management of almost all treatment programs to some extent. Patient-centered issues include patient selection and discharge as boundary management, handling violent patients who have a clear mental status, and working with the homeless patient or prevention of homelessness for the dually diagnosed person. On the levels of staff relations and the larger systems are the recurrent controversies surrounding medication management, the difficulties of developing integrated dual diagnosis treatment teams, and the never-ending task of shaping the culture of a ward and a program as a whole. Each of these issues is discussed briefly below to clarify the need for continual management and administrative vigilance.

Patient Selection, Progress, and Discharge as Organizational and Treatment Issues

The application of program admissions, progress, and discharge criteria is perhaps more crucial in dual diagnosis programs than in many other mental health settings. This is because of the fairly precise assessments and judgments that are required at more than one stage of the treatment process and because of the almost inevitable emphasis that the staff place on having patients whose problems and motivation are appropriate to their particular treatment mission. Therefore, an intake assessment team with representation from several professional and paraprofessional backgrounds involved in routine admissions is highly recommended. The team can be led or organized administratively by a senior mental health professional to ensure that all crucial aspects of preliminary assessment and admission are met and not compromised by the team's need to limit or encourage a given type of admission. Movement from one component to another (such as inpatient treatment to residential housing arrangements) also should be conducted in a responsible manner, respecting that the boundaries between components must be permeable while maintaining essential integrity. Primary control of the boundary should be with those who manage and work in that system component.

Violence and Disruptive Acting Out

Violent acting out is the most damaging activity to occur in a treatment setting. Dual diagnosis patients often rationalize violent behavior, not expecting consequences to themselves or official or legal sanction. Staff can become more bitterly disappointed and divided around violence and sexual predation in the treatment setting than almost any other problem. Prevention of violence requires specific training for the staff to recognize danger signs and initiate early intervention. In addition, solidarity of staff and administration in their attitudes toward violence must be nurtured and communicated clearly to patients. This message is most clearly communicated by prosecuting those patients who break the law in inpatient settings either by possessing illegal drugs or committing violence. Obviously, an institution or agency will carefully choose the cases that are handled in this manner, electing to confine, restrict, or discharge some patients without prosecution, depending on the patient's condition and evidence of criminal intent. At the very least, an executive level committee that reviews every incident of violence against staff or patients must be established in any dual diagnosis program.

Homelessness and the Residential Spectrum

A significant percentage of homeless persons is both mentally ill and chemically dependent. About one-third suffer from severe mental illness, up to 40 percent have alcohol problems, and perhaps another 20 percent have problems with other drugs (Drake et al. 1991). Conversely, without external intervention, many dual diagnosis patients will become homeless due to exacerbation of symptoms, lapses in financial responsibility, or discharge from a treatment setting to an unsupported, untenable housing arrangement. Many homeless patients with substance abuse also have schizoid or avoidant personality traits and a very fragile sense of self-esteem (Bebout and Harris 1990). Such individuals are particularly resistant to mental health treatments, which they view as stigmatizing or which they have experienced in the past as a setup for failure. Addiction-oriented interventions and self-help activities may at times be more acceptable and ego-syntonic to such individuals and may successfully penetrate their isolation and denial of need. However, treatment services are often sought by the homeless dual diagnosis patient more for the housing, security, and basic physical needs that the environment provides for the treatment itself. Homeless dually diagnosed patients are, nonetheless, unlikely to have received recent treatment for either of their disorders (Koegel and Burnam 1987). Even after a successful treatment episode, these patients are more likely to return to an institutional environment if housing and other amenities are not provided in a noninstitutional setting.

Once homeless individuals are engaged in treatment, full residential services are necessary to support progress (Pepper 1985). Several housing characteristics must be considered. The following analysis was based on the combined experience of providing treatment, case management, and residential placement services to dual diagnosis patients in both Washington, D.C., and New Hampshire (urban and rural environments):

> Any residential continuum for the mentally ill must incorporate a range of options that vary along several dimensions simultaneously: pressure for growth (versus

maintenance), level of demand, degree of structure, and length of stay (transition versus long-term). For the dually diagnosed there must be programs with varying levels of tolerance for substance use, ranging from unlimited use to limited use to total abstinence. Component programs may include a stratified apartment program as well as a series of supervised group homes with different lengths of stay: thirty-day crisis residences, intermediate-stay transitional houses, and long-stay group homes with significant levels of structure and support but minimal expectations regarding movement toward more independence. [Klein et al. 1991, p. 102]

Klein and colleagues also identified three major issues in housing for the dually diagnosed patient: safety and security, inclusiveness, and time limits. Access to safe and secure housing is sometimes seen as a priority that competes with the need for treatment-oriented, abstinence-mandated housing. These authors also recommend the availability of residential options with liberal housing rules, abstinence housing for patients who can tolerate this demand, and other settings where gentle confrontation and limit setting provide structure for those less advanced in recovery. Inclusiveness of housing access requires the staff to be sensitive to the full range of dual diagnosis problems so that restrictive discharge criteria do not perpetuate residential instability and convert lapse into relapse and treatment failure. Regarding time limitations, administrative transfers and moves should be avoided because of the stress they cause. Moves should respond to clinical needs. Because dual diagnosis patients demonstrate slow progress and often regress to earlier levels of functioning and behavior, transitional housing arrangements may be required for longer periods of time than for other patients, and programs must maintain a long-term care perspective.

Medication Management

All members of a treatment staff must thoroughly understand the model of medication management adopted by the program and its psychiatry staff and why such a model has been chosen out of several that exist. The model of physician-directed treatment of all aspects of care is increasingly untenable even in programs that prefer the medical model of mental illness. The high cost of psychiatric services results in only limited involvement of the psychiatrist with the ongoing psychosocial treatment of the dual diagnosis patient. As a result, the patient may resist either the medical or psychological treatment components, which can increase the tendency of some patients to split the psychiatrist from the rest of the staff. The nonprofessional staff usually have the most contact hours with a patient. The nonphysician therapist will often have the most intensive intimate contact with the patient. The individual therapist will perhaps have more direct interactive contact minutes than any other person in the patient's life, before, during, or after treatment. Despite these realities of contact hours and direct influence on the patient, responsibility for a suicide or failure of psychotropic medication will fall exclusively on the medical staff.

The split model of medication management, wherein the prescribing physician is by intention someone other than the patient's therapist, was developed to prevent any complications that could arise from the same person being medicator and psychotherapist (Gitlin 1990). The split model must now be applied to a whole range of settings simply because the psychiatric staff is spread thin due to budgetary restraints. Gitlin lists several criteria for evaluating the appropriateness of a given psychopharmacologist for working within the split model. These include:

1. General clinical competence
2. Acceptance and respect for psychotherapy
3. Specific psychopharmacological competence
4. Comfort with the split model
5. Capacity to communicate with therapists
6. Capacity and willingness to educate patients
7. Personal style.

The split model of medication management depends on all staff members holding realistic expectations of medication results on patient behavior. Also, a basic awareness of the psychodynamics of psychopharmacology should be propagated among the entire staff. Educating patients in the basic understanding of their diagnosis, the addictive process, the goals of treatment, and the nature of their possible treatments will greatly enhance compliance to medication regimens. The treatment staff, especially those in recovery themselves, must understand and accept that medication is usually involved in the treatment of choice for the major mental illnesses and that it can be helpful in making detoxification safer, less painful, and less medically complicated. The role of medication in controlling craving and diminishing relapse must be understood as an important temporary support of recovery processes The staff psychiatrist is ideally qualified to assist in providing these understandings and in guiding realistic attitudes toward medication management. In addition to an interest in such work, the psychiatrist must be allowed the time and structured access to patients and staff to provide this support to the program.

Developing and Maintaining Ward Milieu and Culture

A discussion of developing a program or ward culture and its desired nature could easily cover several chapters. Therapeutic community-based programs will view this element as the crucial change mechanism in treatment, much more important than medication or formal psychotherapies. Dual diagnosis workers in recovery or from the substance abuse treatment sector will be more familiar with the therapeutic community than will those with mental health backgrounds. Because this model and its variants are so pervasive, they must be understood by all staff in order to clearly communicate perceptions and expectations of the evolving culture of any specific program. This communication will provide a basis for designing interventions to shape the program culture.

Drug treatment in therapeutic communities originated with Synanon, founded in 1958 by Charles Dederich. Although there is a large degree of agreement on the general approach to treatment among advocates of the therapeutic community, there is some disagreement about specific issues, notably the orientation toward resocialization, and duration and phases of treatment, particularly reentry. These programs are loosely based on AA; they now emphasize personal encounter and confrontation and originally stressed permanent participation. They follow a model of addiction that fits the antisocial or heavily defended narcissistic personality more than other dual diagnosis cases.

The basic goal of therapeutic communities is for drug abusers to undergo a complete change in lifestyle: abstinence, elimination of criminal behavior, development of a work ethic, self reliance, and personal honesty. The programs rely heavily on the use of graduates and peer counselors; they are highly structured and participants must account for nearly every moment. Clearly demarcated stages exist with each indicating increased individual responsibility and liberty. Work duties are established within the community confines and only advanced members are permitted to work outside in the larger society. Authority is more concentrated in these programs than in most mental health cultures. Expectations concerning desired or unacceptable behaviors tend to be explicit, specific, and concrete, and rely much less on the subjective interpretation of general rules of conduct than is often found in mental health programs.

Proponents of the TC (Therapeutic Community) approach to substance abuse treatment, such as DeLeon and Rosenthal, feel that remission can be achieved only if all aspects of lifestyle, attitudes, and behavior that contributed to the drug abuse can be changed. The programs are essentially long-term intensive communal experiences, including group therapy supported with other appropriate services and activities. These activities are often geared toward a major therapeutic role for paraprofessionals who have had experiences similar to those of the residents. Peers provide most of the interventions, with 20 percent of activity time guided by formally trained counselors and only 5 percent by physicians and nurses. Participants are expected to maintain a commitment to reenter the large society through the therapeutic community subculture, meaning that independence from the TC is not a legitimate goal. McLaughlin and Pepper (1990) report the successful modification of the therapeutic community for the treatment of dual diagnosis patients by integrating the TC concept with the less confrontational NA and AA traditions. Harbor House, a forty-five bed program in The Bronx, New York, sponsored by Argus Community, a drug treatment agency, opened in 1985 to serve homeless dual diagnosis patients. The program relies on the integrated or hybrid model of design, with a multidisciplinary treatment team. Twelve Step recovery programs are also integrated into the Harbor House milieu. Abstinence is mandated and drug use is a cause for discharge, as is severe exacerbation of psychosis. Planned discharge is after 18 to 20 months of treatment. The program is very expensive, however— $35,000 per resident per year (one-half the cost of inpatient hospitalization for the year) with only one in three admitted patients completing the program.

Dual diagnosis patients with major mental disorders or with symptomatic dependence have better results in a cultural intervention that is less intense than the therapeutic community and more tolerant of noncompliance. The TC intensity is poorly tolerated by fragile individuals, and the gains accomplished in the TC model are often not generalized by these patients to outside settings. However, the experience gained from the TC model and its variants can be applied to less intensive settings by using the model as a comparison for paying close attention to the program therapeutic milieu as a cultural intervention with the purpose of gradual resocialization.

Whatever the treatment orientation, the administration, clinical and nonprofessional staff, and patients must have open channels to communicate their views about the quality and direction of the ward climate. At the very least, the climate or culture should have the following characteristics:

1. The culture must foster both individual responsibility and responsibility to the group. Behavior should always be viewed as related to personal identity and communication to the group of interpersonal attitudes.
2. The culture must encourage behavior congruent with recovery goals and compatible with treatment activities.
3. The culture must be capable of identifying events, activities, dynamics, or specific behaviors of individuals that are disruptive or unacceptable.
4. The previous items imply explicit expectations, rules, and guidelines for the conduct of administrators, staff, and patients. The potential for significant positive or negative consequences should exist, contingent upon behavior. At a minimum these guidelines must specifically address the management of lapses, relapse, general noncompliance, violence, and sexual acting out by patients. Guidelines for staff should include unacceptable off-duty *public* behavior, relapse intervention for staff, and professional ethics. The staff should also be made aware of exemplary behavior of its members through incentive programs.
5. The milieu must contain an open forum for dealing with disruptive elements and conflicts, within each structural level (e.g., an open forum of patients on a ward, of staff in a treatment component, etc.).
6. The program must have an officially sanctioned mechanism for resolving conflict between structural elements (e.g., between therapists and nursing staff on a ward). Unlike the previous characteristic, this mechanism will usually require a level of supervision above that of the conflict.

7. The program must develop traditions, ceremonies, and an historical awareness that will help to provide continuity and coherence over time and allow for informal disposition of conflicts and tensions.
8. The program as a whole must have the capacity to recruit, indoctrinate, reward, discipline, and remove members from either the staff or patient membership.

Team Development

Staff in a comprehensive, integrated dual diagnosis program must be flexible, well trained, and from a range of professional and paraprofessional backgrounds. The administrators and staff must be prepared for dealing with the problems arising from the conflict of the two cultures of substance abuse treatment communities, that is, conflicts between staff in recovery from their own addictions or illnesses (and/or those of their family members), versus those staff whose interest, motivation, and perspective are more clinical or professional in origin. Training of professionals in dual diagnosis work and providing links between these two cultures should be seen as part of the essential mission of these programs.

Authority for treatment decisions should be centered in the team as a whole. This is not a purely head counting democratic affair, since sound staff development should be based on the concept of natural and rational authority: people who truly know more about a specific aspect of care (by reason of experience or training) or who will have to deal directly with the consequences of a bad decision should be heeded. When individual team members have special responsibility and expertise (such as the psychiatrist in regard to medication management), it should be understood that their responsibility to the treatment team as a whole is also increased accordingly, both in regard to actively listening to staff concerns, providing clear communication of the rationale for any truly unilateral actions, and being available to share in the consequences of these actions for the team as a whole.

In addition to avoiding the problem of the two cultures, dual diagnosis programs must avoid splits between professional and nonprofessional staff and along differences in financial compensation. A common attitude toward nonprofessional staff held by professionals is that they are prone to be less objective and less comprehensive in their views. Alfonso Paredes (1981) expressed this view explicitly:

One important feature might affect the services provided by the alcoholism services enterprise: the system has become increasingly dominated by paraprofessionals. This has important implications. Paraprofessionals usually adopt an intuitive, deductive style in their work. They perceive empirical data as obscure and irrelevant, especially when they conflict with intuitive and experiential understanding. Professionals, on the other hand, tend to adopt an objective, cognitive style and are more likely to respect deductive and empirical reasoning. They possess the skills to interpret and evaluate data. In a system where paraprofessionals are dominant, treatment might be prescribed more in terms of social biases rather than following a scientific assessment. Such a system is bound to become narrowly categorical. [p. 122]

A counterclaim could be made by paraprofessionals that professional staff tend not to understand the experiential side of recovery, have no understanding of AA or NA (two major recovery disciplines), make stunning generalizations based only on the in-treatment behavior of addicts and patients, and form conclusions based on abysmally small samples of patient behavior. Paraprofessionals often view professional staff as co-dependency or enabling in regard to patients. Some dual diagnosis professionals have recognized the wisdom of heeding such observations. According to Kaufman (1989):

> The concept of codependency gives the therapist a frame of reference for changing his or her antitherapeutic countertransference reactions, for example, the over-protective, over-controlling, or over-involved therapist can relate these behaviors to codependency and change them through self-knowledge as well as through Al-Anon or, where appropriate, Adult Children of Alcoholics groups. [p. 17]

The Chemical Dependency Treatment staff at Cambridge Hospital in Massachusetts are all required to attend Al-Anon meetings regularly because it is felt that co-dependency issues are so common in hospital staff working regularly with substance abusers (Vaillant 1981) that such a level of involvement probably also decreases the gulf of understanding and acceptance between staff from the two cultures.

Appendix A

TAT Protocol Illustrating Failures in Self-Regulation

SUBJECT DESCRIPTION

Female, 38-year-old depressed clerical worker. Sees herself as having an "eclectic personality," i.e., creative but with mood swings and depression. Her written self-description (tester elicited) mentions guilt and shame three times, especially in regard to feelings related to her father, whom she described as offering "unconditional love." The patient also spontaneously wrote of the meaning of her father's death in her self-description. This written narrative included a mixture of childlike drawings and symbols within cursive writing that also contained printed capitals for emphasis. Diagnostic impression: Bipolar disorder with borderline/histrionic personality dynamics (see cycloid-affective spectrum, Chapter 7). Parentheses within the narratives indicate tester queries or prominent nonverbal behaviors.

TAT RESPONSES

Card

1. This young boy has just been told that he has to do much better in his music practicing, otherwise he will never fulfill the potential that he keeps being told he has. He doesn't believe that he has potential. The last part would be, uhm, he would decide to practice a little more to please his mother, that being the person who told him about his potential. But it's very important to, not that he will go back to his practice, not so much out of his love for music, but out of love for his mother and to please her.

SFSR Scores:1,1,0,0,1,1,1,1,0,0,0

15. Oh yes, I recognize this. I don't know where I've seen it, uh. This man has just come from a nighttime funeral in a quaint old town where not many people are Catholic. He is visiting a departed friend who was Catholic and is feeling badly because he noticed that besides the one he is in front of, there are only two other crucifixes. What'll happen afterwards is he will desecrate some of the headstones but not the crucifixes. He's also a very interverted, secretive, and uhm, sexually repressed man.

SFSR Scores:3,3,1,2,0,0,3,1,0,3,3

Card

14. What just happened previously is this artist, the man in the picture, has just finished, uhm, doing a, uhm, one of his best paintings and he worked all night uhm . . . he's exhausted but serene because of uh, he feels he put his heart and soul into this painting and he opened the window just to put himself back into the real world, look out into the world. I don't know why I feel this, but the next thing he's going to do is to stare at the painting for several hours, go outside, he lives in a city and he's going to attack a woman and molest her, not to rob her but to physically molest her.

SFSR Scores:3,3,3,0,1,3,3,3,0,3,3

12. OK, what just previously happened is a man who uhm, hasn't seen his son in, say, 20 years, almost since the day he was born. He's just found out that the boy is dying and can't be cured. He uhm, took the boy out of the hospital and brought him to this room, like a hotel room, and sat with him as the boy was dying. The boy never regained consciousness and died. (Thinking or Feeling?) He is thinking, well he's thinking, "I wish I'd been there when he was growing up. I wish I knew what kind of man he'd turned out to be" and he's feeling extreme guilt and shame. As soon as he leaves the boy in the room, he's going to commit suicide.

SFSR Scores:3,3,0,1,3,1,3,3,0,3,3

3BM. This woman just previously tried to slash her wrist with a scissor, being that which it looks like to me, a scissor. She's just tried to slash her wrist. She was unsuccessful and feels more of a failure than she did before she tried to kill herself and right after this she tries when she pulls herself together, which she does, she's going to find out that when she goes into her local grocery store to buy cigarettes, she discovers that the lottery ticket she bought the day before came in and she won a great amount of money. (Thinking or Feeling?) Before or after? In general, she's acting on a feeling level, not a thinking one. She feels invisible, that's the word, invisible.

SFSR Scores:3,2,3,2,2,1,3,2,3,3,3

Card

3. This is easy. What just happened is uhm, there's a little girl playing the piano in her mother's living room, which the mother always tells her to stay out, but she loves the piano. The mother heard the music, came barging through the

door. The little girl turned around when she heard the door open and neither said a word to each other because the look that the mother gave the daughter told her that she did wrong and to leave the room. Immediately afterwards the child goes outside into the woods and sits under a tree and cries, alone. (Thinking or Feeling?) Rejected, the kind that a child feels that really hurts because they don't understand it the way adults might and her one other feeling is that her mother must be jealous of her musical talent.

SFSR Scores:3,3,1,2,3,3,3,3,0,3,1

10. OK, what just happened is two people who met only a few hours before decided that because they both admitted to being lonely and alone, they consented to uh, be physically close, holding and touching and attempting to have inter- course, but it was unsuccessful. Immediately afterward would say that uh, the man promised to visit her again and often, but he never did and the woman's feelings were very trusting and she believed he would contact her again. She believed him.

SFSR Scores:3,3,1,1,3,3,3,3,1,3,1

13MF. What just previously happened was a typical family man picked up a woman in a bar. They went to her apartment, it's not a motel room, its where she lives. She's uhm, very poor, just getting by so uhm, what had happened was he asked her if he could undress her first, uhm, it got him sexually aroused as he was about to uhm, take off his own clothes, she mentioned money, that it would cost him, but she did it in a kind way, not a harsh way. He became enraged. He said, "I've never paid for it in my life" and then strangled her. Now he's standing here, he is feeling no remorse for the loss of another human being, but rather concern for himself and he decides to just leave her there and he goes. That's what happens afterwards, he just leaves. He did pull the sheet up partway over the body.

SFSR Scores:3,3,2,1,3,3,3,3,1,3,3

16. Uhm, alright this is simple. OK, flying a beautiful, impossible blue sky and I'm flying through that sky. The higher up I go the easier it is to fly. I think I'm uhm, catching warm currents, I don't have to flap my arms. I'm able to use the warm air currents to stay aloft. I'm really happy. I'm singing. The lower I fly the harder it gets for me to get back up again. I have to work harder to get up again and I can tell you where it is, it's Scotland.

SFSR Scores:0,0,3,3,0,3,0,2,0,0,2

Appendix B

Arousal-Induced Shifts in Modal Psychological Functioning—Depressed Substance Abusers

FEMALE, AGE 36

Card 1

(Long pause) OK—umm—it's a young boy whose father wants him to learn to play the violin, but the child wants to go out and play with his friends. He doesn't realize it now—but—he's mad at his father, but one day he learns to play beautifully and thanks his father for making him practice. (Thinking?) I would like to go out and play ball with my friends instead of practice this violin.

Card 13MF

This woman got into an argument with this man and he killed her in a fit of rage. He can't believe he did it (laughs). Now he's sorry, he realizes he has to live without her. (Led up?) He thought she did something, but she didn't, he was wrong. (Outcome?) He'll have to live with this guilt. (Feeling?) Loss—very empty—that he has to live without her—despair. (Thinking?) He realizes what he did, he realizes he'll be alone and won't have her again—to touch or anything—and he did it with his own hand.

Low: 4,4,4,4,4,4,4,4,4,3 Mode = 4, or Oedipal
High: 1,2,2,1,2,1,2,2,2,3 Mode = 2, or Borderline

MALE, AGE 38

Card 1

My son and his violin, we have a 6-month-old baby whose parents are splitting up, he is in a situation he doesn't want to be in but can't do anything about it, when he's older he'll be able to do something about it, he's wondering what is going to happen, where am I going from here? (Feeling?) Hopefully, everything turns out all right, he looks like my son's age, he will get . . . whether it has to do with the violin, what he wants.

Card 13MF

This is somebody obviously distraught about the death of someone he cares about, I don't see him killing her, he found her dead and is distraught, how will I live without her? What will I do now? (Thinking and feeling?) Looks like the girl's dead, her body's rigid, he's distraught, whether it is his wife, sister, or close friend, thinking what will I do now?

Low: 3,2,2,2,3,3,2,2,2,3 Mode = 2, or Borderline/Narcissistic
High: 2,2,2,2,2,3,2,2,2,2 Mode = 2, or Borderline

FEMALE, AGE 23

Card 1

This is a child and he's deciding whether or not he should pick up the violin or choose another hobby. His parents, what led up to it is his parents asked him to start the violin and what else? What led up to it is his parents decided that this is the thing for him and he's deciding whether this is the thing he wants. (Feelings?) His feelings are . . . he wants to do what his parents want him to do. He just wants to make them happy. (Outcome?) He goes with it.

Card 13FM

OK, this man is feeling very sad. He got a call from a friend to go to a mutual friend's apartment. When he walked in, the woman was lying unconscious. He doesn't know what to do. He thinks it was his fault because he sold her the drugs she took. She's gonna die. (Pause) OK, what am I missing? (stares at card intently). Let's say also he loved her. (Outcome?) She died. OK, she died and he commits suicide.

Low: 3,3,2,2,4,4,3,2,2,3 Mode = 2, or Narcissistic/Borderline
High: 1,2,2,1,1,1,2,2,1,3 Mode = 2, or Borderline/Psychotic

Appendix C

Summary of an EMP

Summary	Comments

EM 1

I remember a time of total darkness and total deafness; I'm lying in my crib, my body ablaze with pain and burning. I cannot see; I cannot hear; I am utterly alone. No one touches me or reaches out; there is no one.

I have been told that when I was 15 months old I had German measles, which seriously affected both my eyes and ears. I was close to death.

As I recall this early memory, I know that I have remembered and relived that feeling of isolation, loneliness, and terror again and again over my lifetime.

Clearest Part: The blackness and silence.

Strongest Feeling: A feeling of shriveling up, touching no one, feeling nothing.

Change: I would be held, touched, reassured.

Age: 1½ years.

Precis: I am alone, sick, and helpless; no one is there for me.

Perception of Self: Isolated, weak, vulnerable.

Perception of Others: Indifferent, insensitive, uncaring, unavailable.

Major Issue (unfinished business): Trust/security—no one cares enough to meet my needs.

EM 2

My mother and I were lying on the living room sofa listening to the radio; the room was totally dark. Suddenly I was terribly afraid and started to cry.

Precis: When I am left, I feel abandoned and rejected.

Perception of Self: Isolated, unlovable.

387

Summary	Comments

EM 2 (continued)

I was so alone and I knew I was being left. No amount of reassurance could make me stop crying; I cried myself to sleep.

Clearest: The blackness and the feeling that there would be no more light.

Feeling: The terror of the darkness.

Change: There would be light and warmth.

Age: 3

Perception of Others: (Mother) not there for her.

Major Issue: Separation/ individuation (abandonment) – sees self as weak, vulnerable, very much in need of support.

Process Interpretation (the psychological link that connects a series of EMs): For a while mother is there for her in EM 2 but not in EM 1. In EM 2, she seems to be owning the problem – her needs/fears are too great for others to handle. Abandonment concerns connect for two EMs.

EM 3

I was locked in the closet for punishment. I had thrown a rock at my aunt. My father hit me and yanked me by the arm screaming how bad I was and how I needed to be punished. "No one wants you around when you're so bad." He then locked me in the closet and left me there for a long time.

Clearest: The blackness and silence.

Feeling: Feeling rejected, worthless, and abandoned.

Change: Not to be shut away when I was bad.

Age: 5

Precis: When I act out my anger, I am severely punished.

Perception of Self: Not a very nice person (because of her anger and how she is punished).

Perception of Others: (Father) punishing and rejecting.

Major Issues: (1) Problem with impulse control/anger; (2) separation-individuation (abandoned again).

Process Interpretation: The anger over abandonment in EMs 1 and 2 is expressed in EM 3 (counterproductive) and leads to more rejection and abandonment.

EM 4

My father and I went to the hospital to bring my baby sister and mom home. I was excited about having a sister but a little upset because she was going to get half my room. My dad had moved out my double bed,

Precis: (Specific) I was overthrown, replaced, and pushed aside by my baby sister; or (general) if I feel displaced or threatened in a relationship and I express my feelings, I expect no empathy or consideration.

Summary	Comments

EM 4 (continued)

replaced it with a small single bed, and moved a crib in. He told me he was moving my toys to the attic because there wasn't enough room; the baby needed the space. I was upset. When I complained, I was told that I was being selfish and that if I complained any more I would have to move to the basement and give the baby my whole room.

Clearest: Losing my space and being replaced.

Feeling: Rejected and angry toward the baby. I didn't want a sister.

Change: I would have my own room all to myself.

Age: 7

Perception of Self: Needy, deprived of attention, security, and caring.

Perception of Others: (Father) insensitive, punishing, harsh.

Major Issues: (1) Rivalry/jealousy toward new sibling; (2) sharing, cooperation.

Process Interpretation: Expression of anger over abandonment and overly harsh punishment (EM 3) leads to being displaced, abandoned, and rejected again.

EM 5

I went to stay all night at a neighbor's house. It was summer, and I loved to stay over at the G.s—they had six kids, five girls and a boy; we always had lots of fun. The house was always filled with noise and lots of people. we were getting ready to eat supper and the grandmother said to me, "S., you'd better go home to eat. We're heating ham for supper, and Jews don't eat ham."

Clearest: Feeling different and unliked when the grandmother told me to go home.

Feeling: Rejection, not belonging.

Change: To be liked for just being me.

Age: 11.

Precis: I was rejected for being Jewish.

Perception of Self: Different/unlikable.

Perception of Others: (Grandmother of the neighbor's child) rejecting.

Major Issue: Acceptance.

Process Interpretation: Displacement by sister and rejection by parents (EM 4) leads her to seek acceptance outside the family, where she is again rejected, now for being Jewish.

Group Memory: Identifies herself as a Jew. (See Bruhn 1990b, for a discussion of group memories and their function.)

Summary	Comments

Memory 6 (A particularly clear or important memory, lifetime)

When I came home from overseas after being gone for 2 years, I was happy to be back in the U.S., excited about having a month and a half off work before moving to D. to start my new job, happy to be back in my home with M. (my husband) and P. (my dog), and looking forward to seeing friend. The plane ride had been a time of mentally reviewing and reliving the many great times I had in the battalion over the last 2 years, reliving the change-of-command ceremony that had happened just a few hours before I got on the airplane with mixed emotions.

Then, within 2 hr of walking through my front door, my world shattered; I found out my marriage was over, our savings were gone, and we were enormously in debt. It seemed as if my world had ended.

Clearest: Feeling so good and then so bad; feeling so used, deceived, and cheated.

Feeling: Rejection, humiliation, and abandonment.

Change: Feeling worthless and abandoned and keeping it all inside. It took months before I stopped blaming myself, became angry, and began to take care of myself.

Age 45:

Precis: (After thinking that I had finally found acceptance and love), my husband abandoned me.

Perception of Self: Rejected, abandoned.

Perception of Others: (Ex-husband) devious and deceitful, dishonest.

Major Issue: Acceptance.

Process Interpretation: After being rejected because she was Jewish (EM 5), she nevertheless married and was happy until being rejected by her husband (men).

Comment: Thus far, her memories appear to be assessing the basis for why she believes she has been rejected.

Summary of Ratings Scales

	Pleasantness: 7-Point Scale	Clarity: 5-Point Scale
EM 1	2 = *moderately negative*	2 = *somewhat clear*
EM 2	1 = *very negative*	3 = *moderately clear*
EM 3	1 = *very negative*	4 = *clear*

Summary of Ratings Scales (continued)

	Pleasantness: 7-Point Scale	Clarity: 5-Point Scale
EM 4	2 = *moderately negative*	5 = *exceptionally clear*
EM 5	2 = *moderately negative*	4 = *clear*
Memory 6	1 = *very negative*	5 = *exceptionally clear*

Client's rank ordering of significance of memories

1. Most significant: #4
2. Next significant: #3
3. Next significant: #2

Q: Why do you think that you call *these* from all your childhood experiences?
A: They were all negative and in all I was rejected.

Interpretation of Rating Scale Data

Clearest EMs (5s on a 5-point scale) are usually among the most significant memories. Particularly clear memories draw proportionately more psychic energy because the issue illustrated by the memory is currently focal. One can think of such EMs as being spotlighted.

If the clearest memory is also very positive (7 on a 7-point scale), this suggests that a strong need or wish has been gratified—likely a need that is primary in importance for the individual now. Such memories contain a self-message or reminder to the individual that takes the form—"this is what you need most, and here is how this need can be met." If the clearest memory is very negative (1), this suggests that a major issue is being played out, something that the individual is actively trying to work through now.

In this protocol, two members are rated as 5s for clarity—EM 4 and Memory 6 (see Summary of Rating Scales). The client rates EM 4 as her most significant memory, thus providing independent evidence of its importance. Both are also very negative (2,1), suggesting a major issue in process. The common denominator between EMs 4 and 6 involves rejection (Memory 6) or perceived rejection (EM 4). Due to the client's preoccupation with rejection, I wonder whether the client has the energy and self-confidence to commit to establishing a relationship and making it work. Her major issues appears to involve her poor self-concept—"there is something wrong with me that causes me to be rejected." Such self-perceptions often lead to a withdrawal from emotionally meaningful relationships and, eventually, a depressive episode.

Directed memories are requested to determine whether something important was omitted from the spontaneous memories in Part I. There are 15 directed memories in all. Those reported here add to what we have gleaned from the spontaneous memories.

Summary	*Comments*

First School Memory

Once, when I was in kindergarten, I had a new dress, red plaid, and at recess I tore it [on the swings] and started to cry. I knew that my mother would be furious and would spank me for being so careless. I refused to go home, and the teacher called my mother. She had to walk to school to get me and was really mad. She picked up a stick and kept switching me on the back of the legs all the way home.

Clearest: The swings and the switch.

Feeling: I was so proud of my new dress and so upset with myself for tearing it. I knew I deserved to be punished.

Change: Not tear the dress.

Age: 5½

Precis: When I make a mistake, I expect that others will be furious with me and will punish me severely.

Perception of Self: Avoidant and fearful.

Perception of Others: (Mother) critical, demanding, harsh, and unforgiving (see also A Memory of Mother).

Major Issues: (1) Accepting her own fallibility; (2) self-disclosure.

Process Interpretation: I do not ordinarily recommend process interpretations for directed memories due to the intrusive quality of the probes used (e.g., most traumatic memory).

Comment: In mastery situations, she is worried about making mistakes and is fearful and avoidant with significant others when such occur.

First Punishment Memory

I had gotten into a terrible argument with my mother (I don't remember about what). We both were yelling at each other; she threatened that she would lock me in the bedroom until Dad came home to punish me (Mother never spanked, she always got Dad to do it). I was nasty and belligerent and sassy and taunted her, "You can't do it, you can't make me do it." She became angry and picked up the broom and tried to hit me with it. I grabbed the broom away from her and hit her with it and ran out of the house.

Precis: When I defy authority or act out, I expect brutal treatment (see also EM 3).

Perception of Self: Provocative, defiant.

Perception of Others: (Father) brutal, punishing, cruel.

Major Issue: Accepting authority.

Comment: This memory has the same form as EM 3. In both memories, she acts provocatively and ends up feeling hurt, angry, rejected, abandoned, and ultimately responsible for the misery that she brings on herself.

Summary	*Comments*

First Punishment Memory (*continued*)

I stayed away until about 9:00 p.m. and then sneaked back into the house. Dad was waiting for me, grabbed me, and took me to the bathroom to wash out my mouth with soap. I tried to fight him; he began hitting me with his belt. He dragged me into the bathroom and made me eat a bar of soap; he wouldn't let me spit out any and kept hitting me every time I tried.

Clearest: Eating the soap and feeling it burn my tongue and gums.

Feeling: Hating my mother and father, wishing I could hurt them as badly as they hurt me.

Change: I would not have made them so angry at me.

Age: 11

First Sibling Memory

I was going to summer camp. We were all in the car on a Sunday afternoon, Mom, Dad, my sister S., and me. I had a sack lunch for supper that first night at camp. S. began demanding that she get something from my lunch sack. After a while, Mother gave in and gave her half my sandwich and, later, the cookies. I became very angry, and when we got to camp, I refused to take the lunch at all and threw it on the ground when my mother tried to make me. "I don't want any of it, give it all to S.; she always gets everything."

Clearest: Throwing the rest of the lunch on the ground and kicking it.

Feeling: Being very angry at S. and resenting her intrusion into my happy time (going to camp).

Precis: (Specific) I am angry at my sister because I feel she gets what is rightfully mine and is favored over me (cf. EM 4); or (general) when others compromise my sense of entitlement, I become furious.

Perception of Self: Jealous, resentful, insecure with regard to her position in the family.

Perception of Others: (S.) testing, demanding.

Major Issue: Feeling secure about her own value, entitlement.

Summary	*Comments*

First Sibling Memory (*continued*)

Change: Not be so unreasonably
jealous of her.
  Age: 9

First Family Memory

We were on a family fishing trip,
Mom, Dad, my sister, me, and my
aunt, B. (who was 4 years older than
me and was my Dad's little sister).
I always hated the fact that Dad included B. in everything we did
as a family. He felt sorry for her
because her parents were old, and
she was always alone. I wanted to
go out in the boat with Dad. He
said no.

Precis: Nearly identical in form to the
First Sibling Memory.
  Comment: Memories like this, which
repeat an earlier pattern, indicate
through their repetition a highly significant issue. Through repetition a
client tells us in effect. "Let me show
you just how important this is."

A Memory of Mother

I remember all the times when I was
bad and my father would beat me with
his belt and mother would do nothing
to help me. One particular time, I had
lost a dollar bill on the way home from
the store. My father was very angry
and started hitting me with his belt. I
yelled for mother to help me. "It was
an accident, Mom; I didn't mean to.
Help me!" She turned away and went
into the bathroom, and the beating
continued.
  Clearest: The belt hitting my back.
  Feeling: Feeling helpless and alone.
  Change: Not lose the money.
  Age: 8

Precis: (General) When I make a mistake, I expect to be treated (punished)
severely. (NB: Her intention does not
count, and even minor mistakes are
harshly punished). (Specific) I cannot
count on my mother's protection or
support.
  Perception of Self: Unreliable.
  Perception of Others: (Father) punishing, brutal, unreasonable. (Mother)
unsympathetic, unwilling to protect
her.
  Major Issue: Accepting her own
fallibility and trusting others to
deal with her failings/mistakes appropriately.
  Comment: Compare form of
memory to first school memory—the
two are nearly identical.

Summary	*Comments*

A Memory of Father

I had done something bad—not cleaned my room or mowed the front yard. For punishment, my father said I couldn't go to the Saturday birthday party of my best friend. I was very mad and yelled back at him that he wasn't being fair, and I hated him. Dad got mad and hit me and kept on hitting me. I taunted him—"you can't hurt me!" He said I didn't deserve being allowed to be around other people; I had to stay in my room for the whole weekend by myself. I was so angry. After he left and locked the door, I threw myself on the bed, face down, and started kicking and screaming and crying into the pillow. I hated them; I never got to do things other kids did. I stayed in my room all alone Saturday, Sunday, and finally on Monday morning, Mom came and let me out. All I wanted to do was escape and I did, to school.

Clearest: Being so angry at my father for locking me in my room. Not going to the birthday party.

Feeling: Feeling unloved and rejected.

Change: Would not have made my father mad at me.

Age: 10

Precis: When I do something wrong and am punished/disciplined, I become angry and provoke the authority figure who disciplined me (cf. EM 3).

Perception of Self: Acting out, rebellious, defiant. (NB: She is likely to challenge and provoke male authority figures.)

Perception of Others: (Father) punishing, brutal, cruel.

Major Issues: (1) learning to cooperate and to respect authority; (2) learning to handle anger appropriately.

Comment: We now see in retrospect how she constructs being alone in EMs 1 and 2—that she "didn't deserve being allowed to be around other people" (father's statement, internalized).

A Memory of Someone You Admired

I was a junior in college; I had a female professor, Dr. T., who was the Chinese-Japanese faculty expert in the History/ Political Science Department at the university. I was in her class in Far

Precis: Being praised, especially in front of others, has a tremendous impact on my self-esteem.

Perception of Self: Academically competent as a history scholar.

Summary	*Comments*

A Memory of Someone You Admired (*continued*)

East history and had done a special research paper for her on the Meiji restoration in Japan—a topic of great interest to her. I was totally taken with her, considered her absolutely brilliant, and had really knocked myself out on the paper. She praised my work before the rest of the class and asked if I would let her submit it for publication. It was later published (in a scholarly journal). She asked me to assist her in further research she was doing for a book and helped me get a summer scholarship to a seminar led by a China expert. I was absolutely overcome with feelings of pride and self-worth. I was liked and appreciated.

Clearest: Listening to her praise.

Feeling: Feeling good, happy, worthwhile, and appreciated. I took every course she taught and did three independent research projects under her over the next 2 years. Later, I felt somewhat used but also felt I had vindicated an earlier assessment.

Age: 20

Perception of Others: (Teacher) Acknowledging of her accomplishments.

Perception of World: Interesting.

Major Issue: Memories with positive affect do not depict major unresolved issues, rather the satisfaction of major needs. Here, the need is for acknowledgment and recognition.

Happiest Memory

I was graduating from Army Basic Officer Training. I had been in training for over 4 months. I had not consulted my parents before joining the Army. I dropped out of graduate school, quit my teaching job and turned down an assistant professorship, joined the Army, and then told my parents; they were not happy. I had had little contact with them during my training, but had sent them a graduation

Precis: When my father is proud of me, it makes me feel proud.

Perception of Self: Competent in a training situation.

Perception of Others: (Father) Proud of me.

Major Issue: This is a positive affect memory, so there is no unresolved issue. The major needs are acknowledgment, acceptance, and recognition.

Summary	Comments

Happiest Memory (continued)

announcement. They surprised me by driving down to see me graduate. I was the top honor graduate out of 192 officers in my class. I was very proud and pleased they had made such an effort. It was the first time my father ever attended a graduation of mine—he was not at my high school, college, or grad school graduation—but he had made this effort and told me how proud he was of me because I had volunteered to go to Vietnam.

Clearest: Walking across the stage and receiving my certificate and saluting H., the Army's first female general.

Feeling: Feeling immensely proud that I had finally done something for which my father was proud of me.

Change: It was great just the way it was—no change.

Age: 26

Comment: This memory appears to function as an emotional counterweight in that it balances so many perceived slights and rejections from father in addition to the many beatings she received growing up. The memory tells her, in effect, that she finally "passed muster" with her father.

Most Traumatic Memory

I was a battalion commander overseas with 1,100 soldiers for whom I was responsible. We were in the midst of the biggest exercise conducted in the free world. The battalion was fully deployed and operating 24 hrs. a day. I was awakened at 1:30 a.m. in my tent. One of my soldiers, a 19-year-old who had been in the country for 1 month, had just hit and killed a local male on a motorcycle. I dressed and raced to the police station as quickly as possible. My soldier was in total shock; the other two soldiers who had been with him were comforting him. I had just

Precis: When people I am responsible for mess up, I feel so inadequate and guilty.

Perception of Self: Inadequate, culpable, ineffectual.

Perception of Others: (Soldier) Vulnerable, dependent.

Major Issue: Mastery—performing competently so that nothing goes wrong.

Comment: It is understandable how anyone in such a situation would feel bad for all parties concerned. Notice, however, how she blames herself for what occurred even though her degree

Summary	*Comments*

Most Traumatic Memory (*continued*)

come from the scene—blood, brains, and junk all over the road.

The local police refused to release custody, and my soldier was put in jail. The young man was totally terrified and crazy with fear. He had an 18-year-old wife and 2-month-old baby at home. He was sure he would never see them again. I felt so helpless because I could not lighten his burden nor belay his fears. All I could do was try to reassure him with words and make sure that someone stayed with him until we could get him back into U.S. custody.

Clearest: The body on the highway, the total fear of my soldier, and his absolute remorse.

Feeling: I felt so inadequate, so sorry that I was responsible for putting this young man in such a position, and so helpless to make things okay.

Change: I would have prevented the accident, better safety precautions and better supervision.

Age: 44

of personal responsibility was minimal. Her severity with herself appears to carry over from her father's severity (extreme punishment) with her. In other words, just as father physically abused her when she did something wrong, she emotionally abuses herself when something goes wrong. The memory confirms our worst fears, that she has internalized what she perceives as her father's attitudes toward her.

A Memory of a Parental Fight or Argument

My parents had begun arguing during supper. My dad had gotten home late from work and had not called and everything had gotten cold. Mom had started yelling at him about being so inconsiderate, and they both were yelling at each other. After eating, Mom was washing the dishes and I was drying them. Mom and Dad continued fighting and yelling. Dad came storming into the kitchen from the

Precis: The most insignificant event can trigger a conflict that escalates into a life-and-death struggle.

Perception of Self: Vulnerable, victimized.

Perception of Others: (Father) inconsiderate, domineering, aggressive, bullying, out of control. (Mother) unappreciated, victimized.

Major Issue: Learning to deal with conflict and angry feelings appropriately.

Summary	Comments

A Memory of a Parental Fight or Argument (*continued*)

living room yelling at my mother to
shut up and threatening to hit her.
Mom was afraid and threw a glass at
him. I was standing next to the sink in
front of the basement door. Dad
ducked, and the glass missed him; he
grabbed a butcher knife off the
kitchen table and threw it at my
mother. It missed her, went between
us, and stuck in the basement door. I
was crying and screaming at Dad to
stop: "Don't hit Mom, don't hit me, go
away." He hit both of us. I ducked
under the table and ran outside.

Clearest: The knife sticking in the
basement door.

Feeling: Hating my father for always
disrupting everything.

Resolution: I ran to my grandpar-
ents' house and stayed all night. Dad
beat Mom up.

An Incident That Made You Feel Ashamed

My family had gone to M. to visit my
aunt, uncle, and two consins. One
consin was my age, the other 3 years
older. They took me to the neighbor-
hood grocery store to show me how
they stole candy. They had bragged
that they stole all the time and never
got caught. We went in; C. and I
started looking at things in the front
of the store and making lots of noise.
Then we left. D. came out and showed
us all the stuff he had put in his
pockets—candy, gum, a little knife.
They laughed and said they dared me
to go in and steal something—said I
was a chicken if I didn't. I didn't want

Precis: Even though I knew better, I
did something wrong because I was
afraid of being rejected by my friends.

Perception of Self: Sensitive to rejection, insecure.

Perception of Others: (Peers) lacking
scruples, demanding. (Male authority)
judgmental, rejecting.

Major Issue: Acceptance.

Summary	*Comments*

An Incident That Made You Feel Ashamed (*continued*)

to, but I was afraid they wouldn't like
me if I didn't. I went back inside, finally put a package of gum in my
pocket, and ran out. The store owner
caught me, dragged me back inside,
and began yelling at me how terribly
bad I was.

    Clearest: Being grabbed and caught.

    Feeling: Feeling totally ashamed and
mad at myself for letting D. and C.
talk me into stealing.

    Change: Just told them no, I
wouldn't do it and I didn't care what
they thought of me.

    Age: 7

A Memory of Being Physically or Emotionally Abused

I was frequently physically abused as a
child, often whipped with a belt so
badly I couldn't go to school the next
day, and frequently had my mouth
washed out with soap—in fact was usually made to eat a bar of soap, which
caused burns and ulcers on my tongue
and inner mouth, which made swal-
lowing and eating difficult for days.

    One of the last memories of such an
incident happened when I was a sophomore in high school. I can't
remember what triggered the argument
I had with my parents, but I know it
involved money I wanted. My father
and I were screaming at each other,
and he threatened that I would be permanently grounded—would never go
on another debate or tennis trip with
my school teams. I was in an absolute
rage, screaming abusive things and
trying to hit him. He hit me with his

Precis: When I needed something from
my father, he was likely to deny me,
which made me so frustrated and
angry that I became verbally abusive;
he retaliated by abusing me physically
(cf. First Punishment Memory,
Memory of Father).

    Perception of Self: Verbally abusive
when frustrated, worthy of physical
abuse (blames self), unable to tolerate
frustration without exploding or acting
in a self-destructive manner.

    Perception of Others: (Father) ex-
tremely abusive physically when challenged or angered and lacking in control and judgment in such
circumstances.

    Perception of World: Brutal, punish-
ing.

    Major Issues: (1) Tolerating frustra-
tion; (2) resolving conflicts; (3) handling her anger appropriately.

Summary	*Comments*

A Memory of Being Physically or Emotionally Abused *(continued)*

fist as hard as he could, knocked me into a wall. He grabbed me and started hitting me with his belt—the buckle end—anywhere he could—head, arms, body. I cowered down on the floor and rolled into a ball and blacked out. My next recollection is lying on my bed, hurting all over. I fingered the welts on my arms and body—the skin was broken in several places, blood was oozing from a cut over my left eye. I felt numb.

I missed 3 days of school because I was too ashamed to be seen—especially to go to gym class and tennis practice and have people see what a mess I was.

Clearest: The belt buckle—it was silver with a turquoise eagle on it.

Feeling: The deep, deep feeling of shame—wishing I could escape, run away, die.

Change: I would not have lost my temper and made my father so angry.

Age: 15

Comment: Although EM 3 hints at possible abuse, the matter is not completely resolved until directed memories are requested. There appears to be a history of severe physical abuse with her, an issue that needs to be addressed in her therapy. Notice how she blames herself for what happened, thus turning her anger in on herself and damaging her self-esteem. This pattern is common among individuals who have been abused as children.

A Fantasy Memory

"I will be better, richer, more successful than anyone in my family ever was. I'll make them sorry for how they treat me, for how mean they are to me—I'll show them, I'll show everyone."

Over the years, I played out this fantasy hundreds of times in my mind with lots of different scenarios that all always achieved the same ends. After being punished and lying in my dark room, I would make detailed plans about running away and never

Precis: I will express my anger and defiance at those who reject me by successfully competing and through my accomplishments.

Perception of Self: Success at mastery activities expresses defiance.

Perception of Others: Mean, rejecting.

Major Issues: Acceptance (adulation).

Summary	*Comments*

A Fantasy Memory (*continued*)

returning until I was grown and very successful. At about 10 years old, I began writing endless stories always with a hero character who saved others, made great discoveries, received great rewards and adoration, and was much admired.

My writing was my escape from the reality of my day-to-day life throughout junior and senior high school. I fantasized my future as a great writer. I kept detailed journals and poured out the feelings that I could never share. I was the hero, admired and loved. I would make an impact upon the world; it would matter that I had passed through. I would show everyone; no one could hurt me.

As a child and as a teenager, I lived vicariously through my imaginary characters; as long as I had them, as long as I had my dreams, no one could touch me or hurt me; I didn't need anyone.

Your Interpretation of a Memory

(Did not feel comfortable attempting.)

Questionnaire (Selected questions in italics)

2. *Are you being seen for treatment?* Yes
   If yes, briefly describe the reason. Personal relationships are difficult for me. I don't allow myself to get close to people. I am afraid of rejection/abandonment. I have poor self-esteem and feel inadequate in most situations, feel myself to be unlikable/unlovable.
   Do you see any connection between what brought you in for treatment and the earliest childhood memories that you described? I was continually rejected, punished, and made to think that everything was my doing. I was at fault and only getting what I deserved because I was a bad person.

4. *How much did you learn about yourself?* Quite a lot (rated 5 on a 5-point scale).

5. *How much did you learn about yourself from the EMP in comparison to other psychological tests that you have taken?* Somewhat more (rated 4 on 5-point scale).
6. How much time did it take you to complete the procedure? Approximately 8 hrs.
9. *Any other comments about your experience with the EMP?* Writing these was very difficult. When I first started and read through the booklet, I couldn't actually remember much of my childhood before my teenage years. Slowly, over weeks, I forced myself to think back and remember those earlier years.

Summary of Issues (in order of appearance – used to formulate synthesis of issues, below)

1. Trust, security. Feels that no one cares about her enough to want to meet her needs, soothe her, and comfort her (EM 1).
2. Separation-individuation. Feels weak, vulnerable, in need of support (EMs 2 and 3).
3. Impulse control, especially around the expression of anger (EM 3).
4. Jealousy. Feels displaced and overthrown by her baby sister and by father's little sister (EM 4, First Sibling Memory, First Family Memory).
5. Sharing, cooperation. Has difficulty with this issue because she feels threatened and insecure about her position (EM 4, First Family Memory).
6. Acceptance. Is sensitive to rejection because she experiences so little acceptance and is not sure what she needs to do to be accepted. She is concerned that her being Jewish (group memory) is at least partly responsible (EM 5, Memory 6, Incident That Made You Feel Ashamed, Fantasy Memory).
7. Accepting her own fallibility (First School Memory, Memory of Mother, Traumatic Memory).
8. Self-disclosure (First School Memory).
9. Accepting authority (First Punishment Memory, First Memory of Father).

Synthesis of Issues

This is a woman who does not feel loved, valued, important, or special. She feels that she was upstaged and overthrown by her younger sister and as a result feels rejected, abandoned, and pushed aside. This same dynamic operates today in her interpersonal relationships. She expects to be rejected, abandoned, and pushed aside, just as occurred in her marriage. When it is operative, this dynamic also elicits violent feelings of anger that are usually expressed in a provocative, defiant, counterproductive manner. Her actions commonly elicit exasperation, scape-goating behaviors, rejection, and abandonment from significant others. Such reactions close the loop for her, leaving her feeling even more unloved, unimpor-tant, and ultimately despondent. This dynamic confirms her negative expectations and frustrates her need to be loved and valued.

A complicating factor is her belief that she must perform competently and flawlessly at all times to keep this pattern from being activated. This belief generates tremendous internal tension and anxiety and makes interactions with her difficult due to her resentment over what she thinks others expect of her.

This pattern also increases her vulnerability to abuse substances, which can be used to medicate her resentment and tension and provide temporary relief from her expectations of rejection, and depression, which will occur whenever she believes she has failed or been rejected.

What the Client is Looking for Initially in a Therapist and What She Needs From Treatment.

1. Someone who will offer support and provide reassurance and comfort to help weaken her expectation that authority figures will turn their backs on her when she is vulnerable. AA should be used in this regard as an adjunct for substance-abuse problems.
2. Someone who will provide emotional stability, constancy, and acceptance to help balance her experiences with authority figures who are critical, judgmental, and rejecting.
3. Someone to teach her how to deal more appropriately with conflict situations and the violent anger that is aroused.
4. Someone to help her understand how she punishes herself when she thinks she has failed, and the role alcohol plays in this process. Concurrently, new ways to process "failure" experiences must be developed (e.g., as learning experiences rather than as confirmation of her lack of self-worth). Work with Alanon will help her understand how she has learned to think as an alcoholic, which will provide another helpful perspective to her work in individual therapy.
5. Longer term, she will need to reprocess old relationships and examine current ones to better understand what she is doing to sabotage them and thus frustrate her need for love and acceptance. She will learn that all individuals will not be as punitive and punishing with her as her father if she handles conflict situations appropriately.

Awareness

This individual is quite sensitive to certain feelings and patterns but appears to be unaware of others. For instance, she is aware that she has been scapegoated by her parents for things that went wrong, and she has been willing to accept responsibility—perhaps too willing. She is aware that her low self-esteem is related to this dynamic. What she seems to be less in touch with is what she is legitimately responsible for. She appears to be too willing to accept her parents' opinion of her rather than form her own opinion. Her confusion about herself has led to relational problems. For instance, she does not appear to be able to form close relationships without accepting the role of the scapegoat. In sum, she is aware that her relational problems are connected to her problems with her parents, but she does not seem to know what caused these problems. Early in treatment, the therapist can explore with her what went wrong in her family, how she constructed her contribution to this process, and how this construction affects her present relationships.

Appendix D

Addiction Severity Index

ADDICTION SEVERITY INDEX

SEVERITY RATINGS

The severity ratings are interviewer estimates of the patient's need for additional treatment in each area. The scales range from 0 (no treatment necessary) to 9 (treatment needed to intervene in life-threatening situation). Each rating is based upon the patient's history of problem symptoms, present condition and subjective assessment of his treatment needs in a given area. For a detailed description of severity ratings' derivation procedures and conventions, see manual. Note: These severity ratings are optional.

Fifth Edition

SUMMARY OF PATIENTS RATING SCALE

0 - Not at all
1 - Slightly
2 - Moderately
3 - Considerably
4 - Extremely

I.D. NUMBER ☐☐☐☐

LAST 4 DIGITS OF SSN ☐☐☐☐

DATE OF ADMISSION ☐☐☐☐☐☐

DATE OF INTERVIEW ☐☐☐☐☐☐

TIME BEGUN ☐☐ : ☐☐

TIME ENDED ☐☐ : ☐☐

CLASS:
  1 - Intake
  2 - Follow-up ☐

CONTACT CODE:
  1 - In Person
  2 - Phone ☐

GENDER:
  1 - Male
  2 - Female ☐

INTERVIEWER CODE NUMBER ☐☐

SPECIAL:
  1 - Patient terminated
  2 - Patient refused
  3 - Patient unable to respond ☐

GENERAL INFORMATION

NAME _____

CURRENT ADDRESS _____

_____

_____

GEOGRAPHIC CODE ☐☐

1. How long have you lived at this address? ☐☐ ☐☐
   YRS.   MOS.

2. Is this residence owned by you or your family? ☐
   0 - No   1 - Yes

3. DATE OF BIRTH ☐☐☐☐☐☐

4. RACE ☐
   1 - White (Not of Hispanic Origin)
   2 - Black (Not of Hispanic Origin)
   3 - American Indian
   4 - Alaskan Native
   5 - Asian or Pacific Islander
   6 - Hispanic - Mexican
   7 - Hispanic - Puerto Rican
   8 - Hispanic - Cuban
   9 - Other Hispanic

5. RELIGIOUS PREFERENCE ☐
   1 - Protestant   4 - Islamic
   2 - Catholic   5 - Other
   3 - Jewish   6 - None

6. Have you been in a controlled environment in the past 30 days?
   1 - No
   2 - Jail
   3 - Alcohol or Drug Treatment
   4 - Medical Treatment
   5 - Psychiatric Treatment
   6 - Other _____

7. How many days? ☐☐

ADDITIONAL TEST RESULTS

Shipley C.Q. ☐☐☐

Shipley I.Q. ☐☐☐

Beck Total Score ☐☐

SCL-90 Total ☐☐☐

MAST ☐☐

_____ ☐☐

_____ ☐☐☐

_____ ☐☐☐

SEVERITY PROFILE

	PROBLEMS	MEDICAL	EMP/SUP	ALCOHOL	DRUG	LEGAL	FAM/SOC	PSYCH
9								
8								
7								
6								
5								
4								
3								
2								
1								
0								

MEDICAL STATUS

* 1. How many times in your life have you been hospitalized for medical problems? *(Include o.d.'s, d.t.'s, exclude detox.)*

2. How long ago was your last hospitalization for a physical problem   YRS.   MOS.

3. Do you have any chronic medical problems which continue to interfere with your life?
0 - No
1 - Yes _____
Specify

4. Are you taking any prescribed medication on a regular basis for a physical problem?
0 - No   1 - Yes

5. Do you receive a pension for a physical disability? *(Exclude psychiatric disability.)*
0 - No
1 - Yes _____
Specify

6. How many days have you experienced medical problems in the past 30?

FOR QUESTIONS 7 & 8 PLEASE ASK PATIENT TO USE THE PATIENT'S RATING SCALE

7. How troubled or bothered have you been by these medical problems in the past 30 days?

Comments

8. How important to you now is treatment for these medical problems?

INTERVIEWER SEVERITY RATING

9. How would you rate the patient's need for medical treatment?

CONFIDENCE RATINGS

Is the above information significantly distorted by:

10. Patient's misrepresentation?
0 - No   1 - Yes

11. Patient's inability to understand?
0 - No   1 - Yes

EMPLOYMENT/SUPPORT STATUS

* 1. Education completed *(GED = 12 years)*   YRS.   MOS.

* 2. Training or technical education completed   MOS.

3. Do you have a profession, trade or skill?
0 - No
1 - Yes _____
Specify

4. Do you have a valid driver's license?
0 - No   1 - Yes

5. Do you have an automobile available for use? *(Answer No if no valid driver's license.)*
0 - No   1 - Yes

6. How long was your longest full-time job?   YRS.   MOS.

* 7. Usual (or last) occupation.
_____
(Specify in detail)

8. Does someone contribute to your support in any way?
0 - No   1 - Yes

9. (ONLY IF ITEM 8 IS YES) Does this constitute the majority of your support?
0 - No   1 - Yes

10. Usual employment pattern, past 3 years.
1 - full time (40 hrs/wk)
2 - part time (reg. hrs)
3 - part time (irreg., daywork)
4 - student
5 - service
6 - retired/disability
7 - unemployed
8 - in controlled environment

11. How many days were you paid for working in the past 30? (include "under the table" work.)

How much money did you receive from the following sources in the past 30 days?

12. Employment (net income)

13. Unemployment compensation

14. DPA

15. Pension, benefits or social security

16. Mate, family or friends (Money for personal expenses).

17. Illegal

Comments

18. How many people depend on you for the majority of their food, shelter, etc.?

19. How many days have you experienced employment problems in the past 30?

FOR QUESTIONS 20 & 21 PLEASE ASK PATIENT TO USE THE PATIENT'S RATING SCALE

20. How troubled or bothered have you been by these employment problems in the past 30 days?

21. How important to you *now* is counseling for these employment problems?

INTERVIEWER SEVERITY RATING

22. How would you rate the patient's need for employment counseling?

CONFIDENCE RATINGS

Is the above information significantly distorted by:

23. Patient's misrepresentation?
0 - No   1 - Yes

24. Patient's inability to understand?
0 - No   1 - Yes

DRUG/ALCOHOL USE

```
□ □ □ □
```

	PAST 30	LIFETIME USE	
	Days	Yrs.	Rt of adm.
① Alcohol - Any use at all			
② Alcohol - To Intoxication			
③ Heroin			
④ Methadone			
⑤ Other opiates/ analgesics			
⑥ Barbiturates			
⑦ Other sed/ hyp/tranq.			
⑧ Cocaine			
⑨ Amphetamines			
⑩ Cannabis			
⑪ Hallucinogens			
⑫ Inhalants			

⑬ More than one substance per day (Incl. alcohol).   □ □   □ □

Note: See manual for representative examples for each drug class

* Route of Administration: 1 = Oral, 2 = Nasal
3 = Smoking, 4 = Non IV inj., 5 = IV inj.

⑭ Which substance is the major problem? *Please code as above or 00-No problem; 15-Alcohol & Drug (Dual addiction); 16-Polydrug; when not clear, ask patient.*   □ □

15. How long was your last period of voluntary abstinence from this major substance? *(00 - never abstinent)*   □ □ MOS.

16. How many months ago did this abstinence end? *(00 - still abstinent)*   □ □

* ⑰ How many times have you:

Had alcohol d.t.'s   □ □

Overdosed on drugs   □ □

* ⑱ How many times in your life have you been treated for:

Alcohol Abuse: □ □

Drug Abuse: □ □

* ⑲ How many of these were detox only?
Alcohol   □ □

Drug   □ □

⑳ How much would you say you spent during the past 30 days on:

Alcohol   □ □ □ □ □

Drugs   □ □ □ □ □

Comments

㉑ How many days have you been treated in an outpatient setting for alcohol or drugs in the past 30 days *(Include NA, AA)*.   □ □

㉒ How many days in the past 30 have you experienced:
Alcohol Problems   □ □
Drug Problems   □ □

FOR QUESTIONS 23 & 24 PLEASE ASK PATIENT TO USE THE PATIENT'S RATING SCALE

㉓ How troubled or bothered have you been in the past 30 days by these:
Alcohol Problems   □
Drug Problems   □

㉔ How important to you now is treatment for these:
Alcohol Problems   □
Drug Problems   □

INTERVIEWER SEVERITY RATING

㉕ How would you rate the patient's need for treatment for:
Alcohol Abuse   □
Drug Abuse   □

CONFIDENCE RATINGS
Is the above information significantly distorted by:

㉖ Patient's misrepresentation?
0 - No   1 - Yes   □

㉗ Patient's inability to understand?
0 - No   1 - Yes   □

LEGAL STATUS

⬜⬜⬜⬜

1. Was this admission prompted or suggested by the criminal justice system (judge, probation/ parole officer, etc.)

   0 - No   1 - Yes   ⬜

②. Are you on probation or parole?

   0 - No   1 - Yes   ⬜

How many times in your life have you been arrested and <u>charged</u> with the following:

* ⑬ - shoplifting/vandalism
* ⑭ - parole/probation violations
* ⑮ - drug charges
* ⑯ - forgery
* ⑰ - weapons offense
* ⑱ - burglary. larceny, B & E
* ⑲ - robbery
* ⑩ - assault
* ⑪ - arson
* ⑫ - rape
* ⑬ - homicide, manslaughter
* ⑭A - prostitution
* ⑭B - contempt of court
* ⑭C - other

⑮ How many of these charges resulted in convictions?   ⬜⬜

How many times in your life have you been charged with the following:

* ⑯ Disorderly conduct, vagrancy, public intoxication   ⬜⬜
* ⑰ Driving while intoxicated   ⬜⬜
* ⑱ Major driving violations (reckless driving, speeding, no license, etc.)   ⬜⬜
* ⑲ How many months were you incarcerated in your life?   ⬜⬜ MOS.

20. How long was your last incarceration?   ⬜⬜ MOS.

21. What was it for? (Use code 3-14, 16-18. If multiple charges, code most severe)

⑫ Are you presently awaiting charges, trial or sentence?
   0 - No   1 - Yes   ⬜

⑬ What for (If multiple charges, use most severe).   ⬜⬜

⑭ How many days in the past 30 were you detained or incarcerated?   ⬜⬜

Comments

⑮ How many days in the past 30 have you engaged in illegal activities for profit?   ⬜⬜

FOR QUESTIONS 26 & 27 PLEASE ASK PATIENT TO USE THE PATIENT'S RATING SCALE

⑯ How serious do you feel your present legal problems are? (Exclude civil problems)   ⬜

⑰ How important to you now is counseling or referral for these legal problems?   ⬜

INTERVIEWER SEVERITY RATING

⑱ How would you rate the patient's need for legal services or counseling?   ⬜

CONFIDENCE RATINGS

Is the above information significantly distorted by:

⑲ Patient's misrepresentation?
   0 - No   1 - Yes   ⬜

⑳ Patient's inability to understand?
   0 - No   1 - Yes   ⬜

FAMILY HISTORY

Have any of your relatives had what you would call a significant drinking, drug use or psych problem- one that did or should have led to treatment?

Mother's Side	Alc	Drug	Psych	Father's Side	Alc	Drug	Psych	Siblings	Alc	Drug	Psych
Grandmother	⬜	⬜	⬜	Grandmother	⬜	⬜	⬜	Brother #1	⬜	⬜	⬜
Grandfather	⬜	⬜	⬜	Grandfather	⬜	⬜	⬜	Brother #2	⬜	⬜	⬜
Mother	⬜	⬜	⬜	Father	⬜	⬜	⬜	Sister #1	⬜	⬜	⬜
Aunt	⬜	⬜	⬜	Aunt	⬜	⬜	⬜	Sister #2	⬜	⬜	⬜
Uncle	⬜	⬜	⬜	Uncle	⬜	⬜	⬜				

Direction: Place "0" in relative category where the answer is clearly <u>no for all relatives in the category</u>; "1" where the answer is clearly <u>yes for any relative within the category</u>; "X" where the answer is <u>uncertain or "I don't know"</u> and "N" where there <u>never was a relative from that category</u>. Code most problematic relative in cases of multiple members per category.

FAMILY/SOCIAL RELATIONSHIPS

(1.) Marital Status

   1 - Married   4 - Separated
   2 - Remarried   5 - Divorced
   3 - Widowed   6 - Never Married

2 How long have
you been in
this marital status?   YRS.   MOS.
(If never married, since age 18).

(3.) Are you satisfied with this situation?
   0 - No
   1 - Indifferent
   2 - Yes

• (4.) Usual living arrangements (past 3 yr.)
   1 - With sexual partner
     and children
   2 - With sexual partner alone
   3 - With children alone
   4 - With parents
   5 - With family
   6 - With friends
   7 - Alone
   8 - Controlled environment
   9 - No stable arrangements

5. How long have you
lived in these
arrangements.   YRS.   MOS.
*(If with parents or family,
since age 18).*

(6.) Are you satisfied with these living
arrangements?
   0 - No
   1 - Indifferent
   2 - Yes

Do you live with anyone who:
   0 = No   1 = Yes

6A. Has a current alcohol problem?

6B. Uses non-prescribed drugs?

(7.) With whom do you spend most of
your free time:
   1 - Family   3 - Alone
   2 - Friends

(8.) Are you satisfied with spending
your free time this way?
   0 - No   1 - Indifferent   2 - Yes

(9.) How many close friends do you have?

Direction for 9A-18: Place "0" in relative
category where the answer is clearly no for all
relatives in the category; "1" where the answer
is clearly yes for any relative within the
category; "X" where the answer is uncertain or
"I don't know" and "N" where there never was a
relative from that category.

9A. Would you say you have had close, long
lasting, personal relationships with any of the
following people in your life:

   Mother

   Father

   Brothers/Sisters

   Sexual Partner/Spouse

   Children

   Friends

Have you had significant periods in which you
have experienced serious problems getting
along with:

	PAST 30 DAYS	IN YOUR LIFE
0 - No 1 - Yes		
(10) Mother		
(11) Father		
(12) Brothers/Sisters		
(13) Sexual partner/spouse		
(14) Children		
(15) Other significant family____		
(16) Close friends		
(17) Neighbors		
(18) Co-Workers		

Did any of these people (10-18) abuse
you: 0 = No; 1 = Yes

18A. Emotionally (make you
feel bad through harsh words)?

18B. Physically (cause you
physical harm)?

18C. Sexually (force sexual
advances or sexual acts)?

(19.) How many days in the past 30
have you had serious conflicts:

A with your family?
B with other people? (excluding
   family)

*FOR QUESTIONS 20-23 PLEASE ASK
PATIENT TO USE THE PATIENT'S
RATING SCALE*

How troubled or bothered have you been in the
past 30 days by these:

(20) Family problems

(21) Social problems

How important to you now is treatment or
counseling for these:

(22) Family problems

(23) Social problems

INTERVIEWER SEVERITY RATING

(24) How would you rate the patient's
need for family and/or social
counseling?

CONFIDENCE RATINGS

Is the above information significantly
distorted by:

(25) Patient's misrepresentation?
   0 - No   1 - Yes

(26) Patient's inability to understand?
   0 - No   1 - Yes

Comments

PSYCHIATRIC STATUS

☐☐☐☐

* ① How many times have you been treated for any psychological or emotional problems?

In a hospital

As an Opt. or Priv. patient ☐☐

② Do you receive a pension for a psychiatric disablity? ☐

0 - No   1 - Yes

Have you had a significant period, (that was not a direct result of drug/alcohol use), in which you have:

0 - No   1 - Yes

	PAST 30 DAYS	IN YOUR LIFE
③ Experienced serious depression		
④ Experienced serious anxiety or tension		
⑤ Experienced hallucinations		
⑥ Experienced trouble understanding, concentrating or remembering		
⑦ Experienced trouble controlling violent behavior		
⑧ Experienced serious thoughts of suicide		
⑨ Attempted suicide		
⑩ Been prescribed medication for any psychological/emotional problem		

⑪ How many days in the past 30 have you experienced these psychological or emotional problems? ☐☐

FOR QUESTIONS 12 & 13 PLEASE ASK PATIENT TO USE THE PATIENT'S RATING SCALE

⑫ How much have you been troubled or bothered by these psychological or emotional problems in the past 30 days? ☐

⑬ How important to you now is treatment for these psychological problems? ☐

THE FOLLOWING ITEMS ARE TO BE COMPLETED BY THE INTERVIEWER

At the time of the interview, is patient:

0 - No   1 - Yes

⑭ Obviously depressed/withdrawn ☐

⑮ Obviously hostile ☐

⑯ Obviously anxious/nervous ☐

⑰ Having trouble with reality testing thought disorders, paranoid thinking ☐

⑱ Having trouble comprehending, concentrating, remembering. ☐

⑲ Having suicidal thoughts ☐

Comments

INTERVIEWER SEVERITY RATING

⑳ How would you rate the patient's need for psychiatric/psychological treatment? ☐

CONFIDENCE RATINGS

Is the above information significantly distorted by:

㉑ Patient's misrepresentation?
   0 - No   1 - Yes ☐

㉒ Patient's inability to understand?
   0 - No   1 - Yes ☐

Glossary

This glossary includes 123 terms common to the fields of addiction studies, the recovery movement, and psychotherapy, as well as terms introduced for the first time in this text. Most well-known terms included here have been provided with new nuances of meaning or new connotations and connections. *The American Heritage Collegiate Dictionary*, 2nd edition, was used for basic meanings and etymologies, which are useful starting points in thinking about the historical and primary process origins of concepts in basic images and obsolete practices. Words printed in capitals in the body of a definition are defined elsewhere in the glossary. Reading the definitions of related terms referenced this way in the body of a definition, or between parentheses at the end of a definition, will provide additional understanding and insight to the denotations, connotations, and connections among related terms. In most cases the glossary goes somewhat beyond the text of chapters to explicate in detail the meaning of a term.

Abstinence violation effect (AVE): Marlatt's (Marlatt et al. 1985) term describing the tendency to go "whole hog" after having violated an absolute rule. The AVE effect is seen by some practitioners as one rationale for advocating controlled use rather than total abstinence.

Acuity: The degree to which a disorder exhibits a temporary exacerbation that can be expected to subside over time, perhaps without treatment, but for which some immediate attention is required.

Addict, Addiction: From Latin: to give over, or award; same root as dictate. The term *addict* is not used as a pejorative in this text, but as one characteristic of a person given over to the addictive cycle. Addiction is defined as drug dependence in the face of negative consequences, especially when the alternations in self-experience described in the addictive cycle are evidenced. The term *addictive process* is often used in this book as an umbrella word to cover all levels of severity of harmful use of psychoactive substances. The term is valued because of its connotations of loss of control and because it avoids placing a negative connotation on dependency as a trait, which is implied in the terms chemical dependence and substance dependence. The concept of an addictive personality is not endorsed in this text. Addicts are viewed as primarily having only the addictive cycle and its consequences in common (see *ADDICTIVE CYCLE*).

Addictive core: From Wilson and Malatesta (1989), a pre-verbal self-representation based on overwhelming (usually negative) affective components of early infant–caretaker experiences. Forms the basic affective center of the person in later life and drives the addictive cycle. Interpreted by this author as a precursor to the phobic core (see *ADDICTIVE PERSONALITY, PHOBIC CORE*).

Addictive cycle: Changes in self-experience over time due to an addictive process reflecting failures in self-regulation. The phases or positions are modeled on modes of infantile experience, which are assumed to influence adult experience and behavior in the form of primary process distortions. These experiences influence the epigenesis of adult behavior. The three positions are the inflated/grandiose, depleted/depressed, and detached/schizoid. The order of the changes in the cycle are not universal, but individuals demonstrate a preferred position, a typical sequence of position changes, and a typical speed or frequency in moving through the cycle and its positions. Substances are used either to maintain or change position. For the depressed self, the drug helps to unify experience after separation from the caregiver. In the grandiose self, the drug pacifies a globalized sense of threatened bewilderment related to traumatic overstimulation of the infant. For the schizoid self, the drug supports denial of interpersonal dependency related to failed attachment and repressed rage. The individual addict will emphasize one of these aspects of self over others, based on the predominant pathological elements in the mixture of his or her early parent–infant experiences (see *ADDICTIVE CORE; EPIGENESIS; FAILURES IN SELF-REGULATION; POSITION IN ADDICTIVE CYCLE*).

Addictive personality: The view that certain personality types are especially prone to addiction and that substitution of one abused substance or activity for another is more common among these persons than among individuals who develop an addiction due to some other vulnerability. In the author's view, this stance is overly simplistic; the problems that result in addiction are below, or more basic, than the level of personality. Individuals with the same personality style or type often have very different degrees of susceptibility to addiction and addictive substitution. Wilson and colleagues (1989) have proposed failures in self-regulation as central to addiction. These failures have their origin in preverbal experience (prior to personality formation) that is incorporated into the adult person as a preverbal core self (see *ADDICTIVE CORE*).

Agent, Personal agency: Sanskrit root: to drive. The person as prime mover or director of events, especially events affecting the individual's course through a life plan. The experience of personal causation found in "I do," "I will," "I choose," or "I am responsible." Agency is experienced optimally through exercising personal creativity under conditions of liberty. However, preferences and choices made within an externally circumscribed range of options may be attributed to personal agency by the self, or by an external observer, without recourse to using other causal mechanisms to account for the preference or choice. Agency and consciousness are the minimal assumptions that must be made about persons (see *PERSONOLOGY*).

Anxiety complex: A group of symptoms found in addiction and mental illness, which reflects a failure of anxiety management and the experience of manifest anxiety, either due to a greater level of inherent anxiety or a failure of defenses. Anxiety may be experienced as global tension or physical tautness in specific body regions, usually the throat or chest. Patients suffering from this complex of symptoms may exhibit alexithymia, that is, the inability to identify feelings. In these cases, reported anxiety may be low. However, craving for the drug, somatic discomfort, psychosomatic illness, or general apprehension during abstinence usually displaces manifest anxiety and emotional reactions to stress in these cases.

Bipolarity: Meaning or extension of a quality as defined by two opposing extremes, each of which is understood or described, at least in part, by contrast with the other. Bipolarity may be inherent to human thought as a consequence of our segmented brains with their differentially developed hemispheres. Bipolar qualities may be dichotomous or continuous. Bipolar descriptions are minimal extensions of meaning. In most cases, meaningful descriptions require multiple poles. Dialectical relationships usually involve multipolarity.

Central conflicts: Conflicts are opposing motives and wishes, both conscious and unconscious. Central conflicts are repetitive, link and explain a number of important behaviors, and usually contain elements that are hidden from the patient's awareness (Perry et al. 1987). Usually a small number of issues may be identified that are pervasive to the patients' personal histories and to both their adaptive and maladaptive behaviors.

Character, Characterological: Greek: to sharpen, to engrave, to cut; from an earlier root meaning pointed stake, hence engraved mark. A description of behavior that emphasizes long-standing aspects of an individual that are implicit in his or her most basic predispositions, early history, and seminal acts of agency. Character once took on the meaning of morality, as in "moral character." Although not currently popular, it still makes sense to draw the distinction of character as deeper or more ingrained than personality (persona: the mask). Characterological studies, given this line of thought, are similar but not identical with personality descriptions. Personality, linked as it is to affect and constitution, is expected to be somewhat contingent upon external situations and to change somewhat over the lifespan with age. Character is more internally determined. Changes in character tend to be structural, revolutionary, and require habitual decisions made by the person as agent.

Characterological addiction: A level of severity of addiction related to a personality disorder and its related symptoms. (see ADDICT, ADDICTION; INSIDIOUS ADDICTION)

Chronicity: The degree to which a disorder has been long-standing and is ingrained in the individual's adjustment across many areas of life.

Clinical Formulation: A written statement of the patient's problem, which includes a coherent description of presenting problems and symptoms over time, suggests an etiology for these, identifies related dynamic and nondynamic central factors, and provides a prognosis based on pursing a specified optimal treatment strategy.

Cognition and context complex: A group of symptoms found in addiction and mental illness that reflects a failure in information processing. In general, the complex describes deficits in forming and coordinating facts, meanings, emotions, and frameworks of understanding. The normal process of association and resulting belief systems are often impaired, as are the pace and range of thought. Inappropriate contexts are often applied to situations, or a once appropriate context is not relinquished as the situation changes. Organic impairments often contribute to this complex when deficits in lower order cognitive functions are exhibited consistently.

Cognitive orientation: An emphasis on the conscious content of the mind and its products and, therefore, on the various mental representations and functions that influence conscious perception and decision making. The image of the mind as computer or information processor is central to this orientation.

Compulsive accelerating addiction: A level of addiction marked by instability, rapid decline in functioning, and an escalating need for more frequent drug use and higher doses.

Construction, Constructivism: The emphasis on the role of human beings (as a society corporately or singly as individuals) in constructing reality has its roots in Kantian philosophy. Kant's categorical knowledge was "wired-in" to the mind prior to experience and later applied to the objects of experience, thus inescapably shaping reality. Both Jean Piaget (1937) and George A. Kelley (1955) developed more contemporary applications of the principle of construction. For Piaget, adaptation and growth involved the construction of either organic or cognitive structures through reciprocal interaction with the environment. Kelley viewed constructs as anticipatory acts whereby the person actively construed the environment and potential self-environment interactions in terms of predictions based on concepts gleaned from personal experience. As used in this text, constructivism explicates how the person constructs reality and forges a future out of the highly systematized set of concepts that makes up his or her world view, self-concepts, and sense of identity (See *COGNITION AND CONTEXT COMPLEX; DECON-STRUCTION; IDENTITY*).

Cyclicity: A process is cyclical when it exhibits a recurrent, repetitive set of changes, usually in a specific sequence over time. Many behavioral and psychological processes are cyclical due to a dynamic relationship among their parts, or among levels of organization within the same process, and are thus self-sustaining.

Deconstruction: In literary criticism, the act of removing the assumption of a single author-guided message in the text by stressing the potential for creating unintended meanings, which is inherent in language and in the act of creating texts based on conventions such as genre. These meanings are treated without regard to their absurdity, logic, or base in reality. As used in this text, deconstruction involves the process of the patient "letting go" of the authorial sense of ownership over specific constructs and concepts, especially those related to the sense of personal identity, which is inextricably bound with the symptoms of addiction or other manifestations of loss of freedom. This process is both cognitive and emotional and requires psychoeducational interventions, development of insight, and corrective emotional experiences (see *CONSTRUCTION, CONSTRUCTIV-ISM; IDENTITY, RECOVERY PROCESS/PHASE*).

Demonstrative reasoning: (From the Latin to show, give divine portent, or to warn. Contrast these primarily visual, authoritarian root images to the auditory, democratic roots of dialectical in DIALECTICAL REASONING.) Reasoning that is based on unquestioned premises, which are themselves derived from tradition or experience. Concepts and categories are assumed to be exclusive, linear, unidirectional, and noncontradictory. The truth of a matter is proved authoritatively by demonstration based on specific rules of logic and evidence (see Rychlak 1981b).

Depleted/depressed position: An experience of the self during addiction and mental illness that is marked by a sense of inadequacy, frustrated dependency, powerlessness, depression, intense anxiety, and hopelessness. On the primary process level, this mode is similar to the depressive mode of experience (Klein 1952) wherein the infant perceives the temporary loss of the mother and the attendant experience of separation, threat/abandonment, and global distress (see *ADDIC-TIVE CORE, ADDICTIVE CYCLE*).

Detached/schizoid position: An experience of the self during addiction and mental illness, which is marked by the dominance of feelings of alienation, absence of meaningful attachment, depersonalization, and dominance of perception, sensation, or fantasy over cognition/affect. At very low levels of intensity, this position may be experienced as a soothing sense of oceanic merger, which obliterates painful affects or relationships. This experience is related on the primary process level to the autistic/contiguous mode (Ogden 1989), which parallels the infant's experience of self-regulation thorough sensory experience and the blurring of boundaries, such as in sucking or other forms of tactile contact, with the mother. Thus, detachment has as its goal preservation of a minimal, idealized, soothing attachment, as well as escape from painful or problematic attachment. Addicts usually experience this mode during periods of extreme intoxication. When experienced during abstinence, this mode may prompt craving or relapse (see *ADDICTIVE CORE, ADDICTIVE CYCLE*).

Dialectical reasoning: Greek: conversation, discussion, or debate. Reasoning based on the relationship perceived among processes in change. Concepts and categories are reciprocally defined and understood and may be in conflict, contradiction, and opposition. Categories are inclusive and multidimensional. Truth of a matter arises through participation in a negotiation or interchange that challenges rather than assumes the original premises, which are the starting point of investigation or examination. The points of view advanced in this text (like those of Jung, Maslow, and others) are highly consistent with a philosophy of dialectical holism, as opposed to dialectical materialism or dialectical idealism.

Dominance of affect complex: A group of symptoms found in addiction and mental illness that reflects a defect in affect management. This may be due to either an innate predisposition toward a higher baseline intensity and frequency of a specific affect, or to general affective lability. In many cases of addiction, an intense affective response is made only to a particular life situation or theme. In cases where dynamic, rather than nondynamic issues are dominant, negative affects that have been suppressed, repressed, or delayed are most problematic, especially depression, anger, guilt, shame, disgust, and more rarely fear. However, positive affects may trigger and support addictive behavior when these affects are either very intense or serve an unrealistic, defensive response to an aversive situation, such as when the quality of a negative affect is defensively transformed into its opposite (see *ANXIETY COMPLEX, COGNITION AND CONTEXT COMPLEX*).

Drug effects: The direct psychophysiological impacts of the substance, either due to a single dose or habitual use over time. Theoretically, drug effects can be inferred by an analysis of physiological events at the cellular or synaptic level. Drug effects account for only a portion of the total effect of drug use (see *DRUG EXPECTANCIES, DRUG VECTORS, FEEDFORWARD*).

Drug Expectancies: The set of beliefs concerning the consequences of drug use. These beliefs significantly influence the experience of drug effects and the anticipation of withdrawal or the "high" (see *DRUG VECTORS, FEEDFORWARD*).

Drug vectors: The factors other than the chemical properties of the drug that influence the quality, intensity, and duration of its effect. Includes such factors as the means of procuring the substance (e.g., criminal activity, friendship, sexual favors), route of administration, expected consequences of use, and the social context of use (see *DRUG EXPECTANCIES; ROUTE OF ADMINISTRATION*).

Drug(s) of choice: The substance (and/or addictive activity) that would be preferred by the addict during periods of drug use, if cost and availability were no object. The drug of choice (and other drugs of the same class) reliably performs certain biopsychosocial functions to compensate for or moderate specific deficits. The drug of choice is often invested with additional powers and properties (including personifications) through the *PARANOID PROCESS*.

Dual diagnosis: Refers in this book to cases where either the mental illness, the addiction, or their interaction are severe enough to have caused multiple treatment failures or the need for specialized treatment or management. As an approach to addiction generally, the dual diagnosis perspective emphasizes the role that addictions play in addressing either temporary or long-standing deficits and defects in biopsychosocial functions.

Dualism: The view that more than one basic principle is required to explain a given phenomena. Mind–body dualism holds that mental events and biological events are not explainable by the same basic principles of existence. Dualism can be contrasted with monisms such as materialism, idealism, or spiritual universalism. The mental health tradition has been described as adhering to either biological or psychological monism, whereas the recovery tradition has adhered to dualisms.

Dynamic: Greek: strength, basis for the words dynamite and dynasty. A process of change that may be viewed in one of two basic ways: (1) a dynamic may be described as a unity with enough articulation or definition to allow for opposition and contrast (i.e., emphasis on identity and equilibrium), or (2) a dynamic may be viewed as consisting of opponent elements held in relationship by natural co-creation or co-articulation, or by a broader confining context (i.e., emphasis on diversity and disequilibrium). The dynamism of an automobile battery is a good example of a physical dynamic that may be viewed as a continuous current from the first definition above, or as a reciprocal, interactive exchange of individual positive and negative ions at the micro-chemical level, as in the second definition. Dynamics may result in either emergence of new identities or the maintenance of identity within change. Psychological or emotional dynamics always involve conflict, opposition, and exchange, even when this energetic situation leads to apparent equilibrium or stasis (see CENTRAL CONFLICTS; OPPONENT PROCESS).

Ego syntonic/dystonic: The degree of acceptance (syntonic) or rejection (dystonic) by the ego of an impulse, wish, fantasy, or thought. Note that what may be disapproved by the superego may be acceptable and compatible with the ego, an important distinction for addicted individuals who often demonstrate Wurmser's (1985) split identity: some aspects of the self are dissociated from the superego, whereas others are reigned by a harsh, overdeveloped superego. Symptoms and activities may loosely be referred to as syntonic or dystonic with the ego, based on the impulses and thoughts that they tend to evoke. Many users experience drug use as ego-syntonic while condemning (superego) the behavior as wrong, immoral, or evil.

Ego strength(s): The degree to which the ego maintains integrity of functioning under conditions of stress or demand. Bellak has identified the following typical ego functions: reality testing, judgment, sense of reality, regulation and control of drives, object relations, thought processes, adaptive regression, defenses, stimulus barrier, autonomous functions, synthetic functions, and mastery competency functions (Bellak, Hurvich, and Gediman 1973). Wilson has identified ten dimensions of psychological functioning that reflect ego strength: affect tolerance, affect expression, personal agency, centration/ decentration, type of threat to self, defensive operations, empathic knowledge, use of an object, adaptive needs (most pressing psychosocial needs), and temporality (Wilson, Passik, and Kuras 1989). Erikson identified specific ego strengths related to the outcomes of various life crises or critical phases. The ego crisis of autonomy versus shame and doubt, if properly managed, leads to the development of the ego strength of will. The crisis of initiative versus guilt provides the opportunity to develop purpose. The crisis of identity versus role confusion and fragmentation optimally results in the ego strength of fidelity in regard to one's self, one's values, and to a primary reference group. These three ego strengths are often atrophied in substance abusers.

Embedded cognition: A belief or expectancy concerning drug use that is irrational, preconscious, or unconscious, and that fuels the addictive process. These beliefs are referred to as embedded because the patient often consciously holds other more conventional views on addiction and because these beliefs are often strongly associated with larger belief systems. Cognitions related to family, sexuality, aggression, or achievement may appear to be nonpathological or nonpathogenic except for the addictive cognition they contain, or with which they are associated.

Endocept: Arieti's (1976) formulation of emergent psychological contents prior to the split between affect and cognition.

Engagement: An aspect of active treatment or recovery activities that reflects the degree to which the patient is curious about, involved in, interested, invested, or concerned about recovery issues.

Epigenesis: A view of development originating in biology, which postulates a close reciprocity between organism and environment, resulting in progressive changes in structure. Earlier structures differentiate into increased complexity through a series of levels, stages, or modes. Emergent qualities appear at each new level, meaning that the structures have functional qualities that are not predictable (or merely build upon) the functions of earlier structures. When applied to psychological functioning, the epigenetic principle explains the instability within stability of personality. Lower modes (like the layers of an onion) remain as underlying influences on behavior during moments of regression, resulting in continual progressive or regressive shifts in mental function in response to stress, threat, or demand (see *FAILURES IN SELF-REGULATION*).

Escape/avoidance function of addiction: Refers to the ability of psychoactive substances and related activities and relationships to interrupt, cancel, cloud, or help to prevent the expression of some undesired or feared aspect of self experience. Cases viewed from the self-medication hypothesis of addiction are usually examples of this function, such as a patient using heroin to escape intolerable emotions or using alcohol to "forget" a demoralizing life event.

Existential orientation: As an approach to understanding behavior, the existential approach emphasizes the limits, factual reality, and interconnectedness of human existence. Inescapable human experiences such as death, anxiety, radical limitation, meaninglessness, loss, and aloneness, as well as transcendence, are examined (Yalom 1980). An analysis is made of the effect of the conscious or unconscious awareness of these experiences on everyday life and decision making. As an orientation to treatment, responsibility and freedom within these boundaries are stressed. The therapist shares in the patient's experience of limits and shares in affirmation of the patient's freedom and responsibility. Imagery of the person as a responsible agent is central to this orientation.

Extraspective perspective, theory: Understanding built on third-person, external descriptions, as from an unbiased observer (Rychlak 1981a). Extraspective views tend to assume determinism and efficient cause explanations, are accompanied by a subjective sense of psychic passivity or objectivity, and rely on external validation methods as the criterion for truth. Contrasts with *INTROSPECTIVE PERSPECTIVE, THEORY*.

Facilitation function of addiction: Refers to the ability of psychoactive substances and related activities to enable, sanction, provide the catalyst for, or increase the effectiveness of some consciously or unconsciously desired aspect of self-experience or behavior. *REPETITION* is a special case of facilitation.

Failures in self-regulation: An instance of regression, disorganization, or behavioral dyscontrol due to the inability to modulate arousal level, emotional intensity, sense of attachment, or to integrate conflicting aspects of the self. Failures in self-regulation are usually related to the absence or fragility of stable preverbal self-representations. These self-representations are normally established and consolidated through the experience of having internal states regulated by comforting interactions with a trusted caregiver (see *ADDICTIVE CORE*).

Feedback: In cybernetics, a process of regulating input by information related to output, especially by returning part of the output as input. As a home thermostat controls the output of the furnace by using the information of the change in temperature caused by the heat previously generated, behavioral feedback is information concerning behavior in the present or recent past that regulates current or future behavior. Negative feedback decreases specific behaviors. Drug expectancies and direct psychophysiological effects of drugs often prevent users from receiving negative feedback that would otherwise effectively inhibit the addictive process. In addition to the pleasurable reward, the initial rush of a heroin or cocaine user provides positive feedback that the drug is of a certain purity and will accomplish various biopsychosocial functions or goals. Contrasts with *FEEDFORWARD*.

Feedforward: Preparatory regulatory response of a system or organism in anticipation of inputs. For humans, anxiety is a form of feedforward related to demand. Drug expectancies, physiological preparation, and behavioral priming are forms of feedforward related to anticipated use of the drug of choice in addicts or users. Feedforward reactions contribute significantly to withdrawal symptoms, initial responses to drug administration, and reactivity to drug-related cues that may precipitate relapse. Feedforward responses may mirror or mimic the physiological effects of the anticipated drug use.

Felt sense: Genlin's (1979) formulation of the emerging experiential apprehension of a life situation that encompasses the totality of the person's responses. The felt sense later differentiates into thoughts, feelings, behavioral responses, and so on. Failure to differentiate, or rigid, routinized ways of differentiation may result in severe constriction of the personality and in psychopathology or addiction.

Free will: The basis for traditional morality, which states that individuals can make meaningful choices and can choose to act, feel, think, and behave in ways other than those that they exhibit at any given time. In regard to addiction, free will implies that addicts are responsible agents and as such participate willfully, at least in part, in perpetuating their addictive patterns. Belief in free will is congruent with a scientific psychological view of human behavior if we understand that the unconscious mind focuses on the willing of the goal of addictive behavior (addressing a biopsychosocial need) while disassociating and ignoring for the moment the negative consequences of such behavior. In this view, addiction is a form of moral stupidity related to poor integration of conscious and unconscious understandings, rather than essential moral depravity or perversion.

Freedom, subjective: The subjective psychological experience of being able to choose to act or not to act. Basic freedom in this sense is inherent to all creatures that attain to personal agency. The sense of the word *free* as in freeing a ship's anchor line from an entanglement or snag on the river bottom is a useful image. Constriction or anxiety, or feeling stuck, can be increased either though external limitations or though limiting the ability to imagine viable alternatives. Addiction can be defined as a reduction in freedom due to a habitual relationship with substances/activities.

Function of addiction: Describes how an addiction provides a coping mechanism to the patient. Coping mechanisms are learned behaviors that result in either temporary modifications in the self, or the environment causing temporary homeostasis and adaptation. Normally, biopsychosocial aims (adjustments to internal or external demands) are achieved through the coordination of a wide array of physical and mental capacities, emotional competencies, learned behaviors, and social relationships. These capabilities and resources grow and become more efficient and effective over successive adaptations. In addiction, a substance or activity is habitually used to provide a temporary substitute solution (adaptation) to an internal need or external demand, thus undermining adaptation through nonaddictive channels, as well as preventing growth or the viability of long-term adaptation. The ways in which substances are used to provide these solutions are referred to in this book as psychosocial functions of addiction. Five biopsychosocial functions of addiction can be identified: *ESCAPE/AVOIDANCE; FACILITATION; MODULATION; REPETITION;* and *ORIENTATION.*

Helixical steady state: Two or more opponent processes in interaction, such that the resulting process of change is stable, self-correcting, and self-perpetuating. The term points to the double helix structure (DNA) found in the basic protein building blocks of life.

Heuristic: Greek: same root as *eureka*, a find. A "speculative formulation serving as a guide in the investigation or solution of a problem" (*American Heritage Dictionary*, 2nd edition 1982, p. 610), a problem-solving technique. The heuristic system in this book identifies those attributes of a case of addiction that must be addressed in order to arrive at a problem formulation. This heuristic system combined with a holistic focus on the dual diagnosis case together form a PARADIGM: the dual diagnosis perspective on substance abuse treatment.

Hierarchy: Greek: sacred, holy, and ruling, i.e., sacred order. Most easily expressed by rank ordering concepts or principles from the top down. Temporal priority is often confused with logical or causal priority, but hierarchical arrangements of processes are not necessarily limited to those based on temporal sequence. Other principles of hierarchy are logical priority, supremacy of effect, or levels of generality (where higher levels subsume lower levels).

Homeospatial process: From Rothenberg (1988), maintaining more than one image in consciousness at the same time, resulting in a creative synthesis or solution.

Hybrid model: An approach that combines substance abuse treatment and treatment for mental illness in a single program with a staff trained in both areas. Also referred to as the integrated program model (see *LINKAGE MODEL*).

Identity: Latin: it, that one, or sameness. The aspect of a person or self that provides for a sense of sameness and continuity of self-attributes and experiences across time intervals, interruptions in consciousness (such as sleep, forgetfulness, or intoxication), new experiences, and personal change. In Erikson's (1978) view, a specific ego-strength, fidelity, accounted for the ability to form commitments, identifications, or loyalties that are consistent with one's personal identity. Identity is based on the ability to discriminate what is consistent with the self from what is not in an expanding array of contexts and subjects. On the cognitive level, identity consists of the criteria (held either consciously or unconsciously) that are used for this discrimination. On the primary process level, various forms of boundary provide the most basic sense of identity, as when an infant begins to recognize the skin as the boundary beyond which the sense of "me" ends and the "not me" or the "my" begins. Minimally, any benign sense of identity incorporates positive and supportive memories of interactions with other persons, ideals, and ego-involving activities within a well-regulated emotional life. In healthy individuals, this stable and affirming sense of identity gives an anchored and habitually redirected sense of self, despite the buffeting and temporary disorientation caused by external circumstances.

Inflated/grandiose position: An experience of the self during addiction and mental illness that is marked by a sense of mastery, perfection, euphoria, abundant energy, invulnerability, and the absence of perceived limitations. When extreme, the experience may precipitate paranoia, intense anxiety, an attitude of perplexity, and a sense of impending loss of control due to unbridled energy. On the primary process level, this mode is similar to the paranoid-schizoid mode (Klein 1952, Ogden 1989), which is dominated by splitting and projection of unwanted aspects of self-experience, omnipotent reparative fantasies, and denial. This mode parallels the infant's experience of becoming overstimulated and losing boundaries with the mother while experiencing both pleasure and psychological pain (see *ADDICTIVE CYCLE*).

Insidious addiction: An addiction that imperceptibly grows from controlled use to problematic use, primarily though the establishment of physiological dependence. Extremely gradual displacement of formerly adequate, nonchemical coping mechanisms is also common. (see *ADDICT, ADDICTIONS; CHARACTEROLOGICAL ADDICTION*)

Intentions: As subjective thoughts or expressions, intentions are wishes or goals that have become conscious and chosen by the willing agent to be acted upon, either in the immediate present or in the future. Unconscious wishes and ego strength dynamically influence the degree to which various determinants of an intention are available, conscious, or verifiable by the person involved. This book views addictive behavior as goal-directed, intentional behavior.

Introject: A highly energized mental representation (often simplified and censored) of a significant other. The goal of introjection is to contain and carry within one's bodily self (i.e., incorporate) aspects of the original object. In a sense, the introject is the other swallowed whole, remaining as an inner presence. Introjections often have more preverbal and somatic aspects than verbal contents. Introjections can be converted into identifications and thereby assimilated only after a unified sense of self has been solidly established (see *PARANOID PROCESS; PROJECTION*).

Introspective perspective, theory: Understandings built on experience from the inside, i.e., first-person descriptions: "from the outlook of an identity acting within them" (Rychlak 1981a, p. 505). Introspective views assume free will, agency, and the subjective sense of the reality of experience and perception of the self as active.

Janusian process: From Rothenberg (1988), opposites or contradictions held in consciousness, resulting in a creative synthesis or novel product. Optimal cognitive dissonance or optimal approach to a conflict are ways of using the janusian process in therapy (see *HOMEOSPATIAL PROCESS, PARTIAL CONTRADICTION*).

Key dimensions: The aspects of a patient's addiction and mental illness or emotional problems that aid in categorizing a dual diagnosis case, or one that can probably be adequately addressed as a relatively uncomplicated case of addiction or mental health illness.

Lapse, relapse: A return to a less desirable condition, as from a higher to a lower level of functioning as exhibited by use of substances or return to other maladaptive behavior. The true lapse is not in the external act itself, but in the failures in self-regulation, which the behavior expresses or seeks to repair (see *ADDICTIVE CYCLE; FAILURES IN SELF-REGULATION*).

Life space: Kurt Lewin's (1936) use of movement through space as a metaphor for the person's perception and exercise of values in the world.

Linkage model: The aspect of dual diagnosis treatment that stresses forming links of referral, information sharing, training, and occasional staff sharing between substance abuse programs and those dedicated to treating mental illness. Linkage models usually result in parallel, simultaneous treatment of patients in more than one program (see *HYBRID MODEL*).

Modulation function of addiction: Refers to the ability of psychoactive substances and related activities and relationships to provide for the modulation of arousal, affects, or intensity of simple self-states. When the use of a drug is motivated by the need to decrease, increase, or modify a single quality of aspects of experience, the function of modulation is present. Differs from the function of facilitation in that during modulation the aspect of experience is already readily available, although a change in quality or intensity is sought, whereas in *FACILITATION*, the aspect of experience that is the target of drug use is not available to consciousness or behavioral enactment without substance use.

Narcissistic crisis: Coined by Leon Wurmser (1974, 1984, 1985) for the collapse of the defense structure and a return to consciousness of negative affects, painful realizations, and destructive fantasies. These previously denied experiences (from infancy, childhood, and adult life) surface amplified and in a fragmented, disorganized way. This results in a sense of collapse and impending doom, such as the fear of death or going insane, which is itself a severe narcissistic injury that adds to the shame, guilt, and fragmentation. There is an accompanying disorder in the sense of time, an experience of the eerie, or other forms of depersonalization. Suicide attempts, acting out of rage toward others, or incapacitation due to depression are common expressions of the narcissistic crisis.

One-trial dependence: Addictive pattern established on the first dose of the substance. Some substances are purported to lead to one-trial dependence in most persons due to the addictive power of the substance itself. These claims are unfounded. One-trial addiction requires some specific, individual vulnerability to the substance.

Opponent process: A process that acts in opposition to at least one other process to create a movement, change, or system. Hector Sabelli (1989), in his articulation of process theory, identified four major patterns or views of opposition: harmonic, conflictual, separating, and hierarchical. Harmonic opposition is characterized by processes interacting in cooperative, complementary cycles, usually toward the same effect. Conflictual opposition is more familiar and is figured by struggle, competition, or conflicting ends or results. It is more common between processes or actors that are largely similar (such as addiction and mental illness). Separating opposition creates an alteration of a quality with its absence, or an alteration of different qualitative states, such as the alteration of mood states in bipolar disorder or the alternation of the three primary states of self-experience described in the *ADDICTIVE CYCLE*. Hierarchical opposition imposes orderly priority among opposites (one folded into the other), as when fear is subsumed by self-assertion to create the dynamic ego strength of courage (see *DYNAMIC; PROCESS THEORY*).

Process theory: Articulated by Hector Sabelli (1989), a theory that rests on the philosophical assertions of Heraclitus. The theory stress the energy and unity that comes from opposites in interaction and places an emphasis on elements of change that always exist within apparently stable objects, situations, or relationships. Process theory is seen as consistent with Jungian psychology and other psychodynamic views of psychological and social conflicts as attempts at resolution or integration (see *PARTIAL CONTRADICTION*).

Orientation: Refers to the ability of psychoactive substances and related activities to provide or support a sense of identity, direction, interest, values, context of understanding, or system of interpersonal relationships (as in a reference group of other users or dealers). The orientation function of addiction is often relied on by adolescents or young adults who have not consolidated a sense of identity, direction, and belonging, or to individuals in disorienting life passages such as divorce, unemployment, homelessness, or bereavement. Subgroups with limited life options, such as those in poverty or under threat of cultural collapse or genocide, are vulnerable to relying on this function of drug use, as are individuals who have experienced a stripping of values due to an absence of challenge, as the result of narcissistic self-indulgence or from the collapse of a personal value system. Nations suffering humiliating defeat in war or whose economies flounder have high levels of addiction or substance abuse partially related to this function. Orientation through addiction can be combined with orientation through a criminal lifestyle, as in many substance-involved youthful offenders (see *SOCIABILITY AND IDENTITY COMPLEX*).

Paradigm: Latin: to exhibit or to show alongside. A model or illustration, especially one employing the basic consensually held assumptions and acceptable methods of a science or profession. In any ongoing aspect of scientific or clinical work, one or more paradigms are brought into play (shown alongside) the work to guide, direct—and thereby limit—inquiry, investigation, or practice. In this book, the dual diagnosis case is used as a paradigm for working with the addictions generally by illustrating the essential aspects that must be addressed for treatment of cases of addiction with severe complications.

Paranoid process: In Meissner's (1981, 1986) object relations-based theory, the paranoid process is a general, universal aspect of development of the self involving the management of aggression and narcissism. Pathological paranoid process involves the structuring of the personality around the process of externalizing vulnerable narcissistic and threatening aggressive aspects of the self. It, therefore, involves both victim introjects and aggressor–predator introjects. The drug of choice is often invested with special powers, properties, and personifications through the projection of aspects of the self-other dyad into the self-drug situation (see *DRUG[S] OF CHOICE; INTROJECT; PROJECTION; PSYCHOPATHY*).

Partial contradiction: Sabelli's (1989) formulation of an approach to therapy and a specific therapeutic technique based on process theory. Therapy is viewed as a dialogue (dialectic) between the patient in his or her illness and the therapist who opposes equilibrium in this position. As a technique, partial contradiction is an intervention that provides partial affirmation or acknowledgement of the patient's feelings or thoughts, as well as an acceptable, although noticeable, incongruity that is based on a more healthful attitude or response (see *JANUSIAN PROCESS; PROCESS THEORY*).

Partitioned (partial) mental contents: Dissociated aspects of personality or consciousness. The term *complex* is used in Jungian theory to denote dissociated aspects of self that cannot be integrated by the ego. These are often projected onto other individuals or onto the drug use situation. Drug use may facilitate access or enactment of partitioned aspects of self. As such, drug use is a futile attempt at integration, which can only end in further division and repetition of use, because the enabled partial and its opponents are not fully present in consciousness simultaneously, causing no strengthening of the ego and no creative resolution of the conflict. This is the case when drugs provide for disinhibition through dampening higher order functions such as self-criticism (harsh superego contents) and thereby allowing enactment of otherwise taboo behaviors. Drug use may strengthen the partition, thus further aiding splitting of the personality (see *FACILITATION; REPETITION*).

Personality decompensation: Progressive disfunction of the personality, usually related to the interaction of a dominant pathological process (*PROCESS DISORDER*) environmental stress, or demand. Personality decompensation is usually more insidious and debilitating than most Axis I disorders not accompanied by personality decompensation. Once decompensation begins, it may continue throughout life with few periods of spontaneous amelioration. It may become pervasive in every sphere of functioning. The symptom relief that medication provides is apt to be very fleeting. This fleeting relief from drug effects may increase the vulnerability to addiction in individuals suffering from these disorders. Decompensation usually proceeds in the direction of one of three theorotypes: borderline, paranoid, and schizotypal decompensations (see *PROCESS DISORDER; SPECTRUM DISORDER*).

Personality disorder: A highly systematized pattern of maladaptive styles of coping, feeling, thinking, and behaving that are characterized by severe inflexibility, self-defeating or destructive vicious circles, and tenuous stability. Although problematic for self or others, a personality disorder may allow for a tenable lifestyle if it is socially rewarded and if its limitations are accepted by self or others.

Personality style: A highly systematized set of predispositions toward particular styles of coping, feeling, thinking, and behaving that, although ingrained and systematic, do not show the extreme rigidity, exclusiveness, and self-defeating or destructive quality of personality disorders. Although the diversity in personality styles is legion, a limited set of theorotypes can be derived, depending on basic assumptions concerning individual development, culture, and biological constitution.

Personology: Latin: mask, particularly one worn by an actor. The study of persons and personality in the individual case. Persons have the minimal endowments of personal causation (or agency) and consciousness. In addition, they have both stable and unstable attributes or qualities that may in turn be external or internal. Personality theory, which does not usually concern itself with the origins or nature of consciousness or agency, is the study of these attributes. The study of personality, agency, and consciousness as they apply to the unique individual case is referred to by the author as personology (see AGENT, PERSONAL AGENCY; CHARACTEROLOGICAL; PERSONALITY STYLE).

Phenomenology: Greek: to appear or to show or be revealed. An approach to knowledge based on a purely descriptive account of how the object of knowledge presents (shows itself) to consciousness prior to the knower's resorting to previous experience, theory, or received notions. Phenomenology focuses on the experience of the subject–object interaction. It considers the personal reactions of the investigator as valid data but excludes imposed commentary that takes the form of judgments such as subjective, objective, unreal, undeveloped. Introspection and empathy (in regard to sensation, affect, and logic) are the basic tools of phenomenology. Rychlak (1981a) identified two schools of phenomenology: sensory (or perceptual) and logical (or conceptual). Sensory phenomenology, such as relied on by Gestalt therapy, is based on a description of the self–world relationship as experienced in sensation and affect and often proceeds by way of metaphor, assuming that underlying meanings are isomorphic but not identical, with sensations presented to consciousness. Cognitive and constructivist psychology, and to some extent Jung's analytic psychology, rely on logical phenomenology, i.e., the description of the logical content and cognitive structure of the reality as presented to consciousness. Chessick (1991) has shown how the work of philosopher Merleau-Ponty bridged the sensory and logical approaches to phenomenology in the analysis of collectively accepted meanings that form a representation in the physical body of pre-evaluative stances toward the world. Poetry has been described as emotion resurrected in tranquility. Similarly, phenomenological *theories* build on phenomenological descriptions resurrected in the light of preexistent understandings and their resulting judgments. Because of phenomenology's emphasis on what is presented to consciousness, knowledge stemming from this method is referred to by the author as presentational knowledge.

Phobic core: From Wurmser (1985), an unconscious dynamic between phobic fantasies and the abused substance viewed as the end of flight. The addict unconsciously flees superego elements, dependency, and low self-esteem (see ADDICTIVE CORE; ADDICTIVE CYCLE; PARANOID PROCESS; PROJECTION).

Position in addictive cycle: One of three modal states of self-experience in the ADDICTIVE CYCLE, which parallel three modes of infant experience and continue to influence consciousness during adulthood. Although the modes are balanced and synchronic in normal adults, addicts experience extreme expressions, which alternate in relationship to drug use. Any one of these positions may be ego-syntonic and sought out as a drug effect. The most extreme forms result in decompensation to a *NARCISSISTIC CRISIS*, which may be avoided by drug use. The favored position is the most ego-syntonic in the addictive cycle. The drug of choice usually creates or maintains mood states and self-perceptions that support the favored position (see *ADDICTIVE CYCLE*).

Presubjective experience: Preverbal experience that antedates the experience of self-to-other or self-to-object distinctions. Presubjective experience does not contain the not-I experience and is, therefore, prior to identity. When addictions address some aspect of presubjective experience, they often take on a perplexing ego-alien quality of not being one's self. Presubjective experience after infancy may be referred to as psychotic functioning (see *ADDICTIVE CORE; IDENTITY*).

Primary process: The qualities of thought and experience found in unconscious processes such as dreams, infancy and childhood, and psychotic states. Primary process thought serves wish fulfillment and the pleasure principle rather than being oriented toward conformance of self to reality or effective manipulation of the external world, which is the function of secondary process. "Primary process thinking is characterized by the absence of any negatives, conditionals, or other qualifying conjunctions; by the lack of any sense of time; and by the use of allusion, analogy, displacement, condensation, and symbolic representation" (Campbell 1981, p. 484) (see *PSYCHODYNAMIC ORIENTATION*).

Principle of immediate gratification (PIG): Marlatt's term describing the inability of substance abusers to forgo the immediate substitute solution or adaptation presented by drug use or other hedonistic activity. The PIG principle is a construct that can change with intervention, so that the patient grows to understand and predict that positive change and control are possible if gratification is delayed, or if more appropriate gratifications are obtained after additional effort, delay in time, or with acceptance of the unfamiliar.

Process: Movement or change, especially when energized by opposition, interaction, conflict, or alternation of opposites.

Process disorder: A disorder that progressively undermines adaptive personality functions though the intrusion or disruptive influence of symptoms, usually related to an Axis I disorder. A useful analogy is to a computer virus, which in specific ways gradually destroys preexisting programming and thwarts attempts at new program development (see *PERSONALITY DECOMPENSATION; SPECTRUM DISORDER*).

Projection: Perception of others as conditioned by one's own unacceptable characteristics or motives. Using an analogy, the casting of one's own (usually unconscious) mental contents or traits onto another person, as a film is projected onto a screen. Drugs as well as persons may be the repositories of projections. Introjected contents of self may also be later projected in an attempt to reassimilate them in a more integrated form, to rid the self of negative introjects, or to repeat a gratifying or soothing experience by recreating a desired relationship (see *PARANOID PROCESS*).

Psychodynamic orientation: A view of human behavior and experience that emphasizes the interaction of various mental levels and structures in the person, especially when these are in conflict or opposition. This orientation also includes a strongly interpersonal focus, in part because of its emphasis on early childhood experience in the nuclear family, which is viewed as becoming a template for later experience and interactions. A focus on the relationship between a personal unconscious and conscious understandings and intentions is central to the psychodynamic orientation (see *COGNITIVE ORIENTATION; EXISTENTIAL ORIENTATION*).

Psychopathy: A personality disorder resulting from severe pathological narcissism. Cardinal traits include a dominant response set toward reward, sadistic and exploitative object relations, an absence of true empathy, simulation of normal emotion and attachment, which are experienced only in a muted fashion, and an inability to bond. Although psychopaths usually have a very good perception of reality and in narrow circumstances have an unimpaired interpretation of reality, their valuing of it is secondary to the value they place on self-gratification. Psychopaths who are also criminals exhibit irresponsibility, predation or stalking of victims, and violent crime that is neither solely instrumental nor due to emotional dyscontrol. Although psychopathy is usually contraindicative of the major mental illnesses, the two may co-exist (15 percent of forensic populations). The stimulants are the preferred drug class of psychopaths, who use these substances to facilitate narcissistic inflation of the ego. The treatment of psychopathy requires specialized techniques, training, certain inherent personal characteristics of the therapist, and strong environmental supports, constraints, and sanctions. (see *PARANOID PROCESS; PROJECTION*).

Psychotic addiction: A level of addictive severity where reality orientation is severely compromised by the cumulative effects of drug dependence and by an individual's psychosocial resources being totally monopolized by drug-related preoccupations and activities. The individual may become totally identified with addictive behaviors and therefore demonstrate some aspects of presubjective experience during adulthood, although not as pervasively as seen in the general psychotic states of mental illness.

Reciprocal reinforcement: A level of relatedness between two processes such that each may be said to cause the other. Usually increases in one process tend to increase the occurrence and intensity of the other. Addictions and the symptom complexes they address usually demonstrate reciprocal reinforcement, as do treatment activities and recovery phases.

Recovery process/phase: Any one of the natural, modal reparative changes experienced by an individual engaged in recovery from mental illness or addiction. Several typical phases of recovery from addiction have been identified: cooperation, coping with abstinence effects, deconstruction of denial, identity consolidation, establishing balance, challenge, and self-direction of recovery.

Relapse: (see *LAPSE, RELAPSE*)

Relatedness, dimension of: Degree of relationship between two biopsychosocial process, such as addiction and mental illness.

Repetition: Refers to the ability of psychoactive substances and related activities to facilitate an enactment or reexperience of early infantile experience, primitive object relationships, or traumatic experiences. Repetition is a psychologically primitive, relatively ineffective attempt at mastery over trauma or fixation. Repetition is often observed through an analysis of transference in treatment. Repetitions are often related to CENTRAL CONFLICTS and as such are usually special cases of FACILITATION. Improper management of the transference may result in acting it out through substance use (see *ADDICTIVE CORE; ADDICTIVE CYCLE; FACILITATION*).

Resting: Using drugs to remain in one position of self-experience in the addictive cycle. The other positions are present simultaneously but are not dominant in conscious experience (see *ADDICTIVE CYCLE; POSITION IN ADDICTIVE CYCLE*).

Reward—arousal deficits: A group of symptoms found in addiction and mental illness which reflects a vulnerability to poor modulation of the level of psychophysiological arousal and/or abnormal reactivity or learning curves under conditions of reward, punishment, stimulus deprivation, or stimulus enrichment. Individuals who exhibit the following traits can be said to have problems related to this complex: sensation seeking or avoidance, slow extinction of punished behaviors, slow acquisition of rewarded behaviors, slow acquisition of instrumental avoidance behaviors under conditions of punishment (especially when the negative reinforcer is a conditioned stimulus or a weak unconditioned stimulus). Schizophrenia (negative signs) and psychopathy exhibit the two extreme extremes in deficits in this complex (see *PSYCHOPATHY; SYMPTOM COMPLEX*).

Route (method) of administration: All of the prerequisites for introducing the substance into the body through a given boundary. Common routes are oral, inhalant, intravenous, subcutaneous, nasal, and absorption through various mucus membranes or skin abrasions (see *DRUG VECTORS*).

Sadomasochism: An interplay of aggressive and submissive impulses, or of destructive and possessive urges toward the same object simultaneously or cyclically, especially when an erotic or libidinal motive is also present. The slave—master motif is often an sociocultural expression of this psychological dynamic. Drug use is often involved in switching positions within a sadomasochistic relationship, or in facilitating the enactment of this dynamic by providing disinhibition, or by the addiction in itself being a tool of destruction and preservation of the self or other as libidinal object.

Self-protective bias: The defensive habit of people with normal levels of self-esteem that minimizes negative information or memories about the self and optimizes the amount of control and effectiveness attributed to the self in any situation.

Severity: Usually refers to the need for additional treatment for a disorder, but especially to the intensity, comprehensiveness, and degree of coordination of interventions required for effective treatment.

Sociability and identity complex: A group of symptoms found in addiction and mental illness that reflects a failure in basic identity formation, the absence of stabilizing and directing social roles, problems in bonding, or pathological identifications or reactions to social reinforcers. Cultural or family value systems may contribute to the problems in this complex to the extent that values support use of substances as a coping mechanism, or undermine opportunities for personal growth and role diversity (see ORIENTATION; SYMPTOM COMPLEX).

Spectrum disorder: A grouping spanning Axis I and II of the diagnostic system based on relationship to a hypothetical pathological process. The common process is exemplified in a single prototype disorder that is central to the group in severity. Three spectrum disorders are identified in this book: the schizotypal-schizophrenic, the cycloid-affective, and the paranoid-narcissistic, respectively defined by the schizoid/schizotypal, borderline, and paranoid prototypes of personality decompensation.

Split identity: Leon Wurmser's (1985) description of the combination in addicts of an intense vertical split between superego and ego and a horizontal split between aspects of the self that are acceptable and those that are shameful. The addict typically has a harsh superego and a grandiose, archaic sense of self, which is overidentified with the superego. The resulting conflict of an imperfect self and a perfectionistic superego causes a horizontal split in the ego: a repression of the grandiose self and its primitive emotional contents. This split accounts for the pervasiveness of denial of affects and problems in addicts, their typical presentation of a false self (Winnicott 1960), and their reliance on the mechanism of projection.

Stage of treatment: A set of treatment activities or interventions based on an assessment of the patient's current phase of recovery, which are directed at supporting continued recovery and at advancing the individual to the next phase (see RECOVERY PROCESS/PHASE).

State (attribute): An aspect of self or personality that is operative only under certain conditions and at certain times.

State dependent learning effects: The relationship between the physiological or psychological state (such as intoxication, depression) at the time of acquisition or practice of a behavior and the performance of the new learning when some other state is dominant. Usually memory or learning efficiency is better when a subject is tested under the same state of drug influence, mood state, or state of consciousness in which the original learning experience occurred. State dependent learning has been suggested as a powerful component in the development of some forms of pathological processes including alcoholism. Intoxication can provide for the growth and enactment of aspects of self that are not otherwise available to the individual or to public scrutiny (see PARTITIONED (PARTIAL) MENTAL CONTENTS).

State tuning: Coordination or matching intensity and quality of mood or arousal state with others. States may be tuned as identical or as complementary. Seen as a basic process in the mother–infant dyad, leading to nonverbal communication and coordination of behaviors resulting in feeding, soothing, anxiety management, and the generation of joy in interpersonal interaction. Drugs and the context of drug use may provide a similar function in adult users through chemical induction of the same state or through the sharing of activities, "works," and so forth. Nonaddictive methods of state tuning include dancing, music, social contagion (as at a party) (see FACILITATION).

Stuckness: The experience of being determined, living in a world not of one's own making. The absence of options, meaningful volition, or efficacy, or the experience of being stuck in the factual nature of things, that is, of becoming an object in a world of objects. (see FREEDOM, SUBJECTIVE)

Substitute solution (adaptation): A temporary means of coping with a situation or need that does not resolve the situation, fully address the need, or result in growth. Addiction is a substitute solution or adaptation to specific failures in self-regulation.

Switches, mood and drug: Drugs can serve as affective and interpersonal switches, that temporarily modify otherwise stable aspects of personality functioning. The concept of the drug as a switch for personality and affect is adapted from the research on switches between depressive and manic states in the affective disorders. Use of one drug, such as alcohol, may trigger craving for another substance, such as cocaine or heroin, by inducing a problem affect, or through disinhibition.

Symptom cluster: A set of symptoms, often influencing different physical systems or psychosocial spheres, with a common origin in either an addictive process or a mental disorder.

Symptom complex: A number of overlapping symptoms expressing a confluence of addictive patterns with other psychopathology. In a symptom complex, different pathological processes affect more than one psychological, social, or biological system that negatively impacts a basic bio-psychosocial function. Symptom complexes differ from *symptom clusters* because of the divergence of etiology and similarity of impairment of function in the complex. Symptom complexes arise when several clusters interact and reinforce one another, and various unique qualities or characteristics emerge from this interaction. Five symptom complexes are identified: ANXIETY, AFFECTIVE DOMINANCE; COGNITION AND CONTEXT; REWARD–AROUSAL DEFICITS; and SOCIABILITY AND IDENTITY.

Symptomatic addiction: A level of severity addiction that suggests that a clinically significant symptom is supporting the addictive process.

Syndrome(s): Greek: symptoms running together. A coming together of many symptoms indicating some pathological condition. The term is basically statistical in orientation, since the exact cause of all of the symptoms involved in a syndrome are unknown, or multiply determined, with most cases not exhibiting all of the possible symptoms. The SYMPTOM COMPLEX is a syndrome of a specific quality found in many individual diseases and their interactions.

Synergism: Greek: working together. The emergence of new effects or degrees of intensity due to the interaction of two or more processes, drug effects, and so forth.

Theorotype: From Rychlak (1981b), the description of a personality type or style based on a theory of personality, psychological process, or pathology. The pure manifestation of a theorotype is not expected in empirical investigations or clinical work, where actual personalities can only be approximately described by theorotypes or mixtures of them.

Thrownness: A concept in existentialism that points to the randomness and indeterminacy of the universe, but especially in regard to the lack of any inherent connection between human needs, desires, and hopes to the processes of nature and chance. As used in this book, thrownness points to the abandonment of freedom, which is the major symptom of addiction. The experience of thrownness is seen as an expression of the failure of imagination and creativity. Addiction is often a desperate "fetishization of the field" (Ernst Becker 1973), a radical behavioral maneuver designed to limit and control the anxiety of thrownness. Demoralized/detached individuals may use drugs to facilitate a sense of thrownness, thus reducing cognitive dissonance between their sense of self and their perception of the environment.

Trait (attribute): An aspect of self or personality that is pervasive to many situations and is exhibited most of the time. Traits have a dampening, moderating, or potentiating influence on states. New learning must be accommodated within existing trait attributes before it can be consolidated as part of the routine behavioral repertory. Epigenetic approaches to behavior emphasize the instability within stability, or the intrusion of temporary states in typical or trait behaviors (see EPIGENESIS; IDENTITY; STATE).

Urgency: Refers to the combined perceptions of the clinician, patient, and family of the need for immediate intervention in some aspect of the case. Problems that may have a high level of combined urgency may not be crucial to eventual treatment success and may not demonstrate acute exacerbation at the time of highest demand for intervention from the patient, family, or treatment team.

Value: In Maslow's humanistic self-actualization theory, a value is the goal that directs and motivates activity, both globally (as in life goals and aspirations) and specifically (as toward particular objectives). In the case of higher values, the gratification of basic physical or emotional needs are in some way sacrificed, delayed, or modified in order to obtain the approximation of the value that is an ideal and therefore not fully realizable. Beliefs, including religious, moral, and philosophical, are not values until they meet the criterion of motivating activity toward a goal. Values are thus inferred from actions rather than pronouncements.

There is often a wide discrepancy between the stated values and motivated behaviors of addicts, perhaps due to SPLIT IDENTITY, which is common to addicted persons.

Withdrawal effects: The combined short-term effects of abstinence. In addition to physiological effects related to the absence of the dose, active anticipatory biopsychosocial effects related to searching for the dose contribute to withdrawal (e.g., increased craving). The expectancies related to the withdrawal are powerful contributors to the full effect. Anticipation of a *NARCISSISTIC CRISIS* often increases other withdrawal processes. Withdrawal is viewed as an opponent process to the active drug effect. Withdrawal effects may initially either mimic or mirror the effect of the abuse drug, but mirroring the drug effect is more common.

References

Abram, K., and Teplin, L. (1991). Co-occurring disorders among mentally ill jail detainees: implications for public policy. *American Psychologist* 48:1036–1054.

Abramson, L., and Alloy, L. (1981). Depression nondepression, and cognitive illusions: reply to Schwartz. *Journal of Experimental Psychology: General* 110: 436–447.

Abramson, L., and Andrews, D. (1982). Cognitive models of depression: implications for sex differences in vulnerability to depression. *International Journal of Mental Health* 11:77–94.

Adams, J. (1978). *Psychoanalysis of Drug Dependence: The Understanding of a Particular Form of Pathological Narcissism.* New York: Grune & Stratton.

Aichorn, A. (1935). *Wayward Youth.* New York: Harper.

Alexander, B. (1988). The disease and adaptive models of addiction: a framework for evaluation. In *Visions of Addiction: Major Contemporary Perspectives on Addiction and Alcoholism,* ed. S. Peele, pp. 45–66. Lexington, MA: Lexington Books.

Alloy, L. and Abramson, L. (1979). Judgment of contingency in depressed and nondepressed students: sadder but wiser. *Journal of Experimental Psychology: General* 108:441–485.

American Heritage Dictionary, Second College Edition, (1982). Ed. Margerty S. Berube. Boston, MA: Houghton Mifflin.

Ammons, R., and Ammons, C. (1962). *The Quick Test.* Missoula, MT: Psychological Test Specialists.

Andreasen, N. (1982). Negative symptoms in schizophrenia. *Archives of General Psychiatry* 39:784–788.

Andreasen, N., and Olsen, S. (1982). Negative v. positive schizophrenia. *Archives of General Psychiatry* 39:789–794.

Anglin, D., and Speckart, G. (1986). Narcotics use, property crime, and dealing: structural dynamics across the addiction career. *Journal of Quantitative Criminology* 2:355–375.

Arieti, S. (1976). *Creativity: The Magic Synthesis.* New York: Basic Books.

Baker, T. (1988). Models of addiction: introduction to the special issue. *Journal of Abnormal Psychology* 97:115–117.

Bandura, A. (1978). The self system in reciprocal determinism. *American Psychologist* 33:344–358.

Barratt, E. (1959). Anxiety and impulsiveness related to psychomotor efficiency. *Perceptual and Motor Skills* 9:191–198.

Barratt, E., and Patton, J. (1983). Impulsivity: cognitive, behavioral, and psychophysiological correlates. In *Biological Bases of Sensation Seeking, Impulsivity and Anxiety*, ed. M. Zuckerman, pp. 77–116. Hillsdale, NJ: Lawrence Erlbaum.

Bartlett, N. (1989). *The Drug Offender Profiles: Evaluation/ Referral Strategies (DOPERS).* Austin, TX: Adult Probation Commission.

Basch, M. (1976). The concept of affect-A reexamination. *Journal of the American Psychoanalytic Association*, 24:759–778.

Bateson, G. (1971). The cybernetics of "self": a theory of alcoholism. *Psychiatry* 34:1–8.

Bayer, R., and Spitzer, R. (1985). Neurosis, psychodynamics, and *DSM-III*: a history of the controversy. *Archives of General Psychiatry* 42(2):187–196.

Bean-Bayog, M. (1986). Psychopathology produced by alcoholism. In *Psychopathology and Addictive Disorders*, ed. R. Meyer, pp. 335–345. New York: Guilford.

Beardsley, M. (1965). On the creation of art. *Journal of Aesthetics and Art Criticism* 23:291–304.

Bebout, R. R., and Harris, M. (1990). Case management strategies for long-term clients with severe personality disorders. *TIE Lines* 7:4–8.

Beck, A. (1967). *Depression: Clinical, Experiential, and Theoretical Aspects.* New York: Harper & Row.

Beck A., Steer, R., and McElroy, M. (1982). Self-reported preoccupations of depression in alcoholism. *Drug and Alcohol Dependence* 10:185–190.

Beck, A., Ward, C., Mendelson, M., et al. (1961). An inventory for measuring depression. *Archives of General Psychiatry* 4:561–571.

Becker, E. (1973). *The Denial of Death.* New York: The Free Press.

Bellak, L., Hurvich, M., and Gediman, H. (1973). *Ego Functions in Schizophrenics, Neurotics, and Normals.* New York: Wiley.

Berg-Cross, L., Berg-Cross, G., and McGeehan, D. (1979). Experiences and personality differences among breast and bottle feeding mothers. *Psychology of Women Quarterly* 3(4):344–356.

Bibring, E. (1943). The conception of the repetition compulsion. *Psychoanalytic Quarterly* 12:486–519.

Blatt, S., McDonald, C., Sugerman, A., and Wilber, C. (1984). Psychodynamic theories of opiate addiction: new directions for future research. *Clinical Psychology Review* 4:159–189.

Bohman, M., Cloniger, R., von Knorring, A., and Signordsson, S. (1984). A genetic study of somataform disorders: III. Cross-fostering analyses and genetic predispositions to alcoholism and criminality. *Archives of General Psychiatry* 41:872–896.

Bower, G. (1981). Mood and memory. *American Psychologist* 36:129–148.

Bowlby, J. (1969). *Attachment and Loss, vol. 1: Attachment.* London: Hogarth.

_____ (1973). *Attachment and Loss, vol. 2: Separation.* London: Hogarth.

Bradshaw, J. (1988). *Healing the Shame that Binds You.* Deerfield Beach, FL: Health Communications.

Brown, V., and Backer, T. (1988). The substance-abusing mentally ill patient: challenges for professional education and training. *Psychosocial Rehabilitation Journal* 12:42–54.

Brownell, K., Marlatt, A., Lichtenstein, E., and Wilson, G. (1986). Understanding and preventing relapse. *American Psychologist* 41(7):765–782.

Bruhn, A. (1990). *Earliest Childhood Memories: vol. 1: Theory and Application to Clinical Practice.* New York: Praeger.

_____ (1992). The early memories procedure: a projective test of autobiographical memory, part 2. *Journal of Personality Assessment* 58:332–345.

Bunney, W., Murphy, D., Goodwin, F., and Borge, G. (1972). The "switch process" in manic-depressive illness: a systematic study of sequential behavioral changes. *Archives of General Psychiatry* 27:295–302.

Bunney, W., Paul, M., and Cramer, H. (1971). Biological trigger of "switch" from depression to mania may be CAMP. *Roche Reports* 1:1–2.

Bursten, B. (1973). *The Manipulator: A Psychoanalytic View.* New Haven, CT: Yale University Press.

Cadoret, R., O'Gorman, T., Troughton, E., and Heywood, E. (1985). Alcoholism and antisocial personality. *Archives of General Psychiatry* 42:161–167.

Cadoret, R., Troughton, E., and Widmer, R. (1984). Clinical differences between antisocial and primary alcoholics. *Comprehensive Psychiatry* 25:1–8.

Cain, C. (1991). Personal stories: identity acquisition and self understanding in Alcoholics Anonymous. *Ethos: Journal of the Society for Psychological Anthropology* 19:210–253.

Cameron, D. (1963). Addiction: current issues. *American Journal of Psychiatry* 120(4):313–319.

Campbell, R. (1981). *Psychiatric Dictionary.* 5th ed. New York: Oxford University Press.

Cantor, N., Smith, E., French, R., & Mizzich, J. (1980). Psychiatric diagnosis as prototype categorization. *Journal of Abnormal Psychology* 89:181–193.

Carrol, E., and Zuckerman, M. (1977). Psychopathology and sensation seeking in "downers." "speeders," and "trippers": a study of the relationship between personality and drug choice. *International Journal of the Addictions* 12(4): 591–601.

Chaiken, J., and Chaiken, M. (1982). *Varieties of Criminal Behavior*, Santa Monica, CA: Rand.

Chaiken, M. (1989). *In-prison Programs for Drug-involved Offenders*. Washington, DC: National Institute for Justice.

Chaiken, M., and Chaiken, J. (1985). Who gets caught doing crime? Discussion paper. Washington, DC: Bureau of Justice Statistics.

_____ (1990). Drugs and predatory crime. In *Drugs and Crime: Crime and Justice: A Review of Research*, ed. M. Tonry and J. Wilson, pp. 203–239. Chicago: University of Chicago Press.

Chessick, R. (1960). The pharmacogenic orgasm. *Archives of General Psychiatry*, 5:117–128.

_____ (1991). The unbearable obscurity of being. *American Journal of Psychotherapy* 45(4):576–593.

Clark, H. (1987). On professional therapists and Alcoholics Anonymous. *Journal of Psychoactive Drugs* 19:233–241.

Clark, H., and Zweben, J. (1989). Legal vulnerabilities in the treatment of chemically dependent dual diagnosis patients. *Journal of Psychoactive Drugs* 21: 251–257.

Cleckley, H. (1941). *The Mask of Sanity: An Attempt to Reinterpret the So-Called Psychopathic Personality*. St. Louis, MO: Mosby.

_____ (1976). *The Mask of Sanity*. 5th ed. St. Louis, MO: Mosby.

Clendinnen, I. (1991). *Aztecs, An Interpretation*. New York: Cambridge University Press.

Cloninger, C. (1987). A systematic method for clinical description and classification of personality variants. *Archives of General Psychiatry* 44:573–588.

Collins, J. (1984). Treatment characteristics of effective psychiatric programs. *Hospital and Community Psychiatry* 40:659–668.

Collins, J., Hubbard, R., and Rachal, J. (1985). Expensive drug use and illegal income: a test of explanatory hypotheses. *Criminology* 23:23–35.

Compos, J., and Sternberg, C. (1980). Perception of appraisal and emotion: the onset of social references. In *Infant Social Cognition: Empirical and Theoretical Considerations*, ed. M. E. Lamb, and L. R. Sherrod, pp. 273–314. Hillsdale, NJ: Lawrence Erlbaum.

Cowan, J. (1983). Testing the escape hypothesis: alcohol helps users to forget their feelings. *Journal of Nervous and Mental Disease* 171:40–47.

Csikszentmihalyi, M. (1990). *FLOW: The Psychology of Optimal Experience*. New York: Harper & Row.

Csikszentmihalyi, M., and Larson, R. (1984). *Being Adolescent: Conflict and Growth in the Teenage Years*. New York: Basic Books.

Derogatis, L. (1977). *SCL-90 Administration, Scoring, and Procedures Manual-I*. Baltimore, MD: Johns Hopkins University Press.

Derogatis, L. R., Rickels, K., and Rock, A. F. (1978). The SCL-90 and the MMPI: a step in the validation of a new self-report scale. *British Journal of Psychiatry* 128:280–289.

Diagnostic and Statistical Manual of Mental Disorders (1987). 3rd ed.-rev. Washington, DC: American Psychiatric Association.

———— (1990). 4th ed. update. (January/February). Washington, DC: American Psychiatric Association.

Diener, E. (1981). The independence of positive and negative affect. *Journal of Personality and Social Psychology* 17(5):1105–1117.

Diener, E., and Larson, R. (1984). Temporal stability and cross-situational consistency of affective, behavioral, and cognitive responses. *Journal of Personality and Social Psychology* 47:871–883.

Diener, E., Larson, R., and Emmons, R. (1984). Person X situation interactions: choices of situations and congruence of response models. *Journal of Personality and Social Psychology* 47:580–592.

Donovan, D., and Marlatt, A. (1988). *Assessment of Addictive Behaviors.* New York: Guilford.

Dorcerty, J., Fiester, S., and Shea, T. (1986). Syndrome diagnosis and personality disorders. In *Annual Review, vol. 5*, ed. E. Fances and R. Hales. Washington, DC: American Psychiatric Press.

Druck, A. (1989). *Four Therapeutic Approaches to the Borderline Patient: Principles and Techniques of the Basic Dynamic Stances.* Northvale, NJ: Jason Aronson.

Elson, M. (1991). Applying self psychology in different age groups: adolescents. In *Using Self Psychology in Psychotherapy*, ed. H. Jackson, pp. 91–116. Northvale, NJ: Jason Aronson.

Erikson, E. H. (1978). *Adulthood.* New York: W. W. Norton.

Evans, K., and Sullivan, J. (1990). *Dual Diagnosis: Counseling the Mentally Ill Substance Abuser.* New York: Guilford.

Exner, J. (1986). *The Rorschach: A Comprehensive System. Vol. 1: Foundations.* 2nd ed. New York: Wiley.

Eysenck H., (1967). *The Biological Basis of Personality*, Springfield, IL: Charles C Thomas.

Eysenck, H., and Eysenck, S. (1976). *Psychoticism as a Dimension of Personality.* New York: Crane, Russak.

Feinberg, D., and Hartman, N. (1991). Methadone and schizophrenia. *American Journal of Psychiatry* 148:1751.

Fenichel, O. (1945). Neurotic acting out. *Psychoanalytic Review* 32:197–206.

Filstead, W., Reich, W., Parrella, D., and Rossi, J. (1985). Using electronic pagers to monitor the process of recovery in alcoholics and drug abusers. Paper presented at the 34th International Congress on Alcohol, Drug Abuse and Tobacco, Calgary, Canada.

Fitch, G. (1970). Effects of self-esteem, perceived performance and choice on causal attributions. *Journal of Personality and Social Psychology* 16(2):311–315.

Flapan, D., and Fenchel, G. (1987). *The Developing Ego and the Emerging Self in Group Psychotherapy*. New York: Jason Aronson.

Franzoi, S., and Brewer, L. (1984). The experience of self-awareness and its relation to level of self-consciousness: an experiential sampling method. *Journal of Research in Personality* 18(4):522–540.

Freed, E. (1978). Alcohol and mood: an updated review. *International Journal of the Addictions* 13(2):173–200.

Fureman, B., Parikh, G., Bragg, A., and McLellan, A. (1990). *Addiction Severity Index (5th Edition): A Guide to training and supervising ASI interviews based on the past ten years*. Philadelphia, PA: University of Penn/VA Center for Studies Addiction.

Gacono, C., and Meloy, J. (1991). A Rorschach investigation of attachment and anxiety in antisocial personality disorder. *Journal of Nervous and Mental Disorder* 179(9):546–552.

_____ (1992). The aggression response and the Rorschach. *Journal of Clinical Psychology* 48(1):104–114.

Gawin, F. (1991). Cocaine addiction: psychology and neuropsychology. *Science* 251:1580–1586.

Gawin, F., and Kleber, H. (1986). Abstinence symptomatology and psychiatric diagnosis in cocaine abusers: clinical observations. *Archives of General Psychiatry* 143:1283–1286.

Gedo, J. (1979). *Beyond Interpretation: Toward a Unified Theory of Psychoanalysis*. New York: International Universities Press.

_____ (1980). Reflections on some current controversies in psychoanalysis. *Journal of the American Psychoanalytic Association* 28(2):363–383.

_____ (1988). *The Mind in Disorder: Psychoanalytic Models of Pathology*. Hillsdale, NJ: Lawrence Erlbaum.

Gedo, J., and Goldberg, A. (1973). *Models of the Mind: A Psychoanalytic Theory*. Chicago, IL: University of Chicago Press.

Gendlin, E. (1979). Experiential psychotherapy. In *Current Psychotherapies*, ed. R. Corsini, pp. 340–373. Itasca, IL: Peacock Publishers.

Gertsley, L., McLellan, T., Alterman, A., et al. (1989). Ability to form an alliance with the therapist: a possible marker of prognosis for patients with antisocial personality disorder. *American Journal of Psychiatry* 146:508–512.

Gitlin, M. (1990). *The Psychotherapist's Guide to Psychopharmacology*. New York: The Free Press.

Glover, E. (1932). On the etiology of drug addiction. In *On the Early Development of the Mind*. New York: International Universities Press.

Gossop, M. (1986). Drug dependence and self-esteem. *International Journal of the Addictions* 11:741–753.

Gottheil, E., McGahan, J., and Druley, K. (1980). Psychopathy and substance abuse. In *Substance Abuse and Psychiatric Illness*, ed. E. Gottheil, T. McLellan, and K. Druley, pp. 3–27. New York: Pergamon.

Gottheil, E., McLellan, T., and Druley, K. (1980). *Substance Abuse and Psychiatric Illness*. New York: Pergamon.

Gray, J. (1982). *The Neuropsychology of Anxiety*. New York: Oxford University Press.

Greenberg, S. (1977). The relationship between crime and amphetamine abuse: an empirical review of the literature. *Contemporary Drug Problems* 5:101–130.

Greenspan, S. (1979). Intelligence and adaptation: an integration of psychoanalytic and Piagetian development psychology. *Psychological Issues* 47/48.

Grinker, R. (1966). "Open-system" psychiatry. *American Journal of Psychoanalysis* 26(2):115–128.

Grotstein, J. (1982). Newer perspectives in object relations theory. *Contemporary Psychoanalysis* 16:479–546.

Guntrip, H. (1967). The concept of psychodynamic science. *International Journal of Psycho-Analysis* 48(1):32–43.

Hare, R. (1970). Some empirical studies of psychopathy. *Canada's Mental Health* 18(1):4–9.

_____ (1972). Psychopathy and physiological responses to adrenalin. *Journal of Abnormal Psychology* 79:138–147.

_____ (1973). Orienting and defensive responses to visual stimuli. *Psychophysiology* 10(5):453–464.

_____ (1975). Psychophysiological studies on psychopathy. In *Clinical Applications of Psychophysiology*, ed. D. C. Fowles. New York: Columbia University Press.

_____ (1978). Psychopathy and the detection of deception in a prison population. *Psychophysiology* 15(2):126–136.

_____ (1980). A research scale for the assessment of psychopathy in criminal population. *Personality and Individual Differences* 1:11–117.

_____ (1982). Psychopathy and physiological activity during anticipation of an aversive stimulus in a distraction paradigm. *Psychophysiology* 19:266–271.

_____ (1983). Diagnosis of antisocial personality disorder in two prison criminal populations. *American Journal of Psychiatry* 140:887–890.

_____ (1984). Performance of psychopaths on cognitive tasks related to frontal-lobe functioning. *Journal of Abnormal Psychology* 93:133–140.

_____ (1985). Comparison of procedures for the assessment of psychopathy. *Journal of Consulting and Clinical Psychology* 53:7–16.

_____ (1991). *The Hare Psychopathy Checklist-Revised*. Toronto: Multi-Health Systems.

Hare, R., and Forth, A., (1985). Psychopathy and lateral preference. *Journal of Abnormal Psychology* 94(1):541–546.

Hare, R., Harpur, T., Hakstian, A., et al. (1990). The revised Psychopathy Checklist: reliability and factor structure. *Psychological Assessment: A Journal of Consulting and Clinical Psychology* 2:338–341.

Hare, R., Hart, S., and Harpur, T. (1991). Psychopathy and *DSM-IV* criteria for antisocial personality disorder. *Journal of Abnormal Psychology* 100:391–398.

Hare, R., and McPherson, L. (1984). Violent and aggressive behavior in criminal psychopaths. *International Journal of Law and Psychiatry* 7:35–50.

Hare, R., McPherson, L., and Forth, A. (1988). Male psychopaths and their criminal careers. *Journal of Consulting and Clinical Psychology* 56(5):710–714.

Harpur, T., Hakstian, A., and Hare, R. (1988). Factor structure of the Psychopathy Checklist. *Journal of Consulting and Clinical Psychology* 56:741–747.

Harris, G., Rice, M., and Cormier, C. (1991). Psychopathy and violent recidivism. *Law and Human Behavior* 15(6):625–637.

Hart, S., Forth, A., and Hare, R. (1989). Discriminant validity of the Psychopathy Checklist in a forensic psychiatric population. *Psychological Assessment* 1(3):211–218.

———— (1990). Performance of male psychopaths on selected neuropsychological tests. *Journal of Abnormal Psychology* 99:374–379.

Hart, S., Kropp, P., and Hare, R. (1988). Performance of male psychopaths following conditional release from prison. *Journal of Consulting and Clinical Psychology* 56:227–232.

Hartmann, D. (1969). A study of drug-taking adolescents. *Psychoanalytic Study of the Child* 24:384–398. New York: International Universities Press.

Hartocollis, P. (1983). *Time and Timelessness.* New York: International Universities Press.

Hemphill, B., and Werner, P. (1990). Deinstitutionalization: a role for occupational therapy in the state hospital. *Occupational Therapy in Mental Health* 10(2):85–99.

Hesselbrock, M. (1983). "Never believe an alcoholic"? On the validity of self-report measures of alcohol dependence and related constructs. *International Journal of the Addictions* 18(5):593–609.

Hesselbrock, M., Hesselbrock, V., Tennen, H., et al. (1983). Methodological considerations in the assessment of depression in alcoholics. *Journal of Consulting and Clinical Psychology* 42(2):399–405.

Hofer, M. (1984). Relationships as regulators: A psychobiologic perspective on bereavement. *Psychosomatic Medicine* 46:183–197.

Horney, K. (1945). On the criteria for termination of psychoanalysis. *International Journal of Psycho-Analysis* 31:78–80.

Horowitz, M. (1983). *Image Formation in Psychotherapy.* New York: Jason Aronson.

Hurlburt, R. (1979). Random sampling of cognitions and behavior. *Journal of Research in Personality* 13(1):103–111.

Ickes, W., and Layden, M. (1978). Objective self-awareness and individuation: an empirical link. *Journal of Personality* 48(1):146–161.

Jaffe, J., and Ciraulo, D. (1986). Alcoholism and depression. In *Psychopathology and Addictive Disorders*, ed. Roger Meyer. New York: Guilford.

Jellinek, E. (1963). *The Disease Concept of Alcoholism.* New Haven, CT: Hilldale.

Jessor, R., and Jessor, S. (1977). *Problem Behavior and Psychosocial Development.* New York: Academic.

Johnson, A. (1949). Sanctions for superego lacunae of adolescents. In *Searchlights on Delinquency*, ed. K. Eisser, pp. 225–245. New York: International Universities Press.

Jones, M. (1968). Personality correlates and drinking patterns in men. *Journal of Consulting and Clinical Psychology* 36:2–12.

——— (1971). Personality correlates and drinking patterns in women. *Journal of Consulting and Clinical Psychology* 36:61–69.

Jutai, J., and Hare, R. (1983). Psychopathy and selective attention during performance of a complex perceptual-motor task. *Psychophysiology* 20(2):146–151.

Karen, R. (1992). Shame. *The Atlantic* 269:40–85.

Kaufman, E. (1989). The psychotherapy of dually diagnosed patients. *Journal of Substance Abuse Treatment* 6:9–18.

Keeler, M., Taylor, C., and Miller, W. (1979). Are all recently detoxified alcoholics depressed? *American Journal of Psychiatry* 136:386–588.

Kelber, H. (1982). The interaction of a treatment program using opiates for mental illness and an addiction treatment program. *Annals of New York Academy of Sciences* 5:173–177.

Kellerman, H. (1983). An epigenetic theory of emotions in early development. In *Emotion: Theory, Research, and Experience*, vol. 2, ed. R. Plutchik and H. Kellerman. New York: Academic.

Kelley, G. (1955). *The Psychology of Personal Constructs*. New York: W. W. Norton.

Kernberg, O. (1967). Borderline personality organization. *Journal of the American Psychiatric Association* 15(3):641–685.

——— (1975). *Borderline Conditions and Pathological Narcissism*. New York: Jason Aronson.

——— (1984). *Severe Personality Disorders: Psychotherapeutic Strategies*. New Haven, CT: Yale University Press.

Kety, S., Rosenthal, D., Wender, S., et al. (1978). The biological and adoptive families of adopted individuals who became schizophrenic. In *The Nature of Schizophrenia*, ed. L. D. Wynne, pp. 25–37. New York: Wiley.

Khantzian, E. (1980). The alcoholic patient: an overview and perspective. *American Journal of Psychotherapy* 34:4–17.

——— (1985). The self-medication hypothesis of addictive disorders: focus on heroin and cocaine dependence. *American Journal of Psychiatry* 142: 1259–1262.

Khantzian, E., Mack, J., Schatzberg, A. (1974). Heroin use as an attempt to cope: clinical observations. *American Journal of Psychiatry* 131:160–164.

Kilpatrick, D., Sutker, P., Roitzsch J., and Miller, J. (1976). Personality correlates of polydrug abuse. *Psychological Reports* 38(1):311–317.

Kish, G., and Donnenwerth, G. (1972). Interests and stimulus seeking. *Journal of Consulting and Clinical Psychology* 38(1):42–49.

Klein, G. (1976). *Psychoanalytic Theory: A Study of Essentials*. New York: International Universities Press.

Klein, M. (1952). The origins of transference. In *The Writings of Melanie Klein, (Vol. 3): Envy, Gratitude and Other Works.* London: Hogarth.

Kline, J., Harris, M., Bebout, R., and Drake, R. (1990). Contrasting integrated and linkage models of treatment for homeless, dually diagnosed adults. In *New Directions in Mental Health Services: Dual Diagnosis of Major Mental Illness and Substance Disorder*, ed. K. Minkoff and R. Drake, pp. 95–106. San Francisco: Jossey-Bass.

Klinger, E. (1978). Dimensions of thought and imagery in normal waking states. *Journal of States of Consciousness* 4:97–113.

Klopfer, B. (1938). The shading responses. *Rorschach Research Exchange* 2:76–79.

Klopfer B., Ainsworth, M., and Klopfer, W. (1954). *Developments in Rorschach Technique.* New York: World Book.

Koch, J. (1891). *Die Psychopathischen Miderwertigkeiten.* Ravensburg: Maier.

Koegel, P., and Burnam, A. (1988). Alcoholism among homeless adults in the inner city of Los Angeles. *Archives of General Psychiatry* 45:1011–1018.

Kofoed, L., Kania, J., Walsh, T., and Atkinson, R. (1986). Outpatient treatment of patients with substance abuse and coexisting psychiatric disorders. *American Journal of Psychiatry* 143:867–872.

Kofoed, L., and Key, A. (1988). Using group therapy to persuade dual diagnosis patients to seek substance abuse treatment. *Hospital and Community Psychiatry* 39:1209–1211.

Kohlberg, L. (1980). The cognitive-developmental approach to moral education. In *Developmental Counseling and Teaching*, ed. V. Erickson and J. Whitley, pp. 10–26. Monterey, CA: Brooks Cole.

Kohut, H. (1971). *The Analysis of the Self.* New York: International Universities Press.

_____ (1976). *The Restoration of the Self.* New York: International Universities Press.

Kohut, H., and Wolf, E. (1978). The disorders of the self and their treatment: an outline. *International Journal of Psycho-Analysis* 59:413–425.

Kossen, D., Smith, S., and Newman, J. (1990). Evaluation of the construct validity of psychopathy in black and white male inmates: three preliminary studies. *Journal of Abnormal Psychology* 99:250–259.

Kosten, T. & Kleber, H. (1988). Differential diagnosis of psychiatric comorbidity in substance abusers. *Journal of Substance Abuse Treatment* 5:201–206.

Kraepelin, E. (1896). *Psychiatrie: Ein Lehrbuch.* 5th ed. Leipzig: Barth.

Kranzer, M. (1979). Object relations theory: an introduction. *Journal of the American Psychoanalytic Association* 29'7(2):313–325.

Krystal, H. (1975). Affect tolerance. *American Journal of Psychoanalysis* 3:179–219.

Krystal, H., Raskin, H. (1970). *Drug Dependence Aspects of Ego Function.* Detroit: Wayne State University.

Kuhn, T. (1970). *The Structure of Scientific Revolutions.* Chicago: University of Chicago Press.

Kurtz, E. (1979). *Not-God: A History of Alcoholics Anonymous*. Center City, MN: Hazelden Educational Services.

_____ (1982). Why AA works: the intellectual significance of Alcoholics Anonymous. *Journal of Studies in Alcohol* 43:38–80.

Levy, D. (1951). Psychopathic behavior in infants and children. *American Journal of Orthopsychiatry* 21:223–372.

Levy, M., and Mann, D. (1988). The special treatment team: an inpatient approach to the mentally ill alcoholic patient. *Journal of Substance Abuse Treatment* 5:219–227.

Lewin, K. (1935). *A Dynamic Theory of Personality*. New York: McGraw-Hill.

_____ (1936). *Principles of Topographical Psychology*. New York: McGraw-Hill.

Lewinsohn, P. (1974). A behavioral approach to depression. In *The Psychology of Depression: Contemporary Theory and Research*, ed. R. J. Friedman and M. M. Katz, pp. 157–186. Washington, DC: Winston/Wiley.

Little, G., and Robinson, K. (1988). Moral reconation therapy: a systematic step-by-step treatment system for treatment resistant clients. *Psychological Reports* 62:135–151.

Little, G., Robinson, K., and Burnette, K. (1990). Treating drunk drivers with Moral Reconation Therapy: a two year recidivism study. *Psychological Reports* 66:1379–1387.

Loewald, H. (1971). Some considerations on repetition and repetition compulsion. *International Journal of Psycho-Analysis* 52:59–66.

Lopes, L. (1991). The rhetoric of irrationality. *Theory and Psychology* 1(1):65–82.

Loranger, A., and Tulis, E. (1985). Family history of alcoholism in borderline personality disorder. *Archives of General Psychiatry* 44:153–157.

Lykken, D. (1956). A study of anxiety in the sociopathic personality. *Dissertation Abstracts* 16:795.

MacDougall, E. (1976). Corrections has not been tried. *Criminal Justice Review* 1:1–88.

Maier, S., and Seligman, M. (1976). Learned helplessness: theory and evidence. *Journal of Experimental Psychology*, 105:3–46.

Marlatt, A., and Fromme, K. (1988). Metaphors for addiction. In *Visions of Addiction: Major Contemporary Perspectives on Addiction and Alcoholism*, ed. S. Peele, pp. 1–23. Lexington, MA: Lexington Books.

Marlatt, G., and Gordon, W. (1985). *Relapse Prevention: Maintenance Strategies in the Treatment of Addictive Behaviors*. New York: Guilford.

Maslow, A. (1962). *Toward a Psychology of Being*. New York: Harper & Row.

_____ (1964). *Religions, Values and Peak-Experiences*. New York: Viking.

_____ (1970). *Motivation and Personality*. 2nd ed. New York: Harper & Row.

_____ (1971). *The Farther Reaches of Human Nature*. New York: Viking.

McCord, J. (1983). Alcohol in the service of aggression. In *Alcohol, Drug Abuse and Aggression*, ed. E. Gottheil, K. Druley, T. Skoloda, and H. Waxman. Springfield, IL: Charles C Thomas.

_____ (1988). Alcoholism: toward understanding genetic and social factors. *Psychiatry* 51(2):131–141.

McFarland, B., Faulkner, L., Bloom, J., et al. (1989). Chronic mental illness and the criminal justice system. *Hospital and Community Psychiatry* 40:718–723.

McGhie, A., and Chapman, J. (1961). Disorders of attention and perception in early schizophrenia. *British Journal of Medical Psychology* 34:103–116.

McKelvy, M., Kane J., and Kellison, K. (1987). Substance abuse and mental illness: double trouble. *Journal of Psychosocial Nursing and Mental Health Services* 25(1):20–25.

McLaughlin, P., and Pepper, B. (1990). Modifying the therapeutic community for the mentally ill substance abuser. In *New Directions in Mental Health Services: Dual Diagnosis of Major Mental Illness and Substance Disorder*, ed. K. Minkoff and R. Drake, pp. 85–94. San Francisco: Jossey-Bass.

McLellan, A., and Druley, K. (1977). Non-random relationship between drugs of abuse and psychiatric diagnosis. *Journal of Psychiatric Research* 13:179–184.

McLellan, A., Woody, G., and Luborsky, L. (1983). Increased effectiveness of substance abuse treatment: a prospective study of patient-treatment "matching." *Journal of Nervous and Mental Disease* 171:597–605.

McLellan, A., Woody, G., and O'Brien, C. (1979). Development of psychiatric illness among drug users. *New England Journal of Medicine* 310:1310–1313.

McMahon, R., and Davidson, R. (1985). Transient versus enduring depression among alcoholics in inpatient treatment. *Journal of Psychopathology and Behavioral Assessment* 7(4):317–328.

_____ (1986). An examination of depressed vs. nondepressed alcoholics in inpatient treatment. *Journal of Clinical Psychology* 41:177–184.

McNair, D., Lorr, M., Droppleman, L. (1971). *Profile of Mood States Manual*. San Diego, CA: Educational and Industrial Testing Service.

Meel, P. E. (1962). Schizotaxia, schizotypy, schizophrenia. *American Psychologist* 17:827–838.

Megargee, E., and Bohn, M. (1979). *Classifying Criminal Offenders*. Beverly Hills, CA: Sage.

Meissner, W. (1981). Notes on the psychoanalytic psychology of the self. *Psychoanalytic Inquiry* 1:233–248.

_____ (1986). *Psychotherapy and the Paranoid Process*. Northvale, NJ: Aronson.

Meloy, J. (1988). *The Psychopathic Mind: Origins, Dynamics, and Treatment*. Northvale, NJ: Jason Aronson.

Menicucci, L., Wermuth, L., and Sorensen, J. (1988). Treatment providers' assessment of dual prognosis patients: diagnosis, treatment, referral, and family involvement. *International Journal of the Addictions* 23:617–622.

Miczek, K., and Thompson, M. (1982). Opioid-like analgesia in defeated mice. *Science* 215(1539)1520–1522.

Midanick, L. (1983). Alcohol problems and depressive symptoms in a national survey. In *Psychosocial Constructs of Alcoholism and Substance Abuse*, ed. B. Stimmel, pp. 6–28. New York: Haworth.

Milkman, H., and Frosch, W. (1973). On the preferential abuse of heroin and amphetamines. *Journal of Nervous and Mental Disorders* 156:242–248.

Miller, S., and Frances, R. (1986). Psychiatrists and the treatment of addictions: perceptions and practices. *American Journal of Drug and Alcohol Abuse* 12:187–197.

Miller, D., Rosellini, R., and Seligman, M. (1977). Learned helplessness in depression. In *Psychopathology: Experimental Models*, ed. J. D. Maser amd M. Seligman. San Francisco: Freedman.

Millon, T. (1968). *Approaches to Personality*. New York: Pitman.

_____ (1969). *Modern Psychopathology: A Biosocial Approach to Maladaptive Learning and Functioning*. Philadelphia: Saunders.

_____ (1973). *Theories of Psychopathology and Personality*. Philadelphia: Saunders.

_____ (1977). *Millon Clinical Multiaxial Inventory Manual*. Minneapolis: National Computer Systems.

_____ (1981). *Disorders of Personality: DSM-III, Axis II*. New York: Wiley.

_____ (1983). The *DSM-III*: an insider's perspective. *American Psychologist* 38(7):801–814.

Minkoff, K. (1987). Beyond deinstitutionalization: a new ideology for the postinstitutional era. *Hospital and Community Psychiatry* 38:945–950.

_____ (1989). An integrated treatment model for dual diagnosis of psychosis and addiction. *Hospital and Community Psychiatry* 40:1031–1036.

Monroe, R. *Episodic Behavioral Disorders*. Cambridge, MA: Harvard University Press.

Morely, L. (1988). The categorical representation of personality disorder: a cluster analysis of *DSM-III* personality features. *Journal of Abnormal Psychology* 97:314–321.

Mueller, C., and Klajner, F. (1984). The effect of alcohol on memory for feelings: does it really help users to forget? *The Journal of Nervous and Mental Disease* 172:225–227.

Mukherjee, S. (1991). Schizophrenia: more than two disease processes. *American Journal of Psychiatry* 148(12):1756–1757.

Nerviano, V. (1981). Personality patterns of alcoholics revisited: delineation against the MMPI and clinical implication. *Journal of the Addictions* 16:723–729.

Nerviano, V., McCarthy, D., and McCarthy, S. (1980). MMPI profile patterns of alcoholic men in two contrasting settings. *Journal of Studies on Alcohol* 41:1143–1152.

Newlin, D. (1985). Offspring of alcoholics have enhanced antagonistic placebo response. *Journal of Studies in Alcohol* 46:490–494.

Nurco, D., Hanlon, T., Balter, M., et al. (1991). A classification of narcotic addicts based on type, amount, and severity of crime. *Journal of Drug Issues* 21:429–448.

Nurco, D., Schaffer, J., and Kinlock, T. (1984). Trends in the commission of crime among narcotic addicts over successive periods of addiction. *Journal of Drug and Alcohol Abuse* 10:481–489.

Ogden, T. H. (1989). *The Primitive Edge of Experience*. Northvale, NJ: Jason Aronson.

Ogloff, J., Wong, S, and Greenwood, A. (1990). Treating criminal psychopaths in a therapeutic community program. *Behavioral Sciences and the Law* 8:181–190.

Osher, F., and Kofoed, L. (1989). Treatment of patients with psychiatric and psychoactive substance abuse disorders. *Hospital and Community Psychiatry* 40(10):1025–1030.

O'Sullivan, K., Daley, M., Carroll, B., et al. (1979). Alcoholism and affective disorder among patients in a Dublin hospital. *Journal of Studies in Alcohol* 40:1014–1022.

Ottenberg, D. (1980). Clinical and programmatic perspectives. In *Substance Abuse and Psychiatric Illness*, ed. E. Gottheil, T. McLellan, and K. Druley, pp. 55–66. New York: Pergamon.

Paredes, A. (1980). Administrative locus in the delivery of services for alcoholics with psychiatric disorders. In *Substance Abuse and Psychiatric Illness*, ed. E. Gottheil, T. McLellan, and K. Druley, pp. 119–124. New York: Pergamon.

Parker, E., Birnbaum, I., and Weingartner, H. (1981). Retrograde enhancement of human memory with alcohol. *Psychopharmacology, Berlin* 69:219–222.

Pepper, B., Kirshner, M., and Ryglewicz, H. (1981). The young adult chronic patient: overview of a population. *Hospital and Community Psychiatry* 32:470–474.

Perry, S., Cooper, A., Michels, R. (1987). The psychodynamic formulation: its purpose, structure, and clinical application. *American Journal of Psychiatry* 144:543–550.

Petersilie, J. (1985). Probation and felony offenders. *Federal Probation* 49(2):4–9.

Piaget, J. (1937). *The Construction of Reality in the Child*. London: Routledge and Kegan Paul.

Platt, J. (1975). "Addiction proneness" and personality in heroin addicts. *Journal of Abnormal Psychology* 84(3):303–306.

Prichard, J. (1835). *A Treatise on Insanity*. London: Sherwood, Gilbert, and Piper.

Prochaska, J., and DiClemente, C. (1983). Stages and processes of self-change of smoking: toward an integrative model of change. *Journal of Consulting and Clinical Psychology* 51(3):390–395.

Rado, S. (1926). The psychic effects of intoxicants: an attempt to evolve a psychoanalytic theory of morbid cravings. *International Journal of Psycho-Analysis* 7:396–413.

Rapaport D., Gill M., and Schafer, R. (1946). *Diagnostic Psychological Testing*. Vol. 2. Chicago: Year Book Publishers.

Raps, C., Peterson, C., Reinhard, K., et al. (1982). Attributional style among depressed patients. *Journal of Clinical Psychology* 91:102–108.

Reber, A. (1969). Transfer of syntactic structure in synthetic languages. *Journal of Experimental Psychology* 81:115–119.

———— (1968). Implicit learning of artificial grammar. *Journal of Verbal and Learning Behavior* 6(6):855–863.

———— (1976). Implicit learning of synthetic languages: the role of instructional set. *Journal of Experimental Psychology: Human Learning and Memory* 2:88–94.

Regier, D., Farmer, M., Rae, D., et al. (1990). Comorbidity of mental disorders with alcohol and other drug abuse. Results from the Epidemiologic Catchment Area (ECA) Study. *Journal of the American Medical Association* 264(19):2511–2528.

Reich, J., and Green, A. (1991). Effect of personality disorders on outcome of treatment. *Journal of Nervous and Mental Disease* 179(2):74–82.

Reich, W. (1945). *Character Analysis.* 2nd ed. New York: Farrar, Straus & Giroux.

Rest, J. (1984). Research on moral development: implications for training psychologists. *Counseling Psychologist* 12(3–4):19–29.

Rice, M., Harris, G., and Quinsey, V. (1990). A follow-up of rapists assessed in a maximum security psychiatric facility. *Journal of Interpersonal Violence* 4:435–448.

Rothenberg, A. (1973). Opposite responding as a measure of creativity. *Psychological Reports* 33:15–18.

———— (1988). *The Creative Process of Psychotherapy.* New York: W.W. Norton.

Rothenberg, A., and Sobel, S. (1980). Creation of literary metaphors as stimulated by superimposed versus separated images. *Journal of Mental Imagery* 4(1):77–91.

———— (1981). Effects of shortened exposure time on the creation of literary metaphors as stimulated by superimposed versus separated visual images. *Perceptual and Motor Skills* 53(3):1007–1009.

Routtenberg, A. (1968). The two arousal hypothesis: reticular formation and limbic system. *Psychological Review* 75(1):51–80.

Rush, B. (1812). *Medical Inquiries and Observations upon the Diseases of the Mind* Philadelphia, PA: Kimbler and Richardson.

Rychlak, J. (1981a). *A Philosophy of Science for Personality Theory.* 2nd ed. Malabar, FL: Krieger.

Rychlak, J. (1981b). *Personality and Psychotherapy: A Theory- Construction Approach.* 2nd ed. Boston: Houghton Mifflin.

Sabelli, H. (1989). *Union of Opposite: A Comprehensive Theory of Natural and Human Processes.* Lawrenceville, VA: Brunswick.

Sabelli, H., and Carlson-Sabelli, L. (1989). Biological priority and psychological supremacy: a new integrative paradigm derived from process theory. *American Journal of Psychiatry* 146:1541–1551.

Salzman, B., Kurian, M., and Demirjian, A. (1973). The paranoid schizophrenic in a methadone maintenance program. Paper presented at 5th National Conference on Methadone Treatment, Washington, DC, National Association for Prevention of Addiction to Narcotics.

Savin-Williams, R., and Demon, D. (1983). Situational and transituational determinants of adolescents' self-feelings. *Journal of Personality and Social Psychology* 44:824–833.

Schachtel, E. (1966). *Experimental Foundations of Rorschach's Test.* New York: Basic Books.

Schafer, R. (1967). How was this story told? In *Projective Testing and Psychoanalysis.* pp. 114–169. New York: International Universities Press.

Schalling, D., Lidberg, L., Levander, S., and Dahlin, Y. (1973). Spontaneous autonomic activity as related to psychpathy. *Biological Psychology* 1:83–97.

Schmideberg, M. (1949). Some practical problems in the treatment of delinquents. *Psychiatric Quarterly* 23:235–247.

Schneier, F., and Siris, S. (1987). A review of psychoactive substance use and abuse in schizophrenia: patterns of drug choice. *Journal of Nervous and Mental Disease* 175:641–652.

Schuckit, M. (1979). Alcoholism and affective disorder: diagnostic confusion. In *Psychosocial Constructs of Alcoholism and Substance Abuse,* ed. D. W. Goodwin and C. K. Erikson, pp. 9–28. New York: Spectrum.

Schuckit, T. (1983). Alcoholics with secondary depression. *American Journal of Psychology* 140:711–714.

Schutz, W., and Woods, M. (1977). *Manual for the FIRO Awareness Scales.* Palo Alto, CA: Consulting Psychologists.

Schwartz, B. (1981a). Does helplessness cause depression, or do only depressed people become helpless? Comment on Alloy and Abramson. *Journal of Experimental Psychology: General* 110:429–435.

————— (1981b). Helplessness, illusions, and depression: final comment. *Journal of Experimental Psychology: General* 110:448–449.

Sciacca, K. (1990). An integrated treatment approach for severely mentally ill individuals with substance disorders. In *New Directions in Mental Health Services: Dual Diagnosis of Major Mental Illness and Substance Disorder,* ed. K. Minkoff and R. Drake, pp. 69–84. San Francisco: Jossey-Bass

Segal, H., and Bell, D. (1991). The theory of narcissism in the work of Freud and Klein. In *Freud's "On Narcissism: An Introduction,* ed. J. Sandler. New Haven: Yale University Press.

Seligman, M. (1973). Fall into helplessness. *Psychology Today* 7(1):43–48.

Sevy, S., Kay, S., Opler, L., and Van Pragg, H. (1990). Significance of cocaine history in schizophrenia. *Journal of Nervous and Mental Disease* 178:642–648.

Shaw, J., Donley, P., Morgan, D., and Robinson, J. (1975). Treatment of depression in alcoholics. *American Journal of Psychology* 132:641–644.

Shipley, T. (1982). Alcohol withdrawal and its treatment: some conjectures in the context of opponent-process theory. *Journal of Studies in Alcohol* 43:548–567.

Siegel, S., Hinson, R., Krank, M., and McCully, J. (1982). Heroin "overdose" Death: the contribution of drug-associated environmental cues. *Science* 216:436–437.

Siegel, S., Krank, M., and Hinson, R. (1988). Anticipation of pharmacological and nonpharmacological events: classical conditioning and addictive behavior. In *Visions of Addiction: Major Contemporary Perspectives on Addiction and Alcoholism*, ed. S. Peele, pp. 86–116. Lexington, MA: Lexington Books.

Siever, L. and Davis, K. (1991). A psychobiological perspective on the personality disorders. *American Journal of Psychiatry* 148:1647–1658.

Skinner, H., and Allen, B. (1982). Alcohol dependence syndrome: measurement and validation. *Journal of Abnormal Psychology* 19:199–209.

Sobel, R., and Rothenberg, A. (1980). Artistic creation as stimulated by superimposed versus separated visual images. *Journal of Personality and Social Psychology* 39:953–961.

Solomon, R. (1977). An opponent-process theory of acquired motivation: the affective dynamics of addiction. In *Psychopathology: Experimental Models*, ed. J. D. Maser and M. E. Seligman. San Francisco: Freedman.

―――― (1980). The opponent-process theory of acquired motivation: the costs of pleasure and the benefits of pain. *American Psychologist* 35:691–712.

Solomon, R., and Corbit, J. (1974). An opponent-process theory of motivation. I. Temporal dynamics of affect. *Psychological Review* 81:119–145.

Speckart, G., and Douglas, A. (1985). Narcotics and crime: an analysis of existing evidence for a causal relationship. *Behaviorial Sciences and the Law* 3(3):259–282.

Spence, D. (1982). *Narrative and Historical Truth*. New York: W.W. Norton.

Spielberger, C. (1988). *State-Trait Anger Expression Inventory*. Odessa, FL: Psychological Assessment Resources.

Spitzer, R., Endicott, J., and Robins, E. (1978). Research diagnostic criteria: rationale and reliability. *Archives of General Psychiatry* 31:773–782.

Stern, D. (1983). The early development of schemas of self, of other, and of "self with other." In *Reflections on Self Psychology*, ed. S. Kaplan. New York: International Universities Press.

―――― (1985). *The interpersonal world of the infant*. New York: Basic Books.

Stone, M. (1980). *The Borderline Syndromes*. New York: McGraw-Hill.

Svrakic, D. (1985). Emotional features of narcissistic personality disorder. *American Journal of Psychiatry* 142(6):720–724.

Thomas, A., and Chess, S. (1977). *Temperament and Development*. New York: Brunner/Mazel.

Thompson, T. (1990). The evolution of schizoid orality. *The American Journal of Psychoanalysis* 50:231–241.

Tien, A., and Anthony, J. (1990). Epidemiological analysis of alcohol and drug use as risk factors for psychotic experiences. *Journal of Nervous and Mental Disease* 178:473–480.

Tonry, M., and Wilson, J., ed. (1991). *Drugs and Crime: Crime and Justice: A Review of Research*. Chicago: University of Chicago Press.

Trevarthen, C. (1979). Communication and cooperation in early infancy: a description of primary intersubjectivity. In *Before Speech: The Beginning of Interpersonal Communication*, ed. M. M. Bullowa, pp. 307–320. New York: Cambridge University Press.

Tuke, D. (1892). *Dictionary of Psychological Medicine*. Philadelphia, PA.

Tustin, F. (1981). Psychological birth and psycholgical catastrophe. In *Do I Dare Disturb the Universe?*, ed. J. Grotstein, pp. 181–196. New York: Brunner/Mazel.

Vaillant, G. E. (1981). Dangers of psychotherapy in the treatment of alcoholism. In *Dynamic Approaches to the Understanding and Treatment of Alcoholism*, ed. M. H. Bean and N. E. Zinberg, pp. 36–54. New York: The Free Press.

Viglione, D. (1980). A study of the effect of stress and state anxiety on Rorschach performance. Ph.D. dissertation, Long Island University, Greenvale, NY.

von Knorring, A., Cloninger, C., Bohman, M., and Sigvardson, S. (1983). An adoption study of depressive disorders and substance abuse. *Archives of General Psychiatry* 41:943–950.

Wadsworth, M. (1975). Delinquency in a national sample of children. *British Journal of Criminology* 15:167–174.

Walfish, S., Massey, R., and Krone, A. (1989). Conducting psychological evaluations with AA-oriented alcoholism treatment programs: implications for practical treatment planning. In *Advances in Personality Assessment, vol. 8.*, ed. C. Spielberger and J. Butcher, pp. 161–184. Hillsdale, NJ: Lawrence Erlbaum.

Wangeman, J. (1976). *Coping with Stress: Impulsivity Trait-State Reactions under Stressful and Nonstressful Conditions*. Unpublished master's thesis, University of Melbourne, Melbourne, Australia.

Watson, D., and Clark, L. (1984). Negative affectivity: the disposition to experience aversive emotional states. *Psychological Bulletin* 96:465–490.

Weider, H., and Kaplan, E. (1969). Drug use in adolescents: psychodynamic meaning and pharmacogenic effect. *Psychoanalytic Study of the Child* 24:399–431. New York: International Universities Press.

Weinstein, S., and Gottheil, E. (1980). A coordinated program for treating combined mental health and substance abuse problems. In *Substance Abuse and Psychiatric Illness*, ed. E. Gottheil, T. McLellan, and K. Druley, pp. 50–54. New York: Pergamon.

Weissman, M., and Myers, J. (1980). Clinical depression in alcoholism. *American Journal of Psychiatry* 1:372–373.

Whitters, A., Troughton, W., Cadoret, R., and Widmer, R. (1984). Evidence for clinical heterogeneity in antisocial alcoholics. *Comprehensive Psychiatry* 25(2): 158–164.

Widiger, T. A., Hurt, S. W., Frances, A., et al. (1984). Diagnostic efficiency and DSM-III. *Archives of General Psychiatry* 41:557–563.

Wikler, A. (1973). Dynamics of drug dependence: implications of a conditioning theory for research and treatment. *Archives of General Psychiatry* 28:611–616.

Willenbring, M. (1986). Measurement of depression in alcoholics. *Journal of Studies in Alcohol* 47:367–372.

Wilson, A., and Malatesta, C. (1989). Affects and the compulsion to repeat: Freud's repetition compulsion revisited. *Psychoanalysis and Contemporary Thought* 2:265–311.

Wilson, A., Passik, S., Faude, J., et al. (1989). A hierarchical model of opiate addiction: failures of self-regulation as a central aspect of substance abuse. *The Journal of Nervous and Mental Disease* 177:390–399.

Wilson, A., Passik, S., and Kuras, M. (1989). An epigenetic approach to the assessment of personality: the assessment of instability in stable personality organizations. In *Advances in Personality Assessment, vol. 8.*, ed. C. Spielberger and J. Butcher, pp. 63–95. Hillsdale, NJ: Lawrence Erlbaum.

Wilson, J., and Herrnstein, R. (1985). *Crime and Human Nature.* New York: Simon and Schuster.

Windle, M., and Miller, B. (1989). Alcoholism and depressive symptomatology among convicted DWI men and women. *Journal of Studies in Alcohol* 50:406–413.

Winnicott, D. W. (1960). Transitional objects and transitional phenomena. In *Collected Papers: Through Paediatrics to Psycho-analysis*, pp. 229–242. New York: Basic Books.

Woodruff, R., Guze, S., Clayton, J., and Carr, D. (1973). Alcoholism and depression. *Archives of General Psychiatry* 28:97–100.

Woody, G., McLellan, T., Luborsky, L., and O'Brien, C. (1985). Sociopathy and psychotherapy outcome. *Archives of General Psychiatry* 42:1081–1086.

Wurmser, L. (1974). Psychoanalytic considerations of the etiology of compulsive drug addiction. *Journal of the American Psychoanalytic Association* 22:820–843.

—— (1984). More respect for neurotic process: comments on the problem of narcissism in severe psychopathology, especially the addictions. *Journal of Substance Abuse Treatment* 1:37–45.

—— (1985). Denial and split identity: timely issues in the psychoanalytic psychotherapy of compulsive drug users. *Journal of Substance Abuse Treatment* 2:89–96.

—— (1987). Flight from conscience: experiences with the psychoanalytic treatment of compulsive drug abusers: I. Dynamic sequences underlying compulsive drug use. *Journal of Substance Abuse Treatment* 4(3–4):157–168.

—— (1990). The psychoanalytic treatment of severe neuroses. *Issues in Ego Psychology* 13(1):15–31.

Wurmser, L., and Lebling, C. (1983). Substance abuse and aggression: a psychoanalytic view. In *Alcohol, Drug Abuse and Aggression*, ed. E. Gottheil, K. Druley, T. Skoloda, and H. Waxman. Springfield, IL: Charles C Thomas.

Yalom, I. (1980). *Existential Psychotherapy.* New York: Basic Books.

Yochelson, S., and Samenow, S. (1986). *The Criminal Personality: vol. 3: The Drug User.* Northvale, NJ: Jason Aronson.

Yorke, C. (1970). A critical review of some psychoanalytic literature on drug addiction. *British Journal of Medical Psychology* 43:141–159.

Ziegler-Driscoll, G., Sax, P., Deal, D., and Ostreicher, P. (1980). Selection and training of staff to work with the psychiatrically ill substance abuser. In *Sub-*

stance Abuse and Psychiatric Illness, ed. E. Gottheil, pp. 140–145. New York: Pergamon.

Zuckerman, M. (1974). The sensation seeking motive. In *Progress in Experimental Personality Research (vol. 7)*, ed. B. Maher. New York: Academic.

_____ (1979a). *Sensation Seeking: Beyond the Optimal Level of Arousal*. Hillsdale, NJ: Lawrence Erlbaum.

_____ (1979b). Attribution of success and failure revisited, or: the motivational bias is alive and well in attribution theory. *Journal of Personality Theory* 47:245–287.

_____ (1983). *Biological Bases of Sensation Seeking: Impulsivity and Anxiety*. Hillsdale, NJ: Lawrence Erlbaum.

_____ (1984). Experience and desire: a new format for sensation seeking scales. *Journal of Behavioral Assessment* 6(2):101–114.

Zuckerman, M., and Lubin, B. (1990). *Manual for the MAACL-R: The Multiple Affective Adjective Checklist Revised*. San Diego: Educational and Industrial Testing Service.

Zuckerman, M., Lubin, B., and Robins, S. (1965). Validation of the multiple adjective check list in clinical situations. *Journal of Consulting Psychology* 29(6):594.

Zuroff, D., and Mongrain, M. (1987). Dependency and self criticism: Vulnerability factors for depressive affective states. *Journal of Abnormal Psychology* 96:14–22.

Credits

The author gratefully acknowledges permission to quote from the following sources:

Index

459